THE LAW OF TREATIES

Grupo Editorial Nacional

GEN | Grupo Editorial Nacional is the largest publishing platform in the scientific, technical and professional sectors. It is engaged in the publication of works in the fields of health, exact sciences, juridical sciences, applied sciences, human sciences and public competitions. Furthermore, it provides services for the educational area, continuing medical training and preparation for competitions. Visit our catalogue comprised of over five thousand works and three thousand e-books available at www.grupogen.com.br.

The companies that make up the GEN Group, which are highly respected in the publishing market, developed unparalleled catalogues as a result of their published works, which play a key role in the field of academic training and continuing education of several generations of professionals and students of Management, Law, Nursing, Engineering, Physiotherapy, Medicine, Dentistry, Physical Education and many other sciences, having become a synonym for trustworthiness and respect.

Our mission is to provide readership with the best scientific content and distribute it in a flexible and convenient fashion, at fair prices, yielding benefits for, and serving the interest of, authors, teachers, booksellers, officers, employees and shareholders.

Our unconditional ethical behavior and our social and environmental responsibility are strengthened by the educational nature of our activity, without jeopardizing the continued growth and profitability of the group.

VALERIO DE OLIVEIRA MAZZUOLI

THE LAW OF TREATIES

A COMPREHENSIVE STUDY OF THE 1969 VIENNA CONVENTION AND BEYOND

Foreword
PAULO PINTO DE ALBUQUERQUE
Judge of the European Court of Human Rights

Editora FORENSE

Printed in Brazil

■ English translation of the 2nd Brazilian edition by Diego Luis Alonso
Exclusive rights protected in Brazil concerning the English language version

EDITORA FORENSE LTDA.
A publishing house part of GEN | Grupo Editorial Nacional
Travessa do Ouvidor, 11 – CEP: 20040-040 – Rio de Janeiro – RJ (Brazil)
Phone: +55 (21) 3543-0770 – Fax: +55 (21) 3543-0896
faleconosco@grupogen.com.br | www.grupogen.com.br

■ Book cover: Danilo Oliveira

■ Cataloging in publication (CIP) – Brazil.
Sindicato Nacional dos Editores de Livros (Brazilian Union of Publishers), Rio de Janeiro (RJ) – Brazil.

M429L

Mazzuoli, Valério de Oliveira, 1977-

The law of treaties: a comprehensive study of the 1969 Vienna convention and beyond / Valério de Oliveira Mazzuoli; [Translation by Diego Luis Alonso]; foreword Paulo Pinto de Albuquerque – Rio de Janeiro: Forense, 2016.

Original title: *Direito dos Tratados*
Text in English
Includes Bibliography
ISBN 978-85-309-5686-8

1. Public International Law. I. Title.

15-27260 CDU: 341.9

So bene che è merito d'un libro il dar la volontà di sapere più di quello che insegna.

(MANZONI, Alessandro. *Opere varie*, vol. I, Milano, 1845, p. 487).

Foreword

(*to the First Brazilian Edition*)

Dr. Valerio de Oliveira Mazzuoli has published a new title that is added to his long and impressive list of works on Public International Law. This new work is a thematic monograph on the Law of Treaties. The author in the context of this work elaborates on the general theory of treaties following the pattern established by the Vienna Convention on the Law of Treaties of 1969. As a result thereof, the work deals with the procedure of formation, conclusion, formulation of reservations and amendments of international treaties, as well as the entry into force and termination of international acts. Moreover, in a separate part of the work, the author also addresses specific issues related to treaties as set forth in the 1986 Vienna Convention *itself*. The work concludes with the analysis of the procedure for the conclusion of international treaties, and the solutions of the conflicts which may arise between treaties and domestic law under the 1988 Brazilian Constitution. In addition to a refined compilation of bibliographic references, this work contains the most relevant conventional instruments regarding the law of treaties, a table showing the current *status* of the 1969 Vienna Convention amongst the States having ratified it, as well as the *Guide* of the International Law Commission of the United Nations (2011) to Practice on Reservations to Treaties.

Undoubtedly, this is a fundamental work for the Portuguese-speaking world in the field of public international law academic writing. It stands alongside the most valuable contributions made by French, Italian, Anglo-Saxon and German legal scholars. The reasons for this are threefold: firstly, this work does not sidestep discussions of the most sensitive and intractable dogmatic issues of Public International Law relating to international treaties. The author analyses these problems both from a static and a dynamic perspective, asserting his personal positions based upon solid arguments. Secondly, this work constitutes an updated commentary on the entire Vienna Convention on the Law of Treaties. It should also be noted that this is the first Brazilian work of this sort whereby the Convention is analysed in its entirety, after its ratification by the Brazilian government in 2009. *Last but not least*, thirdly, it should be stated that this work stands out as a result of the ideology that reflects the dogmatic options chosen by the author. Following other works already published and, especially, his brilliant doctoral thesis, the author adopts a clearly favourable stance on international law, conceiving the law of nations as a "dialogue of sources", which basically reflects the value of a true "dialogue of differences". The final line of argument regarding the jurisdictional control of conventionality and supra-legality of municipal law puts the finishing touch on a robust dogmatic thinking, which in an immaculate Cartesian logic concludes that "unconventional constitutional norms" exist.

At a time where mankind faces up to significant political, economic and social challenges, international law academic writings become of utmost importance for conventional boundaries of States' action to be pondered over, defined and determined. Treaties at large and, in particular, international treaties on human rights constitute the most progressive source of current Public International Law. On the one hand, the scope of international treaties has been enlarged to encompass any subject matter domain, as evidenced, for instance, by the treaties adopted by Council of Europe, which amount to more than two hundred instruments. On the other hand, treaties have been construed and applied by a wide variety of international tribunals and similar bodies of a quasi-judicial nature as though they were a "living body of law" (*corps vivant*) in the words of the European Court of Human Rights. Given that treaties constitute bodies endowed with a life of their own, and independent of the will of the States, they can be subject to a continuously updated and teleological interpretation, which in turn circumscribes the discretion of Signatory States to determine and rule upon their provisions, while at the same time they can be adapted to the new circumstances of the political and social life of the peoples.

This commendable work of Dr. Valerio de Oliveira Mazzuoli reflects the immense scientific wealth inherent in all international treaties, fully warranting the dogmatic approach adopted by the author in analysing this subject matter in a stand-alone work.

Strasbourg, September 2011.

PAULO PINTO DE ALBUQUERQUE
Judge of the European Court of Human Rights
Doctorate of Law, Catholic University of Lisbon
Associate Professor with tenure, Faculty of Law, Catholic University of Lisbon
Adjunct Professor, *Illinois College of Law*, United States of America,
and visiting Professor, *Jiao Tong University*, Shanghai, China
Member of the International Institute for Human Rights René Cassin
Acted as an *Expert* of the Group of States against Corruption (GRECO),
appointed by the Council of Europe

Information to the Readership

This English edition faithfully reflects the 2nd edition of this book published in Portuguese in May 2014 by the century-old publishing house, *Editora Forense.*

I prepared this edition with great enthusiasm, with a view to addressing every single aspect of the Law of Treaties as it stands today. Furthermore, my purpose was to write this book in the most didactic fashion, subjecting it to any in-depth and scientifically rigorous analyses that may have been necessary. Overall, I focused on examining the very *essence* of each issue under analysis, always linking theory to practice. Furthermore, I organized the entirety of theory of treaties (especially with regard to the formation, continuance in force and termination of international acts) mirroring the 1969 Vienna Convention on the Law of Treaties.[1] Special consideration was given (which pervades throughout the text) to the *Brazilian* practice relating to the conclusion of treaties; moreover, an entire part of the book deals with the procedural steps that must be complied with according to the Brazilian constitution in order to conclude treaties and the ensuing conflicts that may arise between treaties and domestic law.

After several years of working on this book, I feel that I was able to carry out an original study on the theory and practice of treaties, which is also capable of providing practical answers to recurring issues, especially in the current historical context.

The interpretation carried out, with respect to the articles of the Vienna Convention, reflects my own convictions as it could not have been otherwise. Thus, on all topics dealt with throughout this book I expressed my personal understanding, which will be noticed *at first sight* by any attentive

---

1 Throughout the book, reference is made to the Vienna Convention on the Law of Treaties between States and International Organizations or between International Organizations, 1986 (particularly, with respect to *common* issues with the 1969 Vienna Convention). Furthermore, an entire part of the book (Part IV) deals with the 1986 Vienna Convention, without addressing the *theory* of treaties, since in this work such an analysis is carried out only in connection with the 1969 Convention (the study of which is practically used in its entirety to understand the 1986 Conventions, after some minor adjustments). As mentioned Part IV only deals with specific *issues* regarding the 1986 Vienna Convention.

reader. The generous bibliography consulted, which was gathered in various parts of the world and in the most diverse occasions, made me realize that scholarly writings, in general, address some topics from *a widely accepted* perspective, while other topics give rise to a great disparity of opinions and views that goes well beyond reasonable bounds… Nevertheless, in this book, I follow my own line of thought, which sometimes falls in with the majority of legal writers, although very often it carves out its own path, which diverges from what the majority of legal scholars may have elaborated on a particular matter.[2] In short, I have always believed that an author should be accountable for his/her own work, and in this context it should be no different.

Throughout the tables in this book, distinct fonts were inserted in order to either show *peculiarities* about the topic under consideration, or draw attention to a particular *quote* from an author, that is deemed to be important in a given context, or sometimes *set examples* of specific issues that are being dealt with in that part of the book. Furthermore, I added in the first three *Annexes*, which are placed at the end of the book, the official versions of the three conventions governing the study carried out in this work. In the fourth *Annex* I included the current table (officially published by the United Nations) of the 1969 Vienna Convention on the Law of Treaties, where the number of States that has ratified it can be verified, together with the interpretative statements or reservations that have been made, as well as the objections to the reservations raised by several States. The fifth and last *Annex* contains the *Guide* of the International Law Commission of the United Nations (2011) to Practice on Reservations to Treaties.

Lastly, it should be noted that this book is particularly useful not only for law students and practitioners, but also International Relations scholars, diplomats, consular officers, stakeholders involved in commercial activities, political scientists, sociologists, researchers in related fields, etc.

To conclude, I should thank the *GEN Group* for its on-going commitment in the publication of this work, and in particular, Oriene Pavan, Giselle Tapai and Henderson Fiirst, who contributed to the publication of this work without delay. Furthermore, a special thanks goes to Diego Luis Alonso for translating this work into English. Without their contribution, this edition would certainly not have been possible.

São Paulo, January 2016.

THE AUTHOR

---

2 Let us take, by way of example, the subject matter dealt with in Chapter 2, Part III on "Defects in Consent an in International Acts".

Summary

PART II
GENESIS OF INTERNATIONAL TREATIES

Chapter 1
PROCEDURE OF FORMATION AND CONCLUSION OF TREATIES

Chapter 2

Reservations to Multilateral Treaties

Chapter 3

Entry into Force of Treaties

PART III
CONTINUANCE IN FORCE AND TERMINATION OF TREATIES

Chapter 1
TREATIES IN FORCE

Chapter 2
Defects in Consent and in International Acts

Chapter 3
Termination and Suspension of Treaties

Chapter 2

CONFLICT BETWEEN TREATIES AND RULES OF INTERNAL LAW

ANNEXES

Annex I

Annex II

Annex III

Annex IV

Annex V

Abbreviations and Acronyms Used

Add.	–	Addendum
ADECON	–	Ação Declaratória de Constitucionalidade [Declaratory Action of Constitutionality]
ADIn	–	Ação Direta de Inconstitucionalidade [Direct Action of Unconstitutionality]
ADPF	–	Arguição de Descumprimento de Preceito Fundamental [Allegation of Disobedience of a Fundamental Precept]
ALADI	–	Latin American Integration Association
Art.	–	article
Arts.	–	articles
BIICL	–	British Institute of International and Comparative Law
Cf.	–	Confront/compare
Ch.	–	Chapter
cit.	–	cited earlier
coord.	–	coordinator(s)
DAI	–	Divisão de Atos Internacionais do Ministério das Relações Exteriores [International Acts Division of the Ministry of Foreign Affairs]
Doc.	–	Document
ed.	–	editing/editor
Ed.	–	Editora [Publishing House]
eds.	–	editors
e.g.	–	*exempli gratia* (for example)
et all.	–	and others
etc.	–	*et cetera*
fasc.	–	fascicle
GATT	–	General Agreement on Tarifs and Trade
HC	–	*Habeas Corpus*
ibidem	–	same page(s)
ICC	–	International Criminal Court
ICJ	–	International Court of Justice
ICJ Reports	–	Reports of Judgments, Advisory Opinions and Orders of the International Court of Justice
idem	–	same book/work
i.e.	–	*id est* (that is)

ILC – International Law Commission
ILO – International Labour Organization
IMF – International Monetary Fund
j. – judged in
LINDB – Lei de Introdução às Normas do Direito Brasileiro [Law of Introduction to Brazilian Law Rules]
Mercosur – Common Market of the South
MOUs – Memorandum of Understandings
MRE – Ministério das Relações Exteriores [Ministry of Foreign Affairs]
NATO – North Atlantic Treaty Organization
OAS – Organization of American States
op. cit. – *opus citatum* (in the work cited)
org. – organizer
orgs. – organizers
p. – page/pages
RE – Recurso Extraordinário [Extraordinary Appeal]
Res. – Resolution
RTJ – Revista Trimestral de Jurisprudência [Quarterly Review of Jurisprudence]
SCJ – Superior Court of Justice (of Brazil)
SFC – Supreme Federal Court (of Brazil)
t. – tome
UN – United Nations
UNESCO – United Nations Educational, Scientific and Cultural Organization
vol. – volume
vols. – volumes
WHO – World Health Organization
WTO – World Trade Organization

Introduction

Since the establishment of Public International Law as an autonomous discipline, *treaties* have become the most important subject matter. No public international law scholar has ever denied that this is the source *par excellence* of the law of nations, there being nowadays no other set of norms deemed to be more important than a treaty.[3] It is not difficult to realize that there exists a true *primacy of treaties* when the usage of a treaty is compared to that of any other international acts in writing, such as an *agreement* or a *Memorandum of Understanding* between foreign Powers. Said otherwise, all States (and international organizations also) agree that the legal instrument called *treaty* continues to be the *general rule* at an international level, where they aim at setting a specific norm or a body of norms, which effectively regulates their relationship. The astonishing growth of the *United Nations Treaty Series* clearly reflects this fact, demonstrating – beyond all doubt – the significant role played by treaties nowadays.[4]

Unlike municipal law, which has multiple mechanisms to set out legal norms, the means used by International Law to establish rights and obligations amongst States or international organizations are relatively simple. If compared to municipal law, international law is "much more

---

3 See Remiro Brotons, Antonio. *Derecho internacional público*, vol. 2 (*Derecho de los tratados*). Madrid: Tecnos, 1987, p. 28; Dupuy, Pierre-Marie. *Droit international public*, 7. ed. Paris: Dalloz, 2004, p. 257; De La Guardia, Ernesto. *Derecho de los tratados internacionales*. Buenos Aires: Ábaco, 1997, p. 33; and Crawford, James. *Brownlie's principles of public international law*, 8. ed. Oxford: Oxford University Press, 2012, p. 30.

4 In this respect, see Cançado Trindade, Antônio Augusto, Reavaliação das fontes do direito internacional público ao início da década de oitenta, *Revista de Informação Legislativa*, ano 18, n.º 69, Brasília: Senado Federal, jan./mar. 1981, p. 103-113; and Fleischhauer, Carl-August, The United Nations treaty series, in Dinstein, Yoram (ed.), *International law at a time of perplexity: essays in honour of Shabtai Rosenne*. Dordrecht: Martinus Nijhoff, 1989, p. 131-148. For further information on the increasing development of treaties, see Remiro Brotons, Antonio, *Derecho internacional público*, vol. 2, cit., p. 28; and Dinstein, Yoram. The interaction between customary international law and treaties, *Recueil des Cours*, vol. 322 (2006), p. 261.

restricted in regard with the norm-setting mechanisms",[5] but it is not less true that the latter is *more secure than the former*. Furthermore, international norm setting through the conclusion of treaties is also *a more practical mechanism*. Whilst under municipal law there are specific provisions (set out in National Constitutions) to regulate certain specific matters, under the law of nations, subject-matters of the most varied kinds (provided that their objects are *licit*) are regulated by means of the same legal instrument, that is, a *treaty*. Hence, Joseph Nisot's teaching to the effect that treaties are "la source la plus certaine du droit international".[6] It is true that the above statement could seem nowadays rather obvious, except for the fact that Brazil waited for more than 40 years in order to ratify the Vienna Convention on the Law of Treaties, since its signing (that took place at the United Nations Conference on the Law of Treaties, in the Austrian Capital) on 23 May 1969.[7]

Primacy of the legal instrument – *treaty* – still remains over *customs*, which governed the law of nations throughout human history until the beginning of the twentieth century.[8] This assertion is confirmed by the conclusion of the 1969 Vienna Convention itself, which recognized in its *Preamble*, "the fundamental role of treaties in the history of international relations" (*first recital*), "the ever-increasing importance of treaties as a source of international law and as a means of developing peaceful cooperation among nations, whatever their constitutional and social systems" (*second recital*) and, particularly – with respect to the *primacy* of treaties over customs –, "that the rules of customary international law will continue to govern questions *not regulated* by the provisions of the present Convention" (*eighth recital*).[9] The common denominator among such

5 Shaw, Malcolm N. *Direito internacional*. Transl. by Marcelo Brandão Cipolla (*et all.*). São Paulo: Martins Fontes, 2010, p. 670.

6 Nisot, Joseph. A propos du projet de la Commission du Droit International des Nations Unies relative au droit des traités, *Revue Générale de Droit International Public*, n.º 2, Paris (1967), p. 312.

7 *See* Annex IV.

8 See Guggenheim, Paul. Contribution à l'histoire des sources du droit des gens, *Recueil des Cours*, vol. 94 (1958-II), p. 36-53.

9 The eighth recital was a result of the proposed amendment submitted by Switzerland regarding the *draft articles* of the 1969 Conference Drafting Committee, with the support of Brazil. The 1961 Vienna Convention on Diplomatic Relations and the 1963 Vienna Convention on Consular Relations, both concluded prior to the 1969 Vienna Convention on the Law of Treaties, contain an identical recital in their respective Preambles: "... the rules of customary international law continue to govern matters not expressly regu-

recitals is the underlying truth, i.e. the legal instrument – *treaty* overrides customary law as far as *certainty* is concerned. So much so, the matters until then governed exclusively by customary rules are at present (almost all of them) regulated by treaties. Therefore, treaties have been used in order to regulate a great variety of matters, ranging from the exploration of outer space, the establishment of rules governing intellectual property, the protection of living marine resources, the regulation of investments or the effective carrying out of an extradition process.

The conclusion of the Vienna Convention on the Law of Treaties constituted the most significant step in the codification process of contemporary international law, particularly, taking into account the relevance of the subject dealt with, concerning (since the entry into force of the Convention, on 27 January 1980) any and every treaty.[10] Moreover, at a time when governance of the international society is almost exclusively ruled by the conclusion of treaties, the continuance in force of the 1969 Convention represents a safe harbour for the international players regarding the great variety of issues that nowadays are being discussed in the international arena. In the case of Brazil, the ratification of the Convention that took place on 25 September 2009 marks the definitive entry of this country (albeit late) into this *new era* that the international society is going through, and national academic writings shall support these new developments.

Nevertheless, like any other human work, the 1969 Vienna Convention is not exhaustive. In fact, some issues were not dealt with in the Convention, e.g., the effects of treaties in the event of succession of States and under the state of war; furthermore, issues related to treaties concluded between States and international organizations or between international organizations themselves were not addressed either. The Convention, however, did address other matters, but not in a satisfactory manner, such as, especially, the institution of reservations to treaties. In this particular case, some provisions of the Convention had to be left aside many times – although, in a very careful way – in order to acquire a better understanding of the issue concerned, which should be read together with the guidelines laid out in the Guide of the ILC (2011) (see Part II, Cap. 2, below).

---

lated by the provisions of the present Convention". For a comprehensive commentary on the Preamble of the Convention, see Villiger, Mark E. *Commentary on the 1969 Vienna Convention on the Law of Treaties*. Leiden: Martinus Nijhoff, 2009, p. 43-52.

10 See Nascimento e Silva, Geraldo Eulálio do. *Conferência de Viena sobre o Direito dos Tratados*. Brasília: MRE, 1971, p. 5.

It should be noticed that here the analysis of the Law of Treaties – or the *theory of treaties*, as it is also known – is carried out in strictly *formal* terms. Its understanding does not relate, *a priori*, to the object or purpose of any particular agreement, that is, the *content* of a certain norm. The present research deals with any and every treaty, covering the *whole* of the international acts (either bilateral or multilateral ones) concluded by and between States and/or international organizations. Certainly, from time to time, reference will be made to a specific *type* of treaty, such as, a peace treaty, a friendship treaty, an arbitration treaty, a cooperation treaty, an extradition treaty, a navigation treaty, and so forth. Throughout this work, special consideration will occasionally be given to treaties dealing with the protection of human rights, including conventions for the protection of civil and political rights, and economic, social and cultural rights, as well as those conventions dealing with labour and environmental rights.[11] However, this book has not been contrived to make the reader believe that those instruments shall be analysed *in particular* or in their *material* aspects. Such an analysis would go far beyond the scope of the Law of Treaties.[12]

The present study basically examines (*a*) how States or intergovernmental organizations negotiate, (*b*) which are the organs responsible for these negotiations, (*c*) how a conventional text is adopted, (*d*) what the form to ensure the authenticity of the text is, (*e*) how contracting parties express their consent to be bound by an agreement, (*f*) how a treaty (and its provisional application) enters into force (*g*) how a treaty is incorpo-

---

11 This book, however, carries out neither an in-depth study of the *incorporation* and the *hierarchy* of human rights treaties into the Brazilian legal system, nor the techniques for resolving disputes arising between such treaties and domestic law, since such a study was already conducted by: Mazzuoli, Valerio de Oliveira, *O controle jurisdicional da convencionalidade das leis*, 2. ed. (reviewed, updated and extended), São Paulo: Revista dos Tribunais, 2011; and by Mazzuoli, Valerio de Oliveira, *Tratados internacionais de direitos humanos e direito interno*, São Paulo: Saraiva, 2010. The first work discusses the hierarchical prevalence of human rights treaties (as far as constitutional law is concerned) in the Brazilian legal system, as well as the means to control the conventionality (be it the diffuse manner, be it the concentrated one) of municipal laws; the second work, in turn, proposes a (new) method of solving the contradiction between international human rights law and municipal law, based upon what Erik Jayme called (in his Hague Academy Course in 1995) "dialogue of sources".

12 See Mello, Celso D. de Albuquerque. *Curso de direito internacional público*, vol. I, 15. ed. (reviewed and extended). Rio de Janeiro: Renovar, 2004, p. 212. In his view: "Treaties can only be defined through their formal aspect, since any and all matters can be regulated by means of international conventional norms".

rated into the national legal order, (*h*) what the defects capable of nullifying the consent to be bound by a treaty or the treaty itself are, (*i*) what the effects of an agreement on the contracting parties or third parties are, and (*j*) how international acts are terminated.

In addition to these strictly *international* aspects of the theory of treaties, there also exist other aspects related to the *internal* legal systems, to which due consideration will be given, as could not be otherwise, from a *Brazilian* legal system perspective. The latter subject examined throughout Part V of the this book, which begins (Ch. 1) by dealing with the Brazilian constitutional procedural steps for the conclusion of treaties, and ends by addressing the resolution (Ch. 2) of conflicts that may arise between a treaty and a municipal norm, at which point the issue of jurisdictional control of conventionality of domestic laws will also be addressed.

Part I

General Theory of Treaties

Chapter 1

Concept of International Treaty

1.1 Historical background

Treaties have very remote historical origins, their first main features having been outlined more than twelve centuries before Christ. The legal discipline of *jus tractuum* has been gradually built up over more than three thousand years, and even nowadays the procedure carried out to conclude treaties has great similarities with the original manner in which treaties were concluded. That legal regulation of the Law of Treaties was essentially based upon customary rules, since ancient times up to the first half of the twentieth century. Furthermore, it should be noted that no evidence has been discovered dating back to the years before that time period allowing us to know exactly when conventional customary rules started coming into existence in the history of human civilizations.

The first effective framework for the conclusion of an international bilateral treaty relates to that instrument signed between the King of the Hittite, Hattusili III, and the Egyptian pharaoh, Ramesses II, of the Nineteenth dynasty, around 1280 and 1272 before Christ,[1] which put an end to the war in Syrian territory (known as the battle of Kadesh).

K. A. Kitchen transcribed a passage of the Peace Treaty between both peoples in the following terms:

---

1 Some authors consider that, according to the research carried out at the onset of the last century, there exists a precedent, which is even older: the treaty concluded between Eannatum, prince of the City-State of Lagash and the authorities of the neighboring city of Umma, both of them in Mesopotamia, around 3100 BC. In this respect, see Mello, Celso D. de Albuquerque, *Ratificação de tratados: estudo de direito internacional e constitucional*, Rio de Janeiro: Freitas Bastos, 1966, p. 33-34; and Remiro Brotons, Antonio, *Derecho internacional público*, vol. 2, cit., p. 27.

> "Year 21, 1st month of winter, Day 21, under the Majesty of Ramses II. This Day, behold, His Majesty was at the City of Pi-Ramesse, doing the pleasure (of the gods…). There came the (three Royal Envoys of Egypt…) together with the 1st and 2nd Royal Envoys of Hatti, Tili-Teshub and Ramose, and the Envoy of Carchemish, Yapusili, bearing the silver tablet which the Great Ruler of Hatti, Hattusil (III) sent to the Pharaoh, to request peace from the Majesty of Ramses II".[2]

It is believed this was a very moving moment for Ramses II, to sit enthroned surrounded by the splendor of the grand Palace located in the Nile Delta, at the time when his men came and uncovered before his eyes a big shiny silver tablet, with long lines of Babylonian cuneiform writing, bringing in its center (both front and back) a medallion marked with kings, gods and strange hieroglyphs, which neither he nor his court had ever seen before.[3] It was the object that would have sealed the perpetual peace between the two kingdoms.[4]

According to the text of the treaty, both kingdoms considered themselves as equals, and therefore, between them, their kings and their successors, eternal equal rights norms were set out. By means of that treaty clear norms on the special interests of each jurisdiction were laid out, such as those concerning the possession of certain territories and other areas. Furthermore, this treaty contained norms concerning the formation of alliances against common enemies, trade, migration, and extradition. Overall, it can be argued that the Egyptian-Hittite treaty already had the features of modern-day treaties (for instance, that it was based upon the *pacta sunt servanda* principle). Moreover, given that a long period of peace and effective cooperation between both peoples had followed, the treaty seems to have been finally complied with. It also seems that both civilizations became decadent without the aforementioned treaty being breached.[5]

---

2 Kitchen, K. A. *Pharaoh Triumphant: the life and times of Ramesses II*, 2. ed. Cairo, Egypt: American University in Cairo Press (et all.), 1997, p. 75.

3 For a historical perspective on the battles between Egypt and the Hittite empire, see Steindorff, George, "Historia de Egipto", in Goetz, Walter (coord.), *Historia Universal*, t. I, transl. by Manuel García Morente, Madrid: Espasa-Calpe, 1945, p. 420-422.

4 Kitchen, K. A. *Pharaoh Triumphant…*, cit., p. 75-79.

5 See, in this respect, Rezek, José Francisco, *Direito dos tratados*, Rio de Janeiro: Forense, 1984, p. 13-14. One of the reasons for the lasting peace between the two kingdoms may have also been the marriage of Ramesses to the daughter of the Hittite King, when she was conferred the *status* of "Great Queen Consort", as stated by George Steindorff, in "Historia de Egipto", cit., p. 422.

> The text of this instrument as well as the numerous diplomatic documents of oriental antiquity were found in Egypt, in the ruins of Tell el-Amarna, an ancient residence of Pharaoh Amenophis IV, along the Nile River.

Since ancient times, from a historical perspective, the universally recognized principles of *free consent* as well as *good faith* of contracting parties, and the *pacta sunt servanda* rule governed international treaties. However, from 1815 onwards, as a result of intensified international solidarity activities, fundamental changes began taking place at an international level, which was immediately reflected in the conclusion of the so-called multilateral treaties and the coming into existence in the early twentieth century of permanent international organizations, which became entitled to conclude treaties alongside the States. The fundamental cause that brought about this development, explains Paul Reuter, is grounded "in the increasing solidarity that was established amongst the various components of the international society: the mechanical solidarity that exists amongst the States is such that any change of those components alters the balance of power within the entire system; in turn, the solidarity of the general interests of mankind requires that problems be tackled simultaneously and on a community-based approach; and, lastly, one must also take into account the solidarity of individuals in the development of culture and public opinion".[6]

All these factors, together with the increasing recognition of the utmost importance of treaties as a source of public international law brought about the need to establish a genuine *codification,* that is, a compilation of all rules of general international law, whereby every single aspect of the law of treaties was laid down in a precise way. Such law of treaties will thus mean "everything that pervades the whole of the international legal system and serves as a basis of the structure upon which international norms operate".[7] That is, the need has arisen to *codify* the Law of Treaties by further developing its rules and contributing to achieve the purposes of the United Nations, which are essentially the maintenance of international peace and security. However, in order to reach these goals, it was neces-

---

6 Reuter, Paul. *Introducción al derecho de los tratados,* 1. ed. (in Spanish). Transl. by Eduardo L. Suárez. México, D.F.: Fondo de Cultura Económica, 1999, p. 13.

7 Cachapuz de Medeiros, Antônio Paulo. *O poder de celebrar tratados: competência dos poderes constituídos para a celebração de tratados, à luz do direito internacional, do direito comparado e do direito constitucional brasileiro.* Porto Alegre: Sergio Antonio Fabris, 1995, p. 260.

sary to remain focused on the international law principles included in the UN Charter, such as the principle of equal rights and self-determination of peoples, of the sovereign equality and independence of all States, of non-interference in the domestic affairs of States, of the prohibition of the threat or use of force and of universal respect for, and observance of, human rights and fundamental freedoms for all, and the principle of realization of previously mentioned rights and freedoms set out in its Art. 1 (1)(2)(3) and (4).

1.2 Codification of the law of treaties

In the legal sphere, the term *code* means any body of laws in writing, containing a structured set of norms regarding an individual branch of law. A *code* must contain a set of basic rules and principles on a particular branch of law as opposed to a mere compilation of regulations for classification purposes only (such as for instance, when certain rules are gathered by subject matter, by data, etc.).[8]

While it is true that in domestic legal systems codification was necessary in order to achieve a better understanding of the regulations regarding an individual branch of law, it is no less true that codification had the same effects in the sphere of public international law, in general, and in the field of the law of treaties, in particular. Yet with the creation of the United Nations in 1945, its Charter established that the General Assembly shall initiate studies and make recommendations for the purposes of "encouraging the progressive development of international law and *its codification*" (Art. 13(1)(a)).[9] In order to make those goals a reality, the

---

[8] See De La Guardia, Ernesto. *Derecho de los tratados internacionales*, cit., p. 93. In this respect, De La Guardia goes on to say that: "Codification replaces customs with written norms; a variety of norms and customs with a single law; unifies the law, which is a process of consolidation of norms which often precedes, coincides or follows a political centralization process" (Idem, ibidem).

[9] For further details, see Torres Bernárdez, Santiago, La obra de desarrollo progresivo y codificación del derecho internacional llevada a cabo por Naciones Unidas, in *ONU, año XX (1946-1966)*, Madrid: Tecnos, 1966, p. 199-248; Maresca, Adolfo, *Il diritto dei trattati: la convenzione codificatrice di Vienna del 23 maggio 1969*, Milano: Giuffrè, 1971, p. 9-21; Rodrigues, Carlos Calero, O trabalho de codificação do direito internacional nas Nações Unidas, *Boletim da Sociedade Brasileira de Direito Internacional*, n. 101/103, Brasília, jan./jun./1996, p. 23-31; Daudet, Yves, Actualités de la codification du droit international, *Recueil des Cours*, vol. 303 (2003), p. 9-118; and Boyle, Alan, Reflections on the treaty as a law-making instrument, in Orakhelashvili, Alexander & Williams, Sarah

United Nations International Law Commission (ILC) was created, with Headquarters in Geneva, its Statute being approved in 1947 (res.174-II), and the Commission being set up the following year.

It should be noted that the expressions "progressive development of international law" and "its codification" have different meanings. Thus, according to Art. 15 of the Statute of the ILC the expression *progressive development of international law* is used "for convenience as meaning the preparation of draft conventions on subjects which have not yet been regulated by international law or in regard to which the law has not yet been sufficiently developed in the practice of States", whilst the expression *codification* is used "for convenience as meaning the more precise formulation and systematization of rules of international law in fields where there already has been extensive State practice, precedent and doctrine". Consequently, codification, as shown, is inextricably linked to customary international law, since it will be carried out for those fields in which *there already have been* extensive State practice, precedent and doctrine regarding a specific subject.

Since the beginning of its work in 1949, the ILC included the law of treaties amongst the priority topics to be regulated by post-war Public International Law. British jurist, James Leslie Brierly was appointed Special Rapporteur, who was then succeeded by Hersch Lauterpacht in 1952, Gerald Gray Fitzmaurice in 1954 and Humphrey Waldock in 1961.[10]

Brierly prepared three general reports and one special report on reservations to multilateral conventions, upon request by the UN General Assembly through its resolution 478(V). Following Mr. Brierly's resignation to the ILC in 1952, Hersch Lauterpacht was appointed to pursue the work of the Commission. However, in 1954 Lauterpacht took office as Judge of the International Court of Justice, after resigning to the ILC. Gerald Fitzmaurice, legal advisor of the *Foreign Office* was then appointed to take over Lauterpacht's office. Between 1956 and 1960 Fitzmaurice submitted five reports, replacing them with the conventional form, with the inclusion of a certain amount of declaratory and explanatory materials, as he considered inappropriate that a code on the law of treaties should also itself take the form of

---

(eds.), *40 years of the Vienna Convention on the Law of Treaties*, London: BIICL, 2010, p. 22-27.

10 See Sinclair, Ian. *The Vienna Convention on the Law of Treaties*, 2. ed. Manchester: Manchester University Press, 1984, p. 3-4.

a treaty.[11] Fitzmaurice, in turn, was also appointed Judge of the ICJ in 1960. Thereafter, Humphrey Waldock was designated Special Rapporteur of the ILC, maintaining this in a similar fashion – as highlighted by De La Guardia – "a British line of succession in the person of the Special Rapporteur for the subject of treaties".[12] Waldock, in contrast to Fitzmaurice, resumed the work of the Commission following the pattern of the initial Special Rapporteurs, as he considered that "the draft to be a valuable basis for the preparation of a convention on the subject".[13] Waldock prepared six reports[14] (on the subject in its entirety), which served as a basis for the approval of the draft articles by the ILC, until the 1966 final text was concluded, in whose preparation the Italian jurist Roberto Ago also participated.[15]

The final result of the work of the ILC was submitted to the UN General Assembly, which convened (by means of A/RES/2166-XXI, dated 5 December 1966) an international conference that took place during the 1968-1969 sessions in Vienna (Austria). The Vienna Conference was attended by delegates from 103 States and observers from 13 specialized

---

11 See *Yearbook of the International Law Commission* (1959), vol. II, p. 91: "(...) the Rapporteur believes that any codification of the law of treaties, such as the Commission is called upon to carry out, should take the form of a code and not of a draft convention. There are two reasons for this. First, it seems inappropriate that a code on the law of treaties should itself take the form of a treaty; or rather, it seems more appropriate that it should have an independent basis. In the second place, much of the law relating to treaties is not especially suitable for framing in conventional form. It consists of enunciations of principles and abstract rules, most easily stated in the form of a code; and this also has the advantage of rendering permissible the inclusion of a certain amount of declaratory and explanatory material in the body of the code, in a way that would not be possible if this had to be confined to a strict statement of obligation. Such material has considerable utility in making clear, on the face of the code itself, the legal concepts or reasoning on which the various provisions are based".

12 See De La Guardia, Ernesto. *Derecho de los tratados internacionales*, cit., p. 103.

13 See *Yearbook of the International Law Commission* (1961), vol. II, p. 142.

14 Reports I-III (1962-1964) and Reports IV-VI (1965-1966).

15 See, for further information on all these matters, De La Guardia, Ernesto, *Derecho de los tratados internacionales*, cit., p. 102-103. For detailed information on the travaux préparatoires of the Vienna Conference and their various phases, see Nascimento e Silva, Geraldo Eulálio do, *Conferência de Viena sobre o Direito dos Tratados*, cit., p. 11-56; Rosenne, Shabtai, *The law of treaties: a guide to the legislative history of the Vienna Convention*, Leiden: Sijthoff, 1970, p. 29-91; Ago, Roberto, Droit des traités à la lumière de la Convention de Vienne, *Recueil des Cours*, vol. 134 (1971-III), p. 303-311; Wetzel, Ralf Günter & Rauschning, Dietrich, *The Vienna Convention on the Law of Treaties: travaux préparatoires*, Frankfurt: A. Metzner, 1978, 543p.; and Villiger, Mark E., *Commentary on the 1969 Vienna Convention on the Law of Treaties*, cit., p. 28-38.

agencies in the first session (1968), and 110 States and 14 specialized agencies and international organizations in the second session (1969). The final text of the Convention[16] was adopted by 79 votes in favor, one against (France) and 19 abstentions, on 23 May 1969 (in a session chaired by Roberto Ago). The general thrust of the Conference has been to support (almost in its entirety) the efforts made by the ILC throughout its twenty years of work that led to the adoption of the final text, the introduction of any amendment being extremely difficult.[17] Out of all the States that attended the Conference, only 31 (amongst them was Brazil) signed the final text of the Vienna Convention on the Law of Treaties. Ambassador Geraldo Eulálio do Nascimento e Silva was the head of the Delegation of Brazil to the 1968-1969 Conference and signatory of the Convention.

Although international custom has pervaded most of the text of the 1969 Convention, the truth is that the Vienna Code also innovated in regard to the "progressive development of international law" in certain areas.[18] However, identifying the provisions that reflected the *codification* of international law (*lex lata*) and those that represent the *progressive development* of the law of nations (*lex ferenda*) is not an easy task. It is not unusual that a provision of the Convention reflects both the codification and the progressive development of international law.

> "Indeed, it is not easy to identify which parts of the Convention on the Law of Treaties are a reflection of codification and which ones result from the progressive development of international law. As far as issues related to reservations, interpretation and termination of treaties are concerned, rules of customary law and case law have particularly been codified for their most part. Nevertheless, on more than one occasion, the ILC and the Conference detected diverging practices, having felt compelled to choose amongst them (for instance, in respect with reservations the 'Pan-American' system's prevailed; in relation to interpretation, the predominance of text over the determination of the actual intention of the parties); that is, codification did not consolidate *the general* practice but *a* particular type of practice amongst several other options (introducing sometimes additional practices). This forced choice might represent a factor of the progressive development of international law, since codification was carried out following a certain line of thought, rather than another one, that is, codification is based upon a specific legal policy".
> De La Guardia, Ernesto. *Derecho de los tratados internacionales*, cit., p. 97.

---

16 Published in *United Nations, Treaty Series*, vol. 1155, p. 331 (see Annex II of this book).

17 See De La Guardia, Ernesto. *Derecho de los tratados internacionales*, cit., p. 103-104.

18 In fact, the *Preamble* of the Convention itself states that States Parties believe "that the codification and *progressive* development of the law of treaties achieved in the present Convention will promote the purposes of the United Nations set forth in the Charter..." (*seventh recital*) [emphasis added].

By analyzing the 1969 Vienna Convention it becomes clear that most of its provisions are a result of the *codification* of rules of international custom on the law of treaties,[19] which reflects, to a certain extent, an advantage when it comes to their interpretation, while the provisions representing the *progressive development* of international law deal with issues that are much more *recent*, and thus, much less analyzed, leading to greater difficulties in their interpretation.

1.3 The Vienna Convention on the Law of Treaties

The Vienna Convention on the Law of Treaties came into force after more than ten years following its conclusion, on 27 January 1980, as the *minimum number*, according to terms of Art. 84,[20] of thirty-five ratifying or acceding States, has been reached.

> The first country to ratify the Vienna Convention on the Law of Treaties was Nigeria on 31 July 1969, without formulating any reservation. It was followed by Jamaica on 28 July 1970; Barbados on 24 June 1971; United Kingdom and New Zealand, respectively on 25 June and 4 August of the same year; Morocco, Philippines and Argentina, respectively on 26 September, 15 November and 5 December 1972, etc. The Official Status of the 1969 Vienna Convention on the Law of Treaties is available in Annex IV.

Also called *Law of Treaties*, *Code of Treaties* or even *Treaty of Treaties*,[21] the 1969 Vienna Convention constitutes one of the most important in-

---

19 See Villiger, Mark E. *Commentary on the 1969 Vienna Convention on the Law of Treaties*, cit., p. 27: "Up to 1968 the ILC and many States regarded the Convention as combining elements of both codification and progressive development. The turning point came at the 1968/1969 Vienna Conference. With the majority of articles having been adopted with surprisingly high numbers of votes, the delegates and, subsequently, the States in their practice came to regard the Convention as mainly codificatory. Since 1969, States, courts and authors have increasingly relied on the Convention, even before its entry into force, as an authoritative guide to the customary law of treaties".

20 Art. 84 of the 1969 Vienna Convention was the result of a proposal submitted by Brazil and the United Kingdom to the Vienna Conference on the Law of Treaties, which reads: "1. The present Convention shall enter into force on the thirtieth day following the date of deposit of the thirty-fifth instrument of ratification or accession. 2. For each State ratifying or acceding to the Convention after the deposit of the thirty-fifth instrument of ratification or accession, the Convention shall enter into force on the thirtieth day after deposit by such State of its instrument of ratification or accession".

21 See Kearney, Richard D. & Dalton, Robert E. The treaty on treaties, *American Journal of International Law*, vol. 64, n. 3 (July 1970), p. 495-561.

struments in the history of Public International Law. As mentioned above, the convention did not restrict itself to merely codify a set of general rules on treaties concluded between States, but it also dealt with the progressive development of those matters, whose consolidation had not been carried out yet at an international level. The convention regulates a number of matters, ranging from pre-negotiation-related issues (such as the capacity to conclude treaties and full powers) to the procedure for the formation of treaties (conclusion, signature, ratification, accession, reservations, etc.), their entry into force, provisional application, observance and interpretation, as well as their invalidity, termination, or suspension of the operation of a treaty. Amongst the fundamental norms of the law of nations recognized by the Convention, the *pacta sunt servanda* rule (Art. 26) and its corollary should be highlighted, according to which, internal law may not be invoked as justification for failure to perform a treaty (Art. 27); furthermore, the recognition of *rebus sic stantibus* clause should also be recalled, which may be invoked as a ground for terminating or withdrawing from the treaty when a fundamental change of circumstances has occurred with regard to those existing at the time of the conclusion of a treaty (Art. 62), among others.

The 1969 Convention did not deal, however, with the effects of treaties in the event of *succession of States* and under the *state of war*.[22] As far as the first matter is concerned, the Vienna Convention on Succession of States with respect to Treaties was also concluded in the Austrian capital, on 23 August 1978.[23] Another subject that the 1969 Convention also did not address – perhaps because the existence of an international order where States were dispensable was not foreseen – was that of treaties concluded between States and international organizations or between international organizations. In fact, this matter was regulated by a specific convention concluded in 1986, which was entitled: *Vienna Convention on the Law of Treaties between States and International Organizations or between International Organizations*.[24]

---

22 For an insight into these two subjects, see McNair, Arnold Duncan, *The law of treaties*, Oxford: Clarendon Press, 1961, p. 589-691 (effects of treaties in the event of *succession of States*) and p. 693-728 (effects of the state of war on treaties).

23 In relation to this convention, see Remiro Brotons, Antonio, *Derecho internacional público*, vol. 2, cit., p. 378-387; and Aust, Anthony, *Modern treaty law and practice*, 4th printing, Cambridge: Cambridge University Press, 2004, p. 305-331.

24 Regarding this convention, see Part IV.

It is interesting to note that the 1969 Vienna Convention endows itself with legal authority even to those States that are not signatories to it, due to the fact that it is generally accepted as a body of law that is "declaratory of general international law", reflecting the current rules of customary international law, embodied in repeated practice of States regarding the matters contained therein.[25] Also, in this sense, the *Restatement of the Law (Third): the Foreign Relations Law of the United States* expresses that the Vienna Convention on the Law of Treaties constitutes a codification of the *customary international law* on treaties.[26] This does not imply, however, that the 1969 Convention is a higher-ranking set of norms than the other treaties concluded according to its provisions. The convention itself clearly states in a number of passages of its text, at the beginning of any provision, the following formula: "unless the treaty otherwise provides". This means that its provisions (dealing with all those issues that are deemed to be optional) will only become applicable in the event the treaty concerned has not provided a particular solution for the question under consideration, or even, if the treaty remains silent on that respect. Hence, the general understanding is that the application of the 1969 Convention is very often of a "suppletory" nature. But, except for such remarks, the finding that must be reported here is that the Vienna Convention on the Law of Treaties, which codifies and contributes to set out in writing the customary rules on the law of treaties, contains a detailed substantial body of rules, which were carefully thought out and studied for twenty years, concerning the practice and technique of international treaties. Hence, both academic writings and case law make repeatedly reference to the rules of the convention.[27]

In Brazil, the text of the 1969 Convention was submitted to the National Congress by the Executive Power, by means of the Explanatory Memorandum nº. 116, only on 22 April 1992 for its consideration. Said Explanatory Memorandum of the Executive Power was approved by the

---

25 Cf. Buergenthal, Thomas (*et all.*). *Manual de derecho internacional público*. México, D.F.: Fondo de Cultura Económica, 1994, p. 79; and Villiger, Mark E., *Commentary on the 1969 Vienna Convention on the Law of Treaties*, cit., p. 27.

26 See *Restatement of the Law (Third): the Foreign Relations Law of the United States*, do American Law Institute, vol. 1 (1987), p. 145. Regarding international custom, see Mazzuoli, Valerio de Oliveira, Algumas questões jurídicas sobre a formação e aplicação do costume internacional, *Revista dos Tribunais*, vol. 921, ano 101, São Paulo, jul./2012, p. 259-278.

27 See Alland, Denis (coord.). *Droit international public*. Paris: PUF, 2000, p. 218.

Committee of Foreign Affairs of the Chamber of Deputies on 2 December of the same year. Thereafter, and following the unanimous approval of the Opinion of the Rapporteur, Deputy Antônio Carlos Mendes Thame, whereby the adoption of the Convention, albeit with reservations to Art. 25 and Art. 66,[28] was recommended, the Explanatory Memorandum became the Draft Legislative Decree 214/1992. The subject addressed by the Draft Legislative Decree 214-C/92, which had been approved by the Committee of Foreign Affairs of the Chamber of Deputies was ready for its inclusion in the *Agenda*,[29] since October 1995. This situation, however, remained unchanged until 19 June 2007, when the debate on the Draft Legislative Decree was then reopened in a single session, although it was not considered by the Chamber on that date. The matter was reopened again (and closed) on several other occasions during the years 2007 (in the months of July, August and September) and 2008 (in November). Finally, on 14 May 2009, the matter was brought back on the Agenda of the Chamber of Deputies, when it was approved and sent to the Federal Senate. The Convention was approved by the Senate on 15 July 2009, by means of the Legislative Decree 496, which was finally passed on 17 July 2009.[30] That very day, the Secretariat of the Senate transmitted the Message 160/09, by Letter 1.401, to the President of the Republic, whereby the passage of the Convention was notified. Finally, on 25 September 2009 the Convention was *ratified* by the Brazilian Government, being subsequently

---

[28] Art. 25 provides that a treaty or a part of a treaty is applied provisionally pending its entry into force, if the treaty itself so provides or the negotiating States have in some other manner so agreed. The reason for considering this article as incompatible with the provisions of the 1988 Brazilian Constitution is that, according to the latter, the Legislative Power must first state its opinion (*referendum*) when dealing with the approval of international treaties (see Part II, Ch. 3, paragraph 3.1.2, below). Art. 66, in turn, provides that (*a*) any one of the parties in dispute concerning the application or the interpretation of Arts. 53 or 64 (which deal with peremptory norms of general international law (*jus cogens*) may, by a written application, submit it to the ICJ, in the event the parties have not agreed to submit the dispute to arbitration, and that (*b*) in the case of a dispute concerning any of the other articles in Part V, any one of the parties may refer it to the Conciliation Commission specified in the *Annex* to the Convention by submitting a request to that effect to the Secretary-General of the United Nations. Brazil was not pleased with that provision either, which sets forth procedures for the settlement of disputes, since the country considers that it should accept them on a case-by-case basis (see Part III, Ch. 4, para. 4.1, below).

[29] See *Diário do Congresso Nacional (Official Gazette of the Senate)*, Section I, edition 28.10.95, p. 3.386.

[30] Published in *Diário do Senado Federal*, n. 109, edition 18.07.2009, p. 33.326-33.327 (the text of the Convention was published in the same *Gazette*, on 28.05.2009).

promulgated at a national level (with reservations to Arts. 25 and 66) by means of Decree 7030, of 14 December 2009.

As is evident, more than forty years had elapsed (from May 1969 to September 2009) until the Vienna Convention on the Law of Treaties was formally ratified by the Brazilian Government. Nevertheless, even before such ratification, the Ministry of Foreign Affairs (also called *Itamaraty*) has always officially negotiated treaties based upon the rules of the 1969 Convention (and also upon those of the 1986 Convention). This is what came out of the reading of the *Manual on Procedures, International Acts and Brazilian Diplomatic Practice*, which has been released since 1984 by the Consular and Legal Department of the Ministry for Foreign Affairs.[31] Which was the reason behind the official (and appropriate) use of a Convention not had yet been ratified? It should be noted that a number of treaties, albeit not ratified, can constitute customs that have become positive international law. That is, an unratified convention does not *constitute* a treaty, but still can constitute *a custom*.[32] This is exactly the current status (in Brazil) of the Vienna Convention on the Law of Treaties between States and International Organizations or between International Organizations (1986).[33] Although it is not technically in force, its legal value remains, not as *treaty*, but as *customary* international law.

It is noteworthy that according to settled case-law of the Federal Supreme Court (Supremo Tribunal Federal (STF)) international treaties other than human rights treaties (such as the 1969 Convention) are on the same footing as federal common laws in terms of the Brazilian domestic legislation. This view stemmed from the Supreme Court's judgment rendered in *RE* 80.004/SE, j. 01.06.1977 (*v. RTJ* 83/809 et seq.) Thus, regardless of any ongoing current discussion on the hierarchy of ordinary international treaties, the fact remains that *all* the provisions laid down in the 1969 Vienna Convention accepted by the Brazilian State must be fully complied with, just as any other federal law in force in the country.

---

31 See Cachapuz de Medeiros, Antônio Paulo. *O poder de celebrar tratados...*, cit., p. 276.

32 See Eustathiades, Konstantinos Th. *Unratified codification conventions: lecture delivered on 11 July 1973* (Gilberto Amado Memorial Lecture). Geneva: United Nations Publ., 1973, p. 7-13; and Cançado Trindade, Antônio Augusto, Reavaliação das fontes do direito internacional público ao início da década de oitenta, cit., p. 112-113. See, by way of contrast, Sinclair, Ian, The impact of the unratified codification convention, in Bos, Adriaan & Siblesz, Hugo (eds.), *Realism in law-making: essays on international law in honour of William Riphagen*, Dordrecht: Martinus Nijhoff, 1986, p. 211-229, who considers that an unratified codification convention displays symptoms of failure of negotiations, and therefore such an unratified convention should not even be recognized as a custom (p. 229).

33 This is also so in relation with the 1961 Vienna Convention on Diplomatic Relations (for those few Members, which have not yet ratified it).

It should be highlighted, however, that even after the entry into force of the 1969 Vienna Convention in Brazil, the Havana Convention on Treaties is still in force (in so far as its provisions are not incompatible with Vienna Convention). The Havana Convention was concluded on 20 February 1928 on the occasion of the Sixth International American Conference, held in Cuba, and came into force on 29 August 1929. This Convention, which contains 21 articles, was approved by the Brazilian State on 8 January 1929, by means of Decree 5647, and ratified on July 30, and enacted on 22 October 1929 by means of Decree 18956. In addition to Brazil, this Convention was also ratified by Ecuador, Haiti, Honduras, Nicaragua, Panama, Peru and Dominican Republic.

Finally, it should be stressed that the 1969 Vienna Convention is not *retroactive* by virtue of its Art. 4, which sets out that: "Without prejudice to the application of any rules set forth in the present Convention to which treaties would be subject under international law independently of the Convention, the Convention applies only to treaties which are concluded by States after the entry into force of the present Convention with regard to such States".[34] This means that a Convention is valid *ex nunc* for those States when it enters into force with regard to such States.[35] Art. 4 itself, however, excludes the application of any rules *set forth* in the present Convention to which treaties would be subject under international law *independently* of the Convention; this shows that the Convention establishes a number of norms that, in fact, were already accepted as mandatory as a result of an international custom.[36] Thus, treaties concluded before the entry into force of the 1969 Convention with regards to an individual State will continue to be governed by the existing regulations. Nevertheless, nothing will prevent norms set out by the 1969 Convention from being applied to those treaties insofar as they are subject to them by virtue of general international law, regardless of the 1969 Convention.

---

[34] See Villiger, Mark E. *Commentary on the 1969 Vienna Convention on the Law of Treaties*, cit., p. 109-114; and Boyle, Alan, Reflections on the treaty as a law-making instrument, cit., p. 1.

[35] See the precedent provided for in Art. 20 of 1928 Havana Convention on Treaties, which states that: "The present convention does not affect obligations previously undertaken by contracting parties through international agreements".

[36] See Villiger, Mark E. *Commentary on the 1969 Vienna Convention on the Law of Treaties*, cit., p. 110: "In other words, they concern Convention rules which are declaratory of customary international law. Whether such customary rules underlying the Convention exist, is decided according to the usual conditions for the formation of customary law".

Should there be no norms in the Convention (based upon general international law) that are applicable to the specific case, all the consolidated legal situations prior to the entry into force of the Convention with regard to the State concerned will be governed by the existing regulation, to the exclusion of the 1969 Convention, in order to comply with the principle of legal certainty. As noted above, even those treaties concluded after the entry into force of the Convention (which took place on 27 January 1980) are to be governed by the previous regulation in those States that has not yet ratified it,[37] unless certain norms set out in the Conventions are applicable to them as a result of general international law.[38]

1.4 Concept of treaty

One of the first issues the Vienna Convention on the Law of Treaties had to address was the exact definition of *international treaty.* This was due to the lack of accuracy that the most representative international law scholars had used in characterizing this instrument.

It should be noted that McNair once defined, upon the base of the first reports of Lauterpacht for the International Law Commission of the United Nations, a treaty as "a written agreement by which two or more States or international organizations create or intend to create a relation between themselves operating within the sphere of international law".[39]

The final text of the 1969 Vienna Convention, for its part, set out a fairly detailed concept of treaty in Art. 2(1)(a) drafted as follows:

> "1. For the purposes of the present Convention:
> (a) 'treaty' means an international agreement concluded between States in written form and governed by international law, whether embodied in a single instrument or in two or more related instruments and whatever its particular designation".[40]

---

37 Such was the case, e.g., with regard to the United Nations Convention on the Law of the Sea, concluded (on 10 December 1982) *after* the entry into force of the Vienna Convention on the Law of Treaties (on 27 January 1980) and ratified by Brazil (on 12 November 1987, having entered into force at an international level in 1994) *prior to* Brazil's ratification of the Vienna Convention (on 25 September 2009).

38 See Cassese, Antonio. *Diritto internazionale* (a cura di Paola Gaeta). Bologna: Il Mulino, 2006, p. 232.

39 McNair, Arnold Duncan. *The law of treaties*, cit., p. 4.

40 Likewise, the 1986 Vienna Convention on the Law of Treaties between States and International Organizations or between International Organizations defines the term "treaty"

This definition of treaty in the 1969 Convention is set out, as could not be otherwise, in terms eminently *formal*, without taking into consideration neither the *content* nor the *nature* of the conventional provisions.[41] Thus, in light of public international law a treaty is nothing more than an *instrument* serving as a means for expressing legal rules. They have a variable content, which can address matters of a diverse nature. Therefore, following the approach taken here, a treaty means any and all formal agreement concluded between subjects of public international law, governed by the law of nations, and aimed at having *legal effects* for the contracting parties. Furthermore, according to the definition given by Paul Reuter, a treaty is the expression of a meeting of the minds, attributable to two or more subjects of international law, and conceived to have legal effects according to the norms of international law.[42] This formalistic approach of a treaty, however, poses some difficulties when it comes to ascertain whether some international texts are of a real conventional nature and whether or not they are capable of imposing obligations upon the parties concerned. The ICJ on many occasions had doubts about the *substantial* conventional nature of a given instrument. By way of example, the *Ambatielos* case (preliminary objection) rendered on 1 July 1952 could be cited, amongst others, whereby the conventional nature of a Declaration accompanying a treaty concluded between Greece and the United Kingdom in 1926[43] was at issue.

From the definition established in the 1969 Vienna Convention Art. 2(1)(a) five *essential elements* that helped shape the concept of international treaty can be drawn out. In addition to that, one more (*albeit*

(also in Art. 2(1)(a) as "an international agreement governed by international law and concluded in written form: (i) between one or more States and one or more international organizations; or (ii) between international organizations, whether that agreement is embodied in a single instrument or in two or more related instruments and whatever its particular designation".

41 See Klabbers, Jan. *The concept of treaty in international law*. The Hague: Kluwer Law International, 1996, p. 37-64; De La Guardia, Ernesto, *Derecho de los tratados internacionales*, cit., p. 110-120; and Villiger, Mark E., *Commentary on the 1969 Vienna Convention on the Law of Treaties*, cit., p. 74-84.

42 Reuter, Paul. *Introducción al derecho de los tratados*, cit., p. 45. See, to the same effect, Remiro Brotons, Antonio, *Derecho internacional público*, vol. 2, cit., p. 31: "A treaty is a manifestation of a meeting of the minds from where *rights and duties* are deduced for the parties according to the rules of international law" [italics in original].

43 See Alland, Denis (coord.). *Droit international public*, cit., p. 215-216.

non essential) element could also be drawn in relation to the designation, which will be analyzed in the following paragraphs.

1.4.1 International agreement

The Convention states, in the first place, that a treaty means an "international *agreement*". What does that mean? As is commonly known, under public international law the guiding principle of free consent still applies. Such a principle was born with the advent of the French Revolution and later with that of the legal positivism, it became one of the most important factors governing international relations. Accordingly, and since treaties are the main source of public international law, these can only embody what negotiators freely agree to. Therefore, should there exist no meeting of the minds of the contracting parties, no internationally valid agreement is deemed to be concluded.

The volitional component with legal international effects,[44] is thus essential for the coming into existence of that first element that gives shape to the concept of treaty.[45] However, the mere meeting of the minds will not suffice – the term agreement being understood here in its ordinary meaning – for a commitment between subjects of international law to be characterized as a genuine treaty. So, for an international agreement to be considered as a treaty, such agreement, which is about to be concluded, should be understood from a *legal* perspective. That is, it is not enough for an international document to contain a meeting of the minds reflecting the existence of an agreement between the contracting parties. Such an agreement must necessarily be conceived to create a *legally enforceable bond* between the contracting parties in case of non-compliance. Otherwise said, the agreement entered into by the parties must aim at having legal effect.[46] Thus, when reference is made to the fact that a treaty is an "international agreement", what is really meant is that it is an agreement from a strictly legal perspective, as opposed to a moral point of view or any dimension other than the legal perspective. Although the phrase "having legal effect" (as proposed by Chile and Switzerland) has not been added to the Convention by the Drafting Committee of the Vienna Conference, it

44 See Aust, Anthony. *Modern treaty law and practice*, cit., p. 14-15.

45 See Pereira de Araújo, João Hermes. *A processualística dos atos internacionais*. Rio de Janeiro: MRE, 1958, p. 7-8.

46 See Villiger, Mark E. *Commentary on the 1969 Vienna Convention on the Law of Treaties*, cit., p. 77-78.

is clear that the reference made to its legal effect is inherent to the concept of treaty, since this is "an *agreement (...) governed by international law*".[47]

An agreement from a strictly *legal* perspective can only exist when the *animus contrahendi* (that is, the *intention to conclude a contract*) is present. Therefore, the lack of this *animus contrahendi*, namely, the free intention to enter into voluntary relations in order to create mutual obligations for the contracting parties constitutes an insurmountable obstacle for an international treaty to exist under the legal framework of the 1969 Vienna Convention. Moreover, the ICJ dealt with such a question in the case *Qatar v. Bahrain*, concerning the *Minutes* executed on 25 December 1990, signed by the parties and by Saudi Arabia. The ICJ held that the binding or non-binding nature would depend on their "actual terms" and the particular circumstances in which said *Minutes* were drawn up.[48] In this case, the *Minutes* should be "construed as an international agreement giving rise to rights and obligations for the parties concerned, since they contained the commitments the parties had undertaken".[49]

Consequently, having legal effects is inherent to any treaty. Furthermore, they intrinsically present a double nature, this being the reason why they can only be considered as an *act of law* and a *norm* as well. Since they rise out of a *licit act* derived from human will, capable of having legal effect in the field of law and aimed at a specific purpose, treaties are deemed to be an *act of law*. Therefore, as a result of their application in the practice (that is, the application of the *act*) treaties can also be characterized as a *norm*.[50]

In this vein, neither *gentlemen's agreements*, nor *memoranda of understanding*, nor *statements*, nor *joint communiqués*, nor *arrangements* nor other documents lacking *animus contrahendi* can be considered as *treaties* in the full sense of the legal term. The aforementioned is without prejudice to legal relevance that those instruments may have in the sphere of international relations, even from an economic perspective (by way of example, reference should be made to the so-called "*Stand-by Ar-*

---

47 See De La Guardia, Ernesto. *Derecho de los tratados internacionales*, cit., p. 111.

48 See *ICJ Reports* (1994), p. 121-122.

49 Shaw, Malcolm N. *Direito internacional*, cit., p. 673.

50 With regard to the distinction between treaties as *act of law* and as a *norm*, see Reuter, Paul, Le traité international, acte et norme, *Archives de Philosophie du Droit*, t. 32, Paris: Sirey, 1987, p. 111-117, which was also made available in Reuter, Paul, *Le développement de l'ordre juridique international: écrits de droit international*, Paris: Economica, 1995, p. 331-338.

rangements", which are concluded with FMI in order to solve problems revolving around balance of payments, temporary or cyclical deficit[51]). All of these are acts concluded *outside the sphere of treaty law.* They can be defined as "instruments derived from negotiations conducted between State representatives authorized to bind the States concerned and charged with the task of framing their relations, without necessarily having legally binding effects".[52] Therefore, despite being *international* acts, they lack the typical features of *treaties*. Hence, the conclusion to be drawn is that each and every treaty constitutes an international act, while not every single international act can really be deemed to be a *treaty*.[53]

In short, a *treaty* involves the existence of an international *agreement* from a legal perspective between the contracting parties, which enables the effective application of *sanctions or penalties* of a legal nature as well in the event of non-compliance.

1.4.2 Concluded in written form

The second constituent component of the concept of treaty laid down in Convention concerns the *written form*.[54] This is due to the fact that

51 The legal nature of the "*Stand-by Agreements*", which should not be confused with the "Letter of Intent" addressed to the IMF has been analyzed elsewhere (see Mazzuoli, Valerio de Oliveira. *Natureza jurídica e eficácia dos acordos* stand-by *com o FMI*. São Paulo: RT, 2005, 351p.). Those Letters of Intent are documents that *form an integral par*t of the *Stand-by* Agreement (or arrangement) and, therefore, they have a more restricted scope. Consequently, these two instruments have a different legal nature: a Letter of Intent can be characterized as "*gentlemen's agreements*" (coupled with "extralegal" penalties in case of non-compliance), while the *Stand-by* Agreements themselves are to be regarded as "unilateral decisions made by the IMF" aimed at providing its financial resources to support the objectives and policies stated in the Letter of Intent of the Member State concerned.

52 Dinh, Nguyen Quoc; Daillier, Patrick & Pellet, Alain. *Direito internacional público*, 2. ed. Transl. by Vítor Marques Coelho. Lisboa: Fundação Calouste Gulbenkian, 2003, p. 395.

53 See Villiger, Mark E. *Commentary on the 1969 Vienna Convention on the Law of Treaties*, cit., p. 77.

54 The same rule was set forth in the *Projeto de Código de Direito Internacional Público* (1911) (*Draft Code of International Public Law*) by Epitácio Pessoa. It required the written from for the conclusion of any treaties, as well as for their confirmation, renewal, restoration or continuance (Art. 200), and even for their interpretation (Art. 201). Also, the 1928 Havana Convention on Treaties – following the provision proposed by Epitácio Pessoa – set forth that "the written form is an essential condition of treaties", and that "confirmation, prorogation, renewal or continuance, shall also be made in writing unless other stipulations have been made" (Art. 2). On this subject, see Mazzuoli, Valerio

treaties, unlike customs, are basically *formal* agreements. And such formal nature implies (necessarily) a written *form*.[55] Therefore, the written form constitutes the only means by which the contracting parties can put on record their mutually agreed upon purposes after the conduct of negotiations. In fact, this rule had already been set forth in Art. 2 of the 1928 Havana Convention on Treaties, which states that: "The written form is an essential condition of treaties", and that: "confirmation, prorogation, renewal or continuance, shall also be made in writing unless other stipulations have been made".[56]

Consequently, the conclusion of a treaty in verbal form does not satisfy the formality of requirements. Furthermore, this form of conclusion of a treaty lacks the clarity and certainty that a treaty in writing presupposes, and prevents it from being made subject to the democratic control carried out by the Parliament. Only the written form makes it possible for a treaty to become immemorial in relations between peoples.[57] Moreover, it is not democratic that just a few persons conclude an agreement having effects on the entire people of a given Nation, without giving them the chance to be aware of what was agreed upon.[58] The verbal conclusion of a treaty is even incompatible with the historic form of conclusion of treaties itself, taking into account that the first known treaty concluded in human history was engraved in cuneiform writing in silver tablet, between the King of the Hittite, Hattusili III, and the Egyptian pharaoh, Ramses II, of the Nineteenth dynasty, around 1280 and 1272 before Christ, as discussed above. Hence, the 1969 Convention excluded from its scope of application the agreement concluded not in written form. In fact, Art. 3 of the Convention states the Convention does not apply to international agreements not in written forms. However, the same provision adds that this fact shall not affect "the legal force of such agreements", nor "the application to them of any of the rules set forth in the present Convention to

---

de Oliveira, Apontamentos sobre o direito dos tratados no Projeto de Código de Direito Internacional Público de Epitácio Pessoa, in Franca Filho, Marcílio Toscano; Mialhe, Jorge Luís & Job, Ulisses da Silveira (orgs.), *Epitácio Pessoa e a codificação do direito internacional*, Porto Alegre: Sergio Antonio Fabris, 2013, p. 517-518.

55 See Sepúlveda, César. *Derecho internacional*, 26. ed. México, D.F.: Porrúa, 2009, p. 128.

56 See Klabbers, Jan. *The concept of treaty in international law*, cit., p. 49-50.

57 See Sette Câmara, José. *The ratification of international treaties*. Toronto: The Ontario Publishing Company Limited, 1949, p. 48.

58 See Mello, Celso D. de Albuquerque. *Direito constitucional internacional: uma introdução*, 2. ed. (reviewed), Rio de Janeiro: Renovar, 2000, p. 271-272.

which they would be subject under international law independently of the Convention" (Art. 3, *(a)* and *(b)*).

As can be seen, the 1969 Convention *recognizes* the existence of other type of international acts of law, namely, not in written form, which can also be validly embodied in such a way, having *legal* effect at an international level.[59] This is the reason why legal scholars understand that "there appears to be no reason why international law does not recognize the validity of verbal and even tacit and implicit treaties", as ruled upon by the Permanent Court of International Justice in the cases *Free Zones of Upper Savoy and the District of Gex* and *Legal status of the Free City of Danzig*, in 1924 and 1932, respectively.[60] However, the 1969 Convention rules concerning the conclusion, entry into force, operation and termination of treaties falling under the abovementioned Convention[61] shall not apply to verbal (or even tacit or implicit) agreements, since those rules entail a greater level of certainty in the international relations, in addition to more democratic transparency throughout the concluding phases of a treaty.

1.4.3 Concluded between States or international organizations

The 1969 Convention provides that treaties are international agreements concluded "between States".[62] It is obvious that treaties, since they

---

59 See Sinclair, Ian. *The Vienna Convention on the Law of Treaties*, cit., p. 6; Remiro Brotons, Antonio, *Derecho internacional público*, vol. 2, cit., p. 29-30; Klabbers, Jan, *The concept of treaty in international law*, cit., p. 5; Aust, Anthony, Modern treaty law and practice, cit., p. 7; Fitzmaurice, Malgosia & Elias, Olufemi, *Contemporary issues in the law of treaties*, Utrecht: Eleven, 2005, p. 10-11; and Villiger, Mark E., *Commentary on the 1969 Vienna Convention on the Law of Treaties*, cit., p. 101-106. With respect to some types of agreements not in written form, see McNair, Arnold Duncan, *The law of treaties*, cit., p. 7-15. It should be recalled that Henry Wheaton had already recommended that verbal agreements should, to the extent possible, be embodied in the form of a written agreement, so as to avoid future disputes. See Wheaton, Henry. *Elements of international law*, vol. I, 6. ed. rev. London: Stevens & Sons, 1929, p. 488.

60 Pereira, André Gonçalves & Quadros, Fausto de. *Manual de direito internacional público*, 3. ed. (reviewed and extended), (8th reprint). Coimbra: Almedina, 2009, p. 174. Regarding the application of agreements not in a written form by the ICJ, see D'Aspremont, Jean, The International Court of Justice and tacit conventionality, *Questions of International Law*, Zoom-in vol. 18 (2015), p. 3-17.

61 See Fitzmaurice, Malgosia. The practical working of the law of treaties, in Evans, Malcolm D. (ed.), *International law*, 3. ed., Oxford: Oxford University Press, 2010, p. 174.

62 See also Art. 1.º of the Convention which provides that: "The present Convention applies to treaties *between States*".

are international acts, can only be concluded by entities capable of taking on *rights and obligations* in the international sphere. However, not only States enjoy nowadays that prerogative. International intergovernmental organizations such as the United Nations (UN) and the Organization of American States (OAS) have been granted, since the conclusion of the 1986 Vienna Convention on the Law of Treaties between States and International Organizations or between International Organizations, international capacity to conclude treaties (as it shall be analyzed in Part IV). The only difference lies in the fact that whilst States have capacity to conclude treaties dealing with *any* subject matter, international organizations are only entitled to conclude treaties related to their main purposes and needs, having therefore a more *restricted* scope of performance.

The concept of treaty contained in the Vienna Convention also refers to an agreement *concluded* ("*concluded*... in written form..."). This expression, however, should not be construed as having a wider scope of application than its effective and actual meaning. As far as some Romance languages are concerned, such as, Portuguese, Spanish or French, the verb "*concluir*" (to conclude) means that something is *ready or has been finished.* Therefore, the fact that these languages derived from Latin use this verb may lead to some confusion as to the application of public international law. This is so, because this verb "*concluir*" (to conclude) generally denotes that the entire series of required steps for the *execution* of an international agreement has been taken (the given execution being completed through its *ratification* and the subsequent exchange of the instruments constituting the treaty, the point in time from which, as a general rule, the agreement can eventually *enter into force*). Hence, some internationalists understand (including foreign legal scholars such as Paul Fauchille and Dionisio Anzilotti, and Brazilian ones such as Hildebrando Accioly and Francisco Rezek) that a treaty that has only been signed constitutes merely a "draft treaty", in the event it has not entered into force at an international level.[63] This stance is, however, (rightly) put into question by Pontes de Miranda, according to whom, a signed treaty *does constitute a treaty*, even though its *ratification* and effective *entry into force* are still pending at an international level. Otherwise said, a signed interna-

63 See, in this sense, Rezek, José Francisco, *Direito dos tratados*, cit., p. 24, according to whom, prior to its entry into force "there exist no *international agreement* but an executed *draft agreement*, subject to a variety of occurrences that could make it fall into oblivion in the historical archives of international relations, to join the ranks of the draft treaties that died quietly".

tional treaty *has already come into existence*, but before its entry into force it cannot be deemed to be a legal transaction that has been perfected.[64] Furthermore, the point of view of those who argue that a signed treaty constitutes merely a *draft* treaty fails to provide any explanation to justify, for instance, the inclusion of the rule laid down in Art. 18(a) of the 1969 Vienna Convention, according to which a State "*is obliged* to refrain from acts which would defeat the object and purpose of a treaty *when* (...) *it has signed the treaty* or has exchanged instruments constituting the treaty subject to ratification, acceptance or approval, *until it shall have made its intention clear not to become a party to the treaty*".[65] Another example is the inclusion of the rule set forth in Art. 24(4) of said Convention, providing that: "The provisions of a treaty regulating the authentication of its text, the establishment of the consent of States to be bound by the treaty, the manner or date of its entry into force, reservations, the functions of the depositary and other matters arising necessarily before the entry into force of the treaty apply *from the time of the adoption of its text*". To summarize, the previous considerations can only lead to the conclusion that the term "concluded", which appears in the definition of the concept of treaty set out in the Convention, quite simply means a *negotiated and signed* agreement, that is, an agreement *entered into between* the contracting parties, comprising neither the confirmation of such an act at an international level (unless dealing with an agreement in simplified form) nor its entry into force.[66]

It has never been argued that between 23 May 1969 and 27 January 1980 – that is, during those almost 11 years – the Vienna Convention on the Law of Treaties was not a *treaty* itself because it had not *entered into force* yet at an international level. It was evident that the aforementioned Convention was *already a treaty* (just) awaiting its entry into force at an international level. Whenever the text of a given convention is adopted, its subsequent *authentication* and *signature* cast away any doubts as to the

---

64 See Pontes de Miranda. *Comentários à Constituição de 1967 com a Emenda n. 1 de 1969*, t. III, 3. ed. Rio de Janeiro: Forense, 1987, p. 336.

65 As far as Art. 18 of the Convention is concerned, see Part II, Ch. 1, item 1.5.1.6, below.

66 See, in the same sense, De La Guardia, Ernesto, *Derecho de los tratados internacionales*, cit., p. 141-142. It should be noted that during the ILC's work, Special Rapporteur, Gerald Gray Fitzmaurice had also taken a similar stance, in the following terms: "The solution lies in regarding *conclusion* as the process by which the States concerned definitely give their consent to *the text*, though not necessarily their agreement to be bound by it" [emphasis added]. See *Yearbook of the International Law Commission* (1956), vol. II, p. 121.

existence of a treaty "concluded" between States, just for the sake of using the terms set out in the Convention.

In short, what the Vienna Convention really meant in this regard was that an international treaty is an instrument *concluded between* States (or international organizations).

1.4.4 Governed by international law

The concept set forth in the 1969 Convention defines a treaty as being an instrument "governed by international law". This means that for an international act to be deemed a treaty it has to operate within the scope of application of the law of nations, that is, it has to be internationally binding and enforceable. Two States can formally (in written form) conclude an international agreement, and such an agreement (which still has *animus contrahendi*) cannot be deemed a treaty because it is not governed by the law of nations, in the event it is governed by the *internal law* of one of the contracting States.[67] Thus, the phrase "governed by international law" means that the contracting parties intend to create *legal obligations* between each other, which will be governed by public international law. Such an approach can be traced back to the first works of the United Nations International Law Commission (ILC), which are reflected in the *travaux préparatoires* of the Vienna Conference on the Law of Treaties, whereby the view was expressed that it would be obvious that each and every agreement capable of being internationally enforceable would be deemed a *treaty*.[68]

The fact remains that a number of well renowned legal writers did not even highlight the practical importance of this aspect of the concept of treaty, having confined themselves to deal with the *will* and *nature* of the contracting parties, completely disregarding the *governing law* of the commitment they undertake.[69] Nevertheless, the relevance of the phe-

---

67 See De La Guardia, Ernesto. *Derecho de los tratados internacionales*, cit., p. 113-114; Fitzmaurice, Malgosia & Elias, Olufemi, *Contemporary issues in the law of treaties*, cit., p. 20-21; and Villiger, Mark E., *Commentary on the 1969 Vienna Convention on the Law of Treaties*, cit., p. 81.

68 See Remiro Brotons, Antonio. *Derecho internacional público*, vol. 2, cit., p. 32; Klabbers, Jan, *The concept of treaty in international law*, cit., p. 55-62; and Aust, Anthony, *Modern treaty law and practice*, cit., p. 17.

69 See, in this sense, Rousseau, Charles, *Principes généraux du droit international public*, t. I (Introduction, Sources), Paris: A. Pedone, 1944, p. 143.

nomenon cannot be neglected, especially, if it is to differentiate a *treaty* from an *international contract*. The latter also has the first three features of the concept of a treaty, although it should be pointed out that it is not completely *governed* by international law. Whilst it is true that no agreement concluded between States – precisely because it is entered into *between subjects of international law* – can set aside the application of the law of nations, it is not less true that a great number of the international commitments undertaken by the same States are (purposefully) not *completely* regulated by international law, therefore not falling under the scope of application of the Law of Treaties. Consequently, an agreement between States, whereby the national jurisdiction of one of them is chosen for settlement of their disputes, cannot be deemed a *treaty*.[70] A marked difference between an international treaty and an international contract lies in the *governing law* applicable to each of them, given that contracts are primarily governed by rules of an internal legal system of an individual State, whilst treaties are completely governed by public international law principles and rules, as stated in Art. 38 of the Statute of the ICJ.[71]

1.4.5 Whether embodied in a single instrument or in two or more related instruments

In addition to the main text of the treaty there can exist other accompanying instruments, such as, additional protocols and annexes, which may have been simultaneously prepared with the text of the treaty. At this point no issues are present. Nonetheless, issues arise when the instruments that make an integral part of the treaty as a whole are prepared at different points in time, each of them being signed on behalf of just *one of*

---

70 See Reuter, Paul. *Introducción al derecho de los tratados*, cit., p. 50. For an opposite opinion, see Rezek, José Francisco, *Direito dos tratados*, cit., p. 80-81, according to whom, "no agreement between States can avoid the application of the international law, even though, the contracting States, making use of the sovereign powers that that legal system confers upon them, agree that such an agreement be governed by an internal legal system", even in the case that one of the contracting parties "refers to its own judiciary the potential controversies arising out of the application of the treaty" [emphasis in the original]. See also the grounds upon which the rule was based, in: Lauterpacht, Hersch [Special Rapporteur], *Yearbook of the International Law Commission* (1953), vol. II, p. 90-162.

71 See Brichambaut, Marc Perrin de; Dobelle, Jean-François & Coulée, Frédérique. *Leçons de droit international public*, 2. ed. Paris: Dalloz, 2011, p. 268.

the parties, as it is the case when an agreement is concluded through the *exchange of Diplomatic Notes.*[72]

It is clear that the 1969 Vienna Convention was also designed to cover this type of international agreement, which falls under the law of treaties, and is perfectly capable of having legal effect between the contracting parties.[73] In other words, the incorporation of such an element (multiplicity of instruments) into the concept of treaty contributed to the enshrining of the exchange of diplomatic notes as a *suitable* means for the conclusion of treaties.

The recognition provided for in the Vienna Convention to conclude treaties "whether embodied in a single instrument or in two or more related instruments" served to broaden the formal set of international commitments as defined in a broad sense, which were then understood according to the aforementioned formula prepared by Rousseau: international commitments = treaties (agreements, conventions, covenants, protocols, *modus vivendi,* etc.) + agreement in simplified form (exchange of diplomatic notes, letters, statements, etc.).[74]

Finally, an interesting question that must be asked relates to how States express their *consent* to be bound by an agreement through the exchange of diplomatic notes. The response to such an inquiry is to be found in Art. 13 of the 1969 Convention which establishes the following: "The consent of States to be bound by a treaty constituted by instruments exchanged between them is expressed by that exchange when: (*a*) the instruments provide that their exchange shall have that effect; or (*b*) it is otherwise established that those States were agreed that the exchange of instruments should have that effect".[75]

1.4.6 Absence of a particular designation

The 1969 Convention clearly states that the term *treaty* means an international agreement governed by international law, "whatever its particular designation". That is, *treaty* is the generic term, while a number of

---

72 See Klabbers, Jan. *The concept of treaty in international law*, cit., p. 44-46; De La Guardia, Ernesto, *Derecho de los tratados internacionales*, cit., p. 161; Aust, Anthony, *Modern treaty law and practice*, cit., p. 18-19; and Villiger, Mark E., *Commentary on the 1969 Vienna Convention on the Law of Treaties*, cit., p. 80.

73 See Rezek, José Francisco. *Direito dos tratados*, cit., p. 115-116.

74 Cf. Rousseau, Charles. *Principes généraux du droit international public*, t. I, cit., p. 158.

75 For further details, see Maresca, Adolfo, *Il diritto dei trattati...*, cit., p. 167-176.

other designations may also be used, varying according to the form, content, object and purpose of the agreement concerned. Therefore, the term treaty covers any form of agreement in written form concluded between States (or international organizations) and governed by international law. Consequently, in order to establish whether a treaty exists or not, it should be ascertained whether the aforementioned requirements or essential elements have been complied with, regardless of what the specific designation given to the instrument concerned is.

Thus, those are the key elements that the 1969 Vienna Convention takes into consideration in order to define the concept of treaty. This definition, however, is limited to the scope of application of the Convention itself, that is, to those agreements concluded in accordance with the rules of the Convention, given that the aforementioned Convention did not broaden the definition of the term treaty to include other types of agreements, such as those concluded in a form other than in writing (whose legal force, as a matter of fact, is also recognized in Art. 3(a) of the Convention). Hence the need for a broader concept that also applies to agreements concluded outside of the framework set forth in the Convention.

For this reason, an "international treaty" should be defined as a formal meeting of the minds concluded between States or intergovernmental organizations among themselves, governed by the law of nations with the intention to produce legal effects on the contracting parties.

1.5 Treaty terminology

The 1969 Vienna Convention, as stated above, comprises all the different designations under which international treaties may be referred to as. Furthermore, as already discussed, the definition of treaty in the Convention was worded in strictly *formal* terms, regardless of the *content* or the *nature* of its provisions, given that the treaty is nothing more than an *instrument*, whereby legal rules are conveyed. These legal rules laid down in this formal instrument referred to as *treaty* may deal with issues of a varied nature, being logical then, that in the international practice each agreement (dealing with different type of subject matters) is designated the way the negotiators deem most appropriate to the nature of the subject matter concerned. However, the fact remains that, regardless of its designation, the international act will be deemed a *treaty* if it constitutes a formal meeting of the minds (between States or intergovernmental organizations) governed by public international law and aimed at having legal effect between the contracting parties.

The term *treaty* establishes a generic expression, encompassing a number of other designations, as will be seen below. Thus, in the general conventional practice a number of designations can be identified to refer to treaties, depending on the subject matter dealt with, its purpose, the capacity of the parties, the number of the contracting parties, etc.[76] Legal writers, in turn, are making efforts to outline the main aspects of each of these types of instruments, taking into account the designation given to them.[77] Some of them, as stated above, are not *treaties* from a technical point of view (such as the so-called *gentlemen's agreements* and other ones that will be discussed below).

There follow the different terms and specific senses of words (although not all of them are indicative of genuine *treaties*) very often used in the practice of international relations:

a) Treaty. This is the primary generic term set forth in the 1969 Vienna Convention in order to designate each and every international agreement, be it bilateral or multilateral, of utmost political importance, whatever its particular designation (Art. 2(1)*(a)*. Typically, this term has been used to designate solemn commitments concluded between States and/or international organizations, whose object, purpose, number of contracting parties and their corresponding powers are of great importance. These include, for example, peace, friendship, arbitration, cooperation, navigation treaties, and so forth.

Whilst the term treaty (*tractatus*), from an etymological point of view, conveys the idea of laborious debates, transactions or negotiations, the term *convention*, on the contrary, suggests the notion of a conclusion

---

76 Concerning multiplicity of designations for treaties, see Rousseau, Charles, *Principes généraux du droit international public*, t. I, cit., p. 149-154; Accioly, Hildebrando, *Tratado de direito internacional público*, vol. I, 2. ed., Rio de Janeiro: MRE, 1956, p. 543-551; Myers, Denys P., The names and scope of treaties, *American Journal of International Law*, vol. 51, n. 3 (July 1957), p. 574-605; Pereira de Araújo, João Hermes, *A processualística dos atos internacionais,* cit., p. 9-17; McNair, Arnold Duncan, *The law of treaties*, cit., p. 22-30; Rezek, José Francisco, *Direito dos tratados*, cit., p. 83-115; Remiro Brotons, Antonio, *Derecho internacional público*, vol. 2, cit., p. 36-38; Klabbers, Jan, *The concept of treaty in international law*, cit., p. 42-44; and Mello, Celso D. de Albuquerque, *Curso de direito internacional público*, vol. I, cit., p. 212-214.

77 See, in this sense, Brierly, J. L., *Direito internacional*, 2. ed., transl. by M. R. Crucho de Almeida, Lisboa: Fundação Calouste Gulbenkian, 1968, p. 323: "In international law there is no uniformity in the terms to be used to designate the contractual agreements between States. Out of the variety of the terms used, namely, treaty, convention, covenant, act, declaration, protocol, none of them has a very precise meaning".

of an already pre-negotiated agreement amongst the negotiators, which is, in turn, a source of general rules of the law of nations, the fact remains that the Vienna Convention eventually put these terms (*treaty* and *convention*) on equal footing with synonymic value. In this vein, although the different Brazilian Constitutions have always used the term "treaty" alongside other expressions such as "agreement" and "convention", giving the impression that *treaties*, *agreements* and *conventions* designate different things, the truth is that this drafting technique is currently superfluous and has no practical value at all.

Conversely, if this issue is analyzed from a different perspective, it seems understandable that some countries (such as Brazil) include in their Constitutional provisions detailed terminology as to the international acts falling within the competencies of the Executive Power and those of the National Congress. This is to ensure that those branches of State do not evade their responsibilities under the international commitments they undertook, or even, that one of them (the Executive Power, for instance) completely ignores one of the other Powers (the Legislative Power, for instance) and prevents the latter from expressing its opinion on the content of what has been agreed upon at an international level. Despite the fact of the term *treaty* being of a generic nature, the redundant terminology used in the 1988 Brazilian Constitution is aimed at preventing the Brazilian body, which is competent to conclude treaties, from entering into onerous international acts without submitting them to rigorous scrutiny of the Legislative Power, under the fallacious pretext that the given legal transaction did not constitute a *treaty*, but a mere international *act*, or something of that sort, making the need to put the conclusion of that act to the vote of the National Congress to become moot. Thus, the conclusion of treaties would depend solely on the will of the President of the Republic. In this regard, it is worth highlighting the relevant provisions of the 1988 Brazilian Constitution that clearly set forth the specific competences of the Executive Power and those of Legislative Power, as follows: Art. 84(VIII) establishes that the President of the Republic shall have the exclusive power to conclude "*international treaties, conventions and acts, ad referendum* of the National Congress", and Art. 49(I), sets forth that it is the exclusive competence of the National Congress to make final decisions on "*international treaties, agreements or acts* which entail encumbrances or onerous undertakings affecting the national property". Certainly, it was the above mentioned kind of fraud or swindling that the Brazilian constitutional tried to avoid.

In any event, however, treaty is still the generic term that is widely used in practice.

b) *Convention*. This term started to be used in the sense currently used as a result of the proliferation of international congresses and conferences dealing with matters of utmost importance for the international society, which resulted in international acts that created general rules of public international law reflecting a uniform stance of the contracting parting in relation to issues of general interest.

The term *convention* implies a type of solemn (and multilateral) treaty, whereby the will of the parties is not really divergent, as in the case of the so-called *treaty-contracts*, but parallel and uniform, that is termed *law-making treaties*. Examples of the latter include the Vienna conventions on diplomatic and consular relations, as well as the Geneva conventions on humanitarian law, etc. Lastly, it should be noted that the term convention has been used indiscriminately – mainly by the Brazilian constitutions – alongside the generic term *treaty*. Undoubtedly, it is more appropriate to reserve the term *convention* to designate multilateral acts resulting from international conferences dealing with matters of general interest. For this reason, international practice is prone to avoid using the term under analysis to designate *bilateral* acts, whatever their importance, even more so if they formally execute a meeting of the minds with different purposes.[78]

Quite a significant example of the term under consideration, which clearly highlights the above mentioned features, is the Vienna Convention on the Law of Treaties. This is one of the most important multilateral treaties that has ever been concluded throughout the history of international relations. Nevertheless, the distinction between treaty and convention does not stand up to a detailed analysis of the international standard-setting texts, which shows that there still remains some confusion as to the usage of both terms (treaty and convention).

c) *Pact and/or Covenant*. The term Covenant has been used in the Agreement constituting the Covenant of the League of Nations of 1919. On the other hand, the term Pact has been used to restrict the political purpose of a given treaty, whose example is the Pact of Steel concluded in Berlin in 1939. Sometimes, the term pact is used as a synonym of treaty, as in the case of the 1928 *General Treaty for Renunciation of War as an Instrument of National Policy* (also known as Kellog-Briand Pact or Pact of Paris) or the Warsaw Pact concluded in 1955. In the framework of the United Nations the term chosen (in the English version) was *covenant* in order to name

78 See Pereira de Araújo, João Hermes. *A processualística dos atos internacionais*, cit., p. 13-14.

two of the most important treaties concluded under its aegis, namely, the International Covenant on Civil and Political Rights and the International Covenant on Economic, Social and Cultural Rights, concluded in New York in 1966 (and also known as International Covenants of Human Rights). Another peculiar element of this terminology analysis is that in some cases the informal name of the convention is used instead of its technical designation, also in the sphere of the international protection of human rights, as in the case of the American Convention of Human Rights (1969), whose informal name is the Pact of San Jose, Costa Rica).

d) Agreement. The term *agreement* is frequently used to designate treaties of an economic, financial, commercial or cultural nature. These *agreements*, however, may deal with reciprocal protection, disarmament programs, cooperation on border issues, arbitration, public policy issues, etc. Therefore, the term agreement means any bilateral or multilateral acts – very often with a reduced number of contracting parties and of relative importance – that may be of a political, economic, commercial cultural or scientific nature. The origin of the usage of this term *agreement* in this context can be traced back to the *agreement* concluded, under American law, by the President without consultation with the Senate. Nonetheless, this cannot be understood as an *agreement* being an international instrument of lesser relevance, citing as an example of the level of specialty that this term can attain, the *GATT – General Agreement on Tariffs and Trade.*

e) Agreement by exchange of diplomatic notes. The exchange of diplomatic notes is generally used in connection with matters of an administrative nature, as well as with acts aimed at amending or interpreting clauses of acts already concluded. These are agreements signed *at different points in time* and on behalf of just *one of the parties.* The agreements by exchange of diplomatic notes do not differ, as far as their structure is concerned, from agreements in simplified form (or "executive agreements"), which will be discussed in the following paragraphs. Typically, their entry into force occurs right after the exchange of notes, when negotiations are deemed to have definitively come to an end. After the exchange of diplomatic notes, the text of the agreement is published in the Official Gazette without any other formalities.

f) Agreements in simplified form. These agreements are also named *executive agreements,* which is a term of American origin.[79] They desig-

[79] As far as this matter is concerned, see Rodas, João Grandino, Os acordos em forma simplificada, *Revista da Faculdade de Direito da Universidade de São Paulo*, vol. LXVIII, fasc. I (1973), p. 319-340.

nate those treaties concluded by the Executive Power without being necessary to request the consent of the Legislative Power. In most cases, they are concluded by an exchange of diplomatic notes, an exchange of letters or any other similar procedure, with their signature being, as a rule, sufficient for the State to be bound by them. Thus, the main features of these agreements are that their conclusion procedure comes to an end right after negotiations have ended and the instruments are signed, without the need for the Head of State to ratify them. As a general rule, there is no need to ratify the agreements in their simplified form. However, this is not always a valid parameter to differentiate such agreements from the so-called *treaties in due form,* which, in turn, according to the provisions set forth in Art.12 of the 1969 Convention can also enter into force only after being signed. That is why the nature of the executive agreement cannot be in fact ascertained without taking into account their content and form.

There are a number of reasons that prompt the Executive Power to conclude treaties in simplified form, including but not limited to, celerity in the conclusion process, the technical nature of the subject matter of the treaty, the need to keep a certain degree of confidentiality, the diversity of factors related to the contractual transaction, etc. From the Executive Power's perspective, the involvement of the Parliament represents a *delay* in the conduct of the country's international relations, which could turn out to be a factor of hindrance of said international relations. This kind of agreements developed, primarily, in the United States of America, where there is an increasing trend to circumvent the control by the Senate (*fast track* system).[80] The basis for this is contained in the American Constitution itself, whereby the term "treaty" is not accurately defined or determined when such an agreement must be deemed a "treaty". Therefore, in the United States of America, the term "agreement" (in an international context) makes reference to those agreements, which do not require the *advice and consent* of the Senate, whilst the term "treaty" applies to those international commitments requiring the approval of the Senate.[81] The

---

80 Regarding the American procedure for the conclusion of these treaties, see Crandall, Samuel B., *Treaties: their making and enforcement*, 2. ed., Washington, D.C.: John Byrne & Company, 1916, p. 102-120; and Carter, Barry E.; Trimble, Phillip R. & Weiner, Allen S., *International law*, 5. ed., New York: Wolters Kluwer, 2007, p. 159-238.

81 See Wheaton, Henry. *Elements of international law*, vol. I, cit., p. 488, according to whom: "The United States distinguishes for its own purposes treaties which need senatorial assent, and mere agreements, but this is not a question of international law". See also, Soares, Guido Fernando Silva, "Agreements" – "Executive Agreements" – "Gentlemen's Agreements", in França, R. Limongi (coord.), *Enciclopédia Saraiva do Direito*, vol. 5, São

Supreme Court of the United States of America *in re* "United States *v.* Belmont" stated that the binding force of the discussed executive agreements is similar to those of treaties adopted by the Senate. Finally, it is worth clarifying that executive agreements *are treaties* (in simplified form), which are thus of a legal nature, on an equal footing as that of any other international treaty.

Furthermore, it should also be underlined that executive agreements do not always deal with matters of a lesser degree of importance or interest, since they may address complex issues, entailing onerous undertakings affecting national property, etc. Hence some legal scholars understand that the conclusion of executive agreements, which is widely used in the United States because of the peculiarities of the American constitutional system, cannot be justified under the Brazilian constitutional structure. However, in spite of the fact that many constitutions require Parliament approval for all international acts, none of them expressly prohibits the conclusion of executive agreements. It is also crucial to note that, despite the formal differences between the conclusion of international agreements in simplified form and international treaties in the strict sense, there exists no hierarchical difference between them. Consequently, both kinds of agreements have the same legal force and the noncompliance of any of them entails the international responsibility of the defaulting State.

g) Gentlemen's agreements. This term refers to those agreements concluded by gentlemen and governed by moral norms, the observance of which is just a matter of *honor.* These are concluded between Heads of State or Government setting out a policy line to be followed between the parties, being dependent on the time span their parties will remain in office.[82] *Gentlemen*, in this case, means: persons who behave righteously and high-mindedly, which implies the existence of a set of common

---

Paulo: Saraiva, 1977, p. 247-248; and De La Guardia, Ernesto, *Derecho de los tratados internacionales*, cit., p. 158-159. It is important to note that, according to the *fast track* system, the American Legislative Power approves as a whole (with limited debate and within more limited time frames) the trade agreements entered into by the Government of United States of America. Such a system is currently known as *TPA (Trade Promotion Authority)*, whereby the American Legislative branch takes part, *together with* the Executive branch, in the conclusion procedure of trade agreements. This is not applicable to Brazil, where *all the treaties* (even those of a commercial nature) are concluded by the Executive Power with the simultaneous (concomitant) participation of the National Congress (since the Legislative branch in Brazil has a precise time frame, within which it must perform its obligations in the treaty-making process – see Part V, Ch. 1, below).

82 See Rezek, José Francisco. *Direito dos tratados*, cit., p. 73.

moral values among them. As these agreements lack a legal basis, because they do not produce legal effects, they are not deemed treaties.[83] It must be stressed, however, that the gentlemen's agreements do not share the essential features of a treaty, not because of the quality of their parties, who are persons holding high-level offices and taking on "moral" commitments on their account (and not on behalf of the State they represent); such agreements are not treaties because of the *content of the commitment* that the parties take on, since no *animus contrahendi* can be said to exist, which is an essential element for an international agreement to have *legal effects*.[84] Furthermore, gentlemen's agreements are in force as long as one of the parties remains in office. These agreements *could* only be treated as being of a standard-setting nature in that they relate to the *intent* of the parties, but not to their *effects*. Therefore, since they cannot be characterized as being of a legal nature, these *gentlemen's agreements* are not submitted to the democratic control exercised by the Legislative Power.[85]

The purpose of these agreements is to outline the policy lines that their parties intend to follow, which makes them become a deep commitment vis-à-vis the parties concerned. By way of example, reference could be made to the 1907 Root-Takahira Agreement, whereby "Japan undertook the obligation to keep on implementing its policy on limitation of the Japanese immigration to the United States", and the 1917 Lansing-Ishii Agreement, between the same parties.[86] It should be noted that the term gentlemen's agreements differs from the term *Memoranda of Understanding – MOUs*) among States, since the latter are agreements of a more formal nature.[87]

h) Charter. The term Charter is frequently used to establish constituent instruments of international organizations, but it may also be used to designate solemn treaties, whereby rights and obligations for the States parties are set forth. As example of the first modality, reference should be made to the Charter of the United Nations, 1945, and the OAS Charter, 1948; the European Social Charter is an example of the second modality.

---

83 See Kraus, Herbert. Système et fonctions des traités internationaux, *Recueil des Cours*, vol. 50 (1934-IV), p. 325-329.

84 See Rezek, José Francisco. *Direito dos tratados*, cit., p. 74-75.

85 See Mello, Celso D. de Albuquerque. *Direito constitucional internacional...*, cit., p. 273-274.

86 See Klabbers, Jan. *The concept of treaty in international law*, cit., p. 16; and Soares, Guido Fernando Silva, "Agreements" – "Executive Agreements" – "Gentlemen's Agreements", cit., p. 276.

87 For further details on MOUs, see item 1.6, below.

It should be underlined that the usage of the term under analysis to designate a *gentlemen's agreement* (which is not a treaty) called *Atlantic Charter*, 1941, contributed to reinforce the flexibility approach, according to which international acts have been designated in international practice.[88]

i) Protocol. Besides being used to name the results of a diplomatic conference or an agreement less formal than a treaty, the term *protocol* has also been used to designate subsidiary agreements or agreements that maintain a logical relation (e.g., complementation) to an earlier treaty. However, nothing prevents an agreement having no relation whatsoever with another treaty from being named protocol, since the only interest of the terminology of international acts lies in its practical nature. In general, the term "protocol" may refer to agreements that are less formal than treaties, additional agreements, or supplements to existing agreements or agreements already established (e.g., Protocol of Ouro Preto, 1994 additional Protocol to the Treaty of Asunción, 1990, the Kyoto Protocol, 1997 to United Nations Framework Convention on Climate Change, 1992), interpretive agreements of prior treaties or agreements on the prolongation of a pending a legal situation (e.g., Protocol concerning the Prolongation of the Treaty of Alliance (of 31 August 1922) between the Czechoslovak Republic and the Kingdom of the Serbs, Croats and Slovenes, signed in Geneva on 19 September 1928), or even, agreements amending prior treaties (e.g., the Paris Protocol of 25 July 1928 concerning the Agreement revising the Convention of December 18 1923, relating to the organization of the Statute of the Tangier zone). After the closure of an international conference, the documents or instruments adopted during its session are often named *final protocols*. According to Brazilian diplomatic practice the term protocol has been used, preferably, to designate "protocols of intent", which do not contain a meeting of the minds, but only an international commitment at an early stage of development.

j) Act. This term has been used for decades to name a resolution on Inter-American Reciprocal Assistance and Solidarity, also referred as to *Act of Chapultepec*, signed in 1945, at the Inter-American Conference on Problems of War and Peace, held in Mexico City. This term is also used when setting out norms that incorporate the outcome of a conference or an agreement amongst the parties (e.g. the *General Act of Berlin*, 1885). There exist, however, *Acts* that are not treaties (such as, for instance, the so-called *Helsinki Final Act*, 1975, which concluded the Conference on

---

88 See Rezek, José Francisco. *Direito dos tratados*, cit., p. 95.

Security and Cooperation in Europe, and the *Founding Act on Mutual Relations, Cooperation and Security between NATO and the Russian Federation*, 1997). These Acts are not deemed treaties because their binding nature is just moral not legal.[89] The same features are shared by those *acts* encompassing a certain *diplomatic event* of a non-conventional nature (in which case the term normally used is *final act* in order to designate the closure of an international conference, etc.). In this context, it is important to note the indiscriminate use of the terms *final act* and *final protocol* (discussed above).

k) Declaration. This is the term used for those acts that establish certain rules or legal principles, or rules of international law adopting a common policy stance of collective interest. By way of example, reference can be made to the Declaration of Paris, 1856 on maritime law principles in time of war; the Declaration Prohibiting the Discharge of Projectiles and Explosives from Balloons, signed at The Hague in 1907; the Declaration of Mexico, 1945, proclaiming the Inter-American principles. Some of these joint declarations, despite their substantial content, are not *treaties* from a technical point of view, such as, the great Universal Declaration of Human Rights, 1948.[90] Therefore, nothing prevents the term *declaration* from being used as a synonym for treaty. Furthermore, it can also be used to clarify or construe an existing international agreement[91] or set out the viewpoint or the course of action of one or several States on a particular issue. The truth is that when dealing with an instrument named *declaration*, the only way to determine whether it is an act that can be characterized as a *treaty* is to analyze its content (that is, finding out whether its purpose is to set forth rights and obligations between the parties).[92]

---

89 See Brichambaut, Dobelle & Coulée. *Leçons de droit international public*, cit., p. 268.

90 The Universal Declaration of Human Rights was adopted by a United Nations General Assembly (Res. 217 A-III, 10.12.1948) and by means of a conclusion of a multilateral treaty. UN resolutions – though *unilateral acts* of the Organization – are not "treaties" from a technical perspective. A number of scholars, however, consider that the 1948 Declaration (as far as its substantial content is concerned), and despite not being a treaty from a formal perspective, has attained a degree of legal force that goes far beyond (as a consequence of its moral significance, etc.) than that of any international treaty. Moreover, other legal scholars hold (as we also do) than that such Declaration constitutes a *jus cogens* norm (see Part III, Ch. 2, item 2.2.1, below).

91 For more detailed information on the so-called "interpretative declarations" (see Part II, Ch. 2, item 2.7, below).

92 See De La Guardia, Ernesto. *Derecho de los tratados internacionales*, cit., p. 116-117.

l) "*Modus vivendi*". This term is used to designate temporary or provisional agreements, normally, of an economic nature and of relative importance. Their temporary or provisional status is the most characteristic feature of this kind of instrument. The Holy See has made use several times of that type of international agreement to settle pending diplomatic issues with some States. The term *modus vivendi* was also used in other contexts, for instance, to deal with treatment of foreigners (e.g., *modus vivendi* concerning the treatment of Syrian and Lebanese citizens in France, from 6 to 27 December, 1934) and the international regulation of waterways (e.g., *Modus Vivendi* related to the Jurisdiction of the European Commission of the Danube, 13 March 1932). Currently, a *modus vivendi* is deemed to be an agreement entered into by the parties with a view to maintaining the status quo until the final establishment of a state of affairs is materialized, be it by means of the conclusion of a treaty or any other circumstance. In general, such an agreement is established by means of a mere *exchange of diplomatic notes*.

m) *Arrangement*. This term is used to name those temporary agreements that are deprived of any legal nature, such as for instance, those entered into by the IMF (the so-called "*stand-by arrangements*") which, however, cannot be technically deemed treaties because they lack the *animus contrahendi* element necessary for the conclusion of an agreement from a strict legal perspective (see item 1.7, below).[93]

n) *Concordat*. This term is used to designate bilateral agreements of a religious nature concluded between the Holy See and those States, which have a Catholic population. They mainly deal with matters related to the organization of religious cults, the exercising of ecclesiastical administration, etc.[94] From a formal point of view Concordats do not differ at all from treaties *sensu stricto* concluded between subjects of public international law (the Holy See being necessarily one of the parties). Thus, all general principles of the Law of Treaties apply to them; however, from a substantial viewpoint, Concordats differ from treaties in due form in that the first ones strictly deal with *religious* matters. The Holy See, however, in its capacity as a legal entity under international law, is not precluded from negotiating and concluding with the other States agreements un-

---

93 See Mazzuoli, Valerio de Oliveira. *Natureza jurídica e eficácia dos acordos* stand-by *com o FMI*, cit., p. 157-161.

94 Regarding concordats, see, in particular, Prieto, Vicente, *Diritto dei rapporti tra Chiesa e società civile*, Roma: Edizioni Università della Santa Croce, 2008, p. 173-224.

related to the religious matters. In such a case, those agreements will be designated according to any of the designations discussed in this item, with the exception of *concordats*. It should be noted that the Brazilian diplomatic tradition shows that Brazil has never concluded a Concordat with the Holy See.

o) Reversal notes. This term is used for the specific purpose of establishing reciprocal concessions between States or declaring that the grant or special benefit conferred by a State in favor of another party does not override other vested rights or privileges previously accorded. This term is, thus, used as well to specify the meaning of certain provisions of a treaty at the time of its conclusion in order to preserve uses, rights or commitments previously recognized by the parties. This is the reason why *reversal notes* should be exchanged at the exact moment that the agreement is concluded. Finally, it should be stated that they have been less frequently used in international relations practice.

p) Complementary and/or supplemental agreement. These terms are used to designate commitments of a relative or lesser importance, without, however, losing the legal status of a treaty. Both complementary and supplemental agreements are acts aimed at implementing other agreements previously and duly concluded, normally, under a *framework agreement* or *basic agreement*. By way of example, the following agreements can be cited: Agreement concluded by Brazil and Italy on 6 August 1980, complementary to the Basic Agreement of Technical Cooperation concluded in 1972; Agreement concluded between Brazil and Uruguay on 11 September 1980, aimed at implementing the Brazil-Uruguay agreement on Social Security, etc.[95]

q) Agreement (Convention). The term agreement (*Convênio)* is widely used in Brazilian practice and usually refers to agreements involving matters of political interest, although it is also used to designate agreements of a lesser degree of importance, as well as cultural and transport matters. Sometimes the term is confused with contractual instruments of a national nature, which are obviously not deemed *treaties*. Apart from these few cases, the term agreement (*convênio)* is widely used in Brazilian conventional practice, with examples dating back to the times of the Empire of Brazil.

r) Arbitration agreement ("compromis" or "clause compromissoire"). This term is normally used to establish an agreement (almost invariably

---

[95] Cf. Rezek, José Francisco. *Direito dos tratados*, cit., p. 91.

of a bilateral nature), whereby two or more States undertake to refer to arbitration any existing disputes amongst them, or any other disputes that may arise in the future. The term *arbitration agreement* (meaning "*compromis*") is also used when a treaty has already been concluded, setting forth a general provision for the settlement of disputes by means of arbitration proceedings.

s) *Statute*. As a general rule, this term is used to designate treaties setting out norms for tribunals of international jurisdiction (e.g., the Statute of the International Court of Justice (ICJ), 1920; the Rome Statute of the International Criminal Court (ICC), 1998, etc.). From 1919 onward, this term started to be used at a global level to designate international agreement of a constituent nature. At present, this term is frequently used to refer to a body of procedural norms or to specify the jurisdictional scope of international tribunals, either temporary or permanent, created under the aegis of the United Nations or regional organizations (such as, for instance, OAS, etc.).

t) *Regulation* and/or *Rules of Procedure*. Since the term regulation is somewhat rare in the international context, there is no clear-cut definition for it. It was used, for instance, in the Congress of Vienna, 1815 (*Regulation of the Congress of Vienna*) in order to determine the precedence among the heads of mission by date of arrival at post. However, the term rules of procedure is frequently used (although deprived of the meaning of treaty) to name a set of procedural rules governing some international agencies or tribunals (such as, for instance, the *Rules of Procedure of the Inter-American Commission on Human* and the *Rules of Procedure of the Inter-American Court of Human Rights*, etc.).

u) *Code*. This term has not been formally used in the international arena, the only known text named this way being the Pan-American Sanitary Code, signed in Havana, Cuba, on 14 November 1924. However, there was general agreement to name, with the informal designation of *code*, some important international conventions, such as the "Bustamante Code", 1928, whose official designation is Convention on Private International Law. Likewise, the Vienna Convention on the Law of Treaties has been named by a number of internationalists "Code of Treaty Law", etc.

v) *Constitution*. The term *Constitution* is very rarely used to designate international treaties, since it can obviously be easily confused with State constitutions. A well-known treaty named Constitution is the constituent instrument of the International Labour Organization (ILO), named *Constitution of the International Labour Organization*, originally adopted in 1919 and replaced in 1946. More recently, an example of the use of this term in international context was the attempt to establish a "European Constitution", which was signed in Rome on 29 October 2004, but not entered into force as a result of its rejection by France and the Netherlands.

x) Contract. The use of this term has been avoided in international practice, as is closely linked to municipal law, and thus, appropriate to designate those agreements concluded between a subject of public international law and a private entity, as opposed to an international treaty. In this case, the term designates those international agreements entered into – although by two or more States – that are not governed by the rules of public international law. Hence, quite rightly, it is infrequent for the term *contract* to be used to designate an international legal instrument that is deemed a *treaty*.

In any case, in order to conclude the analysis of this topic it should be stated that despite their *formal* diversity (examples of which are the various treaties, according to the different terms cited above), all conventional instruments share the same *legal* nature, since all of them have the same binding force, be it whether they are named treaties, pacts, agreements, conventions, etc.

1.6 The issue of Memoranda of Understanding (MOUs)

The so-called Memoranda of Understanding came into existence in diplomatic practice in the early twentieth century, after the end of World War I, when it became apparent that many issues of the international agenda (many of them of a non-legal nature) would be negatively affected if dealt with in treaties, taking into account the lengthy procedure necessary to conclude formal international instruments. As a result, multilateral diplomacy increasingly fostered the use of these MOUs amongst the States, which are currently widely used.[96]

First and foremost, it should be stressed that MOUs may be used either by States or by companies or non-governmental organizations. However, the only MOUs that will be discussed here are those concluded by

---

96 For further details on this issue, see McNair, Arnold Duncan, *The law of treaties*, cit., p. 15; McNeill, John H., International agreements: recent U.S.-UK practice concerning the Memorandum of Understanding, *American Journal of International Law*, vol. 88, n. 4 (Oct. 1994), p. 821-826; Klabbers, Jan, *The concept of treaty in international law*, cit., p. 15-25; Aust, Anthony, Modern treaty law and practice, cit., p. 26-46; and Fitzmaurice, Malgosia & Elias, Olufemi, *Contemporary issues in the law of treaties*, cit., p. 28-34.

sovereign States, since the present study on the law of treaties has not been conceived to deal with other types of agreements entered into by entities, which are not subjects of public international law. Therefore, the analysis that follows will revolve around the conclusion of MOUs between States (and most probably also, between intergovernmental organizations).

First of all, before moving on to the heart of the question, there follow some excerpts of an MOU signed between Brazil and Peru on the cooperation for the protection and surveillance of the Amazon.

Memorandum of Understanding between the Governments of the Federative Republic of Brazil and the Republic of Peru on Cooperation for the Protection and Surveillance of the Amazon

The Government of the Federative Republic of Brazil

And

The Government of the Republic of Peru,

(hereinafter the "Parties"),

Inspired by the firm intention to continue forging a strategic alliance between the two countries;

Conscious of the need to exercise adequate control over the Amazon region and their respective territories, and to effectively combat any illegal acts that may be carried out in that area, among others, by drug-traffickers;

Firmly committed with the need to preserve natural resources in their respective Amazonian territories and give them a reasonable use for the benefit of both countries, with special emphasis on populations settled in this large space;

Decided to implement the process of cooperation that will lead to the integration of Peru to the System of Protection of the Amazon (SIPAM) and System of Surveillance the Amazon (SIVAM) and its corresponding use for the protection, surveillance and development of Peruvian and Brazilian Amazon; as well as for the strengthening and integration in various fields of mutual bilateral interest;

As a follow-up of the agreements contained in the Communiqué issued by the Presidents of the Federative Republic of Brazil and the Republic of Peru, on 11 April 2003, in Brasilia;

Agree:

ARTICLE 1

The Government of the Federative Republic of Brazil will provide the necessary technical advice and cooperation that enable Peru to have gradual access to the data generated by the SIVAM and its integration to the SIPAM.

ARTICLE 2

As a first step, the Government of the Federative Republic of Brazil, through the Ministry of Defense, will provide the necessary assistance to its Peruvian counterpart in order to initially establish, in the city of Pucallpa, the technical facilities that enable the Peruvian Party to exchange real-time radar data in the common border zone, with a view to monitoring and controlling the airspace in that area, with emphasis on illicit activities.

(...)

ARTICLE 4

The purpose of Government of Peru is to complement the first phase outlined in Article 2, through the gradual acquisition of technological and logistical resources necessary to enable the increasing use of data related to the control and preservation of the environment, meteorological and climatological surveillance, health population, land surveying and land use, education, surveillance of the electromagnetic spectrum and territorial surveillance, amongst other areas of interest relating to the Peruvian territory.

To this end, the Parties shall, by mutual agreement, establish mechanisms and modalities for cooperation and assistance, including training of personnel, computer program projects (software), joint studies, working visits, among other things.

(...)

ARTICLE 7

The Parties agree to observe the principle of confidentiality, which ensures that the data arising from this Memorandum of Understanding are for the exclusive use of the authorities of Brazil and Peru.

The Parties undertake to maintain the same degree of confidentiality of the exchanged data as established by the originating Party.

(...)

ARTICLE 12

This Memorandum of Understanding shall enter into force on the date of the last notification by which the Parties communicate, through diplomatic channels, which they have complied with the established procedures in their respective domestic legal systems.

Done in the city of Lima, on 25 August 2003, in two originals, in the Portuguese and Spanish languages, both texts being equally authentic. [This is an unofficial translation of the Portuguese version].

[In Brazil, this *Memorandum* has been approved by the National Congress (by means of the Legislative Decree 26 of 15.02.2006) and promulgated by Decree 5752 of 12.04.2006].

As a preliminary remark, it should be stated that MOUs do not fall under the classification of *treaties*, nor do unilateral acts of States or some documents signed by State officials on its behalf – such as, for instance the *Letters of Intent* (*lettres d'intentions*) sent to the IMF for a possible withdrawal of monies held by the Fund.[97] Therefore, these instruments do not form part of the *sources* of Public International Law. The difference between MOUs and Letters of Intent addressed to the IMF (the latter are cited here just as an *example*, among many other instruments, which cannot be deemed *sources* of the law of nations) lies only in the number of

[97] To obtain more details about the legal nature of letters of intent sent to IMF, see Mazzuoli, Valerio de Oliveira, *Natureza jurídica e eficácia dos acordos* stand-by *com o FMI*, cit., p. 191-194.

Parties: Letters of Intent only bear the signature of *one* State (that is why the discussion revolves around whether they constitute a *unilateral* act or not – and it is well known that said Letters are not a unilateral act), while MOUs are concluded by *two or more* States.[98]

MOUs should not be confused, either, with *gentlemen's agreements*, although according to some governments both of them fall under the same legal category.[99] In our opinion, it is erroneous to place MOUs on the same footing as *gentlemen's agreements*, since the latter are concluded by the Head of State in a *personal* capacity and their binding effect relies on her/his personal *honor*, unlike the case of MOUs, which are entered into *on behalf of the State itself*. Furthermore, it should be highlighted that MOUs are more formal than gentlemen's agreements. In any case, what really matters here is to demonstrate that as far as purely legal terms are concerned, the response for all of these cases is the same: they are not international *agreements* and, thus, they cannot be deemed *sources* of Public International Law.

Given the legal issues that they give rise to, the decision was made to discuss the matter relative to MOUs under a separate topic. The aim of this analysis is to show the reasons why MOUs cannot be deemed treaties, and consequently, sources of the law of nations. Below will outline some of the reasons warranting the above statement:

a) Drafting of memoranda. The current practice observed by States when drafting MOUs is to make clear that their intent is not to conclude a formal agreement. Therefore, the wording of such memoranda avoids the use of terminology of a contractual nature. MOUs are worded in such a way as to circumvent the use of phrases such as "States *accept*" or "States *sign*", instead using phrases like "States *understand*" or "States *intend to*",

---

98 It should be stressed that in the United States, in the field of private law, the term "letter of intent" may be synonymous with "memorandum of understanding", if signed by both parties. However, labeling a bilateral document as a *letter of intent* is not exact from a strictly legal point of view (since the "intent" should come from *one* of the parties towards the other, as with those letters addressed to the IMF, and not from both parties concurrently). Thus, when dealing with bilateral documents the most appropriate term will always be "memorandum of understanding".

99 See McNeill, John H. International agreements: recent U.S.-UK practice concerning the Memorandum of Understanding, cit., p. 822. A number of writers consider that MOUs and *gentlemen's agreements* are the same. In this sense, see Fitzmaurice, Malgosia & Elias, Olufemi, *Contemporary issues in the law of treaties*, cit., p. 28, according to whom: "Such arrangements, and the documents in which they are recorded, have been referred to variously as, for example, 'gentlemen's agreements', 'memoranda of understanding' or 'informal instruments'".

and so forth. In the English language, as is well known, whenever parties are not willing to undertake an *obligation* the modal verb *shall* is replaced with a more appropriate modal verb such as *may* (denoting just an option or possibility). Likewise, the modal verb *shall* is replaced with *will*, which does not necessarily imply a legal obligation. In any case, it is evident that MOUs are worded in a manner that the use of language with contractual connotation is avoided.[100]

The same holds true for those transactions with the IMF, embodied in the above mentioned *stand-by arrangements*. In its first considerations concerning the legal nature of the discussed arrangements, the IMF insisted on making it clear that any "language having a contractual connotation" will be avoided in their wording.[101] Despite guidelines set forth by the IMF concerning the *wording* of documents, whereby *stand-by* operations are embodied, its instructions are based upon the *nature* of those instruments, showing that the intent of the IMF is not to conclude an international agreement (treaty) with the State member concerned when that international organization approves a *standby arrangement*.[102]

The MOU concluded between Brazil and Peru (see above) states that the Government of the "Federative Republic of Brazil will provide the necessary technical advice and cooperation that enable Peru to have *gradual access* to the data generated by the System of Surveillance the Amazon..." (Art. 1). It goes on to state that "the purpose [that is, the *intent*] of the Government of Peru is to complement the first phase outlined in Article 2, through the *gradual acquisition* of technological and logistical resources necessary to enable the increasing use of data related to the control and preservation of the environment..." (Art. 4). As can be seen, the entire wording of the instrument under analysis is aimed at not creating contractual obligations between the States concerned.

In short, special attention must be given to the *language* used in the texts of certain agreements, which might very often not be international treaties (as in the case of MOUs), when it can be inferred from the examination of the intent of the negotiators that they did not mean *to create any legal obligations* under the instrument that they signed.

---

100 See McNeill, John H. International agreements..., cit., p. 822; and Aust, Anthony, *Modern treaty law and practice*, cit., p. 27.

101 See FMI Decision 2603-(68/132), adopted on 20.09.1968, paragraph 7.º.

102 For further details on this matter, see Mazzuoli, Valerio de Oliveira, *Natureza jurídica e eficácia dos acordos* stand-by *com o FMI*, cit., p. 114-157.

b) Absence of approval by the Parliament. Unlike international treaties, MOUs, as a general rule, need not be approved by the Parliament prior to their conclusion by the government. This particular point is considered as a major advantage when entering into an MOU, since parliaments usually take a considerable amount of time for the consideration and approval of international acts in general. The absence of an obligation to submit an MOU to the Parliament for its consideration is also indicative of the will of the Government to create no formal obligation. As is well known, the lack of parliamentary approval in relation to an international act is a factor that is capable of altering the legal nature of the act concerned. That is why there are treaties that are not (although they should be) subjected to the scrutiny of the Legislative Power. However, in the case of the MOUs, the fact that there is no need for them to be considered by the Parliament is a result of the subject matter involved in these kinds of arrangements (that is, the "understanding" between States), which is under the purview of the exclusive competence of the Executive Branch. It should be noted, however, that nothing prevents an MOU from being approved by the Parliament, as it was the case for the above mentioned MOU signed in 2003 between Brazil and Peru on Cooperation for the Protection and Surveillance of the Amazon. Since the requirements set forth in Art. 2(1) *(a)* of the 1969 Vienna Convention are not fulfilled, the instrument concerned cannot be deemed a *treaty*.

c) Absence of registration with the United Nations. Moreover, MOUs may have the advantage of being confidential, unlike international treaties (except for military treaties). As a general rule, international treaties, after their conclusion, shall be registered with the Secretariat and published by it, according to the provisions of Art. 102(1) of the UN Charter, under penalty of not being able "(to) invoke that treaty or agreement before any organ of the United Nations" (Art. 102(2)). In international relations practice MOUs have not been registered with the UN Secretariat, with rare exceptions,[103] which ensued more likely from a poor interpretation by the State concerned (which does not understand very well what exactly a *treaty* is) than as a result of the State's intention to conclude a legally binding agreement. On this point, however, two remarks should be

103 See some of these cases in Aust, Anthony, *Modern treaty law and practice*, cit., p. 29, note 15 (the author cites only *four* cases). In his turn, John H. McNeill states that "several of these [memoranda of understanding] were registered by the United States pursuant to Art. 102 of the UN Charter, but without specifying which ones, citing just one concrete example (see International agreements…, cit., p. 822, note 2).

made: *1*) the registration of something that is *not* really a *treaty* (such as an MOU) does not award that instrument said legal nature (in which case such a registration will be valid only as a means of *disclosure* of the act), and therefore the Government is presumed not to seek the confidentiality of the instrument concerned; and 2) the *absence of registration* of a *treaty* itself does not make it invalid (it only prevents that treaty from being invoked before any organ of the United Nations, in particular, the ICJ). There is no doubt, however, that the lack of registration of the instrument concerned with the UN Secretariat is a clear indication of the parties' intent not to conclude a treaty.

d) *Confidentiality*. Governments often prefer concluding MOUs rather than treaties, precisely because MOUs are *confidential*. Since they are informal acts, they do not require formal publication. States *may do so* if they wish to make known to the general public the subject matter of the memorandum, but they are not obliged to do so.[104] As is common knowledge, whenever a *treaty* is concluded that instrument is to be published in the *Official Gazette of the (Brazilian) National Congress* (after being approved by the Congress) and also in the *Official Gazette* (after its ratification). Conversely, regarding MOUs there exist no publication requirements through any official means. Therefore, as far as *treaties* are concerned, the rule that applies is that of its publication, whilst regarding *MOUs* the rule to be observed is that of their confidentiality.

Undoubtedly, a number of MOUs have been published, as it was the case in Brazil. But still, depending on certain clauses, it is impossible for the public at large to know the *substantial* obligations contained in the MOUs, when these types of instruments set forth provisions like the following: "The Parties agree to observe the principle of confidentiality, which ensures that the data arising from this Memorandum of Understanding are for the exclusive use of the authorities of Brazil and Peru".[105]

e) *Conclusions on their legal nature*. In short, said MOUs are nothing but a set of stipulations constituting "non-binding agreements".[106] That is, they are intentions (of understanding) of a non-binding nature. Clearly, governments consider that MOUs are much more practical (for the setting-up of their international relations, in particular, the bilateral ones) than other types of legal arrangements of a greater degree of for-

104 See Aust, Anthony. *Modern treaty law and practice*, cit., p. 35-37

105 Art. 7.º of the *Memorandum* between Brazil and Peru (2003), cit.

106 See Crawford, James. *Brownlie's principles of public international law*, cit., p. 371.

mality (as such, for instance, an international treaty). Furthermore, given their informal nature, MOUs are not capable of (legally) binding the State to the terms set out therein. Nonetheless, the fact that MOUs are not *legally* binding does not imply that failure to comply with their terms goes unsanctioned. Indeed, there will be a sanction, but it will not be of a *legal* nature (that is, it will be *extralegal*, almost invariably of an *economic*, *political*, or even *moral* nature).[107] The fact remains that MOUs cannot be deemed international treaties. Thus, since they are not treaties – and, consequently, they are not conventional *sources of* Public International Law either –, the 1969 Convention on the Law of Treaties does not apply to them.

1.7 *Soft law* instruments

In 1983, the *Institut de Droit International*, under the direction of Rapporteur Michel Virally, devoted a significant part of his Cambridge session to the analysis of the distinction between "international texts of a legal nature in the mutual relations between their respective authors" and "international texts devoid of that character". The Members of the *Institut* found that some subjects of international law often adopt, under different designations, the most varied texts under different names, which despite creating obligations in their mutual relations, are deprived, by the express or implied intention of the parties, of any legal nature. At that time, it was also found that, although the intention of the parties is not clear as to the creation of legal effects by such texts, it is very difficult to ascertain if the texts concerned are of a legal nature or not, because all of them present a certain *gray area* between the universe of law and non-law.[108]

One factor in the proliferation of such arrangements, according to Virally, is rooted in the fluctuation of the current international economic situation, which requires a certain degree of flexibility in the implementation of their agreements, and also in the rampant technical progress, whose effects are felt immediately in the field of international relations.[109] Furthermore, the international society has gone through so many trans-

---

107 See Aust, Anthony. *Modern treaty law and practice*, cit., p. 45-46 (especially, in regard to *political* sanctions as a result of non-compliance of MOUs).

108 See *Annuaire de l'Institut de Droit Internacional*, Paris: A. Pedone, 1984, vol. 60, t. I, p. 166-374 e vol. 60, t II, p. 116-153 e 284-291. Regarding the ambiguous character of those instruments, see also Dupuy, Pierre-Marie, *Droit international public*, cit., p. 264; and Fitzmaurice, Malgosia & Elias, Olufemi, *Contemporary issues in the law of treaties*, cit., p. 34-35.

109 See *Annuaire de l'Institut de Droit Internacional*, vol. 60, t. I, cit., p. 191.

formations in recent times that it became difficult to properly ascertain the legal nature of these new instruments, which appear on a daily basis in the context of international relations, as for instance, the above cited, concerning the international economic situation, and also some directly linked to the international protection of human rights and the environment.[110] International practice has shown that many of the *soft law* rules are designed to regulate the future behavior of States, guiding their conduct and that of their agents in multilateral international fora, establishing a joint action program, but without being aimed at falling under the universe of conventional norms, whose main feature is the mandatory fulfillment of what was agreed upon.

Yet the fact remains that the existing need that the new international order should adapt to those emerging issues in international law, coupled with the flexibility that the regulation and the adjusting of the interests contained therein require, causes numerous doubts to arise as to the legal nature of such texts, that came into existence as a result of the practice of the twentieth century multilateral diplomacy and which form an integral part of the so-called *soft law* or *droit doux*,[111] as opposed to the well-known system of *hard law* or *droit dur*.[112]

Despite the fact that legal writers have not yet agreed on a clear conceptualization of what the term *soft law* stands for[113] – which in the Portuguese language can be translated as *"direito plástico"*, *"direito flexível"* or

---

110 See Dupuy, Pierre-Marie. *Soft law* and the international law of the environment, *Michigan Journal of International Law*, vol. 12 (Winter 1991), p. 420-422. It should be reminded, however, that the soft law phenomenon is not an exclusive feature of International Law. As Dupuy explains, a number of States have adopted, also in their domestic legislation, rules on genetic research and assisted reproduction in the form of *ethical guidelines* ("soft law") applicable to scientists and physicists, without having the typical features that laws or other "hard" related-instruments may have (Idem, p. 422).

111 It should be noted that the term *soft norm* has also been used (although less frequently) as, according to some legal theorists, the term "law" would not technically be correct, taking into account that such a term has a mandatory connotation in Anglo-saxon law. On this point, see *Bilder*, Richard B., Beyond Compliance: helping nations to Cooperate, in Shelton, Dinah (ed.), *Commitment and compliance: the role of non-binding norms in the international legal system*, Oxford: Oxford University Press, 2000, p. 71-72.

112 In regard to the difficulties encountered to ascertain the precise legal nature of the *soft law* rules, see Fitzmaurice, Malgosia & Elias, Olufemi, *Contemporary issues in the law of treaties*, cit., p. 37-47.

113 See in this regard, the analysis carried out by *Grnchalla-Wesierski*, Tadensz, A framework for understanding "soft law", *McGill Law Journal*, vol. 30 (1984), p. 44-51.

"direito maleável" (plastic, malleable or flexible law) – it can be argued that its current meaning encompasses all those rules whose normative force is less stringent than the traditional legal standards. This is especially due to the fact that their devices do not directly compel States, or because they create obligations of a much lesser mandatory degree (as they lack elements to ensure its enforcement in practice). However, it cannot be argued that known *soft law* instruments have no relevance at all for the creation and development of public international law; the relevance of these instruments have already been well highlighted by international practice, even though they are not capable of autonomously creating international norms. In fact, such instruments can serve even as *opinio juris* of States concerning a certain area of international law, as was the case with the 1992 Rio Declaration on Environment and Development with regard to the crystallization (still ongoing) of the principle of sustainable development.[114] Still, the current understanding is that it is not possible (at least at present) to characterize a norm of *soft law* as a true *source* of public international law.[115] Thus, *soft law* rules do not oblige States to the effect given by the 1969 Vienna Convention.

Examples of *soft law* norms are, among others, the rules set forth in diplomatic fora in connection with the negotiations that may take place in those instances and the "agenda" to be followed by the States in future sessions to discuss the subject matter of the negotiations. Regarding the "agendas", examples include, those agendas setting forth States' commitments or cooperation for specific purposes, such as the well-know *Agenda 21* for the protection of the environment, adopted at the closure of the United Nations Conference on Environment & Development (Rio de Janeiro, 1992). Other examples of *soft law* rules include "codes of conduct", "joint declarations", "declarations of principles", "final acts" and "action programs".[116]

---

[114] In this sense, see Fitzmaurice, Malgosia & Elias, Olufemi, *Contemporary issues in the law of treaties*, cit., p. 43: "They may not be binding but they may be an element in the process of the formulation of the uniform conviction of States that certain principles are law, such as, in our view, the 1992 Rio Declaration, which assists the ongoing (not yet completed) process of crystallization of the principle of sustainable development".

[115] On this analysis, see Nasser, Salem Hikmat, *Fontes e normas do direito internacional: um estudo sobre a* soft law, São Paulo: Atlas, 2005, p. 143-157.

[116] See Soares, Guido Fernando Silva. *Curso de direito internacional público*, vol. 1. São Paulo: Atlas, 2002, p. 138.

The truth is that these instruments do not share any features with what the 1969 Vienna Convention characterizes as "international treaty" (see item 1.4, above). It should be stressed that, in particular, those instruments lack the contractual element ("treaty" means an "*international agreement...*" as set forth by the Convention), which is necessary for an agreement to be deemed a formal conventional instrument. Furthermore, said instruments are not subject to the municipal law procedures, according to which a treaty must go through until its entry into force, especially, the approval of the Legislative Power prior to the formal ratification by the Executive Power (as set forth, for instance, by the 1988 Brazilian Constitution, Art. 49(I). This is so, especially because the States want deliberately to "avoid" a more precise legal characterization when concluding such an instrument, aiming thereby at preserving a certain degree of flexibility in their application, the possibility to amend it more easily in the future, and to circumvent the potential legal sanctions that may arise from its non-compliance.[117]

Each and every international agreement devoid of legal sanctions – as seems to be the case of *soft law* standards – is not exactly an "agreement" in the sense used in the 1969 Vienna Convention. This does not exclude, however, that said norms might be relevant to the formation and development of the law of nations or serve to crystallize *opinio juris* of States with respect to an issue or matter of their interest.

117 See Grnchalla-Wesierski, Tadensz. A framework for understanding "soft law", cit., p. 41-42; and Fitzmaurice, Malgosia & Elias, Olufemi, *Contemporary issues in the law of treaties*, cit., p. 35-36.

Chapter 2

Classification of Treaties

A myriad of classifications has been used throughout the ages for international treaties. They have already been classified according to their purpose, the historical moment of their conclusion, the special application, etc. In this respect, the 1969 Vienna Convention has adopted a cautionary approach by not making use of any systematic treaty classification, having confined itself to draw some distinctions from a restricted scope of application[118]

In spite of the multiplicity of existing classifications – many of which have no scientific basis – only those that conform to the purposes of this work will be utilized. Therefore, treaties here will be classified according to two methods, namely, the *formal* one and the *substantial* one. The formal method is formed by those classifications taking into account the *number of parties, the type of procedure applied for its conclusion* and the *possibility of accession to the treaty concerned.* The substantial method refers to those classifications based upon the *legal nature*, the *application time frames*, the *territorial application* and the *application structure.*

In addition to those classifications, reference should also be made to the *institutional or constituent treaties* category, which differs from the rest of the treaties in that that they constitute or create international organizations, giving shape to those organizations by conferring them international legal personality, coupled with the prerogative to take on rights and obligations at an international level, such as the Charter of the United Nations, 1945 (and its specialized agencies) and the OAS Charter,1948.

2.1 Formal classifications

Under the *formal classifications* category, these group those classifications that take into consideration the extrinsic characteristics of the

---

118 See Reuter, Paul. *Introducción al derecho de los tratados*, cit., p. 51.

treaties concerned. Under all of these classifications no analysis is made of the *treaty itself*, but the discussions revolve around their extrinsic characteristics.

Under this (formal) extrinsic aspect of treaties, classifications concern the *number of parties*, the *type of procedure for their conclusion* as well as the *possibilities to accede to the treaty in question*. Following is an analysis of each classification in particular.

2.1.1 Considerations regarding the number of parties

As to the number of parties, treaties can be classified as *bilateral* (or *particular*) treaties or *multilateral* (also named *collective*, *general* or *plurilateral*) treaties.

Bilateral treaties are those concluded only by two contracting parties, or between victors and vanquished. These treaties can be entered into by two States or between a State and an international organization, or even, between two international organizations. In the latter case – that is, treaties concluded by a State and international organization or between two international organizations – no multilateral treaty will exist as a result of said international organizations being *formed* by *various States*. The bilateral feature of the act is always represented by its *two parties*, *one of them* being an international organization, which constitutes a *single* and *indivisible* subject under the law of nations, although such an organization is formed by a multiplicity of States.[119] A good example of that type of *bilateral* treaty, albeit multipartite, was the Treaty of Versailles, 1919, among the victors and the vanquished in the World War I.[120]

Bilateral treaties prevailed in an absolute manner until the seventeenth century and their main feature was that they were capable of regulating matters relating to the Crown, regardless of whether such matters were of the sole interest of the State or of the particular interest of the Sovereign.

---

119 See, in this respect, Basdevant, Jules, La conclusion et la rédaction des traités et des instruments diplomatiques autres que les traités, *Recueil des Cours*, vol. 15 (1926-V), p. 555.

120 Some scholars, such as Rezek, consider that such treaties should be referred to as *multilateral* treaties, on the basis of the criterion "that takes into account the exact number of contracting legal entities", arguing that "the ascertainment of the parties that the signatories to an international treaty may be grouped into, besides being a extralegal exercise, will often require a prior and thorough review of the substance of the commitment undertaken" (*Direito dos tratados*, cit., p. 125-156).

The language used for the drafting of bilateral treaties is usually that of the contracting parties themselves. Or to be more precise, if the States do not share the same language, two original versions are adopted, each one written in one of the languages of the parties. Thus, a bilateral treaty between Brazil and France will be drawn up in duplicate, that is, in Portuguese and in French, each version being equally authentic. However, it should be noted that it is also frequent that a treaty be adopted in only one language (normally in English) that is convenient for both parties, in the event that the signatories consider that there might arise future divergences as to the interpretation of the respective versions in different languages.

Multilateral are those treaties concluded by more than two parties, that is, among three or more parties, upon the basis of their reciprocal provisions. As a general rule, any State or international organization without restriction, or even a substantial number of States or organizations can take part in these kinds of treaties, aiming at setting general norms of public international law or addressing matters of common interest.[121] Typically, they are characterized by a meeting of the minds, with a view to regulating the essential aspects of the international society, as well as harmonizing international norms. The *Saint-Alliance* – created in the Congress of Vienna (1815) with the aim of structuring the international society of that time – was the first open multilateral treaty. At present, multilateral treaties are used to regulate matters of common interest for mankind, such as public health, communications, protection of human and environmental rights, air safety, protection against infringement of literary, artistic and scientific property, terrorism, and even, political corruption. In this role of defending the common interests of humanity, as expressed by Paul Reuter, such treaties have less to do with a juxtaposition pattern of State commitments on divergent interests than with that of a balanced combination of efforts to reach a common goal.[122]

The use of the prefix *multi* for treaties concluded by just three, four or five State parties has been much criticized because it is considered that such a prefix would give the impression that the number of parties to the treaty concerned is a lot higher. Although some voices supported the replacement of that term with the term *plurilateral*, the fact is that the first term (*multilateral*) was already rooted in the international practice, being

---

121 See. *Yearbook of the International Law Commission* (1962), vol. II, p. 36.

122 See Reuter, Paul. *Introducción al derecho de los tratados*, cit., p. 14-15.

thus kept unchanged to date. In any event, as Rezek recalls, it is always possible to opt for the use of the former and more appropriate term *collective treaties* to designate multilateral treaties.[123]

Currently, special attention has been drawn to two new multilateral treaty modalities in the international arena, which requires a brief analysis. The first modality, that has not been embodied in written form of international law yet, deals with the so-called *umbrella treaty*, which is a comprehensive treaty. Consequently, this type of treaty does not focus on an individual legal issue, but it is aimed at establishing a set of principle elements for the subject matter concerned, requiring complementation by means of other international treaties which will be concluded under its aegis.[124] For example, under the aegis of the Antarctic Treaty concluded in Washington, on 1 December 1959, two additional international conventions were signed, namely: the Convention for the Conservation of Antarctic Seals (CCAS, London, 1972) and the Convention on the Conservation of Antarctic Marine Living Resources (CCAMLR, Canberra, 1980), as well as the Protocol on Environmental Protection to the Antarctic Treaty (Madrid, 1991), which form the so-called "Antarctic Treaty System". The integration of these instruments into such a *system* of norms creates a regulating framework of the activities related to the Antarctic, based upon the prescriptive guidelines of its *umbrella treaty.* A second modality of a modern multilateral treaty, already embodied in international prescriptive instruments deals with the so-called *framework treaty* or *framework convention*, which is a term that appeared with the adoption of the United Nations Framework Convention on Climate Change, in New York, on 9 May 1992. The translation of the term "framework" into Portuguese, which is *quadro*, is likely to cause confusion, as the appropriate translation of term "framework" into the official languages of the United Nations in which the convention was drafted has not been followed in Portuguese. In the English language the Convention was adopted under the name of *United Nations Framework Convention on Climate Change*; in French, under the designation of *Convention-Cadre des Nations Unies sur la Changement Climatique*; and in Spanish, *Convención Marco de las Naciones Unidas sobre Modificaciones del Clima.* The terms *framework* (in English), *cadre* (in French) and *marco* (in Spanish) have the connotation of a *receptacle* (rather than a *picture (quadro)*, as the connotation of this

---

123 See Rezek, José Francisco. *Direito dos tratados*, cit., p. 122-123.

124 See Boyle, Alan. Reflections on the treaty as a law-making instrument, cit., p. 8-10.

term in the Portuguese language; if that were the case, said conventions would be called convention (*picture*, *tableau* and *cuadro* in those languages, respectively). Therefore, this type of "framework convention" (that in the Portuguese language should be appropriately referred to as "*convenção-moldura*"), instead of using the term "*quadro*" ("picture" in English) set forth the general legal basis of the agreement, as well as the rights and obligations of the parties, leaving its detailed regulation for a later point in time, which will be done through *annexes* and *appendixes* thereto. This new type of international mechanism has repercussions even in the manner multilateral treaties can be *amended*, taking into consideration that it may be much easier to modify and adapt annexes and appendixes to the new circumstances of the international society, without the need to fall back upon *amendments*, requiring to follow a much lengthier procedure, and on occasions, somewhat cumbersome.[125]

2.1.2 Considerations regarding the type of procedure for their conclusion

It is import to know, in respect with this classification, whether the conclusion of an international agreement is to be carried out in a *twofold phase* to express the consent to be bound by it. When the expression of such consent requires the *signature* and the *ratification* (the treaty is characterized as being a *two-phase* treaty); conversely, when *only one* phase suffices for a State to express its final consent to be bound by a treaty, paving the way for conditions enabling the treaty concerned to enter into force and give legal force to what had been previously agreed upon, then such a treaty is characterized as being a *one-phase* treaty). Thus, international treaties are classified, depending on the type of procedure used for their conclusion, in *sensu stricto* (or two-phase) treaties and in *treaties in simplified form* (or one-phase treaties).

Treaties in the strictest sense (*sensu stricto*) are those whose conclusion requires the observance of a complex procedure consisting of internationally distinct phases: the first one begins with negotiations and ends by the signing; and the second one goes from signature to ratification. Besides these two different phases at an international level, there are other steps that need be complied with in relation to the municipal law of the Contracting States to the agreement concerned, such as approval by

---

125 For further details on umbrella treaties and framework treaties, see Soares, Guido Fernando Silva, *Direito internacional do meio ambiente: emergência, obrigações e responsabilidades*, 2. ed., São Paulo: Atlas, 2003, p. 175-178.

the Legislative branch and the internal enactment of the ratified treaty. That is, out of the *four* phases that treaties go through until they reach their final status (signature, parliamentary approval, ratification and enactment) two of them are international phases (signature and ratification). Hence, a treaty in the strictest sense always involves a *two-fold phase*.

In turn, treaties in simplified form (known as executive agreements) are those whose conclusion is completed in only one phase, which consists of the *signature* of the agreement, at which time the parties express their consent to be bound by them. Hence, they may also be named abridged procedure agreements. As a general rule, these kinds of agreements need not be ratified, and consequently, the formal involvement of the Parliament is not necessary. Due to their simplicity, many of them do not even require the involvement of the Head of State, their conclusion being left to government officials or, more often, the Minister of Foreign Affairs.[126]

Treaties in simplified form are generally bilateral. These kinds of treaties are mostly concluded by means of exchange of diplomatic notes, correspondence, reversal notes, protocols or joint declarations. They are executed in a single instrument, without being subject to many formalities or delay. Examples of agreements in simplified form may include the following: Agreement for the Approval of a Special Convention between the National Commission of Nuclear Energy (CNEN) and the Jülich Centre for Neutron Science (JCNS) signed on 23 April 1971 and concluded by exchange of diplomatic notes in Brasilia, Brazil, and the Agreement for Approval of an Addendum to that instrument, signed on 3 October 1973; such agreements are a result of the General Agreement of Cooperation in the Areas of Scientific Research and Technological Development, 9 June 1969, previously adopted by Decree-Law 681, 15 July 1969 and enacted by Decree 65160, 15 September 1969.[127]

The agreements in simplified form are derived from North American practice, according to which certain international acts are not submitted to the scrutiny of the Senate (the so-called *fast-track* system). The rationale behind this lies in the slowness of the legislative chambers and the

---

126 See Rousseau, Charles. *Principes généraux du droit international public*, t. I, cit., p. 157-158; Cachapuz de Medeiros, Antônio Paulo, *O poder de celebrar tratados...*, cit., p. 202-240; and Basdevant, Jules, La conclusion et la rédaction des traités et des instruments diplomatiques autres que les traités, cit., p. 601, note 221.

127 Examples drawn from Soares, Guido Fernando Silva, "Agreements" – "Executive Agreements" – "Gentlemen's Agreements", cit., p. 273.

ever increasing intensification of international relations, which require a rapid response in solving problems of immediate interest that in its turn cannot depend on a parliamentary approval that may ultimately be untimely, implying an obstacle to the normal conduct of foreign relations. As discussed above, in the United States of America, the term "agreement" connotes those agreements, whose approval by the Senate is not necessary, while the term "treaty" means those treaties, whose approval by the Senate is legally constraining. At present, the continued practice of such agreements has led some legal scholars to not even contest its constitutionality.[128] It should be highlighted that Parliamentary intervention, especially in the United States, has implied an *obstacle* to the Executive Power's conduct of its international relations, becoming an additional factor of delay interfering with the sphere of international relations.[129]

Furthermore, the improvement of telecommunications and the establishment of international organizations with permanent State representation (parliamentary diplomacy), as well as the repeated practice of direct contacts between Heads of State (summit diplomacy) fueled by progress in transportation, which made the principles of entry into force of international treaties become obsolete, can be considered as the driving force behind the growth of the agreements in simplified form, as Guido Soares notes.[130]

The Vienna Convention on the Law of Treaties regulates the consent to be bound by treaty expressed only by signature in its Art. 12, while the consent to be bound by a treaty expressed only by an exchange of instruments constituting a treaty is regulated in Art. 13.

In spite of the reaction of most of the legal theorists against the practice of concluding agreements without the approval of the Legislative Power, the fact remains that that great deal of criticism was unsuccessful and that practice cemented itself in the international arena, being nowadays accepted and used by a great number of States. In Brazil, since the early days of the Republic, such practice is being observed by the Executive without changing its orientation. Itamaraty, (as the Brazilian Ministry of Foreign Affairs is known) also considers that Brazil may be a party to

---

128 See Pinto, Roger. La réforme du Congrès, *Revue du Droit Public et de la Science Politique*, t. 66, Paris: LGDJ, 1950, p. 378.

129 See Rodas, João Grandino. Os acordos em forma simplificada, cit., p. 319-321.

130 See Soares, Guido Fernando Silva. "Agreements" – "Executive Agreements" – "Gentlemen's Agreements", cit., p. 255

international agreements, without requiring the approval by the National Congress.[131]

As can be seen, the lack of solemnity is not always a valid criterion to determine the nature of the agreements in simplified form. Such agreements may be even subject to ratification. Conversely, there may exist treaties in due form that enter into force only by signature, this being the reason why characterizing these so-called agreements in simplified form may become somehow difficult. It appears likely that such agreements, besides not being subject to ratification, are also concluded by the body vested with treaty-making power, but under a procedure that is not expressly provided for in the Constitution, or even, according to a procedure which disregards the constitutional rules setting forth the competence of each of the Powers of the Republic on the conclusion of treaties.

2.1.3 Considerations concerning the possibility to access to a treaty

In regard to the possibility that a treaty allows the chance of future *accession* by other States (or international organizations) reference should be made to *open* and *closed* treaties. The first ones (*open* treaties) are those which offer other States (or international organizations) that did not take part in their preliminary negotiations (or that did not ratify the treaty concerned or, that they did ratify it, but afterwards they denounced it and later on they retracted such a denunciation, etc.) the possibility to access to the treaty in question. The Declaration of Paris, 1856 was the first multilateral treaty of its kind. It should be stressed that the characterization of a treaty as open is always expressly stated in its provisions, but without following a standard *template* for all cases, especially when it comes to those treaties whose accession is restricted (see below). Conversely, closed treaties are those whose provisions prohibit a later accession by other States (or international organizations), which have not been initial parties to them, unless a new agreement is concluded between the aforementioned initial parties and that party willing to access to the treaty concerned.[132]

Accession to *open treaties*, in turn, can be of a *limited* or *unlimited* nature. In the case of limited accession, only a restricted group of States may be allowed to accede to the treaty in a later stage, normally based upon *regional* or *geographic* criteria. Examples thereof are the Treaty of Asunción,

---

131 See Rodas, João Grandino. A constituinte e os tratados internacionais, *Revista dos Tribunais*, vol. 624, São Paulo, out./1987, p. 46.

132 See Maresca, Adolfo. *Il diritto dei trattati…*, cit., p. 101.

establishing the Southern Common Market (hereinafter "Mercosur"), whereby only those countries that were parties to the Latin American Integration Association (hereinafter "ALADI") were permitted to access to it (Art. 20); and the Inter-American Convention to Prevent and Punish Torture, 1985, whose Art. 20 provides that the Convention "is open to accession by *any other American State*". Open treaties providing for *unlimited accession*, in turn, allow unrestricted subsequent accession by any State (principle of universal participation).[133] Treaties providing for unlimited accession include the Convention on the Elimination of All Forms of Discrimination against Women, 1979, which sets out that the Convention "shall be open to accession by *all States*" (Art. 25, 4); and also the Convention against Torture and Other Cruel, Inhuman or Degrading Treatment or Punishment, 1984 (Art. 26); the Convention on the Rights of the Child, 1989 (Art. 48); the Inter-American Convention on the Prevention, Punishment and Eradication Violence against Women ("Convention of Belém do Pará"), 1994 (Art. 17), among many others.

Open international treaties providing for limited or unlimited accession may also be of a *conditional* or *unconditional* nature. In the first case, that is, an open treaty (be it limited or unlimited) requires the new State seeking to accede to the treaty to comply with certain conditions. This is the case, for instance, of the UN Charter, which is only open, according to its Art. 4(1), "to other peace-loving states which accept the obligations contained in the present Charter and, in the judgment of the Organization, are able and willing to carry out these obligations". Unconditional treaties, in their turn, are those open treaties (be it limited or unlimited) whereby no obligation is set forth for the later accession by other States, for instance most of the international treaties on the protection of human rights.

2.2 Material classifications

The features relating to the intrinsic aspects of a treaty are subsumed under the rubric *material classifications*. However, this statement should not cause any confusion at all. Indeed, this is not about classifying the contents of the treaties, which could even be done in another context (sorting them, for instance, by the matter they deal with, such as *ordinary treaties* or *human rights treaties*, etc.). This is not what is at issue here. *Material* classifications take account of the *intrinsic* aspects of the treaty *in itself*, that is, the treaty as an *instrument*.

---

133 See De La Guardia, Ernesto. *Derecho de los tratados internacionales*, cit., p. 58-59.

As far as this intrinsic (material) aspect of treaties is concerned, classifications relate to the *legal nature*, *implementation over time*, *territorial implementation* and the *implementation mechanism*.

2.2.1 Considerations concerning the legal nature

According to their legal nature, namely, their object, treaties are classified into *law-making treaties* (also named *normative treaties*) and *contract-treaties.*[134]

Law-making treaties or *normative treaties* are normally entered into by a great number of States with the aim of setting public international law norms of a general and abstract nature, which are objectively valid for the contracting parties. Consequently, these kinds of treaties can be said to amount to genuine *laws* (as the rules set forth by them are of a general and abstract nature).[135] Thus, said *Law-making treaties* establish a real *objective* international law norm, as a result of the converging (parallel) will of the parties concerned, which will be generally applicable to those situations foreseen by agreement, there being no exact correspondence between the obligations that are enforceable and those that have not been complied with. In other words, such treaties impose on the contracting parties an obligation of identical content, as a result of the meeting of the minds of the States concerned, this being the reason why these treaties are considered to be "the core element of the theory of the law of treaties".[136] In this way, the parties undertake the obligation to comply simultaneously with all the provisions agreed upon, in virtue of the *pacta sunt servanda* principle. Therefore, such treaties set forth a *common* purpose for the contracting parties, which are under the obligation to achieve that goal through the same actions. That is, the will of the parties in the framework of law-making treaties is convergent, with identical content, aimed at achieving a common goal.

Such treaties are mandatory only for those States concluding them. These are, as a rule, multilateral treaties, which are open to accession by

---

134 Such a distinction seems to have been drawn for the first time in Bergbohm, Carl, *Staatsverträge und Gesetze als Quellen des Völkerrechts*, Dorpat: C. Mattiesen, 1876, 110p. In the context of that work, the author drew a distinction between those international acts that constitute *legal transactions* for the parties concerned (granting or invalidating subjective rights of States) and those that contain *abstract rules* to the contracting parties (that the latter expressly recognize as common rules governing their future acts).

135 See Rousseau, Charles. *Principes généraux du droit international public*, t. I, cit., p. 136.

136 See Reuter, Paul. *Introducción al derecho de los tratados*, cit., p. 15, whereby Triepel's teachings are cited.

other States that did not participate in the procedure for their formation (these contain a provision on accession, although very often of a *limited* nature). In fact, it is by means of these kinds of treaties that Public International Law is codified. Examples of these types of international acts are the large collective conventions such as the Hague and Geneva conventions on the law of war, the Vienna Convention on the Law of Treaties itself, as well as all other international treaties whose purpose is to establish uniform legal rules of conduct, e.g. the treaty establishing the Organization of Petroleum Exporting Countries – OPEC, according to which all signatory countries had the same purpose, namely, to control international oil trade.

Given their normative nature, which creates rules of general international law, some scholars go on to claim that only *law-making treaties* constitute a formal source of public international law, as they are the most evolved form of setting out international legal standards.

Conversely, in the context of *contract-treaties*, the wills of the parties are divergent, which on the one hand prevents the creation of a general and abstract rule of public international law, and on the other hand, establishes a reciprocal and specific stipulation of their respective rights and obligations with a common object (namely, relating to the individual interests of two or more States).[137] They resemble, therefore, municipal law contracts. Against that background, each party aims precisely at obtaining benefits from the other party. Thus, through a specific legal transaction, a seemingly genuine international contract is perfected, which in its turn is extinguished by complying with the respective obligations therein. These types of treaties are conceived to regulate specific interests in a concrete manner. They are the result of mutual concessions by States, exchange of wills for several purposes, and they appear to be contracts. The difference between these contractual obligations and those deriving from domestic law lies solely in the fact that, the parties in the aforementioned contractual obligations happen to be sovereign States or international organizations. They are, thus, from a formal point of view, ordinary bilateral agreements; from a substantial perspective, they have essentially subjective effects (varying according to the will of the contracting States) or with few contracting parties, given that reconciling different interests of many States is not an easy task.[138]

---

137 See De La Guardia, Ernesto. *Derecho de los tratados internacionales*, cit., p. 64-65.

138 See Rousseau, Charles. *Principes généraux du droit international public*, t. I, cit., p. 135.

Law-making treaties are sub-divided into *executed* and *executory*. The first ones are the so-called *transitory* treaties, which are immediately executed and establish a static legal situation. The second ones are the so-called *permanent* treaties, being so considered because they require regularly executory measures that continue over long periods.[139] Examples of the latter treaty category include treaties concerning international trade, scientific cooperation, technology transfer or transfer of military material subject to certain conditions related to military measures, balance of payments adjustment mechanisms, etc.[140]

As for questions involving contract-treaties extreme care should be taken by courts when ruling on them, especially, not to confuse that type of treaties (these *are* international treaties, which are just named *contract-treaties* for didactical purposes) with typical domestic or international contracts, since otherwise the findings of the court concerned would turn out to be completely wrong, adversely affecting by doing so the party whose rights are guaranteed in the *treaty* itself. In this line of thought, it should be stated that the Supreme Court of the United States of America rendered a decision, on 5 March 2014, in case *BG Group plc v. Republic of Argentina*, whereby it confused a bilateral investment treaty concluded between the United Kingdom and Argentina with a typical domestic contract,[141] when comparing these two completely different legal instruments (rendering its decision on the basis of such a comparison!), which prompted Justice Roberts (joined by Justice Kennedy) – and not without reason- to criticize, albeit partially, such a ruling, in his dissenting opinion.[142]

---

139 See Wheaton, Henry. *Elements of international law*, vol. I, cit., p. 504; and Accioly, Hildebrando, *Tratado de direito internacional público*, vol. I, cit., p. 552-553. Regarding transitory and permanent treaties, see item 2.2.2, below.

140 See Soares, Guido Fernando Silva. Os acordos administrativos e sua validade no Brasil, *Revista Forense*, vol. 272, Rio de Janeiro, 1980, p. 60-61; and Klabbers, Jan. *The concept of treaty in international law*, cit., p. 21-22.

141 See *BG Group plc v. Republic of Argentina*, 12-138, 572 U.S., 5 March 2014 (Opinion of the Court), p. 6: "In answering the question, we shall initially treat the document before us as if it were an ordinary contract between private parties. Were that so, we conclude, the matter would be for the arbitrators. We then ask whether the fact that the document in question is a treaty makes a critical difference. We conclude that it does not". For a detailed critical analysis of this decision, see Mazzuoli, Valerio de Oliveira & Alonso Massa, Diego Luis, Analysis of the Decision rendered by the U.S. Supreme Court in *Re BG Group plc v. Republic of Argentina*: do all roads lead to Rome?, *Journal of International Arbitration*, vol. 32, n. 2 (2015), p. 215-236.

142 *Verbis*: "The 'document before us', of course, is nothing of the sort [that is to say, a contract between private parties]. It is instead a treaty between two sovereign nations: the

Moreover, *Contract-treaties* should not be confused with the so-called State contracts (*contrats d'État*), governed by administrative domestic law of one of the parties and entered into by the State and moral or physical persons, whereby specific provisions are set out that should be complied with by either party. The difference lies in the fact that the *contract-treaties* are governed by public international law and entered into by States with other subjects of the law of nations, while State contracts (which are not *treaties*) are governed by the domestic law of one of the parties (or by that of a third State chosen by mutual agreement of the parties) and are concluded by a State and an individual (be it a moral or physical person). However, as Guido Soares points out, even the involvement of an individual (for instance, a foreign national) into a contractual relationship with a State, or with even stronger reason, between States, does not completely do away with the need to virtually invoke public international law norms, "precisely because one of the parties is a State, as stated in international arbitration precedents or taking into account the fact that certain rules are completely derived from public international norms".[143] Such agreements are suitable, for instance, in the event of sale of goods, arms or a property loan, when third parties that are not subject to public international law norms are closely linked to the transaction; the aforementioned agreements can also serve as a basis for hiring the provision of services (studies, technical and financial assistance, etc.), public works (construction of bridges and ports, airports, highways, etc.), exploitation of natural resources (namely, petroleum), public service management (concession or exploitation agreements), etc.[144] They are not termed in a uniform way, consequently, and they can be named international contracts, trade and development agreements, *State contracts*, financing agreements, investment agreements, etc.[145]

A number of scholars have raised objections to this classification of the *legal nature* of the international agreements under analysis, on the grounds

United Kingdom and Argentina. No investor is a party to the agreement. (…) It should come as no surprise that, after starting down the wrong road, the majority ends up at the wrong place" (*BG Group plc v. Republic of Argentina*, cit.; Roberts, C.J., dissenting p. 1).

143 Soares, Guido Fernando Silva. Os acordos administrativos e sua validade no Brasil, cit., p. 61.

144 See regarding this matter, Pereira, André Gonçalves & Quadros, Fausto de, *Manual de direito internacional público*, cit., p. 176-181.

145 See Soares, Guido Fernando Silva. Os acordos administrativos e sua validade no Brasil, cit., p. 61.

that any treaty, no matter how many contractual features it shares, will always contain normative elements.[146] In fact, even *contract-treaties* contain several *standard-setting* elements, such as, for instance, their final clauses on ratification, entry into force and the possibility of denunciation; or even a most-favored-nation clause or any safeguard provision, etc.[147] Furthermore, certain internationalists consider that this classification should be abandoned, not only for the aforementioned reasons, but also because it has no "legal effect", as there is no hierarchy in the context of public international law among *law-making treaties* and *contract-treaties*. Actually, each and every international treaty prevails over municipal law and no treaty can be repealed by the latter, under penalty of considering that the State incurred international responsibility. In the context of positive treaty law, both law-making treaties and contract-treaties have the same legal value, there being no hierarchical difference between them. Lastly, it should be noted that 1969 Vienna Convention on the Law of Treaties does not even draw a distinction between law-making treaties and contract-treaties.

2.2.2 Considerations concerning implementation over time

As to implementation over time, international treaties can be classified as *transitory* or *permanent*.[148]

Transitory treaties are those treaties that, even though they are long-lasting, their implementation is completed instantaneously and immediately, very often as a result of the mere publication of the treaty entered into by the parties. They are, in fact, agreements whose conclusion takes only one step, with no later or successive implementation clauses being provided for therein.[149] They are also termed *dispositive, real, territorial* or

---

146 For criticism of this perspective, see Kelsen, Hans, *Principles of international law*, New York: Rinehart & Company, 1952, p. 319-320; Holloway, Kaye, *Modern trends in treaty law: constitutional law, reservations and the three modes of legislation*, London: Stevens & Sons, 1967, p. 7; Verdross, Alfred & Simma, Bruno, *Universelles Völkerrecht: Theorie und Praxis*, 3. ed., Berlin: Duncker & Humblot, 1984, p. 339; Reuter, Paul, *Introducción al derecho de los tratados*, cit., p. 42-43; Mello, Celso D. de Albuquerque, *Curso de direito internacional público*, vol. I, cit., p. 220; Xavier, Alberto, *Direito tributário internacional do Brasil*, 6. ed. (updated and extended), Rio de Janeiro: Forense, 2005, p. 132-137; and De La Guardia, Ernesto, *Derecho de los tratados internacionales*, cit., p. 70-73.

147 See Rezek, José Francisco. *Direito dos tratados*, cit., p. 131.

148 See Rezek, José Francisco. Idem, p. 132-135.

149 See Cançado Trindade, Antônio Augusto (org.). *Repertório da prática brasileira do direito internacional público (período 1899-1918)*, 2. ed. Brasília: Fundação Alexandre de Gusmão, 2012, p. 131, citing Counsel Lafayette Rodrigues Pereira's opinion.

executed treaties, creating all of them static legal situations (that is, objective and final situations), such as for instance, those treaties providing for the sale or cession of territories,[150] establishing borders or limits between States, or stipulating the final transfer of certain assets. Despite the legal relationships created by such treaties that remain over time, their implementation is almost immediate, neither extending over long periods of time nor interfering with the everyday activities of their States Parties.

Permanent treaties, in turn, are those treaties whose implementation extends indefinitely over time, including trade and partnership treaties, extradition treaties, scientific and technological cooperation treaties, arbitration treaties, human rights treaties, and so forth. These are international commitments whose implementation does not occur in an *exact* moment, but instead, it develops while they are in force, and may be of long or short-term duration. These are international commitments whose implementation is not exhausted at a *particular* point in time, but quite to the contrary, they extend over time as long as they are in force, and their continuance in force could be of a long or even short duration. It should be stressed, however, that there may exist treaties, which combine the *transitory* and *permanent* features, mentioning by way of example, those treaties, "drawing a boundary line between two States while establishing a joint committee to preserve the natural resources of the border zone".[151]

As can be seen, this classification concerns the *implementation* of treaties over time but not their *effects*. In fact, such effects, although they may persist in time, as in the case of treaties concerning the cession of territories or the demarcation of borders, cannot be deemed *transitory* on the basis of the instrument embodying said treaties, as their implementation is completed upon their conclusion.

2.2.3 Consideration concerning territorial implementation

Some contracts are concluded to have legal force over *the whole* territory of a State, and some others are concluded only to have effects over just *a portion* of the territory of the State concerned.

Art. 29 of the Vienna Convention deals with this matter by setting forth that "unless a different intention appears from the treaty or is oth-

150 Regarding that type of treaties, see Crandall, Samuel B., *Treaties: their making and enforcement*, cit., p. 200-229.

151 Rezek, José Francisco. *Direito dos tratados*, cit., p. 134.

erwise established, a treaty is binding upon each party in respect of its entire territory". That *different intention* as mentioned in the text of the Convention – Rezek explains – "becomes very often united in one common nature with the scope of the so-called 'colonial clauses', whereby the powers of the northern hemisphere expressly set forth their intention that those treaties concerning social progress, economic benefits, and protection of individual rights are not applicable to their overseas territories".[152]

In fact, the conclusion of treaties not having legal effect in respect of the entire territory of a given State has not been occurred frequently in recent times.

2.2.4 Considerations concerning the implementation mechanism

Under this classification, which encompasses only multilateral treaties, treaties are classified into *mutualizable* and *non-mutualizable*.[153]

Mutualizable treaties are those multilateral treaties whose non-compliance by one party or multiple parties among themselves does not have the effect to compromise the implementation of the agreement as a whole. In this case, the failure to perform the treaty by some of the parties does not prevent it from continuing to be applied in relation to the other parties that are fully complying with its terms. A good example thereof is the GATT. In this vein, by way of example, although Brazil and Italy ceased to fulfill the agreement between them, for whatever reason, nothing would preclude the agreement from continuing to be regularly applied in relation to other States Parties. That is, the treaty remains fully effective and can normally be applied by the other contracting parties.

Non-mutualizable treaties are, in turn, those multilateral treaties that have not been conceived to allow non-compliance by any of their contracting parties. Consequently, in the event that one or more contracting parties, for whatever reason, do not comply with terms of the agreement in relation to each other, all the complying parties will be affected by that non-compliance, there being no way to cease to apply the treaty solely vis-à-vis the infringing parties. The Antarctic Treaty is an example of a *non-mutualizable* treaty.

---

152 Rezek, José Francisco. Idem, p. 136. See also on this matter, Sinclair, Ian, *The Vienna Convention on the Law of Treaties*, cit., p. 87-92.

153 See Rezek, José Francisco. *Direito dos tratados*, cit., p. 136-137.

2.3 Plan of the following parts of this work

Having analyzed the *general theory* of international treaties, it is now time to turn to the study of the *special part* of theory of treaties. Therefore, the study will revolve around the procedural aspects of international acts or agreements in light of the international norms concerning this matter (Parts II, III and IV) and under Brazilian Law as well (Part V). This study will essentially cover the treaty-making process, their execution and entry into force of treaties, as well as their termination. This analysis will focus on the modifications that treaties may be subject to (reservations and amendments) and the defects in the consent to be bound by a treaty that may adversely affect their validity. Moreover, Part IV will discuss treaties falling under the framework of the 1986 Vienna Convention on the Law of Treaties between States and International Organizations or between International Organizations. The final part of the book is devoted to understanding the constitutional rules concerning the conclusion of treaties by Brazil, followed by the study of conflicts that may arise between treaties and municipal law.

Part II

Genesis of International Treaties

Chapter 1

Procedure of Formation and Conclusion of Treaties

1.1 Introduction

Having analyzed the concept, the terminology and classification of international treaties, attention should now be turned to the procedural aspects (that is, the procedural steps), which lead to their conclusion.[1] The study of procedural steps that lead to the conclusion of treaties covers the procedure of formation and conclusion of international acts, in accordance with the 1969 Vienna Convention on the Law of Treaties. In short, this section will revolve around understanding the series of acts that enable the *negotiation*, *conclusion* and *entry into force* of an international treaty.[2]

Once again, it should be stated that the analysis of the procedure of formation and conclusion of treaties will be conducted from a strictly *formal* perspective, regardless of the content (or *subject-matter*) the concerned agreement deals with, but focusing on the procedure the instrument went through, from the moment of its conclusion until its entry into force. The problem concerning the matter (or *content*) that the agreement deals with leads to *intrinsic unconstitutionality* of treaties, the solution to such a problem falling within the scope of the constitutional law of the State concerned (although it should be noted that, pursuant to Art. 27 of 1969 the Vienna Convention an international norm shall *always* prevail over internal law – see Part III, Ch. 2, item 2.3.5); the question concerning

1 For further details, see Maresca, Adolfo, *Il diritto dei trattati…*, cit., p. 125-206. See also Balladore Pallieri, G., La formation des traités dans la pratique internationale contemporaine, *Recueil des Cours*, vol. 74 (1949-I), p. 469-542.

2 See Remiro Brotons, Antonio. *Derecho internacional público*, vol. 2, cit., p. 69.

the form (or the procedural aspects) can, in turn, lead to the *extrinsic unconstitutionality* of the agreement – which concerns Public International Law – coupled with a number of practical issues, such as the authorization to conclude treaties and the potential responsibility of the President of the Republic due to the fact that she/he has ratified the treaty without the acquiescence of the National Congress, as will be discussed in due course. (See Part III, Ch. 2, items 2.3.1 to 2.3.4).

The analysis that follows is common to both bilateral and multilateral treaties. When the issue at hand will deal specifically with one of these types of treaties, the reader will be made duly aware of it.

1.2 International and internal stages

The first concept to be defined when analyzing the procedure of formation and conclusion of treaties is that such acts are *solemn*, their completion requiring (as they are legal acts) a series of strictly distinct and successive formalities. International acts can only be completed after the conduct of successive *phases*, which will be interwoven from the moment those acts are executed until they enter into force.

Typically, solemn treaties must go through *four* phases until they can be deemed to be concluded: *a)* preparation of the text (negotiations, adoption, authentication) and signature; *b)* parliamentary approval by each State Member intending to become a party to the treaty; *c)* a ratification or accession to the treaty, carried out by deposit or exchange of the instruments in which the treaty is embodied, and *d)* enactment and publication of the treaty by the Official Gazette. This last step is just a complementary aspect that aims at enabling the internal application of the engagement undertaken at an international level; its non-compliance does not exonerate the State under any circumstance from being held responsible under the terms and conditions of the already ratified treaty and that has come into force. It should be stressed that the Convention when undergoing some of these phases uses its own terminology to refer to States, as follows: *negotiating State*, when the State takes part in the drawing up and adoption of the text of the treaty (Art. 2(1)(e)); *contracting State*, whenever a State has consented to be bound by the treaty, whether or not the treaty has entered into force (Art. 2(1) (f)); and *party*, when a State has consented to be bound by a treaty and for which the treaty is in force (Art. 2(1)(g)).

It should be clarified that the Vienna Convention of 1969 did not address the so-called internal phases for the conclusion of treaties, that is, whether or not the conventional text followed the constitutional rules regarding competence to conclude treaties, unless in this phase of the process to conclude a treaty an internal law provision of fundamental importance has been manifestly violated, as provided for in Art. 46(1) of the Convention, which will be discussed in detail below (see Part III, Ch. 2, item 2.3).

If complementary measures, such as promulgation and publication of international acts are taken into consideration, then the different phases for the conclusion of a treaty (divided into international and national phases) include broadly the following:

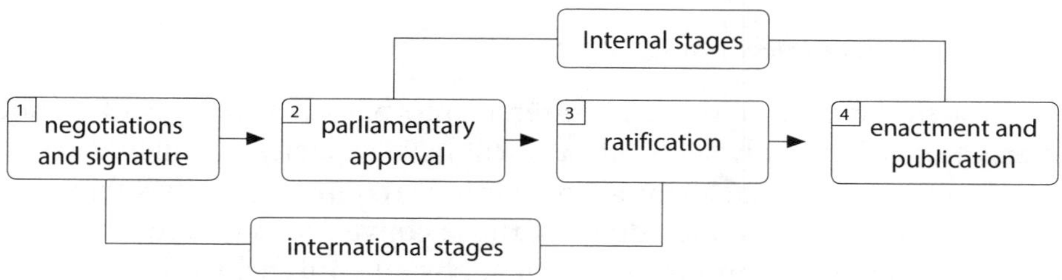

The combination of international phases with internal phases for the conclusion of international acts gives rise to a complex procedure involving two of the Powers of the State, whereby the will of the Executive Power (Tables 1, 3 and 4) and that of the Legislative Power (Table 2) interact in order to achieve a perfect formalization of the treaty concerned, which undoubtedly makes the procedure for the conclusion of treaties more democratic in nature. That is a characteristic tendency of contemporary constitutional texts, in which the involvement of these two Federal Powers is essential to form the will of the State in relation to what has been agreed to at international level.

1.3 Conditions of validity

There exist a number of *conditions* or *essential elements* for a treaty to be valid. Thus, negotiating Parties (States or international organizations) (*a*) must be *competent* enough to conclude a treaty; their respective signatory agents must be (*b*) *legally authorized* to act; there must exist (*c*) *mutual consent* of the parties; and the purpose of the treaty must be (*d*) *licit and materially possible.*

Legal scholars generally agree that the absence of one or many of these conditions invalidates the treaty, which may therefore be declared by the competent international courts (in particular, the ICJ within the UN System). However, it should be noted that as these *conditions* (except for the first one) do not form part of the concept of treaty provided for in Art. 2 (1) (a) of the 1969 Vienna Convention, the treaty as such exists, although it may be declared *invalid*. If those conditions of validity did form an integral part of the concept of treaty, an international agreement that has not been freely agreed to, would not constitute a treaty.[3] It is thus clear that an unintended agreement is deemed to constitute a treaty, although consent to be bound by it may be voidable (Arts. 46-50) or void *ab initio* (Art. 51).

1.3.1 Capacity of negotiating States

If a treaty is an agreement entered into between *subjects* of Public International Law, only such *subjects* will have capacity to conclude treaties. The 1969 and 1986 Vienna Conventions require that only subjects of law of nations should conclude what those conventions define as being a *treaty*. Consequently, an international act by an entity which is not a *subject* of Public International Law cannot be deemed a treaty.[4]

Who are those *subjects* of Public International Law possessing capacity to conclude treaties? It must be emphasized that *physical persons*, albeit subjects of law of nations, do not possess capacity to conclude treaties. Only three of the current subjects of Public International Law have permanent capacity to conclude treaties: sovereign States, the Holy See (as it has international legal personality[5]) and international intergovernmental organizations. The latter, however, have their own rules regarding the issue of competence to conclude treaties, thus, this matter shall be discussed later (see Part IV, Ch 2, item 2.1). Exceptionally, *belligerents* and *national liberation movements* may have capacity (albeit temporary or provisional) to enter into treaties,[6] as well as dependent States (vassal

3 See De La Guardia, Ernesto. *Derecho de los tratados internacionales*, cit., p. 112.

4 See Dinh, Daillier & Pellet. *Direito internacional público*, cit., p. 192. On this subject, especially see Kamto, Maurice, La volonté de l'État en droit international, *Recueil des Cours*, vol. 310 (2004), p. 68-94.

5 On the international legal personality of the Holy See, see Mazzuoli, Valerio de Oliveira, *Curso de direito internacional público*, 8. ed. (reviewed, updated and extended), São Paulo: Revista dos Tribunais, 2014, p. 450-455.

6 For further details, see Mazzuoli, Valerio de Oliveira, *Curso de direito internacional público*, cit., p. 446-448.

and protected States) that have permission to do so from their suzerain or protector States.[7]

Apart from the referred to exceptions, the truth is that *States* are subjects holding the primary (and full) capacity to enter into treaties, since the character of *sovereignty* and the capacity to take conventional obligations (the so-called *jus tractuum*) are implicit. Therefore, the Vienna Convention has established that "every [sovereign] State possesses capacity to conclude treaties", under the exact terms of its Art. 6.[8] Such provision, as explained by Reuter, does not set forth a rule, but only describes *one of the basic attributes* of the character of State, which is the capacity to conclude treaties. Even though the States are not the only subjects of Public International Law, they are the *primary* subjects of the law of nations, then enjoying full legal personality, whose fundamental expression in International Law is the capacity to conclude treaties.[9] Then, no regulation or subject domain is prohibited, *a priori*; at the most, the problem that may arise is that of some States denying the character of *State* to an entity.[10]

Interstate organizations, in turn, have *derivative* capacity to conclude treaties, since it all depends on the provisions of the "rules of [the] organization [concerned]" (Art. 6 of the 1986 Convention).

Dependent states lack the capacity to conclude treaties. This way, colonies, as well as dependent territories, protected lands, vassal States, and others, cannot be included internationally as parties to international treaties.

---

7 See Mello, Celso D. de Albuquerque. *Curso de direito internacional público*, vol. I, cit., p. 214-215.

8 This article does not refer to the character of *sovereign* of States, but this should be inferred. It should be noted that the wording of Art. 6 was the one that caused a lot of debate between 1968 and 1969. For details on those debates, see Nascimento e Silva, Geraldo Eulálio do, *Conferência de Viena sobre o Direito dos Tratados*, p. 63-64; De La Guardia, Ernesto, *Derecho de los tratados internacionales*, cit., p. 131-132; and Villiger, Mark E., *Commentary on the 1969 Vienna Convention on the Law of Treaties*, cit., p. 127-128.

9 See Reuter, Paul. *Introducción al derecho de los tratados*, cit., p. 94. See also Villiger, Mark E., *Commentary on the 1969 Vienna Convention on the Law of Treaties*, cit., p. 128-129, as is: "At the heart of Article 6 lies the capacity which States possess to conclude treaties. Capacity refers to two elements of treaty-making: (*i*) it is an essential requirement for the validity of a treaty since validity depends on the capacity of the contracting parties (*e.g.*, *Articles* 7, 8, 27, 46, and 51, *q.v.*); and (*ii*) in the absence of possessing an inherent capacity to conclude treaties, an international entity cannot be a State. Article 6 is concerned with the latter only".

10 See Dinh, Daillier & Pellet. *Direito internacional público*, cit., p. 193.

Such power is only held by the colonial Powers, or the colonies themselves, with the *express* consent of latter. Therefore, a vassal State, for example, will only have the right to conclude treaties when authorized to do so by the suzerain State, never under any other condition.[11] International Law recognizes, however, legal validity of: *a)* such agreements that, concluded after the dependency relationship, amend the terms of the vassalage relationship, by the free will of the parties; and *b)* such agreements that are aimed at terminating the subordination or colonial dependency relationship.[12]

Regarding federated States,[13] there are two situations: one in which the Federal Union recognizes the power to conclude treaties to these states, and another in which the Constitution does not contain any provision dealing with it, or denies the existence of such possibility.[14] In the first case, as only States (since they have *sovereignty*) can conclude treaties, along with international organizations, the Federal Union (which only has *autonomy*) must be liable for the commitments made, in its name, by its federated States. Since these cannot be held liable for any contingent failure to comply with the agreement, but rather only the sovereign State can be held responsible, thus liability for the international unlawful act by federated States will fall under the latter, which authorized the federated State to make international commitments on behalf of the Nation. Anyway, nothing in the law of nations can prevent a federated State from undertaking international obligations, if authorized by the Federal Constitution (such obligations, however, will not be governed by the 1969 Vienna Convention).[15] In the second case, when the National Constitution states nothing about

---

11 See Calsing, Maria de Assis. *O tratado internacional e sua aplicação no Brasil.* Brasília: UnB, 1984, p. 10; and Mello, Celso D. de Albuquerque, *Curso de direito internacional público*, vol. I, cit., p. 215, which adds: "In order to check whether a dependent State possess or not the right to conclude conventions, it is necessary to review each case, since the dependent situation is set by the dominant State".

12 For details, see Rezek, José Francisco, *Direito dos tratados*, cit., p. 45-46.

13 They (*federated* States) represent the parts into which the *Federal* State is divided.

14 On the problem of international law application in Federal States, see Krüger, Herbert, Völkerrecht im Bundesstaat, *Um Recht und Gerechtigkeit*: Festgabe für Erich Kaufmann zu seinem 70, Geburtstage, September 21, 1950; überreicht von Freunden, Verehrern und Schülern, Stuttgart und Köln: W. Kohlhammer Verlag, 1950, p. 239-248; and Oliver, Covey T., The enforcement of treaties by a Federal State, *Recueil des Cours*, vol. 141 (1974-I), p. 331-412.

15 See Rezek, José Francisco. *Direito dos tratados*, cit., p. 34. See also Sagüés, Néstor Pedro, *Teoría de la Constitución*, Buenos Aires: Astrea, 2004, p. 396-397; and Crawford, James, *Brownlie's principles of public international law*, cit., p. 117.

it, the Federal Union authorizes the federated State to conclude the treaty, which should be construed in the aforementioned manner, being the federal government liable for the contingent unlawful act. When the Constitution expressly denies the power to conclude treaties to federated States, only the federal State (that is, the Republic) can be part of the international treaty, although the agreement proposal has been made by one of the federation members interested in its conclusion. Therefore, the International Law Commission of the UN suggested, at the conference of the Vienna Convention on Law of Treaties, the following provision: "States Members of a Federal Union may possess capacity to conclude treaties if such capacity is admitted by the Federal Constitution, and within the limits there laid down". This provision would be item 2 of Art. 6 of the 1969 Vienna Convention on the Law of Treaties, but it was immediately rejected, because it did not attract the approval of many States that were present.

Art. 52(V) of the 1988 Brazilian Constitution allows the Union, the States, the Federal District, the Territories and Municipalities to carry out foreign transactions of a financial nature, provided that they are authorized by the Federal Senate.[16] Many of such transactions are negotiated with international organizations, such as the IMF and the World Bank, which have international law legal personality. But the constitutional text itself states that the Union shall have the power to "maintain relations with foreign states and participate in international organizations" (Art. 21, I), so it is not possible to understand the conclusion of treaties to which the *Brazilian State itself* is not a party.[17]

Agreements concluded between States and populations with no government of their own or tribes (that are very rare nowadays), as well as conventions between States and foreign persons (remarkably those regarding international loans), lack the legal requirements and aspects of *treaties*, and they are not akin to the latter in any manner. Also, companies do not possess the capacity to conclude treaties, whether public or private, irrespective of their capital, size, or multinationality.[18]

---

16 See Mazzuoli, Valerio de Oliveira. Comentário ao artigo 52, V, in Canotilho, J. J. Gomes; Mendes, Gilmar F.; Sarlet, Ingo W. & Streck, Lenio L. (coord.), *Comentários à Constituição do Brasil*, São Paulo: Saraiva/Almedina, 2013, p. 1054-1058.

17 For details, see Mazzuoli, Valerio de Oliveira, *Natureza jurídica e eficácia dos acordos* stand-by *com o FMI*, cit., p. 231-305.

18 See Rezek, José Francisco.*Direito dos tratados*, cit., p. 29-30; De La Guardia, Ernesto, *Derecho de los tratados internacionales*, cit., p. 127; and Aust, Anthony, *Modern treaty law and practice*, cit., p. 15.

1.3.2 Signatories authorization and full powers

As has been discussed, every sovereign State possesses the capacity to conclude treaties. However, such entities are not identifiable natural persons, this requires the existence of specific principles to guarantee that the natural persons that act on behalf of the State have the authority to conclude the treaty under preparation.[19] How is such procedure carried out in practice? Obviously, it is carried out through *representation*. That is to say, every State holds legally authorized *representation bodies* to represent it at the international level, to act in its name and under its control. Such *persons* acting on behalf of the State are their *representatives*. Therefore, when they are sent to negotiate a treaty and they conclude it with representatives of other foreign Powers, they are *signatories* of the agreement. Then, the question that arises here is under which terms a person is held to be a representative of a given State for the purpose of concluding a treaty.

Under the law of nations, the rule is that every signatory must be duly authorized to perform international acts *in the name* of the State. Such authorization is given (*a*) by the express wording of the Constitution, or (*b*) by the institution of *full powers*. In practice, those agents who effectively participate in the initial steps of the formation of treaties are not Heads of State, but they are those chosen by the State to represent it abroad and in whose favour a "Letter of Full Powers" is granted. That is why their agents are called *plenipotentiaries* (because they hold *full powers*).[20]

The institution of *full powers*, influenced by the *Corpus Juris Civilis*, was developed in the Renaissance period (the first one dating back from 1303) and consisted of a power granted by the Head of State to his representative, establishing the limitations of powers granted to him.[21] It arose by virtue of the intensification of international relations and, consequently, of the incapacity of the Heads of State to be in many places at the same time, for the purpose of negotiating more than one treaty. After the 19th

---

19 See Shaw, Malcolm N. *Direito internacional*, cit., p. 677.

20 On the institution of full powers, see Pereira de Araújo, João Hermes, *A processualística dos atos internacionais*, cit., p. 101-124; and, with a contemporary view, Sinclair, Ian, *The Vienna Convention on the Law of Treaties*, cit., p. 29-33; Aust, Anthony, *Modern treaty law and practice*, cit., p. 57-65; and Villiger, Mark E., *Commentary on the 1969 Vienna Convention on the Law of Treaties*, cit., p. 135-147.

21 See Sette Câmara, José. *The ratification of international treaties*, cit., p. 19-24; and Mello, Celso D. de Albuquerque, *Curso de direito internacional público*, vol. I, cit., p. 217.

century, the letter of full powers (*litera fidei*) turned out to be an instrument of *communication* between the plenipotentiary and its Government rather than an instrument of *validity* of the international act itself. That is why, nowadays, given that the phase of absolute monarchs and inefficient communication is over, the letter of full powers considerably lost is practical relevance.[22] Today, it is understood that, due to the speed of communication between the Government and its plenipotentiary, the existence of fraud is almost impossible regarding the representation of the State abroad.[23] Moreover, the mere signature of the agreement except for Art. 12 of the 1969 Vienna Convention, has no inherent power to generate a valid legal bond to (finally) bind the State at the international level, which will only happen as a result of the later *ratification* of the respective treaty. This is another reason why the institution of *full powers* lost its relevance today. Even its *form* was simplified, being possible (nowadays) to be carried out via *fax, telegram, telex* or *e-mail*, as required by the contemporary international relations dynamics.[24] However, although the international society is today in a totally transformed context, the institution of full powers is still in effect as a "symbol" of sovereignty.[25] Finally, its granting guarantees that a treaty is being negotiated with a duly authorized agent by the State.

It should be noted that the determination of the competent authority to negotiate (and sign) treaties depends on the Constitutional Law of each State,[26] being the same authority (appointed by the Constitution), the competent one to delegate such negotiation competency to others (to plenipotentiaries).[27] In Brazil, pursuant to Art. 84(VIII) of the 1988 Brazilian Constitution, the aforementioned authority is the President of the

---

22 See Brownlie, Ian. *Princípios de direito internacional público*. Transl. by Maria Manuela Farrajota (*et all.*). Lisbon: Fundação Calouste Gulbenkian, 1997, p. 630.

23 See Calsing, Maria de Assis. *O tratado internacional e sua aplicação no Brasil*, cit., p. 26.

24 See Remiro Brotons, Antonio. *Derecho internacional público*, vol. 2, cit., p. 147; and De La Guardia, Ernesto, *Derecho de los tratados internacionales*, cit., p. 123.

25 See Dinh, Daillier & Pellet. *Direito internacional público*, cit., p. 129.

26 See Wheaton, Henry. *Elements of international law*, vol. I, cit., p. 487. See also De La Guardia, Ernesto, *Derecho de los tratados internacionales*, cit., p. 197, who argues that: "As a general rule, when referring to a State, it is the *constitutional norms* that govern such capacity, traditionally referred to as *treaty-making power* (power to conclude treaties). As regards the State unions or international organizations, it is the *constitutive instrument*, which is the one establishing competence to conclude treaties".

27 See Dinh, Daillier & Pellet. *Direito internacional público*, cit., p. 130.

Republic, who is also responsible for delegation of his/her competence (Art. 84).

The Heads of State (or Government, depending on the system adopted in each country) have, by virtue of the position that they hold, *primary competence* to conclude treaties. Typically, at the internal law level, constitutions appoint them as primary responsible persons for the conclusion of treaties in the name of the State, under the chart of general assignment of positions. The Ministries of Foreign Affairs (or of *Foreign Business*, as referred to as in some States, or even the *Foreign Secretary* or *Secretary of State*) have, in turn, *derivative* (or *secondary*) *competence* for the conclusion of treaties, with the same powers that Heads of State or of Government have, once vested in their respective positions; they are plenipotentiaries, who are, *by virtue of their offices and depending on the case*, released from producing the "Letter of full powers", and it cannot be required of them to present it.[28]

According to the 1969 Vienna Convention (Art. 7, item 2), such organs that by virtue of their offices represent the State internationally, without the need to produce full powers, are divided into three groups, each one limited to the practice of *certain acts* regarding the conclusion of a treaty, as follows:

a) Heads of State, Heads of Government and Ministers for Foreign Affairs are released from producing full powers for the purpose of performing *all acts regarding the conclusion* of a treaty, being able to adopt and authenticate their text, sign it, ratify it and agree to it;

b) Heads of diplomatic missions (ambassadors or business responsible persons) are released from producing full powers *only* for the purpose of *adopting* the text (also being understood as previous *negotiations*) of a treaty between the accrediting State and the State to which they are accredited (which means that they cannot participate in *every* act regarding the conclusion of a treaty); and

c) representatives accredited by States to an international conference or to an international organization or one of its bodies are released from producing full powers (only) for the purpose of adopting the text of a treaty in that conference, organization or bodies.[29]

---

28 For details, see Remiro Brotons, Antonio, *Derecho internacional público*, vol. 2, cit., p. 148-149; and Villiger, Mark E., *Commentary on the 1969 Vienna Convention on the Law of Treaties*, cit., p. 140-144.

29 See Rousseau, Charles, *Principes généraux du droit international public*, t. I, cit., p. 164.

In item 1.4.2.3 (see below) a number of criticisms will be made to such provision (especially to paragraph (b) of Art. 7, item 2) of the 1969 Vienna Convention (whose rule is also reproduced in the 1986 Convention). For the moment, it will suffice to say that, in principle, for other plenipotentiaries who are not those referred to above and for performing acts other than the ones therein provided, the letter of full powers, issued by the State competent authority, shall be required.[30] In the event that the representation of the State is done by a delegation or a group of people, it should be pointed out that only the *head* of the delegation or commission will hold full powers, being vested in him/her and in no one else, the execution of acts expressing the will of the State he represents, at the international level.

The President of the Republic, in today's Brazilian practice, when issuing a *full powers letter*, lets the foreign Government or international organization where the treaty is being executed know that such plenipotentiary who is there *representing the Brazilian Government*, will produce full powers to *negotiate, adopt* and *sign* the international treaty under preparation, with its validity subject to the later *approval* of the National Congress and the ratification of the President of the Republic himself/herself.

In the Brazilian case, the competence of the Head of the Executive to conclude treaties is *exclusive*, which enables delegation of powers, which is, in fact, very common in the procedure of international acts, since the President of the Republic has other functions to fulfill apart from concluding treaties. At present, it is very rare to see a Head of State participating in person in the negotiations of a treaty, and this has many reasons (internal and international), both political and practical.[31] That is why the 1988 Brazilian Constitution states that the President of the Republic has exclusive powers to "maintain relations with foreign States and accredit their diplomatic representatives" (Art. 84, VII), as well as to "conclude international treaties, conventions and acts, subject to the approval of the National Congress" (Art. 84, VIII).

---

30 Sinclair reports that in the United Kingdom practice, there are "general full powers" (exercised by the Secretary of State for Foreign Affairs and the British Community, Ministers of State and Undersecretaries of Parliament for the Minister for Foreign Affairs and the British Community and by Permanent Representatives from UN, European Community and GATT, which enable that *any* treaty be negotiated and signed) and "specific full powers" (granted to a specific person to negotiate and sign a certain treaty). See Sinclair, Ian. *The Vienna Convention on the Law of Treaties*, cit., p. 32.

31 See Pereira de Araújo, João Hermes. *A processualística dos atos internacionais*, cit., p. 23.

It should be highlighted that the *sole paragraph* of Art. 84 of the 1988 Constitution gives the false impression that the presidential delegation is only possible in the specific case of the *three items* listed therein, when it states: "The President of the Republic may delegate the duties mentioned in items VI, XII and XXV, first part, to the Ministers of State, to the Attorney-General of the Republic or to the Advocate-General of the Union, who shall observe the limitations established in the respective delegations". The interpretation, however, that should be given to such paragraph is that the President of the Republic can only exercise the delegation in favour of the three entities mentioned in the three items (Ministers of State, Attorney-General of the Republic or to the Advocate-General of the Union), with no further delegation to third parties being possible. Nevertheless, this does not mean that the President of the Republic cannot delegate his/her powers to other persons at his sole discretion, under the other items of Art. 84, for instance, in favour of the Minister for Foreign Affairs in the event of the execution of international treaties (item VIII), etc.

The presidential competence to conclude treaties is generally delegated to the Minister for Foreign Affairs, who exercises the function of assistant to the President of the Republic when performing international acts and foreign policy in Brazil. Such competence may also be delegated to accredited diplomatic agents in foreign countries (when the agreement takes place in the foreign country where such agents are located) or to the heads of diplomatic missions. The latter, when holding a permanent status, have their appointment approved previously by the Federal Senate, which interviews them in a secret session (Art. 52, IV, Federal Constitution /88). It is very rare that the Head of the Diplomatic Mission is not an active official of the government, as it was the case of Professor Haroldo Valladão, former Legal Advisor to Itamaraty and Attorney-General of the Republic, who was many times, in his capacity as university professor and lawyer, Head of Diplomatic Missions at the request of the Brazilian Government.[32] All diplomatic agents, however, accredited or certified by the foreign country, may be a plenipotentiary agent and have the capacity to represent the State to conclude treaties. The reason for this constitutional permission to delegate the presidential competence to conclude treaties is well explained by Basdevant, since according to his opinion "the direct participation of Heads of State in the negotiation and signature of a treaty gives it sometimes a final character, which is ordinarily deemed more convenient to avoid".[33]

In fact, although the formula of certain constitutional texts is literal, for example the Brazilian one, in the sense that the President of the Re-

32 The example was taken from Rezek, José Francisco, *Direito dos tratados*, cit., p. 213, note 369.

33 Basdevant, Jules. La conclusion et la rédaction des traités et des instruments diplomatiques autres que les traités, cit., p. 546.

public shall have the power to "conclude international treaties, conventions and acts", it is perceived, since long ago, that Heads of State only exceptionally will conclude, by themselves, the treaties that the country intended to conclude. Therefore, the regulation of such presidential competence must be in the sense of enabling the *executive body* to conclude treaties (that is, to the government and its assistants, for subjects regarding the foreign relations of the country).

Finally, some thoughts should be expressed about the representation of international organizations at international level, whose regulation is covered by the 1986 Vienna Convention on the Law on Treaties between States and International Organizations or between International Organizations (which turned out to follow the model established by the 1969 Convention for the representation of States). The rule here is also that a person is considered a representative of an international organization for the adoption or authentication of the text of a treaty or to express organization's consent to be bound by a treaty if producing full proper powers (Art. 7, item 3 *a*). In practice, however, it is not common to grant a document whereby a certain person is expressly authorized as a representative of a specific international organization for the purpose of performing acts regarding the formation of a treaty, as it is sometimes difficult to determine which competent body should grant it.[34] The usual thing to do, explains Brotons, is that the representation is deducted from the correspondence previously interchanged or from other created uses within each organization, also being able to arise from *resolutions* adopted by collegiate bodies, etc.[35] Although the 1986 Convention (which followed the 1969 Convention on this subject) has placed the need for *full powers* also for the representation of international organizations, the fact remains that practice has contributed to make this rule more flexible, for the purpose of enabling a higher degree of informality in comparison to that allowed in the field of State representation.[36] The 1986 Convention established, in item *b* of Art. 7, item 3 that the representation will be equally valid where "it appears from the circumstances that it was the intention of the States and international organizations concerned to consider that person as representing the organization for

---

34 See Remiro Brotons, Antonio. *Derecho internacional público*, vol. 2, cit., p. 152.

35 See Remiro Brotons, Antonio. Idem, ibidem.

36 See Remiro Brotons, Antonio. Idem, ibidem.

such purposes, in accordance with the rules of the organization, without having to produce full powers".

1.3.3 Mutual consent

Every treaty corresponds to a *concurrence of wills*, which is premised on the free and unmistakable right of option of States, clearly expressed in writing. Consent of the contracting parties must be *mutual*. What are its features? It is known that every negotiation of a treaty is based on a *promise* (made by some parties) and its *acceptance* (by other parties). The exact match between what is *promised* by one contracting party and what it is *accepted* by the other party, explains Accioly, constitutes the *concurrence of wills* or *consent*.[37] In other words, consent is *mutual* when expressed by *both parties* in agreement (*consensus ad idem*) and without being vitiated by any reason (for example, by mistake, fraud, coercion, etc.). When one of them forces the other, by any reason, to accept its will, or when one party imposes its will, as a result of the vitiated consent of the other party, the consent expressed for the conclusion of the treaty will be *null and void*.

Consent must be expressed on a *free* way in order to be mutual. The most serious cases of violation of such freedom are related to the coercion of the representative of a State, which according to the Vienna Convention (Art. 51) turns the consent *void ab initio*. As Brierly states, the treaty imposed by force "represents a clear violation to the contractual freedom rule, which is the basic principle of every civilized society".[38] Besides, there are many types of *defects* that may affect consent, which may turn it null, or even void *ab initio*, as in the mentioned case of coercion on the representative of a State.[39]

There are plenty of historic examples of treaties concluded without the consent of one of the contracting parties. The 1919 Versailles Treaty is an illustrative example, which was exclusively prepared by the allied States (the victors) and submitted to the losing States for their signature, as though the treaty was, in comparison to internal law agreements, a pre-formulated standard contract.

---

37 Accioly, Hildebrando. *Tratado de direito internacional público*, vol. I, cit., p. 562-563. In the same sense, see Remiro Brotons, Antonio, *Derecho internacional público*, vol. 2, cit., p. 29.

38 Brierly, J. L. *Direito internacional*, cit., p. 325.

39 On this subject, see Ch. 2, Part III, which will fully cover it.

1.3.4 *Lawfulness and material possibility of object or purpose*

The object or purpose of treaties must be *lawful* and *materially possible*. It is clear that the promise of an unlawful, immoral or physically unachievable consideration cannot form a valid legal bond.[40]

Here the lawfulness and the material possibility of the object of a treaty are being analyzed, that is, the content of its consideration. In this case, the treaty as such, *exists* and is in force, but it is *void* for breaching the law and morals (unlawfulness of the object) or for promising something physically unachievable (material impossibility of the subject-matter).[41] A judgment handed down by a post-war international court is an example of the first case (the treaty did not apply for being contrary to accepted principles of morality): "We have no doubt to conclude that, if Laval or the ambassador of Vichy in Berlin concluded any treaty on the use of French war prisoners in the German industry, such treaty is expressly contrary to accepted principles of morality and, therefore, void".[42] An example of the second case (physical impossibility of performing the treaty) is given by Accioly: "(…) Article 1, item 6, of the treaty between Brazil and Bolivia, signed in Petrópolis, on November 17, 1903, laid down that the border between both countries should be established from the main headwaters of the Rapirrán River, by the parallel of the same headwaters, towards the west, until reaching the Iquiri River. However, it was later verified that the Iquiri River runs entirely, north of the mentioned parallel, so it cannot be reached by Rapirrán River. Therefore, such provision had to be amended

---

40 See Mello, Celso D. de Albuquerque. *Curso de direito internacional público*, vol. I, cit., p. 217.

41 See See Wheaton, Henry. *Elements of international law*, vol. I, cit., p. 489.

42 Case "United States *versus* Krupp and others", in *Annual Digest and Reports of Public International Law Cases*, No. 214 (1948), p. 267, quoted by Dinh, Daillier & Pellet, *Direito internacional público*, cit., p. 205. However, the comment made by De La Guardia should be pointed out on this subject: "The problem of the *subject-matter lawfulness* (…) does not have in international law the importance given to it in connection with legal acts of internal law. Firstly, because the limited notion of the free will of the parties (public order) has less importance in the international order, where the concept of *jus cogens* is not finally formed yet, and also because the conclusion of *treaties with unlawful subject-matters* is unachievable (not possible). Secondly, the chance that a treaty be concluded in contravention of positive international law rules, which are mandatory to the interested parties, is more related to the subject of treaties that are incompatible between them than to the relation between mandatory and non-mandatory rules" (*Derecho de los tratados internacionales*, cit., p. 265-266).

in another treaty because, as a result of a physical impossibility, it could not be performed".[43]

However, the case of the treaty whose object is *lawful* and *materially possible*, but that is void *ab initio* is even worse (*a*) for having been concluded by threat or the use of force (Art. 52) or (*b*) for conflicting with an existing peremptory norm of general international law (*jus cogens*) (Art. 53). Due to the intricacies of the subject, it will be studied in a separate Chapter (see Part III, Ch. 2, items 2.1.3 and 2.2.2.1, respectively).

1.4 Preparation of the conventional text

Conventional texts go through a *treaty-making process* at the international level, apart from the existing stages at the internal law level (which the text should also undergo). Even though there is not a predetermined form for its conclusion, it should be noted that treaties may be concluded as understood by negotiators, but the truth is that there are stages where the conventional text should go through, so that in the future the treaty may enter into force for the parties.

There several stages that the treaty must undergo, from the writing of its *draft*, until its effective *entry into force*, so that international legal act becomes an obligation of binding nature.[44] Those *stages* which the treaty must undergo until its entry into force were initially established by international *practice*, and later transformed into *custom*. Acceptance of general practice as law (a necessary element for the creation of international custom under the terms of Art. 38, item 1 *b* of the Statute of the International Court of Justice) in connection with the conclusion of treaties ended up transforming it into *positive* law in the text of the 1969 Vienna Convention.

At this stage, what are known as *international stages* of the conclusion of treaties should be considered, which are carried out (always) by the *government* of States, that is, by the Executive Power. Such international stages are divided into (*a*) the *text formation* and (*b*) the *expression of consent*. The first one (*text formation*) is formed by *negotiations*, by the *text adoption* and its *authentication*. Everything else apart from such acts constitutes the stage known as *expression of consent*, formed by the acts of *signature*, *ratification*, and eventually, *accession* (see item 1.5, below).

---

43 Accioly, Hildebrando. *Tratado de direito internacional público*, vol. I, cit., p. 640.

44 See Shaw, Malcolm N. *Direito internacional*, cit., p. 675.

1.4.1 Negotiations

The treaty-making process starts with *negotiation* acts, which are generally carried out by the Executive Power (that is to say, the President of the Republic or the Minister for Foreign Affairs), with such prerogative able to vary from one country to another. The competence of the Executive to participate in international relations in the name of the State, even though it varies from one country to another, is historical, being its foreign acts (from negotiations of a treaty up to its ratification) preponderant over the rest of the Powers.[45] That is why the Executive *participates more* in international relations than the Legislative, which only gives its opinion in the treaty-making process *once*, when it considers the feasibility of the State to undertake its international commitments (a stage that takes place after the *signature* and before the *ratification*).

The importance of the Executive in conducting the foreign relations of a State, when the subject refers to the execution of treaties, is exactly found at this stage of *negotiations*. Negotiations of a treaty start when the representatives of States meet at a specific place and at arranged time, for the purpose of studying the possibilities to reach an agreement in connection with the conclusion of a specific international instrument in a joint manner. Therefore, the word negotiation has a wide meaning "every action prior to an agreement of any nature, the time of discussion and the concurrence of wills which will or will not be transformed into a legal act".[46] The exchange of expression of wills, offers and counteroffers, concessions done by some States in connection with other States, as well as the final set of positions, are the features of the negotiations of a treaty.

However, it should be pointed out that when outlined that negotiations of a treaty are in charge of the *Executive Power*, this does not mean that the Head of State must *directly* participate in them. It is perfectly possible that the Head of State *delegates* the negotiation of a treaty to another agent (also a private person), as authorized by Art. 84, VIII, of the Brazilian Constitution, which states that the presidential competence to conclude treaties is *exclusive* (that is to say that it may be delegated). Some authors, such as Cachapuz de Medeiros, state that, although the Head of the Executive continues playing a preponderant role in the conclusion of treaties, this would mean to endorse that he/she does *not even participate*

---

45 On the predominance of the Executive in international relations, see Cachapuz de Medeiros, Antônio Paulo, *O poder de celebrar tratados...*, cit., p. 163-185.

46 See Pereira de Araújo, João Hermes. *A processualística dos atos internacionais*, cit., p. 21.

at all in negotiations, since "such attitude can give the appearance that the agreements obtained at the initial stage are of a final nature, which may cause some problems in the event of disapproval by the Legislative".[47]

It should be noted that, maybe due to the lack of systematization, Art. 7 of the Vienna Convention does not refer to the possibility to grant *full powers* to a representative of State for the negotiation of a treaty. However, art 2, item 1 *c*, of the same Convention, expressly contemplates such possibility, by establishing that "full powers" mean a document emanating from the competent authority of a State designating "a person or persons to represent the State for negotiating, adopting or authenticating the text of a treaty...". Then, by virtue of a systematic interpretation of both provisions, it should be understood that the *delegation* to negotiate a treaty is (again) perfectly possible, hence being issued the respective *letter of full powers* to the representative chosen by the President of the Republic in order to act in his/her name (in case of such authorities that are not entitled to be released from producing the *letter*, see item 1.3.2, above).

It should be highlighted that delegations of foreign Powers present at meetings or diplomatic conferences have the authority to accept the offers submitted, reject them, or even amend them, according to what they deem more appropriate in connection with their own interests. Regarding the final wording of the text, the *experts* are usually in charge, since they support negotiators in this area.[48]

1.4.1.1 Distinction regarding the type of treaty

Negotiations of a treaty may give rise to differences according to the type of agreement that is to be signed.[49]

Negotiations involving *bilateral* treaties (typically) start by sending a *diplomatic note*, of an informal nature, from one country to another, from one chancery to another, which will be later developed in the territory of one of the contracting States, although the possibility that such negotiation occurs in the territory of a third State chosen by mutual agreement by negotiators is not discarded. In the event of treaties concluded between a

---

47 See Cachapuz de Medeiros, Antônio Paulo. *O poder de celebrar tratados...*, cit., p. 198-199.

48 See Dinh, Daillier & Pellet. *Direito internacional público*, cit., p. 133.

49 For further details, see Pereira de Araújo, Joao Hermes, *A processualística dos atos internacionais*, cit., p. 27-37; Rezek, José Francisco, *Direito dos tratados*, cit., p. 186-234; Remiro Brotons, Antonio, *Derecho internacional público*, vol. 2, cit., p. 72-82; and Reuter, Paul, *Introducción al derecho de los tratados*, cit., p. 9-84.

State and an international organization, negotiations normally take place in the headquarters of the organization. The *initiative* of a negotiation always comes from the State that expresses more interest in concluding the treaty. *Full powers* have not been required in this type of negotiation anymore for it is assumed that agents of the Ministry of Foreign Affairs are fully authorized by the Head of State to carry out the procedures with the other foreign Power. Regarding the language used for negotiating bilateral treaties, practice has shown that, if contracting States have a different language, a third language is frequently chosen (generally English), which is convenient to both parties, for the purpose of facilitating the understanding of negotiations between the parties.[50] The negotiation of bilateral treaties is usually established between the chancery and the diplomatic mission accredited in the country and, if there is no diplomatic representation, a delegation or special mission *ad hoc* is typically sent to negotiate.[51] The chance that technical commissions of the directly interested body participate in concluding a treaty is not eliminated (the respective Ministry), when this is competent in the subject, such as agriculture, science and technology, public finance, health, education, transport, tourism, etc.

Negotiations of *multilateral* treaties usually take place in the headquarters of an international organization or an *ad hoc* international conference (especially called for the discussion or preparation of one or more treaties) located in the territory of one of the negotiating States.[52] When the multilateral negotiation takes place in the first case (at the headquarters of an international organization) there is no *ad hoc* conference and all discussions are held in the plenary meeting of the Organization. There is one sole limitation for negotiating treaties at the headquarters of an international organization in connection with the specialty principle: conventions concluded in an organization must be in agreement with the purposes thereof. In the event that the negotiation takes place in *ad hoc* specialized conferences, the situation differs. Such conferences are subdivided into special commissions, in charge of preparing the draft treaty to be discussed and voted by the present States, setting the timeframe within which work should be finalized, establishing the rules to be complied with by the contracting parties during negotiations, and following up the final

---

50 For a study on the issue of the language of treaties, see Pereira de Araújo, João Hermes, *A processualística dos atos internacionais*, cit., p. 54-60.

51 See Rezek, José Francisco. *Direito dos tratados*, cit., p. 186-200; and Calsing, Maria de Assis, *O tratado internacional e sua aplicação no Brasil*, cit., p. 29.

52 For details, see Dinh, Daillier & Pellet, *Direito internacional público*, cit., p. 170-177.

stage of discussion. Conferences are endowed with their own will: they start in agreement with the conference rules and end with the drafting of records of all texts adopted, which will turn into future treaties as from their adoption and authentication. States are represented therein by *delegates* with the necessary powers to negotiate and conclude the conventional text. The negotiations procedure, in this case, is highly sophisticated and strict, observing internal rules previously set and normally using one or more of the six official languages of the United Nations (whatever they may be, English, French, Spanish, Arabic, Russian, and Chinese).[53]

1.4.1.2 Procedure followed in international organizations or ad hoc *international conferences*

Negotiations, at the international organization or at the respective *ad hoc* international conference venue, will start based upon a treaty text previously prepared, in the form of a *draft*, which will be used as a basis for discussions, regardless of whether the final text of the approved treaty reflects in any manner the draft text used as *an initial* document for discussions. This system has prevailed in the current international order. Regarding the venue of negotiations of multilateral treaties, it will vary based upon the international legal subject that convenes the conference: if it is a State, it usually takes place in its territory; if they are many States or just an international organization, the venue will be in the territory of the State, which will host the conference.

Treaty negotiators are generally supported by experts in the specific field regarding the treaty, for the purpose of providing the necessary resources to achieve a good negotiation and position taking. In Brazil, every international act negotiation must be supported by a diplomatic officer, and the final agreement text shall be approved based upon its legal terms, by the Legal Consultancy of Itamaraty, and when it comes to its procedural terms, by the Division of International Acts. Also, according to the Brazilian practice, the records of international acts "with advanced status of negotiation, but with reasonable anticipation in connection with the signature date, shall be submitted to the Division of International Acts

---

53 See Rodas, João Grandino. *Tratados internacionais*. São Paulo: Revista dos Tribunais, 1991, p. 15. On the subject regarding the aegis of the League of Nations, see Sibert, Marcel, Quelques aspects de l'organisation et de la technique des conférences internationales, *Recueil des Cours*, vol. 48 (1934-II), p. 387-457; and Rousseau, Charles, *Principes généraux du droit international public*, t. I, cit., p. 159-162.

for technical assessment of its proper writing and legal form, in accordance with the provisions of internal law and international law rules and practices".[54]

Upon termination of negotiations, the treaty is deemed *concluded* (according to the meaning given to the term 'concluded' by the 1969 Vienna Convention, that is to say, the treaty being able to reach the remaining conclusion stages). At this point, there is already a *treaty draft* formed by: *a)* a *preamble*, which lists the names of the contracting parties and expresses the reasons for the conclusion of the agreement;[55] *b)* a part *containing the substantive provisions*, which represents the body of the treaty text, and establishes the principles and rules of the commitment that the contracting parties are making, also including some *final clauses* and *provisions*, for the purpose of applying the technical rules of the treaty itself, for example the rules for its entry into force, time frames, accession, amendments and reservations, etc. and *c)* eventually some *annexes*, which contain supplementary technical elements to the treaty text, serving as assisting instruments for the parties with regards to the regular compliance of the agreement.

1.4.1.3 General rule of good faith negotiations

There is no doubt that negotiations of a treaty shall be held by the general rule of *good faith*, as stated by the International Court of Justice in the Nuclear Tests Case, judgment of 20 December 1974.[56]

Acting in *good faith* means acting in a manner, which is neither fraudulent nor stealthy, with transparency and good purposes. Then, the Vienna Convention sanctions (in Arts. 49 and 50) any expression of consent procured through the fraudulent conduct or corruption of a representative of a State or an international organization.

For the majority of legal scholars the general rule of good faith imposes on negotiators the duty (resulting from customary law) to refrain from performing acts that may defeat the object and purpose of the treaty under analysis. They argue that even though the 1969 Vienna Convention has not expressly dealt with the matter – Art. 18 of the Convention

---

54 MRE. *Atos internacionais – Prática diplomática brasileira – Manual de procedimentos.* Brasília: DAI/MRE, 2008, p. 14.

55 On the legal value of the preamble of treaties in general, and specially of the 1969 Vienna Convention see Villiger, Mark E., *Commentary on the 1969 Vienna Convention on the Law of Treaties*, cit., p. 43-52.

56 See *ICJ Reports* (1974), p. 267-269.

does not refer to *negotiations* themselves, but to subsequent acts, such as the *signature*, etc. –, there exists a well-established *customary* rule on the matter, and they also recall that the 1969 Convention itself imposes the application of customary rules to govern questions not regulated by it.[57] In fact, in the last *whereas* of its preamble, the Convention provides that "the rules of customary international law will continue to govern questions not regulated by the provisions of the present Convention".

1.4.2 Adoption of the text

Treaty negotiations (when concluded successfully) must give rise to a full *concurrence of wills* of the contracting parties. Such *concurrence of wills* must mandatorily be closed through a *legal act*, for it only to be *valid*. Such a legal act that closes the agreement of the parties and ends negotiations consists of the *adoption* of the conventional text, which is governed by Art. 9, items (1) and (2) of the 1969 Convention.

The *adoption* of a conventional text is the legal diplomatic procedure whereby the State bodies in charge of negotiating the treaty understand that *consent* related to the text has been expressed and that the negotiation came to an end (when it is said that the *draft was adopted*).[58] It is an act of will whereby States participating in the treaty preparation procedure accept the final *text* as convenient, which does not mean that States already accept the treaty *in terms of a legal rule* binding per se. In other words, the adoption only closes the final *wording* of the international treaty.[59] Consequently, upon approval of the text wording, negotiations end immediately.

However, some legal *effects* may arise from the adopted treaty, even though the instrument is not imposed as a legal *rule* to the signatory States.[60] One of those effects is in connection with the immediate applica-

---

57 On such opinion, see Remiro Brotons, Antonio, *Derecho internacional público*, vol. 2, cit., p. 75-76. This author, however, seems to accept that view with reservations (by affirming, also, that "it is a constructive opinion"), since to his understanding, it is "de *lege lata, which is arguable*".

58 See Maresca, Adolfo. *Il diritto dei trattati…*, cit., p. 139; Sinclair, Ian, *The Vienna Convention on the Law of Treaties*, cit., p. 33-34; De La Guardia, Ernesto, *Derecho de los tratados internacionales*, cit., p. 145; and Villiger, Mark E., *Commentary on the 1969 Vienna Convention on the Law of Treaties*, cit., p. 156-164.

59 See Remiro Brotons, Antonio. *Derecho internacional público*, vol. 2, cit., p. 82.

60 See Dinh, Daillier & Pellet. *Direito internacional público*, cit., p. 138. Remember Reuter's tenets, for whom the word *treaty* includes "both the *act* and its result, namely the *rule*" (*Introducción al derecho de los tratados*, cit., p. 38).

bility of the *final provisions* of the treaty, as set forth by Art. 24, item 4, of the 1969 Vienna Convention, according to which:

> "The provisions of a treaty regulating the authentication of its text, the establishment of the consent of States to be bound by the treaty, the manner or date of its entry into force, reservations, the functions of the depositary and other matters arising necessarily before the entry into force of the treaty apply from the time of the adoption of its text".

As noted, such final provisions do not establish any *regulatory* aspect of the treaty, but only govern its status as a *legal act*.

1.4.2.1 Rules for the adoption of the text

What are the rules for adopting a treaty? Under the terms of the referred Art. 9, items 1 and 2, of the 1969 Vienna Convention, there are two rules for the adoption of the conventional text, which are as follows:

a) the adoption of the text of a treaty takes place by the consent of all the States participating in its drawing up, or;

b) the adoption of the text of a treaty at an international conference takes place by the votes of *two-thirds* of the States present and voting, unless by the same majority they shall decide to apply a different rule.

Therefore, with the instrument negotiated *out of* an international conference, it is necessary to have the consent of *all of them* for the treaty to be adopted (Art. 9, item 1). The problem is clearer in the case of a *multilateral treaty* concluded out of a conference. It is obvious that in connection with bilateral treaties no other rule could be applied other than the *unanimity* one. However, regarding the issue of multilateral treaties concluded out of an international conference, the Convention establishes that *all* subjects participating therein *shall* accept its adoption. As can be seen, this rule is of an peremptory nature and does not support any flexibility. A State that does not accept voting in favour of the adoption of the conventional text may abandon negotiations, when the remaining ones will carry out the adoption.[61]

When negotiations have been carried out at an international conference, the adoption takes place by the majority of *two-thirds* of States

---

61 See Villiger, Mark E. *Commentary on the 1969 Vienna Convention on the Law of Treaties*, cit., p. 159.

present and voting, except as otherwise provided by the consent of such majority (Art. 9, item 2). Absences and abstentions are not taken into consideration for calculating these two-thirds,[62] since the provision refers to States *present and voting*. Concerning the exception included in Art. 9, item 2, the *conference rules* (to be agreed to by the participants) will determine the adoption procedure of the conventional text. The will of the majority (present at the conference) may also decide by the unanimity rule, or even adopt the text by consensus.[63] It should also be pointed out that "international conference" means *universal* and *regional* conferences, as well as those convened by one or many States or by an international organization.[64] When the adoption takes place at an international conference, it is usually the President of the Meeting or the highest executive of the organization who authenticates the text of the treaty upon termination of negotiations, on behalf of all the parties present therein.[65]

1.4.2.2 Differentiations

The *adoption* of the text of the treaty should be neither mistaken with its *authentication* nor with its *signature*.

The *adoption* of the text is carried out, as earlier discussed, by the consent of *all* States participating in its drafting, other than when it is held at an international conference, in which case it is deemed to be held by the majority of *two-thirds* of States present and voting (such States being also able to decide differently by the same majority). Therefore, it is strictly a legal act: the will of the States that participated in the wording of the treaty to adopt a given *text* as convenient, or the will to adopt such text as a document on which final consensus shall be given at certain time.[66]

The *authentication*, in turn, is only a formality concerning diplomatic documents, which grants *authenticity* and *finality* to the adopted con-

---

62 See UN, *Final clauses of multilateral treaties: handbook* (prepared by the Treaty Section of the Office of Legal Affairs), New York: United Nations, 2003, p. 1.

63 See Dinh, Daillier & Pellet. *Direito internacional público*, cit., p. 174. In that very sense, see Villiger, Mark E., *Commentary on the 1969 Vienna Convention on the Law of Treaties*, cit., p. 162, states: "States may wish to adopt a treaty text by other majorities, for instance, by simple majority, unanimously, or even by means of consensus".

64 See Remiro Brotons, Antonio. *Derecho internacional público*, vol. 2, cit., p. 83.

65 See Reuter, Paul. *Introducción al derecho de los tratados*, cit., p. 84.

66 See Maresca, Adolfo. *Il diritto dei trattati…*, cit., p. 139-140; and Aust, Anthony, *Modern treaty law and practice*, cit., p. 66-71.

ventional text (see above).[67] That is to say, first the text is *adopted* (by the majority will, by consensus) and then it is given legitimacy (authenticity and finality). Only upon adoption and authentication of the conventional text the representatives of States may sign it, and then, continue with the remaining stages of the *treaty-making process*. A State can also disagree on the text of the treaty drawn up at an international conference and adopted by the majority of two-thirds of States present and voting and, however, sign it in the future, if they want to.

1.4.2.3 Full powers for adoption

As has been discussed, Ministers for Foreign Affairs, besides, the Heads of State and the Heads of Government are released from producing *full powers* to perform *all* acts in connection with the conclusion of a treaty (Art. 7, item 2, of the 1969 Convention).With regard to heads of diplomatic missions, however, Art. 7, item 2 (b) of the Convention states that such release concerns only the *adoption* of the conventional text, not including its *signature*. Therefore, *a priori*, such plenipotentiaries (e.g. an ambassador) would be restricted from reaching the *adoption* stage of the text of the treaty, without being able to effectively *sign it* in the name of the State (except if they produce the aforementioned *full powers*).[68]

However, it is true that such a rule cannot be strictly and literally interpreted, and we must agree with Rezek, who lectures as follows:

> "It is hard to believe that [the Vienna Convention] has had the purposes to establish that the ambassador [or other authorized plenipotentiary] is only entitled to lead the negotiation to consensus regarding the conventional text, requiring, however, a letter of full powers to authenticate it by means of a signature. That contradicts the ordinary practice, which shows that such diplomats negotiate and sign bilateral treaties between their home State and the State where they carry out their duties, exclusively based on the permanent creden-

67 SeeMaresca, Adolfo. *Il diritto dei trattati*..., cit., p. 146.

68 See De La Guardia, Ernesto, *Derecho de los tratados internacionales*, cit., p. 136, who explains the provisions of the Convention, but without making any criticisms, stating only that: "The Convention, without making a distinction between the signature to authenticate and the signature to express consent to be bound by the conventional text, limits the powers of heads of diplomatic missions to the adoption of the text of a treaty, without dealing with the authentication by them by means of a signature, a signature *ad referendum* or initialling". See also Villiger, Mark E., *Commentary on the 1969 Vienna Convention on the Law of Treaties*, cit., p. 143: "Thus, heads of diplomatic missions cannot represent their States for the purpose of performing *all* acts relating to the conclusion of a treaty".

> tials held by them. However, that occurs provided that the signature confirms the conclusion of the negotiation process and the authentication of the agreed text, not implying any final consent".[69]

In other words, legally authorized plenipotentiaries (such as heads of diplomatic missions) are allowed to reach the stage of *adoption* of the text, so they can also *sign it* on behalf of the Government, when the signature does not imply final consent (with regards to its effects). It is clear that such discussion will not make sense if the representative of the State (plenipotentiary) has *full powers*, in which case he may also express the final consent of the State (Art. 7, item 1).

1.4.3 Authentication

Another procedure concerning the formation of treaties (which chronologically comes after the adoption) is its *authentication*, which is an act whereby the text of the treaty is deemed "authentic and definitive", under the terms of Art. 10 of the 1969 Vienna Convention.[70] It should be highlighted that the authentication turns the text *adopted* into authentic and definitive for the States, not meaning that the *treaty itself* is already binding as from such an act, which requires the ultimate *expression of consent* (see item 1.5, above).

The authentication of the conventional text is not a legal act *strict sensu*, like adoption is, but a diplomatic formality of a merely *notarial* nature. Both stages (adoption and authentication) are, however, closely related: firstly the text of the treaty is *adopted* (which is about the *consensus* already reached on it), then it is *authenticated*, and finally it becomes *definitive*. The purpose of the authentication procedure is to record that the adoption (which took place at a previous stage) was carried out successfully. That is why Adolfo Maresca refers to authentication as the "documentary manifestation" of adoption.[71]

The provision dealing with conventional authentication is Art. 10 of the 1969 Vienna Convention, which states:

---

69 Rezek, José Francisco. *Direito dos tratados*, cit., p. 207-208.

70 See Sinclair, Ian. *The Vienna Convention on the Law of Treaties*, cit., p. 39; De La Guardia, Ernesto, *Derecho de los tratados internacionales*, cit., p. 146-149; and Villiger, Mark E., *Commentary on the 1969 Vienna Convention on the Law of Treaties*, cit., p. 168-170.

71 Maresca, Adolfo. *Il diritto dei trattati…*, cit., p. 146. See also Remiro Brotons, Antonio, *Derecho internacional público*, vol. 2, cit., p. 86; and Aust, Anthony, *Modern treaty law and practice*, cit., p. 71-74.

> "Art. 10. *Authentication of the text.* The text of a treaty is established as authentic and definitive: *a)* by such procedure as may be provided for in the text or agreed upon by the States participating in its drawing up; or *b)* failing such procedure, by the signature, signature ad referendum or initialing by the representatives of those States of the text of the treaty or of the Final Act of a conference incorporating the text".

This provision must be clearly understood so that authentication is not in any way mistaken for signature. As noted, the Convention states that the authentication of the text of a treaty (act which makes it "authentic and definitive") shall be carried out, *a priori*, "through the procedure provided for in the text or agreed upon by the States participating in its drawing up" (Art. 10 (*a*)). That is the real diplomatic procedure (see above), which "records" the adoption of the text. In other words, negotiators are totally free to choose the authentication procedure of the text that they may deem convenient.[72] For example, a record could be included (as an annex to the treaty), whereby negotiators authenticate the text of the adopted treaty. However, in the event that the text of the instrument does not contain any provision on its authentication, or the States present do not reach any agreement on it, then, the rule established in item *b*, of the same Art. 10. This states that the signature, signature *ad referendum* or the initialling by the representatives of those States of the text of the treaty or of the Final Act of the Conference incorporating the text, shall also be valid as authenticating acts. Furthermore, this is even more obvious, since if the representatives of the States *signed* (or *initialled*) the treaty, this means that they also *accepted* that the text concerned is authentic and definitive.

In summary, the authentication is the procedural diplomatic step whereby the States, present at negotiations of the treaty, declare that the conventional text adopted is exactly the same as the one they intended to adopt, then that text will become definitive. Failing such diplomatic procedure, authentication can also take place as a result of the signature, signature *ad referendum* or initialing by the representatives of such States of the text of the treaty or of Final Act of the Conference incorporating the same text. Once the text is authenticated, no modification (amendment, change, etc.) shall be introduced.[73]

---

72 See Remiro Brotons, Antonio. *Derecho internacional público*, vol. 2, cit., p. 86.

73 See Villiger, Mark E. *Commentary on the 1969 Vienna Convention on the Law of Treaties*, cit., p. 169.

The authentication carried out by the signature, signature *ad referendum* or initialing of the text of the treaty is appropriate, e.g., in the context of bilateral treaties.[74] The case of authentication of a treaty by signing the Final Act of a Conference incorporating the same text has been a frequent practice, e.g., in the field of the International Labour Organization, in which the signatures of the President of the International Labour Conference and the Director-General of the International Labour Organization *authenticate* the conventional texts issued by the organization.[75] It should be pointed out that Art. 10(b) of the 1969 Convention does not refer to the authentication carried out by signing a *resolution* of an international organization body (since it only foresees the assumption, discussed above, of the signature of the *Final Act* of an international conference). As De La Guardia explains this is so because the International Law Commission understood that such authentication modality is foreseen in Art. 5 of the 1969 Convention in connection with the specific rules of international organizations.[76] In fact, Art. 5 of the Vienna Convention provides that: "The present Convention applies to any treaty which is the constituent instrument of an international organization and to any treaty adopted within an international organization *without prejudice to any relevant rules of the organization*".[77] Therefore, it should be also understood that the signature of a *resolution* of an international organization incorporating the text of an adopted treaty serves as an *authentication* act of the treaty. Now, it should be clarified what the difference is between the expressions "signature", "signature *ad referendum*" and "initialing", as featured in Art. 10(b) of the 1969 Vienna Convention.

The difference between a "signature" and a "signature *ad referendum*" mentioned in Art. 10(b), relates to the *legal effects* of the act, since, as a general rule, the signature is always expressed *ad referendum* by the internal bodies of the State, competent to authorize the ratification of the treaty. The signature *ad referendum* (whose effect is not definitive) is also

---

74 See Maresca, Adolfo. *Il diritto dei trattati*..., cit., p. 146-147.

75 See De La Guardia, Ernesto. *Derecho de los tratados internacionales*, cit., p. 148.

76 De La Guardia, Ernesto. Idem, p. 149.

77 On this regard, Mark Villiger outlines that: "Where the international organization contains separate and different rules on a particular subject of the law of treaties, these have priority over the Convention. Article 5 thus provides for a balance between the *lex generalis* of the Convention and the *lex specialis* of the rules of the various international organisations" (*Commentary on the 1969 Vienna Convention on the Law of Treaties*, cit., p. 119).

called *authentication signature*, since it is not aimed at binding the State definitively. Therefore, the reference made to a mere "signature" in Art. 10(b) is related to the exceptional assumption provided for in Art. 12 of the Vienna Convention (analyzed below), in which the signature of the treaty *is valid* as the expression of a State to be bound by a treaty (that is why it is also referred to as *full signature*, *final signature* or *consent signature*); here we are dealing with a simplified procedure (that is, a *fast-track procedure* for the conclusion of treaties). According to Brazilian diplomatic practice the procedure unfolds as follows: the plenipotentiary present at the negotiation stamps his/her "signature *ad referendum*" on the treaty, authenticating it. Since it is a signature *ad referendum*, the instrument is brought to the country for the purpose of being *countersigned* by the National Parliament, and, afterwards, *ratified* by the President of the Republic. Therefore, according to Brazilian diplomatic practice no *full signature* is stamped on international treaties, also due to the existing constitutional prohibition (Art. 49, I, of the 1988 Federal Constitution).[78]

Finally, Art. 10(b) also refers to the "initialling", which is not a signature *per se*, but the stamping of a brief graphic *sign* by the plenipotentiary for mere authentication purposes. It is an old practice that has been followed by diplomats in general. By means of that practice State representatives can simply authenticate the text, without the risk of signing a document which, as from its signature, may eventually bind the States they represent. Therefore, once the text is "initialled", representatives will have more time to consult with their governments such matters that, by chance, may still arise in connection with the treaty therein concluded.[79] The fact is that, as explained by João Hermes Pereira de Araújo, "despite the instructions and powers given to them, plenipotentiaries rarely sign an international act without submitting it, before, to many administrative authorities and to the Head of Government or of State himself/herself", and this is "what happens in Brazil, where treaties are examined by the Legal Consultancy of the Foreign Affairs Department, by the Division of International Acts, by the Minister for Foreign Affairs, and by the President of the Republic", except, obviously, if the treaty is adopted in an international congress or conference, in which case the responsibility of delegates shall be remarkably greater.[80]

---

78 The issue of *signature* of treaties will be discussed more in detail in item 1.5.1, below.

79 See examples in Sette Câmara, José, *The ratification of international treaties*, cit., p. 57-58.

80 See Pereira de Araújo, João Hermes. *A processualística dos atos internacionais*, cit., p. 42. It should be pointed out that when the Legal Consultancy of the Ministry for Foreign Affairs cannot express its opinion *before* the signature of the treaty, as generally occurs

1.5 Expression of consent

The *authentication* act ends the initial stage (*pre-consent stage*) of a conclusion of a treaty, where the drafting of text has been *finalized*. Once the text is concluded, all necessary acts are carried out for States (or international organizations) to become *a party* to it.[81] It is about a procedure (that is often long, due to the lack of time forecasted between one act and another) conducive to the parties *expressing their consent* to being bound by the treaty whose text was adopted and authenticated. Such (broad) a stage concerning *expression of consent* is formed by two major acts: *signature* and *ratification*. Both acts lead to the conclusion of treaties *stricto sensu*, which means accepting the instrument under International Law, with all possible effects under internal Law (e.g., its immediate application, etc.). Eventually, there also exists the possibility to express consent by accession, in the cases that will be duly analyzed (see item 1.5.3, below).

The decision to carry out the final stage of the execution of a treaty rests with the States, more specifically with their *governments*. This decision, as explained by Brotons, requires an opportunity assessment, usually based on perceptive reports of interested Ministerial Departments and of Administration advisory bodies. Sometimes, it requires the prior opinion of the Legislative Power (as it happens in Brazil, where the Legislative Power *authorizes* the President of the Republic to ratify the treaty). Exceptionally, it may require an advisory opinion on the constitutionality of the treaty concerned by an *ad hoc* body.[82]

The 1969 Vienna Convention establishes (in Art. 11) the forms whereby consent to be bound by the treaty may be expressed by the State, under these terms:

> "Article 11. The consent of a State to be bound by a treaty may be expressed by signature, exchange of instruments constituting a treaty, ratification, acceptance, approval or accession, or by any other means if so agreed".

In the quoted article, although it seems that the Convention has opened a series of assumptions in which consent of a State to be bound by

---

in the case of multilateral treaties concluded at international congresses or conferences, it shall give its *opinion* before assessment by the Legislative Power (see Pereira de Araújo, João Hermes. Idem, p. 43).

81 See Sinclair, Ian. *The Vienna Convention on the Law of Treaties*, cit., p. 39-42.

82 See Remiro Brotons, Antonio. *Derecho internacional público*, vol. 2, cit., p. 98.

a treaty is validated, there happen to be only three assumptions: *signature*, *ratification*, and *accession*. Signature expresses definitive consent of the State to be bound by the agreement, in the event of treaties concluded according to Art. 12 of the Convention (see below). The exchange of instruments and its effective transmission, also common to treaties concluded in a simplified form or under a fast-track procedure, implies, in the same manner, the final commitment of the State, which amounts to the signature. *Acceptance* and *approval*, in turn, are terms technically allien to the expression of consent (States use them in practice, in this case correctly, when they want to refer to the Parliament *approval* of treaties) and, therefore, they shall be understood, for the purpose of Art. 11 of the Convention, as being tantamount to ratification (where the treaty was previously signed) or to accession (where the treaty was not previously signed).[83] For the purpose of *reservations* to multilateral treaties, the term *approval* may mean the possibility of making reservations by Parliaments (see Ch. 2, item 2.12, below). Therefore, as well as the signature, in the cases strictly provided for by the Convention in which it has a categorical commitment power, it may be concluded that *ratification* and *accession* are the only ways of definitive commitment of the State, where no other means of expressing consent have been agreed upon.

"The Vienna Convention deals with this topic [*expression of consent*] in Arts. 11-18, which state, in summary, and with some redundancies, that the definitive expression of consent by the State in connection with conventional commitment is carried out, alternatively, by *signature, exchange of instruments constituting a treaty, ratification, acceptance, approval* or *accession*, not excluding other means that the parties may agree to adopt. This final clause, due to the flexibility given to the role of alternatives, would have been an excellent reason for the Vienna text to have refrained from mentioning *acceptance* and *approval*, terms whose accurate meaning cannot be reached. They are both contemporary to the fertile production of treaties in international organizations, and the latter has already been used to define the adoption of a text at a conference as well, something clearly different from the definitive expression of consent of each concerned State. It is probable that those two terms, all the more inappropriate as already used in this very area to depict other legal acts,

[83] This conclusion is reinforced by Art. 14 item 2 of the Convention, which outlines as follows: "The *consent* of a State to be bound by a treaty is expressed by *acceptance* or *approval* under conditions similar to those which apply to ratification". In fact, discussions held in the ILC already showed that drafters intended to give the terms *acceptance* and *approval* the same meaning as *ratification*, in the case of the *definitive commitment* of the State to be bound by the treaty. However, at this point, the work of the ILC did not get away with criticism, especially for having been based on an arguable State *praxis*. In this regard, see De La Guardia, Ernesto, *Derecho de los tratados internacionales*, cit., p. 122.

are the result of the clumsy creativity of those who, in international fora, have intended to generate 'simpler' ways to express consent by the State. Furthermore, it is not possible that that double inventive outburst is motivated by an attempt to facilitate the non-compliance with constitutional requirements concerning Parliament approval upon which, according to the regulations of each country, the definitive decision of governments is dependent". REZEK, José Francisco. *Direito dos tratados*, cit., p. 255-256.

The final sentence of Art. 11 authorizes States to agree to "any other means" of expressing their consent. Then, provided that it is agreed to by the parties, even the oral expression of a Head of State would be valid, e.g., as an expression of State consent. However, it should be pointed out that such a solution provided for in the Convention has not been frequently used in treaties concluded in due and proper form,[84]especially because the classic means of expressing consent – signature, ratification and accession – are more accurate and secure for relations between States (also being easier to prove, etc.).

Arts.12-16 of the Vienna Convention were conceived to regulate the cases mentioned in Art. 11. In light of the above discussions, items below will deal with the *signature*, *ratification* and *accession* of treaties.

1.5.1 Signature

Signature concludes the initial stage of the treaty-making process (started with *negotiations* and followed by *adoption*) and closes the formal act of *authentication* (where such act was not carried out under the terms of Art. 10(a) of the Vienna Convention "by such procedure as may be provided for in the text or agreed upon by the States participating in its drawing up").[85]

Undoubtedly, the signature is a *necessary* stage of international acts procedure, since it puts an end to general negotiations and expresses a *minimum* will by the State to continue to examine the question, for the purpose of (in the future, with the ratification) finally accepting everything that has been agreed upon. In other words, the signature expresses the *future* inten-

---

84 That is why Mark Villiger notes the following: "Clearly, it is intended to embrace treaties in simplified form" (*Commentary on the 1969 Vienna Convention on the Law of Treaties*, cit., p. 177).

85 For further details, see McNair, Arnold Duncan, *The law of treaties*, cit., p. 120-128; Pereira de Araújo, João Hermes, *A processualística dos atos internacionais*, cit., p. 125-145; Maresca, Adolfo, *Il diritto dei trattati…*, cit., p. 159-166; and Aust, Anthony, *Modern treaty law and practice*, cit., p. 75-81.

tion of the party State concerned to be bound by the treaty once and for all.[86] In summary, its relevance arises for being related to "the act of closure of negotiations and the drawing up of its results in an instrument to be submitted to governments for final approval", as explained by José Sette Câmara.[87]

From the signature onwards (more precisely, from *authentication*) any modifications to the text of the agreement are forbidden, as discussed above. However, the possibility that the contracting parties formulate reservations to the adopted text remains open thenceforth, as applicable (which shall also be *formally confirmed* at the time of ratification under the terms of Art. 23, item 2, of the Convention).

1.5.1.1 Concept

What is the concept of *signature* in a legal document in general? The Vienna Convention did not define the concept of signature, but (international and local) practice shows that there is a certain degree of consensus on its concept.

"Signature" means the written sign of a person, in his/her own handwriting,[88] at the end of a document or paper, whose purpose is to record that the preparation of such document or instrument is known by its holder, and that he/she accepts the terms contained therein.[89]

Regarding the signature of *treaties*, there is no conceptual difference, except for the capacity in which the person is acting, since that act is carried out by the *representative* of a given sovereign State (its direct representative or a plenipotentiary).

There are specific rules set forth in the 1969 Vienna Convention (followed by the 1986 Convention) on the signature of international acts (see below).

1.5.1.2 Legal nature

The legal nature of the signature of a treaty is two-fold: it constitutes a *precarious* and *formal* acceptance, which has no binding legal effects (with the exception of Art. 12 of the Convention).

---

[86] See Remiro Brotons, Antonio. *Derecho internacional público*, vol. 2, cit., p. 87.

[87] See Sette Câmara, José. *The ratification of international treaties*, cit., p. 67-68.

[88] Or by any means of body expression, where the person is unable to use his/her own hand.

[89] It should be highlighted that *electronic signature* is also used in legal documents (but still uncommon in international relations practice).

It is of (*a*) *precarious* nature because such an acceptance is provisional, since the treaty may not be ratified and never enter into force, for only the ratification (exchange or deposit of its instruments) can represent the effective *consensus* of the contracting parties to what has been previously agreed upon; and (*b*) it is of *formal* nature because its only purpose is to provide evidence that the text therein contains no formal defects, complying with all the requirements necessary to reach the stage of conclusion.

The formal obligation undertaken by negotiators upon the signature consists of continuing the procedure based upon the adopted text, with no further modifications to its structure (except for of course the possibility of formulating a unilateral reservation). In other words, the signature legally binds States *to the definitive text* of the treaty (especially in the case in which the signature also authenticates the treaty, under the terms of Art. 10(b) of the 1969 Convention).[90] That is why any amendment to the instrument made after being signed, renders the executed agreement void, and opens a new round of negotiations, if the contracting parties so agree. The signature also means the legal obligation of States to refrain from acts which would defeat the *object* and *purpose* of the treaty before being ratified, as provided for in Art. 18(a) of the 1969 Convention (see item 1.5.1.6, below).

The authority of the signature is almost always *ad referendum*, requiring the later approval by the State concerned, which is expressed by means of the ratification.[91] Thus, it means the expression of *consent* of the State to be legally bound by the adopted text until its later confirmation by ratification, which does not mean anything other than the expression of a future (and contingent) commitment of the parties.[92] That is to say,

---

90 See Brichambaut, Dobelle & Coulée. *Leçons de droit international public*, cit., p. 270.

91 In that very sense, see Villiger, Mark E., *Commentary on the 1969 Vienna Convention on the Law of Treaties*, cit., p. 184: "The classical process of concluding treaties was by means of signature followed by ratification. Treaty-making authority was vested in the Sovereign, the plenipotentiary was regarded as the Sovereign's personal agent, and signature by that agent in possession of full powers meant acceptance of a treaty which the Sovereign was bound to ratify. However, rules became wary of being obliged to ratify treaties signed by plenipotentiaries who had perhaps interpreted their powers beyond what might have been intended. To overcome this, signature was affixed on the condition of future approval, and the consent of the Sovereign to be bound was then sealed by ratification".

92 See Sette Câmara, José. *The ratification of international treaties*, cit., p. 61-62; Maresca, Adolfo, *Il diritto dei trattati*..., cit., p. 159-160; and Rodas, João Grandino, *Tratados internacionais*, cit., p. 15.

the signature that concludes negotiations does not bind the State, it only determines the content of its will. Furthermore, it is only a formal expression of consent by the State. By signing, the State accepts the form and the content of the negotiated treaty (without expressing its definitive acceptance) and agrees to continue with (based on the adopted text) the treaty-making procedure.[93]

1.5.1.3 Full powers upon signature

Item 1.3.2. of this Chapter has already discussed the meaning of *full powers* of representatives of States to conclude treaties. Without being repetitive, here certain details of full powers should be analyzed in more detail regarding specifically the matter of *signature* of treaties.

Pursuant to the provisions of Art. 7 item (1) of the 1969 Vienna Convention, for a person to be able to represent the State in the treaty-making process (for example, to perform acts related to adoption, authentication or signature) or to express the final consent of the State to be bound by a treaty, he/she shall have *full powers*. Such full powers must be granted by means of a "letter of full powers", an instrument whereby the chosen plenipotentiaries are granted the power to negotiate and conclude treaties on behalf of the State.

The letter of full powers is signed by the Head of State and countersigned by the Minister for Foreign Affairs. Under the terms of the 1988 Federal Constitution, the President of the Republic is able to conclude international treaties on behalf of the Brazilian State (Art. 84, VIII). In turn, the Minister for Foreign Affairs is authorized to assist the President in the formulation of the Brazilian foreign policy, ensure its implementation and maintain relations with foreign States, international agencies and organizations. Therefore, unless the treaty is signed directly by the President of the Republic or by the Minister for Foreign Affairs (also by the heads of diplomatic missions, according to the broad interpretation of Art. 7 item (2) (b) of the 1969 Convention, as analyzed above), any other authority shall have to produce a *letter of full powers* in order to be able to sign an international treaty. The preparation of such a *letter* is the responsibility of the International Act Division of Itamaraty,[94] which acts upon formal request by the President of the Republic.

---

93 See Rezek, José Francisco. *Direito dos tratados*, cit., p. 201.

94 See MRE, *Atos internacionais – Prática diplomática brasileira – Manual de procedimentos*, cit., p. 15.

Art. 8 of the 1969 Vienna Convention considers that any acts regarding the conclusion of a treaty (negotiations, adoption, authentication, and also *signature* and *ratification*) have *no legal effects,* if carried out by a person who has no power to represent the State under the terms of Art. 7, unless such a State were to *later confirm* the act by validating it (the same rule being applied for the representation of international organizations). This is particularly true regarding (*a*) someone who has no power to represent the State to perform acts concerning the conclusion of a treaty and takes part in an international conference, adopting, signing or even ratifying the treaty; or (*b*) someone who only has express full powers to adopt the treaty, but exceeds such powers and signs it (or ratifies it); or even (*c*) a State that is in dispute by two equally strong Powers and each of them intend to perform such acts in connection with the conclusion of a treaty (or, even, to carry out the final acts to express the consent of the State to be bound by the treaty) without the consent of the other party, with these two Powers convinced that the bodies and plenipotentiaries of the other party do not represent the State.[95] An example of the first situation occurred in 1951, at a convention concerning the naming of cheeses that was signed by a delegate on behalf of Norway and Sweden, when in fact it appeared that they only had authority to do so only on behalf of Norway, although the agreement was eventually ratified (this is, "subsequently confirmed", under the terms of Art. 8 of the Convention) by both parties, and resulted in the entry into force as usual.[96]

Art. 8 allows, as aforementioned, that the State concerned subsequently *confirms* any acts carried out by the unauthorized person, in which case (after confirmation by the State) such acts will be deemed valid and effective. The subsequent confirmation of the acts has effects, as can be seen, *ex nunc.*[97] Such a solution, explains Remiro Brotons, is unorthodox, since most of the legal scholars are of the view that an act *with no legal effect*, taking into account the inclusion of Art. 8 in Section 1, Part II, of the

95 See Remiro Brotons, Antonio. *Derecho internacional público*, vol. 2, cit., p. 150-152.

96 See ILC, *Yearbook of the International Law Commission* (1966), vol. II, p. 194: "Again, in 1951 a convention concerning the naming of cheeses concluded at Stresa was signed by a delegate on behalf both of Norway and Sweden, whereas it appears that he had authority to do so only from the former country. In both these instances the treaty was subject to ratification and was in fact ratified". On the subject, see also Shaw, Malcolm N., *Direito internacional*, cit., p. 675.

97 See Villiger, Mark E. *Commentary on the 1969 Vienna Convention on the Law of Treaties*, cit., p. 151.

Convention, cannot be confirmed; however, adds Brotons, the solution adopted has prevailed because it is *practical*.[98] Nothing hinders the *tacit* confirmation by the State, if the State later expresses (in regular terms) its consent to be bound by the treaty through its ratification. By doing so, the previous defects are immediately resolved.[99]

It should be pointed out that in the event that the power granted to a representative, for the purpose of adopting or authenticating the text of a treaty, has been *specifically restricted* (expressly stated in the letter of full powers) by the competent authority, the fact that the representative does not observe the restriction stated therein *cannot be invoked* as invalidating the consent expressed by him/her, unless such a restriction was notified to the other negotiating States prior to his/her expressing such consent, according to the provisions of Art. 47 of the 1969 Convention.[100] A classic example was the attempt by Persia (currently the Islamic Republic of Iran) in the Council of the League of Nations to reject the Erzerum Treaty (1847), availing itself of the fact that its representative had exceeded his powers by accepting an explanatory note on the exchange of ratifications.[101]

1.5.1.4 Signature with ratification effect

Art. 12 of the Vienna Convention (referred to on several occasions) deals with the assumption – not always accepted by the municipal legislation of a number of countries – that a signature can express the *definitive* consent of a State to be bound by a treaty, requiring no further act to be performed (for example, Parliament approval and ratification) for the treaty to enter into force, and thus, binding the parties to abide by its terms.

Such assumption, which differs from the *signature-authentication* generally used in State practice (see item 1.4.3, above), can be referred to as *full signature*, *final signature* or *consent signature*, being provided as such by the 1969 Convention:

---

98 Remiro Brotons, Antonio. *Derecho internacional público*, vol. 2, cit., p. 151.

99 See Remiro Brotons, Antonio. Idem, ibidem.

100 See Sinclair, Ian. *The Vienna Convention on the Law of Treaties*, cit., p. 171-172; and Villiger, Mark E., *Commentary on the 1969 Vienna Convention on the Law of Treaties*, cit., p. 597-602.

101 See Remiro Brotons, Antonio. *Derecho internacional público*, vol. 2, cit., p. 151.

"Article 12.Consent to be bound by a treaty expressed by signature.

1. The consent of a State to be bound by a treaty is expressed by the signature of its representative when:

a) the treaty provides that signature which shall have that effect;

b) it is otherwise established that the negotiating States were agreed that signature should have that effect; or

c) the intention of the State to give that effect to the signature appears from the full powers of its representative or was expressed during the negotiation.

2. For the purposes of paragraph 1:

a) the initialling of a text constitutes a signature of the treaty when it is established that the negotiating States so agreed;

b) the signature *ad referendum* of a treaty by a representative, if confirmed by their State, constitutes a full signature of the treaty".

Therefore, although *ratification* is the most frequent means of expressing consent, consent by *signature* will be possible (*a*) when the treaty establishes that the signature will have such effect (stating, for example, that "the present treaty will enter into force upon its signature"), (*b*) when negotiating States *agree* (by means of joint declarations, diplomatic documents, etc.) that the signature should have such effect, or also (*c*) when the will of the State to be bound by the signature arises from the *full powers* granted to its representative or was expressed *during* the negotiation (Art. 12 item 1). Furthermore, the Convention does in fact provide that the mere *initialing* of a treaty will amount to a final signature, when it is established that the negotiating States agreed in such a way. It is noteworthy, Art. 12, item 2(a) of the Convention states that "*for the purposes* of paragraph 1" – this is, for *final consent* purposes expressed by signature – "the initialling of a text *constitutes a signature* of the treaty when it is established that the negotiating States so agreed".

It is clear that, except for the case in which the treaty itself provides that the signature has the effect of expressing the final consent by the State, in the remaining cases provided for in Art. 12 of the Convention, the evidentiary question becomes more complex. However, all evidence must be admitted for a State to prove that (1) negotiators agree to grant the effect of final commitment to the signature, or that (2) the intention to give that effect to the signature appeared from the full powers of the representative of the State or was expressed during the negotiation.[102] In summary, once the treaty was signed, for example by a Head of State authorized to do so, and once it has been agreed upon (in any form whatsoever) that, upon its signature, the international act agreed between the parties would enter into force, by virtue of the Vienna Convention on Treaties Law, the treaty is fully *valid* between the parties.[103]

During negotiations of the 1969 Convention, many expressed their opposition to the contents of this provision, on the ground that the participation of the Legislative Power in the treaty-making process, according to purposes of the provisions of Art. 12, would be totally undermined, as a mere stamping of a signature would amount to the expression of consent of the State to be bound by a treaty.[104] Nevertheless, despite the heated debates and the many voices that have been raised in opposition to it, the premise enshrined in Art. 12, which put the signature on an equal footing with the ratification, in the cases provided for therein, prevailed. Drafters of the Vienna text understood that waiting for the ratification, as well as the ratifying procedure itself, may take too long, in addition to overburdening the administrative structure of the government. By means of such provision, States can agree to manage without the approval of other internal bodies so that the treaty concluded by them enters into force at the international level, turning the signature into the first condition to be complied with for the treaty to enter into force. The 1973 Paris Peace Agreement can be cited as an example of such practice. Indeed, this treaty

---

102 For details, see Villiger, Mark E., *Commentary on the 1969 Vienna Convention on the Law of Treaties*, cit., p. 188-190.

103 See ICJ, "Land and Maritime Boundary between Cameroon and Nigeria" (*Cameroon v. Nigeria: Equatorial Guinea intervening*), in *ICJ Reports* (2002), p. 429-430 (§ 264): "The Court cannot accept the argument that the Maroua Declaration was invalid under international law because it was signed by the Nigerian Head of State of the time but never ratified. Thus while in international practice a two-step procedure consisting of signature and ratification is frequently provided for in provisions regarding entry into force of a treaty, there are also cases where a treaty enters into force immediately upon signature. Both customary international law and the Vienna Convention on the Law of Treaties leave it completely up to States which procedure they want to follow. Under the Maroua Declaration, 'the two Heads of State of Cameroon and Nigeria agreed to extend the delineation of the maritime boundary between the two countries from Point 12 to Point G on the Admiralty Chart No. 3433 annexed to this Declaration'. In the Court's view, that Declaration entered into force immediately upon its signature".

104 On that discussion at the Vienna Conference, see Nascimento e Silva, Geraldo Eulálio do, *Conferência de Viena sobre o Direito dos Tratados*, cit., p. 154.

officially terminated the intervention of the United States in the Vietnam War, having entered into force upon its signature.

However, despite the provision under analysis, the fact remains that the ratification is always a better manner to express consent to be bound by a treaty,[105] since it enables the participation of the Legislative Power in the procedures of preparation and conclusion of international acts. In Brazil, for instance, this measure (parliamentary approval) prevails over the provisions of Art. 49 (I) of the 1988 Federal Constitution. But countries in general (Brazil and any other that has a similar rule in their Constitution) must be careful when signing treaties, whereby the signature is given the effect of expressing consent of the State to be bound by a treaty or in whose negotiations it was agreed (for example, by diplomatic documents exchanged between negotiators) to give that effect to the signature, under the penalty of international responsibility of the State. The ICJ, when analyzing an international treaty from a legal perspective, will certainly declare an international act between States to be *into force*, if it observes that (in any way) negotiators agreed to give the signature the effect of expressing the consent of the State to be bound by the treaty.[106] In the case of Brazil, the Legal Consultancy of the Ministry for Foreign Affairs must *notify* the government of any legal consequences of the signature of a treaty that may cause it to enter into force for the country, irrespective of the later ratification.[107]

1.5.1.5 Deferred signature

It should also be mentioned that in diplomatic jargon it was agreed that the signature discussed above, should be referred to as a *deferred* signature, conferring States a longer period of time for the (effective/full) signature of treaties.[108] In this regard, Art. 12 item (2)(b) of the Vienna Convention provides that "the signature *ad referendum* of a treaty by a representative, if confirmed by his State, constitutes a full signature of the treaty".

This advantage began with the plenipotentiaries who did not have full instructions about what was being agreed to and wanted to gain extra

---

105 See Brierly, J. L. *Direito internacional*, cit., p. 326-327.

106 See *ICJ Reports* (2002), p. 429-430.

107 See Art. 7 of Executive Order 7304, dated 09.22.2010 (on competency of the Legal Consultancy).

108 See Mello, Celso D. de Albuquerque. *Curso de direito internacional público*, vol. I, cit., p. 227.

time. Therefore, the stratagem used consisted of stamping only their initials on the text of the treaty, which provided them with certain leeway to previously consult with their respective governments.

This is what in diplomatic practice was called deferred signature, whose disadvantages are outlined by João Hermes Pereira de Araújo as follows: "One of them refers to the possibility of formulating reservations. If the signatory who wants to sign with reservations is not in the presence of the remaining plenipotentiaries, they will not be aware of such reservations till later on". Another problem relates to the ratification: "In fact, signatory States cannot ratify a convention before the term provided for additional signatures elapses. This caused a great delay for the entry into force of a number of conventions, which caused the League of Nations to issue a resolution in such regard".[109] Therefore, the majority of legal scholars are of the opinion that, instead of using the system of deferred signature, it would be better and more convenient to record on the conventional text that accession to the treaty is still open. This offers the States that did not participate in negotiations of the treaty the same opportunity to become a party to it, without the disadvantage of leaving the text open for signature and without the need for ratification (as accession has the same legal nature as the former). This will also enable a more detailed analysis of the matter during the time the government concerned may deem necessary.[110]

In any case, the fact remains that practice of deferred signature, albeit criticized, has been fostered by political considerations.[111]

1.5.1.6 Obligations arising from signature

As discussed earlier (see item 1.5.1.2, above), the formal obligation that negotiators undertake by means of the signature is basically to continue with procedure *based upon* the adopted text, without introducing any changes to its structure (except for the chance to make a unilateral reservation). Besides, a second (and more important) obligation that arises from the signature is that States are not allowed to carry out any act that may defeat the *object* and *purpose* of the treaty before its ratification, as provided for in Art. 18(a) of the 1969 Convention, as follows:

---

109 Pereira de Araújo, João Hermes. *A processualística dos atos internacionais*, cit., p. 134.

110 See Sette Câmara, José. *The ratification of international treaties*, cit., p. 60.

111 See Dinh, Daillier & Pellet. *Direito internacional público*, cit., p. 180.

"A State is obliged to refrain from acts which would defeat the object and purpose of a treaty when it has signed the treaty or has exchanged instruments constituting the treaty subject to ratification, acceptance or approval, until it shall have made its intention clear not to become a party to the treaty".

It is clear that here we are dealing with obligations arising from the signature of *solemn* treaties, those concluded *in due form*, rather than treaties concluded in a simplified form, which enter into force upon its signature. Therefore, the problem under analysis in this section will revolve around the situation in which a signed treaty *depends on its future ratification* to finally bind the State. Indeed, the purpose of this section is to analyze the *effects* that a signature produces – from the moment it is stamped on the conventional text until the ratification of the latter (or non-formal ratification) in light of the provisions of Art. 18 of the 1969 Vienna Convention.

That matter arose especially when the United States of America (during George W. Bush administration, in 2002) formally decided *not to ratify* the Rome Statute of the International Criminal Court that had previously been signed (during Bill Clinton administration, in 2000). Such situation cast doubt on the obligations to which the United States were subject between the years 2000 and 2002, pursuant to the provisions of the Rome Statute of the ICC, which led legal scholars to turn their attention to the provisions of Art. 18 of the 1969 Vienna Convention.

Art. 18 of the Vienna Convention clearly shows that some practical obligations *do arise* for signatory States from the signature of a treaty, whilst the ratification does not take place.[112] In other words, the Conven-

---

112 On the subject, see Zoller, Elizabeth, *La bonne foi en droit international public*, Paris: A. Pedone, 1977, p. 69-71; Rogoff, Martin A., The international legal obligations of signatories to an ungratified treaty, *Maine Law Review*, vol. 32, n. 12 (1980), p. 263-299; Cançado Trindade, Antônio Augusto, Reavaliação das fontes do direito internacional público ao início da década de oitenta, cit., p. 106; Sinclair, Ian, *The Vienna Convention on the Law of Treaties*, cit., p. 42-44; Thirlway, Hugh, The law and procedure of the International Court of Justice, 1960-1989 (Part Four), *British Year Book of International Law*, vol. 63 (1992), p. 48 *et seq*; De La Guardia, Ernesto, *Derecho de los tratados internacionales*, cit., p. 165-166; Bradley, Curtis A., Unratified treaties, domestic politics, and the U.S. Constitution, *Harvard International Law Journal*, vol. 48, n. 2 (2007), p. 307-336; Villiger, Mark E., *Commentary on the 1969 Vienna Convention on the Law of Treaties*, cit., p. 245-253; Palchetti, Paolo, Article 18 of the 1969 Vienna Convention: a vague and ineffective obligation or a useful means of strengthening legal cooperation?, in Cannizzaro, Enzo (ed.), *The law of treaties beyond the Vienna Convention*, Oxford: Oxford University

tion intended to clarify that during the time elapsed between the signature and the ratification (or during the signature and the *non-formal ratification* of the treaty) the signatory State *is not free* to act as it wishes, being bound to refraining from (during the entire period) performing acts that may defeat the *object* or *purpose* of the treaty. As a matter of fact, the Convention addressed that situation because it was felt due to the lapse of time between the signature and the ratification (or the lack thereof) it could take too long (here it should be highlighted that Brazil took *forty years* to ratify the 1969 Convention itself) and thus undermine the expectations that other subjects of the law of nations had in a given State, clearly contravening good faith obligations. Consequently, it becomes clear that the signature of a treaty is not an ancillary act deprived of any effect, as it imposes on the signatory States obligations of security related to the duty to act in good faith.[113]

The idea of good faith here referred to is associated with the behavior of the State when signing an international treaty, as well as the duty to proceed *consistently* with regards to the signed treaty. In fact, when a State *signs* a given treaty it is trying to communicate to the entire international society to the effect that it is "taking a step forward", albeit initial and incipient, towards the formal *ratification* of the agreement. The international society, in turn, expects the ratification to take place within a reasonable amount of time, with no unjustified delays, and that whilst the ratification does not occur, the State at least keeps focused on its initial pledges, without retracting its purpose and disappointing the legitimate expectations of the rest of the international society. Nevertheless, that fair "step" taken by the State (when signing the treaty) "towards" the ratification stage should be *consistent* with the object and purpose of the treaty, since the signature of an international treaty should be view as the predisposition to *move forward* (this is, an *evolutionary step*) with regard to the future will of *accepting* all the provisions laid down in the treaty (which will occur upon ratification). Therefore, a State that, although it had signed a treaty and shown the international society its intention to be finally bound by it, still does perform acts which may defeat the object and purpose of the treaty, would be clearly breaching its obligation to

---

Press, 2011, p. 25-36; and Almeida, Paula Wojcikiewicz & Pereira, Maíra Fajardo Linhares, Revisitando os efeitos da assinatura de um tratado internacional: da obrigação de boa-fé à sujeição internacional do Estado, *Revista Direito GV*, vol. 9, n. 1, São Paulo, Jan./Jun./2013, p. 171-197.

113 See Zoller, Elizabeth. *La bonne foi en droit international public*, cit., p. 69.

act in good faith. This would amount to taking many "steps backwards" regarding all the commitments resulting from the act of signature of the treaty. In summary, this is the spirit of Art. 18 of the Vienna Convention on the Law of Treaties.

There are several reasons why a State may (*a*) delay the ratification of a treaty, for example, the delay caused by an internal competent power (in Brazil, the National Congress) to analyze the instrument and approve it, or even (*b*) not to ratify it, although approved by the Parliament, for reasons of political convenience or opportunity. Whatever the case may be, during the time elapse between the signature and the ratification (or the lack thereof) the signatory State is bound to refrain from performing acts that may defeat the object and purpose of the treaty.

In such regard, for example, it should be stated that a State that signed the 1982 United Nations Convention on the Law of the Sea (but that still did not ratify it) shall, upon its signature, refrain from prohibiting that ships from other States navigate by its watercourses that, according to their internal law, are under their jurisdiction, but which, according to the Convention fall under the control of the so-called international waters. In the same manner, a State that has signed a treaty on the prohibition of certain chemical or nuclear weapons shall of course refrain from proceeding to use it or manufacturing it, for being acts defeating the object and the purpose of such type of agreement. Moreover, a State that has signed an international agreement on the prohibition of fishing shall, as from that time, refrain from continuing to fish the species protected by the specified agreement. In brief, while the State does not formally express its intention to withdraw its signing the treaty, it is bound to fulfill the object and the purpose of the treaty until its ratification.[114] It is a provisional obligation the State shall live up to, under the penalty of international responsibility. Upon ratification, it is clear that any obligations imposed by the treaty (besides the fulfillment of the object and purpose of the agreement) turn final, with the provisions of Art. 18(a) of the Convention being no longer applicable.

---

[114] For the criteria on which acts may be defeating the object and the purpose of a treaty, see Klabbers, Jan, How to defeat a treaty's object and purpose pending entry into force: toward manifest intent, *Vanderbilt Journal of Transnational Law*, vol. 34, n. 2 (2001), p. 283-335; Jonas, David S. & Saunders, Thomas N., The object and purpose of a treaty: three interpretive methods, *Vanderbilt Journal of Transnational Law*, vol. 43, n. 3 (2010), p. 565-609; and Almeida, Paula Wojcikiewicz & Pereira, Maíra Fajardo Linhares, Revisitando os efeitos da assinatura de um tratado internacional..., cit., p. 178-181.

It should be pointed out that the 1969 Vienna Convention neither establishes any *term* for the ratification of treaties, nor does the 1988 Brazilian Constitution, which causes the obligation provided in Art. 18 of the Convention to last during the time that the ratification of the treaty is pending, except that, as discussed before, the State *formally* expresses[115] its intent to withdraw its signature previously stamped on the treaty, in which case the obligation provided for in Art. 18 shall no longer be in effect thenceforth. Since the Convention does not provide any specific rule on the way in which the State should express that intention, it is understood that any means (provided that they are *formal*) admitted by law shall be valid.[116] Maybe *notification* would be the best way to do so, by analogous application of the provision of Art. 25 item 2 of the Convention, which sets forth that such is the way to end the temporary application of a treaty, under these terms: "Unless the treaty otherwise provides or the negotiating States have otherwise agreed, the provisional application of a treaty or a part of a treaty with respect to a State shall be terminated if that State notifies the other States between which the treaty is being applied provisionally of its intention not to become a party to the treaty".

> It was by means of a *notification* that the United States expressed, in 2002, its intention to not become a party to the Rome Statute of the ICC, which had been previously signed by the American government. The notification of the United States of America states as follows: "Dear Mr. Secretary General: "This is to inform you, in connection with the Rome Statute of the International Criminal Court adopted on July 17, 1998, that the United States does not intend to become a party to the treaty. Accordingly, the United States has no legal obligations arising from its signature on December 31, 2000 (...)". (USA. *Letter to UN Secretary General Kofi Annan*. Washington, D.C, 2002).

Taking into account the fact that those obligations arise from the signature of an unratified treaty, some authors have suggested that the States that were concerned about undertaking any kind of obligations upon the signature of the given treaty, should state that their intention is not to be

---

115 Some authors, like Mark Villiger, understand that a State may express its intention to not be part of the treaty, both by express declaration and by implicit behavior, for the purpose of removing the application of Art. 18 (see *Commentary on the 1969 Vienna Convention on the Law of Treaties*, cit., p. 250).

116 See Scott, David C. Presidential power to "un-sign" treaties, *The University of Chicago Law Review*, vol. 69, n. 3 (2002), p. 1475; and Almeida, Paula Wojcikiewicz & Pereira, Maíra Fajardo Linhares, Revisitando os efeitos da assinatura de um tratado internacional..., cit., p. 182-183.

deemed bound by the commitments therein included upon signature, at least, until the final process of ratification has come to an end.[117] However, this type of interpretative declaration (based upon a dubious intention) could be interpreted as being overly restrictive by virtue of an analysis of Art. 18 carried out on the basis of good faith.

1.5.2 Ratification

As a general rule, a State participates in the drawing up of a treaty subject to the reservation of ratification, which means that the mere signature of the instrument does not suffice to bind the State to the treaty concerned.[118] As a matter of fact, *ratification* has been used more frequently as a means for a State to be bound by an international treaty. However, before a treaty can be finally ratified, it is necessary that, after being signed (firstly[119]) by the plenipotentiaries, it is then submitted to the Legislative Power for its approval, before the final (and most important) stage can take place: its *ratification*.[120] In Brazil, the formality concerning the Parliament approval is *necessary* before the treaty ratification by the competent authority.[121] It is known that once the treaty has been signed, the Govern-

---

117 In that very sense, see Bradley, Curtis A., Unratified treaties, domestic politics, and the U.S. Constitution, cit., p. 334. It should be highlighted that the meaning of the text of such author is associated to the quoted American notification to the Secretary-General of the UN, whereby the United States does not recognize any the legal obligations arising from the signature, which enables (according to the American stance) the United States to conclude bilateral agreements with a number of countries for the purpose of preventing the rules of the ICC from being applied to American citizens.

118 See Villiger, Mark E. *Commentary on the 1969 Vienna Convention on the Law of Treaties*, cit., p. 184.

119 According to the practice of States some types of treaties (for example, an agreement in simplified form) need not be approved by the Parliament, as will be seen in Part V. Ch. 1, item 1.3, below (in which cases *ratification* will not take place either).

120 On this subject see Wilcox, Francis O., *The ratification of international conventions: a study of the relationship of the ratification process to the development of international legislation*, London: George Allen & Unwin Ltd., 1935, 349p; McNair, Arnold Duncan, *The law of treaties*, cit., p. 129-147; Maresca, Adolfo, *Il diritto dei trattati…*, cit., p. 177-194, apart from the classic work of Sette Câmara, José, *The ratification of international treaties*, which has already been quoted. See also Atay, Ender Ethem, La conclusion des traités internationaux et les systems constitutionnels, *Journal of the Faculty of Law of Gazi University*, vol. 1, n. 1, Ankara, Jun/1997, p. 166-191, in which it is included an interesting study on the classification of competent bodies with ratification powers.

121 The internal stages and constitutional procedure leading to the conclusion international acts will be studied in detail in Part V, Ch. 1, below.

ment is not bound to submit it to the Parliament for its consideration, being able to discontinue the formalities procedure leading to cause the treaty to enter into force, in the event it has no future intent to ratify it.[122] That is to say, the signature of the treaty does not necessarily mean that it has to be submitted to the Parliament, the President of the Republic is able to discontinue the conclusion procedure of the treaty, even after having been signed, taking into consideration domestic or international reasons in connection with the future obligations of the State arising out of the treaty concerned. Imagine, however, that the Head of the Executive submits the treaty to the National Congress and the latter approves it, as it usually happens in the procedure of international acts. Then, once the treaty has been *approved* by the Parliament, it returns to the Executive Power for its *ratification*. It is at this point that the State, through its representative, has the power (see below that the ratification of treaties is a discretionary power of the States) to express its *final* consent *to be bound by* the international commitment.[123] It is precisely this international step, namely, the *ratification* that will be analyzed below.

Although Art. 12 of the Vienna Convention provides that the State can express its consent to be bound by a treaty by means of a mere signature (see item 1.5.1.4, above), the fact remains that according to the practice of the majority of countries ratification is the most important stage – also the most formal, solemn, etc. – of the conclusion procedure of international acts. This is so because through ratification the intent of the State to take part in the legal relations regulated by the treaty is reaffirmed, especially taking into account the prior legislative consideration of the treaty concerned. Therefore, it can be asserted that the institution of ratification is clearly the *preferred one* in the practice of international relations, as a means of binding the State in connection with a treaty *stricto sensu*, although, from a legal perspective, it is just *one of the means* that allow a State to undertake a final commitment. In brief, ratification, as a means of binding the State definitively, which is much better than the

---

122 In such regard, see Pereira de Araújo, João Hermes, *A processualística dos atos internacionais*, cit., p. 173-174. This principle has exceptions in the conventions concluded under the auspices of the International Labour Organization. On the subject, see Mazzuoli, Valerio de Oliveira, *Curso de direito internacional público*, cit., p. 1115-1121.

123 For an analysis of the politics of ratification, see Lantis, Jeffrey S., *The life and death of international treaties: double-edged diplomacy and the politics of ratification in comparative perspective*, New York: Oxford University Press, 2009, 255p.

so-called "full-signature", reflects an international custom, which has not been abandoned by the States.

It can be said that the custom of States to constantly use ratification results from two main motives: (*a*) because the time that elapses between the stamping of the signature to the ratification is necessary for the government to make absolutely certain that its commitment will be good for the country; and (*b*) because the ratification must be previously *authorized* by the Parliament, therefore encouraging the people's participation (through their elected representatives) in the foreign affairs of the State.[124]

The institution of ratification is governed by Art. 14, items (1) and (2) of the 1969 Vienna Convention, which provides as follows:

> "Article 14.Consent to be bound by a treaty expressed by ratification, acceptance or approval.
>
> 1. The consent of a State to be bound by a treaty is expressed by ratification when:
>   *a)* the treaty provides for such consent to be expressed by means of ratification;
>   *b)* it is otherwise established that the negotiating States were agreed that ratification should be required;
>   *c)* the representative of the State has signed the treaty subject to ratification; or
>   *d)* the intention of the State to sign the treaty subject to ratification appears from the full powers of its representative or was expressed during the negotiation.
> 2. The consent of a State to be bound by a treaty is expressed by acceptance or approval under conditions similar to those which apply to ratification".

The grounds justifying the ratification, according to Angelo Piero Sereni, derive from many factors: (*a*) the subject matters of the treaty are of great importance and shall be approved by the Head of State; (*b*) ratification is used by Heads of State to monitor whether plenipotentiaries exceeded his/her powers in connection with the conclusion of the international agreement; (*c*) Parliaments started to participate in the Executive Power's affairs, leading to the democratization of international relations;

---

124 In that very sense, see Shaw, Malcolm N., *Direito internacional*, cit., p. 677-678.

(*d*) the chance that, before its final acceptance, the text of the treaty is previously submitted to the consideration of the People through its representatives in Parliaments, by means of the parliamentary approval, a step that is necessary for an international commitment to become valid, according to the majority of municipal law of the States, before the consent of the State is expressed to be bound by the agreement at the international level; (*e*) the chance for internal bodies to make a decision quietly and thoughtfully about what has been agreed upon at the international level; and (*f*) the need for internal bodies in charge of forming and expressing the will of the State at the international level to know and assess the reactions of national public opinion regarding the text of the treaty.[125]

According to the Brazilian constitutional framework, the ratification of the treaty constitutes the second time in which the Executive Power expresses itself in the formation procedure of international acts. If the signature legally binds the State to the adopted *text*, the ratification binds the State *to the treaty itself*, under all the mandatory terms contained therein. This additional participation of the Executive Power is justified by the fact that the circumstances under which the treaty was concluded may have changed or the political atmosphere of the State is not the same, making the expression of the State to be bound by the treaty unadvisable.

Looking at the history of international relations, the time in which States expressed their consent to be bound by a treaty was displaced from the act of signature to that of ratification, the latter having become the most important stage of the current treaty-making process.[126]

1.5.2.1 Concept

Etymologically, the expression *ratification* comes from Vulgar Latin *ratificare*, corresponding to Classical Latin *ratum facere*, *ratum esse*, which means "render valid", or *ratum efficere*, *ratum habere*, *ratum ducere*, *ratum alicui esse*, which has the meaning of "approval". Except for the expressions *ratum facere* and *ratum esse*, whose meaning corresponds to the one given today to ratification in public international law, this is, the *confirmation* of a previous act, the other terms lead to the idea of creation

[125] See Sereni, Angelo Piero. *Diritto internazionale*, vol. III, 1962, p. 1403-1404, quoted by Mello, Celso D. de Albuquerque, in *Ratificação de tratados…*, cit., p. 61-62.

[126] See Pereira de Araújo, João Hermes. *A processualística dos atos internacionais*, cit., p. 211.

of a new legal situation, which corresponds to the meaning of *approval*, assigned to the term by Civil Law.[127]

Thus, it is important to define the term ratification according to the meaning given by public international law, rather than the one given by the private law (especially of the Civil Law tradition) of any State.

Therefore, ratification means the act whereby the highest authority of a State, with constitutional competence to conclude treaties confirms the signature of the agreement prepared by his/her plenipotentiaries and finally expresses the consent of the State to be bound by the treaty, at the international level, coupled with the commitment to execute it in good faith.[128] It is the expression of *definitive* consent to be bound by the treaty, which implies the *formal* communication given by the national authority to the authorities of the other States to the effect that the treaty, concluded by their plenipotentiaries, is now *mandatory* for the State represented by such authority at the international level.

This conceptualization does not differ from the classical definition by José Sette Câmara, who stated:

> "Ratification is the act whereby the competent national authority of a State notifies the relevant authorities of the States whose plenipotentiaries concluded a draft treaty with the plenipotentiaries of the notifying State, that the draft treaty was approved, rendering the treaty concerned binding on the notifying State at the international level".[129]

The ratification is the last legal act carried out, in the treaty-making process, before the conventional text being promulgated and published in the *Official Gazette*, which is tantamount to the passage of an Act in the internal legislative process, which also takes place immediately before its promulgation and publication in the official press. It should be pointed out that in the latter case, Art. 84 (IV) of the Brazilian Constitution expressly provides for such legislative promulgation and publication, whilst in the case of treaties, Constitution *remains silent* on this matter.

---

127 See Mello, Celso D. de Albuquerque. *Ratificação de tratados...*, cit., p. 32-33; of the same author, *Direito constitucional internacional...*, cit., p. 278; and Pereira de Araújo, João Hermes, *A processualística dos atos internacionais*, cit., p. 207-208.

128 See Accioly, Hildebrando. *Tratado de direito internacional público*, vol. I, cit., p. 574; Rezek, José Francisco, *Direito dos tratados*, cit., p. 267; Dinh, Daillier & Pellet, *Direito internacional público*, cit., p. 140; and Tavares, Francisco de Assis Maciel, *Ratificação de tratados internacionais*, Rio de Janeiro: Lumen Juris, 2003, p. 35-37.

129 Sette Câmara, José. *The ratification of international treaties*, cit., p. 15.

1.5.2.2 Legal nature

Long discussions were held about the *legal nature* of ratification. There are three main schools of thought regarding its legal nature: (*a*) for some the ratification is the act that exclusively renders the treaty valid; (*b*) others understand that the will of negotiators is the only factor that is valid for the conclusion of a treaty, with the ratification as a mere "act of approval" of the treaty, which only relates to its execution, and its effective validity is not necessary; and (*c*) finally, a third position advocates that the will of the competent body to ratify the international agreement concurs with the will of the plenipotentiaries who signed it, thereby generating a complex act.[130]

The first school of thought, which was defended by Anzilotti, cannot be accepted, since it fully excludes the effects of the signature, the existence of which is known in the procedure of international acts. Frequently treaties include provisions on the timeframe for ratification, which is calculated from the date of signature. Such a provision would be void if the signature would not produce any legal effects. Besides, upon the signature the conventional text *is deemed a treaty*, although it still lacks the ratification to be considered as a perfected legal act. Another piece of evidence indicating its importance is the fact that treaties are always referred to by the date of their signature and not by the date of their ratification, which may vary from one country to another. However, according to the 1969 Vienna Convention, a treaty may also (as discussed earlier) enter into force on the date of its signature, under the terms of Art. 12. Although this provision may give rise to heavy criticism the aforementioned possibility is expressly set forth. Finally, the signature authenticates the conventional text, which is henceforth valid under public international law.

The second position, advocated by Alphonse Rivier, cannot be accepted either. According to the law of nations the ratification act implies the *confirmation* of the signature previously stamped, which differs from the meaning used in the realm of private law, where confirmation means *approval*. That is why Art. 2 item (2) of the Vienna Convention had established that the use of terms in the Convention "are without prejudice to the use of those terms or to the meanings which may be given to them

---

130 For further details see Mello, Celso D. de Albuquerque, *Ratificação de tratados...*, cit., p. 64, and authors quoted therein.

in the internal law of any State".[131] In the absence of the will of the Head of State the signature of the agreement by the plenipotentiaries is not fully materialized. The signature act will only be considered as fully executed when *confirmed* by means of ratification. It would not be possible, for example, to think of a *reservation* formulated upon ratification, if it is understood that such signature expresses a mere act of approval.

The third school of thought is the most realistic one, having been advocated by Balladore Pallieri in Italy. According to this conception, the signature and the ratification contribute to the conclusion of the treaty at the international level, so much so that the international commitment cannot be modified at the stage of ratification, except as otherwise provided for in its text.[132] Although this position has not overlooked the importance of the signature, which is evidenced in international law for several reasons, in our judgment, it seems, however, that ratification is *of greater importance* than the signature, firstly because the former confirms the latter, and secondly because ratification is the means for the State to express its definitive consent to be legally bound by the internationally commitments undertaken by it.

In fact, ratification is of a *sui generis* nature. This renders it difficult to perfectly match any classifications proposed by the above mentioned schools of thoughts. Ratification is undoubtedly the most important stage of the treaty-making process; it confirms the signature without overshadowing its international relevance. It could not be otherwise, since the signature enables the State to reach the ratification stage.[133] In addition, ratification compels the State to fulfill in good faith all the agreements it had entered into under penalty of incurring international responsibility for voluntary breach of the agreement.[134]

Given that ratification expresses the confirmation of the will of the State to become bound at international level, affirming its intention to

---

131 It should be noted that the ILC drafted this rule specifically for the purpose of avoiding the confusion that may be created by the term "ratification" in internal Law (see De La Guardia, Ernesto. *Derecho de los tratados internacionales*, cit., p. 124-125). For more information on the difficulties posed in internal Law by the terminology used in treaties, see Reuter, Paul, *Introducción al derecho de los tratados*, cit., p. 76-78

132 See Balladore Pallieri, G. *Diritto internazionale pubblico*, 6. ed. rifatta. Milano: Giuffrè, 1952, p. 263.

133 See Brownlie, Ian. *Princípios de direito internacional público*, cit., p. 630.

134 For further details see Mello, Celso D. de Albuquerque, *Ratificação de tratados...*, cit., p. 64-67.

abide by all obligations and duties set forth in the instrument concerned, that act is thus one of the *most relevant* stages in the treaty-making process. This statement, however, does not eclipse the importance that the *signature* has, since upon its stamping the State is obliged to refrain from acts contrary to the object and purpose of the treaty it had signed (Art. 18, *a*), by virtue of the good faith principle. Furthermore according to the terms of Art. 12 of the 1969 Vienna Convention, a treaty may enter into force on the date of the signature where the treaty itself expressly provides that the signature shall have such effect, or it is otherwise established that the negotiating States were agreed that the signature should produce that effect, or when the intention of the State to give that the effect to the signature appears from the full powers of its representative or was expressed during the negotiation.

1.5.2.3 Silent treaties

The ratification, as already known, constitutes the stage in which the international acts signed by the government concerned become mandatory for the State, after the exchange or deposit of the instruments with the State or body acting as a depositary. However, the development of the institution of the ratification cast doubts as to whether the ratification was mandatory in the event of the so-called *silent treaties*, this is, those instruments which contain no provisions on the need for ratification for them to become binding on the State.

International practice has shown (since the beginning of the 20th century) that ratification is *implicit* in international treaties in due form, in case these set forth no provision concerning their mandatory nature. That is why the Havana Convention on Treaties (1928) expressly states in Art. 5 that treaties "are obligatory *only after ratification* by the contracting States, *even though this condition is not stipulated* in the full powers of the negotiators or does not appear in the treaty itself".[135]

---

[135] In that sense, see Beviláqua, Clóvis, *Direito público internacional: a synthese dos princípios e a contribuição do Brasil*, t. II. Rio de Janeiro: Francisco Alves, 1911, p. 21; and Mello, Celso D. de Albuquerque, *Curso de direito internacional público*, vol. I, cit., p. 230. An identical provision that contained in Art. 5 of the Havana Convention (and on which it was clearly based) was already included in the *Projeto de Código de Direito internacional público* (1911) by Epitácio Pessoa, which states as follows: "Art. 203. Treaties are obligatory only after ratification by the contracting States, even though this condition is not stipulated in the full powers of the negotiators or does not appear in the treaty itself". On such provision, see Mazzuoli, Valerio de Oliveira, Apontamentos

The multiplication of executive agreements, at international level, has seriously undermined the institution of ratification, what prompted the ILC (since reports issued by Brierly) to stop establishing that ratification should be mandatory for all cases, stating that ratification would only be necessary in principle, the conventional text being capable of providing for exceptions to that rule, especially when dealing with treaties in simplified form. As a matter of fact, these treaties, which have a lower political impact and are executed by means of exchange of notes need not be ratified, and according to international practice their validity has never been challenged due to the absence of ratification. Hence, the 1969 Vienna Convention has dealt with this matter in Art. 13, which reads as follows: "The consent of States to be bound by a treaty constituted by instruments exchanged between them is expressed by that exchange when: (*a*) the instruments provide that their exchange shall have that effect; or (*b*) it is otherwise established that those States were agreed that the exchange of instruments should have that effect". Furthermore, as ruled upon by the ICJ in the *Aegean Sea Continental Shelf Case* (Greece *v.* Turkey), even the exchange of a joint communication may be valid to bind two States (see *CIJ Recueil*, 1978, § 96).

As can be seen, in 1928, at the time of the Havana Convention on Treaties (that provides that "treaties are obligatory *only after ratification* by the contracting States…"), the presumption was in favour of the ratification, while in 1969, under the Vienna Convention on the Law of Treaties (according to which the "[t]he consent of a State to be bound by a treaty is expressed by ratification when […] the treaty provides for such consent to be expressed by means of ratification…"), the presumption is now in favour of the signature.[136] However, despite this provision of the Vienna Convention, the current trend that has been accepted (for example, by the ILC since 1962) is that the silence of the treaty regarding ratification, at least with regard to the agreements *in due form*, does not release the Government from that formality, since every silent international treaty contains a *tacit provision* of ratification.[137]

---

sobre o direito dos tratados no Projeto de Código de Direito Internacional Público de Epitácio Pessoa, cit., p. 521.

136 See Mello, Celso D. de Albuquerque. *Direito constitucional internacional…*, cit., p. 281.

137 See Pereira de Araújo, João Hermes. *A processualística dos atos internacionais*, cit., p. 213; and Remiro Brotons, Antonio, *Derecho internacional público*, vol. 2, cit., p. 106-107. Most authors agree with the sense indicated above, as acknowledged by Brierly: "A difficult question here is to ascertain what solution should be adopted when the terms of the treaty do not allow to conclude which would have been the intention of the parties regarding the need to ratify the treaty or not. The majority of modern legal scholars understand that, in such a case, ratification must be deemed essential" (*Direito internacional*, cit., p. 328). For an opposing view, see Fitzmaurice, Gerald Gray, Do treaties need ratification?, *British Yearbook of International Law*, vol. 15 (1934), p. 129, who advocates the idea that ratification will be mandatory only if it is expressly foreseen by the parties; that was the point of view adopted, for example, by the United Kingdom. See also Sinclair, Ian, *The*

1.5.2.4 Procedure

Ratification is completed with the *formal communication* given by a contracting party to the other (or others) that it accepted to be finally bound by the treaty. That communication is transmitted by the issuance of a document named *Letter of ratification* signed by the Head of State and countersigned by the Minister for Foreign Affairs. By means of such a *Letter* the government of a given State notifies the government of another State (or other States) through the Secretariat of United Nations or through the Organization of American States, and whom it may concern that the text of the treaty was finally accepted and that its provisions will be fully complied with.[138]

The instruments of ratification typically issued by the Brazilian Government essentially follow this pattern:

> (Name of the President)
> President of the Federative Republic of Brazil.
> Please be informed that according to this Letter of Ratification, the Federative Republic of Brazil and (...), by their respective plenipotentiaries concluded and signed on the (...) day of the month of (...) of the year (...), a treaty with the following content (the content of the instrument follows).
> With the National Congress approving the aforementioned treaty, which was transcribed above, I do hereby confirm and ratify it, and I consider it final and binding to produce its due effects, promising that its provisions will be fully complied with.
> I do hereby certify that I had this Letter written, which I sign and is sealed with the Coat of Arms of the Republic and subscribed by the Minister for Foreign Affairs.
> Given at the *Palácio do Planalto*, in Brasilia, this (...) day of the month of (...) of the year (...), after (...) years of Independence, and (...) years of the Republic.

The mere ratification of the treaty, however, does not suffice for it to enter *into force*. The signature of the Letter of ratification is an internal act that has no influence in validating the agreement. The entry into force of treaties is carried out by the *exchange* or *deposit* of the instruments of ratification with a State or body that assumes their custody (for example, the UN or the OAS); in the latter case, the depositary[139] shall give notice to the other contracting parties that the State *has already ratified* the treaty and that it can be potentially applied (when the text does not provide for

---

Vienna Convention on the Law of Treaties, cit., p. 40; and Shaw, Malcolm N., *Direito internacional*, cit., p. 678.

138 See Accioly, Hildebrando. *Tratado de direito internacional público*, vol. I, cit., p. 579.

139 On the *depositary* of treaties, see Part V, Ch. 1, item 1.7.1, below.

vacation legis). Only after the exchange or deposit of the instruments of ratification can the contracting parties effectively express to each other their final will to fulfill the agreements. The *exchange* of the instruments of ratification takes place only when dealing with bilateral treaties and the event of ratification is similar to that of the signature of the agreement.[140] When dealing with *multilateral* treaties the *deposit*, in turn, occurs when each Government prepares a ratification instrument, which is sent to the depositary of the treaty previously designated for that purpose.[141]From this moment onwards States are no longer mere *contracting parties* to become real *parties* to the treaty, in the event the instrument is already in force (see Art. 2 item (1)(g) of the 1969 Convention).[142] Before such supplementary acts (exchange or deposit) the application of the treaties may not be required from the States concerned, except for, indeed, the obligation set forth in Art. 18 of the Convention.[143]

As can be seen, the exchange or deposit of ratifying instruments constitute the last stage of the ratification process of treaties, if understood in *latu sensu*. As clarified, two acts take place: the *ratification itself* and the *exchange* or *deposit*.[144] The aforementioned claims stem from the analysis of the provisions of Art. 16 (a) and (b) of the 1969 Vienna Convention, which governs the subject, under the following terms:

---

140 Art. 13 of the 1969 Vienna Convention deals with the *exchange* of instruments constituting a treaty, under these terms: "The consent of States to be bound by a treaty constituted by instruments exchanged between them is expressed by that exchange when: *a)* the instruments provide that their exchange shall have that effect; or *b)* it is otherwise established that those States were agreed that the exchange of instruments should have that effect".

141 See Accioly, Hildebrando. *Tratado de direito internacional público*, vol. I, cit., p. 594-595; McNair, Arnold Duncan, *The law of treaties*, cit., p. 136; Remiro Brotons, Antonio, *Derecho internacional público*, vol. 2, cit., p. 109; and De La Guardia, Ernesto, *Derecho de los tratados internacionales*, cit., p. 163.

142 See Remiro Brotons, Antonio. *Derecho internacional público*, vol. 2, cit., p. 246; and Villiger, Mark E., *Commentary on the 1969 Vienna Convention on the Law of Treaties*, cit., p. 93: "The ILC Report 1966 emphasized that the term 'party' is employed in the Convention also in respect of treaties which cease to be in force, in particular in Section 5 of Part V of the Convention".

143 This article states as follows: "A State is obliged to refrain from acts which would defeat the object and purpose of a treaty when: *a)* it has signed the treaty or has exchanged instruments constituting the treaty subject to ratification, acceptance or approval, until it shall have made its intention clear not to become a party to the treaty; or *b)* it has expressed its consent to be bound by the treaty, pending the entry into force of the treaty and provided that such entry into force is not unduly delayed".

144 See Mello, Celso D. de Albuquerque. *Ratificação de tratados...*, cit., p. 151-154.

> "Article 16.*Exchange or deposit of instruments of ratification, acceptance, approval or accession.*
>
> Unless the treaty otherwise provides, instruments of ratification, acceptance, approval or accession establish the consent of a State to be bound by a treaty upon:
>
> *a)* their exchange between the contracting States;
>
> *b)* their deposit with the depositary; or
>
> c) their notification to the contracting States or to the depositary, if so agreed".

It should be pointed out that, in Brazil, the *ratification exchange* instrument model (used in bilateral treaties) is as follows:

> The undersigned (...), Minister for Foreign Affairs of Brazil and (...), special envoy and plenipotentiary minister for (...), duly authorized, met in the city of (...), at the *Palácio do Planalto* of (...), this (...) day of the month of (...) of the year (...), in order to exchange the instruments of ratification of the treaty entered into (...) between both countries, concluded and signed in the aforementioned city on this (...) day of the month of (...) of the year (...). Having the two respective instruments of ratification been found acceptable and concluded in due form, they thus are exchanged. In witness whereof, the present record is signed in duplicate, in the (...) and (...) languages, being the respective stamps affixed thereon.

Apart from ratification itself and the exchange or deposit of the instruments of ratification, the 1969 Convention also makes reference to a *third modality* to conclude a treaty, which is provided for in Art. 16 *c*: their *notification* to the contracting States or to the depositary.[145]This is a less formal and more recent means of making known the instruments of ratification, acceptance, approval or accession to the other contracting States or to the depositary.[146]

What are the rules applying to *notification* in the 1969 Vienna Convention? According to the Convention, any notification shall be transmitted, if there are no depositaries, directly to the States for which it is intended, or, if there is a depositary, to the latter (Art. 78, *a*); it shall be considered as having been made by the State in question only upon its receipt by the State to which it was transmitted or, as the case may be, upon

[145] See Remiro Brotons, Antonio. *Derecho internacional público*, vol. 2, cit., p. 111-112.

[146] See Villiger, Mark E. *Commentary on the 1969 Vienna Convention on the Law of Treaties*, cit., p. 233.

its receipt by the depositary (Art. 78 *b*); if it is transmitted to a depositary, it shall be considered as received by the State for which it was intended only when the latter State has been informed by the depositary in accordance with Art. 77, paragraph 1 (e) of the Convention, which requires the depositary to inform the parties and the States entitled to become parties to the treaty of acts, notifications and communications relating to the ratified international instrument (Art. 78 *c*).[147]

In summary, once the agreement has been ratified (including the formality of the exchange or deposit of instruments of ratification), the State becomes bound by the treaty on a definitive basis. From that moment onward, a State can cease to being a party to a treaty only if it denounces it, which is the customary form that was codified in the Vienna Convention to be released from any internationally valid commitment.[148] Once the ratification has been carried out, no other procedure is required at the international level for the commitment signed by the Government to be valid and capable of being executed.

Upon ratification of a treaty, the State undertakes the obligation to fulfill, enforce and guarantee the rights recognized under the conventional text vis-à-vis any person subject to its jurisdiction; adapt its internal legislation to the provisions of the treaty (which, as a rule, is not fulfilled by most States); ensure that its authorities do not take any actions or steps contrary to the provisions of the treaty; and make available effective legal remedies for any person who considers that his/her rights have been violated in order to rectify the situation.

1.5.2.5 Characteristics

The legal institution of ratification has really special characteristics, which must be well known (and understood) by the agents responsible for the international relations of a State. The foregoing is not only applicable to them but also to judges and law enforcement personnel at large, to the extent that the ratification is conclusive for the internal application of treaties. The study of such characteristics provides also the chance – in particular as regards the competent body to express the consent of the State to be bound by the treaty – to understand the eventual limits to its materialization. An analysis thereof follows.

---

[147] See Reuter, Paul. *Introducción al derecho de los tratados*, cit., p. 89-90.

[148] See Magalhães, José Carlos de. *O Supremo Tribunal Federal e o direito internacional: uma análise crítica*. Porto Alegre: Livraria do Advogado, 2000, p. 67.

1.5.2.5.1 Governmental act of international nature

Ratification is *governmental* legal act of *international* nature carried out according to the stringent rules of public international law rather than the internal constitutional provisions of each country. In fact, the constitutional systems of the States contain no rules on the ratification of treaties, there being only a certain State practice concerning the subject – in some cases a well- established practice, in other cases an incipient one.[149] Therefore, no reference should be made, for being fully inappropriate from a technical viewpoint, to "constitutional ratification" or "internal law ratification", as meaning the approval of the international treaty by the Legislative Power or its internal enactment.[150] Any reference to "ratification by Congress" or to "internal ratification" of the treaty is not correct and shall not be understood as such; there exists not even State practice according to which the participation of the Legislative in the procedure of international acts is referred to as ratification. That is why section 9 of the Act of 29 October1891, in which the Congress approval of a treaty was referred to as *ratification*, was criticized by Beviláqua.[151] Furthermore, Art. 2 item 1 (b) of the 1969 Vienna Convention itself adopts the stance that ratification is a legal act of *international* nature. The quoted provision states that "ratification" [...] "mean[s] [...] the international act so named whereby

---

149 See Sepúlveda, César. *Derecho internacional*, cit., p. 131.

150 See McNair, Arnold Duncan. *The law of treaties*, cit., p. 130; and Remiro Brotons, Antonio, *Derecho internacional público*, vol. 2, cit., p. 100. In this regard, we cannot agree with Ian Brownlie, according to whom ratification "implies two different procedural acts: firstly, an act by the competent body of the State, which in the case of the United Kingdom is the Crown, and that may be named *ratification in the constitutional sense*; secondly, the international procedure, which enables the entry into force of a treaty by means of a formal exchange or deposit of the instruments of ratification" [emphasis added]. The author admits, however, that in that latter sense "ratification is an important act that implies the consent to be bound" (*Princípios de Direito internacional público*, cit., p. 631; the same position was maintained in Crawford, James, *Brownlie's principles of public international law*, cit., p. 372-373). Malcolm Shaw also refers (improperly) to "ratification in the internal constitutional sense", to make a conceptual distinction with the ratification provided for in the 1969 Vienna Convention (see *Direito internacional*, cit., p. 677, note 42). Ratification can only be understood as an *internal* act when dealing with its *form*, since this is not governed by the forms prescribe in international law, each country being entitled to establish how the ratification instrument will be from a formal perspective. Besides, this does not mean that there may exist verbal or even tacit ratification. In that sense, see Pereira de Araújo, João Hermes, *A processualística dos atos internacionais*, cit., p. 223-224.

151 See Beviláqua, Clóvis. *Direito público internacional...*, t. II, cit., p. 22.

a State establishes on the international plane its consent to be bound by a treaty". The Convention was fairly straight forward in providing that the aforementioned acts refer to *international* legal acts.[152] At the national level, there only exists the approval by the Parliament, which does not mean ratification in the public international law sense, which is an (exclusive) act of government. Moreover, the competence to ratify always rests with the Power in whose behalf treaties were signed.[153] Therefore, neither Parliament approval nor any similar procedures provided for in internal law concern ratification in the technical sense.

> "The conceptual mistake underlying this last understanding of ratification [according to which the expression also denotes 'the approval of the treaty by the Legislative Power, or other State body whose consent may be necessary'] is even more serious than it seems. In this case, the term enshrined in international law is used to refer to a legal fact that where provided for in internal law, is exclusively governed by the latter. Furthermore, it seems that the idea of 'ratification' of a treaty as an constitutional act of an internal nature by a Parliament or any other body underpins the unclear and serious oversight that the international agreement involves *a number* of sovereign States, being impossible to assume that one or more contracting sovereign Parties, which have already entered into an agreement with the government of the State concerned, had remained in expectation of final approval of the Parliament of the latter.
> That is why ratification can only be understood as an *international act* and as a *governmental act*. The Executive Power, which is usually responsible for the foreign relations of the State appears to be capable of ratifying, which in the legal lexicon means *confirmation*, vis-à-vis other international law legal persons, the question it had left open at the end of the negotiating stage, this is, its consent to be bound by the agreement".
> REZEK, José Francisco. *Direito dos tratados*, cit., p. 264.

Therefore, the validity of an international treaty, as well as the provisions on its continuance in force are found in the rules of the law of nations rather than in the internal constitutional rules on competence to conclude treaties or any other domestic rules.

Here the following question can be posed: who establishes which branch of the State is the competent one to express its consent to be bound by a treaty at the international level? As a quick answer, it could be stated that it is the internal Law itself, which determines the branch of the State that is competent to express its will. However, where that issue is analyzed in the context of the monist theory with the primacy of international law,

152 See De La Guardia, Ernesto. *Derecho de los tratados internacionales*, cit., p. 120.

153 See Pereira de Araújo, João Hermes. *A processualística dos atos internacionais*, cit., p. 217.

the conclusion is drawn that the competence of body/bodies responsible for approving a treaty is established by internal law, but as a result of delegation by public international law. This being the source from which State internal Law derives, is at the same time, the legal system that delegates to the States the power to conclude treaties. Therefore, States must observe the limits imposed on them by international law regarding the ratification of treaties, which according to the 1969 Vienna Convention is the act "whereby a State establishes on the international plane its consent to be bound by a treaty". Even though the Legislative Power participates in the treaty-making process, the discretionary prerogative of ratification, according to international law, rests with the Head of the State, who is responsible to decide whether ratification of the treaty concerned is timely and appropriate. Ratification is a *governmental* act of an *international* nature regulated by the law of nations in all its aspects, States being ultimately unable to modify it by their unilateral will. Therefore, there only exists one form of ratification that is legally valid: the one performed according to the express rules of public international law. It follows that any reference to ratification according to internal law or any internal legal act with such effects should be deemed incorrect.

Moreover, ratification still constitutes an international act, even if it is preceded by the approval of the Legislative Power. Those who deem ratification unnecessary due to the fact that the Parliament *had previously expressed itself* in the treaty-making process are seriously mistaken. Without ratification, the final will of the State is not expressed and thus there is no chance to demand the application of the treaty vis-à-vis the other State Parties to it, except for the exceptional case that the treaty has become legally valid and binding upon its signature (under the terms of Art. 12 of the Convention).

1.5.2.5.2 Express act

Ratification must be always carried out in an *express* form. Such an important act cannot be expressed in a tacit manner. According to the Havana Convention on Treaties (1928), ratification must be "made *in writing* pursuant to the legislation of the State" (Art. 6, first paragraph). The need for ratification to be carried out in writing has been advocated by several authors, on the grounds that evidence is more solid when *in writing*.

Currently, however, the oral expression by a Head of State has already been accepted as a ratifying act, where, he/she has publicly declared the commitment undertaken as final. Although this can be so in certain countries, as regards Brazil, ratification must be expressed in writing on a mandatory basis, due to the fact that the Brazilian State is a Party to the Havana Convention on Treaties and this convention requires ratification to be carried out in writing.

The prevailing opinion is that the requirement that ratification should be carried out in writing should not be easily waived at a national level, particularly due to the fact that ratification in writing implies a higher degree of certainty and security for international relations as to the genuine consent of the State to be bound by a treaty.

1.5.2.5.3 Political and circumstantial act

Ratification is also characterized by being an act of a highly *political* and *circumstantial* nature, as the Head of State – who is almost always, according to constitutional law, responsible for maintain relations with foreign Powers – is under no obligation to confirm the consent of the State to be bound by the treaty concerned vis-à-vis the other contracting parties.

Typically, constitutions establish that ratification of treaties must be carried out after their approval by the Legislative Power. This parliamentary approval represents – in the treaty-making process – an *intermediate* stage between signature and ratification. Yet, parliamentary approval of a treaty puts the Head of State under no obligation to ratify it. Consequently, the Head of State may make a decision on a discretionary basis as to whether or not ratify the treaty concerned. This means that, after the treaty has been approved by the Parliament, the Government *may* still ratify the treaty or *not*, according to what it deems more convenient (political aspect) or, even, the circumstances of the time (circumstantial aspect).

Failure to ratify the treaty by the Executive constitutes a legitimate act (both from an internal and international law perspective) and the President of the Republic may not be held responsibility under no circumstances. In other words, *failure to* carry out the ratification does not imply any unlawful act (at neither the national nor the international level) by the Head of the Executive. The matter in its entirety will depend on the convenience or the circumstances.

Due to the double nature of ratification there exists no *time frame* for it to be carried out at the international, except if the treaty expressly sets a specific term for the ratification to take place. On this regard, modern scholars and international practice have been unanimous. Furthermore, failure by the President of the Republic to ratify an international agreement may result from a final political and discretionary decision that he/she may have made, in addition to exercising an inherent right to sovereignty of the State.

1.5.2.5.4 Discretionary act

As a logical corollary of the aforementioned feature, ratification is also *discretionary*, depending exclusively on the will of the Government, which will base its decision upon convenience and opportuneness criteria. If the Head of the Executive can even "waive" the treaty-making process, ordering the filing of conventional text even before its examination by the Legislative Power, he/she will even be able to not ratify the treaty after having been approved by the Parliament.[154] Moreover, failure to ratify a treaty constitutes a lawful act and is allowed under public international law, without international responsibility being incurred by the State concerned, although such an act may result in political retaliations. It seems then logical that the Executive Power – which may have neither even started negotiations of the treaty nor participated in them, nor even submitted the conventional text to the Parliament for its approval – must also have the authority to decide (based upon opportuneness and convenience criteria) whether it ratifies the agreement or not that it had previously signed. This is the enshrining of the freedom principle to refuse ratification, which is accepted by all internationalists.[155] There is a number of reasons to refuse ratification: political shifts, information that comes to light indicating that other States are not willing to ratify the agreement, the occurrence of subsequent facts, etc.

For example, imagine a treaty concluded for the purpose of enabling the construction of an aqueduct connecting two States that awaited for years its approval by the Parliament. Upon ratification, it is noticed that headwaters, which would be transferred by the aqueduct, dried up. Under such circumstances, the President of the Republic would wonder if it would be convenient for the country to ratify a treaty whose performance is impossible due to the disappearance or destruction of its object? If ratification were not a discretionary act of the Head of the Executive, the

---

[154] See Dinh, Daillier & Pellet. *Direito internacional público*, cit., p. 143; Tavares, Francisco de Assis Maciel, *Ratificação de tratados internacionais*, p. 44-47; and Brichambaut, Dobelle & Coulée, *Leçons de droit international public*, cit., p. 272.

[155] For further information see Pereira de Araújo, João Hermes, *A processualística dos atos internacionais*, cit., p. 218-220.

country would certainly have to live up to agreements that had become obsolete or (as in the case at hand) had become impossible of being performed.

The aforementioned argument of ratification as a discretionary act is expressly enshrined in Art. 7 of the Havana Convention on Treaties, which states as follows:

> "Article 7. Refusal to ratify or the formulation of a reservation are acts inherent in national sovereignty and as such constitute the exercise of a right which violates no international stipulation or good form. In case of refusal it shall be communicated to the other contracting parties".

However this rule whereby the discretion of ratification is established is not valid for *all* treaties, there being exceptions exclusively as far as ILO conventions are concerned.[156] The reason for this lies in the ILO Constitution (the constituent instrument of the Organization), which *requires* the Government to submit (within the period of one year, or no later than 18 months from the closing of the session of the General Conference of the International Labour Organization) the adopted convention for the consideration by the Parliament, under the terms of Art. 19, item 5, *b*: "In the case of a convention: *b)* each of the Members undertakes that it will, within the period of one year at most from the closing of the session of the Conference, or if it is impossible owing to exceptional circumstances to do so within the period of one year, then at the earliest practicable moment and in no case later than 18 months from the closing of the session of the Conference, bring the Convention before the authority or authorities within whose competence the matter lies, for the enactment of legislation or other action". In other paragraph (subparagraph *d*) of the same Art. 19 item (5), the ILO Constitution sets forth that "if the Member obtains the consent of the authority or authorities within whose competence the matter lies, it *will communicate the formal ratification of the Convention to the Director-General* and will take such action as may be necessary to make effective the provisions of such Convention", suggesting that the ratification of the convention

[156] For details, see Mazzuoli, Valerio de Oliveira, *Curso de direito internacional público*, cit., p. 1115-1121. On the application of ILO conventions in comparative law, especially in Argentina, France, Mexico, Netherlands, Switzerland, and United States, see Leary, Virginia A., *International labour conventions and national law*, Dordrecht: Martinus Nijhoff, 1982, 191p.

should be mandatory.[157] For most legal scholars, although the ILO treaty does not expressly refer to the mandatory nature of aforementioned ratification, that mandatory character seems to be a logical consequence thereof. Then, if the President of the Republic is under the obligation to submit a labour international convention to the Parliament, once it *is approved* by the latter ratification should not be viewed as discretionary. Moreover, it should be noted that the ILO constituent instrument states that conventions shall be brought before "the authority or authorities within whose competence the matter lies, for the enactment of legislation". The only body capable of enacting laws is the Legislative Power. This task is not a typical function of the Executive. So the most adequate interpretation of the ILO Constitution is that it requires the submission of the international labour conventions to National Congress for its consideration, and in the event that they have been approved by the latter, they shall be mandatorily ratified by the Executive.[158]

---

[157] It should be pointed out that although the ILO Constitution refers to "ratification" of conventions, the most appropriate thing would be using the term "accession" to refer to the commitment undertaken by the State to become a party to an open multilateral treaty, following the terminology used by the Vienna Convention of the Law of Treaties for the assumption. Indeed, it should be noted that ILO conventions are not signed by the representatives of States adopting them, but only by the President of the session, namely, the General Conference of the International Labour Organization and by the Director-General of the International Labor Office. It should be pointed out that only what has previously been signed can subsequently be ratified, and in the case of ILO conventions there was no previous signature (by State plenipotentiaries). Therefore, there only exists, from a technical viewpoint, the chance to *accede* to the conventional text. In that regard, see Süssekind, Arnaldo, *Direito internacional do trabalho*, 2. ed. (updated and extended), São Paulo: LTr, 1987, p. 211. See also Valticos, Nicolas, Nature et portée juridique de la ratification des conventions internationales du travail, in Dinstein, Yoram (ed.), *International law at a time of perplexity: essays in honour of Shabtai Rosenne*, Dordrecht: Martinus Nijhoff, 1989, p. 987-1004.

[158] In that very sense, see Mello, Celso D. de Albuquerque, *Direito constitucional internacional...*, cit., p. 280; Tavares, Francisco de Assis Maciel, *Ratificação de tratados internacionais*, p. 58-62; and also Rezek, José Francisco, *Direito dos tratados*, cit., p. 162, who considers that: "Once consent has been expressed by the 'competent authority', the government of the State Member *shall be bound to ratify* the international labour convention, by sending to ILO secretariat the respective ratification instrument. Therefore, the usual methodology is not followed in two different stages. Indeed, the government is under no obligation to *submit* the draft treaty to the Parliament in whose execution is not interested, nor is it obliged, in the event that the treaty concerned is approved by Parliament, to live up to its initial intention, by *ratifying* it". On the contrary, see Seitenfus, Ricardo, *Manual das organizações internacionais*, 4. ed. (reviewed, updated and extended), Porto

1.5.2.5.5 Act of non-retroactive nature

Ratification has no retroactive effects, unless otherwise expressly provided for in the treaty.[159] The predominant legal literature throughout the 19th century and at the beginning of the 20th century, in American case law concerning the retroactive nature of ratification is no longer relevant. If ratification or certain acts leading to it, namely, the exchange or deposit of the instruments constituting a treaty, grants binding force to the treaty, it then becomes clear that it is not possible to claim that a treaty may have retroactive effects as from the date of its signature. It does not matter whether the treaty is *known* or *referred to as* by the date of its signature. The only purpose of this is to identify the treaty concerned more easily, as it is not always easy to know the exact date of ratification by each State.[160] Moreover, the signature date of the agreement is better known than the date of entry into force itself. This, however, does not mean that ratification should have retroactive effects back to its date of signature. Consequently, a treaty will only be deemed binding on States *upon* its ratification, this being understood as the exchange of the instruments constituting a treaty or their deposit with a State or body appointed for such purpose. Art. 8 of the Havana Convention on Treaties sets forth, on this regard, that treaties "shall become effective from the date of exchange or deposit of ratification, unless some other date has been agreed upon through an express provision".

In any case, if a State only becomes legally bound by the text of the treaty upon its ratification, it seems obvious that the treaty concerned shall only have effects as from the date of ratification. There is general agreement that this is the prevailing opinion (international legal scholars, practice and case law).[161]

Alegre: Livraria do Advogado, 2005, p. 232, who is of the opinion that: "The obligation imposed on States to submit the convention text to their respective Parliaments does not imply an automatic ratification. States may refuse to do so. However, texts may be deemed guidelines to be followed for subsequent governmental action. From an international law point of view, however, rules arising out of the ILO conventions shall not be put on an equal footing with international norms, as they depend on the expression of consent by the States".

159 See Nascimento e Silva, Geraldo Eulálio do. Le facteur temps et les traités, *Recueil des Cours*, vol. 154 (1977-I), p. 277-279.

160 See Accioly, Hildebrando. *Tratado de direito internacional público*, vol. I, cit., p. 597.

161 See Mello, Celso D. de Albuquerque. *Ratificação de tratados...*, cit., p. 70-71; and Tavares, Francisco de Assis Maciel, *Ratificação de tratados internacionais*, cit., p. 51-52.

1.5.2.5.6 Irrevocable act

Ratification, albeit a discretionary act, once performed it becomes *irrevocable*.[162] It becomes effective even before the commitment enters into force at the international level, the basis for this being the very performance of the act of ratification itself. Nothing could be more accurate than this. Nevertheless, governments can simply not take part in international negotiations, and, even if they did participate in them, they can refuse to send the conventional text for parliamentary approval. Moreover, even if Parliament approves the treaty, Governments can refuse to ratify the agreement, according to their assessment of the situation at that very moment.[163] It would then not be reasonable that, after all the aforementioned opportunities for *withdrawal*, a Head of State could just *withdraw* the consent express on behalf of the State.

The irrevocability of ratification also operates in two lapses of time immediately prior to the entry into force of the treaty at the international level, namely, (1) in those cases in which it is expected to reach the *necessary number* of ratifications under conditional treaties, on the basis of the principles of good faith and legal certainty; and (2) during a possible period of legal vaccum (*vacation legis*) contained in the treaty itself for its entry into force, as the agreement has already been executed.[164]

A ratification that has been completed may, however, be revoked (*a*) in the event of a unilateral denunciation, if permitted, or (*b*) when the entry into force of the treaty is unduly delayed, as stated in Art. 18 (a) and (b) of the 1969 Vienna Convention.[165] Although the Convention has not been clear about the chance to revoke the ratification, it did foresee the performance of acts which would defeat the object and purpose of the ratified treaty, albeit not in force, in the event of undue delay caused by one of the Contracting Parties, which would prevent the agreement from being executed.

1.5.2.5.7 No time limits

There is no rule (not even of a customary nature) that provides a *time limit* for submitting the ratification, following neither time in which ne-

---

[162] See Sepúlveda, César. *Derecho internacional*, cit., p. 133.

[163] See Accioly, Hildebrando. *Tratado de direito internacional público*, vol. I, cit., p. 578.

[164] See Rezek, José Francisco. *Direito dos tratados*, cit., p. 275-276.

[165] For a commentary on the discussions on the aforementioned rule held at the Conference of the 1969 Vienna Convention, see Nascimento e Silva, Geraldo Eulálio do, *Conferência de Viena sobre o direito dos tratados*, cit., p. 67-68.

gotiations end, nor the signature (if deferred) nor after the time in which the Parliament of the State concerned *has approved* the conventional text. Therefore, the subject-matter is dealt with on a case-by-case basis. From time to time, treaties do not contain any provisions concerning time limits for ratification, authorizing thus the governments concerned to ratify them when they deem it convenient. In practice, governments ratify treaties when they understand that the final commitment of the State is timely and convenient taking into consideration their national interests. In other cases, there are treaties establishing that the contracting parties are to ratify them "as soon as possible". However, in practice, this situation does not differ from the previous case.[166]

What cannot be done in that field is to intend to establish a specific time limit for ratification, that is, for the State to express its consent to be bound by the treaty by analogy with the provisions of Art. 66 (1) (3) of the 1988 Brazilian Constitution. Indeed, according to that provision the time limit for the enactment of laws is of *fifteen days*, after which, the silence of the President of the Republic implies the tacit enactment of the law. Even those authors who consider such a solution as correct in other countries, namely, Jorge Miranda, in Portugal, indicate that "perhaps a longer time frame may be justified, given that the conclusion of a treaty may require a much higher weighting than that required for the approval of a law (which the State may repeal at any time)".[167]

However, if the treaty itself establishes a *specific time limit* for the expression of consent to be bound by a treaty, any ratification outside that time limit is forbidden. It should be noted that a great number of those treaties are *open* to accession, then giving a second chance to those States failing to express their definitive consent (see item 1.5.3, below). Consequently, if a State that participated in the drawing up of the treaty misses the time limit specified for its ratification, they may *accede* to the treaty concerned if it is an open instrument. In this case, accession becomes a true *key factor* for that State that failed to comply with the ratification time limit. This was what happened with Brazil in relation with the Convention providing a Uniform Law for Bills of Exchange and Promissory Notes (Geneva Convention), whose Art. 4 sets forth that the instruments of ratification should be deposited *before September 1st, 1932.* Since Brazil

[166] See Rezek, José Francisco. *Direito dos tratados*, cit., p. 271.

[167] Miranda, Jorge. *Curso de direito internacional público*, 5. ed. (reviewed and updated). Cascais: Princípia, 2012, p. 111-112.

did not comply with the aforementioned time limit, it acceded to the convention (under the terms of Art. 5) on August 26th, 1942.[168]

1.5.2.5.8 Possibility or impossibility of carrying out a conditional ratification

The Havana Convention on Treaties rejects the chance of a *conditional* ratification, as its Art. 6 (first paragraph) provides, that ratification "must be unconditional and must embrace *the entire treaty*".[169]

Here we have two situations: the obligation that ratification shall be carried out *without conditions*; and the requirement that it shall cover *the entire treaty*. Regarding the first situation (impossibility of a conditional ratification), no problem arises. However, as for the second one, there exists a conflict between the provisions of Art. 6 of the Havana Convention and Art. 2 item 1 (d) of the 1969 Vienna Convention, which allows the ratification of a treaty with *reservations*.

Therefore, the second situation as provided for in Art. 6 of the Havana Convention (which states that ratification must embrace "the entire treaty") shall be construed with the limitations imposed by the 1969 Vienna Convention, with the only effective portion of Art. 6 being that which states that ratification must be unconditional and must embrace the entire treaty.

1.5.3 Accession

In the event that the State intends to enter into a treaty after its establishment, it may do so (depending on the circumstances) by *accession*.[170]As

---

168 See Rezek, José Francisco. *Direito dos tratados*, cit., p. 273.

169 Such rule came from Art. 204, first part, of *Projeto de Código de Direito Internacional Público* (1911) by Epitácio Pessoa. On the subject, see Mazzuoli, Valerio de Oliveira, Apontamentos sobre o direito dos tratados no Projeto de Código de Direito Internacional Público de Epitácio Pessoa, cit., p. 521-522.

170 On this matter see Balladore Pallieri, G., *Diritto internazionale pubblico*, cit., p. 266-269; Accioly, Hildebrando, *Tratado de direito internacional público*, vol. I, cit., p. 615-621; Pereira de Araújo, João Hermes, *A processualística dos atos internacionais*, cit., p. 261-273; McNair, Arnold Duncan, *The law of treaties*, cit., p. 148-157; Maresca, Adolfo, *Il diritto dei trattati…*, cit., p. 195-206; Remiro Brotons, Antonio, *Derecho internacional público*, vol. 2, cit., p. 102-104; Rezek, José Francisco, *Direito dos tratados*, cit., p. 417-429; and Villiger, Mark E., *Commentary on the 1969 Vienna Convention on the Law of Treaties*, cit., p. 216-223. On expression of consent by means of accession in the framework of the

a matter of fact, even if the State concerned neither participated in the treaty negotiations, nor it signed it, nor it complied with the time limits for ratification, or because it denounced the treaty and afterwards it retracted that denunciation, it can still become a party to that treaty if the instrument constituting the treaty is *open* to accession. In other words, accession consists of the unilateral expression of the will of the State, which reveals its intent to become a party to a certain treaty, which it neither negotiated nor it signed, or, if it did sign it, it did not ratify it for any reason or it denounced it, etc.

There are numerous reasons that lead a State to access to a given treaty, including at least four clear situations: (*a*) having an interest in becoming a party to an international act in whose negotiations the State concerned had not participated; (*b*) regretting not having signed the treaty in due time; (*c*) failure to comply with the time limit set forth for ratification; and (*d*) regretting having denounced the treaty (this case deals with that Party that intends to become a Party to the treaty again).

The legal nature of accession is identical to that of ratification: it denotes the firm and strong will of the State to be bound by the international commitment it had undertaken.[171] The very same practice also applies to international organizations.

Accession is governed by Art. 15 of the 1969 Vienna Convention,[172] under the following terms:

> "Article 15.*Consent to be bound by a treaty expressed by accession.*
>
> The consent of a State to be bound by a treaty is expressed by accession when:
>
> *a)* the treaty provides that such consent may be expressed by that State by means of accession;

---

travaux préparatoires of the Vienna Convention, see ILC, *Yearbook of the International Law Commission* (1966), vol. II, p. 199-200.

171 See De La Guardia, Ernesto. *Derecho de los tratados internacionales*, cit., p. 162; and Brichambaut, Dobelle & Coulée, *Leçons de droit international public*, cit., p. 270.

172 It should be pointed out that in the French version of the Convention the expression used is "accession" (*adhésion*), while in the English version the term used is "accession", also in the official Portuguese version, based on French, the noun "accession" is used. For the purposes of the Law of Treaties, it should be understood that both expressions of "accession" (as used in French, Portuguese, etc., and present in the English version) are synonyms for the Vienna Code.

b) it is otherwise established that the negotiating States were agreed that such consent may be expressed by that State by means of accession; or

c) all the parties have subsequently agreed that such consent may be expressed by that State by means of accession".

By *accession* any State may reach the status of being a *party* to an open multilateral treaty after its conclusion. Among others, advantages of accession include the ease with which a State may become a party to a treaty, without the erosion that negotiations may entail, the reduced waiting period for the instrument to enter into force (in the event that accession has been carried out *before* the treaty entered into force at the international level), and also the immediate application of the treaty in the internal legal system (when consent to be bound by the treaty was expressed *after* its entry into force at the international level). As can be seen, accession may occur *before* or *after* the entry into force of the treaty concerned.[173]

Also, accession maybe the *only* way for a given State to participate in certain treaty, depending on the provisions of the international instrument. There are examples (albeit not many) of treaties that can only be accepted by means of accession by the States, such as the Conventions on the Privileges and Immunities of the United Nations and of the Specialized Agencies, dated January 13, 1945, and November 25, 1947, respectively. Furthermore, the same holds true for the cases in which the conventional text is adopted by an International Organization and authenticated by its agents, being possible to choose accession as the only form for States to participate in this category of treaties.[174]

Accession may only occur in multilateral agreements. It cannot be carried out in bilateral agreements, which are naturally closed to the only two signatory parties. However, it could be argued that there exist "bilateral" agreements open to future accession by third party States.[175] In this case, we are not dealing with *bilateral* treaties themselves, as it may seem at first sight. The fact that the *entry into force* starts with only *two parties* does not mean that the instrument is technically bilateral. As a matter of fact, this is a genuine *collective* agreement, as authorization has been granted to incorporate *other parties* by means of accession.

---

173 See Fitzmaurice, Malgosia. The practical working of the law of treaties, cit., p. 178.

174 See Remiro Brotons, Antonio. *Derecho internacional público*, vol. 2, cit., p. 103.

175 See Remiro Brotons, Antonio. Idem, p. 102.

There is no need for the treaty to enter into force for a State to be able to accede to it.[176] Accession has also been admitted in international practice, even in those cases in which certain a *minimum number* of ratifications is expected for the treaty entry into force. That *minimum number* has been reached by ratifications of States and *also* by accession of those that did not participate in negotiations, but wish to become parties to the agreement. In summary, many treaties today include provisions similar to that of Art. 84 item 1 of the 1969 Vienna Convention, according to which: "The present Convention shall enter into force on the thirtieth day following the date of deposit of the thirty-fifth instrument of ratification or *accession*".

Accession may also be used (as discussed above) in the event that a State has denounced the treaty, but afterwards, regrets having done so and intends to become a party to it again. Although rare, reentry by accession is fully valid (evidently if the treaty concerned is *open* to accession). On 15 December 1983, Spain acceded to the Convention for the establishment of a European Organization for Nuclear Research (CERN), concluded in Paris, on 1 July 1953, to which it had been a Party from 6 June 1962 and 31 December 1968, date on which it withdrew from the treaty by means of denunciation.[177]

An interesting question is to determine whether those treaties signed by accession require ratification, as the latter could be deemed unnecessary. The practice of accession subject to ratification mostly developed during the period of the League of Nations. In general, the prevailing trend in the legal literature on this matter has been that accession does not require ratification. However, this stance is not reflected in international practice, whereby accession may require ratification by the acceding State. The underlying reason for this may be the admittance that the Executive Power quite often does not wait for the *approval of* the Legislative Power and hasten to accede to the text of the treaty, which had been previously

---

176 See Villiger, Mark E. *Commentary on the 1969 Vienna Convention on the Law of Treaties*, cit., p. 219. For an opposing view, but with no further explanations, see Pereira de Araújo, João Hermes, according to whom: "*Accession will be possible if the contracting parties allow it and if the treaty to which it refers has already entered into force*" [emphasis added] (*A processualística dos atos internacionais*, cit., p. 263). According to Rezek's opinion, it is also logical "that accession presupposes the existence of a treaty in force", although he points out that this idea has already been "prescribed by international practice for decades, for reasons of convenience" (*Direito dos tratados*, cit., p. 418).

177 See Remiro Brotons, Antonio. *Derecho internacional público*, vol. 2, cit., p. 103.

signed by other States. In this regard Art 19 of the 1928 Havana Convention provides as follows:

> "A State not participating in the making of a treaty may adhere to the same if none other of the contracting parties be opposed, its adherence to be communicated to all. The adherence shall be deemed final *unless made with express reservation of ratification*".

The same approach has been adopted by the International Law Commission, which considers that accession that is subject to ratification should be viewed as an "anomaly", although it occurs frequently. Brazil, in its turn, has followed both accession procedures, namely, by means of (*a*) final accession, that is, it has acceded to a treaty on a definitive basis, with the Executive Power being authorized by National Congress; (*b*) *ad referendum accession*, that is, it has acceded to a treaty subject to *approval* by the Legislative Power. Therefore, the conclusion that can be drawn is that ratification has been carried out in accession procedures, although it constitutes an "anomaly" and, that sometimes has been criticized by legal scholars.[178]

It should be highlighted that not every international treaty allows accession. Only when dealing with the so-called *open treaties* is accession possible. That is to say, accession to a treaty by a certain State (or international organization) that did not participate in its drawing up, or that had previously denounced it, or also, failed to comply with the term for ratification, will only be possible when the text of the treaty itself expressly or tacitly allows it. The cases of *express* and *tacit* authorization for accession are provided for, respectively, in items (a) and (b) of Art. 15 of the Convention (see above). If a multilateral treaty is *closed* to accession, Art. 15 (c) allows all the parties *to subsequently agree* that an interested State accedes to the treaty; in that case the international instrument becomes "open" for the specific incorporation of the State concerned; in such case, the consent of all the States having participated in the conclusion of the treaty must be *unanimous*.

In Brazil, accession to a treaty is subject to the prior authorization of National Congress, which is an essential condition, as with a signed treaty, which can only be ratified *after* approval by the Parliament. If the President of the Republic needs the authorization of Congress to ratify a treaty, it seems clear that she/he will also need the same congress approval in case she/he

178 For further details see Mello, Celso D. de Albuquerque, *Ratificação de tratados...*, cit., p. 74-77.

intends to access to it. Therefore, the same internal procedure observed for the approval of a signed treaty also applies to accession. In this case, the National Congress, by authorizing accession to a treaty, does not validate an *ad referendum* act, as when it approves an international agreement previously signed by the Head of the Executive and allows its ratification by the latter, but it rather grants from a technical point of view an "authorization", which is always *prior* to any expression of consent by the Executive Power. Nevertheless, nothing prevents accession to the treaty from being carried out prior to the examination by the Congress, which will be performed *subject to ratification*, as mentioned above, when the Congress will consider once again the treaty for its *approval*. Brazilian practice (as discussed above) has followed both procedures, that is, the final accession to the treaty, with the previous authorization by National Congress for the Executive Power to ratify the treaty concerned; and accession *ad referendum*, which means that accession will be subject to the future acceptance by the Congress.[179]

After authorization by Congress, the President of the Republic shall proceed *to deposit* the letter or instrument of accession with the depositary agency or the State appointed for that purpose, as occurs in the case of ratification. The depositary will then inform the other parties to the agreement that accession by a given State has been carried out. The only difference from ratification here lies in the impossibility to *exchange* instruments of accession, since that exchange is done in the framework of bilateral agreements, which, as discussed above, are capable of being acceded because they are *closed* (restricted) to only the two parties concerned. Therefore, when dealing with an accession no letter or instrument is exchanged, but rather the instrument of accession is *deposited* with the organization or State appointed as depositary.

Once the instrument of accession has been deposited, as occurs in the case of ratification of a treaty, the Head of the Executive must issue a promulgation or enactment *decree* and publish it in the *Official Gazette* with the transcription of the text of the treaty as an annex thereto.

1.6 Structure of treaties

It is already clear that international treaties are *formal* agreements concluded by States or international organizations. That *form* of the international instruments requires a *structure*, although it is not immutable

---

179 See Pereira de Araújo, João Hermes. *A processualística dos atos internacionais*, cit., p. 268.

and may vary from one instrument to another.[180] That is to say, international instruments have a *minimum* structure (and not a sole *standard*) which deserves being analyzed, knowing beforehand that any modifications of treaties are the result of the contingencies of international practice, this being also true concerning their form.

Traditionally, without taking into consideration the variations in form of each instrument in particular, international treaties can be said to be structured generally by the following parts:

a) a *title*, which specifies the subject matter dealt with in the agreement or, on a wider basis, the *matter* regulated therein;

b) the *preamble* or *introduction*, which is composed of two types of enunciations: (1) the list of the contracting parties and (2) the reasons that led the States to negotiate the agreement. In International Law, the preamble of treaties is not binding, except as an interpretation element of the agreement.[181] The preamble, as aforesaid, starts with the list of the contracting parties, that is, the States or international organizations that concluded the treaty, with reference to the credentials of the representatives of States. As a general rule, the contracting parties are mentioned by the abbreviated title of the Head of State, which serves as evidence of their competence to maintain international relations. In ancient and medieval times Gods were invoked in the preamble of the instrument concerned, or in a more recent past, the *Holy Trinity* or the *God Almighty* or the *Almighty* were frequently invoked (this was also very frequent during the time of the Brazilian Empire). In treaties with a great number of con-

---

180 On the structure of treaties, see Accioly, Hildebrando, *Tratado de direito internacional público*, vol. I, cit., p. 556; Pereira de Araújo, João Hermes. *A processualística dos atos internacionais*, cit., p. 61-100 (this author even carries out a thorough analysis of each of the parties of the instrument and gathers many useful examples); Maresca, Adolfo, *Il diritto dei trattati...*, cit., p. 103-108; Rezek, José Francisco, *Direito dos tratados*, cit., p. 239-253; and Dinh, Daillier & Pellet, *Direito internacional público*, cit., p. 133-136.

181 The position of some authors should be highlighted, such as that of De La Guardia, who argues that some paragraphs of a preamble "may have *a norm-setting nature*, if they were laid down as legal obligations". Nevertheless, the same author concedes that the most common trend is that which considers preambles "as *elements which may be of help for the interpretation of* treaties" [quotation marks in the original] (*Derecho de los tratados internacionales*, cit., p. 345). In the defense of the norm-setting nature of preambles, see also Corriente Córdoba, José Antonio, *Valoración jurídica de los preámbulos de los tratados internacionales*, Pamplona: Universidad de Navarra, 1973, p. 16, who considers that "the capacity of a given rule must be deduced from its own nature, and not from its systematic arrangement or position in a piece of legislation".

tracting parties, it is common practice that parties thereto are referred as in the preamble as the "High Contracting Parties". The second element of the preamble considers the *reasons* that led the States to negotiate the agreement. This is the specification of *intentions* of negotiators regarding the treaty concerned, which are called *recitals or whereas*. These (which are normally drafted using a gerund) make reference to the intentions of negotiators regarding the conclusion of the treaty (it is sometimes an actual political agenda) and also the possible binding nature of the commitments made by negotiators in connection with what has been agreed to, their compatibility with previous conventional norms, etc. Recitals are a means of expressing the reasons and purposes of the agreement, whereby the philosophy of diplomacy behind the conclusion of the treaty is made known. Recitals, however, are not part of the *legal* provisions of the treaty (which starts with *set of articles*). Recitals may vary from one treaty to another, and there exists no requirement as to a minimum number in each instrument, as this will depend on the sophistication and importance of the subject matter dealt with in the agreement.

c) the *articles* (or *provisions*) are considered the main part of the conventional instrument, made up of a set of numbered articles, in which all the operative provisions of the agreement are set forth (in *legal language*), with the number of articles varying from treaty to treaty. All elements of the provisions of the treaty concerned are legally binding. After the body of the treaty and its subjective right provisions, there follow *final clauses* (of *a procedural* nature) concerning ratification of the treaty and exchange of instruments, its entry into force, conditions for its denunciation or its extension, the term during which it will remain in force, conditions for accession, amendment, etc. After the articles, as a general rule, there appears the set phrase "in witness whereof..." for plenipotentiaries to testify that they participated in the making of the agreement;

d) the final part typically starting with the set phrase *DONE at* (...), which specifies the place and date of conclusion of the treaty, the language in which it was drafted and the number of originals. Reference to the *place* and *date* of conclusion allows for the signature of the representative of the State to be stamped thereon and the seal to be affixed thereto;

e) the *signature* of the Head of State, the Minister for Foreign Affairs, or any other authority that has represented the President of the Republic on the preparation of the instrument. In bilateral acts, signatures are stamped according to *alternation* or *reversal system*, which means that each contracting party will stamp first on the copy they will keep,[182] avoiding the problem of precedence of signatures of a State vis-à-vis the other State, which happened in the old times among Princes and the Pope (whose signatures always preceded those of the rest of plenipotentiaries). As for multilateral treaties, stamping of signatures *in alphabetical order* of the names of the contracting parties has been used, which may vary according to the language in which the instrument was drafted. For a long time, the signature system in alphabetical order followed the *French* name of the respective countries parties to the treaty concerned. In addition, the option of a *draw* regarding the signature order is not ruled out, which is generally performed at the beginning of the conference aimed at negotiating the treaty; and, finally,

f) the *wax seal*, whereby the coat of arms of the High Contracting Parties are affixed, therefore sealing their commitment.

The text of the treaty may also contain *annexes* or *appendixes*, depending on the need of any further explanation in addition to what has been agreed upon in the text, as well as any other complement text that may be deemed necessary. Annexes and appendixes, unlike the preamble, are an integral part of the treaty and their provisions, being of a conventional *legal norm* nature.

182 See Sepúlveda, César. *Derecho internacional*, cit., p. 131.

Chapter 2

Reservations to Multilateral Treaties

2.1 Introduction

The so-called *reservation* is one of the many methods that enable the participation of States in multilateral treaties. Reservations allow States to *participate* in an individual treaty even if they are in *disagreement* with any of its provisions, thus promoting a higher level of participation by States in general multilateral instruments (and other kind of instruments) that are of great interest to the international society, the 1969 Vienna Convention on Law of Treaties being an illustrative example of this. However, this subject is one of the most intricate issues dealt with by the 1969 Convention. *Reservation* is a highly controversial topic, casting doubts and giving rise to discussion. It still draws the attention of legal scholars, who not always offer satisfactory solutions to the issues that may arise therefrom.[183]

---

[183] On the subject, see Bishop Jr., William W., Reservations to treaties, *Recueil des Cours*, vol. 103 (1961-II), p. 245-341; Maresca, Adolfo, *Il diritto dei trattati*, cit., p. 279-305; McNair, Arnold Duncan, *The law of treaties*, cit., p. 158-177; Ruda, J. M. Reservations to treaties, *Recueil des Cours*, vol. 146 (1975-III), p. 95-218; Gamble Jr., John King, Reservations to multilateral treaties: a macroscopic view of State practice, *American Journal of International Law*, vol. 74, n. 2 (April 1980), p. 272-394; Koh, Jean Kyongun, Reservations to multilateral treaties: how international legal doctrine reflects world vision, *Harvard International Law Journal*, vol. 23, n. 1 (1982), p. 71-116; Sinclair, Ian, *The Vienna Convention on the Law of Treaties*, cit., p. 51-77; Remiro Brotons, Antonio, *Derecho internacional público*, vol. 2, cit., p. 206-240; De La Guardia, Ernesto, *Derecho de los tratados internacionales*, cit., p. 169-191; Wei, Su, Reservation to treaties and some practical issues, *Asian Yearbook of International Law*, vol. 7 (1997), p. 105-139; Reuter, Paul, *Introducción al derecho de los tratados*, cit., p. 98-105; Aust, Anthony, *Modern treaty law and practice*, cit., p. 100-130; Kamto, Maurice, La volonté de l'État en droit international, cit., p. 182-194; Riquelme Cortado, Rosa, *Las reservas a los tratados: lagunas y ambigüedades del Régimen*

The practice of accession with reservations became popular as from the second half of the 19th century, when multilateral conventions started to include an increasingly higher number of States. Nevertheless, it was only after the 1899 and 1907 Hague conventions that reservations were granted the *status* of "institution". The conclusion reached was that it is better for the international legal community to have only part of a treaty in effect among States, or even provisions with limited effects, than the lack of any legal norm governing the relations among them. Furthermore, given that, due to the unanimity rule, a treaty could contingently not obtain the consensus required for its approval, it is absolutely fair to think that States may have the chance to formulate reservations to certain provisions of the treaty in order to remove such inconvenience, without imposing an extremely serious sacrifice upon the other parties or waiving their participation in the agreement.[184]

In the beginning, the express or implicit consent of all signatories was required for a reservation to be accepted, according to the so-called "unanimity rule";[185] but, in the latest decades, most multilateral treaties themselves included articles which regulated the possibility to make reservations and their respective scope of application. This is partly due to the Resolution Nr. 598 (VI) of the UN General Assembly, dated January 12, 1952, which approved the *Advisory Opinion* rendered by the ICJ (res. 478-V) regarding the admissibility of reservations to the 1948 Convention on the Prevention and Punishment of the Crime of Genocide.[186]

---

de Viena, Murcia: Universidad de Murcia, 2004, 427p; Villiger, Mark E., *Commentary on the 1969 Vienna Convention on the Law of Treaties*, cit., p. 262-335; and Crawford, James, *Brownlie's principles of public international law*, cit., p. 374-377.

184 See Anzilotti, Dionisio. *Cours de droit international*. Transl. by Gilbert Gidel. Paris: Editions Panthéon-Assas, 1999, p. 401.

185 See *Resolution* of the 1931 General Meeting of the League of Nations, according to which "a reservation may only be formulated at the time of ratification if *all other signatory States* agree to or if the said reservation has been provided for in the Convention text" [emphasis added]. See Koh, Jean Kyongun, Reservations to multilateral treaties..., cit., p. 77.

186 See *ICJ Reports* (1951). On the aforementioned declaration by the *ICJ*, see Koh, Jean Kyongun, Reservations to multilateral treaties..., cit., p. 84-88; Remiro Brotons, Antonio, *Derecho internacional público*, vol. 2, cit., p. 214-216; De La Guardia, Ernesto, *Derecho de los tratados internacionales*, cit., p. 176-177; Wei, Su, Reservation to treaties and some practical issues, cit., p. 111-115; Reuter, Paul, *Introducción al derecho de los tratados*, cit., p. 99-101; Kamto, Maurice, La volonté de l'État en droit international, cit., p. 184-185; Cassese, Antonio, *Diritto internazionale*, cit., p. 247-248; Daudt, Gabriel Pithan, *Reservas*

598 (VI). Reservations to Multilateral Conventions

The General Assembly

Bearing in mind the provisions of its resolution 478 (V) of 16 November 1950, which (1) requested the International Court of Justice to give an advisory opinion regarding reservations to the Convention on Prevention and Punishment of the Crime of Genocide and (2) invited the International Law Commission to study the question of reservations to multilateral conventions,

Noting the Court's advisory opinion of 28 May 1951 and the Commission's report, both rendered pursuant to the said resolution,

1. *Recommends* that organs of the United Nations, specialized agencies and States should, in the course of preparing multilateral conventions, consider the insertion therein of provisions relating to the admissibility or non-admissibility of reservations and to the effect to be attributed to them;

2. *Recommends* to all States that they be guided regard to the Convention on the Prevention and Punishment of the Crime of Genocide by the advisory opinion of the International Court of Justice of 28 may 1951;

3. *Requests* the Secretary-General:

(*a*) In relation to reservations to the convention on the Prevention and Punishment of the Crime of Genocide, to conform his practice to the advisory opinion of the Court of 28 May 1951;

(*b*) In respect of future conventions concluded under the auspices of the United Nations of which he is the depositary:

(i) To continue to act as depositary in connection with the deposit of documents containing reservations or objections, without passing upon the legal effect of such documents; and

(ii) To communicate the text of such documents relating to reservations or objections to all States concerned, leaving it to each State to draw legal consequences from such communications.

360th plenary meeting,
12 January 1952.

Afterwards, a more flexible approach was taken in connection with reservations, so as to increasingly remove the old unanimity rule. In that sense, the aforementioned *Advisory Opinion* of the ICJ (res. 478-V) ended up prompting Humphrey Waldock (last Rapporteur of ICJ) to incorporate the thesis of admissibility of reservations provided that they do not violate the object and purpose of the treaty (see item 2.5, below).

However, it should be pointed out that the 1969 Vienna Convention was unable to solve all the issues raised by reservations, generating ambiguities and uncertainties,[187] which underlined the need to study the problem again in order to solve all pending matters. Therefore, more than

aos tratados internacionais de direitos humanos: o conflito entre a eficácia e a promoção dos direitos humanos, Porto Alegre: Sergio Antonio Fabris, 2006, p. 39-48; and Shaw, Malcolm N., *Direito internacional*, cit., p. 682-683.

187 See Riquelme Cortado, Rosa. *Las reservas a los tratados*..., cit., p. 14.

twenty years after the adoption of the Vienna Convention, the ILC included the following Agenda item (in 1993, in its45th session): "Law and Practice on Reservations to Treaties" (although in its 47th session, in 1995, initial title proposed was amended to just read "Reservations to Treaties"), for which Prof. Alain Pellet was appointed as Special Rapporteur. The pertaining works lasted 17 years, and ended in 2011, when the ICJ (in its 63rd session) published a *Guide to Practice on Reservations to Treaties* (hereinafter, the ILC *Guide*).[188] However, although it is a highly relevant study, the *Guide* on reservations prepared by the ICJ is just a *facilitator* of understandings, and has no authority to revoke contingent rules contrary to the 1969 Vienna Convention on the Law of Treaties; in other words, the *Guide* was created to supplement (better define, etc.) the 1969 Vienna Convention and explain the practice of States and international organizations on the subject, with no power to go beyond the provisions of the Vienna Convention in connection with any conflicting issues.

2.2 Reservations to bilateral treaties?

The *Draft Articles* of the International Law Commission (1966) called what is currently known as Part II, Section 2 (Reservations) of the 1969 Convention, *Reservations to Multilateral Treaties*. But in the final wording of the approved Convention, the same Section 2 was just named *Reservations*, without any specification, thus making it possible (at least in theory) to formulate reservations to bilateral treaties.[189] However, if Arts. 19 to 23 of the Convention are read together, it can be clearly seen that the intention of the text is to apply the institute of reservations only to *multilateral* treaties.

The President of the Vienna Conference, Prof. Roberto Ago, had already expressed himself in that connection, stating that reservations to bilateral treaties are a *contradictio in terminis* not allowed by the scheme provided in the Convention.[190] In fact, as Gerald Fitzmaurice also pointed out during the ICJ works, the contractual element is so strong in bilateral

---

188 See *Report on the work of its sixty-third session* (26 April to 3 June and 4 July to 12 August 2011), General Assembly, Official Records, Supplement n. 10 (A/66/10 and Add.1); and *Yearbook of the International Law Commission* (2011), vol. II, Part Two. The ILC *Guide* can be found in Annex V to this book.

189 See De La Guardia, Ernesto. *Derecho de los tratados internacionales*, cit., p. 171; and Riquelme Cortado, Rosa, *Las reservas a los tratados…*, cit., p. 29.

190 See Remiro Brotons, Antonio. *Derecho internacional público*, vol. 2, cit., p. 207.

treaties that the admissibility of reservations will be deemed contrary to the whole spirit of the negotiation and the basis and balance of the treaty under discussion.[191]

> "By removing [in the 1969 Vienna Conference] the express mention of the multilateral character of treaties subject to reservations, technical accuracy had simply gave in upon the political opportunism of those who preferred to keep any kind of ways open. In any case, the reservation to a bilateral treaty had nothing to do with the reservation to a multilateral treaty. By adopting the text of a bilateral treaty by mutual agreement, reservations are, consequently, unthinkable; their later formulation, upon expression and completion of the consent, as time limit, would reveal, on the other hand, the breach of *consensus ad idem* of the previous agreement on the text. A similar situation may arise of course: an unqualified plenipotentiary, a change in the composition or foreign policy of a Government, the imposition of a Legislative Chamber empowered to amend treaties... may explain their occurrence; however, in this case, the intended *reservation* either leads to renegotiation, or finishes up with the text of the treaty stuck in the limbo where innocents purge the original sin inherited from their parents".
> REMIRO BROTONS, Antonio. *Derecho internacional público*, vol. 2, cit., p. 207.

In summary, no reference should be made to reservations in case of bilateral treaties, since in the aforementioned agreements the will of the parties has to be in perfect harmony. Any statement made as a reservation should be understood as a *new proposal* to be discussed and renegotiated by the States.[192] If the proposal were possibly rejected, it would be considered that the treaty *was not concluded* by negotiators, due to the lack of will necessary for the conclusion of the aforementioned treaty. Therefore, the legal institute of reservations may only be admitted (in a practical way) in the framework of *multilateral* treaties.[193]

However, it should be highlighted that the formulation of *interpretative declarations* to bilateral treaties is allowed. Upon acceptance by the

---

191 See ILC, *Yearbook of the International Law Commission* (1956), vol. II, p. 127.

192 See De La Guardia, Ernesto. *Derecho de los tratados internacionales*, cit., p. 171-172; Alland, Denis (coord.), *Droit international public*, cit., p. 228; Villiger, Mark E., *Commentary on the 1969 Vienna Convention on the Law of Treaties*, cit., p. 266; and Brichambaut, Dobelle & Coulée, *Leçons de droit international public*, cit., p. 274. See also Wei, Su, Reservation to treaties and some practical issues, cit., p. 106.

193 See Guideline 1.6.1 of the ILC *Guide*: "A unilateral statement, however phrased or named, formulated by a State or an international organization after initialling or signature but prior to entry into force of a bilateral treaty, by which that State or international organization purports to obtain from the other party a modification of the provisions of the treaty, does not constitute a reservation within the meaning of the present Guide to Practice".

other party, such declarations will be deemed valid as an *authentic interpretation* of the treaty (see item 2.7, below).[194]

2.3 Concept and formulation of reservations

Art. 2, item 1 (d) of the 1969 Vienna Convention defines *reservation* as "a unilateral statement, however phrased or named, made by a State, when signing, ratifying, accepting, approving or acceding to a treaty, whereby it purports to exclude or to modify the legal effect of certain provisions of the treaty in their application to that State".[195] Likewise, the 1986 Vienna Convention on the Law of Treaties between States and International Organizations or between International Organizations also authorizes the formulation of reservations by interstate organizations (Art. 2 item 1, *d*).[196]

There are three *basic* elements involved when legally defining reservation: *form*, *time* and *content*.[197] The first and the third elements will be examined now, and the second one (*the temporal element*) will be analyzed below (item 2.4).

In formal terms, a reservation is a *unilateral* statement. It aims at excluding the article "chosen" from the text of the treaty so that it is not

---

194 See Guideline 1.6.3 of the ILC *Guide*: "The interpretation resulting from an interpretative declaration made in respect of a bilateral treaty by a State or an international organization part to the treaty and accepted by the other party constitutes an authentic interpretation of that treaty".

195 See also Art. 19 et ssq. of the 1969 Convention. A similar provision was already included in the *Harvard Research in International Law* from 1935, which defined reservation as "a formal declaration by which State, when signing, ratifying or acceding to a treaty, specifies as a condition of its willingness to become a party to the treaty certain terms which will limit the effect to the treaty in so far as it may apply in the relations of that State with other State or States which may be parties to the treaty" (see Bishop Jr., William W. Reservations to treaties, cit., p. 249). According to the ILC *Guide*, reservation means "a unilateral statement, however phrased or named, made by a State or an international organization when signing, ratifying, formally confirming, accepting, approving or acceding to a treaty, or by a State when making a ratification of succession to a treaty, whereby the State or organization purports to exclude or to modify the legal effect of certain provisions of the treaty in their application to that State or to that international organization" (Guideline 1.1 item 1). The *Guide* further provides that a unilateral statement, made by States or international organizations upon consent, which purports to *limit* or execute an obligation *in a different manner, but equal to that imposed by the treaty*, also constitutes a reservation (Guidelines 1.1.1 and 1.1.2).

196 See also Art. 19 of the 1986 Convention.

197 See Wei, Su. Reservation to treaties and some practical issues, cit., p. 109.

valid among the parties. Nevertheless, unlike other unilateral statements (like a *promise* or *denunciation*) whose formulation and production of legal effects are independent, a *reservation* is doubly *dependent*, since: (*a*) its formulation depends on the terms (object and purpose) of the treaty under analysis; and (*b*) its production of legal effects depends on the attitude adopted (towards the reservation) by the other contracting parties.[198] Therefore, it can be said that a reservation is a unilateral statement in *its formulation*, but *not in its effects*.[199] It should also be pointed out that, for being a *unilateral* formulation statement, a reservation does not form *part* of the treaty,[200] not belonging to the text of the instrument (which only *authorizes it* or *not*, either in an express or tacit way); reservations are just a condition for compliance with the treaty formulated in relation to certain provisions thereof.

Even according to the above definition, a reservation lacks its own *phrasing* or *naming* ("...whatever its phrasing or naming may be..."). In other terms, any phrasing or naming that may be given by the State lacks importance whenever the intention to exclude or modify the legal effects of certain provisions of the treaty signed by it may be perceived.

The *instrument* whereby the reservation is formulated has no importance at all.[201] Provided that it is made in *writing*,[202] a reservation may be stated on a diplomatic document (of several kinds) or even by a legal act frequently used in internal orders (although the latter case is quite unusual). In Brazil, for example, a reservation may be stated in the legislative decree whereby the National Congress approves the treaty and authorizes the Government to ratify it, in which case the Executive Power will confirm the deposit of the ratification instrument (for ratification purposes).

The *content* of a reservation is what really matters for its formulation, regardless of its form: Content shall effectively show the intention of the State to be *excluded from* the application of certain provision of the treaty in its relations with the other Parties. The willingness to finally amend the content and scope (whether material, subjective, territorial, or temporal...) of rights and obligations established in certain conventional

198 See Remiro Brotons, Antonio. *Derecho internacional público*, vol. 2, cit., p. 208.

199 See De La Guardia, Ernesto. *Derecho de los tratados internacionales*, cit., p. 170.

200 See Sinclair, Ian. *The Vienna Convention on the Law of Treaties*, cit., p. 51; and Villiger, Mark E., *Commentary on the 1969 Vienna Convention on the Law of Treaties*, cit., p. 88.

201 See Bishop Jr., William W. Reservations to treaties, cit., p. 251.

202 See Guideline 2.1.1 of the ILC *Guide*: "A reservation must be formulated in writing".

provisions, both substantive and adjective or ancillary, shall be clear in the reservation to be formulated (as explained by Remiro Brotons).[203] It is necessary to remember that reservations are State *unilateral acts*, and they should be understood as such, particularly with regard to the need for the party to *express* its will to be *released* from the obligation or to *amend it* internally.[204] In that connection, it is understood that a reservation only implies the will of the reserving State to *amend* the treaty (negatively, i.e., with the *elimination* of provisions) in its relations with the other Parties.[205] In other words, reservations appear in the Vienna Convention as a *condition*: the condition of the State concerned to accept the treaty without being bound by the legal effects of some of its provisions. That is to say, the will of the contracting State when making reservations to the text, constitutes an amendment proposal of the relations of the aforementioned State with the other States Parties as far as the content subject to reservation is concerned, in such a way that, in the relations between the reserving State and the other States, the provisions in respect of which the reservation is formulated do not exist at all.[206]

Reservations shall be *specifically* formulated in respect of one or several provisions of a treaty. No *generic* statements of States indicating the prevalence of their Constitution or their internal laws over the conflicting conventional provisions are included into the regime established in the 1969 Convention.[207]

Even with regard to the *content* of reservations, a distinction should be made between *exclusion* reservations from *amendment* reservations. As stated under Art. 2°, item 1, (d) of the 1969 Convention, a reservation shall be formulated "to *exclude* or to *modify* the legal effect of certain provisions of the treaty in their application to that State". *Exclusion* reservations aim at excluding the application of *certain* provisions of the treaty, some of its paragraphs, subsections or items.[208] Brazil did so upon ratifica-

---

203 Remiro Brotons, Antonio. *Derecho internacional público*, vol. 2, cit., p. 210.

204 See Sinclair, Ian. *The Vienna Convention on the Law of Treaties*, cit., p. 54.

205 See Buergenthal, Thomas (et all.). *Manual de derecho internacional público*, cit., p. 83.

206 See Anzilotti, Dionisio. *Cours de droit international*, cit., p. 400.

207 See Remiro Brotons, Antonio. *Derecho internacional público*, vol. 2, cit., p. 210.

208 See Remiro Brotons, Antonio. Idem, ibidem. Be noted that the Vienna Convention refers to the exclusion or modification of "certain *provisions* of the treaty...". According to Mark Villiger, the said *provisions* may include a *full article*, only *a paragraph* of certain article, or even *one or some words* of the text (see *Commentary on the 1969 Vienna Convention on the Law of Treaties*, cit., p. 226).

tion, for example, of the Vienna Convention on the Law of Treaties, when it declared that it accepted the Convention "with reservations to Articles 25 and 66".[209] Remiro Brotons explains that the articles, paragraphs, subsections and items contemplated by the reservation may be one or more, but there is a limit that the reservation may not exceed if it wishes to keep its condition: the statement may not exclude full *parts* of a treaty. The consent of a State to be bound by *part* of a treaty, as stated in Art. 17, item 1°, "is effective only if the treaty so permits or the other contracting States so agree"; however, this principle starts excepting the "provisions of Articles 19 to 23" which deal exactly with reservations. Therefore, there are no doubts (as Brotons also affirms) that the State that *partially accepts* the treaty by formulating reservations to *parts* of it would breach the 1969 Convention (especially Art. 17, item 1, above quoted).[210] Nevertheless, in this field it is precisely difficult to *define* the meaning of *part* of a treaty, there not being someone who in theory could have quantified an exact proportion... International courts (specially the ICJ) shall be liable for solving the dilemma.

In turn, *amendment* reservations have the purpose of not excluding, but *reducing* or *limiting* the legal effects of certain provisions of the treaty in their application to a certain State. It is true that the Vienna text refers to "*modifying* the legal effect of certain provisions of the treaty", making no specific reference to "reduction" or "limitation". Consequently, it could be considered that the Convention admitted the so-called *expansive* or *extensive* reservations.[211] As regards the verb "to exclude", there is no doubt (its purpose is to *reduce* the text of the treaty by means of the reservation formulated); but, as regards the verb "to modify", literally interpreted, it may also mean the *extension* of the scope of certain conventional provision. Even if it means literally so, at the strictly legal level and in light of the spirit of the 1969 Vienna Convention, expansive or extensive amendments are deemed *inconsistent* with the institution of reservations. If it is true that a reservation "may imply the exercise by the State of a sovereign right that is in line with the purpose of facilitating its participation in a treaty, enabling it to lighten the obligations that it may deem particularly heavy", it is not possible, however, that a State formulates statements that imply "a proposal of new commitments for which the presumption of a

209 See Annex IV.

210 Remiro Brotons, Antonio. *Derecho internacional público*, vol. 2, cit., p. 210.

211 See Remiro Brotons, Antonio. Idem, p. 211.

tacit acceptance – as it happens in the case of *reservations* – is obviously reckless".[212]

2.4 Moment of formulation of reservations

From the analysis of Art. 2, item 1(d), of the 1969 Convention,[213] emerges the need to discuss the *temporal* element of the reservation concept. It is necessary to accurately know *when* a reservation can be formulated by one of the contracting parties.

Upon reading the concept given, it can be observed that the Convention admits reservations at several stages of the conclusion process of treaties: *signature*, *ratification*, *acceptance* or *approval* of the treaty (and, in the latter case, the formulation of reservations is admitted upon Parliament approval of the text), or even upon *accession*.

It is true that reservations made upon *signature* of the agreement (also called *embryonic reservations*) are more of a political than a legal nature, since they intend to avoid the so called *surprise factor* present when they are signed at the time of final consent (ratification).[214] Remiro Brotons points out that in the Inter-American context there has been a practice for many years, regulated later on by resolution AG/RES. 102 of the OAS, on 14 April 1973 (*Standards* on reservations to Inter-American multilateral treaties), which implies the circulation of the draft reservation proposed by one State to the other States concerned, by the Secretary-General of the Organization, for the purpose of receiving their comments before adopting a final decision.[215] The only detail to be noted here (see item 2.6, below) is that reservations made upon signature (according to the 1969 Vienna Convention) shall be *formally confirmed* upon ratification so as to be legally valid. In this case, the reservation will be deemed made on the date of its confirmation (Art. 23, item 2).

What is not admitted is the formulation of reservations during *negotiations*, *adoption* and *authentication* of the text, since making reservations at those stages reveals the intention to *renegotiate* the treaty. As explained by De La Guardia, "a reservation shall be formulated upon the execution of legal acts which express the consent of a State to be bound

212 Remiro Brotons, Antonio. Idem, ibidem.

213 And also from Art.19, above.

214 See Rezek, José Francisco. *Direito dos tratados*, cit., p. 337.

215 Remiro Brotons, Antonio. *Derecho internacional público*, vol. 2, cit., p. 209.

by a treaty, and even if signature means, under certain circumstances, the mere authentication of the text, it is traditionally a solemn act, which may be equated with legally binding acts".[216] That is why the Vienna Convention has allowed the formulation of reservations *as from signature*, when negotiations have ended and the instrument has been perfectly adopted. In practice, however, many negotiators have not complied with the Vienna provision and have made reservations during the first instances of text formation. Once more, we insist that the best understanding is the one which allows the formulation of reservations only *as from* signature, when the text has been already perfectly finished (and has been *already* adopted and *already* authenticated).

Indeed, nothing prohibits that an *interpretative statement* submitted upon signature turns into a true *reservation* upon ratification of the treaty, provided that the Government declares the aforementioned intention formally and in writing on behalf of the State. This is the *conversion* phenomenon of an interpretative statement into a true reservation, which is absolutely possible.

Finally, it should be wondered whether it would be possible that a State reserves, upon *signature* or *ratification* of a treaty, the right to formulate reservations to the treaty in the future.[217] It may happen that a State, upon *signing* a treaty, reserves the right to ratify it with reservations (which does not raise any legal issue, since reservations may be made upon ratification, without further issues). The Federal Republic of Germany did precisely that regarding the 1969 Vienna Convention on the Law of Treaties, and no State raised any objection thereto. In fact, the German statement reads as follows: "The Federal Republic of Germany reserves the right, upon ratifying the Vienna Convention on the Law of Treaties, to (...) make reservations regarding certain provisions of the said Convention". But it may also happen that a State, upon *ratification* of a treaty, intends to *reserve* the right to formulate reservations in the future. In this case, however, the intention of the State should be rejected, since the 1969 Vienna

---

216 De La Guardia, Ernesto. *Derecho de los tratados internacionales*, cit., p. 185-186. Also according to De La Guardia: "In fact, the need that reservations be made in such acts [mentioned in Art. 2 item 1(d), of the 1969 Convention; i.e., going from signature to final commitment] means a guarantee of good faith for the parties, who introduce their amendments at times when they are easy to be accounted for" (Idem, p. 186). See also Villiger, Mark E. *Commentary on the 1969 Vienna Convention on the Law of Treaties*, cit., p. 317-318.

217 See Remiro Brotons, Antonio. *Derecho internacional público*, vol. 2, cit., p. 209-210.

Convention (Art. 2, item 1(d); Art. 19) does not allow States to skip the stages specified therein (*signature*, *ratification*, *acceptance*, *approval* and *accession*) when they intend to make reservations to a text. By reading the rules contained in the Convention, it can be clearly noticed that the so-called *late reservations* (those made after final commitment) are void by operation of law. In summary, the Convention prohibits that contracting parties formulate reservations, at their discretion and will, in any day and at any time *whenever* final consent has already been given.

In addition, it should be noted that the Convention did not use (neither in Art. 2, item 1, *d*, nor in Art. 19 above) the recurrent formula "...unless otherwise provided in the treaty...", or "...when, the negotiating States have in some other manner so agreed...". Therefore, it seems that the Convention has really *prohibited* that the treaty itself or the will of the contracting Parties authorizes the formulation of late reservations. However, the Guideline 2.3 of the ILC *Guide* provides that: "A State or an international organization may not formulate a reservation to a treaty after expressing its consent to be bound by the treaty, *unless the treaty otherwise provides or none of the other contracting States and contracting organizations opposes the late formulation of the reservation*", and Guideline 2.3.1 further states that: "Unless the treaty otherwise provides or the well-established practice followed by the depositary differs, the late formulation of a reservation shall only be deemed to have been accepted if no contracting State or contracting organization has opposed such formulation after the expiry of the twelve-month period following the date on which notification was received".[218] In our opinion, such provisions (that have no binding effect on States) are *contra legem* proposals, which are contrary to the express rules of the 1969 Vienna Convention (Art. 2, item 1 (d), Art. 19); at this point, the ILC *Guide*, which constitutes a set of mere recommendations, may not be accepted, since it directly contravenes provisions of the Convention. Furthermore, it should be clear that ILC guidelines, in this case, did not codify any *good* practice of States, but rather a practice fully deplorable of some States, which causes a great legal uncertainty.[219]

---

[218] With regard to "interpretative declarations", the *Guide* followed the same concept, anticipating the possibility of formulation of a late interpretative declaration unless "none of the other contracting States and contracting organizations objects to the late formulation of the interpretative declaration" (Guideline 2.4.7).

[219] In that regard, see Coulée, Frédérique, La codification du droit international: les cas des réserves aux traités internationaux, in Brichambaut, Dobelle & Coulée, *Leçons de droit international public*, cit., p. 325 (strongly putting into question the actions taken by the

2.5 Limitations on reservations

In general, the text of the treaty already includes the possibility of and the conditions under which reservations can be formulated. If there are no comments in that connection, this obviously means that they are admitted, and it should not be understood otherwise.[220] Nevertheless, the right of the States to formulate reservations is not unlimited. That is to say, there are *limitations* to the possibility of making reservations, which may be of three types:

a) when the treaty itself expressly *prohibits* making reservations to its text, either in full or in part;

b) when the treaty specifies that only *certain* reservations may be formulated, among which the reservation under analysis *is not included*; or when

c) in the cases provided for in paragraphs (a) and (b), the reservation is not compatible with the *object* and *purpose* of the treaty.

Such cases are included in Art. 19 of the 1969 Vienna Convention.[221] As far as the first possibility is concerned, there are no doubts, since the conventional text *prohibits* (in full or in part) the possibility of formulating reservations.[222] In such case, either the treaty states that *the whole text* may not be subject to reservations,[223] or that just *some* reservations will

---

ILC in such regard, especially because it should not "codify the questionable behaviors of States", as in the case of the formulation of late reservations). The author also refutes the argument, which could possibly be used, according to which he who can do more (denounce the whole treaty), can do less (make a late reservation): firstly, the denunciation does not operate in an absolute manner, since it is governed by the final provisions of the treaty; secondly, the denunciation and the "late reservation" do not politically have the same meaning, since the denunciation clearly shows the intention not to be party to a treaty, while the "late reservation" warrants the State all the benefits of being a party, with no disadvantages whatsoever (Idem, p. 325-326).

220 See De La Guardia, Ernesto. *Derecho de los tratados internacionales*, cit., p. 180-181, under these terms: "The governing principle is that *a convention that says nothing* about reservations is open to them" [emphasis in original].

221 Also see Guideline 3.1 of the ILC *Guide*.

222 In practice, that type of provision has been an exception (see Villiger, Mark E. *Commentary on the 1969 Vienna Convention on the Law of Treaties*, cit., p. 269).

223 The 1988 Rome Statute of the International Criminal Court is taken as an example, which states: "No reservations may be made to this Statute" (Art. 120). Art. 39 of the 1952 Convention on Damage caused by Foreign Aircraft to Third Parties on the Surface also states that: "No reservations may be made to this Convention".

be prohibited (including the reservation under analysis)[224] or that *certain categories* of reservations will be prohibited (also including the reservation being discussed).[225] Even the consent of all the parties cannot authorize the formulation of reservations expressly prohibited by the treaty; it would be an inconsistency to think that the parties who negotiated a treaty where reservations were prohibited may, later on, and in contradiction to the agreements reached in the stage of negotiations and adoption of the text, modify their previous will against the *express* provision of the treaty already concluded.[226] *Venire contra factum proprium non valet*. In the second case, the treaty admits the possibility of reservations, but only in *certain* cases, providing that reservations other than the ones agreed thereon will not be valid; in this case, the contracting Parties understand during negotiations that it is good to create a *hard core area* (which will be determined by exclusion) in respect of which reservations are not admissible, leaving the possibility to formulate reservations just to the provisions expressly authorized (usually, provisions of a less importance nature, such as procedural issues, etc.).[227] And, in the third case, in the assumptions established under paragraphs (a) and (b) of Art. 19, the reservations for-

---

224 In this case, a State may formulate reservations to the provisions *not prohibited* by the treaty, but the compatibility with the object and the purpose of the treaty shall be met (see Guideline 3.1.3 of the ILC *Guide*).

225 Here, it will also be possible to formulate reservations in relation to provisions not falling within a prohibited category, provided that the reservation under analysis is compatible with the object and purpose of the treaty (see Guideline 3.1.3 of the ILC *Guide*).

226 For an opposing view, see Remiro Brotons, Antonio, *Derecho internacional público*, vol. 2, cit., p. 219, who states that: "Undoubtedly, the *prohibited* reservation, assuming that a State dares to formulate it, is not effective on its own merits. In order for the reservation to produce effects, the unanimous and express consent of the other contracting parties would be essential, including those that may be a party in the future, unless with regard to the treaties that have not entered into force yet or have just done so recently".

227 The 1982 United Nations Convention on the Law of Sea is quoted as example. Art. 309 thereof sets forth as follows: "No reservations or exceptions may be made to this Convention unless expressly permitted by other articles of this Convention". It is interesting to be note that the same Convention authorizes (in Art. 310) the formulation of *interpretative declarations* to the text: "Article 309 does not preclude a State, when signing, ratifying or acceding to this Convention, from making declarations or statements, however phrased or named, with a view, inter alia, to harmonizing its laws and regulations with the provisions of this Convention, provided that such declarations or statements do not purport to exclude or to modify the legal effect of the provisions of this Convention in their application to that State". On the issue of interpretative declarations, see item 2.7, below.

mulated shall be *void* in case they are not compatible with the *object* and *purpose* of the treaty.

The last case provided for in Art. 19(c) of the Convention deals with the most important (and also more sophisticated) limitation on reservations, which deserves a more thorough analysis.[228] It occurs in the event that the treaty *states nothing* about the possibility of formulating reservations to the text; here, in the cases not provided for in paragraphs (a) and (b) of Art. 19, reservations are *possible*, but subject to the *limitations* set forth in Art. 19(c). Therefore, according to this provision, the formulation of reservations incompatible with the *object* and *purpose* of the treaty is expressly prohibited, consequently establishing the obligation to ensure the compatibility of the reservation with the object and purpose of the treaty concerned.

The drafters of Art. 19(c) of the Vienna Convention based themselves, for the final wording of the text, on the 1951 advisory opinion delivered by the ICJ concerning the admissibility of reservations to the 1948 Convention on the Prevention and Punishment of the Crime of Genocide. In this case, the Court accepted (by the tough majority from seven to five, being McNair among the dissidents) the possibility of reservations in widely open treaties, provided that they do not defeat the *object* and *purpose* of the instrument; the Court understood that if the treaty states nothing about it, its object and purpose should limit, on the one hand, the authority to formulate reservations, and, on the other hand, the authority to make objections to them.[229] It transpired from the Opinion rendered in 1951 that the prohibition of genocide constituted a *jus cogens* norm, which prevented reservations from being made to the Convention. At that time, the so-called "compatibility doctrine" was conceived, whereby the *object* and *purpose* of the treaty are the criteria used to define whether a reservation to the text may be formulated or not.

It should be noted that Art. 19(c), will only be applicable "in cases *not falling under sub-paragraphs* (a) and (b)" of the aforementioned article. Which are those cases? Remiro Brotons, after indicating that Art. 19(c) is applicable to "cases not falling under sub-paragraphs (a) and (b)

---

228 On the subject, see Koh, Jean Kyongun, Reservations to multilateral treaties…, cit., p. 88-99; Klabbers, Jan, Some problems regarding the object and purpose of treaties, *The Finnish Yearbook of International Law*, vol. VIII (1997), p. 138-160; and Villiger, Mark E., *Commentary on the 1969 Vienna Convention on the Law of Treaties*, cit., p. 271-273.

229 See *ICJ Reports* (1951), p. 15.

of Art. 19", explains that reservations not falling under a treaty mean: "1) reservations formulated in relation to provisions of a treaty that does not have an article on reservations; 2) reservations formulated to provisions not mentioned in the provision that without limitation, authorizes the formulation of reservations [this is the case of Art. 20, item 1, which expressly *authorizes* a reservation, without *prohibiting* others, see below]; and 3) reservations formulated to provisions of a treaty not expressly or implicitly included in the provision prohibiting them [this is the case of Art. 19(a) whereby some reservations to a treaty are expressly *prohibited* by it]".[230] In case (1) referred to by the author there appears no problem; it is obvious that a treaty that does not contain a provision on reservations *may* be subject to reservations, provided that its *object* and *purpose* are complied with (compatibility criterion). Also, no problem arises in case (3), since if the treaty only *prohibits* certain reservations, it is clear that the others are *allowed* (in which case they may be formulated provided that the compatibility criterion is also met); however, reservations to *the whole text of a treaty* when it expressly prohibits any reservations will not be allowed, as, for example, provided for in Art. 120 of the Rome Statute of the ICC and Art. 39 of the Convention on Damage Caused by Foreign Aircraft to Third Parties on the Surface. However, in the case (2), presented by Brotons, doubts may arise, thus requiring a more detailed explanation. It is indeed possible for a treaty to expressly *authorize* a specific reservation, without *limiting*, however, its formulation to the provision concerned. What is the consequence of that? If the treaty states that "the reservation to a certain provision is authorized", no other State has to accept it later on for it to be valid (since Art. 20, item 1, states that "[*a*] *reservation expressly authorized by a treaty does not require any subsequent acceptance by the other contracting States*...").[231] This does not mean that reservations to *other provisions* of the treaty that are not expressly referred to are prohibited; the difference lies in the fact that for such *other* provisions acceptance by the other parties is necessary for that reservation to be valid (see item 2.8, below). Therefore, Brotons observes that it is

[230] Remiro Brotons, Antonio. *Derecho internacional público*, vol. 2, cit., p. 220.

[231] The ILC *Guide* defines a "reservation expressly authorized by the treaty" in Guideline 1.1.6 as follows: "A unilateral statement made by a State or an international organization when that State or organization expresses its consent to be bound by a treaty, in accordance with a clause expressly authorizing the parties or some of them to exclude or to modify the legal effect of certain provisions of the treaty with regard to the party that has made the statement, constitutes a reservation expressly authorized by the treaty".

possible to formulate reservations (provided that the compatibility criterion is met) to provisions "not mentioned in the provision that authorizes them, without limitation".[232] This has nothing to do with Art. 19, *b*, of the Convention, which deals with the issue of a treaty providing "that *only specified reservations* [...] *may* be made...". It should be noted that in the case of Art. 20, item 1, the wording is *open*: the treaty establishes that a reservation is expressly authorized (not depending on the acceptance by any other party), without prohibiting other reservations from being made (which *will depend* on the acceptance by the other parties). In the case of Art. 19(b), the wording is *closed*: the treaty states that *only* a certain provision may be subject to reservation, to the exclusion of any other (therefore, it is prohibited that *all the other* provisions be subject to reservations, even if the compatibility criterion is applied). Nevertheless, if the treaty only allows a *specific* reservation, it is because it forbids *all the other ones* (this result being achieved by exclusion, or by an interpretation to the contrary). In this case, it cannot be said that *there is no* prohibitive *provision* of reservations; in effect, there is a prohibition of reservations *not falling under* the treaty in question (prohibition by exclusion), in which case, even if the other parties *accept* such reservations, they may not be formulated. So, Art. 19(b) may not be mistaken with Art. 20, item 1, which provides that "[a] reservation *expressly authorized* by a treaty *does not require any subsequent acceptance by the other contracting States...*"; in this case, it is indeed possible to make reservations beyond the ones *expressly authorized*, provided that they are accepted by the other parties (taking into account the compatibility criterion). As can be observed, this is not the assumption provided for in Art. 19(b) which clearly prohibits the formulation of reservations whenever "the treaty provides that *only specified reservations*, which *do not include* the reservation in question, *may be made*". Thus, a treaty providing that *only specified reservations* may be made would make no sense if it intended to leave the chance open to formulate reservation to all other provisions not falling under the provision dealing with reservations (even if the compatibility criterion is met, etc.). That is the reason why Art. 19(c) establishes that the compatibility criterion should be used (examination of reservations examination according to the *object* and *purpose* of the treaty) only for those cases "not falling under sub-paragraphs (a) and (b)". In summary, when the treaty expressly authorizes a reservation (without prohibiting others), any State

---

232 Remiro Brotons, Antonio. *Derecho internacional público*, vol. 2, cit., p. 220.

may formulate it irrespective of the acceptance by the other parties and any justification; however, when the treaty purports to allow for reservation in relation to a provision not mentioned in the provision authorizing reservations, the *compatibility criterion* shall be met (that is, the other parties shall have to *accept* the reservation made for it to be *valid*).

The greater difficulty in this area (concerning the interpretation of Art. 19(c) of the 1969 Convention) is related to the meaning of "object and purpose" of the treaty.[233] Only by defining the *object* and the *purpose* of a specific international instrument will it be possible to verify whether the reservation formulated meets the compatibility criterion or not. And it is already known that where definitions of expressions have an uncertain content, States always intend to follow their own interests; therefore, their interpretation (about the validity or not of a specific reservation formulated by another State) is always *interested*. In such regard, to avoid divergent interpretations, the ILC *Guide* tried to clarify the issue, by establishing the meaning of a reservation incompatible with the object and purpose of a treaty. According to the *Guide*, a reservation is incompatible with the object and purpose of the treaty "if it affects an *essential* element of the treaty that is necessary to its general tenor, in such a way that the reservation impairs the *raison d'être* of the treaty" (Guideline 3.1.5); the *Guide* adds further that the object and purpose of the treaty "is to be determined in good faith, taking account of the terms of the treaty in their context, in particular the title and the preamble of the treaty", being also possible to "[have recourse to] the preparatory work of the treaty and the circumstances of its conclusion and, where appropriate, the subsequent practice of the parties" (Guideline 3.1.5.1). Although its intention is clearly good, it is doubtful, however, if the *Guide* could solve the interpretative gap relating to the conception that States still have of the terms "object" and "purpose" of the treaty, expressions that can be subject to every kind of case-based approach.

This issue has been particularly focused on by international case law when dealing with instruments on human rights,[234] which have a *distinct* regime of reservations, monitored by permanent jurisdictional bodies

---

233 On such drawback, see Klabbers, Jan, Some problems regarding the object and purpose of treaties, cit., p. 139-144.

234 See Coccia, Massimo. Reservations to multilateral treaties on human rights, *California Western International Law Journal*, vol. 15, n. 1 (1985), p. 1-51; Lijnzaad, Liesbeth, *Reservations to UN-human rights treaties: ratify and ruin?* Dordrecht: Martinus Nijhoff, 1995, 448p; and Simma, Bruno & Hernández, Gleider I., Legal consequences of an impermis-

that control the practice of reservations.[235] In other words, in the case of treaties on human rights, the acceptance of reservations incompatible with their object and purpose may be under the control of the treaty monitoring bodies created by them, unlike the case of ordinary international treaties (which are not subject to international monitoring bodies, with jurisdiction to determine whether the object or purpose of a treaty was defeated or not).[236] In fact, treaties on human rights typically authorize themselves (even implicitly) judicial bodies established by them (for example, the Inter-American Court of Human Rights, in the case of the 1969 American Convention on Human Rights), or their treaty monitoring bodies (namely, the Commission on Human Rights in relation to the 1966 International Covenant on Civil and Political Rights)[237] to declare the invalidity of those reservations clearly incompatible with their protection regime, thus requesting the reserving State to comply with the treaty in its entirety.[238]

---

sible reservation to a human rights treaty: where do we stand?, in Cannizzaro, Enzo (ed.), *The law of treaties beyond the Vienna Convention*, cit., p. 60-85.

235 See Alland, Denis (coord.). *Droit international public*, cit., p. 229; Daudt, Gabriel Pithan, *Reservas aos tratados internacionais de direitos humanos…*, cit., p. 18; Riquelme Cortado, Rosa, *Las reservas a los tratados…*, cit., p. 332-368; and Fitzmaurice, Malgosia, The practical working of the law of treaties, cit., p. 193-195.

236 See Guideline 3.2.1, item 1, of the ILC *Guide*: "A treaty monitoring body may, for the purpose of discharging the functions entrusted to it, assess the permissibility of reservations formulated by a State or an international organization". See also Guidelines 3.2.2, 3.2.3, 3.2.4 and 3.2.5 of the ILC *Guide*.

237 According to Malcolm Shaw, this Commission "has already adopted the opinion that the provisions contained in the 1966 International Covenant on Civil and Political Rights, which has already become customary international law, did not admit reservations; in the event of reservations to mandatory provisions that did not fall under such category, States would bear 'a heavy burden' to justify their reservations. The Commission also made clear that an unacceptable or inadmissible reservation would normally turn the objected reservation valid in connection with the party that made the reservation, rather than that Convention in its entirety become absolutely void for such State Party. Finally, the Commission was the only competent body to establish whether a specific reservation was incompatible or not with the object or purpose of the treaty" (*Direito internacional*, cit., p. 686).

238 For further details, see Lijnzaad, Liesbeth, *Reservations to UN-human rights treaties…*, cit., p. 95-98; Redgwell, Catherine, Reservations to treaties and human rights: Committee general comment n. 24(52), *International and Comparative Law Quarterly*, vol. 46 (1997), p. 390-405; Korkelia, Konstantin, New challenges to the regime of reservations under the International Covenant on Civil and Political Rights, *European Journal of International Law*, vol. 13, n. 2 (2002), p. 437-477; and Daudt, Gabriel Pithan, *Reservas aos tratados in-*

The Inter-American Court of Human Rights, in *Advisory Opinion No. 3*, of 1983, also declared that when interpreting a specific reservation, its compatibility with the object and purpose of the treaty shall be taken into account. On that occasion, the Court held that a reservation which was designed to enable a State to suspend any of the peremptory fundamental rights must be deemed to be incompatible with the object and purpose of the Convention and, consequently, not permitted by it. The situation would be different if the reservation sought merely to restrict certain aspects of a peremptory right without depriving the right as a whole of its basic purpose.[239]

> "The issue in that connection also included the powers of the Commission [on Human Rights concerning the International Covenant on Civil and Political Rights] and of other similar treaty monitoring bodies, which, pursuant to their constitution treaties, were competent to interpret them on a legally binding basis. In 1997, the Commission of International Law [of the UN] adopted the Preliminary Conclusions on Reservations to Normative Multilateral Treaties, including Human Rights Treaties, which reaffirmed the applicability of the reservations regime of the Vienna Convention on the Law of Treaties to all treaties, including those on human rights. The ILC recognized that the treaty monitoring bodies of human rights were competent to comment and make exceptions on the admissibility of reservations to treaties, among other things, but declared that it neither affected the traditional monitoring ways at all by the contracting parties, according to both the 1969 and the 1986 Vienna Conventions, nor it meant that such bodies may exceed the powers conferred to them to carry out their general monitoring role. It was especially pointed out that the State which formulates the reservation is liable for acting in case the reservation concerned is deemed inadmissible; that State may modify or withdraw the reservation, or withdraw from the treaty. However, regardless of such controversy, the question of the high number of reservations to treaties on human rights, many of which have been criticized as contrary to the object and purpose of treaties is still pending".
> SHAW, Malcolm N. *Direito internacional*, cit., p. 686-687.

The truth is that in the specific case of treaties on human rights, the reservation system of the 1969 Vienna Convention (and also that of the 1986 Convention) seems to be inadequate.[240] This is due to the fact that the

---

ternacionais de direitos humanos..., cit., p. 171-199. For a more limited analysis, see Wei, Su, Reservation to treaties and some practical issues, cit., p. 136-138; Shaw, Malcolm N., *Direito internacional*, cit., p. 685-687; and Coulée, Frédérique, La codification du droit international: les cas des réserves aux traités internationaux, cit., p. 316-319.

239 I/A Court H.R., Advisory Opinion OC-3/83 of September 8, 1983 (Restrictions to the Death Penalty) Series A No. 3, paragraph 61.

240 See *General Comment* No.24 (52), dated 11.02.1994, of the UN Commission of Human Rights, which stated that the provisions of the Vienna Convention on the Law of Treaties are "improper to address the issues of reservations to treaties on human rights". As also

logic of treaties on human rights is totally different from that of traditional treaties, including their reservation regime. As previously mentioned, and irrespective of the issues that may arise on the subject,[241] treaties on human rights implicitly authorize (judicial or monitoring) bodies established by them to determine whether a specific reservation is compatible or not with the object and purpose of the treaty; in case of incompatibility, the reservation in question would be deemed void and the treaty would have to be fully complied with.

As it can be easily noted, that system (of questioning the *object* and *purpose* of a treaty) is not free of criticism, in spite of the fact that its purpose is appropriate. The main criticism lies with the difficulty to asses when (in practice) a reservation would be in accordance with the object and purpose of the treaty.[242] This led the General Assembly of the UN, in January 1952, based upon a statement made by the ICJ, to recommend the bodies of the United Nations, their specialized agencies, and its States Members, that during the course of the preparatory work for a multilateral convention arrangements should be made to determine whether reservations are admissible or not and which are the provisions that may be subject to reservations.[243]Since then, few treaties remained silent on the issue of reservations, including the instrument that should be considered as an example to the other international agreements: the Vienna Convention on the Law of Treaties.[244]

Other problem posed by reservations lies in determining who (or which body) is competent to assess its validity (whether the reservation is in accordance with the object and purpose of the treaty). It is obvious that if the treaty contains a provision on the subject, there will be no problem. As discussed above, treaties on human rights typically authorize *judicial* bodies established by them, or their treaty *monitoring* bodies, to declare the inva-

---

stated by Daudt, Gabriel Pithan, *Reservas aos tratados internacionais de direitos humanos…*, cit., p. 199, "the rules of the Vienna Convention are not enough to establish an efficient legal regime in connection with reservations to treaties on human rights".

241 See Korkelia, Konstantin. New challenges to the regime of reservations under the International Covenant on Civil and Political Rights, cit., p. 449-468.

242 See Mello, Celso D. de Albuquerque. *Curso de direito internacional público*, vol. I, cit., p. 250.

243 See Res. 598 (VI)-AG (transcribed in item 2.1, above).

244 See McNair, Arnold Duncan. *The law of treaties*, cit., p. 166; Rezek, José Francisco, *Direito dos tratados*, cit., p. 342-343; and Brownlie, Ian, *Princípios de direito internacional público*, cit., p. 633.

lidity of a reservation clearly incompatible with their protection regime.[245] Other forms of control may be also provided for, as in the case of the 1965 International Convention on the Elimination of All Forms of Racial Discrimination, whose Art. 20, item 2, provides as follows: "A reservation incompatible with the object and purpose of this Convention shall not be permitted, nor shall a reservation the effect of which would inhibit the operation of any of the bodies established by this Convention be allowed. A reservation shall be considered incompatible or inhibitive *if at least two thirds of the States Parties to this Convention object to it*". In the case of treaties on human rights, it is usually considered that the inadmissibility of a reservation renders the reservation in question *void*, and the treaty shall be valid in its entirety for the State that formulated the reservation.[246] What is the scenario, however, when the treaty states nothing about it? In that case, according to the most authoritative legal academic writing "the assessment of the validity of reservations may not be under the control of a judge, except that States so agreed". Therefore, except for the particular case of reservations to the constituent instrument of an international organization, for which an "institutional" solution by the competent organ of the organization concerned may be envisaged (Art. 20, item 3, of the Vienna Convention…), there is only one possible way: each co-contracting State should be entitled to assess the validity of a reservation, and, especially, its compatibility with the object and purpose of the treaty".[247] The 1969 Vienna Convention (apart

---

245 The problem arises when the relevant State does not accept the international jurisdiction or the surveillance of the respective monitoring body, in which case, "unfortunately, nothing else can be done except for the individual reactions of States, especially through objections to reservations" (Daudt, Gabriel Pithan. *Reservas aos tratados internacionais de direitos humanos…*, cit., p. 202).

246 See Shaw, Malcolm N. *Direito internacional*, cit., p. 685. In the case *Belilos v. Switzerland* (1998), the European Court of Human Rights considered that the reservation formulated by Switzerland was *void*, consequently rendering the provision under analysis *full* binding on Switzerland (Art. 6). For more details on the *Belilos* case, see item 2.7, below.

247 Dinh, Daillier & Pellet. *Direito internacional público*, cit., p. 186-187. In that very sense, see Shaw, Malcolm N., *Direito internacional*, cit., p. 685, under these terms: "Currently, unless otherwise provided for in the specific treaty, the decision on admissibility of a reservation must be taken by the States that are a party to the treaty. In other words, it is a subjective application of objective criteria". On the subject, see Remiro Brotons, Antonio, *Derecho internacional público*, vol. 2, cit., p. 222, especially when he indicates that the disadvantage of such system (of individual acceptance of validity of reservations) lies in its result: the same reservation would simultaneously be compatible and incompatible with the object and purpose of the treaty, according to the point of view, tainted by political considerations, which are used by different interpreters; it would be enough that a

from the exception of item 3 of Art. 20,[248] which states that the reservation to the constituent instrument of an organization requires the acceptance of the "competent organ" of that organization) also adopted such position with regard to item 4 of Art. 20.[249] Namely, if the treaty provides nothing on the subject, each contracting party (however questionable that solution may be) shall be entitled to assess the validity and compatibility of a reservation formulated by a State.

Finally, it should be recalled that even when the treaty provides which reservations may be formulated, such permission authorizes under no circumstances that a *jus cogens* rule may be subject to reservations (Arts. 53 and 64 of the Convention). In that very sense, the ILC *Guide* provides that "[a] reservation to a treaty provision which reflects a peremptory norm of general international law (*jus cogens*) does not affect the binding nature of that norm, which shall continue to apply as such between the reserving State or organization and other States or international organizations" (Guideline 4.4.3, item 1). The reservations formulated in relation to a common conventional provision (not related to human rights issues) shall be also deemed invalid when their *effects* imply the breach of a *jus cogens* rule.[250] In this latter case, even if the reservation does not directly breach the *jus cogens* rule, it shall be considered void should its effects conflict with the international *jus cogens* rule.

2.6 Procedure regarding reservations

The 1969 Vienna Convention deals with the procedure regarding reservations in Art. 23. According to such provision, both the *formulation* of

---

State accepts the reservation of another State for the latter to become a contracting party, even if the majority had challenged it as incompatible with the object and purpose of the treaty. See also Korkelia, Konstantin, New challenges to the regime of reservations under the International Covenant on Civil and Political Rights, cit., p. 445-446.

248 See also item 2 of the same article, which requires the acceptance of the reservation by *all the parties* to a treaty, "[w]hen it appears from the limited number of the negotiating States [...] and the object and purpose of a treaty that the application of the treaty in its entirety among all the parties is an essential condition of the consent of each one to be bound by the treaty".

249 During the 1968-1969 Vienna Conference, many proposals were not accepted, including the Japanese, Philippine and Korean ones, for the adoption of a *collegiate* assessment procedure to validate reservations.

250 See Guideline 4.4.3, item 2, of the ILC *Guide*: "A reservation cannot exclude or modify the legal effect of a treaty in a manner contrary to a peremptory norm of general international law".

a reservation, and its *acceptance* or *objection* shall be done *in writing*,[251] and such fact shall be notified to other contracting States and other States entitled to become a parties to the treaty (item 1).[252] The reservation is usually informed to the *depositary* of the treaty, who shall disclose the information to the other contracting parties (who may, in turn, *accept it* or *object it* – see item 2.8, below);[253] if there is no depositary, it shall be directly communicated by the formulating State.[254] In the same way, *withdrawal* of a reservation or an objection shall also be made in writing (item 4); in this case, it shall be notified to the interested parties. According to the ILC *Guide*, apart from being in writing, reservations should also be *justified*, with specification of the reasons that led to their formulation (Guideline 2.1.2).

Determining whether a *pure and simple* ratification of the treaty (i.e., the ratification made with no observations) confirms or not contingent reservations formulated upon signature is a relevant issue. In our opinion, as the meaning of ratification is the same as *confirmation* of signature, the most appropriate interpretation would be that when the State ratifies a treaty and states nothing about the reservations formulated upon signature, it is because it intended to confirm the signature *in totum*, namely, with the reservations then formulated; in that case, silence by the State upon ratification would mean that it did not intend to amend what was done upon signature. However, the 1969 Vienna Convention did not follow such guideline, since item 2, of Art. 23, states that "[i]f formulated when signing the treaty subject to ratification, act of formal confirmation, acceptance or approval, a reservation must be formally confirmed by the reserving State or international organization when expressing its consent to be bound by the treaty";[255] the Convention added that, in such a case "the reservation shall be considered as having been made on the date of its confirmation".[256] Therefore, the *pure*

---

251 See Guideline 2.1.1 of the ILC *Guide*. The *Guide* also enables the communication of reservations by other means, besides diplomatic notes, such as e-mail or fax (Guideline 2.1.6, item 3).

252 See Guideline 2.1.5 of the ILC *Guide*.

253 See Remiro Brotons, Antonio. *Derecho internacional público*, vol. 2, cit., p. 208.

254 See Guideline 2.1.6, item 1 (*i* and *i*), of the ILC *Guide*; the *Guide* understands that the reservation was effectively *made* (formulated) when *received* by the other States or international organizations (Guideline 2.1.6, item 2).

255 It should be highlighted that the formal confirmation of a reservation must be made in *writing*, as stated in Guideline 2.2.4 of the ILC *Guide*.

256 See Sinclair, Ian. *The Vienna Convention on the Law of Treaties*, cit., p. 65; and Villiger, Mark E., *Commentary on the 1969 Vienna Convention on the Law of Treaties*, cit.,

and simple ratification of the treaty, under the terms of the 1969 Vienna Convention, *does not confirm* the reservations formulated upon signature, in which case the treaty will be valid without any reservations previously formulated.[257]

It should be noted that the Convention did not use (also in connection with the confirmation of reservations made upon signature) the formula "...unless otherwise provided by the treaty...", or another formula stating "...as otherwise agreed by negotiating States...". That shows that the Convention when dealing with this matter established a *strict* confirmation rule.[258] But the wording of some treaties contained a different rule. For example, the European Convention on the Suppression of Terrorism (dated 27 January 1977), despite having entered into force prior to the Vienna Convention on the Law of Treaties, which entered into force in 1980, allows to formulate reservations upon signature, without subsequent confirmation being necessary. Indeed, Art. 13, item 1 states that: "Any State may, *at the time of signature* or when depositing its instrument of ratification, acceptance or approval, *declare that it reserves* the right to refuse extradition in respect of any offence mentioned in Article 1 which it considers to be a political offence, an offence connected with a political offence or an offence inspired by political motives...". According to the ILC *Guide*, a reservation formulated when signing a treaty does not require subsequent confirmation when a State *expresses* by signature its consent to be bound by the treaty. (Guideline 2.2.2); however, the *Guide* contemplates the exception, apparently contrary to the strictness of the Vienna Convention, in the event that the treaty expressly provides that a State (or international organization)

---

p. 317-318. On this subject, before the entry into force of the 1969 Vienna Convention, see Accioly, Hildebrando, *Tratado de direito internacional público*, vol. I, cit., p. 592-593.

257 See Guideline 2.2.1 of the ILC *Guide*.

258 However, this is not applicable to "interpretative declarations" formulated upon signature, since the 1969 Vienna Convention does not regulate this subject. Therefore, in the event that the aforementioned *declarations* were formulated upon signature, later confirmation is not necessary (the provision of the Convention expressly applies only in connection with *reservations*). The ILC *Guide* contains a guideline in that very sense by stating in Guideline 2.4.6 that: "An interpretative declaration formulated when signing a treaty does not require subsequent confirmation when a State or an international organization expresses its consent to be bound by the treaty". Then, unlike *reservations*, the lack of subsequent confirmation of an *interpretative declaration* does not render void the declaration formulated after the final commitment by the State.

is authorized to formulate reservations upon signature thereof (as in the example quoted).[259]

Finally, the Convention provided that the "express acceptance of, or an objection to, a reservation made *previously* to confirmation of the reservation *does not itself require confirmation*" (Art. 23, item 3). In this case, the Convention preferred to provide for a rule different from the one established in the preceding provision (Art. 23, item 2). Therefore, if the express acceptance of a reservation, or objection to a reservation, is made *before* confirmation (made upon *ratification*, Art. 23, item 3) of such reservation by the formulating State, the accepting or objecting State shall be released from *confirming* its act at the time of expressing its consent to be bound by the same treaty. The assumption takes place whenever State *X* expressly accepts (or objects) a reservation formulated by State *Y* in the meantime between the signature of the treaty by the latter and its ratification; as provided for in Art. 23, item 3 of the Convention, if the reservation formulated by State *Y* upon signature is confirmed at the time of ratification, the acceptance (or objection) previously formulated by State *X* also becomes automatically confirmed. Evidently, the problem does not arise when the State which formulated the reservation upon signature does not confirm ratification, in which case (under the terms of Art. 23, item 2) the treaty will be fully valid. Thus, the previous act by the third State concerning acceptance or objection will become moot.

2.7 Distinction between reservations and other acts not implying a reservation

Reservations should be distinguished from other acts whose effects are not technically a *reservation*.[260]

In the practice of international relations, the term *reservations* is also frequently (although wrongly) used to name those acts that do not imply a *release* from the application of certain conventional provisions in the relations of a State with the other parties. Basically, two kinds of declarations

---

259 See Guideline 2.2.3 of the ILC *Guide*: "Where the treaty expressly provides that a State or an international organization may formulate a reservation when signing the treaty, such a reservation does not require formal confirmation by the reserving State or international organization when expressing its consent to be bound by the treaty".

260 For an opinion on the subject prior to the 1969 Vienna Convention, see Bishop Jr., William W., Reservations to treaties, cit., p. 303-322. For a current opinion, see Riquelme Cortado, Rosa, *Las reservas a los tratados*..., cit., p. 33-38.

are sometimes confused with reservations themselves: *ratification reservations* and *interpretative declarations*.[261] Nevertheless, both of them deviate from what the 1969 Vienna Convention technically defines as *reservation*. In other words, in order for a reservation to be considered as such, it is necessary to fall under the concept given by the Vienna text, showing the intention to exclude or modify certain provisions of the treaty in connection with a specified State.

Therefore, the so-called *ratification reservations* and *interpretative declarations* (the latter, normally admitted in those treaties where the formulation of reservations is forbidden, or when the Government understands that making a reservation is politically unfeasible) are not exactly *reservations* in light of the 1969 Vienna Convention. Therefore, they cannot be framed in the concept given therein, despite being accepted by international practice and used by almost all States.

The first ones (*ratification reservations*) are not reservations because they express that signatures cannot turn the treaty into a final instrument, which will only occur upon ratification (this sounds even obvious); the second ones (*interpretative declarations*) because, being only interpretative, constituting only a theoretical affirmation of principles or highlighting the special meaning that the State infer from certain provisions of the agreement, do not modify the material content of the text of the treaty in connection with the State.[262] When one party formulates an interpretative declaration it is communicating the other parties that certain provision of the treaty must be interpreted *in according to its own opinion*, among the many possible interpretative options; the party does not *exclude* or *modify* the legal effects of any *provision* of the treaty itself, but it only *interprets* it in his own manner. However, it should be noted, that interpretative declarations may be formulated in the context of a *bilateral* treaty, unlike *reservations* themselves (see item 2.2, above); when formulated in a bilateral treaty, an interpretative declaration will be valid as an authentic (official) declaration of the respective treaty provided that it is accepted by the other party.[263]

---

261 Many examples of such declarations are found in Annex IV.

262 See Rezek, José Francisco. *Direito dos tratados*, cit., p. 338-341. See also the *Temeltasch v. Switzerland* case, on the distinction between reservations and interpretative declarations within the scope of the European Convention on Human Rights, in *European Human Rights Reports*, vol. 5 (1983), p. 417.

263 See Guideline 1.6.3 of the ILC *Guide*; and Shaw, Malcolm N., *Direito internacional*, cit., p. 682.

The most serious legal issues do not arise in connection with *ratification reservations*, which understanding is not difficult to assimilate, but they arise in relation to the aforementioned *interpretative declarations*. That is why their understanding requires greater analysis.

It is very common that States present such "declarations", as "reservations" related to the compatibility of the treaty with domestic laws or previous treaties, or in relation to the solution of disputes that may arise from the application of the treaty, or even, the lack of acknowledgment by other contracting State, etc. However, all of them shall be considered void when the treaty is involved in an international court decision, since they are not genuine *reservations* in light of the 1969 Vienna Convention. They are just the means at the disposal of States to interpret the treaty or some of its provisions at their discretion. In summary, interpretative declarations are unilateral acts of States for the purpose of interpreting (in full or in part) a specified international treaty, but without excluding or modifying any provisions in connection with the State.[264]

> Upon accession to the American Convention on Human Rights (1969), Brazil made the following interpretative declaration: "The Brazilian Government understands that Articles 43 and 48(d) do not include the automatic right of visits and inspections by the Inter-American Commission on Human Rights, which will depend on the express consent of the State". By signing the Antarctic Treaty (1959), Argentina made the following declaration: "The Argentine Republic declares that in as much as the Protocol to the Antarctic Treaty on the Protection of the Environment is a Complementary Agreement of the Antarctic Treaty and that its Article 4 fully respects what has been stated in Article IV, Subsection 1, Paragraph A) of said Treaty, none of its stipulations should be interpreted or be applied as affecting its rights, based on legal titles, acts of possession, contiguity and geological continuity in the region lying south of the 60th parallel, in respect of which it has proclaimed and maintained its sovereignty".

264 See De La Guardia, Ernesto. *Derecho de los tratados internacionales*, cit., p. 187. According to De La Guardia: "(...) the origin of 'interpretative declarations' lies on multilateral treaties that forbid the formulation of reservations; their purpose is not excluding the application of a provision from the treaty or modifying its legal effects, but only assigning *a specified interpretation* in a field of many interpretation possibilities" (Idem, ibidem). According to the ILC *Guide*, the definition of interpretative declaration is the following: "Interpretative declaration" means a unilateral statement, however phrased or named, made by a State or an international organization, whereby that State or that organization purports to specify or clarify the meaning or scope of a treaty or of certain of its provisions" (Guideline 1.2). In Guideline 4.7.1, item 1, the *Guide* itself explains the *effects* of an interpretative declaration, under these terms: "An interpretative declaration does not modify treaty obligations. It may only specify or clarify the meaning or scope which its author attributes to a treaty or to certain provisions thereof and may, as appropriate, constitute an element to be taken into account in interpreting the treaty in accordance with the general rule of interpretation of treaties".

In the framework of ILC works, the adopted approach (proposed by Waldock) consisted of excluding interpretative declarations from the definition of reservation. This approach was actually reflected in the final text of the Convention, whose provisions on reservations did mention such declarations. The Convention referred to interpretative declarations just once in another part of its text, when it established the *General Interpretation Rule* of treaties; thus, Art. 31, item 2(b) of the Convention provided that "[T]he context *for the purpose* of the interpretation of a treaty shall comprise (...) any instrument which was made by one or more parties in connection with the conclusion of the treaty and accepted by the other parties as an instrument related to the treaty". However, such rule reinforces the concept according to which interpretative declarations, which only *help* to interpret treaties, are not formally reservations to the text of the agreement. Nevertheless, if the declaration is accepted by all contracting States, it may constitute an agreement on the interpretation of the treaty.[265]

However, it should be noted that contemporary academic writing (as well as the ILC *Guide* on the subject) has admitted that "stronger" interpretative declarations (or more "emphatic") be deemed to constitute true *reservations*, depending on some conditions.[266] With regard to political declarations or declarations related to principles, there are no further problems;[267] the *intention* of the State is not, in such cases to expressly modify its obligations *beyond* those provided for in the treaty.[268] But, regarding strictly *legal* declarations, they may be considered *reservations* themselves (this is not the case of the declaration made by Brazil to the American Convention) if they really intend to *exclude* or *modify* some terms of the agreement signed,[269] thus losing their *interpretative* character to truly gain the status of *reservation*.[270] This seems to be the only criterion

---

265 See Guideline 4.7.3 of the ILC *Guide*.

266 See Guidelines 1.1.1 and 1.1.2 of the ILC *Guide*.

267 See Remiro Brotons, Antonio. *Derecho internacional público*, vol. 2, cit., p. 212.

268 As an example, it should be pointed out the political statement made by Argentina to the Convention on the Pan-American Union (Havana, 1928): "The Argentine delegation states, according to express instructions of its government, that it approves the project of the convention and that it will sign it; however, it further states that it does hereby make the reservation that it regrets that the economic principles supported within the Commission were not included in the Convention".

269 See Villiger, Mark E. *Commentary on the 1969 Vienna Convention on the Law of Treaties*, cit., p. 89-90; and Cassese, Antonio, *Diritto internazionale*, cit, p. 245-246.

270 See Guideline 1.3 of the ILC *Guide*: "The character of a unilateral statement as a reservation or as an interpretative declaration is determined by the legal effect that its author purports to produce".

(that is, determine whether there is actually an intention to exclude or modify certain provisions of the agreement) to distinguish a mere interpretative declaration from a proper *reservation*.[271] It is evident that such distinction will not occur when the treaty is contrary to *any* reservation, as in the case, for example, of the Rome Statute of the International Criminal Court (Art. 120) and the Convention on Damage Caused by Foreign Aircraft to Third Parties on the Surface (Art. 39); in such cases, any unilateral declaration of the State may only (obviously) be a merely interpretative declaration.[272]

Interpretative declarations with reservation effects have already been characterized as "qualified" declarations, as opposed to "merely" interpretative declarations (thus having no reservation effects).[273] Such "qualified" declarations would be equal to reservations themselves, as they show their intention to exclude or modify the terms of the treaty in connection with the formulating State. There also exist other expressions to name the same thing such as "simple interpretative declarations" and "conditional interpretative declarations".[274] The latter would be those declarations which produce the same effects as reservations.[275]

---

271 See Guideline 1.3.1 of ILC *Guide*: "To determine whether a unilateral statement formulated by a State or an international organization in respect of a treaty is a reservation or an interpretative declaration, the statement should be interpreted in good faith in accordance with the ordinary meaning ascribed to its terms, with a view to identifying the intention of its author, in light of the treaty to which it refers". And Guideline 1.3.2, adds: "The phrasing or name of a unilateral statement provides an indication of the purported legal effects".

272 See Guideline 1.3.3 of ILC *Guide:* "When a treaty prohibits reservations to all or certain of its provisions, a unilateral statement formulated in respect of those provisions by a State or an international organization shall be presumed not to constitute a reservation. Such a statement nevertheless constitutes a reservation if it purports to exclude or modify the legal effect of certain provisions of the treaty, or of the treaty as a whole with respect to certain specific aspects, in their application to its author".

273 See McRae, Donald M. The legal effect of interpretative declarations, *British Yearbook of International Law*, vol. 49 (1978), p. 155-173; and Shaw, Malcolm N., *Direito internacional*, cit., p. 680-681.

274 See Pellet, Alain [Special Rapporteur], "Fifteenth report on reservations to treaties" (Add.), General Assembly/ILC (Sixty-second session), Geneva, 4 May-5 June and 6 July-7 August 2010, p. 2-18.

275 Idem, p. 7 (item 538): "A conditional interpretative declaration produces the same effects as a reservation…" The following paragraph (item 539) reads as follows: "In cases of a simple interpretative declaration, however, the mere fact of proposing an interpretation which is not in accordance with the provisions of the treaty in no way changes the de-

In the *Belilos v. Switzerland* case, of 1988, the European Court of Human Rights examined the effect of a specific interpretative declaration made by Switzerland upon ratification of the European Convention on Human Rights, and indicated that for the analysis of the case recourse should be had to the *travaux préparatoires* of the treaty, when it then determined that the true intention of Switzerland was to "avoid the consequences which a broad view of the right of access to the courts (...) would have for the system of public administration and justice in the cantons and consequently to put forward the declaration as qualifying Switzerland's consent to be bound by the Convention"; as the Court understood that it was a true *reservation*, it concluded that it was a breach of the provision of the European Convention on Human Rights (Art. 57) that allows reservations only to the extent that a law then in force in the territory of the State was in conflict with the conventional provision under analysis, forbidding any "reservation of a general character". Therefore, the European Court considered that the aforementioned declaration by Switzerland was *void*.[276]

In practice, it is obvious that contracting parties to an international agreement, when signing or ratifying it, do not always take care of clearly specifying the reservation nature of a given "declaration". That is why it is hard for international courts (in special, the ICJ) to determine whether the declaration made is "merely" interpretative or a true "reservation". If the court understands that it is a reservation in *stricto sensu*, the solution is to declare the reservation act void in such cases where the treaty does not allow the formulation of reservations. Perhaps, the fact that the 1969 Vienna Convention has left the concept of reservations open was not the best solution in that it allowed for reservations "however phrased or named ...". Anyway, the problem exists and the practical perception shows that the analysis of the specific declaration, in light of the historic time and surrounding circumstances may give an answer to the issue under analysis.

Finally, it should be noted that in order to establish whether a unilateral declaration is of a merely interpretative nature or a reservation in

---

claring State's position with regard to the treaty. The State remains bound by it and must respect it".

276 See Wei, Su. Reservation to treaties and some practical issues, cit., p. 127-128; Shaw, Malcolm N., *Direito internacional*, cit., p. 681-682; and, with more detail, Edwards Jr., Richard W., Reservations to treaties: the Belilos case and the work of the International Law Commission, *University of Toledo Law Review*, vol. 31 (2000), p. 195-207.

itself, it will have to be interpreted "in good faith, according to the current sense of its terms and within the context of the treaty under analysis. Furthermore, the "intention of the declaring State shall be also taken into consideration".[277]

2.8 Acceptance of and objection to reservations

It has already been indicated (item 2.5, above) that in the event of a silent treaty, reservations may be formulated provided that they are compatible with the *object* and *purpose* of the treaty; they may also be formulated in cases not provided in paragraphs (a) and (b) of Art. 19. In addition, as has been discussed, according to legal scholars, and the provisions of Art. 20, item 4 of the 1969 Vienna Convention, the validity of reservations (this is, their compatibility with the object and purpose of the treaty) shall be determined by the contracting States, what may be subject to criticism; in fact, what States do (in practice) is to follow their *own* interests when accepting or opposing a reservation formulated by another State. That is why some authors, such as Remiro Brotons, ironically affirm that "in fact, it is not the compatibility of a reservation with the object and purpose of the treaty what is determined, but rather the free act of acceptance or objection of the other contracting parties, acting like creatures imagined by the famous Defoe, which determines their admission and legal effects".[278] In any case, the fact remains that the 1969 Convention confers States the power to determine whether a reservation formulated by another State is *compatible* or not with the object and purpose of the treaty, thus giving rise to the problem of *acceptance* of and *objection* to reservations.

In *silent texts*, the general rule indicates that reservations shall be *accepted* by the other State Parties to the treaty in respect of which reservations are formulated. With regard to the acceptance of reservations by the other States, there exist no further problems, since, once they are accepted, the treaty is normally valid between the parties, reservations being an integral part of its text. However, apart from express acceptance, the reservation formulated shall be deemed (tacitly) accepted if none of the parties *have raised any objection* to it within 12 months following notice thereof or if the ratification (or accession) were subsequent to the reservation and

[277] Shaw, Malcolm N. *Direito internacional*, cit., p. 682.

[278] Remiro Brotons, Antonio. *Derecho internacional público*, vol. 2, cit., p. 223. *Note*: Defoe (Daniel) quoted in the text was the English novelist author of the classic *Robinson Crusoé* (written in 1719).

there were no objection thereto (Art. 20, item 5);[279] the understanding that prevailed in the Convention was that, in the latter case, a period of 12 months with no objection from the parties or the subsequent ratification (or accession), *sub silentio*, tacitly expresses acceptance of reservations.[280]

Art. 20 of the 1969 Convention deals with the problem concerning the acceptance of and objection to reservations, which provides, in first place, that "[a] reservation *expressly authorized* by a treaty does *not require* any subsequent *acceptance* by the other contracting States (...) unless the treaty so provides" (item 1); in that case, such reservations are not subject to the analysis of compatibility with the object and purpose of the treaty.[281] However, the opposite is not true: as the Convention prescinds from the acceptance of *expressly* authorized reservations, it makes reservations that are *not forbidden* by the treaty depend on the acceptance by the other parties.[282] To affirm that certain reservations are *expressly authorized* does not mean that other provisions of the treaty (not expressly authorized) cannot be also subject to reservations; such *other provisions* may be subject to reservations if they are *accepted* by the other contracting parties (see item 2.5, above). So, unless the treaty provides that "*only* reservations to *certain* articles shall be allowed", nothing forbids the formulation of reservations *other than* those expressly authorized (in which case the treaty *authorizes* a specified reservation, but without prohibiting *others* from being also formulated, as long as such reservations have the *authorization* of the other parties). In summary, to allow the formulation of reservations to *specified* provisions only means that *acceptance* is not required (although *objections* may be raised) by the other contracting parties. Thus, it should be repeated that: Art. 20, item 1, of the Convention aims at pointing out that an expressly authorized

---

279 See Guideline 2.8.2 of the ILC *Guide*. In any case, however, the acceptance of a substantially invalid reservation by a State or an international organization shall not confirm the nullity of the relevant reservation (see Guideline 3.3.3 of the ILC *Guide*).

280 See Sinclair, Ian. *The Vienna Convention on the Law of Treaties*, cit., p. 63; De La Guardia, Ernesto, *Derecho de los tratados internacionales*, cit., p. 183; Wei, Su, Reservation to treaties and some practical issues, cit., p. 120-121; and Villiger, Mark E., *Commentary on the 1969 Vienna Convention on the Law of Treaties*, cit., p. 293.

281 See Sinclair, Ian. *The Vienna Convention on the Law of Treaties*, cit., p. 73-74.

282 Remember that the treaty may provide (Art. 19, *b*) that *only certain reservations* to the text... *may* be made. In this case, other reservations (apart from the ones expressly specified) may not be formulated. In the case of Art. 20, item 1, which is currently being dealt with, the treaty expressly *authorizes* specified reservations, without forbidding, however, the formulation of *other* reservations to the text (provided that they are *accepted* by the other parties).

reservation *does not depend* on any *acceptance* by the other parties; as it is shown, States not agreeing with an expressly authorized reservation can *object* to its formulation (since, in this case, there is no *acceptance*).[283] Nobody questions that a State making a reservation to an expressly authorized provision may comply with the treaty *vis-à-vis* the other parties *without being bound* by the provision under analysis; but that (as explains Brotons) does not imply "that the contracting States have deprived themselves of the power to raise an objection to them and are bound to approve all of them, even if they think that their content may damage their interests".[284] It should be noted that the Vienna Convention did not support the French proposal for the provision under analysis, with the following wording: "A reservation expressly authorized by the treaty may not be subject to objections by other contracting States, unless otherwise provided by the treaty".[285]

Once the analysis of Art. 20, item 1, is over, the two following paragraphs of the same article should be quoted (items 2 and 3). Item 2 provides as follows: [w]hen it appears from the *limited* number of the negotiating States and negotiating organizations or, as the case may be, of the negotiating organizations and the *object* and *purpose* of a treaty that the application of the treaty in its entirety between all the parties is an *essential condition* of the consent of each one to be bound by the treaty, a reservation requires acceptance *by all the parties* (Art. 20, item 2);[286] the ILC *Guide* goes on to state that "[i]n the event of a reservation requiring unanimous acceptance by some or *all* States (...), such acceptance, once obtained, is final" (Guideline 2.8.7). In turn, item 3 of Art. 20 establishes that when a treaty is a constituent instrument of an international organization, a reservation requires the acceptance of the "competent organ" of

---

283 *Objecting to* a reservation means *reacting* against its formulation, for the purpose of avoiding the production of legal effects wanted by the formulating State. According to the ILC *Guide*, an objection to a reservation may be formulated by: *a*) any contracting State; and *b*) any State that is entitled to become a party to the treaty, in which case the objection does not produce any legal effect until the State has expressed its consent to be bound by the treaty (Guideline 2.6.3). It should be highlighted that it is currently understood that States are not required to express the reasons why they object to a specified reservation (see Villiger, Mark E., *Commentary on the 1969 Vienna Convention on the Law of Treaties*, cit., p. 292).

284 Remiro Brotons, Antonio. *Derecho internacional público*, vol. 2, cit., p. 218.

285 See Remiro Brotons, Antonio. Idem, p. 219.

286 There are other conditions provided by the *Guide*, in this specific case, for the reservation to be established: it should be substantially valid and formulated according to the form and procedure provided therefore (see Guideline 4.1.2).

that organization (Art. 20, item 3). Which could be this organ? Under the terms of the ILC *Guide*, "Subject to the rules of the organization, competence to accept a reservation to a constituent instrument of an international organization belongs to the organ competent to: decide on the *admission of a member* to the organization; or *amend* the constituent instrument; or *interpret* this instrument" (Guideline 2.8.9). It should be pointed out that such guideline is only applied in case of *silence* of the constituent treaty of the organization, as excepted by the *Guide* (when it states: "*Subject to the rules* of the organization…"); if the constituent treaty provides that the competent organ of the organization shall accept a reservation, the guideline established in the *Guide* shall not be applicable.

A more serious legal issue arises when some States are *favorable* to the reservation made by the other and some other States *are not*. That occurs when a specified reservation is *accepted* by some States and *not* by others.[287] In the event of a valid reservation, the reserving State becomes a party to the treaty and its obligations towards the other parties are modified to the extent established by the reservation (Art. 21, item 1 (a)).[288] On the other hand, in such situations where reservations are not either expressly forbidden or expressly authorized, the remaining State Parties are free to *accept them* or to *object to them*. If a State *accepts* a reservation, the treaty enters into force (with the reservation formulated) in its relations with the reserving State (Art. 20, item 4 (a)); as from the aforementioned acceptance, there is a "bilateral" relation between the reserving State and the accepting State, irrespective of the relation that such States may have with the other parties.[289] In connection with the relations between a State Party *objecting to* a reservation and the reserving State, there are two options: 1) it may occur that the State Party declares that it objects to the reservation formulated, indicating that it *does not want* to establish a conventional relation with the reserving State, in which case there *will be no* conventional relation between both States;[290] and 2) it may happen that the State Party refuses to accept the

---

[287] For examples of objections (of many States) to reservations formulated in the Vienna Convention on the Law of Treaties, see Annex IV.

[288] See Buergenthal, Thomas (*et all.*). *Manual de derecho internacional público*, cit., p. 85.

[289] See Villiger, Mark E. *Commentary on the 1969 Vienna Convention on the Law of Treaties*, cit., p. 289. According to the ILC *Guide*, the acceptance of a reservation "cannot be withdrawn or amended" (Guideline 2.8.13).

[290] Such authorization is expressed at the end of sub-paragraph *b* of Art. 20, item 4, according to which "an objection by a contracting State or by a contracting organization to a reservation does not preclude the entry into force of the treaty as between the objecting

reservation made by the other State without hindering the establishment of relations with the latter, in which case it will be considered (except with regard to the provision in relation to which the reservation was made) that a valid conventional relation was established between them (Art. 20, item 4, *b*). Consequently, it can be noted that the Convention *does not preclude* the entry into force of the treaty between the reserving State and the objecting State, unless the latter unmistakably expresses a contrary intention.[291]

In the event that the objecting State *disagrees* with the entry into force of the treaty between it and the reserving State, the ILC *Guide* stipulates that for the treaty concerned *not to enter into force* between the parties, as intended by the objecting State, it is necessary that the latter expresses such intention *before* the entry into force of the treaty between the former and the reserving State.[292] In addition, the *Guide* states the objection needs be substantially *valid*, that is to say, that it would not defeat the object and purpose of the treaty in the relations between the reserving State and the objecting State (Guideline 3.4.2, item 2).

When a State objecting to a reservation *has not opposed* the entry into force of the treaty between itself and the reserving State, the provisions to which the reservation relates do not (obviously) apply between the two States, and "to the extent of the reservation" (Art. 21, item 3).[293] Thus, either the objecting State unequivocally expresses its intention that the treaty under analysis *is not applied* to the relations between it and the reserving State, or states nothing and the treaty *becomes valid*

State or international organization and the reserving State or organization *unless a contrary intention is definitely expressed by the objecting State or organization*".

291 See Remiro Brotons, Antonio. *Derecho internacional público*, vol. 2, cit., p. 225.

292 See Guideline 2.6.7 of the ILC *Guide*: "When a State or an international organization formulating an objection to a reservation intends to preclude the entry into force of the treaty as between itself and the reserving State or international organization, it shall definitely express its intention before the treaty would otherwise enter into force between them".

293 See Guideline 4.3.6, item 1, of the ILC *Guide*: "When a State or an international organization objecting to a valid reservation has not opposed the entry into force of the treaty between itself and the reserving State or organization, the provisions to which the reservation relates do not apply as between the author of the reservation and the objecting State or organization, to the extent of the reservation". And also: "All the provisions of the treaty other than those to which the reservation relates shall remain applicable as between the reserving State or organization and the objecting State or organization" (Guideline 4.3.6, item 4).

between both of them, except for the provisions subject to the reservation and to the extent provided by the it.[294] Such "extent" provided by the reservation may have the *effects* of reservations modified case by case, given the more or less wide *extension* of a specified reservation in a specific case. The Convention established, with regard to an objection, the rule that allows the *severability* of the treaty in this case, since only the unaccepted provision in relation to which a reservation was made shall cease being effective between the reserving party and the objecting party (to the extent provided by the reservation itself) and as long as that the nature of the treaty enables such division.[295] Finally, it should be clarified that reservations formulated by a certain State do not affect the relations existing between other acceding States, with no reservations (Art. 21, item 1, *a*).

All such cases of acceptance of or objection to reservations are only evidently valid when the international treaty under analysis is *a mutualizable treaty*, which, as already studied, are not terminated by the fact that their execution is impaired by an act of one of the parties (see above, Part I, Ch. 2, item 2.2.4)

---

294 It can be seen that both in this case of *objection* (Art. 21, item 3) and in the case of *acceptance* (Art. 21, item 1, *a*), the relations will be determined "to the extent provided by the reservation", which led many authors to realize the similarity between both provisions, which would potentially produce the same effects. Also see Ruda, J. M., Reservations to treaties, cit., p. 198; and Sinclair, Ian, *The Vienna Convention on the Law of Treaties*, cit., p. 76-77. The ILC *Guidelines* show, however, that there is a certain difference between the effects of acceptance and those of objection when the reservation intends to *modify* the provisions of the treaty. See ILC, UN-Doc. A/CN.4/L.760, Add. 1 (28May 2010), p. 6, which provides: "3. To the extent that a valid reservation purports to modify the legal effect of certain provisions of the treaty, when a contracting State or a contracting organization has raised an objection to it but has not opposed the entry into force of the treaty between itself and the author of the reservation, the objecting State or organization and the author of the reservation are not bound, in their treaty relations, by the provisions of the treaty as intended to be modified by the reservation".

295 Such rule, by allowing the *severability* of the treaty in this case, is also called "maximum Pan-American rule", since it was developed in the Inter-American context based upon the Havana Convention on Treaties, whose Art. 6, third paragraph, provides that: "In international treaties celebrated between different Sates, a reservation made by one of them in the act of ratification affects only the application of the clause in question in the relation of the other contracting States with the State making the reservation". For details on the discussion regarding this rule in the framework of the ILC, see De La Guardia, Ernesto, *Derecho de los tratados internacionales*, cit., p. 174-183.

2.9 Effects of reservations

The main effect of a valid reservation is to release the reserving State from complying with the reserved provision, without any consequences in terms of international responsability.[296] Therefore, a validly reserved provision is to be understood as *non-existing* in connection with the reserving State in its relations with the other parties. It is clear that this has a double effect, since, the reservation formulated releases the reserving State from complying with a specified conventional provision in its relations with the other parties. The latter will also have a treaty with *less* provisions in their relations with the reserving State (Art. 21, 1, *b*).[297]

In summary, once they have been formulated, effective reservations are valid between the reserving State and the other States according to the modifications established therein. The reserving State is released from the legal effects of certain provisions of the treaty in connection with the other States, as well as they will not (reciprocally) have any rights or obligations under the aforementioned provisions in their relations with the reserving State. This does not mean that the relation of the other States among themselves, which did not formulate reservations to the text of the treaty, will be affected as a result of that fact. A reservation between two States has no power to modify the text of the treaty in connection with the relations with the other States themselves, which were not reserving parties.[298] The reservation accepted (either expressly or tacitly) only binds the reserving State and the accepting State in their mutual relation, to the extent specified by the reservation itself (see item 2.8, above).[299]

---

296 Not even a *void* reservation can generate the international responsability of the State, under the terms of Guideline 3.3.2 of the ILC *Guide*, which provides as follows: "The formulation of an impermissible reservation produces its consequences pursuant to the law of treaties and does not engage the international responsibility of the State or international organization which has formulated it".

297 See Wei, Su. Reservation to treaties and some practical issues, cit., p. 123; and Villiger, Mark E., *Commentary on the 1969 Vienna Convention on the Law of Treaties*, cit., p. 301. In the same sense, Accioly indicates that: "Just like the author of the reservation, which has been accepted by the other contracting parties, is released from the reserved provision, it is natural that, in reciprocity, the said contracting parties may also invoke the same benefit in their favor, in their relations with such State" (*Tratado de direito internacional público*, vol. I, cit., p. 559). See also Guideline 4.2.4, items 1, 2 and 3, of the ILC *Guide*.

298 See Guideline 4.6 of the ILC *Guide*: "A reservation does not modify the provisions of the treaty for the other parties to the treaty *inter se*".

299 See Calsing, Maria de Assis. *O tratado internacional e sua aplicação no Brasil*, cit., p. 46.

As it can be observed, reservations *divide* treaties into a series of different treaties, pursuant to the number of formulations. Thus, as explained by Reuter: the treaty is fully mandatory between the States which did not formulate any reservation; the parts of the treaty not affected by reservation *A* are applicable among the formulating States or international organizations and the other parties; the same applies to the parts of the treaty not affected by reservation *B*, etc.[300]

In addition, if a State *objects* to a reservation made by another State, but it does not oppose the entry into force of the treaty between them, the same solution applies: only reserved provisions shall not be applied between them, and the remaining part of the treaty not affected by the reservation shall be fully observed, as already mentioned.

If the reservation formulated is *void* because it defeats, for example, the object and purpose of the treaty, the reserving State shall continue to be bound by the treaty in its entirety.[301] When a treaty monitoring body (for example, the one provided in a treaty on human rights) makes a statement on the invalidity of a specific reservation formulated and the intention of the reserving State is not to be bound by the treaty without the benefit of reservation, such State shall express its intention to that effect within a period of twelve months from the date at which the treaty monitoring body made its assessment.[302]

2.10 Withdrawal of reservations or objections

Formulated reservations produce effects that last indefinitely, unless the treaty provides for a limited term. Unless the treaty otherwise provides, a reservation may be *withdrawn* at any time by the reserving party and the consent of a State which has accepted the reservation is not required for its withdrawal. Likewise, an objection to a reservation may be withdrawn at any time (Art. 22, items 1 and 2).[303] In that very sense, the ILC *Guide* admits that the withdrawal of reservations or objections may be done at any time.[304]

---

300 Reuter, Paul. *Introducción al derecho de los tratados*, cit., p. 105.

301 See Guideline 4.5.3, item 2, of the ILC *Guide*.

302 See Guideline 4.5.3, item 4, of the ILC *Guide*.

303 See Remiro Brotons, Antonio. *Derecho internacional público*, vol. 2, cit., p. 229; De La Guardia, Ernesto, *Derecho de los tratados internacionales*, cit., p. 184; and Villiger, Mark E., *Commentary on the 1969 Vienna Convention on the Law of Treaties*, cit., p. 306-311.

304 See Guidelines 2.5.1 (withdrawal of reservations) and 2.7.1 (withdrawal of objections) of the ILC *Guide*. In both cases, the withdrawal shall be formulated in writing (see Guidelines 2.5.2 and 2.7.2, respectively).

> "Article 22 received two important additions that did not appear in the Draft: item 2, regarding the withdrawal of objections, and paragraph *b* of item 3 on the effect of such withdrawal; this caused a change in the title: '*Withdrawal of reservations and of objections to reservations*' In fact, if the withdrawal of reservations and its effects are regulated, the withdrawal of objections and its effects should be also provided for. Both the reservation and the objection may be withdrawn at any time; the consent of the accepting State will not be required to withdraw the reservation (...); furthermore, the objecting State, which defends the integrity of the original text, shall have the same right to give up its position and accept a reservation". DE LA GUARDIA, Ernesto. *Derecho de los tratados internacionales*, cit., p. 184.

When will the withdrawal of a reservation or an objection produce effects (this is, when will it enter into force)? According to the Convention, the withdrawal of a reservation becomes operative in relation to another contracting State only when *notice* of it has been received by that State (Art. 22, item 3, *a*).[305] In such case, once reservation is withdrawn, the treaty becomes operative again with its original text for the reserving State and the other parties (both those who had previously accepted the reservation, and those who had objected to it without hindering the entry into force of the treaty vis-à-vis the reserving State; in the event that the objecting State has hindered the entry into force of the treaty between it and the reserving State, upon withdrawal of the reservation, the treaty shall become valid between the parties as from withdrawal[306]). In turn, the withdrawal of an objection to a reservation becomes operative only when the State which formulated the reservation is served notice thereof (Art. 22, 3, *b*);[307] upon withdrawal of the objection, the formulating State *accepts* the reservation *ex nunc*.[308] Although similar, the effects of para-

---

305 See Guideline 2.5.8 of the ILC *Guide*. According to the ILC *Guide*, it is also possible that the withdrawal of a reservation becomes operative *on the date established* by the reserving State or international organization, whenever: *a*) that date is subsequent to the date on which the other contracting States or contracting organizations received the relevant notification; or *b*) the withdrawal does not add to the rights of the withdrawing State or international organization, in relation to the other contracting States or contracting organizations (Guideline 2.5.9).

306 In the latter case, it should be noted that there is a *new* legal relation between the objecting State (which had previously *opposed* the entry into force of the treaty between it and the reserving State) and the reserving State, which starts as from the time when reservation withdrawal produces effects. See Guideline 2.5.7, item 2, of the ILC *Guide*.

307 See Guideline 2.7.5 of the ILC *Guide*.

308 According to the ILC *Guide*, it is a presumption: "A State or an international organization that withdraws an objection formulated to a reservation is *presumed* to *have accepted* that reservation" (Guideline 2.7.4).

graphs (a) and (b) of Art. 22, item 3, are not the same, since, in the first case, the withdrawal of a reservation modifies the relation of the reserving State with all the other parties to the treaty, while, in the second case, the withdrawal of an objection to a reservation modifies the relation only between the objecting State and the reserving State, for which the reservation effects (now accepted, not objected any longer) shall be valid *ex nunc*.

The fact of a State formally withdrawing a reservation or an objection is unusual. However, it is not discarded that constitutional changes, political regime alterations, succession of States and participation in human rights and humanitarian issues may cause the use of the power provided for in Art. 22 of the Convention.[309]

Would it be possible to *partially* withdraw a reservation? Now, if it is possible to withdraw a reservation in *full*, it would also be possible to amend it for the purpose of *limiting* its scope; and it seems logical when it is true that *he who can do more, can do less* ("Cui licet quod est plus, licet utique quod est minus").[310] Although the 1969 Vienna Convention missed the point, the ILC *Guide* understood that the partial withdrawal of a reservation is fully possible, providing as follows: "1. The partial withdrawal of a reservation limits the legal effect of the reservation and achieves a more complete application of the provisions of the treaty, or of the treaty as a whole, in the relations between the withdrawing State or international organization and the other parties to the treaty. 2. The partial withdrawal of a reservation is subject to the same rules on form and procedure as a total withdrawal and becomes operative on the same conditions" (Guideline 2.5.10). The ILC *Guide* provided the following on the *effects* of a partial withdrawal of a reservation: "The partial withdrawal of a reservation modifies the legal effect of the reservation to the extent provided by the new formulation of the reservation. Any objection formulated to the reservation continues to have effect as long as its author does not withdraw it, insofar as the objection does not apply exclusively to that part of the reservation which has been withdrawn. 2. No new objection may be for-

---

309 See Remiro Brotons, Antonio. *Derecho internacional público*, vol. 2, cit., p. 229; and Villiger, Mark E., *Commentary on the 1969 Vienna Convention on the Law of Treaties*, cit., p. 307. This last author takes the example of the fall of the Berlin Wall, in 1989, to show when several Eastern Europe States withdrew their reservations to Art. 66 of the 1969 Vienna Convention (for example, Bulgaria, on 6 May 1994).

310 In that very sense, see Remiro Brotons, Antonio, *Derecho internacional público*, vol. 2, cit., p. 229.

mulated to the reservation resulting from the partial withdrawal, unless that partial withdrawal has a discriminatory effect" (Guideline 2.5.11).[311]

Finally, it should be mentioned that the *notice* required for the withdrawal of a reservation or an objection is usually given by the *depositary* of the treaty (Art. 77, item 1, *e*; Art. 78).

2.11 Interpretation of reservations

At different moments in time, reservations may be made, as already mentioned (see item 2.4, above). They may be formulated upon *signature*, upon *Parliament approval* of the text, upon *ratification*, and upon *accession* as well. At any such moments there is a specific *legal order*, which may not be the same as when the validity of the reservation under analysis is objected before a given court.

It remains to know whether reservations made will have to be interpreted in light of the current law or of the law applicable at the time when they were formulated (or objected).

For consistency and legal certainty reasons, reservations shall be interpreted in light of the law applicable *at the time* of their formulation (or their objection).[312] The current law (at the time of the assessment of reservation validity) does not offer elements to know the *intentions* of the State to be released from the application of a certain provision of the treaty, nor if at the time of its formulation (or objection) that State was breaching any international rule precluding it from formulating the reservation (or objection) concerned. Only by assessing the reservation in light of the law applicable at the time of its formulation may it be determined, more accurately, whether it was (at that time) a true *reservation* or if the statement of the State was a mere *interpretative declaration*, without any legal effect.

In any case, reservations are to be interpreted in good faith, taking into account the intention of the reserving State reflected primarily in the text of the reservation, as well as the object and purpose of the treaty and the circumstances in which the reservation was formulated.[313]

---

311 The ILC *Guide* also allowed the partial withdrawal of an objection upon regulation of the subject in Guidelines 2.7.7 and 2.7.8.

312 See *International Law Reports*, vol. 54 (1979), p. 42; and Shaw, Malcolm N., *Direito internacional*, cit., p. 681, note 62.

313 See Guideline 4.2.6 of the ILC *Guide*.

2.12 The problem of reservations (and amendments) at the internal level

Once the international agreement is signed, it is internally submitted for the approval of the Legislative Power (see Part V, Ch. 1, below). There have been long discussions on the matter in order to determine whether, once the text of the signed treaty is sent to Parliament, this body can reject the approval of certain provisions contained in the agreement, or if it should only accept it or reject it its entirety.[314]

In our judgment, the National Congress can formulate *reservations* to a treaty. The concept of reservation outlined in Art. 2, item 1(d), of the 1969 Convention defines it as "a unilateral statement, however phrased or named, made by a State, when signing, ratifying, accepting, *approving* or acceding to a treaty, whereby it purports to exclude or to modify the legal effect of certain provisions of the treaty in their application to that State". As can be read in the transcribed provision, reservations may be made upon *approval* of the treaty, which is done by the National Congress after the signature of the agreement. Thus, it may be concluded that the 1969 Convention itself authorizes reservations made by the Legislative Power. In its turn, the ILC *Guide* also allows for reservations to be formulated at the internal level, when providing that: "The competent authority and the procedure to be followed at the internal level for formulating a reservation are determined by the internal law of each State..." (Guideline 2.1.4, item 1).

What National Congress cannot do is *to amend* the treaty submitted for its consideration,[315] since it is known in general international law that the signature (which closes the negotiation stage) means that the treaty cannot be modified, unless the parties execute *another treaty* on the same subject.[316] On the other hand, from the point of view of internal law, an amendment made by Congress to the text of a treaty is an undue interference of Parliament in matters falling within the competence of the Executive, which breaches the harmony and independence of Powers (guaranteed by the Constitution). This conclusion seems logical, since one should wonder upon which grounds a State could by itself amend a treaty ne-

---

314 For the discussion on the subject in Spanish law, see Remiro Brotons, Antonio, *Derecho internacional público*, vol. 2, cit., p. 233-238.

315 See Rangel, Vicente Marotta. Emendas dos tratados internacionais, in Cachapuz de Medeiros, Antônio Paulo (org.), *Pareceres dos consultores jurídicos do Itamaraty*, vol. IX (1990-2000), Brasília: Fundação Alexandre de Gusmão, 2009, p. 90-91.

316 See Pereira de Araújo, João Hermes. *A processualística dos atos internacionais*, cit., p. 190.

gotiated with many other subjects of Public International Law. In other words, how would it be explained, from a diplomatic point of view, that the Legislative may (unilaterally) amend provisions of a treaty concluded by the Executive with other foreign Powers? It is clear that the Legislative Power was not entitled to *mutilate* the conventional text submitted for its consideration, which would amount to confer the National Congress the powers to negotiate treaties, removing from such position the officer who is really empowered to perform such an act (this is, the President of the Republic). Now, an international treaty is the result of a great deal of negotiations in which governments participate and reach a final conclusion on all its terms and conditions. After long conferences, discussions and mutual concessions made by the several participating States, having weighed and consolidated the proposals of each of the parties, the international agreement is signed as a consequence of the joint will of *all* the parties. Therefore, the Legislative Power, when called upon to consider the treaty, cannot unduly interfere with the affairs of the Executive, approving with amendments the treaty concluded at the international level.[317] Thus, the amendment to articles, with the replacement of words in the text or the mere elimination of a comma interferes in the task that was carried by *consensus omnium* and constituted the whole homogeneous and unchangeable treaty.[318] The expression contained in Art. 49(I) of the 1988 Brazilian Constitution, namely, "to decide definitively on international treaties" is not to be understood in such a manner. Furthermore, the very nature of treaties does not allow one of the contracting parties to amend it unilaterally. The legal value of a parliamentary approval with amendments is, then, that of a tacit or indirect rejection of the treaty. In other words, the fact that the Constitution reserved to the National Congress the final decision on treaties means that the approval of a treaty with amendments (namely, with articles that were not included in the original text negotiated by the contracting parties) is no longer final, this being understood as a rejection of the agreement, leaving the President of the Republic the chance, at his discretion, to start new negotiations (which is obviously very difficult to occur when dealing with multilateral acts).[319]

---

317 See Campos, Francisco. *Direito constitucional*, vol. II. Rio de Janeiro: Freitas Bastos, 1956, p. 308.

318 See Pereira de Araújo, João Hermes. *A processualística dos atos internacionais*, cit., p. 196-197.

319 Brazil maintain that stance since the first republican Constitution. See Barbalho, João, *Constituição Federal Brasileira: comentários*, 2. ed. (revised and extended), Rio de Ja-

In summary, given that the Executive Power is entitled to entertain international relations, and that the treaty has been negotiated by its Head or its plenipotentiaries at the international level, and is the result of the concurrence of wills of the participating countries, when its text is submitted to the consideration of the Parliament for its approval, there exists no possibility that the latter *amends* its content, since State Parties are not empowered to amend an international agreement, subsequently or unilaterally, because such an act would amount to the renegotiation of the treaty with the participation of the other States Parties, which is only possible from a constitutional point of view, by means of an act of the President of the Republic, who is entitled to "conclude international treaties, conventions and acts" (Art. 84, VIII, Federal Constitution/88). In the United States, in 1936, the Supreme Court decided, in the case "United States *v.* Curtiss-Wright Export Corp", that the Senate, the competent body for the approval of treaties in that country, has no powers to encroach on the competence of the Executive Power, which is entitled to carry out international negotiations. This does not refrain the Executive from requesting an "opinion" from the Senate if necessary, although it is not a constitutional obligation to do so.[320]

However, the scenario changes with regard to *reservations*. As the latter consist of the exclusion or modification of the *legal effects* of certain provisions of the treaty relating to the reserving State, no problem arises if they are made by the Legislative, provided that they are admissible. The President of the Republic shall then decide, at his/her discretion, whether to ratify or not the treaty approved with reservations. Another possible assumption includes the case in which the treaty itself explicitly allows the formulation of reservations upon ratification (as authorized by the 1969 Vienna Convention). In this case, could the National Congress approve the international treaty *sub conditione*, conditioning the President of the Republic to formulate a specified reservation upon final commitment? There is no impediment for the Congress to act like this, but the Head of the Executive will be entitled to ratify the treaty or not in this case, mainly if he understands that the Parliament encroached on her/his discretionary powers regarding the entertaining of international relations of the State.

---

neiro: F. Briguiet Editores, 1924, p. 150. See also Mello, Celso D. de Albuquerque, Os tratados na Constituição, in *Tendências atuais do direito público: estudos em homenagem ao Professor Afonso Arinos de Melo Franco*, Rio de Janeiro: Forense, 1976, p. 158-159.

320 See Mello, Celso D. de Albuquerque. *Direito constitucional internacional*..., cit., p. 307.

Apart from formulating reservations, could the National Congress also *separate* or *eliminate* a specified reservation formulated by the Head of State upon the signature of the agreement? According to Joao Hermes Pereira de Araújo, if reservations were made by the government upon signature "the Congress is not entitled to disregard them".[321] Nevertheless, current Brazilian practice has shown that neither the National Congress is under the obligation to simply approve a treaty, nor the President of the Republic questions the powers of National Congress to formulate reservations or abandon them, as it may deem convenient. In the latter case, if the President of the Republic agrees to the suppression of the reservations by the Congress, he/she will not confirm the reservations in question upon ratification (as she/he should do, under Art. 23, item 2, of the 1969 Vienna Convention, in the event that the Congress did not eliminate the reservations and the President considers that the reservations concerned should be maintained). Therefore, Rezek understands that there is no convincing argument from a legal viewpoint that justifies the thesis that Congress approval can only apply to the treaty concerned in its entirety.[322]

In case the reservation is made by another contracting party, the Executive Power seems entitled to accept it or to validate it, without the approval of the National Congress, since when the Legislative approves an international commitment, it does that in full, including permissive articles of reservations. It would even be rather difficult for the National Congress to consider all the reservations formulated by the other States Parties, particularly when dealing with treaties that have more than one hundred parties. A State reserving a certain provision of the agreement can also withdraw it later, as the case may be, with the conventional text reverting to its original wording. This is because the reservation is a restriction to the agreement and its withdrawal reestablishes the initial content of the treaty. Finally, it would even be incongruous to cause the Parliament to consider conventional text in cases of limited application of the treaty by *other* State Party.[323]

2.13 Addendum: consideration of the matter of reservations and interpretative declarations in case of succession of States

The last item of the ILC *Guide* to Practice on Reservations to Treaties deals with the *Legal effects of reservations, acceptances and objections and*

[321] Pereira de Araújo, Joao Hermes. *A processualística dos atos internacionais*, cit., p. 198.

[322] See Rezek, José Francisco. *Direito dos tratados*, cit., p. 347-348.

[323] See Mello, Celso D. de Albuquerque. *Direito constitucional internacional...*, cit., p. 296-297.

interpretative declarations in cases of succession of States.[324] This is a relevant issue that needs attention, especially for not having been included in the Vienna Convention on the Law of Treaties, which nevertheless clarified that its provisions shall not prejudge "any question that may arise in regard to a treaty *from a succession of States...*" (Art. 73). However, Art. 20 of the Vienna Convention on Succession of States in respect of Treaties, dated August 23, 1978 covered that subject. It is true, however, that the ILC *Guide* went further than the latter in trying to codify the full practice of States on reservations and interpretative declarations in cases of succession of States.

The subjects covered by the *Guide* include matters, which range from newly independent States (Guideline 5.1.1), uniting or separation of States (Guideline 5.1.2), to the irrelevance of certain reservations in cases involving a uniting of States (Guideline 5.1.3), the principle of maintenance of the territorial scope of reservations formulated by the predecessor State (Guideline 5.1.4), the territorial scope of reservations in cases involving a uniting of States (Guideline 5.1.5), the territorial scope of reservations of the successor State in cases of succession involving part of territory (Guideline 5.1.6), the timing of the effects of non-maintenance by a successor State of a reservation formulated by the predecessor State (Guideline 5.1.7), as well as the late formulation of a reservation by a successor State (Guideline 5.1.8). Another part of the Guide touches upon objections to reservations in cases of succession of States (Guideline 5.2), acceptances of reservations in cases of succession of States (Guideline 5.3), legal effects of reservations, acceptances and objections in cases of succession of States (Guideline 5.4), as well as the interpretative declarations in cases of succession of States (Guideline 5.5).

[324] See *Annex V*, item 5 of this book.

Chapter 3

Entry into Force of Treaties

3.1 Entry into force and provisional application of treaties

The entry into force of treaties takes place at the *territorial* and *temporal* levels. At the *territorial* level, the principle established in the Vienna Convention (Art. 34) states that "[A] treaty does not create either obligations or rights for a third State without its consent". Such rule has some exceptions, which will be discussed later (see Part III, Ch. 1, item 1.2, below). At this point only the entry into force of treaties from a *temporal* perspective and its legal regulation shall be studied, followed by an analysis of its *provisional application*.

It should also be clarified that the importance of the analysis that is about to be made is also related to the *entry into force* of treaties at the national level, since it is a *conditio sine qua non* for treaties to be applied at the national level that they have already entered into force at the international level. This subject will be discussed again below (see Part V, Ch. 1, item 1.8).

3.1.1 Entry into force of treaties

Entry *into force* means that the treaty is *fully* applicable (this is, it has *binding force*) between the contracting parties; it means that the commitment meets all the conditions to be legally enforceable, under the terms and conditions provided for in the treaty itself.[325] From a formal perspective, *contracting* States (and international organizations) become true *parties* to

[325] As Mark Villiger says, *tout court*: "With the treaty's entry into force, States are obliged to apply the treaty" (*Commentary on the 1969 Vienna Convention on the Law of Treaties*, cit., p. 343).

the inter national commitment as from the entry into force of the treaty concerned. It is true that the term *parties* has been indiscriminately used by authors to also mean the time when the definitive commitment is made (which is the time of *ratification*); but the 1969 Vienna Convention (in Art. 2, item 1, *g*) textually states that the term *party* means "a State which has consented to be bound by the treaty and *for which the treaty is in force*".

The entry into force of a treaty, which grants *full* applicability to it, does not exclude the effects that treaties have from the time of their adoption. In fact, the Vienna Convention provides that the provisions of a treaty regulating the authentication of its text, the establishment of the consent of States to be bound by the treaty, the manner or date of its entry into force, reservations, the functions of the depositary and other matters arising necessarily before the entry into force of the treaty apply from the time of the adoption of its text (Art. 24, item 4). As already discussed (in this Part II, Ch. 1, item 1.4.2), treaties, although not into force yet, *do produce certain effects* from the time of their adoption, even though they do not have the effect of a legal *rule* on the signatory States. One of such effects relates to the immediate applicability of the *final articles* of the treaty, as provided for in Art. 24, item 4, of the Convention, which does not deal with any *substantive* question of the treaty, but only its status as a *legal act*.[326] Likewise, the statement that the entry into force of a treaty grants full applicability to it does not reduce the chance that the treaty be applied on a *provisional basis* (see item 3.1.2, below).[327]

When does a treaty enter into force? The answer can be found in Art. 24, item 1, of the Vienna Convention, according to which "a treaty enters into force in such manner and upon such date as it may provide or as the negotiating States may agree".[328] As can be seen, the entry into force of a treaty is not a *legal act*, but a *legal fact* resulting from a combination of

---

326 As pointed out by De La Guardia, item 4 of Art. 24 of the Convention is based on logic and reason, given that "a treaty could never enter into force if some provisions, precisely aimed at causing such entry into force, are not applied *before* such entry into force" (*Derecho de los tratados internacionales*, cit., p. 168).

327 See Remiro Brotons, Antonio. *Derecho internacional público*, vol. 2, cit., p. 243.

328 For details, see Maresca, Adolfo, *Il diritto dei trattati...*, cit., p. 229-237; Nascimento e Silva, Geraldo Eulálio do, Le facteur temps et les traités, cit., p. 226-229; Sinclair, Ian, *The Vienna Convention on the Law of Treaties*, cit., p. 44-47; Thirlway, Hugh, The law and procedure of the International Court of Justice, 1960-1989 (Part Four), cit., p. 32 and following ones; and Villiger, Mark E., *Commentary on the 1969 Vienna Convention on the Law of Treaties*, cit., p. 342-348.

legal acts by the parties or the terms provided by them.[329] Therefore, *when* and *how* an international act will enter into force depends on the conventional *provision* itself or the *agreement* reached by negotiating States. Failing any such provision or agreement, the Convention provides (by means of a rule of residual character) that a treaty only enters into force as soon as consent to be bound by the treaty has been "established for *all* the negotiating States" (Art. 24, item 2). Consequently, there exist two basic rules for a treaty to enter into force: (*a*) either the treaty enters into force on the date provided for in its text or agreed upon by negotiating States, (*b*) or, residually, it enters into force (failing any such provision) when *all* the negotiating States express their final consent.

With regards to *bilateral* treaties, the rule for their entry into force is the aforementioned *residual* rule: without the consent of *both* contracting States, there is no entry into force of treaties. The same rule also applies to (almost all, but not exclusively) *closed* multilateral treaties; many of them providing that only the consent expressed by *all* contracting parties to the treaty will cause the treaty to enter into force for all the contracting parties.[330]

Regarding *general* or *open* multilateral treaties, a number of techniques have been used regarding their entry into force. The first one indicates the *exact* date of entry into force in the treaty. The second one provides a *minimum number* of ratifications for the entry into force of the treaty, such as the UN Charter in Art. 110, item 3, which required the deposit of the ratifications of five permanent Members of the future Security Council and of the majority of the other signatory States. The third technique establishes the lapse of a *certain period of time* for the treaty to enter into force at the international level (*vacatio legis*) upon ratification; in this case, the effectiveness of the treaty will not be immediate, but deferred, which means that even if it is internally promulgated and published, the international commitment does not bind yet the State Party, before the expiry of the time period provided for therein. There is still a fourth technique of entry into force, which combines the minimum number of ratifications with certain *vacatio legis*, as in the case of the Vienna Convention on the Law of Treaties, whose Art. 84, item 1 expressly states that the Convention shall entry into force on the thirtieth day following the date of deposit of the thirty-fifth instrument of ratification or accession; the *condition*, in this case, was

---

329 See De La Guardia, Ernesto. *Derecho de los tratados internacionales*, cit., p. 144.

330 See Remiro Brotons, Antonio. *Derecho internacional público*, vol. 2, cit., p. 244.

that the treaty was ratified or acceded at least by *thirty-five* State Parties, plus a period of *thirty days* after implementation of the aforementioned thirty-five instruments of ratification of accession.[331] All such techniques aim at circumventing the *residual* rule set forth in the 1969 Convention, taking into account that consent by all States may be very difficult (or perhaps impossible) to be established in connection with some treaties, which would imply that many of them would *never* enter into force.

When the consent of a State to be bound by a treaty is established on a date after the treaty has come into force, the treaty enters into force for that State on that date, unless the treaty otherwise provides (Art. 24, item 3). This provision adopts, as can be noticed, the system of a staged entry into force, only possible in multilateral treaties. This is very frequent in the event of *accession* of States to a treaty already in force, but where the treaty does not provide otherwise will enter into force on the date of accession of the respective State. This is also the case when a treaty enters into force after reaching the minimum number required and is later ratified by a given State (since the treaty, although into force for the original States, was not already valid for the State that had not ratified it); therefore, the treaty will enter into force for the aforementioned State upon such ratification. Consequently, that is the rule established by the Vienna Convention, but nothing prevents the treaty concerned "from providing otherwise", as authorized by Art. 24, item 3, *in fine*. In such regard, many treaties frequently include a *vacatio legis* provision for the entry into force of the instrument in the State after the date of final commitment (ratification, accession, etc.). This is the case of the Vienna Convention on the Law of Treaties itself, which establishes, in Art. 84, item 2, the following rule: "For each State ratifying or acceding to the Convention after the deposit of the thirty-fifth instrument of ratification or accession, the Convention shall enter into force on the thirtieth day after deposit by such State of its instrument of ratification or accession".

As can be noted, the effectiveness of international treaties produces effects *ex nunc* (*pro futuro*), and these may be: (*a*) contemporary to consent, as it occurs in agreements by exchange of notes or in *executive agreements*; or (*b*) deferred (delayed) to a future time, in those cases in which

---

331 As a more recent example, the Rome Statute of the ICC, of 1998 may be quoted when providing that "[t]his Statute shall enter into force on the first day of the month after the 60th day following the date of the deposit of the 60th instrument of ratification, acceptance, approval or accession with the Secretary-General of the United Nations" (Art. 126, item 1).

(*i*) a certain adequacy period is required before the entry into force of the treaty (*vacatio legis*), or (*ii*) if a certain number of ratifications should be carried for the treaty to enter into force.[332]

3.1.2 Provisional application of treaties

If the treaty itself so provides, or if the negotiating States have in some other manner so agreed, the treaty, or a part of a treaty may be *provisionally* applied until its formal entry into force (Art. 25, item 1, (a) and (b)).[333] This is a common practice at the diplomatic level, widely accepted by States in general, especially by reason of the celerity which allows the fulfillment of the treaty while it is not in force (see below).

However, such permission for the provisional application of a treaty does not convert the treaty into an agreement in simplified form. According to the most authoritative legal academic writing such provisional application "is necessary by virtue of the urgency discretionarily considered by negotiating States, but it still continues to be a lengthy process, with States expressing their consent to be bound by the treaty upon signature".[334]

The importance daily gained by the provisional application of treaties has shown to be a good solution to the problems of entry into force of treaties, particularly with regard to the delay in the obtainment of an internal approval; it is also useful in the case of such treaties whose object attracts the special attention of States, in which case their ratification is deemed practically evident. In addition, international practice has shown that several matters (such as issues relating to transport, cooperation, trade, fishing, technology transfer and many others) need to be quickly solved by States, and cannot depend on the delay or internal bureaucracy of each of the contracting parties. This is why negotiators have the powers to incorporate in the text of treaty (or in some other manner) that it will be *provisionally* applied, while it is not formally in force. As pointed out by Brotons, provisional application of treaties

---

332 See Rezek, José Francisco. *Direito dos tratados*, cit., p. 363.

333 See Maresca, Adolfo. *Il diritto dei trattati…*, cit., p. 239-243; Nascimento e Silva, Geraldo Eulálio do, Le facteur temps et les traités, cit., p. 229-235; Remiro Brotons, Antonio, *Derecho internacional público*, vol. 2, cit., p. 248-253; De La Guardia, Ernesto, *Derecho de los tratados internacionales*, cit., p. 168-169; Villiger, Mark E., *Commentary on the 1969 Vienna Convention on the Law of Treaties*, cit., p. 352-358; and Mertsch, Anneliese Quast, *Provisionally applied treaties: their binding force and legal nature*, Leiden: Brill, 2012, 276p.

334 Dinh, Daillier & Pellet. *Direito internacional público*, cit., p. 166.

still offers a reasonable alternative to *defective ratifications* (see Part III, Ch. 2, item 2.3, below), this being the reason why States such as Netherlands and Switzerland, whose constitutional systems formally establish the Parliament authorization for the conclusion *all* or *almost all* treaties (*negative list* system), are among the first countries to resort to that kind of application.[335] In summary, the provisional application of international treaties, although being a practice not very much used yet by most countries, in many of them (such as Brazil) due to constitutional impediments (see below), serves to solve practical problems involving urgency or need of the State for the treaty to be immediately *applicable* at its internal legal system.[336]

In general, the *provisional* application of a treaty occurs from the date on which of the text was *adopted* or from an immediately subsequent date (for example, after thirty days as from adoption, etc.). According to the Convention, the provisional application of a treaty will be also possible "in some other manner so agreed" (Art. 25, item 1, *b*). Therefore, even if it is not provided for in the treaty itself, its entry into force may occur, for example, through a simultaneous or subsequent protocol or exchange of notes.[337]

It should be noted that such rules of the Vienna Convention (Art. 25, items (1) and (2) do not deal with the possibility that the treaty be provisionally *in force*, but rather with its provisional *application* (more precisely while the treaty has not yet entered into *force*).[338] It is true that the ILC used the expression "provisional entry into force" in the preliminary works of the Convention (having Waldock so defended until the last minute); but the final text of the Convention, following the proposals of Czechoslovakia and Yugoslavia, abandoned the aforementioned expression to refer to the "provisional *application*" of treaties.[339] It seems from the above that, the fact that a treaty is *in force* (always final, permanent)

---

335 Remiro Brotons, Antonio. *Derecho internacional público*, vol. 2, cit., p. 249.

336 See De La Guardia, Ernesto. *Derecho de los tratados internacionales*, cit., p. 168.

337 See Remiro Brotons, Antonio. *Derecho internacional público*, vol. 2, cit., p. 249.

338 Therefore, it is not right to call the case under analysis "provisional *effectiveness*", as Rezek does (see *Direito dos tratados*, cit., p. 368 et seq.). Besides, it is not right to state that a treaty "shall enter into *force*, provisionally, as from the date of signature..." as provided for in the Trade Agreement between the Government of Brazil and the Government of China in 1978, promulgated by Executive Order 83,282, dated 03.13.1979.

339 See De La Guardia, Ernesto. *Derecho de los tratados internacionales*, cit., p. 168.

is clearly differentiated from its *provisional application*; also the intention was to clear up the inaccuracy that treaties enter into force twice.[340]

Each of the contracting parties is entitled to unilaterally *terminate* the provisional application of a given treaty, provided that the other contracting parties are *notified* of its intention *not to become a party* to it. The hypothesis is contemplated under Art. 25, item 2, of the Convention, as follows: "Unless the treaty otherwise provides or the negotiating States and negotiating organizations or, as the case may be, the negotiating organizations have otherwise agreed, the provisional application of a treaty or a part of a treaty with respect to a State or an international organization shall be terminated if that State or that organization notifies the States and organizations with regard to which the treaty is being applied provisionally of its intention not to become a party to the treaty". This provision, as pointed out by Villiger, offers special protection to the State whose Legislative Power did not approve the treaty that is being provisionally applied.[341] Nevertheless, that provision states nothing about the effects (whether they are deemed *ex tunc* or *ex nunc*) of termination of the provisional application of the treaty concerned, although the issue had been raised at the Vienna Conference (by the Argentinean delegate) in the Drafting Commission. How can this issue be solved? According to De La Guardia, "the only solution possible is to regulate the acts performed during the provisional application period of a treaty already terminated by applying general principles of International Law".[342]

In Brazil, the provisional application of treaties, as governed by the 1969 Convention, contravenes the wording of the constitutional text, which imposes the submission of *all* treaties concluded by the President of the Republic to National Congress (Arts. 49, I and 84, Federal Constitution/88), this being the reason by which the Brazilian Congress formulated a reservation in respect of Art. 25 of the Vienna Convention by means of the Legislative Decree 496/2009, which approved the Convention in the country; upon *ratification* of the Convention in Brazil, the same reserva-

---

340 See Remiro Brotons, Antonio. *Derecho internacional público*, vol. 2, cit., p. 250.

341 Villiger, Mark E. *Commentary on the 1969 Vienna Convention on the Law of Treaties*, cit., p. 355.

342 De La Guardia, Ernesto. *Derecho de los tratados internacionales*, cit., p. 169. According to Mark Villiger: "(...) the results of any notification will be *ex nunc* rather than *ex tunc* (unless the treaty provides differently). Article 25 thus corresponds with the general regime of the Convention concerning the effects of termination of a treaty (*Article 70, q.v.*)". (*Commentary on the 1969 Vienna Convention on the Law of Treaties*, cit., p. 356).

tion was confirmed (and notified to the United Nations) by the President of the Republic. What Brazil did, followed by many other States, was to avoid a possible *surprise* as to the commitment (even though provisional) of the country at the international level, which could certainly lead to an extremely uncomfortable situation. In brief, in Brazil a signed (but still unratified) treaty cannot provisionally enter into force, by reason of the Brazilian reservation to Art. 25 of the Convention.

3.2 Registration and publication of treaties

All international treaties, concluded by any member of the United Nations, shall be *registered* and *published* by the Secretariat of the UN.[343] It is what the 1945 UN Charter provides in Art. 102, item 1, according to which "[e]very treaty and every international agreement entered into by any Member of the United Nations after the present Charter [i.e., after October 24, 1945] comes into force shall as soon as possible be registered with the Secretariat and published by it", adding that no party to an unregistered treaty "may invoke that treaty or agreement before any organ of the United Nations" (item 2). It is a widely accepted practice by Member States of the United Nations and it may be considered as a rule of customary International Law.[344]

This rule is clearly aimed at discouraging (and afterwards proscribing) the old diplomatic practice of the so-called *secret agreements*, or even those agreements which, albeit not fully secret, intend to contain certain *secret articles*,[345] seeking to give transparency to international acts and facilitating

343 On the subject, see McNair, Arnold Duncan, *The law of treaties*, cit., p. 178-190; Maresca, Adolfo, *Il diritto dei trattati…*, cit., p. 259-266; Piombo, Horacio Daniel, *Teoría general de la publicidad y tratados internacionales: análisis normativo, fáctico y dikelógico*, Buenos Aires: Depalma, 1977, p. 134; Rodas, João Grandino, *A publicidade dos tratados internacionais*, São Paulo: Revista dos Tribunais, 1980, p. 83-139; Aust, Anthony, *Modern treaty law and practice*, cit., p. 275-284; and Villiger, Mark E., *Commentary on the 1969 Vienna Convention on the Law of Treaties*, cit., p. 972-976.

344 See Villiger, Mark E. *Commentary on the 1969 Vienna Convention on the Law of Treaties*, cit., p. 976.

345 In *Projeto de Código de Direito Internacional Público* (1911) by Epitácio Pessoa, the possibility of secret articles was expressly mentioned in Art. 202, that reads as follows: "Treaties will be published, *except* the part agreed to be confidential". On the subject, see Mazzuoli, Valerio de Oliveira, Apontamentos sobre o direito dos tratados no Projeto de Código de Direito Internacional Público de Epitácio Pessoa, cit., p. 518-519.

access to these sources.[346] It seems that the Brazilian republican constitutionalism has followed such understanding, since Brazilian Constitutions (even the current one) do not include rules releasing such treaties concerning "the interest and safety of State" from being considered by the Legislative Power, as provided for in the Imperial Constitution (of 1824) in Art. 102, item 8.

The rule provided for in Art. 102 of the UN Charter was also contained in Art. 18 of the 1919 Covenant of the League of Nations, which established as follows:

> "Every treaty or international engagement entered into hereafter by any Member of the League shall be forthwith registered with the Secretariat and shall as soon as possible be published by it. No such treaty or international engagement shall be binding until so registered".

The last phrase included in Art. 18 of the Covenant of the League of Nations (which does not recognize treaties not registered with League Secretariat any binding effects) is no longer present in the current system of the United Nations, which only provides that no party to a unregistered treaty "may invoke that treaty or agreement before any organ of the United Nations", without any reference to the non-binding effects of such a treaty or agreement. This means that, in the current system of international acts procedure, unregistered treaties do *not lose* their binding nature (as it was at the time of the League of Nations), the only adverse effect being that they cannot be invoked before any organ of the United Nations.[347] In other words, it does not mean that the treaty which has not been registered with the Secretariat may be disregarded by the parties or that it is void,[348] but that if such treaty were disregarded or breached, those parties might not resort to the United Nations system (such as, for example, the ICJ) to enforce the conventional obligation agreed upon and not complied with, not

---

346 See Brownlie, Ian. *Princípios de direito internacional público*, cit., p. 636. Also on secret treaties, see Remiro Brotons, Antonio, *Derecho internacional público*, vol. 2, cit., p. 253-258.

347 See Brierly, J. L. *Direito internacional*, cit., p. 331-332; and Fitzmaurice, Malgosia & Elias, Olufemi, *Contemporary issues in the law of treaties*, cit., p. 22-25. For an opposing view, see Hurd, Ian, *International organizations: politics, law, practice*, Cambridge: Cambridge University Press, 2011, p. 101, which says: "In other words, no treaty that contradicts the UN Charter *or that is not put on deposit with the Secretary-General is considered legally binding*" [emphasis added].

348 The ICJ, in the case *Qatar v. Bahrein*, confirmed that failure to record the treaty with the UN Secretariat does not affect the factual validity of the treaty, or its binding condition. See *ICJ Reports* (1994), p. 115-121.

being excluded the possibility that the parties have their dispute settled by having resort to other venues, such as, for instance, arbitration.

The subject of binding effects of treaties not registered with the ICJ, was already discussed by such court again and again, and a final solution was never reached.[349] As noted by Rezek, the Court already understood (in the case of the *Minquiers and Ecréhous Islands,* of 1953) that the unregistered convention could be cited by one of the parties, as a supplementary means of shedding light on the legal issue at hand, but not invoked by the same parties, since invoking the treaty at issue before the Court would lead to the idea that that treaty could serve as a basis in support of their arguments. It happens that, years later, in the *South West Africa* cases (1962), when making reference to the registration system of the League of Nations, judges Bustamante and Jessup (in opposition to judges Spender and Fitzmautice) supported that an unregistered treaty could indeed be *invoked* by the parties in proceedings before the Court, provided that, the parties have made it public by any proper means.[350] As can be noticed, the fact remains that the Court may not effectively *apply* an unregistered treaty, since the UN Charter, which has a higher hierarchy than the other treaties, provided such *penalty* for those States which fail to register their treaties with the Secretariat pursuant to the provisions of Art. 103.

The registration of treaties with the UN Secretariat, apart from disclosing the series number and the date of registration of the treaty with the Collection of Treaties (*Recueil des Traités*) of the United Nations, also informs the other parties to the agreement the form of their entry into force. As far as the procedural aspect is concerned, it should be pointed out that such registration is carried out in the official languages of the United Nations, with detailed references to the treaty, being the texts even initialed with the *ne variatur* of the Secretariat.[351]

Reference to the *treaty* and to an *international agreement* made by Art. 102 of the constituent treaty of the United Nations aimed at, as highlighted by Guido Soares, terminating diplomatic practices that had led the world to absolute disasters: for such reasons, by making reference to *treaty* and *international agreement*, it was intended to make it really clear (in the original English text) that any norm-setting act between States,

---

349 See Reuter, Paul. *Introducción al derecho de los tratados*, cit., p. 90.

350 See Rezek, José Francisco. *Direito dos tratados*, cit., p. 378 and note 621; and McNair, Arnold Duncan, *The law of treaties*, cit., p. 186-187.

351 See Pereira de Araújo, João Hermes. *A processualística dos atos internacionais*, cit., p. 283.

ranging from the most formal ones according to the Constitutional Law of countries, to the least formal ones, are subject to registration with the UN Secretariat, under the penalties of not being capable of being invoked before any organ of United Nations.[352]

The rule set forth in Art. 102, item 1, of the UN Charter was confirmed by the Vienna Convention on the Law of Treaties (Art. 80, item 1) under the following terms:

> "Treaties shall, after their entry into force, be transmitted to the Secretariat of the United Nations for registration or filing and recording, as the case may be, and for publication".

Just as the rule established in the UN Charter, the Vienna Convention provision also aims at notifying the other contracting parties that a given State already incorporated the text of the ratified treaty into its internal law. For the purpose of avoiding the registration of treaties that finally do not enter into force, the 1969 Vienna Convention established that only after the entry into force of the treaty (between two or more parties) it may be sent to the United Nations Secretariat for registration, filing, recording or publication. The appointment of a *depositary* constitutes the authorization for it to perform registration, filing acts, etc. (Art. 80, item 2).[353] The provision of the Convention does not make reference either to "United Nations Member", as it can be read in the UN Charter, since the obligation to register the treaty or international agreement with the Secretariat also includes any intergovernmental organization that may possibly ratify an international agreement. Furthermore, the same understanding was also followed by the 1986 Vienna Convention (Art. 81).

The registration system of the United Nations also coexists with other minor systems, which usually occurs within international specialized agencies (such as ILO), considering their competence *ratione materiae*. At the International Labour Organization, labour international conventions are adopted by the International Labour Conference and not in other venues, being competent to register their own conventions, both with the United Nations Secretariat and with the organization, the Labour International Office. Consequently, in this case, ILO Member States are not to proceed to register those conventions with UN Secretariat, since labour

352 See Soares, Guido Fernando Silva. "Agreements" – "Executive Agreements" – "Gentlemen's Agreements", cit., p. 249.

353 See Rodas, João Grandino. *A publicidade dos tratados internacionais*, cit., p. 141-198.

international conventions are adopted *within* the organization and not in other venues.[354]

Finally, it should be highlighted that the possible registration of an international document that is not properly a *treaty*, for example a *memorandum of understanding* (MOU) between States, does not have the status of a formal conventional text (see Part I, Ch. 1, item 1.6, above).[355] In this case, registration shall be valid only as a means of publishing the act.

3.3 Observance and application of treaties

There is no doubt that treaties in force shall be *observed* by the parties; it is not a *discretionary power* of the parties, but an *obligation* imposed by the international legal system. Treaties shall be also correctly *applied*, according to the rules provided by International Law for such a purpose.

Articles 26 to 30 of the 1969 Vienna Convention govern the subject of *observance* and *application* of treaties. Both subjects have a relevant meaning for the Law of Nations, because, in fact, the success of effective execution of the agreement depends on them, which shall not be left to the will of the parties in respect of which the agreement concerned is in force and shall produce its effects.

The following items 3.3.1 and 3.3.2 will discuss issues related to observance (Arts. 26 and 27) and application (Arts. 28 to 30) of treaties, respectively.

3.3.1 Observance (or compliance) of treaties

Among the rules of general international law, the adjective "general" being included because duties are imposed on and rights are granted to *all* States, we find that the *pacta sunt servanda* rule constitutes the basis that supports the legal binding effects of treaties.[356]

---

354 See Rezek, José Francisco. *Direito dos tratados*, cit., p. 380.

355 See Aust, Anthony. *Modern treaty law and practice*, cit., p. 29.

356 See Waldock, Humphrey [Special Rapporteur], *Yearbook of the International Law Commission* (1964), vol. II, p. 7-8; and *ICJ Reports* (1966), reproduced in the *American Journal of International Law*, vol. 61 (1967), p. 334. See also Whitton, John B., La règle *Pacta sunt servanda, Recueil des Cours*, vol. 49 (1934-III), p. 147-276; and, already under the protection of the 1969 Vienna Convention, De La Guardia, Ernesto, *Derecho de los tratados internacionales*, cit., p. 193-195; and Villiger, Mark E., *Commentary on the 1969 Vienna Convention on the Law of Treaties*, cit., p. 363-368.

> "Since men, human groups, tribes, ancient States entered into agreements or treaties among them (*pacts*), morals, human reasoning or natural laws were imposed on them *to be complied with*. In the field of Roman natural law, Cicero (*De oficiis*) is credited with coining the expression *pacta sunt servanda*, soon transmitted to medieval scholastic Christian natural law, as well as to rationalist jus naturalists, being later accepted as a rule of customary law; and, in our time, as an *fundamental rule* of the Law of Treaties".
> De La Guardia, Ernesto. *Derecho de los tratados internacionales*, cit., p. 193.

The 1969 Vienna Convention expressly states in Art. 26 that "[e]very treaty in force is binding upon the parties to it and must be performed by them in good faith".[357] The Convention also explains, in the *third recital* of the preamble, that the above rule is *universally* recognized.[358] Rather than an "essential principle of the Law of Treaties", as described by the ICJ and by academic writing, the rule *pacta sunt servanda* is the governing and most important rule of Public International Law.[359] Its authority appears in the case law of the ICJ, as well as in treaties of utmost importance, such as the 1945 Charter of United Nations itself (Art. 2, item 2).[360]

Based on the language of Art. 26 of the Vienna Convention it can be inferred that the obligation to comply with treaties is a necessary principle of Public International Law. This principle is said to be necessary because, without it, the security of relations among nations and international peace would be unachievable. In addition, reference made to *good faith* clearly shows the need of a balanced co-existence among States, which would not be possible without observing the rules arising from the international society.[361] The observance of a treaty in *good faith* means that subjects

---

357 Before appearing in the Vienna Convention on the Law of Treaties, the rule *pacta sunt servanda* was restricted to academic writing, not being known any text of *positive* international *law* making express reference to it before the Vienna text.

358 The Convention notes in the preamble that "the principles of free consent and of good faith and the *pacta sunt servanda* rule are universally recognized".

359 As Villiger explains, this is the "cornerstone" of international relations: "The rule *pacta sunt servanda*, that is to say, that treaties must be kept, has been applied since time immemorial (*Preamble*, N. 8) and is seen today as the *cornerstone* of international relations. Ulpian referred to it, for Grotius this principle lay at the center of the international legal system. No case is known in which a tribunal has repudiated the rule or questioned its validity" [emphasis added] (*Commentary on the 1969 Vienna Convention on the Law of Treaties*, cit., p. 363).

360 Art. 2, item 2, of the UN Charter provides: "All Members, in order to ensure to all of them the rights and benefits resulting from membership, shall fulfill in good faith the obligations assumed by them in accordance with the present Charter".

361 On the subject, see Kolb, Robert, Principles as sources of international law (with special reference to good faith), *Netherlands International Law Review*, vol. 53, No.1 (2006), p. 14-18.

shall act in such a way that the objectives pursued by the treaty may be achieved, as stated by the ICJ in the case *Gabčíkovo-Nagymaros Project* (Hungary *v.* Slovakia) of 1997.[362] In summary, Art. 26 of the 1969 Convention expressly enshrined the *legal principle* upon which international treaties are based, according to which the obligation to observe them lies in the consciousness and feelings of international justice. Since treaties are the most important source of contemporary International Law, their observance by States is the basis necessary for restoration of peace in the world and for the subsequent political and international organization of the planet.

To the extent that "*[e]very* treaty in force *is binding upon* the parties to it and *must* be performed by them in good faith" the possible breach of a treaty implies State responsibility at the international level (see item 3.4, below). As it can be noticed, the rule must be applied to *every* treaty, as well as its annexes and appendixes, without any exception.[363] It should also be pointed out that, even in countries with a totalitarian regime, there are constitutional rules governing the principle under examination. Thus, Art. 29 of the Fundamental Law of the Former Union of Soviet Socialist Republics established that "the relations of the USSR with other States" should be based "on the compliance with (…) the honest observance of the commitments resulting from universally recognized principles and rules of International Law and from international treaties concluded by the USSR".

The Conference of 1969 Vienna Convention was not satisfied with only establishing Art. 26 whereby the *pacta sunt servanda* principle is enshrined (Section 1 of Part III on *Observance of Treaties*). The general understanding was that Vienna text should not only establish that treaties are binding on *the parties* to them, but also that they should prevail over the internal Law of contracting parties, having regulated that issue in the subsequent provision. In fact, Art. 27 of the Convention, which was the immediate result of an amendment submitted by Pakistan to the UN Conference on the Law of Treaties, provides that "[a] party may not invoke the provisions of its internal law as justification for its failure to perform a treaty. This rule is without prejudice to article 46" (see Part III, Ch. 2, item 2.3.4, below). This means that, with regard to positive Public International Law, the obligation to fulfill treaties in good faith is valid

---

362 *ICJ Reports* (1997), p. 79.

363 See Villiger, Mark E. *Commentary on the 1969 Vienna Convention on the Law of Treaties*, cit., p. 365.

although there is any provision of internal Law to the contrary, whatever it may be, of a constitutional or an infra-constitutional law nature.[364] This stems from the history of Art. 27 of the Convention itself, whose wording, proposed in the UN conference on treaties, had the "declared intention to avoid that a party to a treaty might invoke the provisions of its constitution or its laws as an excuse for its failure to perform the international obligation it had undertaken".[365]

However, Art. 27 of the Convention makes an exception to the provision of Art. 46, according to which "[a] State may not invoke the fact that its consent to be bound by a treaty has been expressed in violation of a provision of its internal law regarding competence to conclude treaties as invalidating its consent unless that violation was manifest and concerned a rule of its internal law of fundamental importance" (item 1). As it can be noticed, the 1969 Vienna Convention (and Public International Law itself) is not unresponsive to the rules of internal law relating to the conclusion of treaties; it is enough to ascertain which such *internal rules* are, that are capable to invalidate the consent regarding a certain treaty.[366] The Constitution of the State is an *essential* internal set of norms, which regulates the competence of each Branch of the State concerning the conclusion of treaties (see Part III, Ch. 2, item 2.3.4, below). The only provision of Brazilian internal Law, of essential relevance, on *competence* to conclude treaties, states that the National Congress is exclusively competent to "decide conclusively on international treaties, agreements or acts which result in charges or commitments that go against the national patrimony" (Art. 49, I, Federal Constitution/88). Therefore, the only and exclusive hypothesis in which the Brazilian State may invoke the fact that its consent to be bound by a treaty was expressed in violation of a constitutional provision of its own about the competence to conclude treaties, seeking, therefore, to void the effects of such international agreement in connection with Brazil, is the one related to the fact that the treaty has been ratified without the approval of the Legislative Power (that is, in the case of *extrinsic unconstitutionality* or *defective ratification*).

---

364 Buergenthal, Thomas (*et all.*). *Manual de derecho internacional público*, cit., p. 87.

365 See *Official Records, First Session*, 29th meeting (Sir Humphrey Waldock). See also document A/Conf. 39/C.1/L. 181, in *Yearbook of the United Nations* (1968), p. 843 and following pages.

366 See Remiro Brotons, Antonio. *Derecho internacional público*, vol. 2, cit., p. 138-139; and Villiger, Mark E., *Commentary on the 1969 Vienna Convention on the Law of Treaties*, cit., p. 585-594.

Apart from this highly special case provided for in Art. 46, which concerns the *form* of the conclusion of treaties, the conflict between treaties and rules of internal Law (when *material*) is always solved by the *prevalence* of the international rule over the internal rule, under the terms provided for in Art. 27 of the Convention. That is to say, except for the hypothesis of the express formal (constitutional) breach of an internal rule that is highly relevant to conclude treaties, a party can never invoke (material) provisions of its internal Law (any of them, including Constitution provisions) as a justification not to comply with the international agreement (Art. 27). As can be seen, the 1969 Vienna Convention does not consider the invalidity of treaties by reason of infringement of the national Constitution regarding basic issues. In light of Public International Law, this is so because it is not possible that the Law of Nations be subjected to the internal law of a given State, therefore undermining its principles, all the more so when taking into account that the State (that generally uses the argument of "a violation of its Constitution rules" not to observe the treaty) expressed its consent to be bound by the agreement upon *ratification* or *accession*, and, *published* it at the national level in its Official Gazette. In fact, as explained by Brotons, the opposite is exactly requested from internal law, that is, to remove the risks of conflict and contradiction between its legal system and the international one.[367]

The lesson of Cançado Trindade is not different, when highlighting that "from the point of view of international law, it is unquestionable that a State *cannot* rely on its own Constitution or its internal law to try to justify the non-compliance with the obligations undertaken by means of treaties in force".[368] In support of his arguments in addition to invoking Art. 27 of the Vienna Convention, he also quotes the *Restatement of the Foreign Relations Law of the United States* (1986), which, in paragraph 115, clearly provides as follows: "The United States remains bound internationally when a principle of international Law or a provision in an agreement of the United States is not given effect because it is inconsistent with the Constitution. (...) A State cannot adduce its Constitution or its law as

---

367 Remiro Brotons, Antonio. *Derecho internacional público*, vol. 2, cit., p. 139.

368 Cançado Trindade, Antônio Augusto. Projeto de decreto legislativo sobre suspensão da vigência dos atos internacionais ainda não aprovados pelo Congresso Nacional: elementos para a tomada de posição do Itamaraty, in Cachapuz de Medeiros, Antônio Paulo (org.), *Pareceres dos Consultores Jurídicos do Itamaraty*, vol. VIII (1985-1990), Brasília: Federal Senate, 2004, p. 493.

defense for failure to carry out its international obligation".[369] In that very sense, André Gonçalves Pereira and Fausto de Quadros also indicate that Art. 27 of the 1969 Convention subordinates *all* the internal legal systems to the observance of international treaties, including their Constitutions, granting "the whole conventional international law a supraconstitutional rank in the internal legal system of States where it may enter into force or by ratification or as an international customary rule".[370]

So, the difference between Arts. 27 and 46 of the 1969 Vienna Convention lies in the fact that Art. 27 is a rule subject to the material conflict between international treaties and the provisions of internal Law, while Art. 46 deals with the matter of the *procedure* to conclude treaties, avoiding the allegation of violation of the constitutional text as a justification for non-compliance with the provisions of a treaty, unless it is a case of a manifest disregard of an essential rule. As a provision concerning the conflict of laws, Art. 27 does not provide for any exception concerning the prohibition to invoke a provision of internal Law as an excuse for non-compliance with treaties, which does not occur in the case of Art. 46 that, covering a procedural topic, makes an exception (and only *one*) to the impossibility of the State to invoke the fact that its consent to be bound by a treaty was expressed in violation of a provision of its internal Law concerning the competence to conclude treaties, and that such violation was of a manifest nature and related to its rule (on the *competence* to conclude treaties) of fundamental importance in its internal Law.

It should be noted that Art. 27 of the Vienna Convention was not opposed by the countries which defended State sovereignty.[371] Although there were some abstentions, no country, voted, however, against the aforementioned rule.

The prevalence of International Law over internal Law may also be justified by Art. 11 of the 1928 Havana Convention on Treaties, which provides as follows:

> "Art. 11. Treaties shall continue in effect even though the internal constitution of the contracting States has been modified. If the organization of the State

---

369 Cançado Trindade, Antônio Augusto. Idem, p. 494.

370 Pereira, André Gonçalves & Quadros, Fausto de. *Manual de direito internacional público*, cit., p. 120.

371 See Nascimento e Silva, Geraldo Eulálio do. *Conferência de Viena sobre o Direito dos Tratados*, cit., p. 72.

should be changed in such a manner as to render impossible the execution of treaties, because of division of territory or other like reasons, treaties shall be adapted to the new conditions".

In fact, the *constitution* (in lower case letter) mentioned in the above article of the Havana Convention makes reference not to the *Magna Charta* of the State, but rather to the *organization of the State* (the form of the State to be more precise), as it can be inferred from the second part of Art. 11 itself. Anyway, even in this case it is not unreasonable to assume that the Havana Convention has adopted a solution of prevalence of International Law over the internal legal system, by not terminating the effects of treaties even when the internal organization of the States is modified.

The solution to be adopted in case of non-compliance with the conventional text shall be found in the body of the treaty itself, which shall provide instruments for the solution of controversies that may possibly arise among the parties. Notwithstanding the foregoing, currently there exists a strong trend for non-defaulting State to resort to certain *reprisals* or *counter-measures* in connection with the alleged defaulting State, being such practice not in line with the current state of Public International Law. However, the dividing lines that separate a fair and balanced answer by the non-defaulting State from unlawful visible hostility at the international level are quite thin.

Under Public International Law, States undertake, in full and free exercise of their sovereignty, many international obligations, and, once undertaken, they cannot (in light of the 1969 Vienna Convention) invoke provisions of their internal Law, even of their Constitutional Law, as a justification for their failure to comply with such obligations. It would even be strange if States could invoke the violation of their own sovereignty after having submitted the treaty by themselves and in total freedom to the Legislative Power for its consideration, which represents the will of the People. The *pacta sunt servanda* rule, which is the corollary to the principle of good faith would also be dishonored if the violation of its own internal law by the international undertaking made by the State itself were held valid. The foregoing aims at showing that the 1969 Vienna Convention effectively intended to enshrine the *supremacy of* rule of International Law over internal Law.[372] Although States have not been compelled to

[372] See Pereira, André Gonçalves & Quadros, Fausto de. *Manual de direito internacional público*, cit., p. 121-122.

adjust their internal rules to internationally assumed obligations, the fact remains that, in order to execute those obligations in good faith, as provided for in Art. 26 of the Convention, the State Party shall make treaties prevail over their domestic provisions.

The 1988 Brazilian Constitution accepts this concept, even though on different grounds, with regard to conventional International Law concerning human rights (Art. 5, items 2 and 3). Regarding other treaties, we considei that the Constitution prevails over them, by reason of the constitutional precept that subjects treaties to the constitutionality control (Art. 102, III, *b*). Only upon lack of such constitutional provision, the rule *pacta sunt servanda*, as well as Art. 27 of the Vienna Convention, establish that all international treaties would prevail over our Constitution.[373] As the Brazilian Constitution allows the declaration of unconstitutionality of treaties, and since our constitutional text does not include an express mention on the hierarchical level to be assigned to common international treaties, there seems to be no other solution but to assign an infra-constitutional value to said common international treaties, even if they are *supralegal*.[374] However, it should be highlighted that the constitutional norms which subject treaties to the constitutionality control do not render such treaties void in any manner whatsoever, since an internal court decision cannot render *void* an undertaking arising from another legal system, especially the international system.

All State Powers, not only the Executive and the Legislative, but also the Judiciary, shall respect and observe Public International Law. Failure to observe it engages the international responsibility of the State, almost always forgotten by judges and courts. An everyday example which materializes the practice of an international unlawful act, can be observed when, an attempt is made to repeal international treaties by means of internal legislative measures, which is an ordinary practice in those countries which put on the same footing the hierarchy of an international treaty and that of an internal law.[375] It is not uncommon to see court decisions rendered by Appellate Courts leading to think that, at the internal level, laws in contravention to the provisions of a previously undertaken treaties, dishonoring commitments made at the international level, would be

[373] See Pereira, André Gonçalves & Quadros, Fausto de. Idem, p. 122.

[374] On hierarchy between (common) international treaties and internal laws, see Part V, Ch. 2.

[375] In Brazil, the understanding that treaties have the same legal ranking than ordinary federal law is still being held by the SFC. See, in such regard, the criticized Resolution No. 80.004-SE, of the SFC, dated 06.01.1977, Report of Judge Cunha Peixoto, published in *RTJ* 83/809-848, still followed by current case law of the Supreme Court.

lawful provided that the country has sufficient resources and is willing to compensate the damages caused by the State at the international level. This line of reasoning holds a fallacious argument that is based on a false and wrong idea. The international legal system order *always* prevails over the internal one, and this is so true that, when the national legislator produces rules contradicting provisions of an already assumed international commitment and, after that, the Judicial Power cannot solve the contradiction, harmonizing such precepts, such final attitude finds a solution in international legal system, through accountability and subsequent condemnation of the defaulting State by an international court. If by mistake or lack of familiarity with international rules, internal judges do not re-establish the previous legal state of affairs, International Law shall always have the last word on the matter, which, by means of the institution of the international responsibility, will condemn the defaulting State, redressing the wrong.[376] This precept was mentioned in the decision held on May 8, 1902, by the Arbitration Court on the case *El Salvador v. United States*, which has been quoted by case law of international instances since then.

According to the current rules of Public International Law (it is important to be highlighted: *Public International Law*, not *domestic Law*) it is not admitted, anyhow, save for the aforementioned exception, that *any* rule of internal Law of States terminates an international treaty, which clearly expresses the option that International Law prevails over internal Law.

3.3.2 Application of treaties

Treaties shall be *applied* under the terms and with the limits provided by them. Insofar as that they are validly concluded and are in force at the international level, international acts may be applied by bodies (internal or international) called upon to make a decision on that regard. The *negotiators* of the treaty are liable for providing the rules on its application. Either for necessity or for practical convenience, the truth is that a great number of current treaties already include in their text well-defined rules on their application. Nevertheless, absence that kind of provisions, the 1969 Vienna Convention (as well as the 1986 Convention) offers *supplementary* rules concerning negotiators' will, which allow for the solutions

376 For further details, see Vignali, Heber Arbuet & Arrighi, Jean Michel, Os vínculos entre o direito internacional público e os sistemas internos, *Revista de Informação Legislativa*, year 29, No. 115, Brasília: Federal Senate, Jul/Sep/1992, p. 417.

of problems concerning the territorial and the temporal scope of application of treaties.[377]

This subject-matter is dealt with in Arts. 28 and 30 of the 1969 Vienna Convention (was followed by the 1986 Convention). The last rule on the application of treaties (included in Art. 30 of the Convention) deals with the application of successive treaties to the same subject-matter; as it is a more sophisticated issue, this topic will be hereinafter dealt with separately (see Part III, Ch. 1, item 1.6, below). Besides these three articles (28, 29 and 30) of the Convention, there are no other rules in positive International Law on the territorial and temporal scopes of application of international treaties

Of course, it should be emphasized that the relevance of the analysis on application of treaties (regarding territorial and temporal scope of application) is specially relevant in the case of those agreements (already studied in the Chapter concerning the classification of treaties) called *norm-setting* treaties, such as agreements on human rights protection, trade, alliance, cooperation, arbitration, etc.

3.3.2.1 *Temporal scope of application*

The general rule given by the 1969 Convention concerning the application of treaties in time is related to its *non-retroactivity*.[378] It consists in the application of the general principle of law according to which legal rules are usually made to govern *future* situations (and not *facta praeterita*). According to Art. 28 of the Convention, "[u]nless a different intention appears from the treaty or is otherwise established, its provisions do not bind a party in relation to any act or fact which took place or any situation which ceased to exist before the date of the entry into force of the treaty with respect to that party".[379] Nothing seems more logical, since treaties, as well as laws are created to produce effects *as from* their entry into force (*ex nunc*), except if the treaty shows a different intention or it is otherwise provided. The former statement means that nothing prevents States from preparing, for example, a treaty or an article repealing the principle of

---

[377] See Remiro Brotons, Antonio. *Derecho internacional público*, vol. 2, cit., p. 284-292.

[378] See Waldock, Humphrey [Special Rapporteur], *Yearbook of the International Law Commission* (1964), vol. II, p. 10-12.

[379] See Nascimento e Silva, Geraldo Eulálio do. Le facteur temps et les traités, cit., p. 273-277; Calatayud, Esperanza Orihuela, *Los tratados internacionales y su aplicación en el tiempo: consideraciones sobre el efecto inicial de las disposiciones convencionales*, Madrid: Dykinson, 2004, p. 21-62; and Villiger, Mark E., *Commentary on the 1969 Vienna Convention on the Law of Treaties*, cit., p. 381-386.

non-retroactivity, either expressly or implicitly.[380] Except for the case in which there is an express provision (also when the retroactivity of the agreement is "otherwise" provided), the *non-retroactivity* rule shall be fully applied; therefore, if there is no express provision in the treaty itself (or even in another one), or if the contracting parties have not otherwise provided in any manner whatsoever, the 1969 Convention presumes the *non-retroactivity* of the treaty in the relations between the parties.

It should be noted that the principle of non-retroactivity of treaties (under the clear terms of Art. 28 of the Convention) exists to avoid that a treaty be applied in connection "with any *previous act or fact* or with a situation which *ceased to exist* before the date of entry into force of the treaty with respect to that party".[381] This provision does not prevent the application of the principle that a situation arising before the entry into force of the treaty, but whose effects *continued* or were produced *after* the entry into force, shall be governed by the treaty. Regional courts of human rights have been declared incompetent to rule upon cases that took place before the entry into force of the respective regional treaties (for example, the American Convention on Human Rights, in the Inter-American system) or on the acceptance by the States of the contentious jurisdiction of such courts, but do not exclude the admissibility of complaints when violations to human rights *continue* after such date and produce effects that are by themselves a *breach* of the treaty.[382] Hence, a State *act* breaching human rights (for example, a murder or disappearance of persons, etc.) occurred *before* acknowledging the contentious competence of the Inter-American Court of Human Rights, may not be judged by it, but the State omission that continued *beyond the date of such acknowledgment* may be perfectly subject to a complaint before the Court (for example, in case that the bodies of the victims, as in the above example of disappearance of persons, are not found yet).[383]

---

380 See Dinh, Daillier & Pellet. *Direito internacional público*, cit., p. 225; and De La Guardia, Ernesto, *Derecho de los tratados internacionales*, cit., p. 203.

381 See Art. 4 of the Convention on non-retroactivity of the Vienna Convention itself: "Without prejudice to the application of any rules set forth in the present Convention to which treaties would be subject under international law independently of the Convention, the Convention applies only to treaties which are concluded by States after the entry into force of the present Convention with regard to such States".

382 See Dinh, Daillier& Pellet. *Direito internacional público*, cit., p. 226.

383 For details, see Mazzuoli, Valerio de Oliveira, *Comentários à Convenção Americana sobre Direitos Humanos (Pacto de San José da Costa Rica)*, 3. ed. (reviewed, updated and extended), São Paulo: Revista dos Tribunais, 2010, p. 326-327.

Finally, it should be pointed out that the 1969 Vienna Convention states nothing (and also the 1986 Convention) on the *duration* of treaties, which is natural, considering that each international instrument has the duration established by its own text. If the treaty provides nothing on its term, it is because it is intended for life, and may be only modified when the parties, by general conviction, understand that it is better to modify its terms and redefine the situation agreed upon. The express provision of final term (as, for example, the Panama Canal Treaty of 1977, which provided, in Art. 2, item 2, that it shall terminate at noon, Panama time, on December 31, 1999) usually avoids the denunciation of the instrument until that date.[384]

3.3.2.2 Territorial scope of application

Again, unless a different intention appears from the treaty or is otherwise established, a treaty is binding upon each party in respect of *its entire territory*.[385] This is the rule on the territorial scope of *application* (or on *territorial execution*) of treaties, which is contained in Art. 29 of the Vienna Convention.

The rule that a treaty is binding upon the parties in respect of its *entire* territory (as well as the rule of temporal scope of application) is *supplementary*, and shall be applied in the event the treaty is silent. If there is a specified *express* provision in the text or a provision that may be otherwise established, the agreements reached by negotiators shall prevail. For example, the 1971 Treaty on the Prohibition of the Emplacement of Nuclear Weapons and Other Weapons of Mass Destruction on the Seabed and the Ocean Floor and in the Subsoil Thereof,[386] expressly excludes the territory of the parties from its scope of application, when establishing that State Parties "undertake not to implant or emplace on the seabed and the ocean floor and in the subsoil thereof *beyond the outer limit of a seabed zone, as defined in article II*, any nuclear weapons or any other types of weapons of mass destruction ..." (Art. I, 1).[387] Evidently, in this case, the

---

384 See Rezek, José Francisco. *Direito dos tratados*, cit., p. 411-413.

385 See Waldock, Humphrey [Special Rapporteur], *Yearbook of the International Law Commission* (1964), vol. II, p. 12-15.

386 Ratified by Brazil on 05.10.1988, promulgated by Executive Order 97.211, dated 12.12.1988.

387 The above Art. II provides, in its turn, that: "For the purpose of this Treaty, the outer limit of the sea-bed zone referred to in Article I shall be coterminous with the twelve-mile outer limit of the zone referred to in part II of the Convention on the Territorial Sea

treaty is applied *outside of* the territory of the State, by virtue of express determination. Only if the treaty is *silent*, its articles shall be applied to the *entire* territory of the State, including its airspace and territorial sea.[388] Here, the expression "territory" shall mean all the space in which the State exercises *sovereignty*.[389]

It is possible that an original treaty be silent in connection with its territorial application and after certain time, States conclude a specific agreement to regulate the matter, providing, for example, that a portion of its territory will not be reached by the effects of the treaty, etc. Such possibility is contemplated under Art. 41, item 1 of the Vienna Convention, which rules on agreements to modify multilateral treaties only among some parties (*inter se* agreements).[390] Art. 29 of the Convention authorizes the conclusion of such type of specific agreement, because an intention is "otherwise provided".

Some treaties contain articles applicable to the federated States relating to issues that fall under the field of their exclusive competence, which is permitted according to Art. 29 of the Convention, as the existence of a different intention is shown in the treaty with regard to its territorial application. However, if such intention is not shown in the treaty, no State, not even a federal State can disregard the scope of territorial application of an international undertaking. Nevertheless, it is possible that a reservation be made in that connection, on account of the lack of an express provision on the limitation of obligations in a given territory.[391]

Even with regard to the territorial scope of application of treaties, it should be pointed out the wise decision reached by the 1969 Vienna Convention when providing a *flexible* article such as Art. 29 (as it also

---

and the Contiguous Zone, signed at Geneva on April 29, 1958, and shall be measured in accordance with the provisions of part I, section II, of that Convention and in accordance with international law".

388 See De La Guardia, Ernesto. *Derecho de los tratados internacionales*, cit., p. 205.

389 See Mazzuoli, Valerio de Oliveira. *Curso de direito internacional público*, cit., p. 476-479. In that very sense, see Villiger, Mark E., *Commentary on the 1969 Vienna Convention on the Law of Treaties*, cit., p. 392, which says: "The territory covers the area over which a party to the treaty exercises sovereignty and thus embraces all that State's land, territorial waters and air space, whether or not these areas are part of the metropolitan area (though not the continental shelf, the exclusive economic zone and the fishery zones). Recognition under international law of the State and its territory is not required".

390 On Art. 41 of the Convention, see Part III, Ch. 1, item 1.4.2, below.

391 See Buergenthal, Thomas (*et all.*). *Manual de derecho internacional público*, cit., p. 87-88.

occurs with the temporal scope of application of treaties regulated in Art. 28 of the Convention).[392] The wise decision of the Convention lies in the fact that it understood that different situations may occur concerning the territorial application of a treaty. Hence, it adopted the provisions of the treaty itself or the agreements otherwise made by contracting parties as a *rule*. It should be noted that there are situations that, even with no conventional provision and no establishment of a different intention of the contracting parties in another way, treaties shall be applied beyond the territoriality presumption provided for in Art. 29. Imagine, for example, a treaty concluded to be applied in territories not subject to the jurisdiction of any State, like the 1959 Antarctic Treaty, or a treaty affecting *concrete* regions of a certain State, like an agreement of limitation of borders or of sale or assignment of territory.[393] This shows that the supplementary rule contemplated under Art. 29 of the Convention is applicable when the chance to apply a specific treaty in space *can be assessed*.

There are still other problems involving the territorial scope of application of treaties, namely: the modification of the State territory (to enlarge or reduce its size); the case of discontinuous territories, with regions separated from the main *core* (for example, the case of France with its Overseas Departments; Denmark with Greenland and the Faroe Islands; Spain with Canary Islands, etc.); the situation of territories occupied by a State through the use of force; the case of non-metropolitan territories (such as colonies and dependent territories), etc. All of them require a case-by-case solution.[394]

3.4 Effectiveness of treaties and international responsibility

The rules analyzed in this Chapter sufficed to understand that the treaty in force *obliges* the parties to comply fully with it, otherwise States may be held internationally responsible.

A diligent reader will notice that frequently (above and below) in the text the same topic is analyzed, always concerning the relations of the parties with the observance or fulfillment of treaties. This topic will only reinforce what it is being said here and there on the subject, which appears in this book strictly in connection with the effectiveness of treaties.

---

392 See Remiro Brotons, Antonio. *Derecho internacional público*, vol. 2, cit., p. 288.

393 See Remiro Brotons, Antonio. Idem, ibidem.

394 For details, see Remiro Brotons, Antonio, Idem, p. 28-292.

Since this is not the right place to study the international responsibility of States,[395] we should only inform the fact that the 1969 Vienna Convention has not regulated *all* the consequences of non-compliance with conventional obligations. Therefore, Art. 73, provided that:

> "The provisions of the present Convention shall not prejudge any question that may arise in regard to a treaty from a succession of States or from the international responsibility of a State or from the outbreak of hostilities between States".

As can be observed, the Convention did not intend to cope with the three topics referred to in Art. 73, which include the succession of States, international responsibility of States, and hostilities. In summary, regarding this topic, the Convention intended to clarify that its provisions do not affect ("shall not prejudge", as indicated in the text[396]) any issues that may eventually arise in connection with a treaty as a result of the international responsibility of a State.

Without doubt certainly, the convergence between the theory of treaties and the topic of international responsibility is clear.[397] Now, the lat-

---

395 On the subject, see Mazzuoli, Valerio de Oliveira, *Curso de direito internacional público*, cit., p. 602-631. For the draft of the ILC on the international responsibility of States, see Crawford, James, *The International Law Commission's Articles on State Responsibility: introduction, text and commentaries*, Cambridge: Cambridge University Press, 2002, 387p.

396 The expression "shall prejudge" was used in the Vienna Convention since it was understood that it was more appropriate in the context under analysis. Other provisions of the Convention (as, for example, Art. 30, item 5) use, however, the expression "without prejudice", which, according to Villiger, "implies that they are establishing one rule without interfering with another" (*Commentary on the 1969 Vienna Convention on the Law of Treaties*, cit., p. 903).

397 In the case entitled *Gabčíkovo-Nagymaros Project* (Hungary *v.* Slovakia) of 1997, the ICJ pointed out the relations between the Law of Treaties and the subject of international liability: "La Cour n'a pas davantage à s'étendre sur la question des relations qu'entretiennent le droit des traités et le droit de la responsabilité des Etats, à laquelle les Parties ont consacré de longs développements. Ces deux branches du droit international ont en effet, à l'évidence, des champs d'application distincts. C'est au regard du droit des traités qu'il convient de déterminer si une convention est ou non en vigueur, et si elle a ou non été régulièrement suspendue ou dénoncée. C'est en revanche au regard du droit de la responsabilité des Etats qu'il y a lieu d'apprécier dans quelle mesure la suspension ou la dénonciation d'une convention qui serait incompatible avec le droit des traités engage la responsabilité de l'Etat qui y a procédé". See *ICJ Reports* (1997), p. 35. On that subject see also Forlati, Serena, *Diritto dei trattati e responsabilità internazionale*, Milano: Giuffrè, 2005, 202p; and Szabó, Marcel (ed.), *State responsibility and the law of treaties*, The Hague: Eleven International, 2010, 208p.

ter covers non-compliance with *obligations*, being its general principles the same, whatever the *source* under analysis may be (treaty, custom or unilateral act).[398] The legal instrument *considered* is, in its turn, the most specific binding *source* of Public International Law, and exactly for that reason the topic of international responsibility (of States and of international organizations as well) is so perfectly vested on it.[399] For example, in the 1969 Vienna Convention, the provision of Art. 60 regarding the termination or suspension of the operation of a treaty as a consequence of its breach (see Part III, Ch. 3, item 3.1.3.1) should be analyzed.

---

398 See Reuter, Paul. *Introducción al derecho de los tratados*, cit., p. 223.

399 See Remiro Brotons, Antonio. *Derecho internacional público*, vol. 2, cit., p. 480-482.

Part III

Continuance in Force and Termination of Treaties

Chapter 1

Treaties in Force

1.1 Effects of treaties on the parties

A universal principle of law states that a commitment among parties to an agreement shall not affect third parties.[1] Since this is a *universal* principle, it also applies to the general theory of treaties. That is to say, treaties only produce effects on the parties who consented to be bound by the relevant international agreement, without affecting third parties. The Law of Nations refers to such principle as the *principle of relativity of treaties*.[2] Likewise, non-member States are strangers to agreements concluded between members and, therefore, they may not demand members to fulfill the agreements, since such agreements are *res inter alios acta* for such third States. This rule refers to the territorial scope of entry into force of treaties, and it has long been established by the State's case law and practice.[3]

The former Permanent Court of International Justice had already confirmed such understanding in Judgment No. 7, dated May 25, 1926, issued on the case *Certain German interests in Polish Upper Silesia*, by declaring that "treaties are only enforceable among States that are a party

---

1 In relation to international treaties, any international law legal entity that is not a *party* thereto is deemed as a *third party*.

2 On this subject, see Cahier, Philippe, Le problème des effets des traités à l'égard des états tiers, *Recueil des Cours*, vol. 143 (1974-III), p. 609-617; Reuter, Paul, *Introducción al derecho de los tratados*, cit., p. 123-154; and Dinh, Daillier & Pellet, *Direito internacional público*, cit., p. 246-248.

3 See Maresca, Adolfo. *Il diritto dei trattati…*, cit., p. 409-427; Rezek, José Francisco, *Direito dos tratados*, cit., p. 399; Danilenko, G. M., *Law-making in the international community*, Dordrecht: Martinus Nijhoff, 1993, p. 58-59; and Villiger, Mark E., *Commentary on the 1969 Vienna Convention on the Law of Treaties*, cit., p. 469-470.

thereto".[4] The Roman principle *pacta tertiis nec nocent nec prosunt* (treaties may not impose *obligations* on or grant *rights* to third parties) was applied in said case.[5]

The Vienna Convention on the Law of Treaties, followed the same path by codifying said principle and setting forth that "a treaty does not create either obligations or rights for a third State without its consent" (Art. 34).[6]

The principle establishing that rights and obligations provided for in treaties only affect the parties may be understood from an *external* point of view (relations among the parties), or from an *internal* point of view (application of the treaty *in foro domestico*), as explained below.

1.1.1 External effects

External effects are those effects produced by treaties on the *relations* among the parties, which may vary depending on the type of international agreement, the scope of the agreement (bilateral treaty or extensive open multilateral treaty) and any reservations to its provisions.

As a general rule, as from *entry into force* of a treaty, any party may request the other to perform the obligations set forth therein (for agreements that impose the performance of *obligations*), or the commencement of the cooperation provided therein (for *cooperation* treaties), or even require such party to take measures to protect, for example, their citizens in transit in the other State (for *guarantee* treaties), etc. As from their entry into force, treaties become *full* applicable among the parties, under the terms and conditions set forth in it (see Part II, Ch. 3, item 3.1.1, above). It is of the utmost importance to determine the *types* of relations established

---

4 Also see the *Chorzow Factory* case, tried by the same PCIJ, in 1928. In relation to arbitration proceedings, see *Island of Palmas* (1928) and *Clipperton Island* (1931) cases. These precedents constitute the basis for Art. 34 of the 1969 Vienna Convention.

5 See Accioly, Hildebrando. *Tratado de direito internacional público*, vol. I, cit., p. 603; McNair, Arnold Duncan, *The law of treaties*, cit., p. 309-321; Sinclair, Ian, *The Vienna* Convention *on the Law of Treaties*, cit., p. 98-106; Dinh, Daillier & Pellet, *Direito internacional público*, cit., p. 246; and Fitzmaurice, Malgosia, Third parties and the law of treaties, *Max Planck Yearbook of United Nations Law*, vol. 6, No.1 (2002), p. 38-39. On preliminary discussions for Vienna provisions, see Waldock, Humphrey [Special Rapporteur], *Yearbook of the International Law Commission* (1964), vol. II, p. 17-26.

6 The concept of *third State* is defined in Art. 2, item 1(h) of the Vienna Convention: "For the purposes of the present Convention (...) '*third* State' means a State not a party to the treaty".

among the parties from such moment, especially if the relevant treaty admits reservations and such reservations have been made. In that case, treaties will have different effects on the different parties. In any case, we can affirm that the entry *into force* of a treaty produces *external* effects on the parties, which may already impose liability on defaulting States (or international organizations).

Countless examples of *external* effects of treaties may be given. We will not list them but it is worth highlighting that treaties in force regulate the parties' mutual relations, and any breach thereof implies international liability for the defaulting State.

1.1.2 Internal effects

Internal effects are those effects produced by treaties on the legal systems of States that are parties thereto. There is a wide range of internal effects, related to the time of internal application, to the hierarchy of treaties under domestic legal systems, the obligations of public powers regarding its performance, etc.

It should be noted that any treaty (provided that it has not been rendered void by any reason under the Vienna Convention) becomes part of the legal system of the parties as an independent set of regulations and with the typical features of *treaties*. Therefore, they revoke any incompatible prior legislation, as it occurs with subsequent laws.[7] Besides revoking any incompatible domestic legislation (like subsequent laws in relation to prior regulations), any subsequent laws shall also comply with treaties. That is to say, in Brazil treaties in general have supralegal status. Although such understanding has not been recognized by the rulings of the Federal Supreme Court yet,[8] it is an undeniable truth (see Part V, Ch. 2).

It should be clarified that treaties incorporated to domestic law are not *laws* (as it is usually said) and they may not be considered equal to them; they are international acts internally *applied as if they were laws*. The typical features of *treaties* that international acts possess do not disappear with their internal application, which is identical to the application of domestic laws. Upon promulgation of the treaty, *common* international instruments ratified by the Brazilian State acquire the *force of an internal rule*, with a

---

7 See Rezek, José Francisco. *Direito dos tratados*, cit., p. 383.

8 Our Supreme Court only recognizes supralegal hierarchy to treaties on *human rights*, and not to the rest of them (see *RE* 466.343-1/SP, j. 12.03.2008).

higher hierarchy than laws, simply because they may not be revoked by subsequent laws (they are not amended by any future ruling), as evidenced by the Brazilian legislation (see, for example, section 98 of the Federal Tax Code) and contemporary international practice. International treaties protecting human rights, which are considered *special* treaties, in turn, enter our legal system with the characteristics and hierarchy of constitutional rules, pursuant to section 5, item 2, of the Federal Constitution of 1988, which states: "The rights and guarantees expressed in this Constitution *do not exclude* others arising from the regime and principles adopted by it, or from *international treaties to which the Federal Republic of Brazil is a party*"). Such a rule was further reinforced by item 3, introduced by Constitutional Amendment No. 45/2004, which has already been analyzed.[9]

International treaties must be applied by law practioners in general the same way as laws are applied, because "although they are not produced by domestic legislative sources, they are identical, as legal provisions, to regulations produced by them".[10] Therefore, they are also applied to individuals and private law legal entities, in the same way as national laws. The question is to know when a treaty must be applied by the State and when it must be applied by individuals or private entities, or by both simultaneously. And the answer will be found on a case-by-case basis, depending on the subject-matter of the international regulation. A treaty regulating the use of cosmic space, has no effects on the general population, for obvious reasons. On the contrary, an agreement on human rights (such as 1969 American Convention on Human Rights) must be complied with on a daily basis by anyone under the jurisdiction of the State.

It should be noted that treaties ratified by the Government must be performed by all the powers of the State (Legislative, Executive and Judicial) and by individuals, since their hierarchy is superior to the other domestic laws.

---

9 For further details, see Mazzuoli, Valerio de Oliveira, O novo § 3.º do Art. 5.º da Constituição e sua eficácia, *Revista Forense*, vol. 378, year 101, Rio de Janeiro, Mar/Apr/2005, p. 89-109, republished in *Revista de Informação Legislativa*, year 42, No. 167, Brasília: Federal Senate, Jul/Sep/2005, p. 93-114; and also Mazzuoli, Valerio de Oliveira, Comentário ao artigo 5.º, § 3.º, in Canotilho, J. J. Gomes; Mendes, Gilmar F.; Sarlet, Ingo W. & Streck, Lenio L. (coord.), *Comentários à Constituição do Brasil*, cit., p. 518-524. An update (and extension) of this text appears in Mazzuoli, Valerio de Oliveira, *Curso de direito internacional público*, cit., p. 896-927. We will deal with this subject further in Part V, Ch. 2, item 2.4, below.

10 Rezek, José Francisco. *Direito dos tratados*, cit., p. 394.

> "When [States] execute an agreement, they undertake a higher rank commitment, in a legal category that is also higher and under the principles of international law. Therefore, such agreements follow the rules governing and guiding said understandings, leaving the laws of each party in a subordinate level. Anything damaging, breaching, or preceding the treaty will be overruled by this regulations issued by a higher authority, agreed among States, and binding on the respective populations. Domestic principles that contradict the content of the international rule expressed in the treaty shall be adjusted to the new regulations contained in the international agreement, especially when it is binding. Even bilateral treaties, in relation to reciprocal obligations and mutual rights, require compliance with internal laws".
>
> Ituassú, Oyama Cesar. *Curso de direito internacional público*. Rio de Janeiro: Forense, 1986, p. 531-532.

In summary, treaties incorporated to domestic legal systems are *legal regulations* equal to any internal law, and they must be complied with by the State and by individuals. Therefore, as from ratification (since they are already in force externally) treaties revoke any provisions to the contrary and they cannot be revoked by subsequent laws. The executive order only certifies that the incorporation formalities for the international agreement were followed, and that the agreement executed is already legally enforceable and binding on everyone. Failure to publish treaties internally does not damage its internal validity and binding force. Art. 4 of the 1928 Havana Convention on Treaties provides that treaties "shall be published immediately after exchange of ratifications", adding that "[t]he failure to discharge this international duty shall affect neither the force of treaties nor the fulfillment of obligations stipulated therein". Such formality, aimed at giving more publicity to a prior commitment before the international society of States and international organizations, does not authorize the State to fail to perform the treaty it ratified as a sovereign State and undertook to perform fully.

1.2 Effects of treaties on third parties

We have already pointed out that the 1969 Vienna Convention provides that "A treaty does not create either obligations or rights for a third State without its consent" (Art. 34). In Art. 2, item 1(h), the Convention defines "thirdy State" as "a State not a *party* to the treaty". Hence, the effects of treaties are *relative*, since they may not, *a priori*, bind or even benefit third parties without their consent.[11] Nevertheless, despite

11 See Remiro Brotons, Antonio. *Derecho internacional público*, vol. 2, cit., p. 355; De La Guardia, Ernesto, *Derecho de los tratados internacionales*, cit., p. 231-241; Fitzmaurice,

the existence of provisions like Art. 34, in practice, there are treaties that establish or modify legal situations among the parties and, as a consequence, they somehow affect third parties that did not accede to the treaty.[12] Therefore, the effects produced by such treaties on third States must be analyzed.

It is possible to distinguish three types of effects of treaties that may affect third States, as described below.[13] The third type of effect (item 1.2.3, below) is divided into the assignment of *rights* and *obligations* to third States, as we will also explain below.

1.2.1 Diffuse effect of recognizing an objective legal situation

This is the case in which a treaty between two or more parties creates an objective legal situation and, as a consequence, it compels the whole international society to acknowledge such situation.[14] In other words, third States are bound to comply with such (objective) legal situation, which is new between the parties. Therefore, a treaty modifying the boundaries between two States creates a new objective legal situation, which must be complied with by third parties, even simply for learning the new cartography of the region from such moment on.[15] In the same way, a treaty between *A* and *B*, States that own river or lake internal waters jointly, granting free civil navigation on said waters for any country, will affect third parties.[16]

It should be highlighted that, during the ILC sessions, this subject – treaties creating *objective regimes* – was discussed from G. Fitzmaurice's report to H. Waldock's third report.[17] According to Fitzmaurice, the gen-

---

Malgosia, Third parties and the law of treaties, cit., p. 44-45; Brichambaut, Dobelle & Coulée, *Leçons de droit international public*, cit., p. 283; and Crawford, James, *Brownlie's principles of public international law*, cit., p. 384-386.

12 See See Wheaton, Henry. *Elements of international law*, vol. I, cit., p. 519-521.

13 For further details, see Rezek, José Francisco, *Direito dos tratados*, cit., p. 402-410.

14 Rezek, José Francisco. Idem, p. 403. On the subject, also see Dupuy, Pierre-Marie, *Droit international public*, cit., p. 297-298; and Salerno, Francesco, Treaties establishing objective regimes, in Cannizzaro, Enzo (ed.), *The law of treaties beyond the Vienna Convention*, cit., p. 225-243.

15 Rezek, José Francisco. *Direito dos tratados*, cit., p. 403.

16 Rezek, José Francisco. Idem, p. 404.

17 For details, see Fitzmaurice, Gerald Gray [Special Rapporteur], *Yearbook of the International Law Commission* (1960), vol. II, p. 73-78; and Waldock, Humphrey [Special Rapporteur], *Yearbook of the International Law Commission* (1964), vol. II, p. 26-27. On

eral principle that governs the so called objective regime, as an exception to the rule *pacta tertiis*, is "performance of lawful, valid or legitimate international acts"; some of the effects that are an exception to the rule are "the recognition and acceptance of valid international acts, especially of rights lawfully acquired by other States, and of the objective validity of any international law, regime or regulation legally applicable *erga omnes*; finally, the passive obligation not to disturb or hinder the operation of a treaty lawfully concluded among other States".[18] In turn, Waldock tried to compile the subject in a report entitled "Treaties providing for objective regimes".[19] However, finally, the theory of "objective regimes" was not accepted by the ILC in general, and the Commission decided to abandon the subject and prepare its final *Proposal*, understanding that Art. 32 and the common law were already providing "a legal basis to establish valid *erga omnes* rights and obligations arising from treaties".[20]

---

the said discussion at the ILC, see Fitzmaurice, Malgosia, Third parties and the law of treaties, cit., p. 72-83.

18 ILC, *Yearbook of the International Law Commission* (1960), vol. II, p. 76.

19 ILC, *Yearbook of the International Law Commission* (1964), vol. II, p. 26-27, as follows: "*Article 63 – Treaties providing for objective regimes* 1. A treaty establishes an objective regime when it appears from its terms and from the circumstances of its conclusion that the intention of the parties is to create in the general interest general obligations and rights relating to a particular region, State, territory, locality, river, waterway, or to a particular area of sea, sea-bed, or air-space; provided that the parties include among their number any State having territorial competence with reference to the subject-matter of the treaty, or that any such State has consented to the provision in question.

2. (*a*) A State not a party to the treaty, which expressly or impliedly consents to the creation or to the application of an objective regime, shall be considered to have accepted it.

(*b*) A State not a party to the treaty, which does not protest against or otherwise manifest its opposition to the regime within a period of X years of the registration of the treaty with the Secretary-General of the United Nations, shall be considered to have impliedly accepted the regime.

3. A State which has accepted a regime of the kind referred to in paragraph 1 shall be:

(*a*) bound by any general obligations which it contains; and

(*b*) entitled to invoke the provisions of the regime and to exercise any general right which it may confer, subject to the terms and conditions of the treaty.

4. Unless the treaty otherwise provides, a regime of the kind referred to in paragraph 1 may be amended or revoked by the parties to the treaty only with the concurrence of those States which have expressly or impliedly accepted the regime and have a substantial interest in its functioning".

20 De La Guardia, Ernesto. *Derecho de los tratados internacionales*, cit., p. 245.

In fact, there is no doubt that the conclusion of a treaty between two States providing, for example, changes to the boundaries between them, or opening (or closing) their joint internal waters to navigation for third States, can generate the diffuse effect of recognition of each objective legal situation on the international society. However, as we mentioned before, the Vienna Convention does not provide any definitions on the theory of objective regimes, since the subject was abandoned by the ILC in the final *Proposal*, leading legal scholars to uncertainty.[21]

Since there are no provisions on the subject, and unlike Private Law, where objective legal situations are enforceable before third parties because they are guaranteed by the State, it is understood that in Public International Law there is no *absolute* obligation to recognize such situations, since the international society (which is decentralized) does not have a supranational authority imposing the compliance of strict rules, like a State Constitution in relation to domestic Law.[22]

1.2.2 Factual impact of a given treaty on third States

This is the case where a third State is directly affected by a treaty (normally a bilateral treaty) due to a prior treaty between such third State and one of the parties.[23] A typical example in such field (although it is not the only one) is the so called *most-favored-nation clause*.[24] By means of such *clause* (generally included in trade bilateral agree-

---

21 De La Guardia then affirmed that "in 1969 there was no general consensus among jurists on the subject" (and still today there is none) (*Derecho de los tratados internacionales*, cit., p. 245).

22 See Rezek, José Francisco. *Direito dos tratados*, cit., p. 404, who states: "Taking into account, however, that the idea of objective situations enforceable on third parties originated in private law, Reuter notes that, in that field, such enforceability is absolute because the agreement generating such situation is verified and guaranteed by a common authority, the State. The scenario is different at the international level, which is not centralized, and where each player is sovereign to recognize or not the allegedly legal and objective situation. After all, as we have described, the most remarkable feature of a State's sovereignty is the prerogative to deny or question the statehood of other states, without any supranational power imposing a compulsory definition on the matter".

23 Rezek, José Francisco. *Direito dos tratados*, cit., p. 405.

24 On this clause, see Wheaton, Henry, *Elements of international law*, vol. I, cit., p. 541-542; Crandall, Samuel B., *Treaties: their making and enforcement*, cit., p. 404-422; Lacharriére, Guy de, Aspects récents de la clause de la nation la plus favorisée, *Annuaire Français de Droit International*, vol. 7 (1961), p. 107-117; Maresca, Adolfo, *Il diritto dei trattati…*, cit., p. 429-448; Remiro Brotons, Antonio, *Derecho internacional público*, vol. 2, cit., p.

ments) the parties undertake to offer each other the same most favorable treatment that may be accorded to any other State in the future. As noted by the ICJ, in a judgment dated August 27, 1952, rendered on the case concerning Rights of Nationals of the United States of America in Morocco, that type of clause intends "to establish and to maintain at all times fundamental equality without discrimination among all of the countries concerned".[25] Then, if *A* and *B* executed a treaty whereby each of them establishes a lower tax rate for products imported from the other party, in the event that one of them grants a lower tax rate for products from any other country, the counterparty (due to the provision of said *clause*) shall have an immediate right to an equal benefit.[26] Therefore, in the most-favored-nation clause, signatories undertake to extend the most favorable treatment offered to a third State to all the other parties to the agreement (an accepted exception is participation in free trade areas). The same rule must be applied to national companies (which, however, may not be subsidized by States, so that free competition is not adversely affected).

295-303; Kamto, Maurice, La volonté de l'État en droit international, cit., p. 308-311; and Sepúlveda, César, *Derecho internacional*, cit., p. 140-141.

25 See *ICJ Reports* (1952), p. 192. However, it should be pointed out that the *Institut de Droit International*, in a session held in Brussels in 1936, clarified that the most-favored-nation clause does not give right to: neither the treatment given or that may be given by any contracting party to a neighboring third State to facilitate frontier traffic; nor the treatment of a customs union concluded or to be concluded; (...) nor the treatment arising from mutual and exclusive agreements among States and that imply the organization of economic regimes of regional or continental nature (unofficial translation).

26 In Brazil, the most-favored-nation clause was already included in the treaty of peace and alliance, dated August 29, 1825, whereby Portugal recognized the independence of Brazil (see the text of the treaty, Part V, Ch. 1, item 1.7.2, below). Art. 5 of the abovementioned agreement states: "citizens of both nations, Brazil and Portugal, shall be considered and treated in the respective States as citizens of the most favored and friendly nation". Today, the *clause* also became one of the leading principles for agreements like the GATT, whose Art. 1 provides that: "With respect to customs duties and charges of any kind imposed on or in connection with importation or exportation or imposed on the international transfer of payments for imports or exports, and with respect to the method of levying such duties and charges, and with respect to all rules and formalities in connection with importation and exportation, and with respect to all matters referred to in paragraphs 2 and 4 of Article III, any advantage, favour, privilege or immunity granted by any contracting party to any product originating in or destined for any other country shall be accorded immediately and unconditionally to the like product originating in or destined for the territories of all other contracting parties".

It is clear then that a subsequent treaty is not binding on third parties as a *legal* rule, but as a mere *fact*.[27] Accordingly a benefit to another State is already the fact-condition previously established in the agreement (where the *clause* is included) concluded by the original parties, being the *clause* a *legal* rule that effectively ensures the benefit to the third State (note: *third State* in connection with a factual situation deriving from a treaty, but *party State* in connection with a treaty-regulation).[28]

1.2.3 Legal effect of imposing obligations and granting rights to third States

Since this third effect is a *legal* effect, the Vienna Convention expressly covers it in Arts. 35 to 38. This is the case where third States – with the exception already mentioned of Art. 34 of the Convention, which sets forth that "A treaty does not create either obligations or rights for a third State without its consent" – become subjects of international *rights* or *obligations*, pursuant to treaties concluded among other parties.[29]

There are two conditions for a treaty to provide for *obligations* or *rights* for a third State: 1) that negotiators have the *common intention* that the treaty produces such effects; and 2) that the third State (or international organization) *accepts* such effects.[30]

Only if a State *does not have the possibility* to be a party to a specific treaty, the parties thereto may stipulate rights and obligations for such third State. If a State *may be a party* to a specific treaty (for example, accession to the agreement is *open* and unrestricted for any State) but it is not a party, there is no discussion as to whether it may be subject to rights and obligations arising from such treaty, as decided by the ICJ on February 20, 1969, in the judgment the concerning the North Sea Continental Shelf cases. Then, as Brotons explains, only when a particular State *cannot be* a party to a specific treaty, the mechanism under analysis "may be used to open a window when a door is closed".[31]

---

27 Rezek, José Francisco. *Direito dos tratados*, cit., p. 405.

28 Rezek, José Francisco. Idem, p. 405-406.

29 On the subject, see Kamto, Maurice, La volonté de l'État en droit international, cit., p. 302-312; and Rezek, José Francisco, Efeitos do tratado internacional sobre terceiros: o artigo 35 da Convenção de Viena, in Tibúrcio, Carmen & Barroso, Luís Roberto (orgs.), *O direito internacional contemporâneo: estudos em homenagem ao Professor Jacob Dolinger*, Rio de Janeiro: Renovar, 2006, p. 491-504.

30 See Remiro Brotons, Antonio. *Derecho internacional público*, vol. 2, cit., p. 357.

31 Remiro Brotons, Antonio. Idem, ibidem.

1.2.3.1 Treaties providing for obligations for third States

An *obligation* arises for a third State from a provision of a treaty if the parties to the treaty intend the provision to be the means of establishing the obligation and the third State expressly accepts that obligation in writing,[32] as set forth by Art. 35 of the 1969 Convention. This obligation does not arise from the existence of the treaty itself, but from the will of the third State to undertake the obligation.[33] In this case, the third State does not *accede to* the treaty for the purpose of being bound by it, becoming a *party* to the instrument, but the treaty imposes obligations to the third State, which simply accepts them, maintaining a *third party* status in relation to the original parties to the agreement. It could also be said that the *nomen juris* of Art. 35 of the Convention ("Treaties providing for obligations for third States") is not properly used from a technical point of view, since the *treaty* itself does not provide for obligations for a third State, but the will of the State to be bound by the treaty.

It should be highlighted that the Convention requires not only an *express* statement of the third State accepting the obligation imposed by a treaty executed by other States; but also that such acceptance be in writing, so as to make clear (free of doubt) its intention to be bound by the provisions agreed upon by other parties. So far, everything is clear. The General Theory of Law, not the Law of Treaties, requires an agreement between parties resulting in obligations to third parties to have the undoubted consent of such third parties to be valid. This "agreement" whereby the third State accepts the obligations imposed on it by the treaty executed among the other States is called *collateral agreement*.[34]

It is really difficult to visualize the *third party* status referred to by Art. 35 of the 1969 Convention. Rezek even questions the following: "If the consent imposed is express and in writing, would not the alleged third party be better defined as a party to the treaty, different from the other

---

32 See Cahier, Philippe. Le problème des effets des traités à l'égard des états tiers, cit., p. 644-657; Rezek, José Francisco, *Direito dos tratados*, cit., p. 407; De La Guardia, Ernesto, *Derecho de los tratados internacionales*, cit., p. 232; Kamto, Maurice, La volonté de l'État en droit international, cit., p. 303-304; and Villiger, Mark E., *Commentary on the 1969 Vienna Convention on the Law of Treaties*, cit., p. 476-480.

33 See Fitzmaurice, Gerald Gray [Special Rapporteur], *Yearbook of the International Law Commission* (1960), vol. II, p. 82.

34 See Waldock, Humphrey [Special Rapporteur], *Yearbook of the International Law Commission* (1964), vol. II, p. 18; and Dinh, Daillier & Pellet, *Direito internacional público*, cit., p. 249.

parties solely for procedural reasons?". The so called *guaranty system* illustrates well a situation where such provision applies, but it is not the only example of the application of Art. 35.[35] Rezek further exemplifies: "At the closing of a collective negotiation, when a particular State expressly accepts the duty of depositary, and for any reason it does not ratify the relevant treaty, it becomes a third party bound by the agreement, pursuant to Art. 35".[36] It should be pointed out that the *guaranty system* is not mentioned in the 1969 Vienna Convention, but it is stated in Art. 13 of the Havana Convention on Treaties:

> "The execution of a treaty may, through express stipulation or by virtue of special agreement, be placed wholly or partly under the guaranty of one or more States. The guarantor State can intervene in the execution of the treaty only by virtue of a request by one of the interested parties and then only under the conditions which were stipulated for intervention. When intervention takes place, only such measures may be employed by the guarantor State as are sanctioned by international law, and without requirements of greater scope than those of the State which has been guaranteed".

As we can see, the quality of *guarantor* assumed (*accepted*) by a State pursuant to the provision above, fits perfectly within the scope of Art. 35 of the 1969 Vienna Convention, and it is clear that an *obligation* accepted by a third State can also differ from the *subject-matter* of the treaty concluded among the State parties.[37]

Note that, for the Convention, obligations arising for third States pursuant to Art. 35, may only be *revoked* or *modified* with the consent of the parties to the treaty and of the third State, unless it is established that they had otherwise agreed (Art. 37, item 1). Construction of Art. 37, item 1, indicates that the obligation can be revoked or modified by *the parties* to the treaty or by the *third State*. When *the parties* intend to revoke or modify an obligation imposed on a third State, the express consent of such State is clearly unnecessary; despite the fact that the text of the Convention may lead to the conclusion that such express consent is necessary. Therefore, the consent of the third party (in the event of reduction or revocation of its obligations by *the parties* to the treaty) may be *tacit*. In fact, the *express* and *written* consent required by Art. 35 of the Convention for undertaking an

---

35 See Rezek, José Francisco. *Direito dos tratados*, cit., p. 408.

36 Rezek, José Francisco. Idem, ibidem.

37 See Rezek, José Francisco. Idem, p. 408-409.

obligation (for logical reasons) is not required when the same obligation is *reduced* or *revoked*. As pointed out by Brotons, there is no reason to require express and written consent when the obligation is *reduced* and, even more, when it is *revoked*.[38] On the other hand, when the *third State* intends to revoke or modify an obligation arising from a treaty among other parties, it is necessary – and Art. 37, item 1 of the Convention is literally applied in this case – for the joint and express consent of the parties to the treaty *and of* the third State (in this case, such collateral agreement must be formalized in a separate treaty).

Finally, we will deal with exceptions to the need of consent by a third State to be bound by a treaty. Art. 75 of the 1969 Convention (and Art. 76 of the 1986 Convention) provides only one exception: a treaty may impose an obligation on a third State (when it is an *aggressor*) in consequence of measures taken in conformity with the 1945 Charter of the United Nations with reference to that State's aggression.[39] However, the problem with the provision of Art. 75 is the *quality* of such aggressor State (mainly because it is difficult for the UN Security Council to formally qualify as aggressions acts that are obvious aggressions). In practice, it is likely that only aggressors *defeated* in a certain international conflict will be subject to application of such provision.[40] Because we all know that the story is always written by the victors…

1.2.3.2 Treaties providing for rights for third States

The contracting parties may expressly accord a *right* or *privilege* to a third party that is not party to the treaty.[41] Although this is not frequent, *it is possible* that the parties to a certain treaty decide to accord such benefit to a third party. Art. 36, item 1, of the Vienna Convention sets forth:

---

38 Remiro Brotons, Antonio. *Derecho internacional público*, vol. 2, cit., p. 363.

39 On the definition of aggression, see Resolution 3314 (XXIX) of the UN General Assembly, dated 12.14.74. For the crime of aggression before the ICC, see Mazzuoli, Valerio de Oliveira, *Curso de direito internacional público*, cit., p. 1043-1045.

40 See Remiro Brotons, Antonio. *Derecho internacional público*, vol. 2, cit., p. 361. For details and reviews on the United Nations system, see Zolo, Danilo, *La justicia de los vencedores: de Nuremberg a Bagdad*, transl. by Elena Bossi, Madrid: Trotta, 2007, 206p.

41 See Waldock, Humphrey [Special Rapporteur], *Yearbook of the International Law Commission* (1964), vol. II, p. 18-19; and Villiger, Mark E., *Commentary on the 1969 Vienna Convention on the Law of Treaties*, cit., p. 483-488.

"A right arises for a third State from a provision of a treaty if the parties to the treaty intend the provision to accord that right either to the third State, or to a group of States to which it belongs, or to all States, and the third-party State assents thereto. Its assent shall be presumed so long as the contrary is not indicated, unless the treaty otherwise provides".

The scope of such statement makes it difficult to list common examples, understanding that *it is a right* granted to a third State from a *provision in favor of other parties* to the possibility to *accede* to multilateral treaties.[42]

The consent set by Art. 36 is considered *presumed*, until it is otherwise indicated.[43] That is to say, the third State, group of States or all the States that benefit from the right granted by the treaty do not need to accept such rights expressly and in writing, and their silence is deemed as an acceptance. Acceptance of *obligations* by a third State, on the contrary, must always be *express* and *in writing*.[44] However, the treaty may provide otherwise and require express consent (Art. 35, item 1, *in fine*). Note that, despite the ambiguous wording of Art. 36, item 1, *in fine*, consent of the third State is not presumed in two situations: *a*) if there is an indication to the contrary; and *b*) if otherwise provided by the treaty (for example, an express consent requirement).[45]

When a third State exercises a right granted to it by a treaty it was not a party to, it must fulfill the conditions provided in the treaty or estab-

---

42 See Rezek, José Francisco. *Direito dos tratados*, cit., p. 406-407. De La Guardia also provides the following examples: (1) *guaranty* treaties (in favor of specified third parties), or *guaranty and assistance* treaties (which either expressly or impliedly conceal an *alliance*); and (2) treaties (in favor of unspecified third parties) related to *communication* (*passages*) among States: Turkish Straits, Suez Canal, Panama Canal, Kiel Canal and Magellan Strait (see *Derecho de los tratados internacionales*, cit., p. 234-235). Villiger, in turn, only provides the example of opening a canal or river for free navigation (see *Commentary on the 1969 Vienna Convention on the Law of Treaties*, cit., p. 484).

43 Pursuant to *Projeto de Código de Direito International Público* (1911) by Epitácio Pessoa, Art. 209, such consent had to be *express*: "Treaty clauses agreed in favor of a third State require the express acceptance of such third State to be valid".

44 See Danilenko, G. M. *Law-making in the international community*, cit., p. 59; De La Guardia, Ernesto, *Derecho de los tratados internacionales*, cit., p. 233; Fitzmaurice, Malgosia, Third parties and the law of treaties, cit., p. 46; and Villiger, Mark E., *Commentary on the 1969 Vienna Convention on the Law of Treaties*, cit., p. 485.

45 We believe that Art. 36, item 1, *in fine*, would be less ambiguous with the following wording: "Consent is presumed until otherwise specified or unless otherwise provided by the treaty".

lished in accordance with it (Art. 36, item 2).[46] An example of such provision is Art. 35, item 2, of the UN Charter, which provides: "A state which is not a Member of the United Nations may bring to the attention of the Security Council or of the General Assembly any dispute to which it is a party if it accepts in advance, for the purposes of the dispute, the obligations of pacific settlement provided in the present Charter".

Therefore, States are entitled to grant rights to one or more third States by means of a treaty, and such third States do not need to give their express and written consent, since silence is deemed as an acceptance as well. But the beneficiary State, as pointed out by Accioly, does not acquire *ipso facto* the right to demand performance, since the contracting parties are free to modify or terminate such treaty in the form they have agreed.[47] For instance, imagine a bilateral treaty granting all States the right to navigate waters adjacent to the territories of both parties. The silence of all third parties will constitute acceptance; but the parties to the treaty may extinguish or modify the benefit, as and when they deem appropriate.[48] Hence, pursuant to Art. 36 of the Convention, States parties to the treaty only "grant" a specific right to third States, without "creating" a subjective legal situation for such States. Third States, in turn, merely "consent" to benefit from the right provided in the treaty, without becoming holders (entitled to) of such right. However, there is an exception to such rule, provided in Art. 37, item 2: "When a right has arisen for a third State in conformity with article 36, the right *may not be revoked or modified* by the parties *if it is established that the right was intended* not to be revocable or subject to modification *without the consent of the third State*". That is to say, consent of the third party will only be necessary (to revoke or modify the right) when the treaty provides or it is otherwise indicated that the intention of the parties was to accord an *irrevocable* or *unchangeable* right to it; in this case, the third State, by will of the parties, becomes the true *holder* of a right, which may not be revoked or modified without its due consent.[49]

---

46 For details, see Cahier, Philippe, Le problème des effets des traités à l'égard des états tiers, cit., p. 620-640; and Kamto, Maurice, La volonté de l'État en droit international, cit., p. 304-308.

47 Accioly, Hildebrando. *Tratado de direito internacional público*, vol. I, cit., p. 610.

48 See related discussions in the third report by Humphrey Waldock at the ILC, in *Yearbook of the International Law Commission* (1964), vol. II, p. 21-22.

49 See Remiro Brotons, Antonio. *Derecho internacional público*, vol. 2, cit., p. 364.

Finally, it should be clarified that a treaty provision may create rights or obligations for third States for reasons different from the will of the parties. A rule set forth by a treaty may also be binding on a third State because it became a *customary rule* of International Law, recognized as such.[50] Pursuant to Art. 38 of the 1969 Vienna Convention, which states "[n]othing in articles 34 to 37 precludes a rule set forth in a treaty from *becoming binding* upon a third-party State as a customary rule of international law, recognized as such".[51] Note that Art. 38 clearly allows an international act to create an international *custom*; therefore, an international customary rule may be created not only by the *practice* of States or international organizations, but also by the provisions of a treaty signed by other States.[52] This makes sense. Since execution of a treaty is a *practice*, we may say that such practice is able to create *precedents* that give rise to certain international customary rules for *third parties* adopting such practice.[53] In this case, the legal effects for third States are not produced by the *treaty*, but by the *custom* created by the treaty, as long as the basic requirements are met: general application, effective performance and belief that such practice is required as a matter of law (*opinio juris*) by the States that comply with the provisions of that treaty (see item 1.3, below).[54]

---

[50] On this subject, see Eustathiades, Konstantinos Th., *Unratified codification conventions…*, cit., p. 7-13; Remiro Brotons, Antonio, *Derecho internacional público*, vol. 2, cit., p. 396-399; De La Guardia, Ernesto, *Derecho de los tratados internacionales*, cit., p. 237-241; and Reisman, Michael W., Unratified treaties and other unperfected acts in international law: constitutional functions, *Vanderbilt Journal of Transnational Law*, vol. 35, No. 3 (2002), p. 729-747; and Villiger, Mark E., *Commentary on the 1969 Vienna Convention on the Law of Treaties*, cit., p. 499-504.

[51] De La Guardia points out the following, in relation to the history of Art. 38: "Due to the difficulties posed by the subject, the ILC inverted the argumentation: instead of affirming or recognizing that customs may arise from treaties, it cautiously stated, but not very clearly for us, that rules codified in Art. 34 'do not prevent' a treaty rule from becoming customary (…)" (*Derecho de los tratados internacionales*, cit., p. 239). The wording of the provision is the result of an amendment made by Mexico, in addition to the final expression "recognized as such", from an amendment made by Syria. According to De La Guardia, the latter amendment "made the ILC text more accurate and fixed a relevant omission, since in the current international community, for a rule to be binding on a third State, such State has to *recognize* it as a customary rule of international law" (*Op. cit.*, p. 240-241).

[52] See Fitzmaurice, Malgosia. Third parties and the law of treaties, cit., p. 58; Villiger, Mark E., *Commentary on the 1969 Vienna Convention on the Law of Treaties*, cit., p. 501-502; and Boyle, Alan, Reflections on the treaty as a law-making instrument, cit., p. 4.

[53] See Reuter, Paul. *Introducción al derecho de los tratados*, cit., p. 131.

[54] See De La Guardia, Ernesto. *Derecho de los tratados internacionales*, cit., p. 237-238.

1.3 Effects of treaties that have not yet entered into force on contracting parties and third parties

The effects of treaties on the contracting parties and third parties were analyzed in items 1.1 and 1.2 above, respectively, when the international act has *already been in force*. Now, it would be interesting to discuss the effects on the contracting parties and third parties when the treaty *has not yet entered into force*. For the avoidance of doubt, a treaty *that has not yet entered into force*, as mentioned herein, is a treaty that has already been *adopted* and *signed* by negotiators. This case does not contemplate the possibility (if any at all) of *treaty draft* effects on contracting parties and third parties.

For signatory *contracting parties*, the effects of a treaty that has not yet entered into force (as mentioned in Part II, Ch. 1, item 1.5.1.2) are basically two: (*a*) negotiators shall be bound by their actions and decisions reflected on the adopted text, so they cannot modify the treaty structure in the future (except for the case of a unilateral reservation); and (*b*) signatories are not allowed to perform any acts that may defeat the object and purpose of the treaty prior to its entry into force. This second effect is expressed in Art. 18, *a*) of the 1969 Convention, as mentioned above, pursuant to which a State "is obliged to refrain from acts which *would defeat* the object and purpose of a treaty *when*: *a*) it *has signed* (...), until it shall have made its intention clear not to become a party to the treaty". This clearly shows that, although the treaty signed has not entered yet into force, it *already produces* effects on the contracting parties; especially, that said parties must refrain from doing any acts that may defeat its object or purpose.

For non-signatory *third parties* (and, obviously, for signatory contracting parties as well) treaties that have not yet entered into force may be deemed *international custom*, depending on the content of the text adopted and the discussions held about it during negotiations. States negotiating a specific treaty are indicated to do it because they are *willing*, *prior* to the negotiation, to see some matters regulated by positive law. Their will prior to negotiations can frequently be translated into the generalized acceptance that certain *practices* are deemed to belong to the world of the law. It was already indicated (item 1.2.3.2, above) that Art. 38 of the Vienna Convention does not preclude "a rule set forth in a treaty from becoming binding upon a third State as a customary rule of international law, recognized as such". Such rule is valid both for treaties in force and for treaties that *have not yet entered into force*. It does not matter if the treaty is in force or not for the rules contained in it to be valid as international *custom*, and, therefore, as a *source* of Public International Law. In relation to this, it should be highlighted that the ICJ has repeatedly understood (for example, in the cases concerning the *North Sea Continental Shelf,* 1969; *Military and Paramilitary Activities in and against Nicaragua,* 1986; *Legal Consequences of the Construction of a Wall in the Occupied Palestinian Territory*, 2004, among others) that a treaty rule may have a *declarative, crystallizing* effect or even be the *generator* of customary rules; and that, by producing one of such effects, the treaty is binding irrespective of its entry into force and in connection with States that are not parties thereto. Therefore, if it can be proved that the adopted treaty is *declaring* a practice that, in fact, had already been deemed mandatory as a result of the custom related to it, or it *crystallizes* a custom generated simultaneously with its creation or, even, it has actually *generated* a new custom after its conclusion, it can be required from a third State (which has not participated in the adopted treaty negotiations and has not signed it) to adopt certain measures regarding compliance with the treaty that has produced effects *vis-à-vis* said State *as a custom.*

1.4 Amendment and modification of treaties

The 1969 Vienna Convention (followed by the 1986 Convention) uses, in different provisions of the text, the expressions *amendment* (Art. 40) and *modification* (Art. 41). Although the purpose of both of them is *reviewing* the text of a treaty, they are different activities, with different effects. While *amendment* includes all formal changes to the provisions of a treaty, irrespective of their number and subject, and valid for all the parties in every specific agreement, *modification* refers to the wording of certain provisions and is valid only between certain parties.[55]

Therefore, both notions should be studied separately. The matter of internal law procedure regarding amending or modifying agreements will also be verified in the last item of this subject (item 1.4.3).

1.4.1 Amendment of treaties

If so agreed by the parties, any treaty can be amended, that is to say, its original text in force can be modified.[56] Such amendments depend only

---

[55] See Remiro Brotons, Antonio. *Derecho internacional público*, vol. 2, cit., p. 408; Dinh, Daillier & Pellet, *Direito internacional público*, cit., p. 301; and Shaw, Malcolm N., *Direito internacional*, cit., p. 692. See also Waldock, Humphrey [Special Rapporteur], *Yearbook of the International Law Commission* (1964), vol. II, p. 47-52.

[56] See Maresca, Adolfo. *Il diritto dei trattati…*, cit., p. 461-478; Sinclair, Ian, *The Vienna Convention on the Law of Treaties*, cit., p. 106-109; Aust, Anthony, *Modern treaty law*

and exclusively on the will (agreement) of the parties, as provided in Art. 39 of the Convention.[57] Such rule is applied to both bilateral and multilateral treaties. This is, however, a rule that *supplements* the parties' will, since the parties "are free to reject it, restrict the possibilities of using it, or clarify its modalities by including special provisions called 'review clauses' in the treaty to establish the treaty amendment process in advance".[58] Such 'clauses' may also be aimed at securing a minimum of stability to the treaty, providing, for instance, that a proposal to review an agreement will be authorized only after a certain period of time, as provided in Art. 312, item 1, of the 1982 United Nations Convention on the Law of the Sea (Montego Bay Convention), which determined that, only after the expiry of a period of 10 years from the date of entry into force, States may propose amendments to the text, other than those relating to seabed activities.

With regard to amendments to bilateral treaties, there is no further issue. Obviously, the parties must negotiate them by mutual agreement, through the appropriate means (mixed commissions as provided for in the treaty, diplomatic means, etc.), but their formulation, again, poses no further issues.[59] The situation differs with amendments to *multilateral* treaties; therefore, the 1969 Vienna Convention dedicated a specific article (under which the general rules of customary origin related to the subject were codified) to regulate the issue. The aforementioned articles provide as follows:

"Article 40. *Amendment of multilateral treaties.*

---

and practice, cit., p. 212-223; Aust, Anthony, Amendment of treaties, in Orakhelashvili, Alexander & Williams, Sarah (eds.), *40 years of the Vienna Convention on the Law of Treaties*, cit., p. 41-54; and Chanaki, Athina, *L'adaptation des traités dans le temps*, Bruxelles: Bruylant, 2013, p. 27-214. See also ILC, *Yearbook of the International Law Commission* (1966), vol. II, p. 231-235. Villiger's opinion on this respect should be pointed out: "There are no unchangeable treaties" (*Commentary on the 1969 Vienna Convention on the Law of Treaties*, cit., p. 512).

57 Art. 39, *in fine*, also provides that the rules laid down in Part II of the Convention shall be applied "to such an [amending] agreement, except in so far as the treaty may otherwise provide". Part II of the Convention (Arts. 6 to 25) provides for the conclusion and entry into force of treaties (capacity of States to conclude treaties, full powers, expression of consent, reservations, entry into force and provisional application of treaties). It is the essential core of the Convention, whose rules must also be followed in the case of amendments, except as otherwise provided by the treaty.

58 Dinh, Daillier & Pellet. *Direito internacional público*, cit., p. 302.

59 On amendments of bilateral treaties, see Remiro Brotons, Antonio, *Derecho internacional público*, vol. 2, cit., p. 410; and Aust, Anthony, Amendment of treaties, cit., p. 43-44.

1. Unless the treaty otherwise provides, the amendment of multilateral treaties shall be governed by the following paragraphs.
2. Any proposal to amend a multilateral treaty as between all the parties must be notified to all the contracting States and all the contracting organizations, each one of which shall have the right to take part in:
   a) the decision as to the action to be taken in regard to such proposal;
   b) the negotiation and conclusion of any agreement for the amendment of the treaty.
3. Every State or international organization entitled to become a party to the treaty shall also be entitled to become a party to the treaty as amended.
4. The amending agreement does not bind any State or international organization already a party to the treaty which does not become a party to the amending agreement; article 30, paragraph 4(b), applies in relation to such State or organization.
5. Any State or international organization which becomes a party to the treaty after the entry into force of the amending agreement shall, failing an expression of a different intention by that State or that organization:
   a) be considered as a party to the treaty as amended; and
   b) be considered as a party to the unamended treaty in relation to any party to the treaty not bound by the amending agreement".

It is reasonable that the Vienna Convention has focused on amendments of *multilateral* treaties, particularly because it is known that *multilateral* treaties *last longer* and govern matters intended to become *stable* in a specific legal field. The number of treaties (though not all of them) that provide for an *express* amendment clause is also growing, especially those treaties whose content (*a*) varies widely or (*b*) is incomplete or fragmented, as they do not cover all the possibilities of regulating the subject.[60]

The first matter to be analyzed relates to the *initiative* to propose amendments to a multilateral treaty. Art. 40, item 2, of the Convention only states that any *proposal* to amend a multilateral treaty as between the parties must be *notified* to all the contracting States… The Vienna Convention has not defined *the legitimate parties* that may propose amendments.[61] There-

60 See Remiro Brotons, Antonio. *Derecho internacional público*, vol. 2, cit., p. 411.

61 As pointed out by De La Guardia, Art. 40, item 2, of the Convention only sought to grant "further guaranties to contracting parties in connection with their participation in amendment proposals and in the negotiation and execution of the new agreement" (*Derecho de los tratados internacionales*, cit., p. 250).

fore, except as otherwise provided in the treaty, it shall be understood that *all* the parties to the treaty may propose amendments to the text.[62] Art. 312, item 1, of the 1982 Montego Bay Convention, as explained before, authorizes "any State" to propose amendments to the Convention, after the expiry of a period of 10 years from the date of its entry into force; Arts. 313 and 314 also contain said authorization. There are some treaties, such as the 1967 Treaty for the Prohibition of Nuclear Weapons in Latin America and the Caribbean (Tlatelolco Treaty), which allow *other* subjects, for instance, an *Agency* created by the treaty itself, to propose an amendment (see Arts. 6 and 7). There are other treaties (such as the 1959 Antarctic Treaty) that restrict the proposal of amendments to the *original* signatories of the Convention (see Art. XII). Therefore, the rules related to amendment proposals vary from treaty to treaty; but, again, if the treaty is silent, *any of the parties* is authorized to propose any amendment, pursuant to the provisions of Art. 40 of the 1969 Vienna Convention.[63]

Items 3, 4 and 5 of Art. 40 of the Convention set forth the *binding* rules for States in relation to the amending agreement, establishing what is called *duplicity of legal regimes* by virtue of which the original treaty and the amended treaty are simultaneously in force.[64] As set forth by item 3 of Art. 40, every State "*entitled* to become a party to the treaty *shall also be entitled* to become a party to the treaty as amended". Such provision only refers to States that became a party to the treaty *after the amending agreement*. In this case, pursuant to the rule of item 5, Art. 40, any State which becomes a party to the treaty after the entry into force of the amending agreement shall, failing an expression of a different intention by that State: *a*) be considered as a party to the treaty as amended; and *b*) be considered as a party to the unamended treaty in relation to any party to the treaty not bound by the amending agreement (in the event that any original States have not acceded to the amending agreement).

There is again a duplicity of legal regimes here, as it allows that a State that will become a party in the future be a party to *one and the same* treaty with *two versions*, and, therefore, with a *double regime*, i.e.: *a*) in connec-

---

62 See Remiro Brotons, Antonio. *Derecho internacional público*, vol. 2, cit., p. 411. See also Villiger, Mark E. *Commentary on the 1969 Vienna Convention on the Law of Treaties*, cit., p. 522-523.

63 See Remiro Brotons, Antonio. *Derecho internacional público*, vol. 2, cit., p. 411-412.

64 See Rezek, José Francisco. *Direito dos tratados*, cit., p. 430-434; Reuter, Paul, *Introducción al derecho de los tratados*, cit., p. 159-164; and Villiger, Mark E., *Commentary on the 1969 Vienna Convention on the Law of Treaties*, cit., p. 524-525.

tion with States parties to the amending treaty and the State becoming a party, the amended treaty will be valid; and *b*) in connection with original States parties (that did not accept the amending agreement) and the State becoming a party, the original treaty with no amendments will be valid.[65] The reason is that, pursuant to item 4 of the abovementioned article, the amending agreement "does not bind any State already a party to the treaty which does not become a party to the amending agreement", adding that "article 30, paragraph 4 (*b*) applies in relation to such State". Under the terms of Article 30, paragraph 4 (*b*), when the parties to the later treaty do not include all the parties to the earlier one, "the relation between a party to both treaties and a party to only one of the treaties, the treaty to which both are parties governs their mutual rights and obligations". Therefore, *duplicity of legal regimes* means that the original treaty may be in force *at the same time* among the parties that have not consented to the amendment, and among them and the parties that have consented to it, notwithstanding the fact that the amended treaty will be fully in force for the latter.[66]

It should be highlighted that, if a State finally expresses its consent to be bound by a treaty that was amended and makes no objection to its content, it is presumed that said State acceded to the amended text. In these cases, the silence of the State implies the acceptance of the amendment. However, the new State *may not want* to accede to the amended treaty, but only to its original text, in which case the treaty (for said specific State) will be valid without amendments. For the avoidance of doubt, when a State becomes a party, generally by *accession*, to an amended instrument, without any objections, said State will be considered a party to said agreement *with the amendments in force* regarding the remaining States parties to the amended agreement. Said State will, however, be considered a party *to the unamended treaty* (that is to say, to the *original* treaty) in connection with the States not bound by the amending agreement, under the terms of Art. 40, item 5, *a*) and *b*) of the 1969 Convention.

Approved amendments must first be *adopted* by States in order *to enter into force*. Even though the Vienna Convention remains silent on the subject, it is understood that amendments (for being a later *agreement*) will be *adopted* in the same way as the original treaty, pursuant to the terms of Art. 9 of the Convention (that provides that the adoption of the text takes place by the consent of *all* the States participating in its drawing up, ex-

65 See De La Guardia, Ernesto. *Derecho de los tratados internacionales*, cit., p. 251.

66 See Calsing, Maria de Assis. *O tratado internacional e sua aplicação no Brasil*, cit., p. 48.

cept if the text was adopted at an international conference, in which case it will take place by the vote of two-thirds of the States present and voting). Evidently, such procedure will only be followed in the event that no other rule has been established by the treaty itself.[67] Once the amendment is *adopted*, its *entry into force* will have to wait. The amendment may, however, enter into force *immediately*, depending on the provisions of each agreement. In some treaties, amendments cannot enter into force immediately, depending on the will of a majority, etc. Art. 108 of the UN Charter, for instance, provides that amendments to the Charter will only enter into force "when they have been adopted by a vote of two thirds of the members of the General Assembly and ratified in accordance with their respective constitutional processes by two thirds of the Members of the United Nations, including all the permanent members of the Security Council".

Nothing precludes the review of a multilateral treaty from being established in *another treaty* executed later. In this case, however, *the same parties* who participated in the original treaty must express their unanimous consent to amend the treaty by means of another international instrument, executed for this same purpose, without which the amendment will not be valid. It does not matter if there are *more parties* to the later treaty than to the original one, but *all* the parties to the original treaty must also be the parties to the later treaty.[68] As explained by Rezek, if this is not the case, that is to say, if the parties to the later treaty were numerically *fewer* than the parties to the original treaty, the original treaty would not be *amended objectively*. Therefore, this would merely be a case of a limited amending agreement, as provided in Art. 41, item 1, of the Convention.[69] In this case, it would not be an *amendment* to the treaty, but a specific *modification* thereof, as it will be analyzed below.

1.4.2 Modification of multilateral treaties

In addition to being *amended*, treaties may also be *modified* (through the so called "*inter se* agreements"). Said expression is only related to *multilateral* treaties (as also set forth by the Vienna Convention). It is a particular way of modifying a treaty, which will be valid only for *specific parties* (not all of them) who consented, by a specific consent among

67 See Remiro Brotons, Antonio. *Derecho internacional público*, vol. 2, cit., p. 413-414.

68 See Rezek, José Francisco. *Direito dos tratados*, cit., p. 434-435.

69 See Rezek, José Francisco. Idem, p. 435, note 719.

them, to modify the terms of the treaty *inter se*.[70] In this way, by means of a *modification* procedure, two or more parties to a multilateral treaty, without proposing any amendment to the other parties, decide by mutual consent to modify the legal effects of a specific treaty in their reciprocal relations.[71]

This is governed by Art. 41, item 1 of the 1969 Vienna Convention, which provides as follows:

> "Article 41. *Agreements to modify multilateral treaties between certain of the parties only.*
>
> 1. Two or more of the parties to a multilateral treaty may conclude an agreement to modify the treaty as between themselves alone if:
>
>   *a)* the possibility of such a modification is provided for by the treaty; or
>
>   *b*) the modification in question is not prohibited by the treaty; and
>
>   i) does not affect the enjoyment by the other parties of their rights under the treaty or the performance of their obligations;
>
>   ii) does not relate to a provision, derogation from which is incompatible with the effective execution of the object and purpose of the treaty as a whole".

It is clear that the 1969 Vienna Convention *authorizes* modifying agreements related to multilateral treaties only between some of the parties, even if the modification under analysis is not *forbidden* by the treaty; in the latter case, however, the Convention requires that the *inter se* agreement (*i*) "does not affect the enjoyment by the other parties of their rights under the treaty or the performance of their obligations"; and (*ii*) "does not relate to a provision, derogation from which is incompatible with the effective execution of the object and purpose of the treaty as a whole" (Art. 41, item 1, *b*).[72] Such conditions (*i* and *ii*) are not alternative,

---

70 See ILC, *Yearbook of the International Law Commission* (1966), vol. II, p. 235-236; and Villiger, Mark E., *Commentary on the 1969 Vienna Convention on the Law of Treaties*, cit., p. 531-538.

71 See Remiro Brotons, Antonio. *Derecho internacional público*, vol. 2, cit., p. 369-370; De La Guardia, Ernesto, *Derecho de los tratados internacionales*, cit., p. 251-255; Shaw, Malcolm N., *Direito internacional*, cit., p. 693; and Aust, Anthony, Amendment of treaties, cit., p. 52-53.

72 According to De La Guardia, the 1991 Treaty of Asunción (which established the Mercosur) would be an example of such type of modifying agreement concluded among four members of ALADI (Argentina, Brazil, Paraguay and Uruguay, with the subsequent

but cumulative ones.[73] Additionally, for the purpose of securing the rights of States that are not a party to the modifying agreement, the Convention provides that, in the case of item 1) a) of Art. 41 – in which case the multilateral treaty itself provides for the possibility of being modified by the conclusion of another instrument between two or more parties, with reciprocal effects –, said parties will *notify* the other parties of their intention to conclude the agreement and of the modifications of the treaty for which it provides (Art. 41, item 2).[74] It should be noted that they are mere *notifications*, which do not secure the notified parties the right to participate in the drawing up of the modifying agreement, as it happens in the case of Art. 40, item 2.[75]

An example of that type of agreement is the agreement executed to modify the territorial application of a treaty, since, under the terms of Art. 29 of the Vienna Convention, a treaty is binding, in principle, "upon each party in respect of its *entire* territory".[76] Consequently, nothing precludes some States from concluding an *inter se* agreement later for the purpose

---

association of Chile, on June 25, 1996). As explained by the Argentine internationalist De La Guardia: "Pursuant to Art. 41 of the Vienna Convention, from a formal point of view: *a*) a modification (separate agreement) among some parties to the 1980 Treaty of Montevideo *was not forbidden by it*; *b*) the Mercosur does not affect the enjoyment of rights that belong to the other parties to the ALADI; on the contrary, they can accede to the Mercosur (...) five years after the entry into force of the Treaty of Asunción. From a material point of view, the Mercosur is not incompatible with the purpose of ALADI (Latin American integration), and also promotes the integration of four of its members as effectively as possible [it should be highlighted that Venezuela is currently participating in the Mercosur too.] Even though the Treaty of Asunción does not contain any provision related to institutional relations with ALADI, one of its provisions states as follows: 'We are aware that this Treaty must be viewed as a further step in efforts gradually to bring about Latin American integration, in keeping with the objectives of the Montevideo Treaty of 1980'; and the relation with ALADI is important under the Trade Liberalization Program, either by modifying agreements in force, recognizing them or establishing limitations and conditions to the trade management by States parties. Thus, for example, Art. 8 states the recognition to abide by the commitments undertaken in the framework of ALADI etc". (*Derecho de los tratados internacionales*, cit., p. 251-252, note no. 8).

73 See De La Guardia, Ernesto. *Derecho de los tratados internacionales*, cit., p. 253; and Villiger, Mark E., *Commentary on the 1969 Vienna Convention on the Law of Treaties*, cit., p. 534: "(...) the two further conditions in subparagraph 1(b) (N. 8-9) apply cumulatively".

74 See Remiro Brotons, Antonio. *Derecho internacional público*, vol. 2, cit., p. 370.

75 See De La Guardia, Ernesto. *Derecho de los tratados internacionales*, cit., p. 253.

76 In relation to Art. 29 of the Convention, see Part II, Ch. 3, item 3.3.2.2, above.

of excluding a portion of their territory from the application of a treaty, as long as said agreement does not affect, as provided in Art. 41, item 1, *b*, the enjoyment by the other parties of their rights under the treaty or the performance of their obligations, and does not relate to a provision, derogation from which is incompatible with the effective fulfilment of the object and purpose of the treaty as a whole.

It should be pointed out that legal scholars have recognized that *custom* may also modify treaties, as well as a *tacit agreement*. In fact, in Art. 38 of the Draft Articles on the Law of Treaties, the ILC had proposed that a treaty "may be modified by subsequent practice in the application of the treaty establishing the agreement of the parties to modify its provisions". Although such rule, entitled "Modification of treaties by subsequent practice", was not approved at the Vienna Conference,[77] the truth is that the most important legal scholars have recognized the possibility of such type of treaty modifications.[78] According to Dinh, Daillier and Pellet, the Vienna Conference "rejected this provision, but without excluding the possibility of a modification by the subsequent behavior of the parties", being concluded by said authors that practice has accepted "this practice undoubtedly, which is established by case law".[79] There are no doubts that a treaty may be modified by a subsequent norm of *jus cogens*. Although the Vienna Convention has no provisions in such regard – Art. 64 of the Convention has only regulated the termination of a *treaty* in conflict with a new peremptory norm of general international law (see below Ch. 2, item 2.2.2.2) –, it may occur that the contradiction only relates to *one provision* of a treaty; in this case, as pointed by Dinh, Daillier and Pellet, there is "no reason to presume the termination of the treaty as a whole; only the article contrary to the new peremptory norm disappears, subject to the provisions of Art. 44, item 3 of the Convention. This solution implicitly arises out of paragraph 5 of said article, which does not exclude treaties contrary to a new norm of *jus cogens* from the possibility of 'separating' the provisions thereof".[80]

---

77 At the Conference, the elimination of the rule was decided by 53 negative votes, 15 positive votes, and 26 abstentions.

78 In that regard, see Cot, Jean-Pierre, La conduite subséquente des parties a un traité, *Revue Générale de Droit International Public*, vol. 70, Paris (1966), p. 632-666. On the topic, see also De La Guardia, Ernesto, *Derecho de los tratados internacionales*, cit., p. 253-255.

79 Dinh, Daillier & Pellet. *Direito internacional público*, cit., p. 303.

80 Dinh, Daillier & Pellet. Idem, p. 304.

Finally, it should be noted that item 5 of Art. 30 of the Convention, which governs the case of successive treaties on the same subject, provides that rules set forth in item 4 of Art. 30 are applied "without prejudice to Art. 41" (see item 1.6.4, below).

1.4.3 Internal law procedure

Any changes made to a treaty, as Malcom Shaw explains, "must be performed pursuant to the same formalities used when the original treaty was created", since "rights and obligations of a legal nature can be involved, and any changes to them involve considerations on sovereignty and the States' consent, all of which require careful interpretation and attention".[81] There would be no reason why the internal law procedures for amendments should be abandoned, if this procedure was used at the time the original treaty was approved. In fact, amending or modifying agreements related to treaties must comply with the *same stages* of the original treaty, at the internal law level. This is a logical point, since any *amendment* or *modification* of the original treaty in practice represents a *new* treaty, which does not mean that the internal law procedures may be disregarded for the approval and final consent thereof.

In Brazil, amending or modifying agreements related to treaties must be necessarily approved by the Legislative Power, as it happens in the case of a treaty ratification and accession, except that none of them required consultation with the Congress. Therefore, if a State required a Parliamentary approval for said ratification or accession, the aforementioned approval will also be necessary to accept the amending or modifying agreement. By a Parliamentary approval of the amending or modifying agreement, the President of the Republic is then *authorized* to deposit (generally, with the same depositary body or State of the treaty) the Brazilian acceptance of the change made in the agreement.

Nowadays, under the provisions of the 1988 Federal Constitution, Legislative Orders ordinarily approve treaties signed by the Executive Power, pursuant to which "*any acts* that may result in reviewing the referred Convention, as well as any *supplementary adjustments* that may, under the terms of Art. 49, I, of the Federal Constitution, result in charges or commitments encumbering the national patrimony, are subject to the approval of the National Congress". This is the case with Legislative Order

---

81 Shaw, Malcolm N. *Direito internacional*, cit., p. 692.

1/1999, which approved the text of the Convention on Protection of Children and Co-operation in Respect of International Adoption, concluded in The Hague, on May 29, 1993, among many others.

Once the modification or the amendment is approved by the Parliament, the President of the Republic must *promulgate* the amending (or modifying) agreement by means of an *executive order* (as when a treaty is ratified or acceded to) and have it published in the Brazilian Official Gazette.

1.5 Interpretation of treaties

The provisions of a treaty are not always drawn up clearly and accurately, for them to be applied immediately without any doubts. Sometimes, it is not easy to establish the scope and clarify the obscurities (in some cases, left by negotiators on purpose) of a rule, a set of rules or even the whole agreement. In most cases, in order to be properly applied, a treaty must first be correctly *interpreted*. Therefore, interpretation is a procedure required for the proper *application* or *execution* of treaties.[82]

---

[82] On the subject, see Crandall, Samuel B., *Treaties: their making and enforcement*, cit., p. 371-403; Ehrlich, Ludwik, L'interprétation des traités, *Recueil des Cours*, vol. 24 (1928-IV), p. 1-145; Accioly, Hildebrando, *Tratado de direito internacional público*, vol. I, cit., p. 623-638; McNair, Arnold Duncan, *The law of treaties*, cit., p. 345-489; Berlia, G., Contribution à l'interprétation des traités, *Recueil des Cours*, vol. 114 (1965-I), p. 283-333; Maresca, Adolfo, *Il diritto dei trattati*..., cit., p. 333-348; Yasseen, Mustafa Kamil, L'interprétation des traités d'après la Convention de Vienne sur le Droit des Traités, *Recueil des Cours*, vol. 151 (1976-III), p. 1-114; Rezek, José Francisco, *Direito dos tratados*, cit., p. 445-456; Remiro Brotons, Antonio, *Derecho internacional público*, vol. 2, cit., p. 306-324; De La Guardia, Ernesto, *Derecho de los tratados internacionales*, cit., p. 216-230; Reuter, Paul, *Introducción al derecho de los tratados*, cit., p. 117-121; Brownlie, Ian, *Princípios de direito internacional público*, cit., p. 650-656; Rodrigues, Luís Barbosa, *A interpretação dos tratados internacionais*, 2. ed. (reviewed), Lisboa: Associação Acadêmica da Faculdade de Direito, 2002, 165p; Engelen, Frank, *Interpretation of tax treaties under international law*, Amsterdam: IBDF, 2004, 590p; Aust, Anthony, *Modern treaty law and practice*, cit., p. 184-206; Linderfalk, Ulf, *On the interpretation of treaties: the modern international law as expressed in the 1969 Vienna Convention on the Law of Treaties*, Dordrecht: Springer, 2007, 414p; Gardiner, Richard K., *Treaty interpretation*, New York: Oxford University Press, 2008, 407p; Villiger, Mark E., *Commentary on the 1969 Vienna Convention on the Law of Treaties*, cit., p. 421-462; and Fitzmaurice, Malgosia; Elias, Olufemi & Merkouris, Panos (eds.), *Treaty interpretation and the Vienna Convention on the Law of Treaties: 30 years on*, Leiden: Martinus Nijhoff, 2010, 382p.

In a legal sense, interpreting means rationally determining the precise sense of the rule, rendering the text or any of its provisions more clear and comprehensible, so that the parties are sure about the scope and meaning of the context, smoothing the way for doubts, obscurities, contradictions or ambiguities that may exist.

During the Vienna Conference, the problem of treaty interpretation was basically divided into two currents of opinion: one which understood that a treaty interpretation is aimed at achieving the actual and common intention of the parties and, the other one which considered that the true purpose of a treaty interpretation was determining the meaning thereof. That is to say, the first current prioritized the intention of the parties, while the second one took into consideration the study and analysis of the text.[83] In practice, the divergence was based on the importance that each current gave to the *travaux préparatoires* for interpreting treaties.[84] The second opinion was finally applied, as the 1969 Vienna Convention gave more importance to the *text* of the treaty (based on the fact that it is the true intention of the parties) than to the *travaux préparatoires* (which must be used only as a *supplementary means* of interpretation).

This subject has been regulated in Arts. 31 to 33 of the 1969 Convention, which turned widely known customary rules into law, both in relation to national legal systems and international case law. In fact, such provisions contain interpretative methods, such as grammatical, contextual (systematic) and teleological ones.

1.5.1 General interpretation rule

Art. 31, item 1, of the 1969 Convention provides a "general rule of interpretation "of treaties, by establishing that any international treaty "shall be interpreted in good faith in accordance with the ordinary meaning to be given to the terms of the treaty in their context and in the light of its object and purpose".[85]

---

83 See Berlia, G. Contribution à l'interprétation des traités, cit., p. 295-305.

84 For a view prior to the Convention discussions, see Lauterpacht, Hersch, *The development of international law by the International Court*, London: Stevens & Sons, 1958, p. 116-141.

85 For more details, see Gardiner, Richard K., *Treaty interpretation*, cit., p. 141-202; and Maresca, Adolfo, *Il diritto dei trattati…*, cit., p. 349-360. For ILC discussions relating to this subject, see Bernhardt, Rudolf, Interpretation and implied (tacit) modification of treaties: comments on Arts. 27, 28, 29 and 38 of the ILC's 1966 Draft Articles on the Law

It is clearly seen that the starting point for interpreting treaties is focused on the *text*, since it is the *authentic* expression of the parties' intention. The reference made by the Convention "to the terms of the treaty in their context" means that the *text* is the main core of the interpretative activity,[86] to which not less important supporting elements will be added, such as *good faith*, *common sense*, *object* and *purpose*.[87]

From the very beginning, Art. 31 item 1 states that treaties must be interpreted in *good faith*. This is an integral element of the rule *pacta sunt servanda*,[88] which is based on the respect and loyalty commitments by any persons whose actions are questioned, always assuming that said persons will refrain from acting with concealment, fraud or willful misconduct in relation to others; good faith ends when such persons become aware (or *should* be aware) that there is no justification (legal base, foundation, etc.) for their claim.[89] The same provision states that treaties must be interpreted according to the *common meaning* attributed to their terms, i.e., that the words of the text must be interpreted in their own and usual meaning, that is to say, the most *common* meaning in which certain expression or

---

of Treaties, *Zeitschrift für ausländisches öffentliches Recht und Völkerrecht*, vol. 27, No. 3, Berlin (1967), p. 491-506.

86 See Bernhardt, Rudolf. Interpretation and implied (tacit) modification of treaties..., cit., p. 495-497. On the contrary, as an expression of criticism towards the textual method of interpretation proposed by the ILC, see McDougal, Myres S., The International Law Commission's Draft Articles upon interpretation: textuality *redivivus*, *American Journal of International Law*, vol. 61, No. 4 (Oct. 1967), p. 992-1000, whose text starts with the following comment: "The great defect, and tragedy, in the International Law Commission's final recommendations about the interpretation of treaties is in their insistent emphasis upon an impossible, conformity-imposing textuality. This unhappy emphasis makes an appearance in, and dominates, the goal for interpretation which the Commission implicitly postulates but never critically examines; the deprecatory appraisal which the Commission offers of the potentialities that inhere in the rational employment of principles of interpretation; and the content and ordering of the particular principles which the Commission puts forward for canonization as 'obligatory' rules of law" (p. 992). *Obs.*: Myres McDougal was the American delegate at the Vienna Conference.

87 See Sinclair, Ian. *The Vienna Convention on the Law of Treaties*, cit., p. 114-115; and Remiro Brotons, Antonio, *Derecho internacional público*, vol. 2, cit., p. 310-311.

88 See Fitzmaurice, Malgosia. The practical working of the law of treaties, cit., p. 181: "Good faith is itself a legal principle and forms an integral part of the *pacta sunt servanda* principle".

89 See Linderfalk, Ulf. *On the interpretation of treaties...*, cit., p. 45.

term is used.[90] Common meaning must not be used when it is incompatible with the provisions of the treaty or when it is expressly used with another meaning. The common meaning attributed to a term, and which must serve as a guide to understand the accurate meaning attributed to a treaty, is the meaning related *to the time* the treaty was concluded,[91] except when it may be understood, from its content, that the intention of the parties was different. In the case *Competence of the General Assembly for the Admission of a State to the United Nations*, the ICJ pointed out, in a request for an *Advisory Opinion*, that "the first duty of a tribunal which was called upon to interpret a text was to endeavor to give effect to the words used in the context in which they occurred, by attributing to them their natural and ordinary meaning".[92]

The exception to this common meaning rule is provided in item 4 of Art. 31, when the Convention also recognizes that certain terms may be assigned *special meanings*, as long as it can be evidenced that it was the actual intention of the parties at that time.[93] This rule *confirms* the opinion according to which the meaning attributed to a treaty provision, for interpretation purposes, is always the *common* or *ordinary* meaning. The meaning intended to be attributed to a treaty provision will be *special* when it does not agree with what is normally (ordinarily) understood by such provision. In this case, the *intention of the parties* to attribute a special meaning to a provision must be proved, if the treaty does not explain the special meaning of the expression by means of an authentic interpretation.

The Convention also provides that treaties must be interpreted in their context, that is to say, *systematically*. For interpretative purposes, the *context* of a treaty also includes, apart from its text, preamble and annexes, (*a*) any agreement relating to the treaty which was made between all the parties in connection with the conclusion of the treaty, and (*b*) any instrument which was made by one or more parties in connection with the con-

---

90 That would be the case, according to De La Guardia, since "international agreements are not always written by jurists, who might use a more technical terminology" (*Derecho de los tratados internacionales*, cit., p. 221).

91 In order to assess the meaning assigned at the time the treaty was concluded, the *travaux préparatoires* of the treaty are used (see item 1.5.2, below).

92 Opinion dated March 3, 1950.

93 For criticism on Art. 31, item 4, see Rodrigues, Luís Barbosa, *A interpretação dos tratados internacionais*, cit., p. 82, who sustains that "this precept has a very limited importance, considering its basically strengthening or even pleonastic nature".

clusion of the treaty and accepted by the other parties as an instrument related to the treaty (Art. 31, item 2, *a* and *b*). The intention expressed by the Convention is that treaties have to be interpreted contextually, *as a whole*, offering the treaty interpreter a vast amount of research material to delimit the common meaning of words.[94] The introduction of such interpretation (or hermeneutics), which is called *contextual*, to the 1969 Convention was important, and it refers to the associations that different parts of the text have among each other ("as a whole"), The "context" itself may be, on the other hand, *intrinsic* or *extrinsic*, depending on whether it specifies, respectively, the meaning of a rule within the regulating text or it shows the interpreter the relations of said rule with the *extratextual* world.[95] By reading Art. 31, item 2, *a* and *b* of the Vienna Convention, it seems that it only admitted, for interpretative purposes, the use of the *intrinsic* context, since (1) the Convention refers to the text, the preamble and annexes *to the treaty*; (2) it provides for any agreement relating to the *treaty* executed among all the parties in connection with *the conclusion thereof*; and, finally, (3) it refers to any instrument established by one or many parties *in connection with the treaty conclusion* and accepted by the other parties *as an instrument relating to the treaty*.[96] That means that the "context" referred to by the Convention is not the *extratextual* context, such as, for example, the political, social, economic or cultural context in which the treaty was executed, but its *intrinsic* context (its elements, related agreements, etc.). In summary, for the Convention, the context should be the *set* of rules related to the treaty itself, taking into consideration every and all parts mutually interrelated, as well as all agreements related to the text.

Apart from the preamble and the remaining parts that belong to the treaty itself, *annexes* to each convention are also integral and indivisible parts, and they cannot be excluded from the examination, analysis and control of governmental powers. When a treaty is ratified, the annexes thereto are also (obviously) included. It means that the conclusion and entry into

---

94 See Gardiner, Richard K. *Treaty interpretation*, cit., p. 203-216.

95 See Palmer, Richard E. *Hermenêutica*. Transl. by Maria Luísa Ribeiro Ferreira. Lisbon: Issue 70, 1969, p. 34; and Silva, José Afonso da, *Comentário contextual à Constituição*, 2. ed., São Paulo: Malheiros, 2006, p. 16-17.

96 This last provision (set forth in line *b* of Art. 31, item 2) allows for the so called "interpretative declarations" of treaties, which, provided they are not *reservations* to the text, serve as an auxiliary means to interpret the instrument. On such "interpretative declarations", see Part II, Ch. 2, item 2.7, above).

force of a treaty are deemed, both by virtue of the Law of Nations and of internal law, the conclusion and entry into force of the relevant annexes.[97]

Furthermore, pursuant to the Convention, the following shall be taken into account together with the context: (*a*) any *subsequent agreement* between the parties regarding the interpretation of the treaty or the application of its provisions; (*b*) any subsequent *practice* in the application of the treaty which establishes the agreement of the parties regarding its interpretation; and (*c*) any relevant *rules* of international law applicable in the relations between the parties (Art. 31, item 3).[98]

This last element, regarding any rule of International Law applicable to the relations between the parties, may raise major doubts, "since later agreements concluded by the parties on the interpretation of the treaty become mandatory only in compliance with the *pacta sunt servanda* rule; and subsequent practices followed by the parties regarding the application of the treaty must be taken into consideration because they reflect the parties' intention and comprehension of the agreement. However, the doubt disappears when we think that the text of a treaty may not exist separately, independently, in a vacuum", and it "has to be considered within the legal framework where it was drawn up and on which it depends. This is the reason why a treaty is always governed by International Law and its rules will always be the sources to which interpreters will resort when necessary".[99] It should be highlighted that the Convention's reference to "any relevant rule of International Law applicable in the relations between the parties" shows one of the strange cases in which the Vienna Code referred to the relations between the law of treaties and customary law.[100]

---

97 See Rangel, Vicente Marotta. Integração das convenções de Genebra no direito brasileiro, *Revista do Instituto de Pesquisas e Estudos Jurídico-Econômico-Sociais*, year II, No. 3, Bauru, Jan/Mar/1967, p. 203-204.

98 For a comprehensive analysis of such provision, see Gardiner, Richard K., *Treaty interpretation*, cit., p. 216-298. See also Fox, Hazel, Article 31(3) (a) and (b) of the Vienna Convention and the *Kasikili/Sedudu Island* Case, in Fitzmaurice, Malgosia; Elias, Olufemi & Merkouris, Panos (eds.), *Treaty interpretation and the Vienna Convention on the Law of Treaties…*, cit., p. 59-74; and Rodrigues, Luís Barbosa, *A interpretação dos tratados internacionais*, cit., p. 95-110.

99 Calsing, Maria de Assis. *O tratado internacional e sua aplicação no Brasil*, cit., p. 54.

100 See Rodrigues, Luís Barbosa. *A interpretação dos tratados internacionais*, cit., p. 100. According to the author: "The following, among others, shall be demed as 'rules of International Law': the principles of good faith, sovereign equality of States, pacific resolution of conflicts, prohibition of threats or use of force, non interference, inviolability of bound-

Finally, pursuant to the final part of Art. 31, item 1, treaties must be interpreted in light of its *object* and *purpose* (teleological interpretation). The *Object* of a treaty means the goals intended to be reached by its rules, through the rights and obligations arising from them, pursuant to what negotiators freely established (principle of *ratio legis*); while *purpose* means the goals intended to be reached by said parties, their common ideal, etc. For example, the *object* of a treaty may be to eradicate massive destruction weapons, with the subsequent *purpose* of reaching peace. Thus, the *object* and *purpose* of a treaty are not mistaken, although they are closely connected. Therefore, saying that the interpreter must take into account the treaty object and purpose when interpreting the treaty means that the interpreter must search the *ratio legis* of the international commitment when looking for the actual intention of the parties as regards the meaning of the text or any of the provisions thereof.

1.5.2 Supplementary means of interpretation

Besides a "general rule of interpretation" (Art. 31), the 1969 Convention also describes (in Art. 32) "supplementary means of interpretation" that can be resorted to if Art. 31 has not been successfully applied. The Convention allows resorting to such supplementary means of interpretation, including the travaux préparatoires of the treaty[101] and the circumstances of its conclusion, for the purpose of (1) *confirming* the meaning resulting from the application of Art. 31, or (2) *determining* said meaning, when the interpretation, in accordance with the same article, (*a*) leaves the meaning *ambiguous* or *confusing*, or (*b*) leads to an obviously *absurd* or *unreasonable* result (*useful effect* rule).[102]

---

aries and territorial integrity of States, lawful defense, self-determination, cooperation, and also, increasingly, respect for human rights" (Idem, p. 104),

101 See Lauterpacht, Hersch. Les travaux préparatoires et l'interprétation des traités, *Recueil des Cours*, vol. 48 (1934-II), p. 709-817. For criticism on the apparent "exaggeration" by Lauterpacht with regard to the defense of the travaux préparatoires as a method of treaty interpretation, see Accioly, Hildebrando, *Tratado de direito internacional público*, vol. I, cit., p. 634-635, for whom "resorting to the travaux préparatoires does not often produce satisfactory results and, in some cases, as stated by the International Court of Justice, is not admissible".

102 See Maresca, Adolfo, *Il diritto dei trattati*..., cit., p. 361-365; Villiger, Mark E., *Commentary on the 1969 Vienna Convention on the Law of Treaties*, cit., p. 445-449; and more widely Gardiner, Richard K., *Treaty interpretation*, cit., p. 301-350. See also Remiro Brotons, Antonio, *Derecho internacional público*, vol. 2, cit., p. 314-315; Sbolci, Luigi, Supplementary means of interpretation, in Cannizzaro, Enzo (ed.), *The law of*

The Convention does not specify said "supplementary means", but it states that the *travaux préparatoires* of a treaty and the *circumstances* of its conclusion are – "including", as pointed out by the Vienna Convention – at least two of those means of interpretation (certainly the most important ones).[103]

The *travaux préparatoires* start with preliminary negotiations and continue until the signature stage. They are based on the *written* documents[104] issued during the treaty creation period, such as *minutes*, *reports*, *studies* and *opinions* arising in the negotiation stage, issued by negotiators or specialists *ad hoc*. *Oral* statements may be taken into account when *referred* to in written documents (for example, a diplomatic communication, etc.). In summary, *travaux préparatoires* are any written documents prepared during the treaty creation period, either published or not; they are the historical memory related to a treaty creation period, including all discussions and deliberations on each matter as well as each issue and provision thereof. In this book, for instance, the *Yearbook of the International Law Commission*, officially published by the UN, is quoted many times in relation to the *reports* issued by jurists called to support the negotiations of a treaty; all those *studies* contained in the *Yearbook* may be considered the *travaux préparatoires* of a specific treaty.

The *travaux préparatoires* are useful for the interpreter to clarify the *origin* of any ambiguity or confusion of any provision contained in the instrument. Their use as a means of interpretation, however, must be moderate, cautious, seeking to reflect not the parties' *agreement*, but their *dissent*. There are no *travaux préparatoires* of a treaty that have not evidenced

---

treaties beyond the Vienna Convention, cit., p. 145-163; and again Gardiner, Richard K., The role of preparatory work in treaty interpretation, in Orakhelashvili, Alexander & Williams, Sarah (eds.), *40 years of the Vienna Convention on the Law of Treaties*, cit., p. 97-116.

103 See Bernhardt, Rudolf. Interpretation and implied (tacit) modification of treaties…, cit., p. 502.

104 In such regard, the Decision of May 16, 1980, by the Arbitration Court in relation to the Agreement on German External Debts between Germany and Belgium, United States, United Kingdom and Switzerland, as mentioned by Treves, Tullio, Une nouvelle technique dans la codification du droit international: le comité de redaction de la conference sur le droit de la mer, *Annuaire Français de Droit International*, vol. 27 (1981), p. 83, states as follows: "D'après un arrêt récent d'un tribunal international, les travaux préparatoires d'un traité doivent, en premier lieu, être des 'données fixées *par écrit*, auxquelles on peut avoir recours par la suite'…" [emphasis added].

how difficult it is to reach a consensus on the object of the agreement to be concluded.

In turn, the *circumstances* related to the conclusion and signature of the treaty may also be useful when looking for the parties' actual intention, in connection with any ambiguous or divergent provision of the instrument, since such circumstances generally influence the drawing up of the treaty final text. The nature of said circumstances may vary; they may be, for instance, political, social, cultural, etc.[105] Consequently, circumstances "either arising from the nature of things, or based upon the provision of the Vienna Convention, become one of the primary factors in providing clarity, even surpassing the *travaux préparatoires*, which are formally conceived to shed light on more doubtful regulation issues".[106] The ICJ, for instance, in item 100 of the decision of December 19, 1978, relating to the case entitled *Aegean Sea Continental Shelf*, made reference to the "circumstances of the meeting",[107] as provided for in Art. 32 of the 1969 Convention.

> 100. Cette divergence de vues sur l'interprétation du communiqué de Bruxelles oblige la Cour à rechercher si les circonstances entourant la réunion du 31 mai 1975 et la rédaction du communiqué peuvent en éclairer le sens. D'après le dossier, la Cour est mentionnée pour la première fois dans une note verbale grecque du 27 janvier 1975, c'est-à-dire quatre mois environ avant la rencontre des deux premiers ministres à Bruxelles. Dans cette note, le Gouvernement de la Grèce proposait que "les divergences au sujet du droit applicable ainsi que sur le fond de la question" soient soumises a la Cour, ajoutant:
> "A vrai dire, et sans préjudice de son droit de saisir unilatéralement la Cour, le Gouvernement grec verrait de très grands avantages à ce qu'un compromis soit *établi de concert* avec le Gouvernement turc..." (Requête, ann. II, n. 9. Les italiques sont de la Cour).

Although the Convention has expressly mentioned only those two supplementary means of interpretation, others may also be used (under the terms of Art. 32) for the purpose of (1) *confirming* the meaning resulting from application of Art. 31, or (2) *determining aforementioned meaning*, when the interpretation, in accordance with said article, (*a*) leaves the

[105] See Villiger, Mark E. *Commentary on the 1969 Vienna Convention on the Law of Treaties*, cit., p. 445.

[106] Rodrigues, Luís Barbosa. *A interpretação dos tratados internacionais*, cit., p. 123. The same author also points out: "In fact, there are social, historic and legal conditions that influence, many times after its termination, the specific time the treaty is concluded, and they must also be included in the notion of circumstances" (Idem, p. 124).

[107] See *ICJ Reports* (1978), p. 41.

meaning *ambiguous* (double meaning) or *confusing* (without clarity, misleading), or (*b*) leads to an obviously *absurd* (without logics, without good sense) or *unreasonable* (contrary to reason, absurd) result. This last provision (Art. 32, *b*) establishes the so called rule of "useful effect", whereby the treaty provisions must always be interpreted in such a way that they produce as much sense and effectiveness as possible relating to their object.[108] In other words, based on the rule of useful effect, any interpretation leading to an absurd or unreasonable (useless) result should be rejected. The idea contained in the rule is that a treaty must always reflect a wise, cautious, rational and fair regulation, that is, reasonable and not absurd.[109] It is an interpretative rule of special relevance aimed at confirming or determining the meaning of a treaty, whenever the application of the general rule of Art. 31 of the Convention has not been successfully applied.

The possibility of using other supplementary means of interpretation should be pointed out; for example, the rule of *functional interpretation*, whereby treaties will be interpreted consistently with their intention, as much as possible for the sake of the treaty effects, as well as *analogy, custom, general principles of law* and the rule *contra proferentem*, especially applied to treaty-contracts and pursuant to which any obscure or ambiguous provision will be interpreted *against the interest* of the proposing party or the party who provided the wording, giving the other party the benefit of doubt.[110]

---

108 The rule of *useful effect* was especially used, under International Economic Law, in a case between Brazil and Venezuela against the United States. The case related to the questioning by Brazil and Venezuela (in 1995) of discriminatory aspects of North American environmental legislation, which restricted the fuel import from those two countries because the amount of lead in the fuel was considered excessive. Finally, based on the rule of *useful effect*, the Appellate Body understood that, by establishing different marketing criteria for fuel produced in the USA and for imported fuel, the *Clean Air Act* breached the principle of "national treatment" of the WTO. The panel and the Appellate Body ruled in favor of Brazil and Venezuela. See OSC/OMC, "United States – Standards for Reformulated and Conventional Gasoline", decision dated 04.29.1996 (WT/DS2/AB/R).

109 See Rodrigues, Luís Barbosa. *A interpretação dos tratados internacionais*, cit., p. 127.

110 See Rezek, José Francisco. *Direito dos tratados*, cit., p. 456. The position of Luís Barbosa Rodrigues should be highlighted as, for him, it is not true that interpretation principles may vary depending on norm-setting treaties or treaty-contracts, since they are necessarily the same, being understood that it would be more correct to state that such distinction was not accepted by the Vienna Convention (see *A interpretação dos tratados internacionais*, cit., p. 141).

1.5.3 Interpretation of treaties authenticated in two or more languages

Treaties concluded in the same language do not generate so many problems, as long as such as version (to the exclusion of others) is to be used by the parties in the event of any doubts or uncertainties relating to the treaty text. A greater problem arises when a treaty is authenticated in two or more languages, which occurs when negotiators do not share the same language and do not want to give preference to any of them, or resort to a different language.[111] It is known that one expression may have diametrically opposite connotations depending on the language used; expressions with a very strong contractual connotation in Common Law (such as *in consideration* clause) do not even have a moral value in Latin languages, etc.[112] Therefore, in the case of treaties authenticated in two or more languages, the 1969 Convention provides that "the text is *equally authoritative* in each language, unless the treaty provides or the parties agree that, in case of divergence, a particular text shall prevail" (Art. 33, item 1).[113]

In bilateral treaties, the treaty text is concluded in the official languages of the contracting States. But this solution has the disadvantage of not solving some interpretative problems arising from the use of terminology with doubtful meanings, in the event both versions of the text are equally valid in both languages. For example, the expression *may* contained in some treaties could, in the official version of the other State, be understood as *shall* and vice versa. In the same way, the expression "in consideration", with a very strong contractual connotation in Common Law countries, is also mistaken in international agreements, generating many interpretation problems (especially in the field of international trade). A good solution for such problems would be concluding a bilateral treaty in the languages of the States parties, adding a third version in another language (usually English or French) to clarify interpretation doubts.

---

111 See Remiro Brotons, Antonio. *Derecho internacional público*, vol. 2, cit., p. 316.

112 On the *consideration* clause in English law, see Sèroussi, Roland, *Introdução ao direito inglês e norte-americano*, transl. by Renata Maria Parreira Cordeiro, São Paulo: Landy, 2001, p. 40-42.

113 For further details, see Gardiner, Richard K., *Treaty interpretation*, cit., p. 353-385. See also Maresca, Adolfo, *Il diritto dei trattati...*, cit., p. 367-371; Remiro Brotons, Antonio, *Derecho internacional público*, vol. 2, cit., p. 316-317; Villiger, Mark E., *Commentary on the 1969 Vienna Convention on the Law of Treaties*, cit., p. 456-457; and Rodrigues, Luís Barbosa, *A interpretação dos tratados internacionais*, cit., p. 136-138. For ILC works on the subject, see Bernhardt, Rudolf. Interpretation and implied (tacit) modification of treaties..., cit., p. 505-506. For an opinion prior to the 1969 Convention, see McNair, Arnold Duncan, *The law of treaties*, cit., p. 432-435.

In connection with multilateral treaties, interpretation problems are multiplied, due to the different meanings that may be assigned to some expression of the text in different languages. So, when a treaty is written in different languages, it is advisable to expressly establish the prevalence of only *one language* in the treaty for interpretation purposes, which solves many problems involving terminology differences (or, at least, they are reduced). The IMF, for example, pursuant to Rule C-13 (Language) of its Rules and Regulations, provides that the working language of the Fund will be *English*, and documents, discussions and reports of meetings will ordinarily be in English. If they are presented in other languages, they will be translated into English.

Under the terms of the 1969 Vienna Convention, only when authorized by the treaty or by the parties, a version of the treaty in a language other than one of those in which the text was authenticated will be considered an authentic text (Art. 33, item 2). It should be noted that the Convention refers, in Art. 33, item 1, to the treaty "text" authenticated in two or more languages, while, in item 2 of the same provision, it refers to a treaty "version" written in a different language; this happened because the ILC understood that, having the Convention established a special regime for authentication in the execution of treaties, such distinction (between a treaty *text* and *version*) should be very clear, being "text" only the document that has been *authenticated*.[114] Hence, the mere "version" of a treaty, as explained by De La Guardia, is not *valid*, whether it is official or not.[115]

The terms of a treaty are presumed to have the *same meaning* in each authentic text (Art. 33, item 3); be noted that this is a (*juris tantum*) *assumption* that may be rebutted when a serious *discrepancy* is shown between authentic texts.[116] Consequently, except where a particular text prevails, as provided by the treaty or decided by the parties (Art. 33, item 1, *in fine*), when a comparison of authentic texts discloses a difference of meaning which the application of Arts. 31 and 32 cannot remove, the meaning which best reconciles the texts, having regard to the *object and purpose* of the treaty, will be adopted (Art. 33, § 4.º).[117] The arbitra-

---

114 See De La Guardia, Ernesto. *Derecho de los tratados internacionales*, cit., p. 228-229.

115 De La Guardia, Ernesto. Idem, p. 229. On this issue, in general terms, see Bernhardt, Rudolf, Interpretation and implied (tacit) modification of treaties…, cit., p. 505.

116 See Remiro Brotons, Antonio. *Derecho internacional público*, vol. 2, cit., p. 316.

117 For details, see Remiro Brotons, Antonio, Idem, p. 317. For criticism on Art. 33, item 4, see Rodrigues, Luís Barbosa, *A interpretação dos tratados internacionais*, cit., p. 138; it is surprising for him that the Convention makes "exclusive reference to the object and

tion related to the case *Young Loan* is an example of the application of Art. 33, item 4, of the Convention, in which the meaning assigned to the expressions *Abwertung*, "depreciated" and *dépréciée* in the German, English and French versions of Art. 2, e, of Annex I-A of the *1953 London Debt Agreement* was discussed,[118] which, under the terms of the last clause of the Agreement, would be equally mandatory ("...all three text being equally authoritative"). The issue arose because, in English and in French, the referred expression (*depreciated/dépréciée*) connotes the economic devaluation of a currency, while the term *Abwertung* in German means the reduction in the currency value by a Government act (that is, a formal devaluation).[119] The Court understood that the rule under analysis should be interpreted "pursuant to the common meaning assigned to the terms of the treaty". However, pursuant to Art. 33, item 4, of the Vienna Convention, in the event of a substantial discrepancy of meaning between authentic texts, the *object* and the *purpose* of the treaty must be taken into consideration, which means that the Convention is also showing that the "technical language" used by the treaty is relevant;[120] in the case of interpretation of the *London Debt Agreement*, it involved the knowledge of technical banking and financial language; therefore, in this case, the object (German external debt) and the *purpose* (debt write-off) of the abovementioned agreement would be the elements necessary for the *reconciliation* of authenticated texts in different languages.

1.5.4 Interpretation systems

Interpretation of a specific treaty may be made both at *international* level and at the contracting parties' *internal* level.[121] Equally, it may be based only on the opinion *of legal scholars*. However, in any case, it is not

---

purpose, without mentioning other already known hermeneutic elements", also pointing out that "conciliating texts under the terms set forth in the Vienna Convention – that is, integrally – will also imply to darken the principle of indivisibility of the treaty".

118 Specifically, it referred to the following terms: "...Währung mit der geringsten *Abwertung*..." (German); "...least *depreciated* currency..." (English); and "...devise la moins *dépréciée*..." (French).

119 See Sinclair, Ian. *The Vienna Convention on the Law of Treaties*, cit., p. 150-151; and Linderfalk, Ulf, *On the interpretation of treaties*..., cit., p. 71-73. See also Creifelds, Carl, *Rechtswörterbuch*, 17 ed., München: C. H. Beck, 2002, p. 24 [headword: *Abwertung*].

120 See See Linderfalk, Ulf. *On the interpretation of treaties*..., cit., p. 72-73.

121 For further details, see Rezek, José Francisco, *Direito dos tratados*, cit., p. 446-452.

absolutely necessary that a *concrete case* should involve a specific treaty. The Law of Treaties general principles allow for the interpretation of a given international act irrespective of its application *in concreto*. It is not uncommon, and international practice has increasingly shown this, that treaties are interpreted by States even *before* they enter into force so that, once into effect, treaties do not cause further damages or setbacks. The subject of treaty interpretation in relation to a concrete case is clearly different, since its interpretation (with an effective result) would lead to the success of one party against the other party.

This item includes the problem of knowing *to what extent* and by means of *which bodies or agents* a treaty may be interpreted, apart from *how* such interpretation is to be performed. There is no doubt that the Law of Treaties interpretation rules, codified under the 1969 and 1986 Vienna Conventions, are directed to *international* bodies (such as courts, monitoring committees, conciliation commissions, etc.) A greater problem arises when the intention of *the parties*, or even of the *internal* bodies of a specific State (such as Assemblies, Ministries of Foreign Relations, Judicial Power, etc.), is to interpret a given treaty. With regard to the work of *legal scholars*, there is (clearly) no problem at all, since their main function is interpreting legal rules.

In summary, the abovementioned interpretation systems (*international, internal and legal scholars*) have characteristics of their own, which should be analyzed separately.

1.5.4.1 International interpretation

At the international level, there are basically four means of interpretation applicable to international treaties:

a) First, there is interpretation jointly made by *all the parties* who acceded to the treaty, through an interpretative statement, which is very common, or through a new treaty specifically for such purpose.[122] This is known as *authentic interpretation* in the General Theory of Law, based on the *same source* that served as a basis to draw up the treaty text; therefore, it is binding on all the parties to the treaty. In the Law of Treaties, this type of interpretation is also called *collective interpretation*. It may occur (*a*) simul-

---

[122] The last case, as Rezek stated, is one of the few cases "in which a constitutional system like the Brazilian may accept an executive order, not subject to the approval of the National Congress" (*Direito dos tratados*, cit., p. 446).

taneously with the conclusion of the international treaty, or (*b*) after its conclusion (when a *specific* treaty is commonly concluded for that purpose). It should be considered that "there is authentic interpretation provided that the parties to the treaty decide on the meaning and scope to be assigned to the rule, with less importance given to the time of such exercise".[123]

b) Interpretation of a treaty may also be made jointly by two or more contracting parties. Here, however, not *all* States interpret the text, but just *some* of them, by means of a formal agreement between them. This may be achieved by the conclusion of a specific interpretative treaty on the points to be clarified or, even, by a *joint statement* made between such parties. Irrespective of the case, there must always be a *formal* agreement between the parties. It is obvious that such interpretation made by only some of the parties to the treaty (two or more contracting parties) is only valid *for those parties* who agreed to give the treaty text a particular meaning, and it is not binding on the remaining parties.

c) Besides, an international treaty may be interpreted by an external judicial body, or by a non judicial body specified by the parties. Interpretation made by international judicial bodies of a permanent nature is certainly stronger than interpretation made by those with a temporary jurisdiction, such as *ad hoc* courts. Being the UN's judicial body, the ICJ clearly has greater moral authority on inferior international courts, when referring to the interpretation of a specific treaty.[124] Therefore, Art. 36, item 2, *a*) of its Statute states that said court is competent to judge, among others, "controversies of a legal order aimed at interpreting a treaty".[125] Interpretation of the Inter-American Court on Human Rights should also be highlighted with regard to international treaties for the protection of

---

123 Rodrigues, Luís Barbosa. *A interpretação dos tratados internacionais*, cit., p. 40. The same author adds: "Rejecting that solution would mean that formal criteria prevail, without cause, over substantial criteria" (Idem, ibidem).

124 Strictly, the interpretation by an international court restricts its binding force to the parties to the case *sub judice*. In that regard, see De La Guardia, Ernesto, *Derecho de los tratados internacionales*, cit., p. 218; and Rodrigues, Luís Barbosa, *A interpretação dos tratados internacionais*, cit., p. 41.

125 On the role of the ICJ on interpretation of treaties, see Lauterpacht, Hersch, *The development of international law by the International Court*, cit., p. 26-31; and Sohn, Louis B., Settlement of disputes relating to the interpretation and application of treaties, *Recueil des Cours*, vol. 150 (1976-II), p. 195-294 (this author, however, despite the wide field of study, examines the matter under analysis, "solution of controversies relating to the interpretation and application of treaties", only with regard to the systematic regulations of the 1958 Law of the Sea.)

human rights under the OAS system, especially the 1969 American Convention on Human Rights.[126] As examples of non judicial international bodies, with technical or political capacity to interpret treaties, the following may be mentioned: UN Security Council, OAS Permanent Council or any international organization (even if it is not a party to the treaty) responsible for the application of the treaty or monitoring its application.[127] The interpretation of treaties resulting from the so-called *advisory function* of international courts (International Court of Justice, Inter-American Court on Human Rights) is also deemed non jurisdictional when a non-binding advisory opinion is issued (therefore, beyond the *contentious* competence of the relevant court.) The authority of such bodies is always granted by the parties, who wish to have the exegetic conflict resulting from the interpretation of the treaty duly resolved. And, once the parties have agree to refer the aforementioned conflict to the decision of such bodies, that becomes binding on them. Finally, there is the matter related to the legal nature of *individual opinions* and *dissenting opinions* issued by international court judges. Although some of the legal scholars understand that such opinions do not fall into case law, but are only the *opinion of legal scholars,* [128] the best position is to consider that they are (despite their inferior binding value) part of the decision, as they actually are, especially when detailing and developing the final *decisum*.[129]

d) Finally, the interpretation of a treaty at international level may even be made by only *one* of the parties to the treaty, when said interpretation is notified by said party to the others. This is called *unilateral interpretation*. But, obviously, such type of interpretation does not bind the other parties. They are just the so called *interpretative statements*, very common in those treaties in which the formulation of reservations is forbidden (see Part II, Ch. 2, item 2.7, above).

---

[126] However, the Inter-American Court may apply (and interpret) other treaties on human rights apart from the American Convention, as it did in the case entitled *Gómez Palomino v. Peru*, dated November 22, 2005, controlling the conventionality of the Inter-American Convention on Forced Disappearance of Persons, approved in Belém do Pará (Brazil) in 1994. In the European regional system, the interpretation held by the European Court on Human Rights (headquartered in Strasbourg, France) concerning the 1950 European Convention on Human Rights should be pointed out.

[127] See Reuter, Paul. *Introducción al derecho de los tratados*, cit., p. 117.

[128] See Farinha, João de Deus Pinheiro. Interpretação dos tratados e das convenções, *Tribuna da Justiça*, Fundão (Portugal), Feb/1985, p. 9.

[129] See Rodrigues, Luís Barbosa. *A interpretação dos tratados internacionais*, cit., p. 43.

1.5.4.2 Internal interpretation

Under internal Law, interpretation of treaties must comply with the rules set forth in the Vienna Convention on the Law of Treaties (since it *is part of* the national regulation patrimony and *governs* the Law of Treaties) and, on a supplementary basis, with the regulations of the State under analysis. It would be against the law to think that a State that *ratified* the 1969 Vienna Convention and *incorporated* it to its legal system, was not bound to fulfill it. Now, as the Convention includes the *interpretation rules* of treaties, the States have to interpret said treaties based on said Convention (and their internal bodies.) However, for that to be satisfactorily achieved, it is evident that the State's bodies and agents must *know well* all interpretation rules included in the Convention, which rarely occurs in practice; as regards *internal* interpretation of treaties, what we can see (including in Brazil) is almost complete unawareness, by the State's bodies and agents, mainly in the Legislative and Judicial Powers, of treaty interpretation rules included in the Vienna text.

In summary, it is necessary to make clear that internal interpretation of treaties is to be made in compliance with the provisions set forth by the 1969 Convention, and the domestic legislation rules of the State must be used only *supplementarily*. It should also be made clear that internal interpretation of treaties is valid only when it is not objected by the other States parties; in other words, the interpretation of a treaty by a State, at the internal law level, is not enforceable in relation to the other parties to the treaty, since "it comes from a body that is not competent to issue an internationally binding legal rule".[130]

Generally, *internal* interpretation of a treaty is carried out by the Executive Power (*governmental interpretation*), which regulates it, and by the Judicial Power (*judicial interpretation*), which resolves conflicts of interest resulting from the application of the treaty to a specific case. Therefore, it can be said that internal interpretation of treaties varies, in practice, from a (*a*) *political* dimension (the Executive Power) to another (*b*) *judicial* dimension (the Judicial Power). The first (*political*) dimension is constantly seen at the level of the Ministry for Foreign Affairs (Itamaraty). This Ministry includes a *Legal Advisory Body* responsible, among other things, for "giving advice and consultancy to the Minister of State in questions of a legal nature", as well as "determining the interpretation of

[130] De La Guardia, Ernesto. *Derecho de los tratados internacionales*, cit., p. 218.

treaties and other regulating acts to be regularly followed in the Ministry's areas of expertise and coordination when there is no ruling guide by the Attorney General of the Union".[131] The Internal Regulations of the Secretary of State's Office are clear when they grant the Legal Advisory Body the power to express an opinion on "interpretation and application of international acts". In summary, it is obvious that treaties submitted to the consideration of Itamaraty's Legal Advisory Body need to be *interpreted* before the opinion of the Legal Advisor is issued on, for example, the feasibility of Brazil to accede or not to a specific international act. In turn, the second (*judicial*) *dimension* is seen both at the level of the Supreme Court and in the ordinary jurisdiction courts. There is no doubt that the Judicial Power, in daily cases involving international treaties, exercises the role of (internal) interpreter of treaties more than the Executive Power. Labor judges and courts, for instance, daily hear cases requiring, in one way or another, the interpretation of the LIO conventions under analysis. However, it should be said again that both the Executive and the Judicial Powers *must* take into account, when interpreting a treaty, the provisions of the 1969 Vienna Convention regulating the interpretation of international acts (Arts. 31 to 33).

The Legislative Power, which participates in the process of execution of treaties at *one stage* only – which authorizes (or not) the President of the Republic to ratify the treaty – is not entitled to give an opinion on its interpretation once the treaty *has entered into force*; this is why the Legislative Power is not, *a priori*, part of the process of internal interpretation of treaties. However, the Legislative Power may express an opinion on the interpretation of a treaty during the *stage it may act*: the *approval* of an international treaty, when it may formulate reservations to the text; obviously, said *reservations* are also performed by means of international act *interpretation*, together with the rules of internal law, especially the Federal Constitution.

Finally, it should be pointed out that *internal* interpretation of treaties is made pursuant to the text version published in its own language in the *Official Gazette of the Union,* independently of being, or not being, one of the authentic texts at international level.[132] It should be borne in mind that Art. 33, item 2, of the 1969 Convention provides that "a ver-

---

131 Art. 7, items I and III, of Executive Order 7,304/2010. See also Art. 11, III, of LC 73/1993, which provides for the Union's Attorney General Organic Law and other rules.

132 Remiro Brotons, Antonio. *Derecho internacional público*, vol. 2, cit., p. 320.

sion of the treaty in a language other than one of those in which the text was authenticated shall be considered an authentic text only if the treaty so provides or the parties so agree". Since this seldom occurs in practice, the texts published (translated into their own language) by countries *are not authentic.*

1.5.4.3 Interpretation by legal scholars

Treaties may also be interpreted by *legal scholars*. Hence, there is no need of a *concrete* case of litigation between parties or involving, in any manner, a specific treaty. There is no need to say again that the role of legal scholars is essentially the *interpretation* of rules.

In comparison to the previous two means of interpretation, we can see that interpretation made by legal scholars is not so effective regarding the *immediacy* of application. In other words, interpretation of legal scholars does not produce, unlike others, immediate legal effects.[133] Anyway, as set forth by Art. 38, item 1, *d*, of the Statute of the ICJ, the teaching of legal scholars is an "auxiliary means for the determination of rules of law", a rule which already existed at the time of the Permanent Court of International Justice in that sense.[134]

An example of treaty interpretation by legal scholars is the one made in relation to the 1920 Peace Treaty of Trianon, executed between Hungary and Romania.

1.5.5 Interpretation of treaties on human rights

With regard specifically to treaties on protection of human rights, it should be pointed out that interpretation always needs to take into account the *most favorable* rule for human beings.[135] This means that treaties on human rights must always be interpreted taking into consideration the principle *pro homine*, by means of which the interpreter must choose the rule that, in each particular case, best protects human beings as subjects

---

[133] See Rodrigues, Luís Barbosa. *A interpretação dos tratados internacionais*, cit., p. 43.

[134] See Ehrlich, Ludwik. L'interprétation des traités, cit., p. 8.

[135] On this subject, see Mazzuoli, Valerio de Oliveira, *Direitos humanos, Constituição e os tratados internacionais: estudo analítico da situação e aplicação do tratado na ordem jurídica brasileira*, São Paulo: Juarez de Oliveira, 2002, p. 272-286; and Mazzuoli, Valerio de Oliveira, *Tratados internacionais de direitos humanos e direito interno*, São Paulo: Saraiva, 2010, p. 105-128.

of law. It should be noted that contemporary treaties on human rights already contain "dialog provisions" (for instance, see Art. 29, *b*, of the 1969 American Convention on Human Rights) aimed at establishing a "dialog" between international and internal rules conducive to *increasingly* protect the individual. That is to say, treaties on human rights provide for their *own* rules of interpretation, always contemplating the prevalence of the *most favorable* rule for the citizen. For example, see the wording of Art. 29, *b*, of the American Convention, pursuant to which no provision of the Convention may be interpreted to the effect that "restricting the enjoyment or exercise of any right or freedom recognized by virtue of the laws of any State Party or by virtue of another convention to which one of the aforementioned States is a party".

The principle *pro homine* (or "prevalence of the most favorable rule") is a *mandatory* principle of interpretation for all treaties on human rights, without which the result of applying an international protection rule (with prejudice to another one, either international or internal) may turn undesirable for being a *less protecting* rule. The principle of *prohibition of regression* should also be mentioned here (for being closely related to the principle *pro homine*), pursuant to which (international or internal) protection rules must *always* secure *more* rights to the individuals, without reducing the maximum effectiveness of human rights as one of their goals.[136]

1.6 Conflict between successive treaties

One of the most sophisticated subjects in the Law of Treaties, maybe the most confusing one, i.e., the conflict between international rules, arises when two successive treaties rule on the same matter.[137] In fact, nowadays

---

136 See Mazzuoli, Valerio de Oliveira. *Curso de direito internacional público*, cit., p. 886.

137 On this subject, see Salmon, Jean, Les antinomies en droit international public, in Perelman, Chaïm (ed.), *Les antinomies en droit*, Bruxelles: Bruylant, 1965, p. 285-314; Nascimento e Silva, Geraldo Eulálio do, Le facteur temps et les traités, cit., p. 242-264; Sinclair, Ian, *The Vienna Convention on the Law of Treaties*, cit., p. 93-98; Remiro Brotons, Antonio, *Derecho internacional público*, vol. 2, cit., p. 326-330; Roucounas, Emmanuel, Engagements parallèles et contradictoires, *Recueil des Cours*, vol. 206 (1987-VI), p. 21-280; De La Guardia, Ernesto, *Derecho de los tratados internacionales*, cit., p. 206-216; Reuter, Paul, *Introducción al derecho de los tratados*, cit., p. 157-159; Pauwelyn, Joost, *Conflict of norms in public international law: how WTO law relates to other rules of international law*, Cambridge: Cambridge University Press, 2003, p. 5-23; Sadat-Akhavi, Seyed Ali, *Methods of resolving conflicts between treaties*, Leiden: Brill Academic Publishers, 2003, p. 45-248; Aust, Anthony, *Modern treaty law and practice*, cit., p. 173-183;

it is common to find that treaty rules overlap, as a result of the increasing number of rules that Public International Law has been experiencing at different levels – bilateral, regional and global – of international cooperation.[138] In fact, in recent times – and the ILC had already succeeded in discussions for drawing up the Vienna Convention, Public International Law has started to deal with a variety of subjects on an increasingly continuous basis, especially due to the increasing multilateralization and institutionalization of international life. As a direct consequence of such phenomenon, there arises a legal problem, based on the *pacta sunt servanda*, related to the conflict of contradictory rules set forth in successive treaties that have simultaneously entered into force, which calls for a proper solution. This subject has been little examined by internationalists in general, since many of them, when doing so, consider the subject generally, as one of the causes of treaty termination (which we think is not correct).

The problem was deeply discussed by the ILC from 1953 to 1966, from five different angles,[139] and Art. 30 of the 1969 Vienna Convention was finally adopted (the same rule was repeated in Art. 30 of the 1986 Convention).[140]

Art. 30 and the paragraphs thereof, of the 1969 Vienna Convention, deal with antinomies between treaties under the following terms:

---

and Villiger, Mark E., *Commentary on the 1969 Vienna Convention on the Law of Treaties*, cit., p. 399-411.

138 See Remiro Brotons, Antonio. *Derecho internacional público*, vol. 2, cit., p. 326; and Roucounas, Emmanuel, Engagements parallèles et contradictoires, cit., p. 21-23.

139 Said angles were: 1) validity of treaties (Lauterpacht); 2) effects of treaties (Fitzmaurice); 3) priority of provisions (Waldock); 4) incompatibility (provisional text adopted in 1964); and 5) successive treaties (1966 Commission draft). See Nascimento e Silva, Geraldo Eulálio do. Le facteur temps et les traités, cit., p. 258. For the last discussion on the subject at the ILC, see *Yearbook of the International Law Commission* (1966), vol. II, p. 214-217. On the points of view of Fitzmaurice and Waldock at the ILC, see De La Guardia, Ernesto, *Derecho de los tratados internacionales*, cit., p. 207-210.

140 It should be noted that the ILC did not contemplate *parallel treaties* between States, only covering *successive* ones, which was deemed insufficient by legal scholars. Among some of the observations made there is, for instance, the one derived from a conflict between a previous treaty already adopted, but not already into force, and a later treaty which has already entered into force (in which case, these would not be, technically, *successive* treaties, but the obligation of the first treaty, contained in Art. 18 of the Convention, not to frustrate the object and the purpose of the treaty). For all criticism, see Roucounas, Emmanuel, Engagements parallèles et contradictoires, cit., p. 35-37.

"Article 30. *Application of successive treaties relating to the same subject-matter*

1. Subject to Article 103 of the Charter of the United Nations [*verbis*: "In the event of a conflict between the obligations of the United Nations Members under the present Charter and their obligations under any other international treaty, their obligations under the present Charter shall prevail"], the rights and obligations of States parties to successive treaties relating to the same subject-matter shall be determined in accordance with the following paragraphs.
2. When a treaty specifies that it is subject to, or that it is not to be considered as incompatible with, an earlier or later treaty, the provisions of that other treaty prevail.
3. When all the parties to the earlier treaty are parties also to the later treaty but the earlier treaty is not terminated or suspended in operation under article 59, the earlier treaty applies only to the extent that its provisions are compatible with those of the latter treaty.
4. When the parties to the later treaty do not include all the parties to the earlier one:
   a) as between States parties to both treaties the same rule applies as in paragraph 3;
   b) as between a State party to both treaties and a State party to only one of the treaties, the treaty to which both States are parties governs their mutual rights and obligations.
5. Paragraph 4 is without prejudice to article 41, or to any question of the termination or suspension of the operation of a treaty under article 60 or to any question of responsibility which may arise for a State from the conclusion or application of a treaty, the provisions of which are incompatible with its obligations towards another State under another treaty".

Many rules have been used through time for resolving temporary law conflicts or even those involving international treaties. Consequently, some concepts such as *lex specialis derogat legi generali* or *lex posterior derogat priori*, have already been applied since long time ago under the General Theory of Law, influencing interpretation relating to conflicts of laws through time. As we can see, the 1969 Vienna Convention has not strictly stuck to such rules, and it has established its own methods (which are not always precise) related to the problem of applying successive treaties on the same matter. However, it is essential to understand one point of the Convention procedures: there should be, at least, two simultaneously effective and successive treaties on the same matter, and the relevant State must be a party to *both*; treaties associated to different parties cannot be deemed in conflict.[141]

Before commenting on the application rules related to successive treaties on the same matter, it should be made clear that such conflicts will only exist in the case of a *multilateral* treaty. Strictly, there are no temporary conflicts involving bilateral treaties, even when their provisions seem to be incompatible.

1.6.1 Prevalence of the UN Charter and norms of jus cogens

The first rule to be analyzed relates to Art. 103 of the UN Charter referred to by the first paragraph of Art. 30 of the 1969 Convention. When stating that rights and obligations of States parties to successive treaties related to the same matter will be determined in accordance with the following paragraphs, said Convention first makes a *reservation* to Art. 103 of the UN Charter, whose rule provides that in case of conflict between the obligations assumed by any Member of the United Nations under the Charter and their obligations assumed under any other international treaty, the obligations imposed by the UN Charter will prevail.[142] By formulating such reservation, the Vienna Convention on the Law of Treaties clearly recognized *a hierarchical prevalence* of the UN Charter in connection with other international agreements, achieving the category of *higher rank law* or "supreme law" at the international level.[143] In doing so, the 1969 Convention ratified the rule according to which *all* conflicts between treaties and the UN Charter (when the parties to the later treaty were also parties to the Charter) must always be resolved in favor of the Charter.[144]

---

141 See Roucounas, Emmanuel. Engagements parallèles et contradictoires, cit., p. 79.

142 The 1986 Vienna Convention also refers to Art. 103 of the UN Charter in Art. 30, item 6, confirming the prevalence of obligations imposed by the United Nations Charter in case of a conflict with the obligations assumed by virtue of another treaty.

143 See Nascimento e Silva, Geraldo Eulálio do. Le facteur temps et les traités, cit., p. 244 e 259-260; Roucounas, Emmanuel, Engagements parallèles et contradictoires, cit., p. 66; Seidl-Hoenveldern, Ignaz, Hierarchy of treaties, in Klabbers, Jan & Lefeber, René (eds.), *Essays on the law of treaties: a collection of essays in honour of Bert Vierdag*, Dordrecht: Martinus Nijhoff, 1998, p. 16-18; Kamto, Maurice, La volonté de l'État en droit international, cit., p. 152-153; and Brichambaut, Dobelle & Coulée, *Leçons de droit international public*, cit., p. 267.

144 See Rezek, José Francisco. *Direito dos tratados*, cit., p. 460.

Along with the UN Charter, the 1969 Vienna Convention also raised the norms of *jus cogens* to a higher level than those of other international treaties, establishing, in Art. 53, that a treaty is *void* if, at the time of its conclusion, it conflicts with a peremptory norm of general international law, and, in Art. 64, that a treaty is *terminated* if it conflicts with a subsequent norm of *jus cogens* (see Ch. 2, item 2.2, below).

Both in the case of Art. 103 of the UN Charter and of treaties incorporating norms of *jus cogens*, the Vienna Convention established a *hierarchical* criterion for resolving antinomies between successive treaties, assigning prevalence to the superior treaty rule over the inferior one.

Then, except for cases of temporary conflicts involving international treaties and provisions of the United Nations Charter, as well as those involving peremptory norms of general International Law (*jus cogens*), any other legal problems and antinomies will be resolved under Art. 30 of the 1969 Vienna Convention.

1.6.2 The problem of compatibility clauses

Compatibility clauses are clauses aimed at *adapting* or *adjusting* the provisions of a given treaty to the provisions of another treaty. They are clauses set forth in a treaty for the purpose of establishing how the treaty will relate to other previous or subsequent treaties.[145] Such provisions are very common in treaties on human rights; for example, the provision establishing the application of the *most favorable* rule to meet the purposes of a treaty on human rights. For instance, Art. 44 of the 1966 International Covenant on Civil and Political Rights provides as follows: "The provisions for the implementation of the present Covenant shall *apply without prejudice* to the procedures prescribed in the field of human rights by or under the constituent instruments and the conventions of the United Nations and of the specialized agencies and *shall not prevent* the States Parties to the present Covenant from having recourse to other procedures for settling a dispute *in accordance with general or special international agreements* in force between them". Such clauses are also formulated, in other cases, to determine the application of a *more special* regime on a given subject, as the case of Art. 237, items 1 and 2, of the 1982 United Nations Convention on the Law of the Sea (on *special* agreements on the sea

---

145 See Remiro Brotons, Antonio. *Derecho internacional público*, vol. 2, cit., p. 328-329 (in which the following examples were given); and Roucounas, Emmanuel, Engagements parallèles et contradictoires, cit., p. 86-93.

protection and preservation).[146] There are also fully *generic* compatibility clauses, as the one contained in Art. 23, item 1, of the 1972 Convention on International Liability for Damage Caused by Space Objects, which provides as follows: "The provisions of this Convention shall not affect other international agreements in force in so far as relations between States Parties to such agreement are concerned".

In summary, such *compatibility clauses* may be expressed by virtue of the provisions of Art. 30, item 2 of the 1969 Vienna Convention. Pursuant to such provision, "when a treaty specifies that it is *subject* to, or that it is not to be considered as *incompatible* with, an earlier or later treaty, the provisions of that other treaty prevail". This rule sets forth *two* different clauses: one related to *subordination* of one treaty to another, and the other related to *compatibility* of one treaty with another. [147] The first case is about a treaty (*X*) that is *subordinate* to another earlier or later treaty (*Y*), and the provisions of the latter (*Y*) prevail (irrespective of treaty *Y* being earlier or later than treaty *X*); in the second case, relating to the subject under analysis here, the clause sets forth that a treaty (*X*) will not be deemed *incompatible* with another earlier or later treaty (*Y*), when the same solution is adopted, that is, the provisions of the latter treaty (*Y*) prevail (irrespective of the treaty *Y* being earlier or later than treaty *X*). However, if the provisions of Art. 30, item 2, cannot be objected with regard to the subordination clause, the situation is different with the compatibility clause (whose removal from the text of the Convention was suggested by the Japanese delegation at the 1968/1969 Vienna Conference, but not approved by the Drafting Commission).[148] In fact, Art. 30, item 2, of the Convention, as regards compatibility provisions, literally provides for

---

146 They provide as follows: "1. The provisions of this Part are without prejudice to the specific obligations assumed by States under special conventions and agreements concluded previously which relate to the protection and preservation of the marine environment and to agreements which may be concluded in furtherance of the general principles set forth in this Convention. 2. Specific obligations assumed by States under special conventions, with respect to the protection and preservation of the marine environment, should be carried out in a manner consistent with the general principles and objectives of this Convention".

147 They can appear in the treat *body*, *preamble* or any *annex thereto* (see Villiger, Mark E. *Commentary on the 1969 Vienna Convention on the Law of Treaties*, cit., p. 404).

148 See Remiro Brotons, Antonio. *Derecho internacional público*, vol. 2, cit., p. 328. Without criticism in such regard, see De La Guardia, Ernesto, *Derecho de los tratados internacionales*, cit., p. 210-211.

the unquestionable prevalence of the provisions of the treaty-paradigm[149] (earlier or later *treaty Y*) in relation to the provisions of the treaty providing for the clause (*treaty X*). Compatibility between the provisions of two or more treaties, as pointed out by Remiro Brotons, cannot be imposed, *a priori*, by means of *imperium*, but only after a logical analysis and comparison of texts.[150] It would be wrong to expect that a compatibility clause should grant *automatic* priority to another treaty, which could also have a similar compatibility clause in connection with a third treaty, and so on.[151] Anyway, although the Convention has provided for the prevalence of the treaty-paradigm provisions over the provisions of the treaty providing for the clause, nothing prevents the application body from seeking the actual *intention* of the parties at the time of setting forth the clause to resolve a contingent conflict of rules.

Finally, it may occur that an earlier treaty *forbids* that the parties conclude a later treaty contradicting it.[152] Such clause, however, may not produce any effect in practice, in case all the parties to the earlier treaty are also parties to the later one. In fact, if such is the case, the forbidding clause of the earlier treaty will be totally invalid if the later treaty provides for the same matter differently, since, speaking of treaties, the last *will* of the parties always prevails, as they are fully free to change their minds in relation to what they had decided before (*jus dispositivum*).[153] As nothing prevents a later treaty even from *abrogating* an earlier treaty, we should not say that a later treaty is *subordinate* to an earlier one only by virtue of the provisions of the latter (see item 1.6.3, below); for instance, even though the Geneva Conventions on the Law of the Sea (1958) forbade incompatible clauses of a later treaty, that would never preclude the United Nations Convention on the Law of the Sea (1982) from stating that it "prevails, as regard the relations between States Parties, over the Geneva Conventions on the Law of the Sea of April 29, 1958" (Art. 311, item 1).

---

[149] We thought this is the best nomenclature to name such "earlier or later treaty" (or "another treaty") mentioned in Art. 30, item 2, of the Convention.

[150] Remiro Brotons, Antonio. *Derecho internacional público*, vol. 2, cit., p. 328.

[151] See Remiro Brotons, Antonio. Idem, ibidem.

[152] See the provisions of Art. 8 of the North Atlantic Treaty, dated April 4, 1949: "Each Party declares that none of the international engagements now in force between it and any other of the Parties or any third State is in conflict with the provisions of this Treaty, *and undertakes not to enter into any international engagement in conflict with this Treaty*".

[153] See De La Guardia, Ernesto. *Derecho de los tratados internacionales*, cit., p. 213.

1.6.3 *Successive treaties relating to the same subject-matter with identical parties*

The following rule, contained in item 3 of Art. 30, resolves the problem of successive treaties relating to the same subject-matter and with *identical parties* to the ones of the earlier agreement, by applying the rule *lex posterior derogat priori*. It is about successive treaties relating to the same subject-matter with identical law creation source, in which case there will be no conflict *between* treaties. In the event of treaty succession, classic hermeneutics rules are applied to give prevalence to the earlier or later treaty, in case one or the other is *general* or *special*.[154] If both treaties are *general*, the latter prevails, for materializing the common (and latest) will of the parties, which annuls or derogates the earlier treaty. According to item 3 above, when all the parties to the earlier treaty are parties also to the later treaty but the earlier treaty is not terminated or its application has not been suspended under Art. 59, the earlier treaty *applies only* to the extent that its provisions are *compatible* with those of the latter treaty. Let us assume that the parties to the earlier and later treaties are *identical*, and they could (if they wanted to) have the earlier treaty expressly revoked by the later one, it is obvious that, if they *did not revoke it*, it would be because they wish to *continue applying* the earlier treaty to those provisions that are compatible with the provisions of the later treaty.[155] In this case, it should also be noted that other States may be signatories of the later treaty, as long as *all signatories of the first* treaty are parties to the second treaty In both cases, the second treaty prevails. In the event the second treaty has the sole purpose of interpreting or clarifying certain rules of the first one, such treaty will only prevail over the earlier one to the extent and under the limitations of the restricted relations it regulates, by application of the principle *lex posterior specialis derogat lex priori generalis*.[156]

The provisions of item 3 of Art. 30 and item 1, *b* of Art. 59 of the Vienna Convention are quite similar, according to which a treaty will be considered terminated if all the parties conclude a later treaty relating to the same subject-matter and "the provisions of the later treaty are so far incompatible with those of the earlier one that the two treaties are not capable of being

---

154 See Reuter, Paul. *Introducción al derecho de los tratados*, cit., p. 157; Alland, Denis (coord.), *Droit international public*, cit., p. 242; and Kamto, Maurice, La volonté de l'État en droit international, cit., p. 153-154.

155 See De La Guardia, Ernesto. *Derecho de los tratados internacionales*, cit., p. 211-212.

156 See Accioly, Hildebrando. *Tratado de direito internacional público*, vol. I, cit., p. 572.

applied at the same time". The difference between one provision and the other one is the *extent* of the incompatibility between earlier and later treaties. Item 1, *b* of Art. 59 refers to the case in which incompatibility between two treaties is *complete* (the only case in which the earlier treaty may be terminated), while item 3 of Art. 30 refers to the case in which incompatibility between treaties is just *partial*, as it allows for the application of the earlier treaty to the provisions that are compatible with the provisions of the later treaty.[157] Hence, in the case of item 1, *b* of Art. 59, the earlier treaty is *terminated* while in the case of item 3 of Art. 30, the treaty *may be applicable* to the provisions that do not conflict with the new treaty.[158]

Art. 30, item 3 of the Convention is not, however, resistant to criticism. The main criticism is maybe that it is unfair (especially regarding treaties on human rights) to apply the later treaty when it is not *more special* or *more favorable* than the earlier one. Also Remiro Brotons wonders if a later treaty should be applied, by any means, when it is *less favorable* or *more generic, incidental* or *incomplete* to regulate the subject. He states: "But, can we hold the same when the later treaty is not *more special* or *more favorable*? Should it be preferred by any means, even if we are convinced that it is *less favorable* or more generic, incidental or incomplete to regulate the subject?[159] The provisions of Art. 30, item 3, clearly set forth that when all the parties to the earlier treaty are parties also to the later treaty "the earlier treaty *applies only* to the extent that its provisions are *compatible* with those of the latter treaty". Drafters of the Vienna Conference were not sensitive or perceptive towards especial matters, mainly involving treaties on human rights, which, due to their own set of principles, do not permit a *regression* concerning the protection of rights.[160] Even the last will of the parties (in such "new" legislative intention) cannot *go back* in terms of human rights… In summary, the best interpretation of the provision under analysis is that the later treaty is *presumed* to be the last will of the parties, which presumption (of a *relative* nature) is destroyed when it can be proven that it was not the *real intention* of the parties to dispense with the earlier treaty which was *more specific* or *more favorable* than the later treaty.[161]

---

157 See Sinclair, Ian. *The Vienna Convention on the Law of Treaties*, cit., p. 184-185; and De La Guardia, Ernesto, *Derecho de los tratados internacionales*, cit., p. 215-216.

158 See Roucounas, Emmanuel. Engagements parallèles et contradictoires, cit., p. 94.

159 Remiro Brotons, Antonio. *Derecho internacional público*, vol. 2, cit., p. 329.

160 See Mazzuoli, Valerio de Oliveira. *Curso de direito internacional público*, cit., p. 886.

161 See Remiro Brotons, Antonio. *Derecho internacional público*, vol. 2, cit., p. 330.

1.6.4 *Successive treaties relating to the same subject-matter with different parties*

When the parties to the later treaty do not include all the parties to the earlier treaty, that is, when there is a *different law creation source* between the earlier treaty and the successive one, the following rule is applicable: *a*) in relations between States parties to both treaties, the provisions of item 3 apply (that is, the *later* treaty prevails, being the earlier treaty applied only to the extent that its provisions are compatible with the provisions of the first treaty); and *b*) in relations between one State party to both treaties and one State party to only one treaty (whether an earlier or later treaty), the treaty to which both States are a party governs their mutual rights and obligations (Art. 30, item 40).[162]

The Convention adds, in Art. 30, item 5, that item 4 applies without prejudice to (*a*) Art. 41, which relates to the case of agreements to modify multilateral treaties only between some parties, or (*b*) any question of the termination or suspension of the operation of a treaty under Art. 60, or (*c*) any question of responsibility which may arise for a State from the conclusion or application of a treaty, the provisions of which are incompatible with its obligations towards another State under another treaty.

When the existing conflict is between multilateral treaties (common right) and bilateral treaties (particular right) relating to the same subject-matter, with different legal solutions, the solution mentioned by Anzilotti based on the rule *in toto jure genus per speciem derogatur*, must be applied, according to which the particular rule will prevail over the general rule. In this case, the agreement between two States (bilateral treaty) will prevail over the collective agreement (multilateral treaty) and this one, in turn, over customary law.[163] Such solution, however, is not absolute, since it is possible for the general rule itself to prevent the application of the particular rule, as in the case of Art. 20, item 1, of the Covenant of the League of Nations, pursuant to which "the members of the League severally agree that this Covenant is accepted as abrogating all obligations or understandings inter se which are inconsistent with the terms thereof, and solemnly undertake that they will not hereafter enter into any engagements inconsistent with the terms thereof".

---

[162] See Villiger, Mark E. *Commentary on the 1969 Vienna Convention on the Law of Treaties*, cit., p. 406-407. On the ILC works relating to Art. 30, item 4, see Roucounas, Emmanuel, Engagements parallèles et contradictoires, cit., p. 95-102.

[163] Anzilotti, Dionisio. *Cours de droit international*, cit., p. 103.

1.6.5 *Conclusion on the Convention system*

After studying the items above, it can be concluded that, based on the brief submitted by Ernesto De La Guardia, the system of the 1969 Vienna Convention on conflicts between successive treaties is as follows:

1) in case of two successive treaties relating to the same subject-matter, it should first be determined whether the later treaty *expressly* terminates the earlier treaty (Art. 54, *b*);

2) if that is not the case, the provisions of Art. 59 will be applied in both cases, as follows: (*a*) it appears from the later treaty or is otherwise established that the parties intended that the matter should be governed by that treaty; (*b*) or it is verified that the provisions of the later treaty are so far incompatible with those of the earlier one that the two treaties are not capable of being applied at the same time;[164] in one case or the other, the earlier treaty will be terminated by the later treaty;

3) If that conclusion is not reached, it must be verified if there is any *clause* in one of the treaties providing for the relation between both treaties (*subordination* or *incompatibility* relation regarding the other treaty, under the terms of Art. 30, item 2);

4) if there is no such clause, and assuming that the parties to both treaties are the same, the later treaty prevails, while the earlier treaty survives only to the extent that its provisions are compatible with those of the later treaty (Art. 30, item 3);

5) if the parties to both treaties are not the same, the rule of Art. 30, item 4, applies, that is: (*a*) in relations between States parties to *both* treaties, the same rule applies as in paragraph 3, and (*b*) in relations between a State party to both treaties and a State party to only one of the treaties, either earlier or later, the treaty to which *both States are parties* governs their mutual rights and obligations.[165]

It should be recognized that this sequence of acts (and interpretations) established by the 1969 Vienna Convention, for the purpose of resolving the delicate problem of conflicts between successive treaties, was

---

164 On Art. 59, see item 3.1.1.2.2, below.

165 For further details, see De La Guardia, Ernesto, *Derecho de los tratados internacionales*, cit., p. 215.

not optimal, and has been (until today) the target of fierce criticism by legal scholars.[166] Practical difficulties arising from this subject, related to the confusing manner in which the Vienna text intended to resolve them, will surely be factors that will hinder legal decisions (especially by the ICJ) regarding the subject, in the cases still pending. Perhaps, the solution to the problem would be that the ICJ prepared, as it did with *reservations*[167], a Guide on conflict resolution between successive treaties relating to the same subject-matter...

1.7 Concurrence of treaties with a later customary rule

The statement of legal scholars affirming that there is no hierarchy between international treaties and customs is well known.[168] Consequently, a treaty in force can derogate, as between the parties concluding said treaty, a given earlier customary rule, in the same way as a supervening custom may derogate a rule set forth in a treaty (in which case, it is commonly said that the treaty fell into *disuse*, as it is no longer observed or it does not meet current needs anymore.) In summary, even if it is true that both treaties and customs have a prevalent position over the remaining sources of Public International Law, it is not less true that both (treaty and custom) enjoy the same authority at internal and international levels.

There are no problems when a treaty comes *after* an international custom since, in this case, it is understood that the *strongest will* of the international society (or the parties to the treaty under analysis) is also *better qualified* to revoke the *earlier* custom. But the opposite case, when a treaty has been concluded before a *later* custom, is more complex. In practice, international courts have given priority to *specific* provisions of international treaties in force between the parties relating to international customary rules, based on the fact that treaties offer more *security* and *stability* to international relations (which qualities are hardly found in customary law). This may be the reason why "international conventions,

---

166 See Remiro Brotons, Antonio. *Derecho internacional público*, vol. 2, cit., p. 328-330; and De La Guardia, Ernesto, *Derecho de los tratados internacionales*, cit., p. 216, note 48.

167 See *Report on the work of its sixty-third session* (26 April to 3 June and 4 July to 12 August 2011), General Assembly, Official Records, Supplement n.º 10 (A/66/10 and Add.1); and *Yearbook of the International Law Commission* (2011), vol. II, Part Two.

168 See Akehurst, Michael. The hierarchy of the sources of international law, *The British Yearbook of International Law*, vol. 47 (1974-75), p. 273-285; and Mazzuoli, Valerio de Oliveira, *Curso de direito internacional público*, cit., p. 125-126.

whether general or particular, establishing rules expressly recognized by the contesting States" precede "international custom" as set forth by Art. 38 of the ICJ Statute, which does not mean (again) that there is any technical hierarchy between such rules.

The prevalence of custom over treaties, which could be mentioned as an exception, relates to the case in which custom is a norm of *jus cogens*, in which case it prevails (hierarchically) over any international rules (whether they are treaties or even customs of another nature).[169]

---

[169] On conflicts between treaties and norms of *jus cogens*, see Ch. 2, item 2.2, below.

Chapter 2

Defects in Consent and in International Acts

We will now examine the defects that may invalidate (*a*) the consent of a State to be bound by a treaty, and (*b*) an international act as such. In other words, we will examine defects in *consent* as well as defects related *to the treaty itself*.[170] These two types of defects (in consent and in the treaty) have completely different consequences (however, legal scholars in general still mistake them) which must be duly analyzed. This Chapter systematizes the subject in an unusual form, which may even be considered *new*. It intends to clarify which are the cases of defects in *consent* and which situations invalidate *the treaty itself* (which no legal literature has done clearly). We believe this classification of the subject (see below) is the only one that fits the 1969 Vienna Convention, and it also answers practical doubts more accurately.

It should be said that defects capable of affecting the consent of a State to be bound by a treaty, or the treaty itself, are an *exception* to the theory of international acts, since every treaty in force is clearly *presumed* valid.[171] This rule is also included in Art. 42, item 1 of the 1969 Vienna Convention, which states that "The validity of a treaty or of the consent of a State to be bound by a treaty may be impeached only through the application of the present Convention".

---

170 See Mazzuoli, Valerio de Oliveira. Vícios do consentimento e nulidade dos tratados à luz da Convenção de Viena sobre o Direito dos Tratados de 1969, *Revista dos Tribunais*, vol. 914, year 100, São Paulo, Dec/2011, p. 185-197.

171 See Villiger, Mark E. *Commentary on the 1969 Vienna Convention on the Law of Treaties*, cit., p. 545: "Thus, Article 42 contains a presumption of the validity of a treaty. (…) As such, Article 42 represents the 'other facet of the *pacta sunt servanda* rule' (N. 12)".

2.1 Defects in consent and invalidity of treaties

The Law of Treaties borrowed the theory of defects capable of invalidating a legal act from the General Theory of Civil Law. The Law of Treaties is concerned with defects invalidating the *consent* of the State to be bound by a treaty, and with facts invalidating *the treaty itself.*

Section 2 of Part V (which covers Art. 46 through Art. 53) of the 1969 Vienna Convention (and also the 1986 Convention) is entitled *Invalidity of Treaties.*[172] However, such name is incorrect, since the Convention only deals with the *invalidity of treaties* in two provisions of that Section: Arts. 52 and 53, which cover the cases of "coercion of a State by the threat or use of force" and of "treaties conflicting with a peremptory norm of general International Law (*jus cogens*)", respectively.[173] The case of *supervening* termination of the treaty, governed by Art. 64 (out of Section 2) is also related to the conflict of treaties with a norm of *jus cogens*. In the first two cases (Arts. 52 and 53) invalidity is *ab initio*, this is, has effect *ex tunc*; in the second case (Art. 64) termination is supervening (*ex nunc* effect).[174] Except for those articles, the other provisions of the Convention (Arts. 46 to 51) deal with cases of defects related to the *consent* of the State to be bound by the treaty (not of invalidity *of the treaty* itself). The Convention allows consent to be *voidable* (depending on the will of the State victim) in the cases of Arts. 46 to 50; and only mentions *one case of invalidity* (*strictly speaking*) *of consent*, ruled by Art. 51: when there is coercion *of a representative of a State* (*or an international organization*).

However, it is not technically correct to refer to *Invalidity of Treaties,*[175] as referred to in the 1969 Vienna Convention (and the 1986 Convention) and supported by most legal scholars.[176] The name used by

---

[172] See Waldock, Humphrey [Special Rapporteur], *Yearbook of the International Law Commission* (1966), vol. II, p. 9.

[173] Articles 69 and 71 of the Convention explain the consequences (or *effects*) of invalidity of a treaty (which we will analyze in Ch. 4, item 4.2, below).

[174] Here we will only deal with the invalidity *ab initio* of treaties. *Supervening* invalidity will be studied later (see item 2.2.2.2, below).

[175] *Invalidity of Treaties*, in the original English version.

[176] Such as, for example, Remiro Brotons, Antonio, *Derecho internacional público*, vol. 2, cit., p. 428 *et ssq.*; De La Guardia, Ernesto, *Derecho de los tratados internacionales*, cit., p. 257 *et ssq.*; Accioly, Hildebrando & Nascimento e Silva, Geraldo Eulálio, *Manual de direito internacional público*, 13. ed., São Paulo: Saraiva, 1998, p. 36 *et ssq.*; Meira Mattos, Adherbal, *Direito internacional público*, 2. ed. (updated and extended), Rio de Janeiro: Renovar, 2002, p. 126 *et ssq.*; Mello, Celso D. de Albuquerque, *Curso de direito interna-*

another part of the legal literature, *defects in consent*, is not accurate either, especially when the invalidity results from the conflict between the treaty and a norm of *jus cogens*.[177] Perhaps due to such terminological inaccuracy of the Convention, legal scholars have been confused on the subject for several years. The Convention, although under an incorrect name, governs both situations: (1) defects that may influence the *consent* of a State to be bound by a treaty, divided into *voidable* (Arts. 46 to 50) and *void* (the only case of Art. 51);[178] and (2) the cases of *invalidity of the treaty* itself (Arts. 52 and 53). Section 1 of Part V of the Convention (entitled *General Provisions*) begins with Art. 42, item 1, which provides that "The validity of a *treaty* or of the *consent* of a State to be bound by a treaty may be impeached only through the application of the present Convention", adequately distinguishing the problem of invalidity *of a treaty* from the issue of invalidity *of the consent* of a State to be bound by a treaty. Art. 42 has the *nomem juris* "*Validity and Continuance in Force of Treaties*", without referring to the matter of consent, a mistake repeated by Section 2, entitled "*Invalidity of Treaties*". In summary, the Vienna Convention did not entitle Part V properly. Therefore, it is necessary to study the subject under the most appropriate name "Defects in Consent and Invalidity of Treaties".

---

cional público, vol. I, cit., p. 263 *et ssq.*; Shaw, Malcolm N., *Direito internacional*, cit., p. 698 *et ssq.*; and Fitzmaurice, Malgosia, The practical working of the law of treaties, cit., p. 178-180.

177 Among authors who refer to the issue under analysis just as "defects in consent", see Rezek, José Francisco, *Direito dos tratados*, cit., p. 350 *et ssq.*; Dupuy, Pierre-Marie, *Droit international public*, cit., p. 278 *et ssq.*; and Amaral Júnior, Alberto do, *Curso de direito internacional público*, 2. ed., São Paulo: Atlas, 2011, p. 62 et seq.

178 Adherbal Meira Mattos, for instance, places Art. 51 of the Convention (that governs the *only* case of invalidity *of consent*) among the cases of absolute invalidity *of treaties*. He mistakenly states that: "*Treaties* resulting from coercion exercised on the representative of a State, by means of actions or threats, will be *void by operation of law*" [italics ours] (*Direito internacional público*, cit., p. 127). Similarly, Malgosia Fitzmaurice mistakenly states: "The grounds for invalidity of treaties within the VCLT can be divided into two groups: relative grounds in Articles 46-50 and absolute grounds in Articles 51-53. The main difference between these grounds is that the relative grounds render a treaty voidable at the insistence of an affected State whereas the absolute grounds mean that *the treaty* is rendered void *ab initio* and without legal effect" [italics ours] (The practical working of the law of treaties, cit., p. 178). Still on "degree of invalidity", see Verhoeven, Joe, Invalidity of treaties: anything new in/under the Vienna Conventions?, in Cannizzaro, Enzo (ed.), *The law of treaties beyond the Vienna Convention*, cit., p. 300 *et seq.*

Then, pursuant to the provisions of Section 2 of Part V of the 1969 Convention (again, wrongly named *Invalidity of Treaties*), the issue under analysis may be divided into three parts: *a) avoidability of consent*; *b) invalidity of consent;* and *c) invalidity of treaties*. The first case refers to *relative invalidity* of consent; the other two refer to *absolute invalidity* (*pleno jure*) of consent and absolute invalidity of the treaty, respectively. Note that the 1969 and 1986 Conventions did not include any case of *avoidability* of treaties. *Consent* may be *avoidable* (when validation is possible) or *invalid* (when it may not be validated). On the other hand, the Convention only mentions cases of *invalidity* of treaties but not of *avoidability* (Arts. 52, 53 and 64).

Now we will analyze each case of defect in consent (*avoidability* and *invalidity* of consent) and invalidity of treaties.

2.1.1 Avoidability of consent

Pursuant to the Convention, there are four cases of *avoidability* of consent of a State to be bound by a treaty: when a Government expresses its consent to a treaty in violation of a provision of its internal Law (Art. 46); due to error (Art. 48); due to fraud (Art. 49); or due to corruption of a representative of a State (Art. 50).[179] The first ground for avoidability (irregular consent of a party) occurs when the Executive ratifies an international agreement in violation of a constitutional rule regarding competence to conclude treaties, also called *imperfect ratification*. This issue will be further analyzed below (see item 2.3). Apart from that case, consent rendered void by *error, fraud or corruption of the representative of a State* (*or international organization*) is also *avoidable*. These other grounds for avoidability will be studied under this subject (see items 2.1.1.1, 2.1.1.2 and 2.1.1.3, below).

First, it should be noted that only the State (or international organization) that was a *victim* of any of such causes of avoidability of consent may *invoke them* in its favor, and no other party, since these grounds have been established solely for its interest. Therefore, the State (or the relevant international organization) may not invoke those grounds if, after take cognizance of them, it agreed, expressly or tacitly, on the validity of the consent previously given.

---

[179] See Elias, Taslim Olawale. Problems concerning the validity of treaties, *Recueil des Cours*, vol. 134 (1971-III), p. 346; Barile, Giuseppe, La structure de l'ordre juridique international: règles générales et règles conventionnelles, *Recueil des Cours*, vol. 161 (1978-III), p. 87-90; Reuter, Paul, *Introducción al derecho de los tratados*, cit., p. 201-208; and Aust, Anthony, *Modern treaty law and practice*, cit., p. 252-257.

It should also be highlighted that the avoidability of consent (due to error, fraud or corruption of a representative of the State) produces effects *ex nunc* on the State victim, this is, the statement of avoidability only starts producing effects as from its declaration, without modifying the past effects that the international act already produced in connection with the party. Besides, since these are grounds for *avoidability* of consent, if they are not invoked, the State victim *continues* to be fully bound by the relevant treaty.

2.1.1.1 Error

Error is considered "the clearer case of defect in consent in a traditional sense".[180] A State (or international organization) may invoke that an error has invalidated its consent to be bound by the treaty, if the error relates to a *fact* or *situation* that was *assumed* by that State (or international organization) to exist at the time when the treaty was concluded and formed an *essential* basis of its consent to be bound by the treaty (Art. 48, item 1).[181] That is to say, in order for an error to invalidate consent, the error must be essential, related to the nature of the act. This is obviously an *error of fact*, since an *error of law* is unable to invalidate consent, either in domestic Law or in International Law).[182] It is clear that an essential error completely *distorts* consent, and it would not have existed if the treaty provided what the parties intended. An error not complying with such conditions – it must be related to a fact or situation whose *existence* was *assumed* by the State at the time of conclusion of the agreement; such fact or situation must be *essential* for the consent of the State; it must not be an *error of law* – is totally unable to invalidate consent.[183]

---

180 Reuter, Paul. *Introducción al derecho de los tratados*, cit., p. 204.

181 See ILC, *Yearbook of the International Law Commission* (1966), vol. II, p. 243-244; Sinclair, Ian, *The Vienna Convention on the Law of Treaties*, cit., p. 172-173; and Villiger, Mark E., *Commentary on the 1969 Vienna Convention on the Law of Treaties*, cit., p. 605-612.

182 See Dubouis, Louis. L'erreur en droit international public, *Annuaire Français de Droit International*, vol. 9 (1963), p. 191-227; and De La Guardia, Ernesto, *Derecho de los tratados internacionales*, cit., p. 273, who states: "In international law errors of *law* and errors of *fact* should be distinguished. It is generally agreed that errors of law *are not* defects in consent; and errors of fact are only admitted if they relate to an event or fact that has been the essential reason for the agreement".

183 See De La Guardia, Ernesto. *Derecho de los tratados internacionales*, cit., p. 274-275: "An error not meeting these conditions, by no means could be accepted as an error by competent international organizations to decide on such ground for invalidity".

It should be pointed out that an error may be made by one or more of the parties.[184] However, the rule of the Convention (that allows an error to invalidate consent) is not applied if the State (or international organization) contributed by its own conduct to the error, "*nemo auditur propriam turpitudinem allegans*"[185] or if the circumstances were such as to put that State or organization on notice of a possible error. (Art. 48, item 2).[186]

Currently, there are very few cases of substantial errors in treaties, and it is difficult (but not impossible) to think that in the era of fast communications and immediate access to information negotiators may conclude an international agreement based on an error of fact about the essential reasons that led the State (or international organization) to execute the agreement.

The most relevant examples of *error* known appear in treaties on limits, involving cartographic matters (maps, etc.) or delimitation of boundaries.[187] In the case *Preah Vihear Temple*, between Cambodia and Thailand, the ICJ disregarded the allegation of Thailand that a map contained an essential error and that, therefore, it was exempt from fulfilling the treaty attaching the map.[188] The Court pointed out that an error may not invalidate consent if the alleging party contributed to the error with its own conduct, or if such party could have avoided the error, or even if the circumstances were such as to put that party on notice of a possible error.[189]

Finally, the Convention provides that "an error relating only to the *wording of the text* of a treaty does not affect its validity; Art. 79 then applies [which provides on the correction of errors in texts or in certified copies of treaties]" (Art. 48, item 3). The ILC correctly understood that a wording error is not *substantial* in the agreement, and may be corrected without prejudice to the validity of the treaty.[190]

---

184 See Reuter, Paul. *Introducción al derecho de los tratados*, cit., p. 205.

185 "No one may allege his own turpitude for his own benefit".

186 See Villiger, Mark E. *Commentary on the 1969 Vienna Convention on the Law of Treaties*, cit., p. 609-610.

187 See McNair, Arnold Duncan. *The law of treaties*, cit., p. 211-213; and De La Guardia, Ernesto, *Derecho de los tratados internacionales*, cit., p. 273-274.

188 See *ICJ Reports* (1960), p. 6.

189 See *ICJ Reports* (1960), p. 26.

190 See ILC, *Yearbook of the International Law Commission* (1963), vol. II, p. 50; De La Guardia, Ernesto, *Derecho de los tratados internacionales*, cit., p. 275 and 342; and

2.1.1.2 Fraud

There is *fraud* when a State (or international organization) is induced to conclude a treaty by the *fraudulent conduct* of another negotiating State or negotiating organization (Art. 49).[191] *Frauds omnia corrumpit.* Then, fraud necessarily implies an unlawful *scam* or *deceit* (for example, false statements, document alteration, omission of substantial information, etc.). In addition to the *fraud*, the *intention* to damage the other party to the treaty is also necessary, which intention is consummated with the *expected* result.[192]

Fraud implies a more severe punishment than error in light of Public International Law, because it is a *crime*. That is why Reuter understands that a treaty rendered void due to fraud is, in fact, an unlawful act, carrying all the relevant legal consequences.[193] However, there is no fraud if the conclusion of the treaty resulted from a mistake generated by wrong information provided in *good faith* by the other party (which could be simply a case of *error*).

There are almost no examples of *fraud* when concluding treaties.[194] As pointed out by De La Guardia, it is difficult "for a State to execute a treaty without adoption of all the regular information, precaution and caution measures by the different bodies exercising the treaty-making power".[195] A very old example of fraudulent act in the process of execution of a treaty was documented at the colonial times, in the special context of

---

Villiger, Mark E., *Commentary on the 1969 Vienna Convention on the Law of Treaties*, cit., p. 610-611.

191 See ILC, *Yearbook of the International Law Commission* (1966), vol. II, p. 244-245.

192 See Remiro Brotons, Antonio. *Derecho internacional público*, vol. 2, cit., p. 435; De La Guardia, Ernesto, *Derecho de los tratados internacionales*, cit., p. 276; and Villiger, Mark E., *Commentary on the 1969 Vienna Convention on the Law of Treaties*, cit., p. 615-620.

193 Reuter, Paul. *Introducción al derecho de los tratados*, cit., p. 206. Also see Elias, Taslim Olawale, Problems concerning the validity of treaties, cit., p. 372-374.

194 See Sinclair, Ian. *The Vienna Convention on the Law of Treaties*, cit., p. 173.

195 De La Guardia, Ernesto. *Derecho de los tratados internacionales*, cit., p. 275. Mark Villiger, in turn, justifies the fact that fraud is rare in international treaties as follows: "Fortunately, cases of fraud are rare in international law. Of course, this may also be explained by the fact that charges of fraud between States are not to be taken lightly, and would even suggest a certain naiveté or incompetence on the part of the diplomatic services of the defrauded State" (*Commentary on the 1969 Vienna Convention on the Law of Treaties*, cit., p. 620).

relations between European powers and chieftains of Central Africa, who were shown intentionally manipulated maps.[196]

2.1.1.3 Corruption of a representative of a State

Finally, consent may also be voided when it was obtained by means of *corruption* of a representative of a State or international organization through direct or indirect action of another negotiating State or negotiating organization (Art. 50).[197]

The Vienna Convention expressly uses the term "corruption" (despite it not defining the term) to clarify that only acts executed to influence substantially the disposition of a representative of a State to conclude a specific treaty may be invoked as *defects* in consent expressed by the representative on behalf of its State.[198] In general, corruption of a state representative is closely related to *bribery*, but there are other similar means of corruption.

Concrete examples of this type of defect are also very rare in diplomatic and treaty practice, but they are frequent at the internal level of States, where it occurs increasingly, followed by all sort of scandals. This practice is actually as old as mankind and the first political systems. Corruption at the diplomatic and treaty level (which constitutes *special* fraud[199]) fully invalidates acceptance of the disloyal representative, even

---

196 See Dinh, Daillier & Pellet. *Direito internacional público*, cit., p. 200. For details on such precedent, see Paisant, Marcel, Les droits de la France au Niger (avec trois cartes), *Revue Générale du Droit International Public*, vol. 5, Paris (1898), p. 31-33.

197 See Elias, Taslim Olawale. Problems concerning validity of treaties, cit., p. 375-378; Sinclair, Ian, *The Vienna Convention on the Law of Treaties*, cit., p. 173-176; Remiro Brotons, Antonio, *Derecho internacional público*, vol. 2, cit., p. 436-437; De La Guardia, Ernesto, *Derecho de los tratados internacionales*, cit., p. 276-277; and Villiger, Mark E., *Commentary on the 1969 Vienna Convention on the Law of Treaties*, cit., p. 623-628.

198 See ILC, *Yearbook of the International Law Commission* (1966), vol. II, p. 245: "(4) The strong term 'corruption' is used in the article expressly in order to indicate that only acts calculated to exercise a substantial influence on the disposition of the representative to conclude the treaty may be invoked as invalidating the expression of consent which he has purported to give on behalf of his State. The Commission did not mean to imply that under the present article a small courtesy or favor shown to a representative in connexion with the conclusion of a treaty may be invoked as a pretext for invalidating the treaty".

199 Many authors understand that the provision of Art. 50 is unnecessary, precisely because *corruption is* a type of *fraud* (covered by Art. 49). De La Guardia, for extample, states that "corruption is just a fraudulent procedure to obtain the consent of a representative of a

if it refers to one or a few clauses of the treaty, and if they are not *essential* for the treaty.[200]

As an example of corruption of a representative of a State, Brotons cites the interesting case of a Norwegian high officer who was a *spy* for the former USSR, who played a key role (in 1978) in the execution of a preliminary agreement on the limits and fishing in the Barentz sea. This agreement was considered by many Norwegian sectors as highly favorable to the Soviet Union (obviously, due to corruption).[201] Brotons also explains that most of the times corruption is much more subtle than in the abovementioned case, combining several signals and amounts with cautious interruptions between the corrupting party and the corrupted party, especially in the field of economic and security relations.[202]

2.1.2 Invalidity of consent

The Vienna Convention only provides for one case of (*absolute*) *invalidity of consen*t of a State to be bound by a treaty (Art. 51). It is the case where consent is obtained by *coercion* of a representative of a State:

> "The expression of a State's consent to be bound by a treaty which has been procured by the coercion of its representative through acts or threats directed against him shall be without any legal effect".

The UN International Law Commission and the 1968-1969 Vienna Conference considered such *coercion* more serious than *corruption* of a representative of a State, *error* or *fraud*, to the extent of *invalidating* consent *ab initio* (since such consent shall not produce "any legal effects").[203] Therefore, unlike the cases of invalidity analyzed above (specially corruption of a representative of a State), coercion exercised on a representative of a State invalidates consent *ex tunc*, as if it had never existed.[204]

State, constituting one of the possible forms of '*fraudulent conduct*' provided in Art. 49" (*Derecho de los tratados internacionales*, cit., p. 277).

200 See Reuter, Paul. *Introducción al derecho de los tratados*, cit., p. 207.

201 Remiro Brotons, Antonio. *Derecho internacional público*, vol. 2, cit., p. 436.

202 Remiro Brotons, Antonio. Idem, ibidem.

203 See ILC, *Yearbook of the International Law Commission* (1966), vol. II, p. 245-246. See also Ago, Roberto, Droit des traités à la lumière de la Convention de Vienne, cit., p. 319-320; Elias, Taslim Olawale, Problems concerning the validity of treaties, cit., p. 378-380; Shaw, Malcolm N., *Direito internacional*, cit., p. 701; and Villiger, Mark E., *Commentary on the 1969 Vienna Convention on the Law of Treaties*, cit., p. 631-637.

204 See Reuter, Paul. *Introducción al derecho de los tratados*, cit., p. 209.

"Coercion" means any unlawful act able to constrain the representative of a State (physically or mentally) to act against its will and in accordance with the intention of the party exerting coercion. In other words, it is an act performed to force the behavior of a person, which was necessary to obtain his expression of consent. An example of coercion of a representative of a State would be a threat to his life (direct coercion) or to his family's life (indirect coercion); or threat to restrict his physical freedom (or his family's freedom). *Extortion* against the representative of the State is also frequent. Coercion may also be exercised not on the person of the representative of a State or his family but on his *property*, which also prevents the consent expressed from producing any legal effect. In any case, *coercion* of a representative of a State implies that the act of the party exerting coercion *leads* the person constrained – due to an imminent threat for him, his family or his property – to express the consent of a State to be bound by the treaty.

The Vienna Convention does not state who may be the *active subject* of coercion, as Art. 50, which provides that corruption of a representative of a State occurs by the action of a "negotiating State". Therefore, the Convention opened a menu of possibilities, which range from a negotiating State (as in the case of Art. 50) to a Head of State or even an individual (irrespective of its interest). Since the Convention does not provide any specification, we may conclude that any person (individual, head of State, etc.) or negotiating State may be the active subject of coercion, generating, therefore, (absolute) invalidity of consent of the representative of a State constrained.

If coercion on the representative of a State is recognized (for instance, by the ICJ), only the *consent* to be bound by the treaty of the *relevant State* is voided *ab initio*, and the *treaty* itself is not invalidated and remains in force for the other contracting parties, if it is multilateral (Art. 69, item 4).[205] It is clear that in the case of bilateral treaties, for a *de facto* reason, recognition of invalidity of consent terminates the relation between both parties (since the treaty cannot survive for only one of the parties). Again, the relevant treaty *remains in force* when consent of a representative of State was voided by *coercion*; it is not a defect of the *treaty*, but only a defect of *consent* of the State to be bound by the treaty. Historical examples (see historical examples below) are normally found in bilateral treaties,

---

205 See Villiger, Mark E., *Commentary on the 1969 Vienna Convention on the Law of Treaties*, cit., p. 635: "In the case of a multilateral treaty, only the consent of the State procured by the coercion of its representative is vitiated; the situation of other contracting States remains unaffected (*Article 69, paragraph 4*, No. 21)". On Art. 69, item 4 of the Convention, see Ch. 4, item 4.2, below.

as a consequence, most legal scholars are under the wrong impression that the treaty is voided *ab initio*.[206] Bilateral treaties are terminated, again, solely due to *a de facto* reason, since they may not survive for one party only, as any other *valid* treaty.

The rule contained in the 1969 Vienna Convention states that coercion must be exercised on the "representative" of the State, through acts or threats directed "against him", in order to invalidate consent. We think that the *representation* of a State must not be attributed solely to the *head of State*, as the authority entitled to express the *final* consent of the State. "Representative" must include any person *involved* in the process of formation and conclusion of a specific treaty. It is clear that a plenipotentiary admitted in an international conference *represents* his State to *negotiate* and even *sign* the relevant treaty. In other words, the *representatives* of States, for the purposes hereof, are those directly involved in the formation process of a treaty, or those who somehow *influenced* its conclusion. For instance, imagine a treaty freely ratified by the President of the Republic who *trusted* his plenipotentiary negotiator (who had been *forced* to diplomatic consent). In this case, it is clear that consent of the State, even if finally expressed by someone who did not suffer any coercion, was indeed affected by coercion and is *void* by operation of law.[207]

To prove the coercion exerted on the representative of State, the circumstances of conclusion as well as the contents of the treaty itself shall be taken into consideration. As pointed out by Villiger, such contents may indicate the use of acts or threats to induce an authorization that would not otherwise have been given.[208]

A classic example of consent rendered void by coercion on the representative of a State is the event of 1526 after the Pavia defeat, when King Francis I of France, imprisoned in Madrid by order of Charles V, was forced to sign the Treaty of Madrid to recover his freedom, giving all of Burgundy. After he was released, he refused to execute it invoking violence exerted against him.[209]

---

206 Throughout its explanation on the subject, Remiro Brotons says, for instance, that it is a ground for "invalidity of treaties" (see *Derecho internacional público*, vol. 2, cit., p. 437-439).

207 See Remiro Brotons, Antonio. *Derecho internacional público*, vol. 2, cit., p. 438-439.

208 Villiger, Mark E. *Commentary on the 1969 Vienna Convention on the Law of Treaties*, cit., p. 633: "In particular, the content may indicate the use of acts or threats to induce a consent which would not otherwise have been given".

209 See Dinh, Daillier & Pellet. *Direito internacional público*, cit., p. 201. According to Remiro Brotons, Francis I did not invoke *coercion* to be exonerated from compliance with the

2.1.3 *Invalidity of treaties*

In addition to the case of invalidity *of consent* of a State to be bound by the treaty provided in Art. 51, the Convention also provides two cases of absolute invalidity *of the treaty itself*, with effects *ex tunc* as well. They are: coercion on a sovereign State by the threat or use of force (Art. 52) and conflict of a subsequent treaty with a norm of *jus cogens* (Art. 53).[210]

The Convention states that coercion on the State and non-compliance with preexisting *jus cogens* are grounds for absolute invalidity of the treaty *ab initio* (non-compliance with subsequent *jus cogens*, however, has effects *ex nunc* and not *ab initio*, as explained in item 2.2.2.2, below). In both cases, the treaty shall be considered as if it did not exist for all the contracting parties.[211] Such grounds for treaty invalidity also arise directly from Art. 45 of the Convention, which separates them from the so-called "confirmation rule" (both express and tacit).[212] In fact, Art. 45 of the Convention[213] sets forth that a State "may no longer invoke a ground for invalidating, terminating, withdrawing from or suspending the operation of a treaty under Arts. 46 to 50 or Arts. 60 and 62 if, after becoming aware of the facts", it has (*a*) expressly accepted validity (force or execution) of the treaty, or (*b*) tacitly accepted (by reason of its conduct) such validity (force or execution), therefore excluding from application of said rule Arts. 52 and 53 relating to absolute invalidity of the treaty *ab initio*.

---

treaty, but refusal by the Burgundy Assembly of Notables to approve the treaty, invoking that the King was not competent to bind French provinces (see *Derecho internacional público*, vol. 2, cit., p. 438).

210 See ILC, *Yearbook of the International Law Commission* (1966), vol. II, p. 246-249. See also Elias, Taslim Olawale, Problems concerning the validity of treaties, cit., p. 380-404; Barile, Giuseppe, La structure de l'ordre juridique international: règles générales et règles conventionnelles, cit., p. 88-92; Rezek, José Francisco, *Direito dos tratados*, cit., p. 355-358; and Villiger, Mark E., *Commentary on the 1969 Vienna Convention on the Law of Treaties*, cit., p. 640-678.

211 See Barile, Giuseppe. La structure de l'ordre juridique international: règles générales et règles conventionnelles, cit., p. 87.

212 See Dinh, Daillier & Pellet. *Direito internacional público*, cit., p. 214.

213 This provision refers to the doctrine of estoppel in the Law of Treaties: *venire contra factum proprium non valet*. On this issue, see ILC, *Yearbook of the International Law Commission* (1963), vol. II, p. 45; Sinclair, Ian, *The Vienna Convention on the Law of Treaties*, cit., p. 168-169; De La Guardia, Ernesto, *Derecho de los tratados internacionales*, cit., p. 262-265; and Villiger, Mark E., *Commentary on the 1969 Vienna Convention on the Law of Treaties*, cit., p. 574-579. For a view prior to the Vienna Convention, see McNair, Arnold Duncan, *The law of treaties*, cit., p. 485-489.

We will now examine the case of coercion on a State established by the Convention; invalidity of treaties due to non-compliance with *jus cogens* (both preexisting and subsequent) will be studied in item 2.2 below.

First, it is necessary to differentiate (mainly regarding invalidity *effects*) between coercion as provided by Art. 51 of the Convention and coercion as ruled by Art. 52 under analysis. The Vienna Convention sets forth that "the expression of a State's consent to be bound by a treaty which has been procured by the coercion of its representative through acts or threats directed against him shall be without any legal effect" (Art. 51); and that "a treaty is void if its conclusion has been procured by the threat or use of force in violation of the principles of international law embodied in the Charter of the United Nations" (Art. 52). What is the difference between both rules, regarding the extent of invalidity effects? The difference, again, is that coercion exerted on the representative of a State does not invalidate the treaty itself, but only *consent* of the State to be bound by it, and its effects apply solely to the *parties* involved, this is, the party that exerted coercion and the party subject to coercion. Coercion of a State by threat or use of force, in turn, affects the *treaty itself*, and invalidity is enforceable *erga omnes*, since it is an unlawful act committed against all the members of the whole international society.[214]

In the cases of Art. 51, Art. 52 and Art. 53 of the Convention (the latter provides for the case of conflict between a treaty and a preexisting norm of *jus cogens*), the provisions of the treaty may not be *separated* (44, item 5). Therefore, in these three cases invalidity contaminates the international act *as a whole*.

> "Finally, as pointed above, the general regime of separability coexists, in the Vienna Conventions, with specific regimes clearly based on the idea of penalty. When fraud or corruption only affect certain clauses, which in accordance with the abovementioned criteria may be normally separated from the rest of the treaty, the victim may choose to invoke fraud or corruption only for such clauses, applying separability, or for the whole treaty; although termination of the treaty as a whole might affect the interests of such party. However, severability may not be applied to cases of unlawful coercion of a State or of its representative, or violation of a peremptory norm of international law (Article 44, item 5). Such a strict solution does not necessarily benefit the victim, and it can only be explained as a penalty imposed on behalf of the interests of the international community as a whole".
>
> Reuter, Paul. *Introducción al derecho de los tratados*, cit., p. 198.

[214] See Barile, Giuseppe. La structure de l'ordre juridique international: règles générales et règles conventionnelles, cit., p. 88.

Now we will examine Art. 52 of the 1969 Convention. Clearly, the rule causing invalidity *pleno jure* of a treaty concluded by means of coercion of the State itself (Art. 52) is more difficult to interpret than the rule invalidating consent due to coercion of the representative of a State (Art. 51), and, therefore, it deserves a more thorough analysis.

First, it is not easy to determine the scope of the terms "threat" and "use of force", used in Art. 52 of the Convention. There were simmering discussions during the Vienna Convention on the accurate meaning of these terms.[215] Many countries (especially those of the Third World, like Afghanistan) wanted the expression to cover economic and political pressures, in addition to strictly *armed* force.[216] Other delegations understood that the expression was too vague and it could cover any type of pressure exercised by one country over another country, compromising the stability of international relations in terms of treaties.[217] But such proposals were not accepted and the article remained unchanged. However, some authors understand that adoption of the final phrase "International Law embodied in the Charter of the United Nations" extends application of the provision to economic and political pressures, as intended by some delegations. In fact, at the end of the Conference two texts were incorporated in the final minutes to such effect: a *Declaration* "solemnly" condemning any military, political or economic coercion in the conclusion of treaties, and a *Resolution* requesting the Secretary-General of the UN to bring such *Declaration* to the attention of all member States, participating States, as well as to main organs of the United Nations.[218] There follow the texts of the abovementioned *Declaration* and *Resolution*[219]:

---

215 See Nascimento e Silva, Geraldo Eulálio do. *Conferência de Viena sobre o Direito dos Tratados*, cit., p. 78-79.

216 See Sinclair, Ian. *The Vienna Convention on the Law of Treaties*, cit., p. 177-179; De La Guardia, Ernesto, *Derecho de los tratados internacionales*, cit., p. 287-288; and Shaw, Malcolm N., *Direito internacional*, cit., p. 701-702. The Rapporteur on the subject at the ILC (Waldock) understood otherwise, and even affirmed that "the application of economic and political pressures are part of the *ordinary* game of relations between States (...)" [italics are ours]. See Waldock, Humphrey [Special Rapporteur], *Yearbook of the International Law Commission* (1963), vol. II, p. 60.

217 See Calsing, Maria de Assis. *O tratado internacional e sua aplicação no Brasil*, cit., p. 52.

218 See Ago, Roberto. Droit des traités à la lumière de la Convention de Vienne, cit., p. 319-320; and Dinh, Daillier & Pellet, *Direito internacional público*, cit., p. 203.

219 For a comment on both texts, see especially Villiger, Mark E. *Commentary on the 1969 Vienna Convention on the Law of Treaties*, cit., p. 651-660.

Declaration on the Prohibition of Military, Political or Economic Coercion in the Conclusion of Treaties
The United Nations Conference on the Law of Treaties,
Upholding the principle that every treaty in force is binding upon the parties to it and must be performed by them in good faith,
Reaffirming the principle of the sovereign equality of States,
Convinced that States must have complete freedom in performing any act relating to the conclusion of a treaty,
Deploring the fact that in the past States have sometimes been forced to conclude treaties under pressure exerted in various forms by other States,
Desiring to ensure that in the future no such pressure will be exerted in any form by any State in connection with the conclusion of a treaty,
1. *Solemnly condemns* the threat or use of pressure in any form, whether military, political, or economic, by any State in order to coerce another State to perform any act relating to the conclusion of a treaty in violation of the principles of the sovereign equality of States and freedom of consent,
2. *Decides* that the present Declaration shall form part of the Final Act of the Conference on the Law of Treaties.

Resolution relating to the Declaration on the prohibition of military, political or economic coercion in the conclusion of treaties
The United Nations Conference on the Law of Treaties,
Having adopted the Declaration on the prohibition of military, political or economic coercion in the conclusion of treaties as part of the Final Act of the Conference,
1. *Requests* the Secretary-General of the United Nations to bring the Declaration to the attention of all Member States and other States participating in the conference, and of the principle organs of the United Nations,
2. *Requests* Member States to give to the Declaration the widest possible publicity and dissemination.

Since the expression "force" was not accurately delimited, it must be interpreted in accordance with generally accepted rules of international hermeneutics. Clearly not every "force" can invalidate an international agreement: if that were the case, as Reuter said, "every peace treaty would be void".[220] Besides, legal scholars have always questioned whether *peace treaties* would be *void* or not since they are concluded through the use of force by the winner against the defeated party. All German legal scholars, for example, considered the 1919 Treaty of Versailles void, since it was imposed on Germany by the victors of the First World War. However, if such understanding is strictly applied, "unequal treaties",[221] which are those

220 Reuter, Paul. *Introducción al derecho de los tratados*, cit., p. 209.

221 The classification between "equal" and "unequal" treaties has a Marxist origin. On this subject, see Marković, Milan, Les traites inegaux en droit international, *Jugoslovenska Re-*

executed by totally unequal States in terms of power hierarchy, would also be void, since the *weak* State is assumed to be fully dependent on the *strong* State, etc.[222] In summary, the *unlawful* use of force only, in the light of the principles of International Law embodied in the UN Charter, may invalidate a treaty, even if such force is exercised *without arms*.[223] For contemporary Public International Law, political, economic, or any other kind of pressure, are also forbidden when exercised "to constrain another State in order to subordinate it in relation to the exercise of its sovereign rights".[224] In turn, the *lawful* use of force (duly proven) cannot invalidate an international act. Then, a peace treaty imposed on an *aggressor* State (not on an *attacked* State) using force shall be deemed fully valid between the parties (even pursuant to the norm of *jus cogens* preventing aggression acts). In this case, the defeated aggressor State could not invoke its *lack of freedom* as a ground for invalidity of consent, because Art. 52 of the Convention does not set forth a ground for invalidity *of consent*, but for invalidity of the *treaty itself* (included in the Vienna text precisely for *sanctioning* States using threat or force in international relations).[225] An example of an international act executed by unlawful coercion on a State

---

vija za Međunarodno Pravo, Nos. 2-3 (1970), p. 264-284; and Nozari, Fariborz, *Unequal treaties in international law*, Stockholm: S-Byran Sundt & Co., 1971, 333p.

[222] See Rezek, José Francisco. *Direito dos tratados*, cit., p. 357-358. Rezek points out that: "In international relations, like in any human relation, every interest leading to a treaty results from a need, and, eventually, from some kind of pressure. The typical scenario when negotiating peace treaties is an unavoidable consequence of war, and if the international legal system could not avoid it, there is no way to defeat the damage it inflicts on the ideal of free consent" (Idem, p. 358).

[223] See Remiro Brotons, Antonio. *Derecho internacional público*, vol. 2, cit., p. 442; and Reuter, Paul, *Introducción al derecho de los tratados*, cit., p. 209.

[224] Res. 2625 (XXV), of the General Assembly of the UN, dated October 24, 1970, attaching the *Declaration on Principles of International Law concerning Friendly Relations and Cooperation among States in accordance with the Charter of the United Nations*. However, Remiro Brotons points out the "difficulty to establish such *intentional* element, essential to qualify conduct and distinguish between unlawful use of force (not armed) and use of resources and power of a State to lawfully *influence* the rest of them" (*Derecho internacional público*, vol. 2, cit., p. 442). According to Villiger, however: "(...) coercion within the meaning of Article 52 does not comprise economic or political coercion. This is confirmed by the *travaux préparatoires*, *inter alia*, the proceedings at the Vienna Conference" (*Commentary on the 1969 Vienna Convention on the Law of Treaties*, cit., p. 644).

[225] See Remiro Brotons, Antonio. *Derecho internacional público*, vol. 2, cit., p. 443; and Reuter, Paul, *Introducción al derecho de los tratados*, cit., p. 198.

is the 1938 Treaty between Germany and Czechoslovakia, concluded under the threat of bombing Prague, where coercion exercised on the former Czechoslovakia was evident.

It should also be highlighted that Art. 52 of the Vienna Convention does not require the threat or use of force to be used by a subject *participating* in the relevant treaty. That is to say, it is perfectly possible for the unlawful act to be committed by a party *not participating* in negotiations of the international agreement. According to Remiro Brotons, this emphasizes the seriousness of this kind of conduct, while depriving powerful States of the advantage of hiding behind figureheads and clients (States, international organizations or other entities) their own violence, looking formally *clean* during the formation of a treaty.[226]

Finally, we will examine the *effects* of the declaration of invalidity of a treaty concluded by coercion on a State by threats or use of force. We will now discuss the subject briefly, since it will be further analyzed (see Part III, Ch. 4, item 4.2, below). Such consequences are governed by Art. 69 of the Convention. Here we will only say that the provisions of a void treaty do not have any *legal effect*. Such invalidity has effects *ab initio* and not as from its allegation by any of the parties; that is to say, the treaty signed using threat or force is void as from its conclusion, and not only as from the time the ground for invalidity was discovered.[227] Therefore, the declaration of invalidity of a treaty terminates the invalid international agreement with effects *ex tunc*. That is to say, the declaration of invalidity is retroactive to the agreement conclusion date, removing all effects it produced since then.

2.2 *Jus cogens* and invalidity of treaties

As we have seen, a treaty may be invalid *ab initio* in two cases: *a*) in the event of coercion on a State by threat or use of force; or *b*) if at the time of conclusion it was in conflict with a peremptory norm of general International Law (conflict between a treaty and a preexisting norm of *jus cogens*). A treaty may also be terminated (invalidity is not *ab initio*) when it conflicts with a subsequent norm of *jus cogens* (Art. 64). Conflict of the treaty with a preexisting norm of *jus cogens* differs from coercion on a State, since it does not imply absolute invalidity resulting from a *defect of*

---

226 Remiro Brotons, Antonio. *Derecho internacional público*, vol. 2, cit., p. 443.

227 See Dinh, Daillier & Pellet. *Direito internacional público*, cit., p. 217.

the act, but absolute invalidity resulting from the *unlawful subject-matter of the treaty*. Conflict of the treaty with a subsequent norm of *jus cogens*, in turn, is a ground for *termination* of the international act. Then, consequences will vary, depending on the case.

Consequences of invalidity involving coercion on a State are governed by Art. 69 of the Vienna Convention; and consequences of invalidity (Art. 53) and termination (Art. 64) of a treaty due to violation of a norm of *jus cogens* are governed by Art. 71, items 1 and 2. Note the importance given to *jus cogens* by the 1969 Vienna Convention, as its procedure is regulated in a separate provision from other defects of a treaty. So, what do items 1 and 2 of Art. 71 provide on *jus cogens* procedure? In the event of a treaty *void* pursuant to Art. 53 (conflict with a preexisting norm of *jus cogens*), the parties shall: *a*) eliminate as far as possible the consequences of any act performed in reliance on any provision which conflicts with the peremptory norm of general international law; and *b*) bring their mutual relations into conformity with the peremptory norm of general international law (Art. 71, item 1). Then, when a treaty is void due a conflict with a preexisting norm of *jus cogens*, the *status quo ante* shall be reinstated and, in addition, States shall *adjust* to the earlier norm of *jus cogens*.[228] In the case of conflicts under Art. 64 (conflict with a subsequent norm of *jus cogens*), termination of the treaty: *a*) releases the parties from continuing to fulfill the treaty; and *b*) does not damage any right, obligation or legal situation of the parties, created by execution of the treaty, before its termination. However, such rights, obligations or situations may thereafter be maintained only to the extent that their maintenance is not in itself in conflict with the norm of *jus cogens* (Art. 71, item 2).

In summary, conflict between treaties and norms of *jus cogens* may occur under two circumstances: (*a*) the norm of *jus cogens* may be *prior* to entry into force of the treaty (invalidity *ab initio*), or (*b*) it may be *subsequent* to its entry into force (the treaty will lose effects *ex nunc*). Those two situations will be examined in items 2.2.2.1 and 2.2.2.2. We will also refer to a third case, relating to the conflict between a treaty and a norm of *jus cogens* existing before entry into force of the Vienna Convention (item 2.2.2.3). However, before studying the *conflict* between treaties and norms of *jus cogens*, we should understand *what* such rules are and their

[228] See Viegas, Vera Lúcia. *Ius cogens* e o tema da nulidade dos tratados, *Revista de Informação Legislativa*, year 36, No. 144, Brasília: Federal Senate, Oct/Dec/1999, p. 188.

characteristics. Finally, we will deal with the hierarchic position of norms of *jus cogens* in the Law of Treaties (item 2.2.3).

2.2.1 What are norms of jus cogens*?*

The notion *jus cogens*, as explained by Antonio Cassese, comes from the end of the sixties, as a result of the pressure of developing socialist countries to establish the idea that some essential rules, formed by custom, should be in a position hierarchically superior to treaty rules, turning such treaties in conflict with them void. Among those rules, said countries emphasized those on self-determination of peoples, prohibition of aggression, prohibition of genocide, slavery, racial discrimination, and in particular, racial aggression (or apartheid).[229] However, according to André Gonçalves Pereira and Fausto de Quadros, the origin of norms of *jus cogens* is older, as evidenced by fifteen references to such norms by Hugo Grotius, under the name of *jus strictum*, in Book I of *De Jure Belli ac Pacis*, based on *jus divinum*.[230]

Such norms of *jus cogens* are absolutely peremptory and, therefore, opposite to the old Roman *jus dispositivum* – composed by rules arising from the free statement of will of the parties – which structured International Law for many years. But the existence of rules that may not be altered by the will of the parties has been invoked since Roman times: *Jus publicum privatorum pactis mutari non potest* (Digest 2;14;38). Romans used the term *jus publicum* for what is nowadays called binding law, this is, law that may not be altered by the exercise of private autonomy,[231] which originated the so called *public policy* rules. *Jus publicum* would then be the opposite or the antithesis of *substantive law*, that is to say, binding laws that preclude any other legal rule to the contrary. Currently, the trend is to abandon the old voluntarism doctrine, which deemed the will of States as the sole foundation for valid rules of International Law, and the modern trend is to consider certain international rules not coming directly from a formal statement of the State as mandatory. In other words, the structure of the old Law of Nations must be replaced by hierarchization

---

229 See Cassese, Antonio. *Diritto internazionale*, cit., p. 199.

230 See Pereira, André Gonçalves & Quadros, Fausto de. *Manual de direito internacional público*, cit., p. 278. On the historic evolution of the notion of *jus cogens*, see Friedrich, Tatyana Scheila, *As normas imperativas de direito internacional público jus cogens*, Belo Horizonte: Fórum, 2004, p. 25-29.

231 See Viegas, Vera Lúcia. *Ius cogens* e o tema da nulidade dos tratados, cit., p. 182.

and verticalization of the rules of Public International Law. And norms of *jus cogens* are on top of Public International Law.

The Vienna Convention on the Law of Treaties regulated the subject in Arts. 53 and 64, which read as follows:

> "Article 53. *Treaties conflicting with a peremptory norm of general international law* (jus cogens). A treaty is void if, at the time of its conclusion, it conflicts with a peremptory norm of general International Law. For the purposes of the present Convention, a peremptory norm of general international law is a norm accepted and recognized by the international community of States as a whole as a norm from which no derogation is permitted and which can be modified only by a subsequent norm of general international law having the same character".

> "Article 64. *Emergence of a new peremptory norm of general international law* (jus cogens) If a new peremptory norm of general international law emerges, any existing treaty which is in conflict with that norm becomes void and terminates".

There is much criticism of these provisions, the first point is the lack of accuracy of the Convention when dealing with the subject, since it only: *a*) describes such "peremptory norm" (without explaining its legal content and without giving leads to determine its scope); *b*) requires it to be "accepted and recognized by the international society of States as a whole"; and *c*) imposes the penalty of *invalidity* or *termination* on all treaties (prior or subsequent) contrary to their provisions.[232]

Before making any analysis, it should be pointed out that *jus cogens* must be deemed as the quality of a specific *rule*. Rules may be substantive, or peremptory of general International Law. Only the latter are *jus cogens*, since they are *peremptory* norms. Both Art. 53 and Art. 64 of the Convention refer to "peremptory *norms* of general international law" to define *jus cogens*.[233] Such *norm* qualified as *jus cogens* may arise from a *treaty*, a *custom*, a *general principle of law*, etc.

---

232 See Pereira, André Gonçalves & Quadros, Fausto de. *Manual de direito internacional público*, cit., p. 281. On this subject, also see Paulus, Andreas L., *Jus cogens* in a time of hegemony and fragmentation: an attempt at a re-appraisal, *Nordic Journal of International Law*, vol. 74 (2005), p. 297-334; and Villiger, Mark E., *Commentary on the 1969 Vienna Convention on the Law of Treaties*, cit., p. 665-678.

233 See Linderfalk, Ulf. The effect of *jus cogens* norms: whoever opened Pandora's Box, did you ever think about the consequences? *European Journal of International Law*, vol. 18, No. 5 (2007), p. 856.

Saying that *jus cogens* is "a peremptory norm of general International Law" does not mean that its precepts are *mandatory*, since even those resulting from *jus dispositivum* are mandatory, but it means that they *may not be derogated by the will of the parties*. Generally speaking, any legal norm is *mandatory*, but not all are absolutely *peremptory*, like the case of *jus cogens*. The total, absolute peremptoriness of norms of *jus cogens* is based on the fact that they may not be derogated. The 1969 Vienna Convention defines norms of *jus cogens* "*...as a norm from which no derogation is permitted*".[234] *Derogation* means the conclusion of an agreement (treaty) not complying with the peremptory norm of general International Law. This means that "agreements contrary to" norms of *jus cogens* are not admitted, which is the corollary to its peremptory quality. Finally, also according to the Convention, *jus cogens* rules "can be modified only by a subsequent norm of general international law having the same character"; that is to say, only a subsequent norm of *jus cogens* revokes an prior norm of *jus cogens*, and rules not having such status may not revoke norms of *jus cogens* under any circumstance.[235]

There are no examples of norms of *jus cogens* in the Vienna Convention, as we have already mentioned. The Convention recognized the "existence" of *jus cogens*, without specifying its content,[236] suggesting that its rules are similar to public policy rules in International Law. However, there seems to be consensus on the view that a rule allowing genocide, traffic of slaves, break of peace, use of force in relations between States, aggression war, torture or piracy, and all prohibitions of the United Nations Charter, for example, shall be deemed void for being contrary to *jus cogens*.[237] Likewise, rules prohibiting discrimination, securing self-deter-

---

234 See Shelton, Dinah. Normative hierarchy in international law, *American Journal of International Law*, vol. 100, No. 2 (April 2006), p. 300.

235 See Gaja, Giorgio. *Jus cogens* beyond the Vienna convention, *Recueil des Cours*, vol. 172 (1981-III), p. 283-284.

236 As pointed out by De La Guardia, the ILC intended not to give examples of norms of *jus cogens* "because it is difficult to provide a list of such rules, which could lead to the construction rule *expressio unius exclusio alterius*" (*Derecho de los tratados internacionales*, cit., p. 290).

237 See Jenks, Clarence Wilfred. *A new world of law? A study of the creative imagination in international law*. London: Longmans, 1969, p. 169-170; and Spinedi, Marina, From one codification to another: bilateralism and multilateralism in the genesis of the codification of the law of treaties and the law of State responsibility, *European Journal of International Law*, vol. 13, No. 5 (2002), p. 1102-1103. Especially on the prohibition of use of

mination of peoples and principles of Humanitarian International Law would also be *jus cogens*.[238]

Some legal scholars have posed the question of which sources of Public International Law can create norms of *jus cogens*. It is currently understood that norms of *jus cogens* come from or may come from either international custom and treaty law, or general principles of law.[239]

We consider that they integrate the *jus cogens* or the international public order, broadly speaking: (*a*) general or common international custom, for example norms protecting the foundations of international order, such as the prohibition to use force other than for self-defense; norms on peaceful cooperation to protect common interests, such as free seas; norms prohibiting slavery, piracy, genocide, torture and racial discrimination; norms protecting religious freedom; norms of humanitarian law, which apply to cases of armed conflicts to protect civilians in times of war, soldiers out of combat, wounded, imprisoned, sick and shipwrecked, as well as norms prohibiting aggression war; norms protecting the rights of States and peoples (such as norms on equality, territorial integrity, free

---

force, see Linderfalk, Ulf, The effect of *jus cogens* norms: whoever opened Pandora's Box, did you ever think about the consequences?, cit., p. 859-867.

238 See Cassese, Antonio. *Diritto internazionale*, cit, p. 205-206. There are also discussions on the possible *jus cogens* nature of the 1948 Universal Declaration of Human Rights. According to John P. Humphrey, for instance, the Universal Declaration is part of customary law of nations, and, therefore, binding on all States (see The implementation of international human rights law, *New York Law School Review*, vol. 24, 1978, p. 31-33). Other authors, such as Jorge Miranda, go further to state that the Declaration is *jus cogens*, especially due to "the increasingly generalized belief of inviolability of human rights and repeated references to the Declaration –sometimes meaningless, but many other times, as a reference or foundation– in Constitutions, treaties, laws and court decisions". See Miranda, Jorge. Nos 60 anos da Declaração Universal dos Direitos do Homem: uma perspectiva constitucional portuguesa, *Polis – Revista de Estudos Jurídico-Políticos*, No. 17, Lisbon, 2009, p. 18. In the same sense, see Lindgren Alves, J. A., *Os direitos humanos como tema global*, São Paulo: Perspectiva, 1994, p. 48, according to whom: "Regardless of the doctrine adopted, in practice the Universal Declaration is generally invoked as an adopted norm of *jus cogens*, and such statement has not been objected even by the States with more accusations of violating its provisions". On the subject, see Pereira, André Gonçalves & Quadros, Fausto de, *Manual de direito internacional público*, cit., p. 282-284; and Mazzuoli, Valerio de Oliveira, *Curso de direito internacional público*, cit., p. 938-940.

239 In that regard, see Gómez Robledo, Antonio, *El* ius cogens *internacional: estudio histórico-crítico*, México, D.F.: UNAM, 2003, p. 79-89.

determination of peoples), etc.;[240] (*b*) treaty norms belonging to general International Law, for example, principles contained in the Charter of the United Nations, such as rules on peaceful solution of conflicts, preservation of international peace, security and justice; rules on contractual freedom and inviolability of treaties (such as *pacta sunt servanda* and good faith), etc.; and (*c*) special International Law, originated unilaterally or from a treaty on essential human rights and warranties, such as the 1948 Universal Declaration of Human Rights, the two 1966 Covenants of New York (International Covenant on Civil and Political Rights and International Covenant on Economic, Social and Cultural Rights) and, within the Inter American regional system, the 1969 American Convention on Human Rights (*San José of Costa Rica Pact*).[241]

It should be noted that the three groups of norms mentioned are somehow related to the subject of "human rights" (by prohibiting slavery, piracy, genocide and racial discrimination; by safeguarding international peace, security and justice; or by standardizing, as hard law, the protection of civil and political rights and economic, social and cultural rights). Therefore, it may be concluded that there is an intrinsic relation between *jus cogens* and norms protecting human rights, considered the most common example of this kind of peremptory norm of Public International Law.[242]

In summary, the ruling procedure of *jus cogens* indicates the existence of a new and independent source of Public International Law, formed by peremptory norms recognized by the international society as a whole and not included in the list of classical sources of International Law set forth in Art. 38 of the Statute of the ICJ. Their recognition by the 1969 Vienna Convention was another factor that contributed to the crisis of voluntarism and strengthened the foundations of Public International Law.[243] Then, the traditional theory of sources in the Law of Nations changed in relation to norms of *jus cogens*, since there are norms higher than treaties and customs in the legal rank that prevail over any other rule.

---

[240] See "*Jus Cogens*", in *Encyclopedia of Public International Law*, vol. 7, Bernhardt, Ed., 1984, p. 327.

[241] See Shelton, Dinah. Normative hierarchy in international law, cit., p. 302-304; and Pereira, André Gonçalves & Quadros, Fausto de, *Manual de direito internacional público*, cit., p. 283-284.

[242] See Bianchi, Andrea. Human rights and the magic of *jus cogens*, *European Journal of International Law*, vol. 19, No. 3 (2008), p. 491-508.

[243] See Pereira, André Gonçalves & Quadros, Fausto de. *Manual de direito internacional público*, cit., p. 285.

2.2.2 *Conflict between treaties and norms of* jus cogens

Since the concept and features of *jus cogens* have already been understood, we will now examine the relations (conflicts) between international treaties and said norms of *jus cogens*. As said before, such conflict may occur under two circumstances: (*a*) the norm of *jus cogens* may be *prior* to entry into force of the treaty (invalidity *ab initio*), or (*b*) it may be *subsequent* to its entry into force (the treaty will lose effects *ex nunc*).

Both cases will be studied in this item, as well as (in third place) the case of conflict between a treaty and a norm of *jus cogens* existing before entry into force of the Vienna Convention.

2.2.2.1 *Conflict between a treaty and an earlier norm of* jus cogens

Pursuant to Art. 53 of the 1969 Vienna Convention, a treaty is *void* if, at the time of its conclusion, it conflicts with a peremptory norm of general international law (*jus cogens*). A treaty the invalidity of which is established under the Convention is *void*. The provisions of a void treaty have no legal force (Art. 69, item 1). Art. 53 of the Convention means that States or international organizations concluding treaties *must* know the prior *jus cogens*, so they do not execute international acts conflicting with higher principles and norms of interest for all mankind (like norms of *jus cogens*). That is why the Vienna Convention has not admitted treaties conflicting with peremptory norms of general International Law.[244]

In order to invoke the invalidity of a treaty, the procedure provided in Art. 65 of the Vienna Code shall be followed (see Ch. 4, below). Pursuant to such norm, the *party* invoking invalidity of a treaty based on an earlier norm of *jus cogens* shall *give written notice* of its claim to the other States, specifying the measure it intends to take in connection with the treaty considered void, as well as its reasons.[245] The notice provided in Art. 65, item 1 must be given in writing.

Only States *parties* to the international treaty are entitled, under the terms of the Vienna Convention, to invoke the invalidity of the treaty conflicting with the earlier norm of *jus cogens*. Despite criticism by le-

---

244 See ILC, *Yearbook of the International Law Commission* (1966), vol. II, p. 266.

245 See Fiorati, Jete Jane. *Jus cogens: as normas imperativas de direito internacional público como modalidade extintiva dos tratados internacionais*. France: Ed. Unesp, 2002, p. 67; Aust, Anthony, *Modern treaty law and practice*, cit., p. 259; and Villiger, Mark E., *Commentary on the 1969 Vienna Convention on the Law of Treaties*, cit., p. 807-808.

gal scholars (including ourselves), pursuant to the Convention, only the *parties* may invoke a violation of the norm of *jus cogens*.[246] That is to say, only the States *participating* in the agreement are entitled to invoke (for instance, before the ICJ) that certain norm of *jus cogens* was violated, and other players of the international society who are not parties are not entitled to such allegation, although the norms of *jus cogens* seek the protection of the *whole* international society. It should be pointed out that this case is also different from the case of defects in consent (Arts. 48 to 52), in which only the State that had its consent affected may void the international act.

In this case, the parties must (*a*) eliminate as far as possible the consequences of any act performed in reliance on any provision which conflicts with the peremptory norm of general international law, and (*b*) bring their mutual relations into conformity with the peremptory norm of *jus cogens* (Art. 71, item 1).

The invalidity of a treaty conflicting with a norm of *jus cogens* has effect *ex tunc*. However, during the minimum term of notice (three months), the party is bound to continue fulfilling the relevant treaty, except in cases of extreme urgency, if no other party filed objections. However, it would be better to consider the treaty as invalid immediately, and later determine whether the party's allegation must be accepted, preventing a State

---

[246] For criticism, see Fiorati, Jete Jane, *Jus cogens...*, cit., p. 108-109, who explains: "Art. 65 introduces a huge and unrepairable contradiction with the norms of Arts. 53 and 64 of the Convention. In said articles, the Peremptory Norm of General International Law recognized by the International Community aims at protecting said Community and its values from unfair Treaties. So the Convention should provide that not only the parties, but also any country of the International Community, could file for invalidity of the treaty derogating a norm of *jus cogens* before the International Court of Justice. Now, this is not the case: Art. 65 says that only one of the parties or all of them may invoke a conflict between the Treaty and the *Jus Cogens*. Note that Art. 65 distorted the nature of *Jus Cogens*, which instead of a guarantor of the value of International Law, peremptory by nature, is defined as a mere implicit clause in treaties, since the party affected by the violation of the *Jus Cogens*, which is the International Community, is not entitled to invoke and prove the invalidity of the unfair treaty. (...) Therefore, we may conclude that the Delegates to the Vienna Conference were not right when entitling only contracting parties to request the invalidity of treaties contrary to *Jus Cogens*". In that very sense, see Sztucki, Jerzy, *Jus cogens and the Vienna Convention on the Law of Treaties: a critical appraisal*, New York: Springer-Verlag, 1974, p. 188-189; Hannikainen, Lauri, *Peremptory norms (jus cogens) in international law: historical development, criteria, present status*, Helsinki: Finnish Lawyers' Publishing, 1988, p. 297-298; and Simma, Bruno, From bilateralism to community interest in international law, *Recueil des Cours*, vol. 250 (1994-VI), p. 288-289.

from continuing to fulfill a treaty that it considers to be void by operation of law. If the claim of the party is eventually not accepted, such party would be liable for breach of the treaty.

The party can request before the ICJ a *provisional measure* to suspend execution of the treaty that it considers void.

It should be remembered that the will of the parties may not alter a norm of *jus cogens*, which means that a treaty conflicting with a peremptory norm of general International Law is not validated by individual agreements.

Pursuant to Art. 44, item 5 of the Convention, which establishes the *separability* of provisions of a treaty in these cases, the *whole* treaty will be invalid *ab initio* and it will have no legal force for the international society, the validity of part of its clauses is not permitted.[247] In other words, since treaties are not *separable*, the invalidity affects the whole treaty, and not only a part of it. But it should be highlighted that this solution only applies to the specific case under analysis: conflict between a treaty and an earlier norm of *jus cogens* (preexisting). However, as noted by Vera Lúcia Viegas, by means of a systematic interpretation of the Vienna Convention, "potential *effects of acts executed based on 'clauses not rendered void' for conflicting with a norm of jus cogens* must be taken into consideration. In this case, item 2, paragraph 'b' of Art. 69 of the Convention applies: *acts performed in good faith before the invalidity was invoked are not rendered unlawful by reason only of the invalidity of the treaty*" [italics from original].[248]

2.2.2.2 Conflict between a treaty and a subsequent norm of jus cogens

Pursuant to Art. 64 of the Vienna Convention, any treaty conflicting with a *new* peremptory *norm* of general International Law (*jus cogens*) becomes void and terminates.

It should be pointed out that Art. 64 of the Convention provides for a *ground for termination of treaties*, and not for *invalidity* (the latter, contained in Section 2, Part V of the Convention, already examined in item

---

247 See De La Guardia, Ernesto. *Derecho de los tratados internacionales*, cit., p. 292; Reuter, Paul, *Introducción al derecho de los tratados*, cit., p. 53; and Villiger, Mark E., *Commentary on the 1969 Vienna Convention on the Law of Treaties*, cit., p. 674-675.

248 Viegas, Vera Lúcia. *Ius cogens* e o tema da nulidade dos tratados, cit., p. 189.

2.1.3, above).[249] This occurs for two reasons: first, because item 2 of Art. 71 of the Convention, which determines the consequences of invalidity and termination of treaties, refers to Art. 64; second, because paragraphs *a* and *b* of Art. 71, item 2, repeat, in general terms, the content of Art. 70 of the Convention, which governs the consequences of *termination of treaties*, and not the content of Art. 69, which relates to *invalidity*. Therefore, despite Art. 64 stating that the relevant treaty "becomes *void* and terminates", the underlying cause of Art. 64 relates to termination rather than to invalidity of treaties.

Unlike the previous case, the effects of a treaty in conflict with a subsequent norm of *jus cogens* are suspended *ex nunc*, this is, as from the time of emergence of the new peremptory norm of general International Law, and not as from execution of the agreement.[250] This is provided in Art. 71, item 2, *b*, of the Vienna Convention:

> "2. In the case of a treaty which becomes void and terminates under article 64, the termination of the treaty:
>
> (...)
>
> *b*) does not affect any right, obligation or legal situation of the parties created through the execution of the treaty prior to its termination; provided that those rights, obligations or situations may thereafter be maintained only to the extent that their maintenance is not in itself in conflict with the new peremptory norm of general international law".

As explained by Vera Lúcia Viegas, "rights and obligations arising from the treaty prior to the new norm of *jus cogens* are not affected because they are based on the good faith of the parties at the time of conclusion and beginning of execution of the treaty (the defect only arises when the new peremptory norm emerges, and it is retroactive, suspending the effects of the treaty only as from the time the new subsequent peremptory norm emerges)".[251]

---

[249] See ILC, *Yearbook of the International Law Commission* (1966), vol. II, p. 266; Sinclair, Ian, The *Vienna Convention on the Law of Treaties*, cit., p. 225; Remiro Brotons, Antonio, *Derecho internacional público*, vol. 2, cit., p. 326; and Gómez Robledo, Antonio, *El* ius cogens *internacional...*, cit., p. 99-100.

[250] See Ronzitti, Natalino. La disciplina dello *jus cogens* nella Convenzione di Vienna sul Diritto dei Trattati, in *Comunicazioni e Studi*, vol. 15, Milan: Giuffrè, 1978, p. 276-278; and De La Guardia, Ernesto, *Derecho de los tratados internacionales*, cit., p. 290.

[251] Viegas, Vera Lúcia. *Ius cogens* e o tema da nulidade dos tratados, cit., p. 189.

The termination procedure, in that case, as permitted by the Vienna Convention, may be described by the treaty itself, or by the Convention itself. The procedure set forth in Art. 65 *et seq.* of the Convention shall only be used, in the second case. When the treaty itself provides for the grounds for termination due to a conflict with a norm of *jus cogens*, the procedure provided by the treaty must be followed. This means that the rules of the Convention are *supplementary* to the provision of any other rules in force binding on the parties in connection with dispute resolution (Art. 65, item 4).

In this case, the parties do not lose the right to request termination of the treaty based on the violation of a norm of *jus cogens*; and any agreement between the parties to the contrary is invalid (rule of unenforceability of the parties' will against a norm of *jus cogens*). In the event of incompatibility of a treaty with a subsequent norm of *jus cogens*, the parties *are obliged* to start the treaty termination procedure; moreover, such obligation is evidenced in the case of an arbitration or judicial body, which must judge the issue *ex officio*.[252]

Unlike the case of conflict between an international treaty and an earlier norm of *jus cogens*, in the event of conflict between a treaty and a subsequent norm of *jus cogens*, the Vienna Convention allows *separability* of the treaty.[253] This may be inferred from interpretation *a contrario sensu* of Art. 44, item 5, which provides: "In cases falling under articles 51, 52 and 53, no separation of the provisions of the treaty is permitted".

Allowing a treaty to be *separated* means authorizing the removal of void clauses of the treaty only. Pursuant to the provision transcribed above, only in the cases provided in Arts. 51 (coercion of a representative of a State), 52 (coercion of a State by threat or use of force) and 53 (treaty in conflict with a preexisting norm of *jus cogens*) separation of the provisions of a treaty *is not permitted*. Therefore, such provision did not make reference to Art. 64 of the Convention (which deals with conflicts between treaties and subsequent norms of *jus cogens*) because it is an exception, allowing *separation* of such treaties. Then, in case of conflict between an international treaty and a subsequent norm of *jus cogens*, only the provisions in conflict with the peremptory norm of general International Law will be terminated (not the whole treaty, as in the case of

---

252 See Remiro Brotons, Antonio. *Derecho internacional público*, vol. 2, cit., p. 498.

253 See De La Guardia, Ernesto. *Derecho de los tratados internacionales*, cit., p. 292; and Gómez Robledo, Antonio, *El* ius cogens *internacional...*, cit., p. 104-107.

conflict with a norm of *jus cogens* existing before the time of conclusion of the agreement).

2.2.2.3 *Conflict between a treaty and a norm of* jus cogens *existing before entry into force of the Vienna Convention*

The Vienna Convention was not created to govern previous situations. Its provisions only apply to events that occurred after it entered into force. However, the Convention makes an exception in relation to rules provided in its own text that *would apply to treaties pursuant to preexisting general International Law*. This rule, proposed by Brazil and Sweden, was adopted by the Convention in Art. 4 (rule of irretroactivity of the Convention), which provides as follows: "Without prejudice to the application of any rules set forth in the present Convention to which treaties would be subject under international law independently of the Convention, the Convention applies only to treaties which are concluded by States after the entry into force of the present Convention with regard to such States".[254] Therefore, "considering that international *jus cogens* was not created by the Vienna Convention, which just introduces identification criteria, conventional provisions relating to compulsory international Law also apply to treaties existing before the Convention".[255]

In order to know if a certain provision of the Convention may be applied to an earlier treaty, the interpreter must verify if such provision comes from treaty law or from custom law, prior to the Convention. Therefore, since Arts. 53 and 64 of the Convention, as well as Art. 71, do not arise from treaty law, but from general International Law, they also apply to treaties concluded *before entry into force* of the Vienna Convention. The reason is that such rules were not created by the Vienna Convention (which only codified them), but by general International Law.

Despite Art. 44, item 5 (which provides for separability of treaties) refers to Art. 53 of the Convention, which is a codified norm of general International Law, since this rule arises from treaty law only, it does not apply to treaties concluded before entry into force of the 1969 Convention. Likewise, the procedure provided by the Convention for the declaration of invalidity or termination of treaties does not apply to treaties con-

---

254 See Villiger, Mark E. *Commentary on the 1969 Vienna Convention on the Law of Treaties*, cit., p. 109-114.

255 Viegas, Vera Lúcia. *Ius cogens* e o tema da nulidade dos tratados, cit., p. 191.

cluded before the Convention, since these norms also arise from treaty law, and not from general International Law.[256]

Arts. 53 and 64 of the Convention did not specify the *core* of incompatibility between the international treaty and the norm of *jus cogens*. Therefore, only the *content* of the treaty must be taken into account to determine if it is incompatible with a peremptory norm of general International Law. Therefore, "if the treaty's content is compatible with the *jus cogens*, but it is concluded by means of an act that violates an international peremptory norm, the treaty is valid. However, the parties concluding the treaty in a manner contrary to mandatory law commit an international unlawful act".[257]

To determine incompatibility of the treaty with a norm of *jus cogens*, its subject-matter as well as its *scope* must be taken into account, this is, the purpose of the treaty, inferred from the content of its clauses.

2.2.3 Hierarchy of norms of jus cogens *in the law of treaties*

From the analysis above, it can be concluded that the Vienna Convention places *jus cogens* on the highest hierarchical position among norms. In other words, since the 1969 Convention sets forth that *jus cogens* prevails over subsequent (Art. 53) and prior (Art. 64) treaties, it established a peremptory norm that prevents the application of *specialty* and *chronological* criteria to solve conflicts between the *jus cogens* and treaties, only enabling a *hierarchical* solution where norms of *jus cogens* prevail. Therefore, as exemplified by Ian Brownlie, "an agreement concluded by a State enabling another State to stop and search its ships at high sea is valid; however, an agreement executed with a neighbor State to carry out a joint operation against a racial group that is at the boundary of both States is void, and, if concluded, it would constitute genocide, since the treaty is incompatible with a prohibition of *jus cogens*".[258] In this context, norms of *jus cogens* are universal and superior to any international treaty or custom, and even superior to Public International Law itself, being at the top of the hierarchy of the international society rules. Then, there is a *minimum legal* guarantee of world order, evidencing the increasing insti-

---

256 See Ronzitti, Natalino. La disciplina dello *jus cogens* nella Convenzione di Vienna sul Diritto dei Trattati, cit., p. 295-296; and Viegas, Vera Lúcia, *Ius cogens* e o tema da nulidade dos tratados, cit., p. 191.

257 Viegas, Vera Lúcia. *Ius cogens* e o tema da nulidade dos tratados, cit., p. 190.

258 Brownlie, Ian. *Princípios de direito internacional público*, cit., p. 538.

tutionalization of the international society. The practical consequence is that, unlike mandatory norms (whose breach only implies international liability of the State), the violation of a norm of *jus cogens* has the effect of invalidating (Art. 53) or terminating (Art. 64) norms conflicting with it.

In brief, the provision on *jus cogens* in the 1969 Vienna Convention *limits* the free will of international sovereign entities (*jus dispositivum*), in order to ensure global public order (*ordre public*).[259] Public policy, a synonym for *jus cogens*, is then the most complex limit to free consent of the States, pursuant to Arts. 53 and 64 of the Convention. It has been the master key for the great progress of Public International Law, because it includes provisions forbidding States to conclude treaties in favor of particular interests to the detriment of common interests of the whole international society, which certainly threatens the firm development of peaceful relations between States.

2.3 Unconstitutionality of treaties

When the power to conclude treaties was changed from a prerogative of the Sovereign to a power of the Head of the Executive, resulting from the transition from the *Ancien Régime* to the democratic and representative regime, the problem of *extrinsic* or *formal* unconstitutionality of treaties became worthy of consideration (in fact, *consent* of the State to be bound by the treaties) in relation to Constitutions of States parties.[260]

While Constitutions assigned competence to conclude treaties to the Head of the Executive Power, with subsequent approval by the Legislative Power, to express the Nation's consent to be bound by a treaty, the problem (not existing at the time of Sovereigns) of *formal* unconstitutionality of treaties in the light of internal Law arose, if the Head of the Executive internationally expressed the will of the State in violation of constitutional rules on competence to conclude treaties (such as the rule requiring Parliamentary approval *before* the final commitment of the State). Then, the Executive Power may ratify a treaty without the consent of the Legislative power, or even sign agreements through a simplified process, when that

---

[259] See Fiorati, Jete Jane. Jus cogens..., cit., p. 47-48; and Gómez Robledo, Antonio, *El* ius cogens *internacional*..., cit., p. 99.

[260] On this subject, see especially Cachapuz de Medeiros, Antônio Paulo, *O poder de celebrar tratados*..., cit., p. 243-281. Also see Pereira de Araújo, João Hermes, *A processualística dos atos internacionais*, cit., p. 200-206; Remiro Brotons, Antonio, *Derecho internacional público*, vol. 2, cit., p. 136-138; and Tavares, Francisco de Assis Maciel, *Ratificação de tratados internacionais*, cit., p. 47-51.

is not permitted by the Constitution. In brief, the Government may bind the State in relation to a treaty without following the legal (constitutional) procedures provided by its own internal Law. This problem is called *extrinsic* or *formal unconstitutionality* of treaties in the light of internal law, also called *imperfect* or *irregular ratification*. This analysis is relevant because internal Law, in this specific case, is important for Public International Law. However, the issue is clearly not "unconstitutionality" in relation to Public International Law (this expression may only be used at the domestic level), but a *defect in consent* of the State (in this case, only *voidable*) to be bound by the treaty (see item 2.1, above).

The issue here is if constitutional limitations to treaty-making power have influence on the international field. That is to say, does International Law question whether the will expressed for an international act by someone who seems to be competent to do so violated any constitutional rule on competence to conclude treaties? What is more important for the Vienna Convention on the Law of Treaties, the way the representative of a State expresses its will, or the constitutional provisions of such State on competence to conclude treaties? In other words, are constitutional limitations to the treaty-making power important in light of the Law of Treaties?

In order to answer said questions, two main theories were conceived: the constitutional approach and the international approach.[261] Let us see:

2.3.1 Constitutional approach

This doctrine argues that if the Head of State could disregard the constitutional procedure to conclude treaties, for instance, not submitting the agreement to the approval of Parliament, and International Law considered such violation of internal Law irrelevant, the democratic principle would be completely set aside. For supporters of this doctrine, the authority vested with the power to conclude treaties does not *validly* express the will of the Nation to be bound by the agreement if the constitutional rules on competence for such conclusion were not followed, since the Constitution determines the organs and procedures to establish and state the will of the State to be bound by treaties.[262]

---

[261] See Sinclair, Ian. *The Vienna Convention on the Law of Treaties*, cit., p. 169-171; and De La Guardia, Ernesto, *Derecho de los tratados internacionales*, cit., p. 198-201.

[262] See Cachapuz de Medeiros, Antônio Paulo. *O poder de celebrar tratados…*, cit., p. 245-251; and Remiro Brotons, Antonio, *Derecho internacional público*, vol. 2, cit., p. 155-156; and De La Guardia, Ernesto, *Derecho de los tratados internacionales*, cit., p. 199.

Many jurists consider that contracting Nations should know each other's constitutional procedures to conclude treaties. Then, compliance of constitutions of the different States with norms of Public International Law should be taken into account. According to Lafayette, a State wishing to execute a treaty with another State must "know the competent power or powers to make treaties and the limits and restrictions imposed, pursuant to such State's Constitution", since "lack of competence or violation of applicable limits and restrictions render the whole treaty or the clauses violating such restrictions void".[263] Therefore, in accordance with this doctrine, before signing any agreement, the contracting States must refer to the Constitutions of other States for the purpose of knowing the restrictions imposed by each domestic legal system on the treaty-making power, because non-compliance with a party's internal provisions may invalidate the consent of that State to be bound by the treaty. In addition, in accordance with the constitutional approach, no international norm validates consent to the detriment of constitutional provisions.

The constitutional approach considers compliance with constitutional norms of contracting States essential for consent expressed to be *valid*, since the Constitutional Law of each contracting party establishes competent powers and procedures for the expression of the will of the State to be bound internationally to be valid. That is to say, in this field internal Law would *prevail* over International Law, since the commitment will only be effective if internal provisions are fully complied with. Hence, if the constitution provides for participation of Parliament in the process of establishment of the will of a State, lack of such participation may cause invalidity of the ratification.[264]

In summary, in accordance with constitucionalism, competence to conclude treaties is determined by internal Law of States, and, when such rules are violated, the consent expressed may be voided, releasing (with effect *ex nunc*) the State from continuing to fulfill the treaty.

---

263 Pereira, Lafayette Rodrigues. *Princípios de direito internacional*, vol. 1. Rio de Janeiro: Jacintho Ribeiro dos Santos, 1903, p. 271. In fact, as explained by Lafayette, the *treaty* is not considered void as a whole but rather *consent* of the State to be bound by the treaty is voidable.

264 See Fraga, Mirtô. *O conflito entre tratado internacional e norma de direito interno: estudo analítico da situação do tratado na ordem jurídica brasileira*. Rio de Janeiro: Forense, 1998, p. 35-37. This author, in her text, mistakenly refers to "invalidity of the treaty", when she should refer to "invalidity of ratification" or "invalidity of consent".

2.3.2 International approach

The international approach is based on the opposite idea. It was inspired in the old rule that the Head of State, at the international level, is the competent organ to conclude valid treaties with other sovereign States, since it has *jus representationis omnimodae* granted by International Law. For this doctrine, failure to submit a treaty to the Legislative power is an internal Law issue not taken into account by International Law. The assumption that the Head of State is the authorized organ to conclude treaties would then be contrary to a State supervising another State in relation to the fulfillment of internal requirements for conclusion of treaties. Besides, another argument of supporters of the international approach is that it would not be reasonable to require all States parties to a treaty to know in detail the Constitutional Law of each contracting party. Therefore, States must accept in good faith the statement of the counter party, otherwise, minimum security in treaty relations could never be achieved.[265] As pointed out by Cachapuz de Medeiros, supporters of the international approach argue that "a State, when negotiating a treaty with another State, cannot consider the internal process of establishment of the will of that State, but only the competent organ to express its will at the international level, which is the Head of State, in accordance with a universally accepted rule".[266] Then, the consent expressed by the Head of State, to whom International Law grants competence to act in the name of the State at the international level, shall be deemed valid and mandatory, even when constitutional norms on treaty conclusion are not complied with.

Note that the international approach seeks to reduce as much as possible the influence of constitutional provisions on the validity of consent. It argues that, since the Head of State (or its plenipotentiaries) is normally competent to represent the State internationally, the other members of the international society should not be concerned with whether such State violated its internal rules on competence to conclude treaties.[267] In accordance with this idea, the contracting parties cannot be affected by the fact that a Head of State did not comply with constitutional limitations to the

---

265 See Remiro Brotons, Antonio. *Derecho internacional público*, vol. 2, cit., p. 154-155; and Reuter, Paul, *Introducción al derecho de los tratados*, cit., p. 33.

266 Cachapuz de Medeiros, Antônio Paulo. *O poder de celebrar tratados...*, cit., p. 251.

267 See De La Guardia, Ernesto. *Derecho de los tratados internacionales*, cit., p. 199-200; and Fraga, Mirtô, *O conflito entre tratado internacional e norma de direito interno...*, cit., p. 39.

treaty-making power in force in its country. On the other hand, admitting that a State may invoke the invalidity of ratification for not complying with constitutional rules on competence to conclude treaties would imply that Constitutional Law has *influence* on International Law, which would constitute denial of the autonomy of International Law.

Therefore, for the international approach, the sole statement of the Head of State certifying that all internal procedures were followed for the execution of the treaty is enough for consent to be deemed valid internationally, and International Law is not concerned with constitutional provisions of each State party to the agreement. In other words, if the Head of State undertakes an international commitment on behalf of the State, it is *presumed* that all internal constitutional formalities for executing treaties were followed, and it is not adequate to grant the other party the right to investigate whether such formalities were complied with or not.[268]

2.3.3 Conciliatory approach

Due to the wide divergence among legal scholars caused by the constitutional approach and the international approach, some authors, for the purpose of conciliating both conceptions, adopted intermediate solutions, based on a *moderate* constitutional approach (or international approach).[269] Such current explains that the allegation of a State that consent is invalid for having been given in violation of its constitutional rules on competence would only be legitimate if such violation is *manifest*, this is, *evident* enough. Then, if the violation by the Executive of constitutional limits to treaty-making power is apparent and easily proven by the other parties, the State may invoke such breach as a defect in consent.[270]

Accordingly, in order not to jeopardize international relations, only *apparent* limitations to treaty-making power that should be reasonably known by the other States must be taken into account to release one of the parties from the internationally undertaken agreement.[271]

---

268 See Accioly, Hildebrando. *Tratado de direito internacional público*, vol. I, cit., p. 600.

269 See, among others, Pereira de Araújo, João Hermes, *A processualística dos atos internacionais*, cit., p. 205-206.

270 See Cachapuz de Medeiros, Antônio Paulo. *O poder de celebrar tratados...*, cit., p. 256-260; and Remiro Brotons, Antonio, *Derecho internacional público*, vol. 2, cit., p. 156-157.

271 See Cachapuz de Medeiros, Antônio Paulo. *O poder de celebrar tratados...*, cit., p. 257.

2.3.4 Solution adopted by the 1969 Vienna Convention

The Vienna Convention on the Law of Treaties adopted the conciliatory solution, according to which the allegation of a State that its consent to be bound by the treaty was invalid for violating its internal Law will have no international value, unless such provision of internal Law is of fundamental importance and it deals with competence to conclude treaties. It is based on the theory of *extrinsic* or *formal unconstitutionality* of treaties against Constitutions of States, since it only refers to *internal* (*constitutional*) rules on *competence to conclude treaties*, which may render consent of the State void if they are not complied with. This is called *imperfect* or *irregular ratification*, because the agreement was concluded in *manifest* violation of rule of internal Law of *fundamental importance* on *competence* to conclude treaties.[272] That is to say, in this case, the Government ratifies a treaty without submitting it for parliamentary approval, breaking an internal principle of fundamental importance, this is, the constitutional rule requiring Congress approval of treaties (in Brazilian Law, Art. 49, I, of the Federal Constitution of 1988). Therefore, for the 1969 Vienna Convention (Art. 46 on this subject will be analyzed below) consent to be bound by a treaty expressed by a Government is internationally valid *prima facie*, even if such a consent is expressed in violation of any provision of internal Law on competence to conclude treaties. However, if the violation of an internal rule is *manifest* and relates to a rule of *fundamental importance* (such as constitutional rules) on *competence* to conclude treaties, ratification of the agreement may be declared *void*. It is understood that if the legal procedure to conclude treaties was not followed, there is no valid consent to bind the State internationally.[273]

However, such ratification invalidity statement does not impose international liability on the State. In other words, imperfect ratification is not an *international unlawful* act and may be unlawful only internally (for instance, in Brazil, it would be an offense committed by the President of

---

272 See Cahier, Philippe. La violation du droit interne relatif à la competence pour conclure des traités comme cause de nullité des traités, *Rivista di Diritto Internazionale*, vol. 54, part 2 (1971), p. 226-245; Meron, Theodor, Article 46 of the Vienna Convention on the Law of Treaties (*ultra vires* treaties): some recent cases, *British Yearbook of International Law*, vol. 49 (1978), p. 175-199; Remiro Brotons, Antonio, *Derecho internacional público*, vol. 2, cit., p. 157-162; Cachapuz de Medeiros, Antônio Paulo, *O poder de celebrar tratados…*, cit., p. 263-269; and De La Guardia, Ernesto, *Derecho de los tratados internacionales*, cit., p. 201-202.

273 See Reuter, Paul. *Introducción al derecho de los tratados*, cit., p. 203.

the Republic as it is an act against "free exercise of the Legislative Power", pursuant to Art. 85, II, of the Federal Constitution of 1988). That is to say, upon the formal violation of the Constitution (disregard for the procedure to conclude treaties) the State is not internationally *liable* for such violation, but consent will be declared *invalid* and the State will not be *held liable* at the international level.

Art. 46 of the 1969 Vienna Convention deals with this subject, as follows:

> "Article 46. *Provisions of internal law regarding competence to conclude treaties*
>
> 1. A State may not invoke the fact that its consent to be bound by a treaty has been expressed in violation of a provision of its internal law regarding competence to conclude treaties as invalidating its consent unless that violation was manifest and concerned a rule of its internal law of fundamental importance.
>
> 2. A violation is manifest if it would be objectively evident to any State conducting itself in the matter in accordance with normal practice and in good faith".

Art. 46 of the 1969 Vienna Convention then provided a *middle-ground* between the constitutional and international approaches examined above, preventing allegation of an internal Law rule to justify failure to fulfill the treaty (international approach), except in the case of the *manifest violation* of a constitutional rule of *fundamental importance* (constitutional approach). Here, a *manifest* violation is a violation objectively evident to any State acting in accordance with normal practices and in good faith.[274] That is, Art. 46 of the Convention intends to maintain a balance between legal certainty, necessary for sound operation of the international society, and respect for democracy, since the *jus representationis omnimodae* is no longer recognized when there is a violation of a fundamental internal rule.[275] Currently, both legal literature and international practice have accepted this solution without reservations.[276]

---

274 See Elias, Taslim Olawale. Problems concerning the validity of treaties, cit., p. 350-361.

275 See Mello, Celso D. de Albuquerque. *Direito constitucional internacional...*, cit., p. 343.

276 See Pereira, André Gonçalves & Quadros, Fausto de. *Manual de direito internacional público*, cit., p. 212. The Plenary Commission of the Vienna Conference, however, approved the article with 55 votes and 30 abstentions, and at the Conference Plenary with 73 votes against 2 and 27 abstentions. The number of abstentions, at the time, indicated wide rejection of the rule by the States (see De La Guardia, Ernesto. *Derecho de los tratados internacionales*, cit., p. 202). Later, the situation changed and the solution proposed by the rule was accepted without objections.

A treaty's ratification (consent), pursuant to the 1969 Convention, will only be invalid when an internal rule of fundamental importance is evidently violated. The Convention clearly refers to *constitutional rules* of the country, and it is not likely that it meant to give *fundamental importance* to the remaining internal rules as well, such as ordinary laws, executive orders, resolutions, etc.[277] As a consequence, failure to comply with any *secondary* regulation could not be invoked as a ground to invalidate ratification of a treaty, for example, internal Parliament regulations, such as lack of submission of the treaty to a special commission on the subject of the agreement, or failure to meet the term to submit an expert opinion, etc. In such cases, the violation is not manifest and, therefore, ratification by the President of the Republic may not be considered void internationally.[278]

The Convention also provided the concept for *manifest violation*. As explained by Cachapuz de Medeiros, Art. 46 defines a manifest violation "as a violation that is evident for any State acting in accordance with normal practice and in good faith, that is to say, reasonably. But, practical application of the concept of *manifest violation* may be really difficult. (…) Diplomatic practice follows a path that is not always the path established by the Constitution. However, for the allegation of invalidity of a treaty to be accepted [*in fact*: of consent of the State to be bound by the treaty], due to non-compliance of a rule of internal Law, the violation must be evident for any State acting in *good faith*. The inclusion of *good faith* in Art. 46, item 2 prevents the State from arguing the violation of its own internal Law. There is also a second limitation to invoke manifest violation pursuant to the Vienna Convention: lapse of time, since the State loses the right to invoke this ground for invalidity if it was aware of the facts and

---

277 See Nahlik, S. E. The grounds for invalidity and termination of treaties, *American Journal of International Law*, vol. 65, No. 5 (Oct. 1971), p. 740-741. For an opposite opinion, see Cachapuz de Medeiros, Antônio Paulo, *O poder de celebrar tratados…*, cit., p. 265, who states that legislation below the constitution "may also be considered of *fundamental importance*, especially if there are special laws on the competence of powers of the State to conclude treaties". Also see Villiger, Mark E., *Commentary on the 1969 Vienna Convention on the Law of Treaties*, cit., p. 588-589: "Internal law on the competence to conclude treaties embraces written and unwritten constitucional law and practice, subordinate legal and administrative provisions, and obligations in internal law derived from treaties which that State has concluded with other States".

278 See Pereira de Araújo, João Hermes. *A processualística dos atos internacionais*, cit., p. 206.

it agreed, or if it can be inferred from its conduct that it agreed, with the validity of the treaty [*in fact*: of consent]".[279]

However, after the final text of Art. 46 of the Convention was released, some jurists who supported the international approach stated that the consent expressed by Heads of State, Heads of Government, Ministers of Foreign Affairs or Ambassadors would be valid in any case, because Art. 7, item 2 of the Convention would *prevail* over Art. 46.[280] In other words, if the treaty had been ratified by any of such authorities, Art. 46 could not be invoked to invalidate consent, even if expressed in manifest violation of internal Law.

Art. 7 of the Convention provides that:

> "Article 7. *Full powers.*
>
> (...)
>
> 2. In virtue of their functions and without having to produce full powers, the following are considered as representing their State:
>
> *a*) Heads of State, Heads of Government and Ministers for Foreign Affairs, for the purpose of performing all acts relating to the conclusion of a treaty;
>
> *b*) heads of diplomatic missions, for the purpose of adopting the text of a treaty between the accrediting State and the State to which they are accredited;
>
> *c*) representatives accredited by States to an international conference or to an international organization or one of its organs, for the purpose of adopting the text of a treaty in that conference, organization or organ".

However, other legal scholars have understood that the most appropriate interpretation for this obvious contradiction is that Art. 46 would impose a *limit* to the application of Art. 7 of the Convention; that is to say, Art. 46 of the Convention would be *wider* than Art. 7 and it would prevail over it, invalidating consent expressed by the Government in manifest

---

279 Cachapuz de Medeiros, Antônio Paulo. *O poder de celebrar tratados*..., cit., p. 265-266. The author also mistakes grounds for invalidity of *consent* with grounds invalidating *the treaty itself*. Art. 46 of the 1969 Vienna Convention (as we have seen in item 2.1. of this Chapter) does not deal with invalidity *of the treaty*, but with avoidability of *consent* of the State (expressed by its representative) to be bound by the treaty.

280 See Cachapuz de Medeiros, Antônio Paulo. Idem, p. 263. On the relation of Art. 46 with Art. 7 of the Convention, see Sinclair, Ian, *The Vienna Convention on the Law of Treaties*, cit., p. 32; and Remiro Brotons, Antonio, *Derecho internacional público*, vol. 2, cit., p. 158-159.

violation of internal Law.[281] In fact, if there was an absolute presumption in favor of the authorities listed in Art. 7, item 2 of the Convention, Art. 46 would have almost no practical application, since, in most cases, such authorities are directly responsible for expressing consent of the State in relation to a treaty.

In summary, as a general rule, the Vienna Convention does not allow a State to invoke its internal (material) Law to be released from the obligations arising from a commitment undertaken (Art. 27). However, it provides an exception to such wide rule: if consent to be bound (this is a matter of *form*, clearly) was expressed in violation of an internal provision on *competence* to conclude treaties, and provided that the violation is *evident* and relates to a rule of *fundamental importance*, the State may be released from complying with the agreement (Art. 46).[282]

The ICJ dealt with the rule of Art. 46 of the Convention in the case *Cameroon v. Nigeria*, heard on October 10, 2002. Nigeria alleged that the *Maroua Declaration*,[283] signed in 1975 with Cameroon, was invalid for conflicting with its constitutional rules on competence to conclude treaties. In item 265 of the judgment, the Court stated that "rules relating to the power to sign treaties on behalf of a State are constitutional rules of fundamental importance", and then it pointed out that a (constitutional) restriction to the power of the Head of State to conclude treaties is "manifest" (pursuant to Art. 46, item 2 of the Convention) only when it has been properly publicized.[284] In relation to the Nigerian argument that Cameroon knew or should have known that the Head of State of Nigeria did not have the power to bind Nigeria without the approval of its internal bodies, the Court stated (in item 266) that "a State is not legally obliged to know the legislative or constitutional measures adopted by other States that are or may be important for the international relations of such States".[285] Then, the ICJ understood that the *Maroua Declaration* was valid and that it legally bound Nigeria (item 268).

---

281 See Cachapuz de Medeiros, Antônio Paulo. *O poder de celebrar tratados...*, cit., p. 264; and Remiro Brotons, Antonio, *Derecho internacional público*, vol. 2, cit., p. 158-159.

282 See Fraga, Mirtô. *O conflito entre tratado internacional e norma de direito interno...*, cit., p. 36.

283 It should be pointed out that, although it is called *Declaration*, it is actually an *international treaty* concluded by the parties, and also recognized as such by the ICJ (item 263 of the judgment).

284 See *ICJ Reports* (2002), p. 430.

285 Idem, ibidem.

265. The Court will now address Nigeria's argument that its constitutional rules regarding the conclusion of treaties were not complied with. In this regard the Court recalls that Article 46, paragraph 1, of the Vienna Convention provides that "[a] State may not invoke the fact that its consent to be bound by a treaty has been expressed in violation of a provision of its internal law regarding competence to conclude treaties as invalidating its consent". It is true that the paragraph goes on to say "unless that violation was manifest and concerned a rule of its internal law of fundamental importance", while paragraph 2 of Article 46 provides that "[a] violation is manifest if it would be objectively evident to any State conducting itself in the matter in accordance with normal practice and in good faith". The rules concerning the authority to sign treaties for a State are constitutional rules of fundamental importance. However, a limitation of a Head of State's capacity in this respect is not manifest in the sense of Article 46, paragraph 2, unless at least properly publicized. This is particularly so because Heads of State belong to the group of persons who, in accordance with Article 7, paragraph 2, of the Convention "[i]n virtue of their functions and without having to produce full powers" are considered as representing their State. (...).

266. Nigeria further argues that Cameroon knew, or ought to have known, that the Head of State of Nigeria had no power legally to bind Nigeria without consulting the Nigerian Government. In this regard the Court notes that there is no general legal obligation for States to keep themselves informed of legislative and constitutional developments in other States which are or may become important for the international relations of these States.

In this case the Head of State of Nigeria had in August 1974 stated in his letter to the Head of State of Cameroon that the views of the Joint Commission "must be subject to the agreement of the two Governments". However, in the following paragraph of that same letter, he further indicated: "It has always been my belief that we can, both, together re-examine the situation and reach an appropriate and acceptable decision on the matter". Contrary to Nigeria's contention, the Court considers that these two statements, read together, cannot be regarded as a specific warning to Cameroon that the Nigerian Government would not be bound by any commitment entered into by the Head of State. And in particular they could not be understood as relating to any commitment to be made at Maroua nine months later. The letter in question in fact concerned a meeting to be held at Kano, Nigeria, from 30 August to 1 September 1974. This letter seems to have been part of a pattern which marked the Parties' boundary negotiations between 1970 and 1975, in which the two Heads of State took the initiative of resolving difficulties in those negotiations through person-to-person agreements, including those at Yaodé II and Maroua.(...)

268. In these circumstances the Maroua Declaration, as well as the Yaoundé II Declaration, have to be considered as binding and as establishing a legal obligation on Nigeria. (...)

International Court of Justice, *Case Concerning the Land and Maritime Boundary between Cameroon and Nigeria (Cameroon v. Nigeria: Equatorial Guinea Intervening)*, j. 10.10.2002, in *ICJ Reports*, p. 303 et ssq.

In Brazilian case law, in turn, the Federal Supreme Court has never declared a treaty unconstitutional due to the lack of *approval* from the Legislative Power. In order to avoid problems created by imperfect ratifications, some Constitutions provided *conditions* for the validity of treaties ratified in violation of an internal rule of fundamental importance on competence to conclude treaties.

2.3.5 *Intrinsic unconstitutionality of treaties*

A more frequent problem is *intrinsic* unconstitutionality of international treaties, that is to say, when a treaty, although it *formally* complies with any constitutional procedures established by internal Law, contains rules in violation of constitutional provisions (this is, *substantially* violates the Constitution). This is not a violation of a rule on *competence* to conclude treaties established by internal Law, but a conflict between a formally valid treaty and the Constitution, which is earlier (there is *material* incompatibility between the treaty and constitutional internal Law). In this case, Art. 46 of the Vienna Convention does not apply, since the agreement was not concluded in *manifest* violation of a rule of internal Law on *competence* to conclude treaties of *fundamental importance* and, therefore there was no *imperfect ratification* (or *extrinsic* unconstitutionality). But, despite the treaty having complied with constitutional rules on competence for its conclusion, it contains provisions materially in conflict with the Constitution of the State.

The study of *conflicts between a treaty and the Constitution* must take into account the constitutional provisions of each country. Therefore, if the Constitution of the State sets forth that international treaties prevail over its own text, any conflict between constitutional provisions and an international agreement must be resolved in favor of the treaty. This is the case of the Dutch Constitution, which was revised in 1956 and set forth in Art. 63 that, in furtherance of the development of International Law, conclusion of a treaty in conflict with the Constitution will be valid as long as it is subsequently approved by a majority of 2/3 of General States. That is to say, in certain circumstances, the Constitution of the Netherlands allowed international treaties to derogate constitutional provisions and it even set forth that "courts may not examine the constitutionality of treaties" (Art. 60, 3). In another provision, the Dutch Constitution of 1983 states: "Legal provisions in force in the Kingdom will cease to apply when they are in conflict with treaty provisions binding on everyone or with decisions of international organizations" (Art. 94). If there is no express reference in the Constitution to the possibility of conflict with a treaty, the Higher Law will prevail over the common treaty provision. However, the State may be held liable internationally.

Art. 102, III, *b* of the Brazilian Constitution of 1988 deals with such rule providing that the Federal Supreme Court is competent, as guardian of the Constitution, to judge, through an extraordinary appeal, cases decided in sole or last instance, "when the decision appealed declares the unconstitutionality of the treaty or federal law". By means of this provision, the Constitution intended to establish the possibility to examine the constitutionality of treaties. Strictly speaking, however, international treaties may not be subject to a constitutionality *control*, because internal judicial decisions may not review the constitutionality of a rule that belongs to another legal system (or international legal system); especially in relation to human rights treaties, which have a hierarchic privilege (constitutional rule status) in the the Brazilian legal system.[286] The constitutionality control or fiscalization must examine the *internal approval* of the treaty (for instance, the legislative order approving it), and not the international *instrument* itself.[287] That is why in some countries, such as the Netherlands, judges may not control the constitutionality of a treaty in force (Art. 120).

In some countries, the ratification of treaties violating constitutional provisions must be preceded by a constitutional amendment. In Brazil, in particular, since there is no constitutional provision governing the subject, only treaties prior to the Constitution prevail over it. Such prevalence of treaties over the subsequent Constitution is based on the *principle of identity*, which states that international agreements limit the freedom of the original constituent power, which, however, may be recovered by denouncing the treaty. In other words, if the existence of a State depends on the existence of a Constitution that governs its form and organiza-

---

286 See Art. 5, items 2 and 3, of the 1988 Constitution. On the constitutional status of human rights treaties, see Mazzuoli, Valerio de Oliveira, *O controle jurisdicional da convencionalidade das leis*, cit., p. 25-71; and Mazzuoli, Valerio de Oliveira, *Curso de direito internacional público*, cit., p. 896-927.

287 See Clève, Clèmerson Merlin. *Abstract fiscalization of constitutionality in Brazilian law*. São Paulo: Revista dos Tribunais, 1995, p. 142, who explains: "It is clear that, since a treaty is a bilateral or multilateral international law act, a declaration of unconstitutionality does not invalidate it. An internal judicial decision may not affect acts that belong to another legal system, whether it is an international system or a foreign domestic system. (...) However, once a treaty is declared unconstitutional (in fact, approval, ratification and promulgations acts), the fact that the treaty is not applicable in domestic law may imply international liability for the country. In this case, the Federal State must denounce the treaty and it will be eventually subject to penalties imposed by international law". Also see Mendes, Gilmar Ferreira, *Jurisdição constitucional: o controle abstrato de normas no Brasil e na Alemanha*, 5. ed., São Paulo: Saraiva, 2005, p. 210-211.

tion and grants minimum rights to its citizens, it is clear that this Constitution must comply with the rules of the bigger society where the State is included, which is the *international society*. The original constituent power, which creates a new Constitution, and, consequently a new State, is only independent in relation to internal Law rules, but not in relation to Natural Law (as noted by Emmanuel Joseph Sieyès, in *Qu'est-ce que le tiers État?*) and to Public International Law, where its own existence originates.[288] On the other hand, if the treaty is *subsequent* and it conflicts with the Fundamental Law, it is internationally valid but it does not prevail domestically}. However, this opinion is arguable in the light of Art. 27 of the 1969 Vienna Convention. In Brazil, it is currently understood that, except for international human rights treaties, which have constitutional hierarchy, an international agreement ratified after the Constitution was issued may not prevail over the Constitution, since it would imply a constitutional amendment without following the procedure set by the Constitution for such purpose. However, in order not to incur international resonsibility due to failure to comply with the treaty, it is necessary to *denounce* the agreement. The States, in spite of establishing the prevalence of the Constitution as the product of their sovereign power, must be well aware of the practical consequences of violating an international rule.[289]

But it should be pointed out that there are convincing opinions, of world class internationalists, sustaining the superiority of treaties over *any* internal Law rules and under all circumstances. Accioly, based on Georges Scelle, clearly affirms that the international rules of a regularly concluded treaty may never be considered as non mandatory in a specified State because they conflict with its constitutional principles; therefore, these principles are modified or revoked by the treaty, *ipso facto*. Note that Accioly believes in hierarchical superiority of treaties over the Constitution, even if the treaty is *subsequent*. He explains that "a government may not take

---

288 See Sagüés, Néstor Pedro, *Teoría de la Constitución*, cit., p. 280-281, who states that International Law governs "the conduct of such State, including its constituent power". And he further explains: "Of course, an original constituent power could consider itself exempt from fulfilling international rules in force. However, it would be acting in conflict with international codified law, generating, in turn, serious liability for the relevant State" (Ibem, p. 281). For the opposite opinion, see the reviews of Gözler, Kemal, La question de la supériorité des normes de droit international sur la Constitution, *Ankara Üniversitesi Hukuk Fakültesi Dergisi*, vol. 45, Nos. 1-4, 1996, p. 195-211, who states that "such arguments are refutable".

289 For further details, see Fraga, Mirtô, *O conflito entre tratado internacional e norma de direito interno...*, cit., p. 115-126.

advantage of its constitution to refuse to fulfill obligations under a treaty *subsequent to the Constitution*" [italics are ours].[290]

As regards conflicts between *human rights* treaties and the Constitution, we think that such international protection rules and the Constitution must be combined in order to find the *best rule* for the specific case, solving contradictions between them by a "dialog of sources" (as expressed by Erik Jayme, in its 1995 Hague Course).[291] The idea is to move away from the traditional criteria to solve contradictions by choosing "one rule *or* the other" to allow *joint* application of international and internal rules, taking the best of each one for protecting subjects of rights, applying the criteria "one rule *and* the other". However, this book, devoted to the theory of treaties, is not concerned with the study of this subject, already widely developed in another book.[292]

---

[290] Accioly, Hildebrando. *Tratado de direito internacional público*, vol. I, cit., p. 547-548.

[291] Jayme, Erik. Identité culturelle et intégration: le droit international privé postmoderne, *Recueil des Cours*, vol. 251 (1995), p. 259.

[292] See Mazzuoli, Valerio de Oliveira. *Tratados internacionais de direitos humanos e direito interno*, cit., p. 129-226.

Chapter 3

Termination and Suspension of Treaties

The Vienna Convention on the Law of Treaties provides a series of modalities whereby treaties may be *terminated* or *suspended*.[293] It is regulated in Arts. 54 and 64 of the Convention, which will be studied below. This is a case different from *invalidity of treaties*, already examined in item 2.1.3 above. Here, the causes *supervening* the conclusion of treaties are studied, even though they may have already been provided by the parties (as in the case of predetermined abrogation), unlike the subject of invalidity, in which the facts taking place (for instance, coercion on a State by the use of force, or the violation of the *jus cogens*) vitiate the roots of the treaty itself.[294]

The *procedure* whereby termination and suspension of treaties operate, as well as the consequences of such termination or suspension, will be analyzed in Chapter 4 below.

---

293 See Crandall, Samuel B. *Treaties: their making and enforcement*, cit., p. 423-465; McNair, Arnold Duncan, La terminaison et la dissolution des traités, *Recueil des Cours*, vol. 22 (1928-II), p. 459-538; Cavaglieri, Arrigo, Règles générales du droit de la paix, *Recueil des Cours*, vol. 26 (1929-I), p. 531-534 ; Accioly, Hildebrando, *Tratado de direito internacional público*, vol. I, cit., p. 638-657; Maresca, Adolfo, *Il diritto dei trattati…*, cit., p. 683-723; Capotorti, Francesco, L'extinction et la suspension des traités, *Recueil des Cours*, vol. 134 (1971-III), p. 417-587; Remiro Brotons, Antonio, *Derecho internacional público*, vol. 2, cit., p. 465-524; Rezek, José Francisco, *Direito dos tratados*, cit., p. 477-523; Vamvoukos, Athanassios, *Termination of treaties in international law: the doctrines of* rebus sic stantibus *and* desuetude, Oxford: Clarendon Press, 1985, 325p; De La Guardia, Ernesto, *Derecho de los tratados internacionales*, cit., p. 297-323; and Brownlie, Ian, *Princípios de direito internacional público*, cit., p. 640-645.

294 See Remiro Brotons, Antonio. *Derecho internacional público*, vol. 2, cit., p. 465.

3.1 Termination of treaties

International treaties may terminate in different ways: by the *common will* of the parties (for example, by expiration of the term agreed, condition subsequent or later treaty), or by the *unilateral will* of one party (for example, denunciation), or by *acts independent of* the will of the parties (for example, subsequent impossibility of complying with the treaty, fundamental change of circumstances, etc.). In all these cases, unlike the case of invalidity, the effects of termination always operate *ex nunc*, being the treaty termination effective *as from* the time in which a given circumstance (for instance, the agreed term, the integral execution of the subject-matter, the new treaty, etc.) comes into existence.

This item does not refer to treaties called real or dispositive, which are valid between the parties as a legal title (for instance, treaties delimiting boundaries and ceding territory). Such instruments (to which the parties are related *ad æternum*) are not terminated by the ordinary means of treaty termination, except when that is the will of *all* the parties, being still impervious to unilateral denunciation or fundamental changes of circumstances. In fact, in the latter case, the Convention provides, for example, that the rule of fundamental change of circumstances will not be applied "if the treaty establishes a boundary" (Art. 62, item 2, *a*).[295]

3.1.1 Termination by consent of the parties

The same parties concluding a specific treaty may wish to terminate it, whether by pre-established agreement (when the term, condition or means of termination has already been set forth in the treaty itself) or by subsequent agreement (with the consent of all the parties). The parties' meeting of the minds leads, in any case, to the *abrogation* of the treaty. This is, like *derogation*, a type of *revocation*, though the difference (between abrogation and derogation) lies on whether a given rule revocation is *total or partial*. In abrogation, *there is tota*l revocation of a given legal rule, which does not occur in the case of derogation, in which revocation is *partial*.

Abrogation (*total* revocation) of treaties is regulated by Art. 54 of the 1969 Vienna Convention, which provides as follows:

---

[295] Such *limits* are *territorial*, as it will later be seen (see item 3.3.1.3, below).

"The *termination of a treaty* or the withdrawal of a party may take place:

a) in conformity with the provisions of the treaty; or

b) at any time by consent of all the parties after consultation with the other contracting States".

It should be noted that in both cases (paragraphs *a* and *b*), there is always *consent of the parties*. There is consent of the parties when they have set forth the means of termination *in the treaty itself*, when the parties *later* decide to *terminate* it, when they conclude a *later treaty*, etc. *Abrogation* applies to all these cases.

In the following items (3.1.1.1 and 3.1.1.2), both abrogation methods will be analyzed: *predetermined* and *supervening* abrogation.

3.1.1.1 Predetermined abrogation

Predetermined abrogation (first method of treaty termination by *agreement of the parties*) occurs when the treaty itself already provides for its termination, or its termination may be inferred from the text of the treaty (as in the case of full performance of the treaty object and purpose).

There are three cases predetermining treaty termination: *a*) when there is a *specific term* setting forth the end of the treaty; *b*) when there is a *condition subsequent*; and *c*) when there is *complete performance of the treaty subject-matter*. The first two are expressly set forth in the treaty itself and the last one is *implied*. Let us see each of the cases abovementioned:

3.1.1.1.1 Expiration of the agreed term

It is the simplest way of predetermined abrogation of treaties. It always occurs when the treaty provides for a *specific term* for its termination. With a final term set forth, the treaty will automatically terminate at that time.[296]

It does not matter if the term of the treaty is five, ten, twenty or more years. Many times, by specifying its final term, the treaty itself already opens the possibility of being extended by the will of the parties, for another or other periods of time equal to the original term. If agreed by the parties, the treaty is extended; otherwise, it will terminate as soon as the agreed term expires.

296 See McNair, Arnold Duncan. La terminaison et la dissolution des traités, cit., p. 465.

The time limitation of treaties with a specific term is counted as from the date of *entry into force*, in case it is not otherwise provided. It may even start as from its *temporary application*, in the event there is an express provision. Instead of providing a term in years (five, ten, twenty, etc.), the treaty may also determine a specific date for its termination (for example, January 1 of a specific year). In both cases, there is a *specific term* for the termination of the treaty by the will of the parties.

This case (expiration of the agreed term) differs from the case of a *condition subsequent* (see the following item); while, in the former case, the term is specific, in the case of a condition subsequent, the ground for termination will depend on a future and *uncertain* event.

3.1.1.1.2 Condition subsequent

The text of the treaty may provide for its termination or extinction of its obligations in the event that certain fact may, in the future, occur (*affirmative* condition) or no longer occur (*negative* condition).[297] That is to say, a given *condition subsequent* (affirmative or negative) may be contained in the international instrument as ground for its termination. This occurred with the Treaty of Warsaw, whose Art. 11 provided for its termination when the General Treaty on Collective Security in Europe entered into force (affirmative condition subsequent).

Another kind of condition subsequent that is frequently formulated occurs in multilateral treaties when there is considerable reduction of the number of parties to the treaty. For example, in Art. 8, item 2, of the Convention on the Political Rights of Women (1952) states that the Convention "shall cease to be in force as from the date when the denunciation which reduces the number of parties to less than six becomes effective". In addition, the Convention on the Prevention and Punishment of the Crime of Genocide (1948) provides that: "If, as a result of denunciations, the number of Parties to the present Convention should become less than sixteen, the Convention shall cease to be in force as from the date on which the last of these denunciations shall become effective" (Art. 15).

It should be noted that the condition subsequent must always be related to a future and *uncertain* event. The resolution *clause* will also be *expressed* in the international treaty, since the Convention does not admit

[297] See Accioly, Hildebrando. *Tratado de direito internacional público*, vol. I, cit., p. 639.

a *tacit* condition subsequent. Therefore, the reduction in the number of States parties below the number necessary for its entry into force may not terminate the treaty, if that (condition) is not expressly set forth in the agreement. That is why the Vienna Convention has established that, unless the treaty otherwise provides, "a multilateral treaty does not terminate by reason only of the fact that the number of the parties falls below the number necessary for its entry into force" (Art. 55).[298]

3.1.1.1.3 Full performance of treaty object and purpose

A treaty may even be terminated as soon as its object and purpose are fully executed, since, in this case, there is no reason why it should continue into force. If the parties, by mutual agreement, had agreed on a specific object and purpose which were finally fully met, the object and purpose of the treaty would be lost, and, consequently, the treaty would naturally be terminated. This is, like the previous ones, a case of pre-established abrogation, and, therefore, executed by the *previous* agreement of the parties, however *implicitly* stated. Therefore, for example, the treaty provides for the payment of a given amount or its purpose is fulfilling a given obligation; once the amount fixed is paid or the respective obligation fulfilled, it is considered that the object and purpose of the treaty (by the previous and implicit agreement of the parties) have been fully executed, and the provisions agreed therein terminated.[299] Let us imagine an agreement between a State and an international organization to grant privileges and immunities to the participants of an international conference; once the conference ends, the respective treaty ceases to be in effect immediately.[300]

Such case should not be mistaken for the case of *transitory* treaties, whose effectiveness is static, which *continue into force* after being concluded, even though its execution takes place at a specific time (see Part I, Ch. 2, item 2.2.2, above). In the case analyzed herein, we are referring to such *permanent* treaties which, for any reason, have complied with the object and purpose for which they were executed, being terminated only by virtue of that fact.

---

298 See Villiger, Mark E. *Commentary on the 1969 Vienna Convention on the Law of Treaties*, cit., p. 692-694.

299 See Accioly, Hildebrando. *Tratado de direito internacional público*, vol. I, cit., p. 638.

300 See Remiro Brotons, Antonio. *Derecho internacional público*, vol. 2, cit., p. 492.

"On August 27, 1927, the Special Agreement between France and Brazil submitting to Arbitration (to the Permanent Court of International Justice) the Dispute relating to the Payment in Gold of Brazilian Federal Loans contracted in France was signed in Rio de Janeiro. The parties fulfilled their mutual obligations and, in 1929, the Court decided on the petition. The treaty was terminated, not by an act of God, but because the operative program provided by the parties had ended. The same way of termination adopted the 1930 Agreement between Brazil and Colombia relating to instructions on the delimitation of the boundary between both countries, which the Collection of Itamaraty pointed out as terminated 'by virtue of the termination of demarcation works'; as well as of treaties, of the same kind, with Great Britain and with the Netherlands, both in 1931. The construction of the bridge over the Uruguay river gave origin, between 1935 and 1943, to three agreements between Argentina and Brazil, all of them terminated due to their full performance at the end of the works".

REZEK, José Francisco. *Direito dos tratados*, cit., p. 480.

Therefore, as regards *execution*, treaties are terminated when they are fully performed; but, as regards *legal title*, treaties are considered permanent, despite the fact that they may imply potential performance measures, as in the case of a treaty related to onerous territorial cession or boundary demarcation.[301] Such treaties, in general bilateral treaties, are, due to their own nature, immune even to unilateral denunciation, as it is difficult to understand that the will of only one of the parties, for instance, may fix a term for an agreement on onerous territorial cession or common boundary definition.[302]

3.1.1.2 Supervening abrogation

Supervening abrogation means that the treaty does not provide for any pre-established means of termination, and it occurs after its clauses have been drawn up.[303] Therefore, unlike pre-established abrogation, in which case the will of the parties *sets forth* in the treaty *when* and *in which circumstances* (even implicitly) the treaty will be *terminated*, there is no anticipation of the parties' consent to terminate the treaty in the supervening abrogation, but – except that the treaty is silent, when it is thus possible to terminate it by the will of *all* the parties or by means of a subsequent treaty – only the provision is that *most* of the parties may terminate it when deemed appropriate.

---

301 See Rodas, João Grandino. *Tratados internacionais*, cit., p. 22.

302 See Rezek, José Francisco. *Direito dos tratados*, cit., p. 486.

303 See Fiorati, Jete Jane. Jus cogens…, cit., p. 38.

In general, treaties state nothing about their termination, in which case they may be terminated by the will of *all* the parties. Such unanimous consent, also known as *mutual agreement* or *common consent*, derives from a rule of Gregory IX era, pursuant to which *Omnis res per quascunque causas nascitur, per easdem dissolvitur* ("Everything that has come into being through certain causes can also be dissolved by the same causes"). That is to say, as the will of the parties is necessary for a treaty to be effective, it is also necessary for it to be terminated. Therefore, no treaty is immune to the will of all the parties to terminate it, even those treaties whose effectiveness is static or whose execution is automatic. Whether in relation to multilateral or bilateral treaties, the supervening will of *all* the parties is always entitled to assign a term.

While treaties may always be terminated by the vote of all the parties, we should analyze the case of treaties terminated by the vote of a *given number* of parties, as well as the case of termination by the conclusion of a *later treaty*.

3.1.1.2.1 Termination by the vote of a given number of parties

If expressly provided in the treaty text, the treaty may be terminated by the vote of *a given number* of contracting parties, in which case dissenting parties will have to agree. It should be noted that, in this case of supervening abrogation, the will of *all* the parties (expressed at the time of assuming the undertaking) allowed the treaty to terminate the treaty by the vote of *some of* the States. That is, when the parties concluded the treaty, all of them expressed their consent to terminate it, in the future, by the act of some of the parties (without providing, as we said before, *when* and in *which circumstances* such termination will occur).

The subject was governed in Art. 54 of the 1969 Convention, which provides that States may terminate a treaty in two cases: *a*) in conformity with the provisions of the treaty; or *b*) at any time by consent of all the parties after consultation with the other contracting States. Now, if the consent "of all the parties" is necessary pursuant to Art. 54 (b) (in case of termination of the treaty "at any time…"), it is clear that in Art. 54 (a) (in case of termination "in conformity with the provisions of the treaty"), the treaty may be terminated by the will of a given number of parties, being *a contrario* interpretation of the text. Therefore, if the treaty provides for the possibility that some States (which may be the majority) may terminate the treaty, it is understood that all the parties agreed with said provision during negotiations, adoption and later execution of the treaty. That means that, by adopting and signing (and then ratifying) the treaty whose text provides for the possibility of termination, the other dissenting parties have already accepted the possibility of terminating the treaty by the will of a given number of parties, depending on the provisions of the treaty.

Again, the will of such number of States (or international organizations), which may win over the opinion of dissenting parties, is inferred from the *a contrario* interpretation set forth in item *b* of Art. 54 of the Vienna Convention, which refers to termination of the treaties by the consent of all the parties.

In the event that a treaty is denounced by most of the States, with the purpose of being released from the obligations thereof, this does not affect the treaty effectiveness regarding the minority group, even if there remained only *two* States in the treaty.

It is clear that Art. 54, *a*, of the Convention does not *exclusively* cover the case of treaty termination by the vote of *a given number* of parties; it may provide for other events of termination, such as the expiration of a specific term (see item 3.1.1.1.1, above) and the condition subsequent (see item 3.1.1.1.2, above). In the last cases, however, abrogation is pre-established; in the event of termination by the vote of a given number of parties, which is being analyzed now, abrogation is supervening.

3.1.1.2.2 (Implicit or tacit) Termination by a later treaty

It may occur (1) that the parties to a specific treaty decide to draw up a *new* instrument, *expressly* terminating the earlier treaty; it may also occur (2) that through the *intention* of the parties to the new treaty, it may be verified that they are willing to revoke the earlier treaty; and also (3) that a new treaty is concluded (also between the same parties) and it is fully *incompatible* with the earlier treaty. In any case, the earlier treaty will be *terminated by the express* (*first case*), *implicit* (*second case*) or *tacit* (*third case*) incompatibility with the new treaty.

The case of *express* abrogation of an earlier treaty by the will of all the parties is regulated by Art. 54, *b*, of the Vienna Convention (see above). On the other hand, cases of *implicit* and *tacit* abrogation of an earlier treaty are governed by Art. 59, item 1, of the Convention, according to which a treaty is considered as terminated "if *all the parties to it* conclude a later treaty relating the same *subject-matter* and: *a*) it appears from the later treaty or is otherwise established that the parties intended that the matter should be governed by that treaty [*implicit termination*]; or *b*) the provisions of the later treaty are *so far incompatible with* those of the earlier one that the two treaties are not capable of being applied at the same time [*tacit* termination]".

As we can see, the provisions of Art. 59 relate to cases in which the parties, *without terminating* the earlier treaty or without *expressly* modifying it, conclude a new treaty (*a*) from which *intention* it causes their will to regulate (totally) the subject regulated by the earlier treaty, or (*b*) whose provisions are so *incompatible* with the provisions of the earlier treaty that it is impossible to apply them at the same time.[304]

For an earlier treaty to be revoked (implicitly or tacitly) by another later treaty, the parties to the second one must *be the same* parties to the earlier treaty. Despite that in the second treaty there are *more parties* than the parties to the first treaty, *all the parties* to the earlier instrument must be parties to the second treaty.[305] The 1969 Convention does not admit the possibility that a treaty may be terminated by the will of *some* States if it is not expressly set forth in this regard (see item 3.1.1.2.1, above).

It should be pointed out that, in current practice related to treaties, it is frequent that new treaties already include an express provision related to earlier treaty termination, so as to avoid any confusion and doubts.

3.1.2 Termination by unilateral will (denunciation)

Legal scholars usually include denunciation among the ways to terminate treaties. However, it may be more accurate to state that denunciation is the typical way a given State (or *international organization*) terminates a treaty just because it is the result of a *unilateral act* by the State Party concerned. Then, except for the case of bilateral treaties, it is not correct to say, technically speaking, that denunciation is a *form of treaty termination*, since it is a unilateral act and it does not affect the rest of the parties to the mutualizable treaty.

Denunciation was regulated in the 1969 Vienna Convention, but it does not solve all the problems related to it. There are *internal* problems relating to denunciation that also deserve the attention of internationalists. In the following items, we will study denunciation under the 1969 Convention, as well as the problems related to it under Brazilian Law.

---

304 See Remiro Brotons, Antonio. *Derecho internacional público*, vol. 2, cit., p. 470-473; De La Guardia, Ernesto, *Derecho de los tratados internacionales*, cit., p. 214-216; and Villiger, Mark E., *Commentary on the 1969 Vienna Convention on the Law of Treaties*, cit., p. 726-727.

305 See Rezek, José Francisco. *Direito dos tratados*, cit., p. 483.

3.1.2.1 *Denunciation in the 1969 Vienna Convention*

Denunciation means the unilateral act whereby a party to a specific treaty firmly expresses its will to withdraw from the treaty. It differs from *abrogation* by the fact that denunciation is held *unilaterally* by a given party to the treaty, and not by all of them.

Denunciation by one of the parties to a bilateral treaty terminates the treaty, obviously based on a *de facto* matter while, in multilateral treaties, the terms of the treaty cease to be effective only *for the denouncing party*, and they continue into effect for the other parties (when the treaty is *mutualizable*).

First, it should be highlighted that denunciation cannot refer to a *part* of the treaty, but only to the whole text (except as otherwise provided by the treaty or the parties). It refers to the application of the rule of *separability* or *integrity* of treaties, as provided in Art. 44, item 1, of the 1969 Convention: "A right of a party, provided for in a treaty or arising under article 56, to *denounce*, withdraw from or suspend the operation of the treaty may be exercised only with respect *to the whole* treaty unless the treaty otherwise provides or the parties otherwise agree".[306]

Materialization of the denunciation does not differ much from the procedure adopted for ratification of treaties, being formalized, in the case of multilateral treaties, in an instrument delivered to the other parties, or to the depositary for that purpose, who will notify the other parties of the denouncing State's intention to withdraw from the treaty under analysis. In the case of bilateral treaties, there will be denunciation when one of the parties notifies the other party of its intention to withdraw from the treaty.

Treaties establishing a permanent legal situation (called *real* or *dispositive* treaties) cannot be denounced. However, not all treaties admitting denunciation provide for the possibility of unilateral denunciation.[307]

We should distinguish two cases of denunciation in international treaties: the case in which the provisions of a treaty expressly provide for the possibility of denunciation; and the case in which its provisions state nothing about it. In the first case, no problem arises since denunciation is *already provided for* in the treaty itself. Some treaties frequently provide

---

[306] For further details, see Villiger, Mark E., *Commentary on the 1969 Vienna Convention on the Law of Treaties*, cit., p. 563-564.

[307] Rodas, João Grandino. *Tratados internacionais*, cit., p. 22-23.

for a specific term, as from its entry into force, for denunciation before which the treaty may not be denounced in any way; other treaties allow for denunciation, but they provide for a time period for denunciation to be effective (such period generally varies from six months to one year, and only at the end of said period the denouncing State may consider the treaty as terminated).[308] In the second case, the treaty *does not provide for anything* related to the possibility of denunciation, so it is impossible to know if, in this case, it is possible to materialize it. The Vienna Conference adopted the position that denunciation would be possible in silent treaties, provided that (*a*) the possibility of denunciation is inferred from the *intention of the parties* or (*b*) it is deduced from the *nature* of the treaty. Consequently, item 1 of Art. 56, of the Convention set forth a supplementary rule that sought the possibility of admitting unmotivated denunciation in silent treaties in the intention of the parties and in the treaty nature. The quoted rule provides as follows:

> "Article 56. *Denunciation of or withdrawal from a treaty containing no provision regarding termination, denunciation or withdrawal.*[309]
>
> 1. A treaty which contains no provision regarding its termination and which does not provide for denunciation or withdrawal is not subject to denunciation or withdrawal unless:
>
> *a*) it is established that the parties intended to admit the possibility of denunciation or withdrawal; or
>
> *b*) a right of denunciation or withdrawal may be implied by the nature of the treaty".

The first case, as explained by Rezek, refers to the quite uncommon case "in which the intention of the parties can be found, without any doubts, out of the treaty text. The second paragraph brings into consideration the *nature* of a silent treaty, so as to determine if the treaty may be denounced or not. Major doubts may arise with collective agreements: it is certainly simpler, between bilateral treaties, to distinguish *by their nature* the treaties which are immune to denunciation from all others,

---

308 See Calsing, Maria de Assis. *O tratado internacional e sua aplicação no Brasil*, cit., p. 66.

309 Some authors (like Remiro Brotons) understand that the terms *denunciation* and *withdrawal* affect different kinds of treaties: *denunciation* would be for treaties in general, while *withdrawal* would be for treaties constituting international organizations (see *Derecho internacional público*, vol. 2, cit., p. 466). However, international practice has used both terms as synonyms in relation to any kind of treaties.

obviously falling under the second class treaties relating to trade and payments; cultural, scientific and technical cooperation; extradition; covenants on fishing activities, postal services, taxes, sea and air navigation, migration, passports, diplomatic bags, telecommunications, tourism, and many other subjects. (...) When the force of the political scenario compels a given State to submit itself to the perpetual acceptance of a commitment which, *based on its nature*, could be denounced, the political circumstances, some way or another, tend to correct such distortion".[310]

In summary, in those cases in which the treaty is *silent* regarding the possibility of denunciation, it is necessary to find out the *nature* of the treaty rule, for the purpose of investigating its possibility of denunciation (peace, disarmament, boundary delimitation treaties, for example, could not be denounced based on their nature.) Such cases, however, do not occur most of the time. Frequently, international treaties already include provisions and procedures for their own denunciation. Many international treaties, as explained by Rezek, "authorize unilateral withdrawal *at any time*, which means that, in theory, one of the parties may withdraw right after the treaty enters into force; the only condition required is the lapse of an adaptation term in favor of the other contracting parties. It is ordinarily called notice, despite it most frequently having the form of a deferment term of the denunciation effects. (...) In relation to treaties, twelve months will probably be the most common adaptation term to adapt to the denunciation. But a six month term is also frequent, and there are examples of considerably lower or higher terms. (...) Treaties with five year, ten year or similar terms usually establish either an automatic extension, in the event the parties do no express their intention to withdraw in advance; or an automatic termination when the parties do not expressly decide for the extension. However, there are treaties with indefinite terms that may be denounced, but not at any time; only as from a given date and, always, in compliance with the adaptation term".[311] There are, however, some treaties without provisions on the possibility of denunciation, like the Vienna Conventions on Diplomatic (1961) and Consular (1963) Relations, apart from the Vienna Convention on the Law of Treaties itself (1969) and the Vienna Convention on the Law of Treaties between States or International Organizations or among International Organizations (1986);

---

310 Rezek, José Francisco. *Direito dos tratados*, cit., p. 487-488.

311 Rezek, José Francisco. Idem, p. 489-492.

as explained by De La Guardia, it shows "that there was no intention to facilitate denunciation of such relevant regulation agreements".[312]

For denunciation to operate under the terms of art, 56, item 1, of the Convention (that is, when the treaty *does not provide* for the possibility of denunciation), the State must deliver a notice or a *letter* in writing expressing its will to denounce the treaty; said notification will be delivered to the Government of the other contracting party, if the treaty is bilateral, or to the depositary of the instrument, if the treaty is multilateral, twelve months in advance of denunciation becoming effective. Art. 56, item 2 of the Convention provides that: "A party shall give not less than twelve months' notification of its intention to denounce or withdraw from a treaty under paragraph 1". In the case of multilateral treaties, the depositary will inform the other parties that the State concerned has expressed its formal will to withdraw from the respective treaty; in treaties constituting international organizations, the depositary is always the organization's *secretary* for denunciation purposes, even if the depositary was one of the founding States for ratification purposes. It may even occur, though infrequently, that the depositary of a multilateral treaty is a State not party to the treaty, as said State has not ratified the treaty after accepting the duty of depositary during negotiations.[313]

What happens if after the aforementioned twelve months (which is called "adaption term") the State concerned *is already released* from the treaty automatically or not? Why do we wonder this? The question is made considering that in Section 4 (of the same Part V containing rules on denunciation) the Convention provides a *procedure* relating "to invalidity, termination, withdrawal or suspension of the operation of a treaty" (Arts. 65 to 68), without which the treaty is not terminated by the unilateral will of the parties (see Ch. 4, item 4.1.1, below). That section provides that the notifying party (and the term established for such notification is *three months*, and not *twelve* as in denunciation; the reader will understand the imbroglio soon) may only take the proposed measure (in this case, *denunciation* of the treaty) if there is no *objection* of any party; in case there is, a solution will be sought by the means provided in Art. 33 of the UN Charter (Art. 65, item 2). Since the Convention has established a term of *twelve months* and not *three months* for denunciations, as set forth in Section 4 relating to the procedure of invalidity or termination

312 De La Guardia, Ernesto. *Derecho de los tratados internacionales*, cit., p. 300.

313 See Rezek, José Francisco. *Direito dos tratados*, cit., p. 493.

of treaties, an unwary interpreter could understand that the Vienna Code has excluded, for denunciation, the termination procedure provided for in Arts. 65 to 68, granting the denouncing party the power to withdraw from the treaty by itself after the notice term.[314] However, this is not true. By a systematic and teleological interpretation of Arts. 65, item 2, and 56, item 2, we can conclude that, in the specific case of denunciation, the term of *three months* provided for in Art. 65, item 2, was *extended* to the term provided for in Art. 56, item 2, which establishes a *twelve months' prior notice* for the State to notify the other parties its intention to denounce the treaty... After such term, if no objections occur, the State may take the proposed measure, that is, withdraw from the treaty due to denunciation.[315] However, in case of any objections, the procedure to be studied along Ch. 4 will be followed to arrive at a solution by the means provided in Art. 33 of the UN Charter, etc. (see below).

Finally, it should be clarified that the denouncing State, within the adaptation term, may *withdraw* the denunciation, confirming its intention to continue to be bound by the treaty, but the other contracting parties, who may also denounce the treaty if they wish, will not have the right to *object* to the decision of the repentant State. It is true, however, that "if the effects of denunciation are already consummated, that is, if the bilateral treaty is already terminated, or if the withdrawing State is no longer subject to the treaty regulations, there is no possible withdrawal. In the latter case, return by accession may be considered.[316]

3.1.2.2 *The problem of denunciation in Brazilian Law*

When we study treaty denunciation, we must discuss an internal law procedural problem related to it which deserves our attention. The issue to be clarified is if the Head of the Executive may, by means of an act

---

314 In that very sense, see Remiro Brotons, Antonio, *Derecho internacional público*, vol. 2, cit., p. 496, for whom "it would be total nonsense to reach a conclusion, taking literally the wording of Art. 65.1 and the procedures set forth in article 56, by virtue of which, in the case of unmotivated denunciation, a party has the power to enforce its purpose unilaterally, which purpose will be subject exclusively to a notice term".

315 See Remiro Brotons, Antonio. Idem, p. 496-497. Nothing is mentioned about this in Rezek, José Francisco, *Direito dos tratados*, cit., p. 493-494 (the same applies to the "Procedure" relating to denunciation); and Mello, Celso D. de Albuquerque, *Curso de direito internacional público*, vol. I, cit., p. 259 (on denunciation) and p. 265 (on the procedure for termination, withdrawal, etc.).

316 Rezek, José Francisco. *Direito dos tratados*, cit., p. 494.

issued by it, denounce international treaties, agreements or conventions for which ratification the Head of the Executive had depended on the approval of the National Congress. In other words, if the Executive Power is required authorization by the Legislative Power to denounce treaties.

This matter appeared among us, for the first time, in 1926 when it was decided, during the last months of Artur Bernardes's administration, that the country would no longer be part of the League of Nations.[317] Clóvis Beviláqua, a Legal Advisor of Itamaraty at that time, when called to express an opinion, answered affirmatively, in an opinion issued on July 5, 1926, but without grounds, as pointed out by Pontes de Miranda.[318] The truth is that since then, without any doubt, the power to denounce treaties started to belong exclusively to the Executive Power, and this has been (since 1926) the official interpretation of the Brazilian Government.

Clóvis understood that the constitutional legal rule requiring the approval of Congress did not refer to *denunciation*; it only mentioned that ratification required the Congress' approval. And if the Constitution said nothing about it, it is because the intervention of Congress in the denunciation process would not be needed. In addition, according to Beviláqua: "If there is a clause in the treaty providing for and governing withdrawal, when Congress approves a treaty, it is also approving that the said treaty may be denounced; therefore, in practice, the Executive Power only exercises a right that has been declared in the text approved by Congress. The denunciation act is merely administrative. Denunciation of a treaty is a way to enforce it; therefore, the right to terminate it is contemplated in one of its clauses. (...) If the principle of prior deliberation by Congress prevailed in order for Brazil to withdraw from the League of Nations, logically, the same formality should be required for fulfilling the other clauses of the Convention and, in that case, Congress would be responsible for executing the treaty and not the Power to which the Constitution entrusts such role. (...) What we want to know is if the Executive Power is competent to denounce treaties, which provide for and condition denunciation. The power to denounce is recognized; the law does not expressly state which is the competent Power to do so; but it clearly arises from its pro-

---

317 On the episode of Brazil´s withdrawal from the League of Nations, see Garcia, Eugênio Vargas, *O Brasil e a Liga das Nações (1919-1926)*, 2. ed., Porto Alegre: Ed. UFRGS, 2005, p. 117-135; and also Rodrigues, José Honório & Seitenfus, Ricardo, *Uma história diplomática do Brasil (1531-1945)*, Rio de Janeiro: Civilização Brasileira, 1995, p. 268-346.

318 See Pontes de Miranda. *Comentários à Constituição de 1967 com a Emenda n.º 1 de 1969*, vol. III, 3. ed. Rio de Janeiro: Forense, 1987, p. 109 et seq.

visions that the competent Power is the Executive. Or it is the Executive Power, or no Power would have such competence, because the Constitution does not state clearly which power is entitled to denounce treaties".[319]

According to Beviláqua, although constitutional provisions have been silent regarding denunciation, only referring to the procedure of *creation* of international legal acts, the authority of the Executive Power to denounce the treaties concluded by the Government itself would be granted by virtue of the combination of constitutional precepts granting the authority of the Powers in which national sovereignty is divided. The competence of the Executive Power to denounce treaties concluded by it, with the approval of Congress, would result from the combination of these precepts, along with their dominating spirit. In Clóvis' opinion: "Such competence is properly attributed, since the Executive power is the body to which the Constitution grants the right to represent the nation in its relations with the other nations. And the Executive Power holds such representative function, making contact with foreign States; concluding treaties, agreements and conventions; appointing members of the diplomatic and consular office; declaring war directly, per se, in cases of foreign invasion or aggression; finally, running the international life of the country, with the collaboration of Congress. Said collaboration is, however, exceptional. It is only required in the cases so established. When the Constitution is silent, it will be understood that the authority of the Executive Power, relating to international relations, is exclusive to said Power".[320]

---

[319] Beviláqua, Clóvis. Denúncia de tratado e saída do Brasil da Sociedade das Nações, in Cachapuz de Medeiros, Antônio Paulo (org.), *Pareceres dos consultores jurídicos do Itamaraty*, vol. II (1913-1934), Brasília: Federal Senate, 2000, p. 347-348. In that very sense, see Pereira de Araújo, João Hermes, *A processualística dos atos internacionais*, cit., p. 295-297.

[320] Beviláqua, Clóvis. Denúncia de tratado e saída do Brasil da Sociedade das Nações, cit., p. 349-350. Besides, as explained by Beviláqua: "It is objected, however, that, after being approved by the Legislative Power, treaties assume the category of law of the country, and laws may only be revoked by other laws. In general, this is the case, but, if the law establishes a term of duration, there is no need to revoke it in order to lose effectiveness. It is the same in relation to treaties. If a term of duration is fixed, it terminates upon its termination, irrespective of any denunciation. The same should be said about the treaty term and condition. If a treaty provides for a condition subsequent, it will lose efectiveness provided that the condition is executed. In the case of the Covenant, Art. 1, final clause sets forth a condition [that] determines, in relation to any Member of the League, its status as such: any Member may withdraw from the League after delivering a notice thereof, provided that all its international obligations and all its obligations under this Convenant will have been fulfilled at the time of its withdrawal In the event that a

Even though Rezek also thinks that the President of the Republic may, due to the President's own authority, denounce treaties without the approval of Congress, he disagrees, however, with the legal foundation of Beviláqua's opinion. According to him: "Clóvis Beviláqua's thesis, despite his wit to develop it, is inconsistent. It is based on the treaty provision of denunciation, as a clause that 'does not differ from others'. This would mean that by denouncing a treaty, the State Party concerned is not subject anymore to its provisions, which is not different from exercising any provision among the operative provisions themselves. And whoever may think that such proposal is not basically unacceptable, due to the great gap that separates a denunciation clause from the operative clauses of treaties, will agree to consider that the thesis under analysis makes us admit, *a fortiori*, that Government does not depend on Congress to *amend* or *reform* treaties in force, as long as that has been provided for in the original text. And such claim, as far as we know, has never been stated by the Brazilian Government, or by another party subject to a similar constitutional law. After all, there are no quantitative or qualitative restrictions on what a reform may, in theory, mean to a treaty: by way of amendments, it is possible to turn a sport interchange agreement into a military alliance agreement or into an agreement to freely cede part of the national territory". And he concludes: "Besides, it is not correct that the recognized authority of foreign relations dynamics by the Executive, which is entitled to 'keep relations with foreign States', implies by itself the exclusive power to denounce treaties. Based on their importance, the power to denounce treaties was included by constituents in a separate item from the item related to general international relations, and they made clear that Congress control was imperative. On the other hand, if denunciation is understood as a condition subsequent provided for in the convention, nothing explains why it is intended to find, in that matter, an answer to the question of knowing which power of the State is competent to denounce".[321]

---

similar clause was found in any law, it would not be necessary for the same Power that sanctioned the law to revoke it. Its publication serves a basis for its effectiveness. Therefore, if a treaty is a law, because the Congress approved it, and as a consequence of said approval, it is applied to the cases it refers to, and if the treaty contains a clause stating when its application will cease for any of the contracting parties, such law does not need to be revoked by the Power approving it, since such Power also approved the way said obligation would be terminated" (Idem, p. 350).

[321] Rezek, José Francisco. *Direito dos tratados*, cit., p. 500-501.

According to Pontes de Miranda, who also denied the validity of Beviláqua's thesis, "to approve a treaty, convention or agreement, entitling the Executive Power to denounce it, without consultation or approval [of the Parliament], is contrary to constitutional principles", so the President of the Republic, as in the case of ratification, must "submit a denunciation proposal, or denounce the treaty, convention or agreement *ad referendum* of the Legislative Power".[322]

Furthermore, Peru's Constitution of 1993 states in such regard, in compliance with Art. 57 (3), that: "Denunciation of treaties is within the power of the President of the Republic, who has the duty to notify the Congress", adding that "in the case of treaties subject to approval by Congress, such denunciation requires its previous approval". Peru's Constitution, it should be pointed out, provides that, *except* for cases of treaties relating to the subjects contained in its Art. 56 (human rights; sovereignty, State domain or integrity; national defense; and State financial obligations), the President of the Republic *does not need* the approval of the Congress to ratify treaties, only having to "notify Congress" of said ratification.(Art. 57).[323] The provisions of Art. 64, item 3, of the Principality of Andorra's Constitution are similar: "The previous agreement of the absolute majority of the Chamber shall be required for the repeal of the international treaties affecting the matters enumerated in epigraph 1". In the Spanish Constitution of 1978, in turn, there is a similar rule setting forth that "the same procedure shall be used for denouncing international treaties and agreements as that, provided in Article 94, for entering into them" (Art. 96, item 2).[324] The same happened with the French Constitution of 1946, whose Art. 28 provided that denunciation should be authorized by the National Assembly in those cases in which the treaty required the approval of Parliament for its ratification.

The need of legislative approval for the (authorization of) denunciation of treaties is not peacefully accepted yet. In fact, some authors, like

---

322 Pontes de Miranda. *Comentários à Constituição de 1967 com a Emenda n.º 1 de 1969*, vol. II, cit., p. 109. In that very sense, see the case entitled *Cafés La Virginia*, judged by the Argentinean Supreme Court in 1994; see, especially, the vote of judge Boggiano, in *CSJN, LL*, 1995-D-277.

323 See the text: "Article 57. The President of the Republic may formalize or ratify treaties or accede to them without previous approval by the Congress in matters not contemplated in the preceding article. In all such cases, the President must notify the Congress".

324 On such provision, see Remiro Brotons, Antonio, *Derecho internacional público*, vol. 2, cit., p. 506-507.

Rezek, understand that the Government does not depend on the Legislative Power's authorization to denounce. He thinks as follows: "I believe that the Head of Government is, based on its own authority, entitled to denounce international treaties, as it has been doing, without restrictions, since 1926. (...) It seems quite reasonable that, where a meeting of the minds between the Government and the Congress is necessary to *bind* the State, engaging the State in an international contractual relation, the decision of one of the powers will be sufficient to *release* it by means of denunciation. In light of the principle of the *acte contraire*, if both minds were necessary to conclude the agreement, both of them would be necessary again to withdraw from it. It should be understood that the minds of both the Government and the Congress are presumed final and unaltered, as from the time of conclusion of the treaty, and during its effective term, as two pillars of the national will. This will lead to the conclusion that no treaty, among those that may be rejected by means of denunciation, will continue in force *against the will* of the Government or the Congress. The negative spirit of one of the two political powers in connection with the treaty may determine its denunciation, since it means the disappearance of one of the basis on which the consent of the State was based".[325]

As can be seen, Rezek admits that the will *of Congress* is also competent to denounce an international convention, even when it is not consistent with the intentions of the Executive Power. In this sense, he concludes: "At this stage, it is necessary to recognize the imbalance between the Government's and Congress' instruments concerning governmental acts If the intention to denounce belongs to the Government, the relevant international act will immediately cause the decision of the President of the Republic, to whom are subordinated all mechanisms of foreign relations and all official communication channels with foreign nations and other Law of Nations' legal entities. If the intention to denounce belongs to the Congress, the responsibility for its formulation at the international level will fall on the Executive Power. In addition, the way in which the Congress expresses its will before the Government cannot be a legislative order of 'rejection' of the agreement in force, if such an act has not been provided for in the field of exclusive competence of the Congress. By exclusion, it should be understood that an *ordinary law* is the appropriate means for the Legislative Power to order the Executive Power to denounce a treaty, as it occurred in 1911 in the field of extradition. (...) The ordinary law,

325 Rezek, José Francisco. *Direito dos tratados*, cit., p. 501-502.

meanwhile, is not an exclusive element of the Parliament, since it depends on the Head of Government to sanction it. The Head of Government will veto the project, in case it disagrees with the idea of denunciation; the project will be promulgated, against the Head of Government's will, in case that two thirds of all members of each Congress' House agree.[326] This is the greatest evidence of the imbalance between the Government's expression of will and the Congress' expression of will, in terms of releasing the country from an international convention. The Congress' expression of will goes, as regards formality, through oblique ways: above all, it needs the largest *quorum* demanded by our Constitution, i.e., the quorum necessary to reject the presidential veto".[327]

According to us, the National Congress may denounce international treaties through a law, having to *reject, if necessary, the veto* of the President of the Republic, in the event the Executive Power does not accept the denunciation proposed by the Congress. In such regard, we agree with the thesis proposed by Rezek. We consider, however, that it is not reasonable to grant to the President of the Republic alone the power to denounce international treaties, whose ratification required authorization by the National Congress. It should be noted that, in case of denunciation by an act of Congress (by means of an *ordinary law*), the President of the Republic *participates* in creating the Nations' will, sanctioning or vetoing the bill under analysis; the National Congress, in the opposite case (denunciation of the treaty by the exclusive act of the President), following the thesis defended by Rezek, is absolutely silent, not even being aware of the presidential will to denounce the treaty. That is where our disagreement lies with regard to the thesis expressed. Therefore, according to our opinion, in the same way the President of the Republic needs the approval of the National Congress, giving him "full powers" to ratify the treaty, it would be more in line with the rules of the Constitution of 1988 in force that the same procedure were applied in connection with denunciation,

---

326 That refers to the previous Brazilian Constitution, which provided as follows: "Upon notifying the veto to the President of the Federal Senate, it will convene both Houses in a joint session to be informed of that, considering that the project which obtains the vote of two thirds of Representatives and Senators present is approved, by secret vote. In this case, the project will be sent to the President of the Republic for promulgation" (Art. 62, item 3, of the 1967 Federal Constitution with the Constitutional Amendment No. 1/1969. In the current Constitution (1988), rejection of the presidential veto needs the *absolute majority* of the national Congress, also in a joint session (Art. 66, item 4).

327 Rezek, José Francisco. *Direito dos tratados*, cit., p. 502-504.

in which case we could not speak about denunciation of a treaty by means of an act issued by the Head of the Executive Power. In this way, the parallelism needed between legal acts of assumption of international agreements and those relating to their denunciation is maintained. We should consider the constitutional provision (Art. 1, sole paragraph) according to which *all the power comes from the people*, also including therein the power to denounce treaties. Thus, an international practice is modified for the effective establishment of democracy, which practice had, until then, been considered uniform and pacific in several countries, among which is Brazil. Therefore, we understand that Pontes de Miranda's position is correct; pursuant to said position, as we mentioned before, denunciation of treaties without the consent of the Congress is contrary to constitutional principles.[328] But it should be pointed out that both cases are not valid regarding denunciation of treaties on protection of human rights, which, for having been incorporated to the Brazilian laws with the *level* and the *type* of constitutional rules, become ingrained as eternal clauses in our internal Law, and they cannot be denounced by the Government (see Art. 5, items 1, 2 and 3, of the 1988 Federal Constitution).[329]

The legal matter discussed here reached the FSC on June 16, 1997, when the *Confederação Nacional dos Trabalhadores na Agricultura* (CONTAG) and the *Central Única dos Trabalhadores* (CUT) filed a Direct Action of Unconstitutionality seeking to obtain the declaration of unconstitutionality of Executive Order 2100/1996,[330] which made public the

---

328 See Pontes de Miranda. *Comentários à Constituição de 1967 com a Emenda n.º 1 de 1969*, vol. II, cit., p. 109. In the same sense, see Capaldo, Giuliana Zicardi, *La competenza a denunciare i trattati internazionali: contributo allo studio del treaty power*, Napoli: Edizioni Scientifiche Italiane, 1983, p. 97; Mello, Celso D. de Albuquerque, Constituição e relações internacionais, in Dolinger, Jacob (org.), *A nova Constituição e o direito internacional*, Rio de Janeiro: Freitas Bastos, 1987, p. 28; and Garcia, Márcio Pereira Pinto, *A terminação de tratado e o Poder Legislativo à vista do direito internacional, do direito comparado e do direito constitucional internacional brasileiro*, Rio de Janeiro: Renovar, 2011, p. 405 and 420 (the author, however, understands "that the Constitution should contain a specific provision with the cases in which the Congress should express its position", p. 423).

329 We will not go deeper into this subject here, as it has already been done in other works. For details, see Mazzuoli, Valerio de Oliveira, *O controle jurisdicional da convencionalidade das leis*, cit., p. 25-71; and also Mazzuoli, Valerio de Oliveira, *Curso de direito internacional público*, cit., p. 896-927.

330 This Executive Order reads as follows: "The President of the Republic makes public that, as from November 20, 1997, LIO's Convention 158, relating to the Termination of the Labor Relationship by Initiative of the Employer, adopted in Geneva on June 22, 1982, will cease to be effective in Brazil, since it has been denounced by means of a Note of the

denunciation of Convention 158 of the LIO, duly approved and promulgated by Legislative Order 68/1992 and by Executive Order 1855/1996, respectively. The complaint also defended the impossibility of denunciation of international treaties without the previous consent of the National Congress, having the petitioners argued that Art. 49, I, of the 1988 Federal Constitution "provided that any denunciation filed by the Brazilian government shall be duly approved by the National Congress, without violating the referred constitutional provision".[331] See, complaint referred to as ADIn, number 1,625/DF, originating in the Office of Reporting Judge Maurício Corrêa, whose final decision by the FSC is still pending.[332]

3.1.3 Extrinsic grounds for termination

There are grounds for termination of treaties that are neither related to the unilateral will of one of the parties nor to any agreement (preordered or supervening) conducive to terminate an international act, irrespective of any expression of will aimed at terminating the treaty, which may occur only as a *consequence* of a specific act or fact (the material breach of the treaty by one of the parties, a substantial change of circumstances, the severance of diplomatic relations, state of war, etc.) Therefore, they are *extrinsic* grounds for *termination*. They are called so because they operate in relation to *any treaties*, including those containing clauses on their termination or denunciation. As pointed out by Remiro Brotons, such (extrinsic) grounds belong to the field of international Public Policy, in the sense that a treaty provision preventing the parties from invoking said grounds must be deemed inoperative.[333] It should be noted that a case of *material breach of a treaty* has to also be considered an *extrinsic* ground for termination of the international act, not held for the purpose of terminating the treaty, for which case the State concerned could resort to *denunciation*. The breach of a treaty (or an agreement, at the internal Law level) is an act not directly aimed at having the effects of the respec-

---

Brazilian Government to the Labor International Organization, having the denunciation been recorded by said Organization on November 20, 1996".

331 See *Petição Inicial*, p. 14, *in fine*, signed by lawyers Marthius Sávio Cavalcante Lobato, José Eymard Loguercio and Ericson Crivelli.

332 For the first comment to the case at that time, see Mazzuoli, Valerio de Oliveira, STF, Poder Legislativo e denúncia de tratados internacionais, *Jornal Correio Braziliense*, supplement "Direito & Justiça", dated 10.30.2006, p. 3, which already defended the fact that government could not denounce treaties without the approval of the Legislative Power.

333 Remiro Brotons, Antonio. *Derecho internacional público*, vol. 2, cit., p. 479.

tive instrument cease, which terminates only as the (extrinsic) result of performing the act.

It is possible to divide extrinsic grounds for termination (the purpose of the division, however, is not practical at all) into two groups: (*a*) grounds operating due to *independent facts* of the parties' will (such as, supervening impossibility to perform a treaty, fundamental change of circumstances and survival of the norm of *jus cogens*) and (*b*) grounds occurring due to *dependent acts or facts* of the parties' will (such as material breach of the treaty, severance of diplomatic and consular relations, state of war and disuse).

In this topic, we will follow the order of topics exposed in the 1969 Vienna Convention (which excluded *state of war* and *disuse*). In the sequence, we will examine *material breach of a treaty, supervening impossibility to perform a treaty, fundamental change of circumstances, severance of diplomatic and consular relations, state of war and disuse*. The last extrinsic ground for termination to be studied would be relating to the survival of a norm of *jus cogens*, which has already been analyzed in the previous topic (see Part III, Ch. 2, item 2.2.2.2, above).

3.1.3.1 Material breach of a treaty

A treaty may terminate when one of the States parties ceases to perform one or more of its provisions, resulting in a material (unjustified, serious) breach of its text. Such breach does not terminate the treaty immediately (that is, *ipso jure*); it only grants the *non-defaulting* parties affected by the breach, among others, the right to terminate the treaty in force with the defaulting State or even to terminate the treaty among all the parties (see below).[334] If that were not the case, the party responsible for the breach would easily violate the commitment as an effective means of being released from the obligations undertaken by said party.

The 1969 Vienna Convention rules on the topic in its Art. 60, which deals with the *principle of reciprocity* of international treaties.[335] It re-

---

334 For a detailed analysis of the subject, see Gomaa, Mohammed M., *Suspension or termination of treaties on grounds for breach*, The Hague: Martinus Nijhoff, 1996, 201p.

335 See Reuter, Paul. *Introducción al derecho de los tratados*, cit., p. 225-231; and Fitzmaurice, Malgosia, The practical working of the law of treaties, cit., p. 196-197. For a view of preparatory work relating to Art. 60, see Spinedi, Marina, From one codification to another..., cit., p. 1105-1106; and Villiger, Mark E., *Commentary on the 1969 Vienna Convention on the Law of Treaties*, cit., p. 736-737.

fers to the application of the principle *exceptio non adimpleti contractus* (exception of breach of an agreement) to the theory of treaties, which authorizes a party to the treaty to invoke the breach as a ground for terminating the treaty or suspending its operation in whole or in part We should highlight the concern of the Vienna Convention to include a series of requirements conducive to avoid that a party arbitrarily terminates the treaty, as said party understands that it is being "damaged" by the intended breach of the agreement by the other State. That was the consequence of the manifest concern of many authors in the sense that a State would be able to arbitrarily terminate the treaty and generate legal uncertainty.[336]

The final text of Art. 60 of the Convention made a distinction between bilateral treaties (item 1) and multilateral treaties (item 2), and it also explained the meaning of *material (or serious) breach* of a treaty (item 3), the only basis to permit its termination or suspension of its operation.

A material breach of a *bilateral* treaty by one of the parties, according to the Convention, entitles the other to invoke the breach as a ground for terminating the treaty or suspending its operation in whole or in part (Art. 60, item 1). In turn, a material breach of a *multilateral* treaty by one of the parties, under the terms of Art. 60, item 2, authorizes (*a*) the other parties, by unanimous consent, to *suspend* the operation of the treaty, *in whole or in part*, or to *terminate* the treaty (in this case, always *in whole*), either between the parties and the defaulting State, or among all the parties; (*b*) a party especially damaged by the breach to invoke it as a ground for *suspending* the operation of the treaty, *in whole or in part*, between itself and the defaulting State;[337] and, finally, (*c*) any party *other than* the defaulting State to invoke the breach as a ground for *suspending* the operation of the treaty *in whole or in part* with respect to itself if the treaty is of such a character that a material breach of its provisions by one party *radically changes* the position of every party with respect to the further per-

---

336 See De La Guardia, Ernesto. *Derecho de los tratados internacionales*, cit., p. 305.

337 In this case, as pointed out by De La Guardia, the treaty "will continue operating *among all the parties*, including the defaulting State, except for the 'specially damaged' State, whose *legal interest* is protected and whose right is limited to simply request (argue) total or partial suspension between itself and the defaulting party, so as not to damage the general economy of the treaty, in whose maintenance the international community may be interested as a whole" [italics of the original] (*Derecho de los tratados internacionales*, cit., p. 307).

formance of its obligations under the treaty.[338] It should be noted that such consequences do not prevent the parties damaged by the breach of the treaty from requesting compensation for damages caused by the wrong conduct of the breaching State, or the performance of the corresponding obligation by the breaching State.[339]

As we can see, the 1969 Vienna Convention introduces three rules for cases of material breach of a *multilateral* treaty: 1) for the treaty to be *terminated*, the consent of *all the parties* is required (as we can see, the Convention excepted, for cases of material breach of a treaty, the procedure to resolve disputes provided for in Arts. 65, item 2, *et seq.*); in this case, one party *by itself* may not terminate the treaty in the event of a material breach, even in its relations with the defaulting State, and said party must *propose the measure* to the other parties' consideration (whose collective decision is *sovereign* and may not be appealed by the defaulting State); 2) a party *especially damaged* by the breach of the treaty may invoke such breach only to *suspend* the operation of the treaty, in whole or in part, as regards the defaulting State; and 3) any party (except for the defaulting State) may invoke a material breach of the treaty also to *suspend* (never *terminate*) the operation of the treaty, in whole or in part, *if the nature of the treaty is such* that a material breach of its provisions by one party *radically modifies* the situation of each of the parties relating to the later performance of its obligations resulting therefrom. It should be noted, however, that all such rules (under the terms of Art. 60, item 4) are *subsidiary* to the provision, under the treaty itself, of the consequences of its breach; that is, in the event the treaty has *already established* in its text the consequences (for instance, separation of a mem-

338 On this paragraph *c*, De La Guardia explains: "This complex paragraph *c* was conceived by the ILC taking into account several considerations by the governments, concerned about a very special type of treaties, *disarmament* treaties, for example, 'in which the breach by one of the parties tends to undermine the treaty regime among all the parties.' In this case, it could happen that the provisions set forth in items *a* and *b* of the paragraph 'do not suffice to protect the interests of a particular party, which may not suspend the performance of the obligations imposed by the treaty relating to the defaulting State without breaching, in turn, its own obligations in connection with the other parties', as further explained by the ILC. To foresee critical cases as this one, the article entitles '*any party*' to allege a material breach as a ground for suspending the treaty in whole or in part, in connection with itself, without the need to obtain the previous consent of the other parties, as required in item *a* of the same paragraph" (*Derecho de los tratados internacionales*, cit., p. 308).

339 See Calsing, Maria de Assis. *O tratado internacional e sua aplicação no Brasil*, cit., p. 70.

ber, etc.) of any material breach, such rules will *prevail* over the rules of the *Convention*.[340]

In any case, the breach of a treaty must always be *material*[341] for its termination to operate under the terms of Art. 60 of the Convention.[342] Material breach (as set forth in Art. 60, item 3) means (*a*) rejection of a treaty not permitted by the Vienna Code, or (*b*) breach of a fundamental provision to perform the object or purpose of the treaty.[343] Examples of the first case are unilateral declarations of invalidity or termination, made beyond the rules established by the Convention, for the purpose of self-excluding the State concerned from performance of the treaty; for the second case, the breach of a treaty is considered material when it jeopardizes the performance of its *object* or *purpose*.[344]

An exception to the principle of reciprocity appears in Art. 60, item 5, of the Convention, according to which the rules regarding termination or suspension of treaty operation "are not applied to the provisions *relating to the protection of the human person* contained in treaties *of a humanitarian nature*, in particular to provisions *prohibiting any form of reprisals against persons protected* by such treaties".[345] That is to say, international humanitarian treaties and provisions prohibiting any form of reprisals against persons protected by such treaties are excluded from the rules of termination or suspension relating to the operation of treaties, being im-

---

340 See Remiro Brotons, Antonio. *Derecho internacional público*, vol. 2, cit., p. 497.

341 In the English text, the expression used is *material* ("material breach of a treaty..."); the term *substantial* ("violation substantielle d'un traité...") appears in the French version of the Convention (and also in the Portuguese version: "substancial"); in the Spanish version the expression *grave* was used ("violación grave de un tratado...").

342 In the case entitled *Gabčíkovo-Nagymaros Project* (Hungary *v.* Slovakia) of 1997, the ICJ made it clear that "seule une violation substantielle du traité lui-même par un Etat partie audit traité peut mettre l'autre partie en droit de s'en prévaloir pour mettre fin au traité. La violation d'autres règles conventionnelles ou d'autres règles du droit international général peut justifier l'adoption par l'Etat lésé de certaines mesures, y compris des contre-mesures, mais elle ne saurait justifier qu'il soit mis fin au traité sur la base du droit des traités". See *ICJ Reports* (1997), p. 62.

343 See Villiger, Mark E. *Commentary on the 1969 Vienna Convention on the Law of Treaties*, cit., p. 742-743.

344 See Remiro Brotons, Antonio. *Derecho internacional público*, vol. 2, cit., p. 481-482.

345 Clear examples of such type of treaty are the 1949 Geneva Conventions and their 1977 Additional Protocols. On the subject, see Daniel, José, La Convention de Vienne de 1969 sur le droit des traités et le droit humanitaire, *Revue Internationale de la Croix-Rouge*, vol. 54 (July 1972), p. 401-414.

mune, for instance, to the effects of a war. Therefore, in the cases set forth in Art. 60, item 5, not even a *material* breach of a treaty by one of the parties authorizes the others to terminate (or suspend) the treaty among them; this is clearly reasonable in the light of that type of treaties, which in general do not depend (for their performance) on the performance of the remaining parties. It should be pointed out that, even though the Convention has expressly mentioned treaties of *humanitarian nature* (those applicable in cases of armed conflicts), the most suitable current interpretation of such expression must be to the effect that it should be extensive to all treaties on *human rights*, since the Vienna Convention said less than it intended to say: *lex minus dixit quam voluit*.[346] Therefore, conventions on civil, political, economic, social and cultural rights, and even conventions on environment protection (regional or global) would not be excluded from such clause.

The principle of reciprocity is not applied (for obvious reasons) either to treaties equivalent to a *legal title* (such as treaties delimiting boundaries or ceding territories).

3.1.3.2 Supervening impossibility of performance

This topic is governed by Art. 61 of the 1969 Convention, according to which a party may invoke the *impossibility* of performing a treaty as ground for terminating it if the impossibility results from the permanent disappearance or destruction of an *object indispensable* for the execution of the treaty.[347] It should be noted that the Convention never used the expression *force majeure* in the text of Art. 61, even though it is partially related to it. In the *travaux préparatoires* of the Convention, the ILC preferred to remove the expression *force majeure* and refer to the "impossibility" of performing a treaty, divided into two cases: when such impossibility results (*a*) from the destruction of an object indis-

---

[346] See Barile, Giuseppe. The protection of human rights in article 60, paragraph 5 of the Vienna Convention on the Law of Treaties, in *International law at the time of its codification: essays in honour of Roberto Ago*, vol. II, Milano: Giuffré, 1987, p. 3-14. Remiro Brotons also understands that the "reference to the *humanitarian nature* of treaties shall be understood in such a way to enable the inclusion of all treaties containing rules on protection of fundamental rights recognized to the human being" (*Derecho internacional público*, vol. 2, cit., p. 482).

[347] See Villiger, Mark E. *Commentary on the 1969 Vienna Convention on the Law of Treaties*, cit., p. 754-761.

pensable for the execution of the treaty, or (*b*) from the permanent *disappearance* of said indispensable object.

Such treaty termination modality is *instrumental*, since it is related to the *indispensable object* for the execution of the agreement. We must not think, however, that the impossibility of performance, in this case, is always *physical* or *material*. A *legal* impossibility to perform the treaty may cause its termination, under the terms of Art. 61 of the Convention.[348]

Such impossibility may be (*a*) *physical* to perform a treaty when there is physical absence (*a1*) of the *object* of the treaty (for instance, submersion of an island, drying of a river, destruction of an embankment or hydroelectric facility, etc.[349]), and (*a2*) of *one of the contracting parties* (for example, disappearance of a State by the loss of one of its constituent elements). There is (*b*) *legal* impossibility when there is (*b1*) incompatibility of operation of a treaty in connection with the other State or (*b2*) antagonism between the provisions of a treaty rule and other international rules in effect. An example of the first case is (*b1*) when a State (*A*) executes an alliance treaty with other two States (*B* and *C*) and said State cannot legally perform the agreement due to a war between said two States. An example of antagonism between the provisions of a treaty rule and other international rules in effect (*b2*) occurs when two States (*A* and *B*) execute a given treaty to govern certain legal matter between them and one of such States (*A*) concludes an identical agreement with another State (*C*), while the treaty concluded with the first State (*B*) is still in force, providing for the matter differently. In that case, the treaty *A-C* does not prevail over the previous treaty *A-B*as it is legally impossible to execute it.[350]

It should be noted that, in order to invoke the impossibility of performance of a treaty, such impossibility should be, under the provisions of Art. 61, item 1, of the Convention, (*a*) *supervening* to the conclusion of a treaty (should it be earlier, the treaty is legally *nonexistent*, having only the *form* of a treaty, revealed by the error of the parties); (*b*) *final* or *irreversible* (should it be temporary or provisional, only *suspension* of the treaty execution, and not its termination, is permitted); and (*c*) it should affect (physically or legally) an *object indispensable* for the per-

---

348 See Remiro Brotons, Antonio. *Derecho internacional público*, vol. 2, cit., p. 484; and Reuter, Paul, *Introducción al derecho de los tratados*, cit., p. 215-216.

349 See ILC, *Yearbook of the International Law Commission* (1966), vol. II, p. 256.

350 The examples are of Accioly, Hildebrando, in *Tratado de direito internacional público*, vol. I, cit., p. 640-641.

formance of the agreement.[351] Under such conditions, the affected party has *two options* relating to the treaty: requiring *termination* of the agreement or *withdrawing* from it. In the first case, the request is submitted for the consideration of the other parties, who may approve it (so the treaty terminates *erga omnes*) or reject it (resulting in the procedure set forth in Arts. 65 and 66); in the second case, the treaty continues in force for the other parties.[352]

Finally, the Convention states that impossibility of performance may not be invoked by a party as a ground for terminating, withdrawing from or suspending the operation of a treaty if the impossibility is the result of a breach by that party either of an obligation under the treaty or of any other international obligation owed to any other party to the treaty(Art. 61, item 2). This is based on a[353] precept according to which "no one can be heard to invoke his own turpitude", which has also been followed, *mutatis mutandis*, by the Convention when it referred to a fundamental change of circumstances (Art. 62, item 2, *b*). However, it should be noted that, with regard to the last case (fundamental change of circumstances), it is understandable that the defaulting party be excluded from the right to claim a change of circumstances as a means to terminate or suspend the treaty; nevertheless, with regard to the supervening impossibility of performance (as pointed by Remiro Brotons) the Convention was wrong since, if a treaty *cannot* be performed (it is a *factual* matter), it cannot be irrespective of being the invoking party responsible for the facts leading to such result.[354] Whether right or wrong, the truth is that the rule approved at the Vienna Conference (Art. 61, item 2) was reproduced by the Convention, and it must be fulfilled; even if a treaty *cannot* be performed, such impossibility may not be invoked by the defaulting party responsible for complying with an obligation resulting from the treaty or any other international obligation in connection with any other party to the treaty.

---

351 See Remiro Brotons, Antonio. *Derecho internacional público*, vol. 2, cit., p. 483-484; and Villiger, Mark E., *Commentary on the 1969 Vienna Convention on the Law of Treaties*, cit., p. 755-758.

352 See De La Guardia, Ernesto. *Derecho de los tratados internacionales*, cit., p. 310.

353 See, for example, Art. 48, item 2 (first part).

354 Remiro Brotons, Antonio. *Derecho internacional público*, vol. 2, cit., p. 498-499. According to Brotons: "This circumstance is relevant to harden the consequences of its unlawful act; however, nothing can be done to change the situation. It is absurd to propose that termination be ignored when it is invoked by the defaulting party" (Idem, p. 499).

3.1.3.3 Fundamental change of circumstances

Art. 62 of the Convention provides for a case of termination (or suspension) of a treaty when there is a *fundamental change* of the circumstances.[355] Under the Vienna Code, a fundamental change of circumstances which has occurred with regard to those existing at the time of the conclusion of a treaty, and which was not foreseen by the parties, *may not be* invoked as a ground for terminating or withdrawing from the treaty *unless*: *a*) the existence of those circumstances constituted an essential basis of the consent of the parties to be bound by the treaty; and *b*) the effect of the change is radically to transform the extent of obligations still to be performed under the treaty (Art. 62, item 1). The Convention adds that a party may invoke a fundamental change of circumstances as a ground for terminating or withdrawing from a treaty it may also invoke the change as a ground for suspending the operation of the treaty (Art. 62, item 3).

The referred provision of the Vienna Code deals with the application of the clause *rebus sic stantibus*[356] to international treaties, restrictively admitted, as we can see by reading it.[357] The *clause* has been considered an implicit condition subsequent of treaties for a long time, but now (after the 1969 Convention) it became an *autonomous* cause for non-application of international acts.[358] However, it differs from the supervening impossibility of performance (see item 3.1.3.2, above) because it does not have the characteristic of *irresistibility*.[359]

---

355 See De La Guardia, Ernesto. *Derecho de los tratados internacionales*, cit., p. 310-322; Reuter, Paul, *Introducción al derecho de los tratados*, cit., p. 217-222; Fitzmaurice, Malgosia & Elias, Olufemi, *Contemporary issues in the law of treaties*, cit., p. 173-200 (chapter entitled: "The doctrine of fundamental change of circumstances revisited"); Villiger, Mark E., *Commentary on the 1969 Vienna Convention on the Law of Treaties*, cit., p. 766-781; Crawford, James, *Brownlie's principles of public international law*, cit., p. 392-394; and Blaser, Cornelia Rabl, *Die* clausula rebus sic stantibus *im Völkerrecht*, Zürich: Dike, 2012, 570p.

356 It means "things thus standing". The clause *Omnis conventio intelligitur rebus sic stantibus* ("Any convention shall be understood as things thus standing") was originally formulated by St. Thomas Aquinas, in *Summa Theologica* (1273), later incorporated to International Law by Alberto Gentili, in its *De Jure Belli* (1598).

357 For an analysis of such rule prior to the 1969 Vienna Convention, see McNair, Arnold Duncan, La terminaison et la dissolution des traités, cit., p. 467-480.

358 See Reuter, Paul. *Introducción al derecho de los tratados*, cit., p. 218.

359 See Reuter, Paul. Idem, ibidem.

An unavoidable result of the conservation right, the clause *rebus sic stantibus* was inspired on canonical contractual law, which subjected contracts to the prevalence of circumstances that would have determined them: *Contractus qui habent tractum successivum de futuris rebus sic stantibus intelligitur*. Upon modification of the circumstances that conditioned the agreement, the contracting party, whose obligations were modified by the event, could claim the termination of the agreement. Similarly, if the circumstances determining the conclusion of a treaty were modified so as to obstruct the purpose sought by the contracting parties or they have even caused (unpredictably) the disappearance of the mutual trust which motivated the parties in the beginning, the solution would be, pursuant to the referred *clause*, termination or suspension of the operation of a treaty or the withdrawal of the damaged party.[360]

However, under the Vienna Convention, invoking the clause *rebus sic stantibus* will always be the *exception*, never the *rule*. In fact, the Convention provides that a fundamental change of circumstances "*may not* be invoked as a ground for terminating a treaty or withdrawing from a treaty, *if...*". The care with which the theory *rebus sic stantibus* was incorporated to the Convention is particularly justified in view of the fact that circumstances relating to international life change very easily, which may result in abuses by some States to be internationally disengaged from the obligations they assumed, based on fundamental changes of said circumstances. In addition, States with higher political force and international representation may use, at their own discretion, the concept of "fundamental change of circumstances" to refrain from performing international obligations contrary to their will, etc. Besides, it should be noted that the clause *rebus sic stantibus* is opposite to the rule *pacta sunt servanda*, one more reason to be careful with its application.[361]

---

360 See Martins, Pedro Baptista. *Da unidade do direito e da supremacia do direito internacional*. Rio de Janeiro: Forense, 1998, p. 41-42; and Pereira, André Gonçalves & Quadros, Fausto de, *Manual de direito internacional público*, cit., p. 253-255. Also see Caviedes, Antonio Poch de, De la clause *rebus sic stantibus* à la clause de révision dans les conventions internationales, *Recueil des Cours*, vol. 118 (1966-II), p. 105-208; and Haraszti, György, Treaties and the fundamental change of circumstances, *Recueil des Cours*, vol. 146 (1975-III), p. 1-94.

361 On this topic, see the criticism of De La Guardia, Ernesto, *Derecho de los tratados internacionales*, cit., p. 310-311, with a transcription of the explanation by Michel Taube: "It refers, above all, to the opinion of legal scholars on the clause *sic stantibus* which, during modern times, it is said to provide invaluable services to whom, in theory or practice, wishes to get rid of the absolute consequences of the fundamental principle of inviolability of treaties".

For the first time, the ICJ interpreted *fundamental change of circumstances* following Art. 62 of the Vienna Convention, in a judicial order dated February 2, 1973, concerning a *Fisheries Jurisdiction Case* (Germany v. Iceland). At that time, the court admitted that Art. 62 could be considered "a codification of customary law existing with regard to the termination of treaty relations by virtue of a change of circumstances" (item 36).

To invoke a fundamental change of circumstances as a ground to terminate the treaty, the following conditions are required, as provided in Art. 62, item 1, of the Convention: *a*) the change should affect circumstances, whether *factual* or *legal*, existing *at the time of the conclusion* of the treaty;[362] *b*) the existence of those circumstances should constitute a *material basis* for the consent of the parties to be bound by the treaty; without which the treaty would not have been concluded; *c*) the change of the circumstances has not been foreseen by the parties (even though it was foreseeable…) at the time of execution of the treaty; that is to say, failure of the parties to foresee those circumstances suffices, the *unpredictability* of such circumstances not being required;[363] *d*) the change of circumstances should be *fundamental* on the scope of the obligations of the parties, not just an insignificant detail; *e*) the new scenario under these circumstances should *radically transform* the obligations of the parties, obliging them (one or another) excessively compared to the original provisions; in this case, it is not required that performance of the treaty should become *impossible* as a result of the change of circumstances (in which case Art. 61 would also be applicable), but it should become *excessively onerous* for any of the parties; and, finally, *f*) the fundamental change of circumstances should refer to the obligations still *to be performed* in accordance with the treaty, and not to obligations already performed.[364]

Obviously, alleging a fundamental change of circumstances will be useless if the treaty contains a denunciation clause, or if denunciation is

---

362 See Caviedes, Antonio Poch de. De la clause *rebus sic stantibus* à la clause de révision dans les conventions internationales, cit., p. 170.

363 In this case, the parties must prove that despite being *foreseeable* at that time to any other individuals, the truth is that the parties could not foresee (for specific, determined, particular reasons, etc.) a future change of such circumstances.

364 On such conditions, see Balladore Pallieri, G. *Diritto internazionale pubblico*, cit., p. 282-287; Calsing, Maria de Assis, *O tratado internacional e sua aplicação no Brasil*, cit., p. 68-69; Remiro Brotons, Antonio, *Derecho internacional público*, vol. 2, cit., p. 486-488; De La Guardia, Ernesto, *Derecho de los tratados internacionales*, cit., p. 320; Reuter, Paul, *Introducción al derecho de los tratados*, cit. P. 218-222; and Villiger, Mark E., *Commentary on the 1969 Vienna Convention on the Law of Treaties*, cit., p. 771-776.

inferred from the intention of the parties or the nature of the treaty, under the terms of Art. 56 of the Convention (see item 3.1.2.1, above). Therefore, in practice, alleging a fundamental change of circumstances would be indispensable only relating to treaties which cannot be denounced due to its nature, or which contain clauses of termination or denunciation not applicable immediately (such as, for instance, treaties authorizing termination or denunciation, but only after a given period of time, before which the circumstances could suffer a fundamental change, turning performance of the agreement excessively onerous to any of the parties…).[365]

The Vienna Convention introduces two cases in which it *is not possible* to invoke a fundamental change of circumstances as a means to terminate a treaty or withdraw from it. Which are they? The answer is expressed in Art. 62, item 2, of the Convention, as follows: *a*) if the treaty establishes a boundary; or *b*) if the fundamental change is the result of a breach by the party invoking it either of an obligation under the treaty or of any other international obligation owed to any other party to the treaty.

The first case relates to treaties establishing *territorial limits*,[366] which cannot be terminated by invoking a fundamental change of circumstances.[367] Some authors, like Remiro Brotons, however, wonder if this rule should be applicable only to *still pending* treaties regulating territorial cessions or delimitations, or boundary demarcation, since, if it were not the case, "it would be difficult to imagine how abstention and surveillance duties arising from the execution of such obligations may be modified by a change of circumstances, once cession, delimitation and the corresponding demarcation have already been completed".[368] The *de facto* pur-

---

365 See Remiro Brotons, Antonio. *Derecho internacional público*, vol. 2, cit., p. 488.

366 It should be noted that the French version of the Convention uses the word *boundary*, and not *limits* as the English, German, Portuguese texts, etc. ("… s'il s'agit d'un traité établissant une *frontière*").

367 On this topic, note the following comment by Rezek: "Item *a* of the second paragraph of article 62 of the Vienna Convention refers obviously to all dispositive treaties, or those with static effectiveness. Unfortunately, drafters of the text only mentioned the most obvious type among such gender: the treaty of limits. An unwary interpreter could then have, *a contrario sensu*, the abstruse idea that a fundamental change of circumstances may, in principle, be invoked as a ground for termination of a convention on onerous territorial cession, like the French-American Louisiana Purchase Treaty of May 3, 1803" (*Direito dos tratados*, cit., p. 521).

368 Remiro Brotons, Antonio. *Derecho internacional público*, vol. 2, cit., p. 489. Celso de Albuquerque Mello also explains that: "The clause would be applied to perpetual treaties,

pose of the exception provided for in Art. 62, item 2, of the Convention should also be questioned. There is no doubt that the purpose of including such rule (which excludes the clause *rebus sic stantibus* of treaties fixing territorial limits) was preserving the *stability* of such limits.[369] But it is well known that the provision under analysis was the result of mainly political reasons, very well defended by the powers which dominated a great part of territories all over the world, and it is clear that they did not want to lose all their conquers. That is why many States (for instance, Afghanistan, Morocco, etc.) declared that Art. 62, item 2, *a*, does not apply to "unequal or unlawful treaties, or any other treaties contrary to the principle of self-determination";[370] consequently, taking into account that self-determination is a norm of *jus cogens*, the problem raised (on how to declare the invalidity of or how terminate a treaty on limits) would be solved by invoking Arts. 53 or 64 of the Convention... The second case analyzed in Art. 62, item 2, *mutatis mutandis*, repeats the precept according to which *nemo auditur propriam turpitudinem allegans*, already established by Art. 61, item 2 (see item 3.1.3.2, above), forbidding the allegation of a fundamental change of circumstances when said change results from a breach, *by the invoking party*, of an obligation arising from the treaty, or of any other international obligation in connection with any other party to the treaty.

---

treaties 'under implementation' (in which execution extends in time, that is, they are not executed at once) and treaties with a term (if the term is short and there is little possibility to apply the clause). Generally, it is applied to treaties-agreements, but nothing prevents it from being applied to treaties-laws" (*Curso de direito internacional público*, vol. I, cit., p. 261-262).

369 In that regard, see Bardonnet, Daniel, Frontières terrestres et frontières maritimes, *Annuaire Français de Droit International*, vol. 35 (1989), p. 56, according to whom: "La justification d'une telle exception à la règle de la caducité instituée par ces deux dispositions [the author speaks about *two provisions* because the 1969 Vienna Convention also provides an identical rule] est évidente. En effet, s'il en était autrement, comme l'a souligné la Commission du droit international dans son commentaire, 'au lieu d'être un instrument d'évolution pacifique, la règle pourrait devenir la cause de dangereux froissements'. C'est qu'en effet, en dernière analyse, au regard de cet article 62, 'l'effet de la qualité de «frontière» est un effet stabilisateur'". See also Villiger, Mark E. *Commentary on the 1969 Vienna Convention on the Law of Treaties*, cit., p. 775-776.

370 See *interpretative statements* of this provision and other provisions of the Convention in Annex IV to this book.

3.1.3.4 Severance of diplomatic or consular relations

The 1969 Convention, in a very simple rule, provides that severance of diplomatic or consular relations between parties to a treaty "does not affect the legal relations established between them by the treaty except in so far as the existence of diplomatic or consular relations is *indispensable* for the application of the treaty" (Art. 63).[371] So, we should not say that severance of diplomatic or consular relations between *A* and *B* (for whatever reason) may affect the relations connected to, for example, human rights established between the parties by a specific protective treaty. But, in the case of treaties of cooperation regarding military matters, it seems clear that it is *indispensable* to maintain diplomatic or consular relations for the correct application of the treaty between the same parties. In summary, a treaty between the parties will be affected, or not, by severance of diplomatic or consular relations depending on whether such relations are indispensable for the treaty application.

The spirit that encouraged the Vienna Convention to draft Art. 63 is visibly related to the matter of indispensability of maintaining friendly relations between the Nations, even though they may be affected by the severance of diplomatic or consular relations. That is why the Convention provided that treaties will continue in force between States with severed diplomatic or consular relations, except when such relations are *indispensable* for the application of the agreement. In relation to this, it should be highlighted that, nowadays, severance of diplomatic or consular relations is many times symbolic, implying less severe effects, both from a legal and the economic point of view.[372] In such regard, as the case may be, severance of a given diplomatic or consular relation, which, *a priori*, would be "indispensable" for the application of a treaty, may even be insufficient to affect the legal relations established between the parties by means of the agreement.

Severance or absence of diplomatic or consular relations between two or more States does not prevent the conclusion of treaties between those States, as set forth by Art. 74 of the Convention.[373] According to this provision, the conclusion of a treaty, *per se*, "does not produce effects on diplo-

---

371 See Villiger, Mark E. *Commentary on the 1969 Vienna Convention on the Law of Treaties*, cit., p. 784-789.

372 See Dinh, Daillier & Pellet. *Direito internacional público*, cit., p. 759.

373 See Villiger, Mark E. *Commentary on the 1969 Vienna Convention on the Law of Treaties*, cit., p. 908-909.

matic or consular relations".[374] Therefore, two States with severed diplomatic or consular relations *may* execute, between them, a specific international agreement (especially a treaty conducive to *recover* the diplomatic or consular relations between them); in the same way, States that *do not* maintain diplomatic or consular relations between them *may* conclude treaties between them. It shows that maintaining, or not maintaining, diplomatic or consular relations between two or more States does not affect, *a priori*, treaties concluded by such powers, except (in the specific case of *severance* of diplomatic or consular relations, not in the case of mere *absence* of such relations) in so far as the existence of diplomatic or consular relations is indispensable for the application of the treaty (Art. 63).

3.1.3.5 State of war

The 1969 Vienna Convention did not even mention the effects of *war* on international treaties. The Convention only stated that its provisions do not affect "any matter that may arise in connection with a treaty by virtue (…) of the *outbreak of hostilities* between States" (Art. 73; Art. 74, item 1, of the 1986 Convention). This does not, however, prevent the study of this phenomenon, and does not exclude *war* as a ground for termination of international acts.[375] However, it should be pointed out that the issue regarding the effects of war on treaties is more closely related to *suspension* of treaty execution than to treaty *termination* (see item 3.2.3, below).

Some treaties executed between States are *immune* to war, like treaties with static effectiveness, treaties equivalent to a *legal title*, treaties relating to loans, and obviously, treaties exactly prepared to be in effect during the period of belligerence, like The Hague Conventions of 1899 and 1907, and The Geneva Conventions of 1949. The latter, for instance,

---

374 Art. 74 originated in a proposal by Chile, which reads as follows: "Severance or absence of diplomatic or consular relations between two or more States will not prevent the conclusion of treaties between those States. The conclusion of a treaty does not, *per se*, affect the status of diplomatic or consular relations". See De La Guardia, Ernesto. *Derecho de los tratados internacionales*, cit., p. 302-303.

375 On this topic, see McNair, Arnold Duncan, Les effets de la guerre sur les traités, *Recueil des Cours*, vol. 59 (1937-I), p. 523-585. McNair had also analyzed the subject – "effects of war on treaties" – in the above referred study "La terminaison et la dissolution des traités" (*Recueil des Cours*, vol. 22, p. 496-512). About the effects of war on treaties, also see Wheaton, Henry, *Elements of international law*, vol. I, cit., p. 508-509. For a view on the impact of war on general International Law, see Del Vecchio, Giorgio, *El derecho internacional y el problema de la paz*, Barcelona: Boch, 1959, p. 68-151.

provide that denunciation made during the period of hostilities will be considered as such only after termination of said period.[376] In particular, treaties on protection of human rights (including environment protection instruments) and treaties creating international organizations fall under this category.[377] On the other hand, there are treaties which may be terminated (or suspended) between the opposing States during the period of war, which makes the issue to be analyzed on a case-by-case basis.

The general rule is that war, today considered by the UN Charter an international unlawful act, causes the termination of bilateral treaties (which are commonly *treaties-agreement*) between States in conflict, such as treaties relating to protections, alliances, guarantees, subsidies, and, in general, treaties with a political nature. The same rule is applied to agreements whose object or purpose is maintaining or consolidating peaceful relations between two States. The *attacked, never the aggressor*, State is entitled to request termination (or suspension) of the treaty under analysis. In turn, multilateral treaties (in general, *treaties-law*) are *suspended* between opposing belligerent States during the conflict, but they continue to operate normally (*a*) between belligerent States and neutral States, or (*b*) among neutral States.[378] Again, the *attacked* State is entitled to request suspension. However, such suspension will be possible only if the treaty under analysis is *mutalizable*, that is, treaties that may not be invalidated as a result of their non-execution by one or some States (see Part I, Ch. 2, item 2.2.4, above).

In practice, the problem arises with *undeclared* wars In contemporary practice, this situation produces the mere *suspension* of bilateral treaties during the conflict. It is different in the case of *declared* wars, whose effect, in said bilateral treaties, is always *termination*. Upon suspension of the bilateral treaty, there commonly follows abrogation or denunciation, which shows that war alone is not enough to terminate a treaty. This is what happened with denunciation of a treaty dated 1965 executed by Argentina on scheduled airline flights, as well as with the

---

376 See Art. 63 (paragraph 3) of the First Geneva Convention 1949: "(...) Should the denouncing Power be involved in a conflict, the denunciation will not take effect until peace has been concluded, or even, where applicable, until the release and repatriation of protected persons is complete".

377 As decided by the *Institut de Droit International*, in its 1985 Helsinki meeting, at which Mr. Bengt Broms was Rapporteur ("Les effets des conflits armés sur les traités", Arts. 4 and 6).

378 See Rezek, José Francisco. *Direito dos tratados*, cit., p. 511-512.

Cultural Convention of 1961, both adopted with the United Kingdom due to the Falkland Islands war.[379]

Many times war is not, *by itself*, the ground for termination or suspension of a treaty, being, however, the *triggering event* of one of them. In fact, war may cause the impossibility (final or temporary) of performance of a treaty or a fundamental change of circumstances, in which case the rules already analyzed on those matters should be followed (see items 3.1.3.2 and 3.1.3.3, above).

3.1.3.6 Disuse (obsolete)

The Vienna Convention (as already noted) does not provide for all the ways of termination of treaties. Another common way of terminating treaty rules, not mentioned by the Convention, is the so called *disuse*.[380] As it may happen with any legal rules, treaties can also cease to be applied and fall into oblivion. In many cases, there are treaties which become obsolete with the lapse of time, and the States that are parties to said treaties deliberately cease to use them, and their performance is not demanded by any means.

A treaty may fall in *disuse* when a supervening *international custom* originates, since there is no hierarchy between conventional and customary rules.[381] But it may also fall in disuse when the parties *no longer use* it, and there is not any subsequent customary modification of understanding, etc. There are many changes of circumstances that can reveal a mutual lack of interest of the parties on the agreed regime, causing the treaty to fall in complete obsolescence.

Diplomatic practice has shown a wide acceptance of the possibility of treaties being terminated by disuse. The cases of agreements with the Saint Alliance (1815) and the German-Soviet of Brest-Litovsk (1918) terminated by *disuse*.[382] Finally, it should be noted that disuse occurs more easily (but not exclusively) in *bilateral* treaties.[383]

---

379 See Rezek, José Francisco. Idem, p. 514-515.

380 See McNair, Arnold Duncan. La terminaison et la dissolution des traités, cit., p. 465-467; Vamvoukos, Athanassios, *Termination of treaties in international law*..., cit., p. 221-229; and De La Guardia, Ernesto, *Derecho de los tratados internacionales*, cit., p. 298.

381 See Mazzuoli, Valerio de Oliveira. *Curso de direito internacional público*, cit., p. 135-136.

382 See Remiro Brotons, Antonio. *Derecho internacional público*, vol. 2, cit., p. 472.

383 See De La Guardia, Ernesto. *Derecho de los tratados internacionales*, cit., p. 298.

3.2 Suspension of the operation of treaties

Suspension of the application (execution) of a treaty has the effect of *provisionally interrupting* its performance.[384] The topic is closely related to *termination* of treaties, which we have seen above (see item 3.1, above), to such an extent that the 1969 Convention (and also the 1986 Convention) deals with them jointly.[385] However, the events triggering both institutes are not *completely similar*; there are reasons (like the survival of a norm of *jus cogens*) which inexorably lead to the *termination* of treaties (Art. 64), while other factors (for instance, *temporary* impossibility of performance) only lead to their *suspension* (Art. 61, item 1, *in fine*).

The possibility of *suspending* the operation of a treaty was the feasible alternative found by the Vienna text for the consequences (always more severe) resulting from *termination* of international acts. However, unlike the last case, suspension always presumes a *temporary* interruption of the effects of all or some clauses of the agreement, ceasing to operate when the circumstances which encouraged it disappeared or when the will which caused it was altered.

First, it should be pointed out that suspension of the operation of a treaty may only be exercised in connection with the *whole* treaty, except as otherwise provided by the instrument or the parties (Art. 44, item 1); also a ground for suspension recognized by the Vienna Convention should be alleged in connection with the *whole* treaty, except in the conditions provided for under items 3 and 4 of Art. 44 or in Art. 60.

In this topic, we will study suspension of treaties *by the agreement of the parties* (item 3.2.1), suspension by *unilateral will* (item 3.2.2) and *extrinsic grounds for suspension* (item 3.2.3). However, as the 1969 Convention analyzed termination and suspension of treaties jointly, that will not be repeated here because it was already studied in relation to termination of international acts (whose comprehension is used for this study). In a separate Chapter, we will study the *procedure* of suspension (also common to *termination* of treaties) and its specific *consequences* (see below, Ch. 4, items 4.1 and 4.2.3, respectively).

---

384 On this subject, see ILC, *Yearbook of the International Law Commission* (1966), vol. II, p. 251-255; Capotorti, Francesco, L'extinction et la suspension des traités, cit., p. 473-558; and Remiro Brotons, Antonio, *Derecho internacional público*, vol. 2, cit., p. 509-524.

385 See Capotorti, Francesco. L'extinction et la suspension des traités, cit., p. 467.

3.2.1 Suspension by the agreement of the parties

The parties are free to agree how and when a treaty may be suspended. Such agreement may be already expressed *in the text* of the treaty or arise from a *later agreement* between all the parties, after consultation with the other contracting States. Art. 57 of the Vienna Convention provides that the operation of a treaty in regard to all the parties or a particular party may be suspended (*a*) in conformity with the provisions of the treaty, or (*b*) at any time by consent of all the parties after consultation with the other contracting States. Both cases deal with the suspension of the operation of a treaty *expressly* provided for (either under the treaty itself or by a later agreement) by the contracting States. With regard to the conclusion of a later treaty, the *implicit* agreement of the parties is also possible for the purpose of suspending the earlier treaty, as set forth in Art. 59, item 2, of the Convention (see below).

There are no further doubts when the treaty itself provides for its suspension, regarding all the parties or a particular party (Art. 57, *a*).[386] However, this is not a common practice. The most common cases relating to suspension of the operation of treaties normally result from the conclusion of a later treaty, which, under the terms of the Convention, may be *express* (Art. 57, *b*) or *implied* (Art. 59, item 2) in such regard. In the last case, the Convention provides that it is possible to suspend an earlier treaty when " it appears from the later treaty" or even "otherwise", i.e., the *real intention* of the parties It is interesting to note that the Convention has not, contrary to what it did in the case of *termination* of treaties by later agreement (see item 3.1.1.2.2, above), dealt with the third possible case of suspension, relating to a later *tacit* agreement between the parties (arising from the absolute incompatibility of applying two treaties on the same subject-matter). Therefore, while termination of a treaty may be express, implied or *tacit*, suspension of its operation (as it seems) will only be express or implied (*tacit* suspension has not been included).[387]

---

[386] The UN Charter, for instance, provides that a State may be *suspended* from exercising membership rights and privileges by the General Assembly upon the recommendation of the Security Council, if any "preventive or enforcement action has been taken by the Security Council" against said State, granting the Council the power to *restore* the "exercise of these rights and privileges" (Art. 5).

[387] See Remiro Brotons, Antonio. *Derecho internacional público*, vol. 2, cit., p. 511. According to Brotons, such omission was "improper, because there are cases (*ad ex.*, when the later treaty sets forth a limited duration or was executed for an exceptional circumstance)

In addition, nothing prevents *some parties* only from concluding a particular agreement to temporarily suspend the execution of the provisions of a multilateral treaty between them. But this will only be possible (under the terms of Art. 58 of the Convention) if: *a*) the possibility of such a suspension is provided for by the treaty; or *b*) the suspension in question is not prohibited by the treaty and (*i*) does not affect the enjoyment by the other parties of their rights under the treaty or the performance of their obligations; and (*ii*) is not incompatible with the object and purpose of the treaty.

Unless the treaty otherwise provides, the parties in question will notify the other parties of their intention to conclude the agreement and of those provisions of the treaty the operation of which they intend to suspend (Art. 58, item 2). As we can see, Art. 58 of the Convention reflects, with little variation, the provisions of Art. 41, relating to agreements to modify multilateral treaties between some parties, known as "agreements *inter se*" (see in this Part III, Ch. 1, item 1.4.2, above).[388] The ILC justified the rule stating that both situations are analogous.[389]

3.2.2 Suspension by unilateral will

The 1969 and 1986 Vienna Conventions do not even mention the case of suspension of a treaty by unilateral will of the parties. Only *Termination* by unilateral will (denunciation) was set forth by the Vienna texts (Art. 56). Would there be, however, a justifiable reason forbidding the unmotivated suspension of a treaty in the same case and conditions established for denunciation set forth in Art. 56? If suspension of a treaty

---

in which suspension may give a more satisfactory solution than termination, and, therefore, it should not be understood as peremptory" (Idem, p. 511-512).

388 See Capotorti, Francesco. L'extinction et la suspension des traités, cit., p. 510; Sinclair, Ian, *The Vienna Convention on the Law of Treaties*, cit., p. 185; De La Guardia, Ernesto, *Derecho de los tratados internacionales*, cit., p. 322; and Villiger, Mark E., *Commentary on the 1969 Vienna Convention on the Law of Treaties*, cit., p. 716-717.

389 See ILC, *Yearbook of the International Law Commission* (1966), vol. II, p. 252, as follows: "At the present session the Commission considered that the question is analogous to that raised by the *inter se* modification of multilateral treaties but that, as the situation is not identical in the two cases, the *inter se* suspension of the operation of a treaty could not be completely equated with its inter se modification. The Commission decided that it was desirable to deal with it in the present article and to attach to it the safeguards necessary to protect the position of other parties".

is understood as an *alternative* to its termination, the answer must be negative.[390]

Cui licet quod est plus, licet utique quod est minus ("He who can do more can do less"). Therefore, if a State may unilaterally disengage from a treaty by means of denunciation (*the most…*), in identical conditions, it may also unilaterally *suspend* the operation of the agreement (*…the least*). With this understanding, the spirit of the Convention which considers suspension of the operation of treaties as a feasible alternative for its termination is preserved (always implying more severe consequences than the other one), while the States are secured the *right* to continue operating the treaty in the future, after the suspension period.

3.2.3 Extrinsic grounds for suspension

As it occurs with termination of treaties, there are also *extrinsic* grounds for suspension of international acts which operate beyond the provisions of the treaty or of the later agreement of the parties.[391]

Such extrinsic grounds that may suspend the operation of a treaty are, in principle, *material breach of a treaty* (Art. 60), *supervening impossibility of performance* (Art. 61) and *fundamental change of circumstances* (Art. 62, item 3).

The material breach of a treaty and the fundamental change of circumstances are factors that always imply the suspension of the treaty as an option for the party to terminate the treaty. The principle of *conservation* of treaties, whose spirit pervades the whole 1969 Convention, also leads to the conclusion that suspension is the best alternative to terminate a particular international act in these cases.

With regard to the supervening impossibility of performance, the meaning of the rule provided for by the Convention is authorizing the *suspension* of the agreement only when the impossibility is *temporary* (Art. 61, item 1, *in fine*), since, in the event of a *permanent* impossibility, the parties may invoke it exclusively as a ground for *terminating* the treaty or *withdrawing* from it. The purpose of the Convention is to differentiate the consequences of permanent impossibility of performance

---

390 In that very sense, see Remiro Brotons, Antonio, *Derecho internacional público*, vol. 2, cit., p. 513.

391 See Remiro Brotons, Antonio. Idem, p. 512-513.

(in which case *termination* of the treaties applies) from temporary impossibility (in which case only *suspension* is possible).

However, the grounds listed above do not exhaust the possibilities of suspending a treaty beyond the agreement of the parties. Such are the cases, for example, of severance of diplomatic or consular relations whose existence is *indispensable* for the application of the treaty (Art. 63 – see item 3.1.3.4, above) and state of war. The latter case also is more closely related to the topic of *suspension* of treaties than to *termination* (see item 3.1.3.5, above).[392]

3.2.4 Suspension of treaties and the Brazilian Law

The constitutional rule pursuant to which "he National Congress shall have exclusive powers to decide definitively on international treaties, agreements or acts that result in charges or commitments encumbering the national patrimony" (Art. 49, I, Federal Constitution/88) is equally applied to *suspension* of the application of treaties. It will be duly studied in detail (see Part V, Ch. 1, item 1.5.2, below) that the reference to "*severe* charges or commitments encumbering the national patrimony", as set forth in Art. 49, I, *in fine*, of the Constitution, will be interpreted along with Art. 84, VIII, of the said Charter, which submits *all* treaties executed by Brazil to the approval of the Congress. For the time being, it suffices to say that *any* treaty which the Brazilian Government intends to suspend (and not only those implying such "severe charges or commitments encumbering the national patrimony") will be previously submitted to the approval of the Legislative Power, which, supporting the will of the Executive, authorizes the *suspension* under analysis. In practice, it is true that many States completely forget rules such as the rule of Art. 49, I, of the Brazilian Constitution, especially in situations in which suspension of a particular treaty is held as an *emergency* measure. In any case, in Brazil, congressional authorization is *mandatory* for the Executive to operate the intended suspension, except in cases in which ratification of the treaty under analysis (whose operation is now intended to suspend) has not required the prior consultation with the Parliament.

Publishing the suspension of the operation of a treaty in the *Official Gazette of the Union* immediately prevents the powers of State (Legislative, Executive and Judicial) from continuing applying the treaty. Upon

---

392 For further details, see Remiro Brotons, Antonio, Idem, p. 518-524.

termination of the suspension term (if any) or upon revocation of said suspension, the treaty operation will continue in the whole national territory and it must again be performed by the powers of the State and by individuals.

Chapter 4

Procedure to be Followed with respect to Defects, Invalidity, Termination or Suspension

In the previous Chapters, we have already analyzed defects of consent and of the treaty itself (Ch. 2) and the means of termination, withdrawal or suspension of the operation of treaties (Ch. 3). Now, we must verify *the procedure* for a State (or international organization) to invoke such defects, invalidity, *means* of treaty termination or suspension of its operation. Such means of invoking a defect of consent by any State to be bound by a treaty or a ground for invalidating the treaty itself, terminating it, withdrawing from it or suspending its application were provided for by the Vienna Convention in Section 4 of Part V, under the headline *Process* (which is better called *Procedure*). Such rules are expressed in Arts. 65 to 68 (and in the *Annex*) of the Convention. In Section 5, of said Part V, in turn, the Convention dealt with the *consequences* of vitiated consent, invalidity, termination and suspension of the operation of a treaty (Arts. 69 to 72).

4.1 Procedure relating to defects in consent, invalidity, termination, withdrawal or suspension of the operation of a treaty

In this topic we will study in detail the procedure relating to defects and invalidity provided for in the 1969 Vienna Convention (item 4.1.1), and also followed by the 1986 Convention. However, the 1986 Convention introduces certain characteristics which deserved some comprehension, and they will be analyzed in a separate subject (item 4.1.2).

Before starting to study the subject, a remark should be made: when the Convention establishes the procedure relating to treaty defects, it expressly leaves out (when stating that "*nothing* in the foregoing paragraphs shall affect…") the rights or obligations of the parties "under any provisions in force binding the parties with regard to the settlement of disputes" (Art. 65, item 4).[393] This means that a *specific* provision of a particular treaty on the settlement of disputes *prevails* over the rules of the Vienna text, and the parties will have to follow what *they* have established in another instrument by themselves. In other words, the rules of the Convention are *supplementary* to the will of the parties, which will always prevail (in case of *termination*, *suspension*, etc.) if there is a conflict with any rule established by the Convention. Now, we will follow with the procedure relating to defects and invalidity.

4.1.1 Procedure under the 1969 Vienna Convention

The procedure relating to defects of consent, invalidity, termination, withdrawal or suspension of the operation of a treaty is governed by Art. 65 of the 1969 Vienna Convention.[394] Under the provisions of item 1 of Art. 65, a party which "invokes either a defect in its consent to be bound by a treaty or a ground for impeaching the validity of a treaty, terminating it, withdrawing from it or suspending its operation, must notify the other parties of its claim [in *writing*, under the terms of Art. 67, item 1]", and the notification will indicate "the measure proposed to be taken with respect to the treaty and the reasons therefor".[395] This procedure is valid for all cases of invalidity or termination of a treaty set forth by the Convention,[396] including the unmotivated denunciation regulated under Art. 56.[397] Only a *material breach* of a treaty follows a specific procedure which is different from the procedures studied in this Chapter (see Ch. 3, item 3.1.3.1, above).

---

393 At the 1986 Convention, see Art. 65, item 5.

394 See Ronzitti, Natalino. La disciplina dello *jus cogens* nella Convenzione di Vienna sul Diritto dei Trattati, cit., p. 267-268; De La Guardia, Ernesto, *Derecho de los tratados internacionales*, cit., p. 327-334; Fiorati, Jete Jane, Jus cogens..., cit., p. 67-68; Gómez Robledo, Antonio, *El* ius cogens *internacional...*, cit., p. 136-140; Friedrich, Tatyana Scheila, *As normas imperativas de direito internacional público* jus cogens, cit., p. 38-39; and Villiger, Mark E., *Commentary on the 1969 Vienna Convention on the Law of Treaties*, cit., p. 803-815. For a report on discussions on Art. 65 at the ILC, see Remiro Brotons, Antonio, *Derecho internacional público*, vol. 2, cit., p. 449-451.

395 See Ronzitti, Natalino. La disciplina dello *jus cogens* nella Convenzione di Vienna sul Diritto dei Trattati, cit., p. 272-273.

396 Only a *material breach* of a multilateral treaty is submitted to a *special* regime of invalidity, since in this case the *unanimous* agreement of the parties is required, excluding the presumed defaulting party (Art. 60, item 2).

397 On this case, see an explanation in Ch. 3, item 3.1.2.1, above.

As we can see, the 1969 Convention *authorized* the parties to invoke a defect in the consent or in the treaty itself based *on the belief* that either the consent or the treaty has any defect, but with the obligation to *notify* their claim to other parties, also indicating in the notification (with the *reasons* therefor) the measure proposed to be taken with respect to the treaty. Therefore, for the Convention, this is how the parties exercise their *right* to invoke a particular treaty defect.

It should be highlighted that any *of the parties* which consider themselves *victims* of a particular treaty defect are entitled to *invoke* a defect in consent or any invalidity of the treaty, for the purpose of invalidating such consent or the treaty itself. At least, with regard to *invalidity of consent*, the Convention is clear on conferring legitimacy to the *affected* party for such invocation (Arts. 46 to 50). However, both in the case of *invalidity of consent* (sole case under Art. 51, see Ch. 2, item 2.1.2, above) and in the case of invalidity *of treaties* itself (Arts. 52 and 53), the Convention does not limit the right to invoke such invalidity to any particular subject, as they are cases relating to the *international public* policy; in these cases, Remiro Brotons says, "any party to a treaty would be legitimated to start a procedure of invalidity, including, though very unlikely, the author of the unlawful act, whose responsibility would anyway remain undamaged".[398] In particular, when a new norm of *jus cogens* (Art. 53) is at stake, any of the parties has the *obligation* to start a procedure of invalidity of the treaty as provided in Art. 65 *et seq*. In any case, the truth is that only *the parties* to the treaty are entitled (whether they are the *damaged party* or not, as the case may be) to invoke one of the treaty defects; *third parties* are not allowed to do so.

Once again, it should be pointed out that the *claim* of a party to prove any of the defects mentioned will be *founded* with an explanation of the measure proposed to be taken with respect to the treaty; the Convention is clear on binding the party invoking a defect to prove the "reasons therefor", through the referred *notification*. The Convention was right on requesting such notification from the State which is considered a victim or damaged by virtue of any defect in the treaty; in this way, the other parties are guaranteed that the State alleging a defect is acting seriously with regard to its purposes.

If after *three months* of the receipt of notification, no party has raised any objection, the Convention states that the State making the notification may take "the measure which it has proposed" (Art. 65, item 2). Such

---

398 Remiro Brotons, Antonio. *Derecho internacional público*, vol. 2, cit., p. 451.

measure will be taken as provided for in Art. 67, which requires that the other parties be notified by means of an *instrument* (see below). However, Art. 65, item 2 provides for an exception to the three month period when the case is of "special urgency"; in this case, the damaged State may take the measure proposed in the notification. The problem is that the Convention does not explain the meaning of "special emergency", so it seems that the meanings of "special" and "emergency" have been left at the discretion of the parties.[399] However, nothing prevents that an intention (of emergency) evidently contrary to reason (that is, not special) may be invalidated or not recognized by the ICJ in any judicial dispute.

Except the case of special emergency, before the three month' notice, *nothing* may be done to release the notifying State from performing the treaty; the treaty may not even be *suspended* (since notification of a treaty defect is not among the extrinsic grounds for suspension of treaties).[400] The only legal possibility would be that the notifying State may obtain the express acceptance of *all* the parties to the agreement to release the notifying State from performance. Save for this exceptional case, the damaged State may only take the measure proposed if there are no *objections* by any of the other parties within the term of three months after receipt of the notification.

Upon expiration of the three month period with no objections, the notifying State then formally *declares* the defect or the invalidity of the treaty, being entitled to take the measure proposed in the notification. How is such statement materialized? According to the Convention, any act declaring the invalidity, termination, withdrawal or suspension of the operation of a treaty, under the provisions of the treaty or of items 2 and 3 of Art. 65, will be materialized by means of an *instrument* to notify the other parties. Such instrument will be signed by the Head of State, Head of Government or by the Minister of Foreign Affairs; if this is not the case, the representative of the State who delivered the notification may be invited to produce full powers (Art. 67, item 2). In countries like Brazil, the instrument formalization will be preceded by a Congress *referendum*, as it happens with denunciation (see Ch. 3, item 3.1.2.2, above).

Nothing prevents, however, both the *notification* (delivered by the State alleging a defect in a treaty, Art. 65) and the *instrument* (which ef-

---

399 According to Villiger: "Such cases could be, *inter alia*, the sudden and serious breach of a treaty (*Article 60, q.v.*) or where unexpectedly a treaty can no longer be performed (*Article 61, q.v.*)" (*Commentary on the 1969 Vienna Convention on the Law of Treaties*, cit., p. 809).

400 See Remiro Brotons, Antonio. *Derecho internacional público*, vol. 2, cit., p. 452.

fects the measure proposed in the notification, Art. 67) from being *revoked* by the State at any time, before they take effect (Art. 68). It should be pointed out that revocation should operate before the notification or instrument takes effect; *after* the other parties (*a*) receive the notification or instrument, or (*b*) start measures (for instance, of a legislative nature) to consider the treaty terminated with regard to the requesting State, it will no longer be possible to revoke the notification or instrument.[401] Consequently, this is a kind of preclusion that exhausts the legal effects of the act that the party intends to revoke. Nevertheless, the Convention is silent on the *ways* of revocation; thus, any way is valid, and it should not be similar to the act intended to be revoked. It should also be highlighted that the possibility of revoking the notification or instrument clearly shows that the Convention decided for the *conservation* of treaties,[402] being the declarations of consent or treaty invalidity *exceptions* in the Vienna text.

If *objections* have been raised, within a three month's period as from receipt of the notification, item 3 of Art. 65 states that "the parties *shall* seek a solution through the means indicated in Art. 33 of the Charter of the United Nations", as follows:

> "Article 33 (Chapter VI – *Pacific settlement of disputes*):
>
> 1. The parties to any dispute, the continuance of which is likely to endanger the maintenance of international peace and security, shall, first of all, seek a solution by negotiation, enquiry, mediation, conciliation, arbitration, judicial settlement, resort to regional agencies or arrangements, or other peaceful means of their own choice.
>
> 2. The Security Council shall, when it deems necessary, call upon the parties to settle their dispute by such means".[403]

---

[401] See Villiger, Mark E. *Commentary on the 1969 Vienna Convention on the Law of Treaties*, cit., p. 848, as follows: "Revocation is thus only possible: (*i*) until the other party has received the notification or instrument (which will normally be within a few days); and, cumulatively, (*ii*) until the other party has started undertaking measures, *e.g.*, initiating domestic legal changes, in view of the imminent termination or suspension of the treaty (which may also happen relatively soon). It is irrelevant here whether the claimant State has undertaken any measures. Any other States parties which followed the first State and also gave notification of termination or withdrawal are, under the conditions of Article 68, equally free to revoke their notification or instrument".

[402] See Remiro Brotons, Antonio. *Derecho internacional público*, vol. 2, cit., p. 453.

[403] For a detailed study of such means of dispute settlement, see Mazzuoli, Valerio de Oliveira, *Curso de direito internacional público*, cit., p. 1133-1172.

The dispute between the parties will be settled within *twelve months* as from the date of the objection filed. In no solution has been reached within a period of 12 months following the date on which the objection was raised, the following procedures shall be followed (art 66):

a) any one of the parties to a dispute concerning the application or the interpretation of Arts. 53 or 64 [relating to the pre-existing and supervening *jus cogens*, respectively] may, by a written application, submit it to the International Court of Justice for a decision unless the parties by common consent agree to submit the dispute to arbitration;

b) any one of the parties to a dispute concerning the application or the interpretation of any of the other articles in Part V of the present Convention [Arts. 42 to 72, except for Arts. 53 and 64] may set in motion the procedure specified in the *Annex* to the Convention by submitting a request to that effect to the Secretary-General of the United Nations [the referred *Annex* provides for a procedure of *conciliation* of the parties, followed by a commission of conciliation].[404]

> It should be pointed out that Brazil ratified the 1969 Vienna Convention with a *reservation* to Art. 66, not accepting the subsidiary jurisdiction of the ICJ in the case of norms of *jus cogens* (Art. 66, *a*) and the procedure of conciliation provided for in the *Annex* to the Convention (Art. 66, *b*). In relation to this subject, directive 3.1.5.7 of ILC's *Guide* on reservations, provided that: "A reservation to a treaty provision concerning dispute settlement or the monitoring of the implementation of the treaty is not, in itself, incompatible with the object and purpose of the treaty, unless: *i*) the reservation purports to exclude or modify the legal effect of a provision of the treaty essential to its raison d'être; or *ii*) the reservation has the effect of excluding the reserving State or international organization from a dispute settlement or treaty implementation monitoring mechanism with respect to a treaty provision that it has previously accepted, if the very purpose of the treaty is to put such a mechanism into effect". Then, considering that Art. 66 of the 1969 Vienna Convention is not the "raison d'être" of the Convention, and said Convention is not a specific convention on dispute settlement, the reservation made by Brazil to Art. 66 shall be considered valid. It should be pointed out that many States also made a reservation to Art. 66 of the Vienna Convention (see the Annex IV to this book).

---

404 See Villiger, Mark E. *Commentary on the 1969 Vienna Convention on the Law of Treaties*, cit., p. 820-822. For all discussions on Art. 66 at the Vienna Conference, see Dupuy, René Jean, Codification et règlement des différends: les débats de Vienne sur les procédures de règlement, *Annuaire Français de Droit International*, vol. 15 (1969), p. 70-90; and Rosenne, Shabtai, The settlement of treaty disputes under the Vienna Convention of 1969, *Zeitschrift für ausländisches öffentliches Recht und Völkerrecht*, vol. 31 (1971), p. 1-62. The following observation of Alan Boyle should be noted on not using Art. 66 in the practice: "The most notable addition was article 66, providing for compulsory dispute settlement procedures in respect of Part V of the convention, although ironically these procedures have never been used" (Reflections on the treaty as a law-making instrument, cit., p. 1-2).

An important consequence of item *a*) of Art. 66 is the assignment of *mandatory* competence to the ICJ in cases of disputes on the application or the interpretation of norms of *jus cogens*, if the parties have decided not to solve the matter by arbitration.[405] In this case, in order to request an answer from the Court concerning the application or interpretation of Arts. 53 and 64 of the Convention, the consent of the other party is not required; only one of the parties, through a unilateral appeal, may initiate the procedure (since the norm refers to "*any party* to the dispute…").[406] In fact, once the procedure is filed before the ICJ, the essential requirement of the other State's consent is satisfied by the fact that said State has participated in the Vienna Convention; by accepting the rules of the treaty, the State is already accepting *pro futuro* the court jurisdiction.[407]

Upon such request, through a unilateral appeal of one of the parties to the treaty, the ICJ must *determine* whether the nature of a particular norm is *binding* and whether the treaty that was objected is breaching said norm.[408] It should be noted that what the Court does is just *determining* if the norm under analysis is or is not *jus cogens*, without invalidating the treaty. That is to say, the *consequences* of invalidity and termination of a treaty contrary to the norm of *jus cogens* (provided for in Art. 71) do not fall under the mandatory jurisdiction of the ICJ; therefore, the Court may not declare the treaty *invalid* or *terminated*.[409]

Despite the jurisdiction of the ICJ is not mandatory when there is an agreement between the parties concerning the submission of the cause to arbitration, if there is no such agreement, the jurisdiction of the Court becomes mandatory *ipso jure*, granting one of the parties the right to raise the matter to the consideration of the court. Such system adopted by the 1969 Vienna Convention (which is called "mandatory jurisdiction of a subsidiary nature") represented an advance against other conventions,

---

405 See Fiorati, Jete Jane. Jus cogens…, cit., p. 67-68.

406 See Viegas, Vera Lúcia. *Ius cogens* e o tema da nulidade dos tratados, cit., p. 191; Gómez Robledo, Antonio, *El* ius cogens *internacional*…, cit., p. 142; and Friedrich, Tatyana Scheila, *As normas imperativas de direito internacional público jus cogens*, cit., p. 40. On the mandatory competence of the ICJ in this case, also see Rodas, João Grandino, *Jus cogens* em direito internacional, *Revista da Faculdade de Direito da Universidade de São Paulo*, vol. LXIX, part II (1974), p. 131.

407 See De La Guardia, Ernesto. *Derecho de los tratados internacionales*, cit., p. 333.

408 See Viegas, Vera Lúcia. *Ius cogens* e o tema da nulidade dos tratados, cit., p. 191.

409 See Ronzitti, Natalino. La disciplina dello *jus cogens* nella Convenzione di Vienna sul Diritto dei Trattati, cit., p. 285-286.

like the Vienna Convention on Diplomatic Relations (1961), which has not even provided for the subsidiary obligation of the Court, but only a protocol of intentions concerning pacific dispute settlements.[410]

4.1.2 Particularities of the 1986 Vienna Convention

The 1986 Convention followed the same steps of the 1969 Convention with regard to the procedure to invoke a defect in consent, or a ground for invalidity of the treaty to which an international organization is a party. Nevertheless, it introduced some particularities as the one relating to the settlement of disputes on treaty incompatibilities with the preexisting *jus cogens* (Art. 66, item 2).[411]

As we have just studied (item 4.1.1, above), the 1969 Convention has established the competence of the International Court of Justice (Art. 66, *a*) for these cases, as the last option and unless the parties decide to settle the dispute by arbitration. During the *travaux préparatoires* of the 1986 Convention, this solution found technical problems, particularly related to the impossibility of international organizations to be a *party* in contentious cases before the Court.

After long discussions held in the ILC,[412] the winning case was that the ICJ (at the request of the UN's General Assembly or the Security Council, as well as by certain specialized bodies[413] – for instance, the ILO, UNESCO, WHO, etc.) was entitled to issue an *advisory* opinion with *final* effects (that is, *binding*) for all the parties. The final text of Art. 66, item 2, approved at the 1986 Conference by forty-seven votes against twenty-three and twenty-one abstentions, reads as follows:

> "2. With respect to a dispute concerning the application or the interpretation of article 53 or 64:

---

410 See Fiorati, Jete Jane. Jus cogens..., cit., p. 68.

411 In relation to all cases, see Remiro Brotons, Antonio, *Derecho internacional público*, vol. 2, cit., p. 457-458.

412 On such articles, see Remiro Brotons, Antonio, Idem, p. 458.

413 Such legitimacy comes from Art. 96 of the UN Charter, which reads as follows: "1. The General Assembly or the Security Council may request the International Court of Justice to give an advisory opinion on any legal question. 2. Other organs of the United Nations and specialized agencies, which may at any time be so authorized by the General Assembly, may also request advisory opinions of the Court on legal questions arising within the scope of their activities".

(...)

b) if a State is a party to the dispute to which one or more international organizations are parties, the State may, through a Member State of the United Nations if necessary, request the General Assembly or the Security Council or, where appropriate, the competent organ of an international organization which is a party to the dispute and is authorized in accordance with Article 96 of the Charter of the United Nations, to request an advisory opinion of the International Court of Justice in accordance with article 65 of the Statute of the Court;

c) if the United Nations or an international organization that is authorized in accordance with Article 96 of the Charter of the United Nations is a party to the dispute, it may request an advisory opinion of the International Court of Justice in accordance with article 65 of the Statute of the Court;

d) if an international organization other than those referred to in sub-paragraph (c) is a party to the dispute, it may, through a Member State of the United Nations, follow the procedure specified in sub-paragraph (b);

e) the advisory opinion given pursuant to sub-paragraph (b), (c) or (d) shall be accepted as decisive by all the parties to the dispute concerned;

f) if the request under sub-paragraph (b), (c) or (d) for an advisory opinion of the Court is not granted, any one of the parties to the dispute may, by written notification to the other party or parties, submit it to arbitration in accordance with the provisions of the Annex to the present Convention".

> This model of dispute submission with the ICJ, so that it may issue an advisory opinion (with binding value for the parties) with the proper solution, had already been used by other treaties concerning international organizations, for instance, by the 1947 Convention on the Privileges and Immunities of the Specialized Agencies of the United Nations, whose Section 32 provides as follows: " All differences arising out of the interpretation or application of the present Convention shall be referred to the International Court of Justice unless in any case it is agreed by the parties to have recourse to another mode of settlement. If a difference arises between one of the specialized agencies on the one hand, and a member on the other hand, a request shall be made for an advisory opinion on any legal question involved in accordance with Article 96 of the Charter and Article 65 of the Statute of the Court and the relevant provisions of the agreements concluded between the United Nations and the specialized agency concerned. The opinion given by the Court shall be accepted as decisive by the parties".

The 1986 Convention also excepted the application of the provisions of Art. 66, item 2, if all the parties to a dispute, by common consent, agree to submit the dispute to an arbitration procedure, including the one specified in the *Annex* to the Convention (Art. 66, item 3). It also established that with respect to a dispute concerning the application or the interpretation of any of the articles in Part V, other than Arts. 53 and 64, of the present Convention, any one of the parties to the dispute may set in motion the conciliation procedure specified in the *Annex* to the Convention by submitting a request to that effect to the Secretary-General of the UN (Art. 66, item 4).

4.2 Consequences of vitiated consent, invalidity, termination and suspension of the operation of a treaty

The Vienna Convention deals with the consequences of *vitiated consent, invalidity, termination* and *suspension* of the operation of a treaty in Arts. 69, 70 and 72, respectively. Art. 71 of the Convention provides for the consequences of invalidity of a treaty (later or earlier) in conflict with a norm of *jus cogens* (see Ch. 2, item 2.2, above). Except the latter case, in respect of which it cannot be set forth otherwise, the other rules of the Convention are *supplementary* and cannot prevail over the will of the parties expressed in the treaty itself or agreed upon by them by any other means (Arts. 70, item 1, and 72, item 1).

With regard to the subject under analysis, it should be remembered that the provisions of Art. 43 of the Convention, according to which the invalidity, termination or suspension of operations of a treaty, as a result of the application of the present Convention or of the provisions of the treaty, will not *impair the duty* of any party ("in any way", as stated by the text) to fulfill any obligation embodied in the treaty to which that State or that organization *would be subject under international law* independently of the treaty. In other words, even though a treaty is void, terminated, denounced or suspended, by reason of the application of the Vienna Convention, the States still have the duty to perform those obligations (which, coincidentally, also are "mentioned" in the void, terminated, denounced or suspended treaty) to which they are subject by virtue of non conventional International Law.[414]

---

414 On the subject, see Villiger, Mark E., *Commentary on the 1969 Vienna Convention on the Law of Treaties*, cit., p. 553-554, under these terms: "Whatever the consequences of the invalidity, termination, etc., this shall not in any way impair the duty of any State to fulfill any obligation which is independent of the treaty and in particular of a contractual obligation. Article 43 refers namely to any other obligations to which the State would be subject under international law. Such obligations derive in particular from customary international law, possibly also from general principles of international law. As the formulation 'embodied in the treaty' indicates, Article 43 envisages identical, underlying customary law. The provi-

Let us see, separately, the consequences of (*a*) invalidity and vitiated consent, (*b*) termination, and (*c*) suspension of the operation of a treaty:

4.2.1 *Consequences of invalidity of a treaty and vitiated consent*

As provided for in item 1 of Art. 69, a treaty "the invalidity of which is established under the present Convention" is void, adding that the "provisions of a void treaty have no legal force". It is the consequence *par excellence* of invalidity of a treaty: the lack of *any* legal force. Such invalidity is *ab initio* (that is, *ex tunc*) and not from its invocation by any party or from the time in which it appeared.[415] This means that the treaty is void from the time it was adopted, and not only from the time in which the ground for invalidity was found.[416]

Art. 69, item 1, of the Convention implicitly deems that *no acts were performed* concerning the treaty under analysis (a treaty whose invalidity resulted from the provisions of the Convention); the reason for that is that the Convention, in item 2 of Art.69, establishes the consequences concerning *acts already performed* by virtue of the treaty.[417] In this case, when the acts were performed under a void treaty, the referred rule (Art. 69, item 2) provides that: *a*) each party may require any other party to establish as far as possible in their mutual relations the position that would have existed if the acts had not been performed (note "as far as possible…"); and *b*) acts performed in good faith before the invalidity was invoked must be maintained (that is, they are not rendered *unlawful* by reason only of the invalidity of the treaty.)[418]

---

sion thus refers to declaratory treaty rules (…), but does not concern other, non-identical customary rules. This result is generally acknowledged in case-law and doctrine".

415 See ILC, *Yearbook of the International Law Commission* (1966), vol. II, p. 264-265: "The Commission considered that the establishment of the nullity of a treaty on any of the grounds set forth in section 2 of part V would mean that the treaty was void *ab initio* and not merely from the date when the ground was invoked". See also Remiro Brotons, Antonio, *Derecho internacional público*, vol. 2, cit., p. 463; De La Guardia, Ernesto, *Derecho de los tratados internacionales*, cit., p. 293; Viegas, Vera Lúcia, *Ius cogens* e o tema da nulidade dos tratados, cit., p. 188; and Villiger, Mark E., *Commentary on the 1969 Vienna Convention on the Law of Treaties*, cit., p. 859.

416 As explained by De La Guardia: "Absolute invalidity, unlike relative invalidity, implies that invalidity goes back *to the date of the void act*, as if it had never existed (…)" (*Derecho de los tratados internacionales*, cit., p. 293).

417 See De La Guardia, Ernesto. *Derecho de los tratados internacionales*, cit., p. 293.

418 With regard to this, see the explanation given by De La Guardia: "In paragraph *b* [of Art. 69, item 2] another important nuance is considered, always under a regime of *good faith*

With regard to cases relating to Arts. 49, 50, 51 or 52 (that is, when there is no presumption of *good faith*), the Convention provides that paragraph 2 of Art. 69 does not apply with respect to the party to which the *fraud*, the act of *corruption* or the *coercion* is imputable (Art. 69, item 3); in these cases, interpreting item 2 of Art. 69 *a contrario*, it is considered that the party to which the fraud, the act of corruption or the coercion is imputable (*a*) may not require the return of the *status quo* prior to the conclusion of the treaty and (*b*) the acts performed by said party before the invocation of invalidity will not be maintained.[419]

With regard to the invalidity of *consent* of a State to be bound by a treaty, there are two rules to be considered: one concerning *bilateral* treaties, and another one concerning *multilateral* treaties. In the first case, it is obvious that, if it is a bilateral treaty, the recognition of invalidity of consent makes the relation between both parties come to an end (since it is not possible that the agreement may survive for one of them); in this case, termination occurs for a *de facto* reason resulting from the practical impossibility of the treaty survival (see Ch. 2, item 2.1.2, above). In the case of multilateral treaties, the rule is that the invalidity of a particular State's consent only affects the legal relations between said State with a vitiated consent and the other parties to the treaty, and *not* to the relations among the other parties. (Art. 69, item 4). This is also one of the reasons (we have already discussed it in Ch. 2, item 2.1, above) by virtue of which the Vienna Convention *makes a mistake* when calling Section 2 of Part V (related to *defects in consent*) *Invalidity of Treaties*, since it does not deal with invalidity of *international acts*, so much so they will be normally applied between the other parties.

4.2.2 Consequences of the termination of a treaty

Concerning the consequences of the *termination* of a treaty, the Convention provides that, unless the treaty otherwise provides or the parties otherwise agree, the termination of a treaty under its provisions or in accordance with the present Convention: *a*) *releases the parties* from any

of the parties concerning invalidity of a treaty; it seeks to protect the acts performed by the parties in *good faith* before the invalidity was invoked, so as to prevent said acts from being rendered unlawful only by reason of the later invalidity of the treaty" (*Derecho de los tratados internacionales*, cit., p. 294).

419 In this way, the Vienna Convention enshrines the principle *ex injuria jus non oritur* (whereby "law does not arise from injustice").

obligation *further to perform* the treaty; *b*) *does not affect* any right, obligation or legal situation of the parties created through the execution of the treaty *prior* to its termination (Art. 70, item 1).

However, it should be highlighted again that such consequences will only be valid in case the treaty does not provide or the parties do not agree "otherwise". Under the Convention, If a State or an international organization denounces or withdraws from a multilateral treaty, paragraph 1 applies in the relations between that State or that organization and each of the other parties to the treaty from the date when such denunciation or withdrawal takes effect. (Art. 70, item 2).

As we can see, the Convention (in Art. 70) was very careful in relation to the *non-retroactivity* of termination of treaties.[420] In this way, the parties are released, *ex nunc*, from continuing to perform the treaty; however, *ex tunc*, termination of the agreement *does not affect* the exercise of any right, obligation or legal situation resulting from the execution of the treaty *prior* to its termination. In other terms, termination of a treaty *preserves* the rights and obligations (or legal situations) implemented prior to its end. Nothing is more consistent. After a treaty is terminated, it is clear that any right, obligation or legal situation of the parties created as a consequence of execution of the treaty *prior* to its termination will survive. The only exception relates to the supervening *jus cogens*, which conditions the validity of the said rights and obligations (or legal situations) to its *compatibility* with the new peremptory norm of general International Law (Art. 71, item 2, *b*).[421] This means, for instance, that a territorial cession established by a treaty executed through the *lawful* use of force at the time of its conclusion, but not of today, must be complied with (Art. 70, item 1, *b*) if it does not breach any norm of *jus cogens* concerning the free determination of nations (Art. 71, item 2, *b*).[422]

When are the parties released from the obligation to continue performing the treaty in case of termination? The question does not raise any problems in the case of treaties with a *specific date* of termination, or when the parties expressly *fix a term* to the agreement, or even when a *later treaty* revokes an earlier one in whole. It is also common that treaties providing for the possibility of denunciation *include* a date (six months,

---

420 See Villiger, Mark E. *Commentary on the 1969 Vienna Convention on the Law of Treaties*, cit., p. 871-872.

421 See Ch. 2, item 2.2, above.

422 See Remiro Brotons, Antonio. *Derecho internacional público*, vol. 2, cit., p. 502.

one year, etc.) as from which the instrument will no longer produce effects for the denouncing party after notification; there is no problem either in the case of an unmotivated denunciation, under the provision of Art. 56, item 2, of the Convention.[423] Nevertheless, as inquired by Remiro Brotons, what should we do when the parties are silent and we have to face a breach of a treaty, a fundamental change of circumstances relating to its execution or the incompatibility of its clauses with peremptory norms of general International Law? The author understands that there are three possible dates to be taken as a reference: 1) the date in which the alleged motive is deemed to have occurred (*date of occurrence*); 2) the date of notification by one party of its intention to terminate the treaty (*invocation date*); and 3) a later date in which the invoking party may adopt the proposed measure or it was admitted by a judge or an international arbitrator (*appraisal date*), according to the applicable procedure rules. According to Brotons, the first possibility should be applied to the incompatibility of a treaty with the supervening *jus cogens*, which opinion is also shared by the ILC in its comment on the final draft on articles; in turn, in cases of termination due to a material breach of the treaty or by a fundamental change in circumstances, the *invocation* or *appraisal* dates would be the best options.[424]

4.2.3 Consequences of the suspension of the operation of a treaty

Art. 72 of the Convention deals with the consequences of the *suspension of the operation* of a treaty. According to this provision, unless the treaty otherwise provides or the parties otherwise agree, the suspension of the operation of a treaty under its provisions or in accordance with the present Convention: *a*) *releases the parties* between which the operation of the treaty is suspended *from the obligation to perform the treaty* in their mutual relations during the period of the suspension; and *b*) does not otherwise affect the legal relations between the parties established by the treaty (item 1).[425]

It should be also pointed out that such consequences will only be valid in case the treaty does not provide or the parties do not agree "otherwise". Hence, except as otherwise provided, the parties are released (*a*)

---

[423] See Remiro Brotons, Antonio. Idem, p. 502-503.

[424] See Remiro Brotons, Antonio. Idem, p. 503.

[425] See Villiger, Mark E. *Commentary on the 1969 Vienna Convention on the Law of Treaties*, cit., p. 886-891.

from continuing to perform the treaty during the suspension period, but this (*b*) does not affect the *legal relation* between the said parties established by the treaty, which remains, in any case, *undamaged.*[426] During the suspension period (as also provided in Art. 72) the parties will refrain from acts tending to obstruct the resumption of the operation of the treaty (item 2).

In principle, the suspension of the operation of a treaty only affects *some* of the parties, but nothing precludes that in the specific case of a *serious breach* of a treaty, the innocent parties, by unanimous agreement, suspend the application of the agreement as between *all the parties* (Art. 60, item 2, *a*, ii). With regard to a supervening impossibility of performance (Art. 61) and a fundamental change of circumstances (Art. 62), the suspension only affects the damaged parties as a result of one of those facts.

We should remember what we have already seen (see Ch. 3, item 3.2, above) on the impossibility, *a priori*, of separating the provisions of a treaty (Art. 44, items 1 and 2): a ground for suspension recognized by the Convention itself should be argued in connection with the *whole* treaty, *except* under the provisions of items 3 and 4, of Art. 44 *or in Art. 60*. As the provisions *of Art. 60 were excepted*, the Convention allowed (in the event of *material breach* of a treaty) the innocent party to decide for the *total* or *partial* suspension of the operation of the treaty (see Ch. 3, item 3.1.3.1, above). Art. 60 insistently repeats (item 2, *a*, *b* and *c*) that a material breach of a treaty entitles the parties to suspend the operation of the treaty "in whole or in part". Therefore, based on a systematic interpretation of the Convention, it seems that the provisions of Art. 60 *excluded* those of Art. 44, item 3, in case of *partial* suspension of the operation of a treaty.[427] In fact, conditions for separability of the provisions of a treaty, under the terms of Art. 44, item 3, are that (*a*) said clauses are separable from the remainder of the treaty with regard to their application; (*b*) it appears from the treaty or is otherwise established that acceptance of those clauses was not an essential basis of the consent of the other party or par-

---

[426] See ILC, *Yearbook of the International Law Commission* (1966), vol. II, p. 267, as follows: "Paragraph 1(*b*), however, emphasizes that the suspension of a treaty's operation 'does not otherwise affect the legal relations between the parties established by the treaty'. This provision is intended to make it clear that the legal nexus between the parties established by the treaty remains intact and that it is only the operation of its provisions which is suspended".

[427] See Remiro Brotons, Antonio. *Derecho internacional público*, vol. 2, cit., p. 516-517.

ties to be bound by the treaty as a whole; and (*c*) continued performance of the remainder of the treaty would not be *unjust*. Nevertheless, Art. 60 does not include (not even require) any such conditions, which really seems to entitle the *non-defaulting* party to decide for a *partial suspension* of the operation of the treaty (never a partial *termination*, which will be effective *only under* the rules of Art. 44, item 3).

When are the parties released from performing the treaty in case of suspension? When it refers to a *factual* matter, like temporary impossibility of performance; the effects of suspension begin when the fact occurred. In other cases, except as provided by the parties in the treaty itself or in a later agreement, the solution entitling the party to suspend the operation of the treaty seems feasible "as from the same date in which that party notifies its intention to the other parties, without prejudice to its obligation of settling, by peaceful means, the disputes raised on the adjustment of its statement to the presumed purposes of the ground for suspension alleged and of accepting the responsibility incurred if it is determined that such adjustment has not taken place".[428]

Once the ground for suspension terminates, the treaty must return to be *operative* between the parties. By requiring that, during the period of the suspension, the States refrain from acts tending to obstruct the *resumption of the operation* of the treaty (Art. 72, item 2), the Convention sought to *recover* the same force of the international act as it had prior to the suspension period.

---

[428] Remiro Brotons, Antonio. Idem, p. 517.

Part IV

Treaties in the 1986 Vienna Convention

Chapter 1

General Rules of the 1986 Convention

1.1 Introduction

The Vienna Convention on the Law of Treaties of 1969, as previously stated, only dealt with the law of treaties between States, but it did not include any provisions for treaties concluded between States and international organizations or between international organizations. In order to regulate this matter, namely those treaties to which international organizations are parties, in 1969, the UN General Assembly suggested that the International Law Commission endeavored to carry out studies on this subject. Thirteen years later, the ILC approved the first draft of the Convention on the Law of Treaties between States and International Organizations or between International Organizations, appointing Prof. Paul Reuter, from the University of Paris II, as Special Rapporteur for the work.[1]

---

1 See, for further information on all these matters, Nascimento e Silva, Geraldo Eulálio do, The 1986 Vienna Convention and the treaty-making power of international organizations, *German Yearbook of International Law*, vol. 29 (1987), p. 68-85; Morgenstern, Felice, The Convention on the Law of Treaties between States and International Organizations or between International Organizations, in Dinstein, Yoram (ed.), *International law at a time of perplexity: essays in honour of Shabtai Rosenne*, Dordrecht: Martinus Nijhoff, 1989, p. 435-447; De La Guardia, Ernesto, *Derecho de los tratados internacionales*, cit., p. 355-456; Cançado Trindade, Antônio Augusto, Direito das organizações internacionais, 2. ed. (reviewed and updated), Belo Horizonte: Del Rey, 2002, p. 199-251; and Bernardes, Maurício da Costa Carvalho (*et all.*), A Convenção de Viena de 1986 sobre direito dos tratados entre Estados e organizações internacionais e entre organizações internacionais: estado atual da matéria no direito internacional público, in Cançado Trindade, Antônio Augusto (org.), *A nova dimensão do direito internacional, Brasília: Instituto Rio Branco*, 2003, p. 173-199.

At the end of its work, the ILC advised the UN General Assembly to convene a Conference to carry out the conclusion process of the future Convention. The Conference convened for such purpose was held in Vienna, from February 18 to March 21, 1986, and was presided over by the Austrian professor Karl Zemanek, who had published in 1959 the work Law of treaties of international organizations.[2] Ambassador Mohamed El-Taher Shash (Egypt) was appointed chairman of the Committee of the Whole, Ambassador Geraldo Eulálio do Nascimento e Silva (Brazil) acted as vice-chairman, and Ambassador Awn Al-Khasawneh (Jordan) was appointed chairman of the Drafting Committee.[3]

The Vienna Convention on the Law of Treaties between States and International Organizations or between International Organizations was finally concluded, after long debates, on March 21, 1986, by 67 votes to 1 and 23 abstentions.[4] It should be noted that the Convention (up to this date) has not entered into force at the international level yet, as it has not reached the minimum number of 35 State ratifications (according to Art. 85).[5]

Part IV shall briefly introduce some aspects of the 1986 Vienna Convention that must be highlighted, reminding the reader that the study on the 1969 Convention shall be absolutely useful to understand the conclusion of treaties which involve international organizations.

1.2 History and current situation of the 1986 Convention

The historical origin of the codification of the Law of Treaties involving international organizations is confused with the appearance of such organizations on the international scene, when it was noticed that the international capacity of these entities inexorably brought them to the condition of holders of the power to conclude treaties (*treaty-making power*).

---

2 Zemanek, Karl. *Das Vertragsrecht der internationalen Organisationen*. Wien: Springer, 1957, 159p.

3 See *United Nations*, Doc. A/CONF.129/16 (vol. I): Summary records of the plenary meetings and of the meetings of the Committee of the Whole (Vienna, 18 February-21 March 1986), p. 3-8. As regards the 1986 Conference, see De La Guardia, Ernesto, *Derecho de los tratados internacionales*, cit., p. 366-369.

4 Text of the Convention in *United Nations*, Doc. A/CONF.129/15 (see Annex III to this book).

5 International organizations may also ratify the Convention, but these ratifications are not taken into consideration in the general count necessary for the Convention to enter into force.

This matter has been discussed from the time of the League of Nations, when discussions were intensified after the creation of the UN, in 1945.[6]

In the *travaux préparatoires* of the 1986 Convention, the basic idea of the authors was not to establish a universal *standard* for all international organizations, which have very different characteristics, but to "identify and formulate the rules necessary for the consolidation and development of a solidly based practice recognizing the legal value of the treaties of international organizations, irrespective of the special features which may characterize each organization".[7]

In the discussions for the formulation of the 1986 Convention, the participation of Brazil must be emphasized, which was represented by Ambassador Geraldo Eulálio do Nascimento e Silva, who had already presided over the Brazilian delegation to the Second Session of the 1969 Vienna Conference, and by Prof. Antônio Augusto Cançado Trindade, Legal Consultant of Itamaraty[8] of that time.

Upon the conclusion of the Convention, there were a significant number of signatures, mainly between 1986 and 1987, but which were not executed through the relevant ratifications. The United Nations is still making great efforts to reach the minimum number of 35 State ratifications necessary for the Convention to enter into force at the international level (according to Art. 85). Among the international organizations that have already ratified the Convention, apart from the United Nations (which ratified it on December 21, 1998), the following entities may be mentioned: International Atomic Energy Agency (IAEA), International Civil Aviation Organization (ICAO), International Criminal Police Organization (INTERPOL), International Labour Organization (ILO), International Maritime Organization (IMO), Organization for the Prohibition of Chemical Weapons (OPCW), United Nations Industrial Development Organization (UNIDO), World Health Organization (WHO) and World Intellectual Property Organization (WIPO). According to Art. 85(3) of

---

6 See Bernardes, Maurício da Costa Carvalho (*et al.*). A Convenção de Viena de 1986 sobre direito dos tratados entre Estados e organizações internacionais e entre organizações internacionais..., cit., p. 175-176.

7 See Reuter, Paul [Special Rapporteur], *Yearbook of the International Law Commission* (1974), vol. II, Part One, p. 143.

8 The opinion of the Legal Consultant on the position of Brazil as to the Vienna Convention of 1986 is stated in: Cachapuz de Medeiros, Antônio Paulo (org.), *Pareceres dos consultores jurídicos do Itamaraty*, vol. VIII (1985-1990), Brasília: Senado Federal, 2004, p. 210-236.

the Convention, "for each international organization depositing an instrument relating to an act of formal confirmation or an instrument of accession, the Convention shall enter into force on the thirtieth day after such deposit, or at the date the Convention enters into force pursuant to paragraph 1, whichever is later".

It must be admitted that the 1986 Convention critics were somewhat right since it has not yet entered into force at an international level, which shows that States and international organizations are not interested in ratifying the Convention.[9] Whatever the case may be, it is important to study the 1986 Vienna Convention, as it represents the basis upon which the law of treaties between States and international organizations or between international organizations must operate.

1.3 Similarities between the 1969 and 1986 Conventions

During the discussions to conclude the 1986 Convention, it was agreed that it should be organized according to the 1969 Convention, which may be easily noticed when handling both conventions, which have the same, mostly identical, order of provisions (see the first 72 articles of both conventions). What the 1986 Convention did in such provisions was merely add the reference to "international organizations" while the 1969 Convention refers to "States". The difference between the provisions of one of the Conventions and the other only appears (in the text of 1986) in the item related to the capacity of international organizations to conclude treaties.[10]

Even though the Vienna Convention of 1986 was based on the 1969 Convention, the ILC insisted on emphasizing that it intended to prepare a project that was "completely independent as to its formalities" when compared to the 1969 Convention, so that the whole text would constitute a "complete unit (...) [with] (...) legal effects independent from the legal effects produced by the Vienna Convention"; it also pointed out that the intention of the commission was that the 1986 Convention stated "completely the proposed provisions, without referring to the articles of the Vienna Convention, even when such norms were formulated on identical

---

9 Cf. De La Guardia, Ernesto. *Derecho de los tratados internacionales*, cit., p. 369.

10 Cf. Bernardes, Maurício da Costa Carvalho (*et al.*). A Convenção de Viena de 1986 sobre direito dos tratados entre Estados e organizações internacionais e entre organizações internacionais..., cit., p. 178-179.

terms as those of the Vienna Convention".[11] Whatever the case may be, the truth is that the 1986 Convention (as it can be easily noticed) followed exactly the methodology and almost all the provisions of the 1969 Convention, just making the adjustments required.[12]

It should be noted that, according to Art. 3 of the 1986 Convention, "the fact that the present Convention does not apply: *i*) to international agreements to which one or more States, one or more international organizations and one or more subjects of International Law other than States or organizations are parties; *ii*) to international agreements to which one or more international organizations and one or more subjects of International Law other than States or organizations are parties; *iii*) to international agreements not in written form between one or more States and one or more international organizations, or between international organizations; or *iv*) to international agreements between subjects of International Law other than States or international organizations; shall not affect: *a*) the legal force of such agreements; *b*) the application to them of any of the rules set forth in the present Convention to which they would be subject under International Law independently of the Convention; and *c*) the application of the Convention to the relations between States and international organizations or to the relations of organizations as between themselves, when those relations are governed by international agreements to which other subjects of International Law are also parties". Such "other subjects of International Law" are new to the 1986 Convention, which finally incorporated the modern tendencies of the Law of Nations in the regulation of the Law of Treaties to include intergovernmental organizations, providing legal support to international agreements concluded by the *new subjects* of International Law when the Convention enters into force.[13]

Apart from the similarities, there are also important differences between the 1969 and 1986 conventions, such as, *for instance*, Art. 74(3) of the 1986 Convention, which sets forth that a treaty signed by an organization shall not affect its members, unless they accept the corresponding treaty (see Chap. 2, item 2.3, below). Another important difference lies in

---

11 De La Guardia, Ernesto. *Derecho de los tratados internacionales*, cit., p. 364.

12 Cf. De La Guardia, Ernesto. Idem, p. 365.

13 Cf. Bernardes, Maurício da Costa Carvalho (et al.). A Convenção de Viena de 1986 sobre direito dos tratados entre Estados e organizações internacionais e entre organizações internacionais..., cit., p. 179-181.

the dispute settlement method adopted by the 1986 Convention.[14] Whereas disputes related to the 1969 Convention are settled by conciliation or proceedings before the ICJ, disputes falling within the scope of the 1986 Convention – as they cannot take part in contentious cases before the Court – may also be settled, apart from conciliation, through a binding *opinion* rendered by the ICJ,[15] in cases involving these organizations and peremptory norms of general international law (*jus cogens*); such opinion shall be accepted as decisive (in the cases set forth by the Convention) by all the parties to the dispute (Art. 66, 2, *e*). If no advisory opinion is requested, or if the Court does not accept the request, the dispute shall be settled by compulsory arbitration.[16]

1.4 Relationship between the 1986 Convention and the 1969 Convention

Art. 73 of the 1986 Vienna Convention entitled *Relationship to the Vienna Convention on the Law of Treaties* set forth a rule whereby the 1969 Vienna Convention shall prevail over the text of 1986 with regard provisions concerning States.[17] In fact, it establishes that as between States Parties to the Vienna Convention of 1969, the relations of those States under a treaty between two or more States and one or more international organizations shall be governed by that Convention.[18]

This provision is completely *new* to the 1986 Convention, as it was not included in the 1982 Project. It ended the symmetry existing between the first 72 articles of both Conventions; thus, Art. 74 of the 1986 Convention corresponds now to Art. 73 of the 1969 Convention, Art. 75 to Art. 74, and so on through the end.[19]

---

14 See Morgenstern, Felice. The Convention on the Law of Treaties between States and International Organizations or between International Organizations, cit., p. 440.

15 According to Art. 65 of the Statute of the ICJ.

16 See Shaw, Malcolm N. *Direito internacional*, cit., p. 711.

17 Cf. Morgenstern, Felice. The Convention on the Law of Treaties between States and International Organizations or between International Organizations, cit., p. 436.

18 This articles states as follows: "As between States parties to the Vienna Convention on the Law of Treaties of 1969, the relations of those States under a treaty between two or more States and one or more international organizations shall be governed by that Convention".

19 See De La Guardia, Ernesto. *Derecho de los tratados internacionales*, cit., p. 439.

De La Guardia[20] considers that Art. 73 of the 1986 Convention must be construed following specific cases, as specified below:

Treaties between a State party to the 1969 Convention and one or more international organizations	Relations shall be governed by the 1986 Convention, whenever both a State and an international organization are parties thereto.
Treaties between two or more States parties to the Vienna Convention of 1969 and one or more international organizations	Relations between States shall be governed by the 1969 Convention. Relations between such States and organization/s shall be governed by the 1986 Convention, if all of them were parties to that Convention.
Treaties between two or more States which are not parties to the Vienna Convention of 1969 and one or more international organizations	Relations between States shall be governed by customary law rules previous to the 1969 Convention, or by this Convention, if they decide to apply it, The relations between States and international organizations shall be governed by the Vienna Convention of 1986, if all of them were parties thereto, and if they were not, by the rules of international customary law, or by the 1986 Convention, if they decide to apply it.
Treaties between international organizations	The 1986 Convention should be applied if they were parties thereto; otherwise, customary practice should apply.

Several legal scholars have criticized Art. 73 particularly because such a provision could break the conventional uniformity established under the 1986 Vienna Convention. As explained by Morgenstern, it may occur that, in practice, in the framework of contentious proceedings between them before the ICJ, the termination of a treaty may be ordered by the latter pursuant to Arts. 53 and 64 of the 1969 Convention (treaties conflicting with a preexisting and supervening peremptory norm of general international law (*jus cogens*), respectively), without the organizations that are also parties to the treaty being heard.[21] In that connection, Malcolm Shaw also states that it is not clear "whether this clause (which reaffirms the ap-

20 De La Guardia, Ernesto. Idem, p. 440.

21 Morgenstern, Felice. The Convention on the Law of Treaties between States and International Organizations or between International Organizations, cit., p. 436-437.

plication of the 1969 Convention when dealing with States) shall affect, in practice, the interests of international organizations".[22]

The truth is that, in the Vienna Conference of 1986, the voice of the States (in favor of the provision of Art. 73) prevailed to the detriment of the position of international organizations; at the most, they could express their hopes that such provision is never used to aggravate a situation related to them.[23]

1.5 Situation of the Vienna Convention of 1986 in Brazil

Brazil signed the 1986 Vienna Convention on March 21, 1986,[24] but to date has not yet ratified the Convention, although it has accepted the capacity of international organizations to conclude treaties. The current Brazilian practice – also followed by Itamaraty – accepts the rule that provides that the capacity of intergovernmental organizations to conclude treaties is governed by "rules of that organization", as stated by Art. 6 of the Convention (see Chap. 2, item 2.1, below).

The (unjustified) delay of Brazil to ratify the 1986 Convention represents not only a step backward for the country, but also prevents it from participating more actively in treaties of interest to the Nation, adopted in the context of important intergovernmental organizations before the international society.

Even though to date the 1986 Convention has not entered into force at the international level, the Brazilian Government should have ratified the Convention, as it ratified (also with some delay) the Vienna Convention on the Law of Treaties of 1969.

In any case, it is possible to advocate (as it already occurred in the case of the 1969 Convention) the full force of the 1986 Convention in Brazil, even without the formal ratification of the Brazilian Government, since it is generally accepted as a declaratory norm of current international custom (which is a source of International Law according to Art. 38, *b*, of the Statute of the ICJ).[25]

---

22 Shaw, Malcolm N. *Direito internacional*, cit., p. 710.

23 Cf. Morgenstern, Felice. The Convention on the Law of Treaties between States and International Organizations or between International Organizations, cit., p. 437.

24 The Brazilian government formulated no reservations upon signature of the Convention.

25 Cf. Buergenthal, Thomas (*et all.*). *Manual de derecho internacional público*, cit., p. 78-79; and even *Restatement of the Law* (*Third*), vol. 1 (1987), p. 145. As regards Art. 38, *b*, of the Statute of the ICJ, see Mazzuoli, Valerio de Oliveira, *Curso de direito internacional público*, cit., p. 128-141.

Chapter 2

Treaties under the Convention of 1986

2.1 Capacity of international organizations to conclude treaties

The capacity of international organizations to conclude treaties is stated in Art. 6 of the 1986 Convention, which regulates this matter, but without conferring international organizations the capacity of an absolute nature (regarding the conclusion of treaties) that States were granted by the Vienna Convention of 1969. However, it is true that even before the establishment of this international regulation, the most authoritative legal scholars (such as Lord McNair) already recognized the capacity of international organizations to conclude treaties.[26]

Art. 6 of the 1986 Convention – according to which "the capacity of an international organization to conclude treaties is governed *by the rules of that organization*" – diminished the importance of the power of these organizations to conclude treaties, giving them a *minimum capacity* for such a purpose. In other words, the capacity of international organizations to conclude treaties was *limited* by the same organizational rules set forth in their constituent instruments. This means that it is the will *of the States* which create the organization which *determines* the scope of its *competence* to conclude treaties, when drafting the *rules* of the or-

---

26 See McNair, Arnold Duncan. *The law of treaties*, cit., p. 50-52. In relation to this matter, see also the ground-breaking studies of Schneider, J. W., *Treaty-making power of international organizations*, Genève: Droz, 1963, 154p; and Chiu, Hungdah, *The capacity of international organizations to conclude treaties, and the special legal aspects of the treaties so concluded*, The Hague: Martinus Nijhoff, 1966, 225p.

ganization.[27] Therefore, these rules grant the relevant international organization the capacity to conclude treaties. Art. 2, item 1(j) of the 1986 Convention defines what must be understood by "rules of the organization": these rules mean, in particular, *constituent instruments*, *decisions* and *resolutions* adopted in accordance with them, and established practice of the organization. Consequently, the 1986 Convention understood that the capacity of international organizations to conclude treaties is derived from their own constituent instruments, from the exclusive law applicable to that organization, there being no uniform rule for all organizations in that connection.[28]

The non-standardization of the law related to the capacity of international organizations to conclude treaties arose from the impossibility of giving the same legal treatment to international organizations that are completely different, both in their structure and scope of operation. Hence, Special Rapporteur Paul Reuter proposed a solution: finding a formula flexible enough, relating to the capacity of international organizations, which could "cover all possible solutions and respect the great diversity" among them.[29]

2.2 Some treaties included in the 1986 Convention

There are many possibilities for applying the Vienna Convention of 1986. Our purpose here is to list some practical examples of this application. According to a current study on the matter,[30] it is possible to highlight some types of agreements to which the 1986 Convention is applied. Some of them include:

2.2.1 Headquarters agreements

The so-called *headquarters agreements* are international treaties concluded between the relevant international organization and the State

---

27 Cf. Schneider, J. W. *Treaty-making power of international organizations*, cit., p. 135-136; and Remiro Brotons, Antonio, *Derecho internacional público*, vol. 2, cit., p. 57.

28 For examples, see De La Guardia, Ernesto, *Derecho de los tratados internacionales*, cit., p. 377-378.

29 See Reuter, Paul [Special Rapporteur], *Yearbook of the International Law Commission* (1974), vol. II, Part One, p. 149-150.

30 See, for further information on all these matters, Bernardes, Maurício da Costa Carvalho (*et al.*), A Convenção de Viena de 1986 sobre direito dos tratados entre Estados e organizações internacionais e entre organizações internacionais…, cit., p. 188-195.

where the *organization headquarters* shall be located.[31] By means of these agreements, the *locations* of organization headquarters are established, which may open their specialized agencies in other places, in relation to which new agreements shall be concluded with the foreign nations that will host them.

Consider the following example: the main headquarters of the UN is in New York, but its office is located in Geneva (Switzerland) and its International Court of Justice in The Hague (Netherlands).

2.2.2 Agreements on privileges and immunities

Headquarters agreements usually include rules on the privileges and immunities of international organizations in the territory of the host State. In general, the agreements on privileges and immunities of international organizations complement headquarters agreements. However, they may be independently concluded when organization officials participate in temporary delegations or visit places where the organization does not have permanent headquarters.

Many privileges and immunities are granted to intergovernmental organizations through these agreements such as, for example, those related to the inviolability of delegation headquarters location, including its property, jurisdiction and execution immunities, and fiscal and tax privileges, which exempt the organization from paying certain taxes or charges in the territory of the State where it is located, etc.

2.2.3 Agreements for the creation of bodies related to the organization in States

Other examples of treaties concluded between international organizations and States are those concerning the creation of bodies related to the organization in States.

In the 1990's, by means of these kinds of agreements, as a result of the decision of the UN Security Council, with the participation and favorable vote of Brazil, two international tribunals of non-permanent nature having jurisdiction on humanitarian law-related issues were established: one to judge the atrocities committed in the territory of the former Yugoslavia from 1991, and the other one to judge the equally serious violations of

---

[31] On this subject, see Cahier, Philippe, *Étude des accords de siège conclus entre les organisations internationales et les États où elles résident*, Milano: Giuffrè, 1959, 449p.

human rights committed in Rwanda, respectively headquartered in the Netherlands and Tanzania.[32]

2.2.4 *Agreements to organize meetings and promote cooperation between international organizations*

The agreements to organize meetings and promote cooperation between international organizations are treaties signed by interested organizations (which generally have complementary purposes and objectives) in order to promote meetings with other international bodies to discuss matters of their interest, usually involving cooperation between them.

Here, it is worth mentioning the agreements concluded by the ILO with other international bodies, for example the International Civil Aviation Organization (ICAO), in order to promote meetings where officials related to the relevant organization field of activity (in this case, civil aviation workers) seek alternatives for common problems.

2.2.5 *Agreements to give conferences of international organizations in States*

One last example of a treaty that may be concluded by an international organization is the treaty signed to organize *conferences* of international organizations in different States. Both the United Nations and its specialized agencies (for example, the IMF, IBRD and ILO) have signed these kinds of treaties with States hosting conferences of such agencies. As far as the environment is concerned, there are examples of conferences of intergovernmental organizations held in different States all over the world.

These agreements are provisional (despite their enormous substantial complexity) and are only effective while the conference is being held in the territory of the State.

2.3 Questions not prejudged by the 1986 Convention

Art. 74 (1), (2) and (3) of the 1986 Convention, includes many questions (divided into the three groups of paragraphs mentioned) not affected by the Convention provisions.[33]

---

32 In relation to these tribunals, see Mazzuoli, Valerio de Oliveira, *Tribunal Penal Internacional e o direito brasileiro*, 3. ed. (reviewed, updated and expanded), São Paulo: Revista dos Tribunais, 2011, p. 33-34.

33 For detailed information on the ILC debates related to this matter, see De La Guardia, Ernesto, *Derecho de los tratados internacionales*, cit., p. 441-446.

The first item states that the provisions of the Convention shall not prejudge any question that may arise in regard to a treaty between one or more States and one or more international organizations (*a*) from a succession of States (*b*), from the international responsibility of a State or (*c*) from the outbreak of hostilities between States (Art. 74, 1).

The second item establishes that the provisions of the Convention shall not prejudge any question that may arise in regard to a treaty, (*a*) from the international responsibility of an international organization, (*b*) from the termination of the existence of the organization or (*c*) from the termination of participation by a State in the membership of the organization (Art. 74, 2).

Finally, the third and last item states that the provisions of the Convention shall not prejudge any question that may arise in regard to the establishment of obligations and rights for States members of an international organization under a treaty to which that organization is a party (Art. 74, 3).

Part V

Treaties and Internal Law

Chapter 1

Constitutional Procedural Aspects on the Conclusion of Treaties in Brazil

1.1 Introduction

Apart from the *international* procedure to conclude treaties (regulated by the Vienna Conventions of 1969 and 1986), there are *internal* procedural steps to conclude international acts.[1] States are responsible for maintaining, within their internal Law, a system to integrate international norms signed by them. These procedural aspects are either governed by law or regulated by the constitutional text, the latter being the case of Brazil. Therefore, the aim is to study the competence of different branches of the State to conclude treaties – also referred to as *treaty-making power*[2] – and the procedure to incorporate these instruments into the Brazilian legal system.[3]

---

1 See, in this sense, McNair, Arnold Duncan, *The law of treaties*, cit., p. 58-77.

2 The expression *treaty-making* power was literally used, for the first time, by Henry Wheaton in the work *Elements of International Law* (2 vols.), originally published in 1836. In this book, the English 6th edition (1929) of Wheaton's work was used, which was, in its turn, updated and extended by A. Berriedale Keith (where the expression *treaty-making power* appears, for instance, in page 497). In relation to this matter, see also Tucker, Henry St. George, *Limitations on the treaty-making power under the Constitution of the United States*, Boston: Litte & Brown, 1915, 420p; and Blix, Hans, *Treaty-making power*, London: Stevens & Sons, 1960, 414p.

3 See, for further information on all these matters, Cachapuz de Medeiros, Antônio Paulo, *O poder de celebrar tratados...*, cit., p. 339-473. See also Soares, Guido Fernando Silva, The treaty-making process under the 1988 Federal Constitution of Brazil, *Chicago-Kent Law Review*, vol. 67, n.º 2 (1991), p. 495-513; Mazzuoli, Valerio de Oliveira, O poder legislativo e os tratados internacionais: o *treaty-making power* na Constituição brasileira de 1988, *Revista de Informação Legislativa*, year 38, No. 150, Brasilia: Federal Senate,

Historically, within the absolutist doctrine, the Executive Power (then called *Sovereign*) was always considered the highest organ of international relations. The Monarch, who represented the State itself, had the so-called *jus representationis omnimodae*, that is, the embodiment of absolute State power. However, as time went by, political changes (as a result of the victory of the bourgeois revolution in France) entailed *limitations* on the competency of the Executive Power concerning its power to conclude treaties. The assent of the Legislative Power was added to the will of the Executive Power, thus giving birth to the internal separation of State powers in order to democratize the procedure concerning the conclusion of treaties.[4] Consequently, it became usual in democracies to submit treaty to the Parliament for its consideration, even in countries with presidential government systems, affirming the theory that the combination of wills of the Executive and Legislative Powers is always necessary for a treaty to be valid as an effective act of law. For that reason, even though the participation of the Legislative Power in the treaty-making process democratizes international relations, preventing the Executive Power from conducting foreign policy at its own discretion, there is no State where the powers to conclude treaties are exclusively exercised by the Parliament.[5]

The regulation of the participation of the Legislative Power in the conduct of foreign affairs was resumed, in modern times, as a result of the American Constitution of 1787 and the French Constitution of 1791. In fact, the American Constitution set forth, in Art. II, Section 2, Clause 2, that the President "shall have Power, by and with the Advice and Consent

---

Apr/Jun/2001, p. 27-53; Gabsch, Rodrigo d'Araujo, *Aprovação de tratados internacionais pelo Brasil: possíveis opções para acelerar o seu processo*, Brasilia: Fundação Alexandre de Gusmão, 2010, p. 43-122; and Mazzuoli, Valerio de Oliveira, Comentário ao artigo 49, I, in Canotilho, J. J. Gomes; Mendes, Gilmar F.; Sarlet, Ingo W. & Streck, Lenio L. (coord.), *Comentários à Constituição do Brasil*, cit., p. 1018-1022. As regards the incorporation of treaties into Portuguese Law, see Pereira, André Gonçalves & Quadros, Fausto de, *Manual de direito internacional público*, cit., p. 201-208; and Gouveia, Jorge Bacelar, *Manual de direito internacional público*, 3. ed. (updated and extended), Coimbra: Almedina, 2008, p. 327-369.

4 See Pereira de Araújo, João Hermes. *A processualística dos atos internacionais*, cit., p. 147. As this internationalist points out: "The great concern of new legislators was undoubtedly international policy, taking into account the spectrum of dynastic wars, secret agreements and the whole apparatus of the absolutist diplomacy. This concern had naturally to be reflected in the procedural aspects of the conclusion of treaties and conventions so as to limit the sovereign powers, uncontested until that time" (Idem, ibidem).

5 See Rodas, João Grandino. A constituinte e os tratados internacionais, cit., p. 43-44.

of the Senate, to make Treaties, provided two thirds of the Senators present concur". This was the first constitutional text in the world to establish the control of foreign relations by the Legislative Power, even though it was subsequently interpreted so as to allow the conclusion of other international acts (not included in the expression *treaties*, corresponding to the term *tratados* in Portuguese) by the unilateral will of the Executive Power, regardless of any parliamentary expression, when the understanding concluded was a mere *agreement* (that is, a simple *commitment*, whose meaning, in the American practice – which, at this point, is contrary to the meaning of treaty embodied in the Vienna Convention of 1969 –, as opposed to a *treaty*, which is the only instrument that requires Senate assent in such country). However, the development of legislative control over international acts was a result of the constitutional and democratic ideals of the French Revolution. At the proposal of Mirabeau, the French Constitution of 1791 welcomed the idea that the expression of consent by the Executive Power should be complemented by the Legislative Power assent. In fact, the French Constitution of 1791 in Art. 3, Section 1, Chapter III, stated "Ratification of treaties of peace, alliance, and commerce appertains to the legislative body; and no treaty shall be effective without such ratification"; it was further stated, in Art. 3, Section 3, Chapter IV, that "conclusion and signature, with all foreign powers, of all treaties of peace, alliance, and commerce, and other conventions that he deems necessary for the welfare of the State appertain to the King, subject to ratification by the legislative body".[6] The intervention of the Parliament in the conduct of foreign policy affairs was also included in the subsequent French constitutions: the Girondin Constitution, and the constitutions of 1793, that of the year III and that of the year VIII.

As can be seen, as a result of passage of these two constitutional texts, that is, the American and French constitutions, the legislative control over foreign relations became of utmost importance for the conduct of the foreign policy by the Executive Power, bringing about significant changes in the treaty-making process practice throughout the world. Therefore, the previous regime, in which the absolutism prevailed and the prerogative to conclude treaties was of the exclusive competence of the Monarch was left behind. As the Monarch embodied the State, there was no reason for

---

6 A technical impropriety should be pointed out in the aforementioned documents, to the effect that a Legislative Body ratifies treaties. As is well-known, Parliaments *do not ratify* international treaties, as ratification is an (exclusive) act of the Government, being not a few the authors that use that expression improperly (see below).

his/her acts to be approved by any other Power. Upon approval of the American and French revolutions certain "international provisions" were introduced into Constitutions, which developed and finally gave birth to what Mirkine-Guetzévitch named *International Constitutional Law*, consisting of a set of constitutional provisions whose contents have international meaning and force.[7] Among several procedural stages, the so-called *legislative stage* was then introduced, which came *after* the signature and precisely *before* the ratification, making such ratification conditional on the Parliamentary acceptance of the treaty concerned.[8] This fact, in turn, contributed to promoting the democratization process of international relations, which intensified during the 19th century.[9]

The constitutional texts that came after the French Charter, and were based on it, had two modalities: *a*) those that subject to parliamentary approval any and all international agreements, such as (in principle) the Brazilian constitutional text of 1988; and *b*) those that expressly set forth which treaties need parliamentary approval and which do not (system of *positive list* or *limited enumeration*). This last system, named *Belgian system*, as it appeared with the Belgian Constitution of 1831, was also subsequently adopted in France, and examples can be found up to this date.[10] In the current French system (Art. 53 of the Constitution of October 4, 1958), only some treaties must be subject to parliamentary approval, namely, "[p]eace Treaties, Trade agreements, treaties or agreements relating to international organization, those committing the finances of the State, those modifying provisions which are the preserve of statute law, those relating to the status of persons, and those involving the ceding, exchanging or acquiring of territory, may be ratified or approved only by an Act of Parliament".[11] The Brazilian constitutional text of 1824, the Venezuelan constitution of 1961 and the Peruvian constitution of 1979 followed the same line.

---

7 See Mirkine-Guetzévitch, Boris. Droit international et droit constitutionnel, *Recueil des Cours*, vol. 38 (1931-IV), p. 307-465.

8 See Pereira de Araújo, João Hermes. *A processualística dos atos internacionais*, cit., p. 148.

9 See Mello, Celso D. de Albuquerque. *Ratificação de tratados...*, cit., p. 81-85.

10 On the subject of the so-called Belgian system, see Cachapuz de Medeiros, Antônio Paulo, *O poder de celebrar tratados...*, cit., p. 101-112.

11 In relation to the French system, see Dinh, Daillier & Pellet, *Direito internacional público*, cit., p. 154-162; Carreau, Dominique, *Droit international*, 8. ed., Paris: A. Pedone, 2004, p. 115-120; and Combacau, Jean & Sur, Serge, *Droit international public*, 6. ed., Paris: Montchrestien, 2004, p. 121-124.

The truth is that, up to this moment, the rules that govern legislative approval of international treaties have not undergone significant formal changes, having also stabilized in the Brazilian constitutional system, in spite of some complications that affected said system related to the material contents of some treaties which, in the opinion of some legal scholars, do not require parliamentary approval, as discussed below.

1.2 The 1988 Brazilian Constitution and the treaty-making power

Documents signed by the Brazilian Government on behalf of the Republic are, according to Brazilian internal law, subject to a complex procedure. Consequently, within the scope of the powers of the Republic, the aforementioned procedure consists of a series of acts that are carried out by the Executive Power in collaboration with the Legislative Power.[12]

The study of Brazilian Republican Constitutions, under the perspective of the internal norms concerning the treaty-making process, shows that the several subsequent Brazilian Constitutions contain few provisions on this matter and that they share similar features, both from a procedural and substantial perspective. From the time of the First Republic onwards, the system adopted by Brazil as to this matter establishes the participation of the Legislative Power in the treaty-making process, having had no major changes in the Brazilian constitutional texts up to the present time.

The competence to conclude treaties was intensely discussed in the Constitutional Convention of 1987-1988. Due to an inexcusable error of the legislator, during the conclusion of works, the Drafting Committee did not respect the will of the Plenary and gave rise to two apparently contradictory provisions: Arts. 49, I and 84, VIII.[13] These articles provide as follows:

> "Article 84. The President of the Republic shall have the exclusive power to:
>
> (...)
>
> VIII – conclude international treaties, conventions and acts, subject to the approval of the National Congress;"

---

12 See Martins, Estevão Rezende. A apreciação de tratados e acordos internacionais pelo Congresso Nacional, in Cançado Trindade, Antônio Augusto (ed.), *A incorporação das normas internacionais de proteção dos direitos humanos no direito brasileiro*, 2. ed., San José, Costa Rica/Brasilia: IIDH (*et all.*), 1996, p. 263-264.

13 For detailed information on this matter, see Cachapuz de Medeiros, Antônio Paulo, *O poder de celebrar tratados...*, cit., p. 339-382.

> "Article 49. It is exclusively the competence of the National Congress:
>
> I – to decide conclusively on international treaties, agreements or acts that result in charges or commitments encumbering the national patrimony;"

From the analysis of the above articles it may be inferred that the will of the Executive Power, expressed by the President of the Republic, shall not be fully effective until the National Congress makes a decision as to the possibility to accede to a given treaty. Therefore, without the Parliament's *authorization*, the Brazilian Government cannot, in principle, *ratify* or *accede* to an international treaty. The 1988 Constitution, however, following the national tradition on the matter (the only exception was the Empire's Constitution of 1824), no longer listed the treaties subject to parliamentary approval. For this reason, doubts emerge as to whether Brazil can accede to certain treaties without congressional approval, including, in particular treaties in simplified form.

1.3 The issue of treaties concluded in simplified form

For a long time, notably from the entry into force of the Constitution of 1946, the Brazilian legal literature has discussed the matter concerning the need of *all* international acts signed by Brazil to be subject to the approval of the National Congress. This discussion, which not only takes place in Brazil, shows the need for contemporary constitutional texts to mitigate the participation of parliaments in the treaty-making process, particularly as a consequence of the development of international relations and the popularization for international agreements of less importance.[14] Some legal scholars, led by Haroldo Valladão, understood that the National Congress should approve each and every international act concluded by the Executive Power, since the expression *treaty* is generic, and the successive Brazilian Constitutions made no distinctions as to its possible different types.[15] Other internationalists, on the contrary, recog-

---

14 See Pereira de Araújo, João Hermes. *A processualística dos atos internacionais*, cit., p. 148-149.

15 See Valladão, Haroldo. Aprovação de ajustes internacionais pelo Congresso Nacional, *Boletim da Sociedade Brasileira de Direito Internacional*, Rio de Janeiro, Jan/Dec/1950, p. 95 *et seq.*; Marotta Rangel, Vicente, A Constituição brasileira e o problema da conclusão dos tratados internacionais, *Problemas Brasileiros*, No. 31, São Paulo: Conselho Regional do Serviço Social do Comércio, Oct/1965, p. 11 *et seq.*; Melo Franco, Afonso Arinos de, Poder legislativo e política internacional, in *Estudos de direito constitucional*, Rio de

nized as valid some international agreements concluded only by the Executive Power, considering the internal and international practice on this matter, notably the American practice.[16] Hildebrando Accioly supported this last current, since according to his opinion it was possible to conclude international agreements without the approval of the National Congress. In Accioly's opinion, the *cornerstone* to solve this question was not the *formalities* of the act, but the *matter* discussed in the treaty. He stated: "If the matter dealt with in the treaty is of the exclusive competence of the Legislative Power, it is clear that such act cannot be valid without the legislative approval; and, if the matter depends on that approval, it must be subject to ratification".[17] According to Accioly, the following acts would not be subject to formal approval by the Legislative Power:

a) agreements on matters that are of the exclusive competence of the Executive Power;

b) agreements concluded by agents or officials with competence to do so, on matters of local interest or limited importance;

c) agreements that merely provide for the interpretation of clauses of a treaty already in force;

d) agreements arising, logically and necessarily, out of a treaty in force and constitute a complement to that treaty;

e) *modus vivendi* agreements, to the extent that they only aim at leaving things as they are or simply lay the foundations for future negotiations;

Janeiro: Forense, 1957, p. 257 *et seq.*; Pontes de Miranda, *Comentários à Constituição de 1946*, 2. ed., vol. II, São Paulo: Max Limonad, 1946, p. 404; Cavalcanti, Themistocles Brandão, *A Constituição Federal comentada*, vol. II, Rio de Janeiro: José Konfino, 1952, p. 127 et seq; and Maximiliano, Carlos, *Comentários à Constituição brasileira*, 5. ed., Rio de Janeiro: Freitas Bastos, 1954, p. 242 *et seq.*

16 See, to that effect, Accioly, Hildebrando, A ratificação e a promulgação dos tratados em face da Constituição Federal brasileira, *Boletim da Sociedade Brasileira de Direito Internacional*, No. 7, Rio de Janeiro, Jan/Jun/1948, p. 5-11; Carneiro, Levi, Acordo por troca de notas e aprovação pelo Congresso Nacional, *Boletim da Sociedade Brasileira de Direito Internacional*, No. 13/14, Rio de Janeiro, Jan/Dec/1951, p. 129 *et seq.*; and Pereira de Araújo, João Hermes, *A processualística dos atos internacionais*, cit., p. 160-173. See also, on this matter, Rodas, João Grandino, *Tratados internacionais*, cit., p. 29; and Mello, Celso D. de Albuquerque, *Direito constitucional internacional...*, cit., p. 288.

17 Accioly, Hildebrando. A ratificação e a promulgação dos tratados em face da Constituição Federal brasileira, cit., p. 6-8.

f) agreements that provide for the extension of a treaty, before its expiration date; and

g) the so-called *extradition declarations*, that is, reciprocity commitments concerning extradition matters.

Accioly supported his position by making reference to the American practice of "executive agreements", which cover the most important matters and whose validity is not subject to the approval of the American Senate. He also advocated that the Constitutions of 1934 and of 1946, when deleting the word "agreements", which appeared in the Constitution of 1891, restricted the field of operation of the Legislative Power. Thus, when analyzing this problem consideration should be given to the matter discussed in the agreement: if the "act" is of the competence of the Executive Power, pursuant to the Constitution, the act as such can take the form of an executive agreement.[18]

Opposed to the argument asserted by Accioly, Haroldo Valladão, in his capacity of Legal Consultant of Itamaraty, in his *Opinion* on the consultation made by the Minister of Foreign Affairs of that time, Raul Fernandes, regarding the need of legislative approval of a payment agreement concluded with France, explained that it is unacceptable that treaties which are not subject to ratification be immune to congressional approval, since this would amount to solving a constitutional exegesis based upon international law. In Valladão's opinion, the extent of the powers that the Government of a State has to negotiate and sign international acts constitutes a typical question of internal law, exceeding the scope of application of international law. He also stated that Brazil is signatory to the Havana Convention on Treaties of 1928, which imposes the absolute need for ratification for *all* international treaties, without exception [see Art. 5]. Finally, he added that the American rule (cited by Accioly) would not be applicable in Brazil, since the Brazilian Constitution [he was referring to the Constitution of 1891, Art. 48, No. 16] did not distinguish, as American constituent members did, between *treaties* and *agreements of less importance*, only stating "agreements, conventions and treaties", all subject to the approval by the Legislative Power, as being a prerequisite (*sine qua non* condition) for their validity and consequent effectiveness

---

[18] See Accioly, Hildebrando. Ainda o problema da ratificação dos tratados, em face da Constituição Federal Brasileira, *Boletim da Sociedade Brasileira de Direito Internacional*, N°. 11/12, Rio de Janeiro, Jan/Dec/1950, p. 95-108.

at the national level. The only exception admitted by Haroldo Valladão would be related to "pacts established by military leaders, within the limits of their competencies".[19]

Accioly replied to these considerations mainly arguing that within the force of the Constitution of 1891, international agreements were concluded without the Congress approval, as evidenced by the *Code of Foreign Affairs*, published in 1900. He considered the argument that Brazilian constituent members aimed at subordinating the Executive Power to the Legislative Power was unjustified, as even in countries with parliamentary regimes, the Head of the Nation or Government is in charge of conducting the foreign policy. He asserted that in international academic writings and case law there is no principle stating the absolute need of ratifying all treaties, without exceptions. Examples of exceptions to the principle of absolute need of ratification would be the so-called *agreements concluded in simplified form*, which enter into force upon their signature. According to Accioly, even the Havana Convention of 1928 recognizes the contrary principle, stating that "treaties shall become effective from the date of exchange or deposit of ratification, unless some other date has been agreed upon through an express provision" [see Art. 8]. Finally, Accioly insisted on the thesis of *reasonability* of the exclusive competence: with the matter having exclusive competence of the Executive Power, there would be no reason for the agreement, once approved, to be authorized by the Legislative Power, in order to enter into force. In his opinion the custom of many years' standing – even if established, as claimed, *extra legem* – never required the approval of the Parliament for certain international acts, as shown by the modern current and the most authoritative legal academic writing.[20]

In spite of all these different opinions, the fact remains that the practice of the Brazilian Ministry of Foreign Affairs, as well as the opinion

---

19 See Valladão, Haroldo. Aprovação de ajustes internacionais pelo Congresso Nacional, cit., p. 95-108. The following authors supported the thesis of Valladão, taking into consideration the wording of the constitutional text of 1946: Melo Franco, Afonso Arinos de, Poder legislativo e política internacional, cit., p. 257 *et seq.*; Pontes de Miranda, *Comentários à Constituição de 1946*, vol. II, 2. ed., cit., p. 404; Marotta Rangel, Vicente, A Constituição brasileira e o problema da conclusão dos tratados internacionais, cit., p. 11 *et seq.*; and Cavalcanti, Themistocles Brandão, *Constituição Federal comentada*, vol. II, cit., p. 127 *et seq*. Both authors recognized the need that any and all international agreements be approved by the Legislative Power, without exceptions.

20 See Accioly, Hildebrando. Ainda o problema da ratificação dos tratados, em face da Constituição Federal Brasileira, cit., p. 20-23.

of many of its legal consultants, always followed the trend mentioned by Accioly. João Hermes Pereira de Araújo, for example, understood that the fact that Brazilian Constitutions subsequent to the 1891 Constitution did not mention the words "always" and "agreements", included in it, created conditions for the appearance of an *extra legem* customary rule capable of allowing a broad interpretation, to the effect that international acts of less importance would be exempt from approval by the Legislative Power. He did not consider the constitutional text so rigid as to avoid exceptions, this fact being shown by the large number of international acts concluded by Brazil without the participation of the Parliament. Therefore, we would be in the presence of a common case in International Law, and odd in our Public Law, of a norm of *customary* origin.[21] This position even has European advocates as important as Paul Reuter, who, referring to Latin American Constitutions, asserts that they include constitutional rules so rigid – as seems to be the case of one Brazilian constitutional text after the other – that make the conclusion of treaties unfeasible.[22]

The controversy intensified even more with the drafting of the constitutional text of 1967, whose Constitution referred to "treaties, conventions and international acts", which served as a basis for Haroldo Valladão to reaffirm his opinion on the impossibility of approving any type of international act without the authorization of the National Congress.[23] In this respect, Francisco Rezek stated that defending the validation of international acts without any kind of parliamentary consent based on the existence of an international custom, as Accioly and Pereira Araújo did, becomes an exercise *contra legem* and no longer *extra legem*, as it was in the republican Brazil before 1967. According to Rezek, it is not possible to understand the formation of a "constitutional custom *against the letter of the Constitution*", which is incomprehensible as it contradicts the legal

---

[21] See Pereira de Araújo, João Hermes. *A processualística dos atos internacionais*, cit., p. 168-169. This internationalist concludes as follows: "In view of these arguments, I consider perfectly defensible not only the constitutional possibility, but also the existence, among us, of a customary rule according to which, within the scope of the exclusive competence of State powers, international acts dealing with matters that are the competence of the Executive Power dispense with the National Congress *referendum*" (Idem, p. 172-172).

[22] Reuter, Paul. *Introducción al derecho de los tratados*, cit., p. 33.

[23] See Valladão, Haroldo. Necessidade de aprovação pelo Congresso Nacional de acordo internacional, *Boletim da Sociedade Brasileira de Direito Internacional*, No. 49/50, Rio de Janeiro, Jan/Dec/1969, p. 111 and following pages. See also Rodas, João Grandino, *Tratados internacionais*, cit., p. 39-40.

logic. There is no doubt as to the existence of the psychological element of custom, which is highly questionable, however, because the mere silence as to official publications does not constitute *opinio juris*; apart from what, at times, there were expressions contrary to the practice. He also criticized the opinion of those that argue the practice of executive agreements due to the need to make rapid decisions, concluding that the possible delay in the approval by the Legislative Power originates either from the little importance of the object of the agreement or the indifference of the Executive Power itself. Thus, not considering the obscure reference to "agreements on matters that are of the exclusive competence of the Executive Power", and those "concluded by agents or officials with competence to do so, on matters of local interest or limited importance" (first and second categories listed by Accioly[24]), Rezek understands – in accordance with the current Brazilian constitutional text – that such commitments concluded without congressional approval may only be validated in the other three hypotheses presented by Accioly, namely: 1) in the cases in which those agreements "merely set forth the interpretation of clauses of a treaty already in force"; 2) when they "arise, logically and necessarily, from a current treaty and are a complement to such treaty", and finally;

24 The second category (from which only separate examples are obtained) is so obscure that it is pointless to discuss it abstractly. In this sense, see Rezek, José Francisco, *Direito dos tratados*, cit., p. 310. In relation to the first case ("agreements on matters that are exclusive competence of the Executive Power"), a brief comment should be made. The fact that the Executive Power has competence to issue regulatory decrees, exclusively, within the scope of internal Law, does not empower it to act at the international level with identical powers, even when dealing with very similar matters. At the internal level, the right of the Executive Power to make certain decisions *sponte sua* is based on the law. And such law, formulated by the Legislative Power, may change at any time, in which case the decrees previously issued by the President of the Republic shall completely lose their value. For that reason it is dangerous to apply the same reasoning used at the internal level, in parallel, to the scope of International Law, because even if the executive competence on matters that may be negotiated through treaties were set forth in law, it would still be possible for the Congress to change (or repeal, etc.) that law. Therefore, the fact that the President may issue decrees on matters of his competence does not empower him to conclude international treaties related to the same matter, without the approval of the National Congress. To conclude, it is worth mentioning the good example formulated by Rezek: "The President of the Republic, by virtue of his singular constitutional authority, freely appoints and dismisses State ministers, and also exercises supreme command over the armed forces. However, nobody shall consider that he is authorized to conclude executive agreements, for example, with Ecuador or the Holy See, temporarily sharing that supreme command, and subjecting the appointment and dismissal of ministers to the opinion of the Roman Curia" (*Direito dos tratados*, cit., p. 311-313).

3) when they are *modus vivendi*, understood as those agreements "that only aim at leaving things as they are or simply lay the foundations for future negotiations". In these cases, the basis for validity of such agreements would be found in the constitutional text itself. In the first and third hypotheses, such treaties would merely be the performance of the diplomatic duty of properly understanding a treaty concluded by parliamentary approval; this case is about executive agreements as an expression of ordinary diplomacy (this means they are "included in the diplomatic routine"), whose authorization for conclusion is based on subsection VII of Art. 84 of the 1988 Constitution, according to which the President of the Republic has the exclusive powers to "maintain relations with foreign States…", as it occurs in *truce agreements* and similar pacts, in *cease-fire*, in the agreement to *preserve certain areas*, or to *exchange prisoners*, apart from other agreements made by military commandos (which, however, shall not be confused with agreements to *make peace*, for which, as stated by the Constitution, the President of the Republic shall need the approval or authorization of the Congress, in accordance with Art. 84, XX). Nevertheless, Rezek draws attention to the fact that these agreements shall only be recognized, according to subsection VII of Art. 84 of the Constitution, if two essential elements are present: *reversibility* (by which these agreements shall be terminated unilaterally, stated in a communication to the other party, without delays – contrary to what would normally occur in case of denunciation) and *preexistence of budgetary coverage* (that is, such agreements shall depend, only and exclusively, on budgetary resources *allocated to foreign relations*, and never on others). In the second hypothesis of Accioly's list (treaties that "arise, logically and necessarily, from a current treaty and are a complement to such treaty"), the justification of Rezek is that there would be an anticipation of the Congress consent, which is already aware, when approving the main agreement, of the fact that there may be new treaties (executive agreements) as a consequence of the previous treaty (nothing prevents this formula from being expressly rejected in the legislative decree of approval, as occurred in the Basic cooperation agreement Brazil-Libya, which established that "all the amendments or changes introduced in the text mentioned in the previous article shall only be effective and binding on the Country after the respective approval by the National Congress").[25]

---

[25] See Rezek, José Francisco. Parlamento e tratados: o modelo constitucional do Brasil, *Revista de Informação Legislativa*, year 41, No. 162, Brasilia: Federal Senate, Apr/Jun/2004, p. 130-138.

However, the Brazilian practice of making agreement in simplified form, concluded without the express and specific authorization of the Legislative Power in their different modalities, is very intense in Brazil, as shown by the numerous agreements concluded by our country in this way. A proposal was submitted by the Subcommittee of Nationality, Sovereignty and International Relations, during the formulation of the Constitution of 1988 to regulate the problem at a constitutional level. Subsections VI and VIII of Art. 26 of the proposed text stated that the President of the Republic had the exclusive powers to "negotiate and conclude treaties and other international commitments when authorized by law or a previous treaty, subjecting them, in any other cases, to the approval of the National Congress, before their ratification"; and also "communicate to the National Congress the contents of all treaties and commitments negotiated without the need for prior approval by the Legislative Power", what would be made, in accordance with Art. 28 within the term of up to *three months* from the conclusion of the treaty.

The Brazilian Constitution of 1988, which introduced innovations as compared to previous Constitutions, asserts that the National Congress shall have exclusive powers to decide definitively (apart from *treaties*) on *international agreements* and *acts* (Art. 49, I). As it may seem, the discussion related to the approval by the Parliament of agreements in simplified form may have come to an end as a result of the new wording of the current Brazilian constitutional text. However, even with the modification of wording of the provisions of the 1988 Constitution, a number of Brazilian jurists still argue that executive agreements are fully admissible in Brazil and do not require the approval of the National Congress.[26] Furthermore, even with the current drafting of the Constitution of 1988, it must be acknowledged that there is an established diplomatic practice, beyond the wording of the constitutional text, by which the Executive Power concludes many types of agreements, without the assent of the Legislative Power, with the consequent undermining of the popular power.[27] The problem, as it can be perceived, is very difficult. Even though there is a closed constitutional norm for such kinds of agreements, there is also concern for determining which orientation shall better satisfy the interests of Brazil in the international arena. This customary practice *extra legem*

---

26 See Soares, Guido Fernando Silva. The treaty-making process under the 1988 Federal Constitution of Brazil, cit., p. 506-507; and Rezek, José Francisco, *Direito internacional público: curso elementar*, 9. ed. (reviewed), São Paulo: Saraiva, 2002, p. 62-64.

27 See Cachapuz de Medeiros, Antônio Paulo. *O poder de celebrar tratados...*, cit., p. 199.

is also applied – apart from countries such as the United States of America – in several Latin American countries, such as Argentina, Chile, Bolivia, Colombia, Mexico, Paraguay, Uruguay and Venezuela.[28] The truth is that, without ignoring the constitutional text, a better basis must be found to justify the agreements concluded in simplified form than the mere pseudo-concern about the protection of Brazilian interests abroad. The doctrine that advocates the full possibility of such agreements among us is certainly better grounded in the current tendency to reduce the level of strictness of the constitutional rule (which states that *all* international treaties concluded by the Brazilian State shall be subject to Parliamentary approval) in favor of a smaller avalanche of treaties that excessively encumbers the Legislative Power, giving rise to an actual *back-log* of treaties pending approval.[29] For this reason, the current Brazilian Constitution (of 1988) permitted exceptions to the principle of mandatory legislative *approval* for all treaties, exceptions based on the previously mentioned *extra legem* custom (which, however, cannot become *contra legem*).

Finally, this constitutional relaxation permitting the conclusion of agreements in simplified form is consistent with contemporary principles of Public International Law (especially, the principle of *international solidarity*). Nowadays, as Reuter points out, international life (based on solidarity) requires that, under certain circumstances, some agreements be concluded and applied rapidly, rendering impracticable those rigid constitutional norms that subject *all* international acts to legislative approval.[30]

Perhaps, the solution to the problem is for the Constitution to determine (through a Constitutional Amendment, in the future) those cases in which agreements in simplified form are permissible, as well as those cases in which the Parliamentary approval would not be necessary in relation to certain agreements concluded by the Executive Power (thus using the so-called *Belgian system*). However, while this does not occur, that is, while the constitutional text is not amended, and it is no longer possible to prevent the proliferation of these agreements, it must be considered to (*a*) prefer the wording of the constitutional text, which subjects *all* international treaties, agreements or acts to the approval of the National Congress, or (*b*) value the

---

28 For detailed information on this matter, see Pereira de Araújo, João Hermes, *A processualística dos atos internacionais*, cit., p. 158-160.

29 See Nascimento e Silva, Geraldo Eulálio do. Direito internacional no projeto de reforma da Constituição, *Boletim da Sociedade Brasileira de Direito Internacional*, No. 43/44, Rio de Janeiro, Jan/1966, p. 13-14.

30 See Reuter, Paul. *Introducción al derecho de los tratados*, cit., p. 33.

practice of international acts that has (long) been followed by the Brazilian diplomacy in this area. The intentional scope of the current Brazilian Constitution (which affects any and all types of international acts concluded by the Government) is well perceived when reading the provisions stating that the President of the Republic and the National Congress shall unite forces, respectively, to conclude "international treaties, conventions and acts" (Art. 84, VIII) and approve "international treaties, agreements or acts" that result in charges or commitments encumbering the national patrimony (Art. 49, I), which makes the position of the interpreter very difficult in the consideration of values between the constitutional text and the mentioned *extra legem* custom already adopted by us.

1.4 The relationship between the Executive Power and Legislative Power in the treaty-making process

According to the Constitution of 1988, "the Union shall have the power to maintain relations with foreign States and participate in international organizations" (Art. 21, I). However, in spite of the clarity of this constitutional provision, the interpreter cannot be confused as to its actual meaning, as the *Union* is only a legal entity of *internal* law, never of International Law; the legal entity of International Law is the *Federative Republic of Brazil* and not the Union, which is only one of its components. The President of the Republic, in turn, has the exclusive powers to "conclude international treaties, conventions and acts, subject to the approval of the National Congress" (Art. 84, VIII).[31] The expression "*conclude* treaties" includes from the *negotiations* to the *signature* of the agreement, not involving (or being able to involve) its *ratification*, a matter not dealt with by the Constitution. The Congress, in turn, has exclusive powers to "decide definitively on international treaties, agreements or acts that result in charges or commitments encumbering the national patrimony" (Art. 49, I).

The truth is that, while the Executive Power conducts the foreign policy of the country, the Legislative Power exercises control over acts of the Executive, as the former is in charge of defending the Nation in the international arena.[32] As a treaty involves the commitment of national

---

31 See Mazzuoli, Valerio de Oliveira. Comentário ao artigo 84, VIII, in Canotilho, J. J. Gomes; Mendes, Gilmar F.; Sarlet, Ingo W. & Streck, Lenio L. (coord.), *Comentários à Constituição do Brasil*, cit., p. 1241-1246.

32 Sometimes, the Executive Power tries to take away from the Legislative Power the internal control of international acts, by means of some well-known resources, such as execu-

sovereignty, it cannot produce effects if it is not followed by the approval of the Congress, which represents the national will. The President of the Republic, with the exclusive competence granted by the Constitution, acts by his own right, and not by delegation of the Parliament.

Once the negotiation stage of a treaty is concluded, the President of the Republic – who could have not participated in it, if such negotiation would have been of a collective nature, or could have withdrawn from it, thus interrupting the participation of the country, if the negotiation would have been bilateral – has the door open to carry out, or not, the process leading to the expression of consent by the State to be bound by an international commitment.[33] Being satisfied with the agreement concluded, the Head of the Executive Power *may* subject it, when he/she deems appropriate, to the consideration of the Parliament (as it represents the will of the Nation) for its approval. He may also order more in-depth studies within the scope of the Executive Power before sending the conventional text to the Legislative Power. In case the President of the Republic is not satisfied with the result of a bilateral or collective negotiation – except for labor international conventions, concluded within the scope of the ILO, whose constituent treaty (Art. 19, No. 5, *b*) *establishes the obligation* to subject such acts to parliamentary approval[34] – he may even order that it be archived.

The file to submit the treaty to the National Congress is prepared by the Ministry of Foreign Affairs. The committees (*ratione materiae)*, or negotiators, prepare the text of the *statement of reasons* by which the Minister of Foreign Affairs, after stating the reasons why the government signed the treaty, justifies the need for its ratification. Thereafter, he/she requests the President of the Republic to submit the treaty to the Legislative Power, as provided for by the Constitution. Itamaraty, at the same time, prepares the text of the *presidential message* for the submission of the treaty to the Congress, as well as a notice to the Secretary of the Chamber of Deputies, sending the whole file.[35]

---

tive agreements and clauses of acceptance or approval of treaties, which notably arose after the Second World War.

33 See Rezek, José Francisco. *Direito dos tratados*, cit., p. 325.

34 From this fact the obligation also arises to ratify ILO conventions approved by the Parliament, according to the prevailing doctrine understanding. This is the only known exception to the ratification discretion (see Part II, Ch. 1, item 1.5.2.5.4, above).

35 See Pereira de Araújo, João Hermes. *A processualística dos atos internacionais*, cit., p. 182.

The National Congress, in turn, when requested to give its opinion, materializes what was decided on international treaties, agreements or acts, by preparing a *legislative decree* (Art. 59, VI, Federal Constitution/88). Through this instrument, the Congress approves the treaty internally and then authorizes the President of the Republic to ratify it. If the treaty is *rejected*, no such regulation is issued, in which case the decision is only communicated, through a *message*, to the Head of the Executive Power. Among the cases of treaty disapproval, which are not very common, it may be pointed out, for example, the Argentine-Brazilian treaty of January 25, 1890, on the border of the Missions territory, rejected by the Plenary Session of the National Congress on August 18, 1891, by one hundred and forty-two votes against five.[36]

The Brazilian model of *legislative decree* to approve international treaties is included below:

> I hereby inform that the NATIONAL CONGRESS approved, in accordance with Art. 49, item V, of the Constitution, and I, MAURO BENEVIDES, President of the Federal Senate, promulgate the following
>
> **LEGISLATIVE DECREE NO. 27, OF 1992**
>
> *Approves the text of the American Convention on Human Rights (Pact of San José) concluded in San José de Costa Rica, on November 22, 1969, during the specialized Inter-American Conference on Human Rights.*
>
> The NATIONAL CONGRESS decrees as follows:
>
> Art. 1. It is hereby approved the text of the American Convention on Human Rights (Pact of San José) concluded in San José de Costa Rica, on November 22, 1969, during the specialized Inter-American Conference on Human Rights.
>
> Art. 2. Any acts that may result in the review of this convention, as well as those that establish complementary agreements, are subject to the approval of the National Congress.
>
> Art. 3. This legislative decree enters into force on the date of its publication.
>
> Federal Senate, May 26, 1992.
>
> **SENATOR MAURO BENEVIDES**
> President

From the Constitution of 1946, eliminating the great imprecision existing in the use of the term "legislative decree", it was established, in the Internal Regulations of the Houses of the National Congress, the use of such expression to refer to those acts that are the "exclusive competence" of the Legislative Power, that is, those acts that are not subject to presidential approval. Thus, the legislative decree is a regulation approved by the Legislative Power on a matter of its exclusive competence (Art. 49, Federal

---

36 See Rezek, José Francisco. *Direito dos tratados*, cit., p. 333.

Constitution/88), such as approving international treaties or reviewing accounts rendered by the President of the Republic. Only one decree may approve more than one treaty; but, if the treaty previously approved and duly ratified is later claimed, a *new* legislative decree shall be necessary in case of new approval of the same treaty.[37] In Brazil, legislative decrees for treaty *referendum* do not make *expressis verbis* reference to subsequent ratification, contrary to what happens in France, where the corresponding decree states the President of the Republic is "authorized to ratify the treaty" after being issued.[38]

As the legislative decree is exclusive competence of the National Congress, it is not subject (be said again) to presidential approval, being subject only to promulgation by the President of the Senate. In addition, the reasons why – as stated by Francisco Campos – the Constitution does not subject decisions voted by the Legislative Power to the approval of the President are obvious. The futility of the presidential approval or its inconvenience may arise from the fact that the Head of State already expressed his position in favor of a matter, or because it is a mere approval of acts already practiced by the President, or because the decisions only grant to the President an authorization requested by him before the Legislative Power.[39]

Finally, in relation to the Brazilian State, international treaties, agreements and conventions, for them to be included in the internal law, that is, to be ratified and then promulgated, *need* prior approval of the Legislative Power, which controls and oversees acts performed by the Executive Power. Therefore, it must be pointed out that treaties have, at least, status of internal law, and as such they must be respected in the same way current legislation in domestic law is obeyed. On the other hand, the Parliamentary approval of international treaties also complies with the provisions of Art. 2 of the Constitution, which states that the Legislative, Executive and Judicial Powers are independent and harmonious with each other. Therefore, the National Congress approves the text of the treaty and *authorizes* (not compels) the Head of the Executive Power to ratify it, which shall only happen (or not, depending on the discretionary will of the President) at a later time. The ratification formality would be completely pointless

---

37 See Rezek, José Francisco. Idem, p. 334.

38 See Pereira de Araújo, João Hermes. *A processualística dos atos internacionais*, cit., p. 181-182.

39 Campos, Francisco. *Direito constitucional,* vol. II, cit., p. 308.

if it was a compulsory (unchallengeable) act and not a discretionary act as it should be.[40] This means that the President, when negotiating and adopting a treaty in the international arena, only commits the country potentially, as such instrument still depends on the legislative *approval* and subsequent *ratification*. There are many examples in diplomatic files of treaties which were not ratified, either due to loss of its subject-matter, or lack of interest from the Nation at the time of its ratification, or even because the agreement is not timely ratified after years of being processed in the National Congress, when it became obsolete.

Our Federal Parliament, as can be noted, also participates in foreign policy without affecting the performance of the Executive Power at an international level. In addition, it should be emphasized that the Brazilian Constitution contains the following provision:

> "Article 49. It is exclusively the competence of the National Congress:
>
> XI – to safeguard preservation of its legislative authority in the face of rule-making powers of the other Branches".

The fact that the Executive Power is the main branch responsible for the conduct of foreign relations (even in countries with parliamentary democracy) does not prevent the Legislative Power at all from also playing its role, which is passive but equally important, in foreign relations. Hence, the general understanding is that the balance between the two Powers of the Union participating in the treaty-making process (Executive and Legislative Powers) is more apparent than concrete, merely considering the fact that historically (notably in federative regimes) the Head of the Executive Power was always the main one responsible for the conduct of State foreign affairs. Indeed, the *direct* intervention of the Legislative Power in international business would result in important issues affecting the dynamism required by foreign policy and other diplomatic actions, but it is impossible to deny the right of the National Congress *not to approve* international acts it considers as *harmful* to national interests.

It should be clarified that the *ad referendum* competence of the Congress is only limited to the *approval* or *rejection* of the conventional text, being inadmissible any interference with its content. Therefore, amendments are not allowed. What the Congress may do (as already discussed in Part II, Ch. 2, item 2.12) is to formulate *reservations*. If the Congress agrees with the signature of the international treaty, through a legislative

[40] See Beviláqua, Clóvis. *Direito público internacional...*, t. II, cit., p. 22-23.

decree, the President of the Republic is given the green light to ratify the signature already deposited, or even accede to it if he had not done it.

Parliamentary approval may be *retracted*, as long as the treaty has not been ratified. If the treaty was not ratified yet, that is, if the State did not make a definitive commitment at an international level (regardless of the fact that the treaty has entered into force internationally or not), the Congress, through a legislative decree, may revoke any act that has approved the agreement.[41] This may not happen if the State already made a definitive commitment.

Even though the *legislative decree* is included within the regulations of Art. 59 of the Constitution, that is, in spite of being included in the "legislative process", it is not capable of transforming a treaty *signed* by the government into a norm to be observed, whether at a national or international level.[42] This shall only occur with the subsequent ratification and promulgation (through an execution decree) of the text of the treaty by the Head of the Executive Power. What happens is that, as the Constitution grants the President of the Republic exclusive competence to conclude treaties, and the President being the representative of the State at an international level, he has the last word on ratification matters, and only then will the State be considered *definitively* committed to the corresponding agreement. The expression (*referendum*) of the National Congress is only definitive when it *disapproves* the text of the treaty submitted to it, in which case the President of the Republic shall not be able to continue with the conclusion of the agreement, ratifying it. Therefore, international treaties do not enter into force within Brazilian internal law from the issuance of the legislative decree. They become effective after their subsequent *ratification* (and consequent *promulgation*) by the President of the Republic, who has exclusive competence to conclude international treaties, conventions and acts (Art. 84, VIII, Federal Constitution/88).[43] The

---

41 See Rezek, José Francisco. *Direito dos tratados*, cit., p. 335. As mentioned by Rezek, there is a precedent in such regard: the Legislative Decree 20, of 1962, which revoked the previous Legislative Decree 13, dated October 6, 1959, which approved the Redemption Agreement signed in 1956 between the Governments of Brazil and France (Idem, p. 335-336).

42 See Fraga, Mirtô. *O conflito entre tratado internacional e norma de direito interno...*, cit., p. 56.

43 See Pereira de Araújo, João Hermes. *A processualística dos atos internacionais*, cit., p. 251, for whom: "The fact that the treaty has been approved through a legislative decree shall not excuse its promulgation, since an approved act may never enter into force because, if the legislative approval conditions the ratification, it shall not render it bind-

ratification is essential for a treaty to be applied at an internal level, even because the internal force of a foreign agreement depends on the *prior* international force of the act, which is only achieved through it. Therefore, it cannot be conceived that an international act becomes binding internally before becoming binding at an international level, even if the State ratifies and promulgates the treaty before such date.[44]

> "(...) it could not be conceived that an international act became binding internally before becoming binding at an international level. Indeed, a treaty can only bind one of the States when it also binds the other, and since the effectiveness or entry into force of treaties only begins with the exchange of ratifications, it is clear that the internal publication of the ratification act of the treaty by one of the contracting parties cannot generate for such party or within the limits of its territory the entry into force or effectiveness of a treaty, which shall only become effective after the contracting parties have exchanged the respective ratification instruments. It would be unconceivable that a contract, before being concluded or perfected in all its elements, was already effective or binding as a contract. An international treaty only becomes perfect at the time and in the place in which ratifications are exchanged or deposited. Before being perfect or complete, a contract is not binding, it is not even a contract. However, were this odd theory to be admitted, it should be accepted that, ratifications made by contracting States, at different times and sometimes separated by long periods of time, would only be effective in the country where the ratification was first published, while the treaty, which is not yet a treaty for the other State, would however, be effective for the more diligent party only as to its obligations, and for the negligent party or the party performing a late ratification there would only be advantages and no obligation".
>
> Campos, Francisco. *Direito constitucional*, vol. II, cit., p. 318-319.

The Brazilian Constitution of 1988, when it set forth the competence of the established powers to conclude treaties, in Arts. 49, I ("It is exclusively the competence of the National Congress: I – to decide conclusively on international treaties, agreements or acts which result in charges or commitments that go against the national property") and 84, VIII ("The President of the Republic shall have the exclusive power to: VIII – conclude international treaties, conventions and acts, subject to the approval of the National Congress"), did so taking into consideration only the first two stages of the common process to conclude international agreements, namely, the *signature* (implied in the expression "*conclude* treaties...") and the *Congress approval*, not having set forth the other subsequent stages (*ratification* and *exchange* or *deposit* of their

ing, let alone affect the other contracting party that, up to the exchange of ratifications, is free to do so".

44 See Pereira, André Gonçalves & Quadros, Fausto de. *Manual de direito internacional público*, cit., p. 111.

instruments), which our constitutional legislator did well when he decided not to interfere in foreign affairs. For this reason, the fact that the Constitution did not deal with the *ratification* – which, as already seen, is an act of essentially *foreign* interest – does not mean that with the Congress approval of the treaty it is ready to generate effects internally. For this to occur, first the international instrument must enter into force at an international level.

In brief, the Legislative Power is entitled to analyze the feasibility of adhering to what the President of the Republic (or its plenipotentiary) signed with other sovereign entities. It is not important to inquire the reason of this constitutional choice, if to prevent a vulnerable Head of State from easily surrendering to tensions or threats from a foreign power, or only to respect the democratic principle of Parliamentary participation in the acts of the Executive Power. The truth is that, in the presence of a complex procedure of the powers of the Union, in which, in order to formalize treaties the Legislative Power and the Executive Power must always participate. Without the participation of these two Powers the act is not complete. Thus, it can be said that the Constitution of 1988 adopted the *theory of complex acts*, which in this area best reflects the public law and democratic regime principles.

In this process, the Judicial Power acts only after the international treaty has been duly incorporated into our law, and the SFC, as guardian of the Constitution, is entitled to decide on *extraordinary appeal* cases decided in sole or last instance, "when the appealed decision declares a treaty or a federal law unconstitutional" (Art. 102, III, *b*, Federal Constitution/88). The Constitution of 1988, in turn, grants the SCJ competence to decide on *special appeal* cases decided, in sole or last instance, by the Federal Regional Courts or by Courts of the States, "when the appealed decision is contrary to a treaty or federal law, or denies the effectiveness thereof" (Art. 105, III, *a*, Federal Constitution/88). Finally, Art. 109 of the Constitution states that federal judges have the power to hear and to decide "cases based on a treaty or a contract of the Union with a foreign State or international organization" (item III), as well as "crimes covered in international treaties or conventions, when their commission has begun in the Country and their results have to take place or should have taken place abroad, or reciprocally" (item V).

What the President of the Republic cannot do is to give the definitive consent of the State to be bound by the treaty without the approval of the National Congress. Even though the President is in charge of the dynamics of international relations, being entitled to decide both on the convenience of starting negotiations and of ratifying an international act already concluded,[45] the authorization of the Legislative Power, in the form of congressional approval, is necessary.[46] The approval of the Congress in relation to the conventional text completes only *one stage* of the whole treaty-making process. The legislative decree of the Congress shall have no value if the treaty is not ratified and promulgated by the President of the Republic.[47]

1.5 The role of the National Congress in the treaty-making process

There is great confusion, on the part of doctrine in general, as to the true role of the National Congress in the treaty-making process, certainly caused by the wrong interpretation of the constitutional text.

The Constitution of 1988 states that the National Congress has exclusive powers to "decide definitively on international treaties, agreements or acts that result in charges or commitments encumbering the national patrimony" (Art. 49, I).

From this provision, a large part of the legal scholars holds that, first of all, the Congress *ratifies* international treaties and, secondly, only treaties "that result in charges or commitments encumbering the national patrimony" must be approved by the Parliament. Others even maintain that the President of the Republic is *obliged* to ratify treaties (*definitively*) approved by the Parliament. These are gross mistakes. The interpretation of the phrase "decide definitively" and what are considered "charges or commitments encumbering the national patrimony", in relation to the role of the Congress in the treaty-making process, must be compared to the competence of the Head of the Executive Power to "conclude international treaties, conventions and acts", set forth by Art. 84, VIII, of the Constitution of 1988.

Therefore, we are going to analyze separately the meaning of "decide definitively on international treaties" (item 1.5.1) and the interpretation of the expression "charges or commitments encumbering the national patrimony" (item 1.5.2) used in Art. 49, I, of the Federal Constitution.

---

45 See Crandall, Samuel B. *Treaties: their making and enforcement*, cit., p. 93-101.

46 See Rezek, José Francisco. *Direito dos tratados*, cit., p. 326-331.

47 See Fraga, Mirtô. *O conflito entre tratado internacional e norma de direito interno...*, cit., p. 68-69.

1.5.1 The expression "decide definitively" used in the Constitution

As is well-known, only the Head of the Executive Power is entitled to *ratify* international treaties, and nobody else. In this area, he has the last word. The Parliament, in turn, has powers to *approve* or *reject* a treaty signed by the Executive Power, and nothing else. Thus, the expression "decide *definitively* on international treaties" used in the constitutional text must be duly understood, not being possible to interpret such phrase with a broader meaning that extrapolates its actual scope. What is the meaning of aforementioned expression set forth in Art. 49, I, of the Constitution? Does such definitiveness involve a *definitive consent* of the State? Clearly, the response is in the negative. It is wrong and incorrect to refer to the *ratification* of the treaty *by the National Congress*, as Levi Carneiro, then Legal Advisor to Itamaraty, did in his *Opinion* dated February 7, 1947, entitled "*Acordos sobre compra de tecidos: necessidade de ratificação pelo Congresso Nacional*", and in another document, dated September 9 of the same year, entitled "*Acordo mediante notas reversais para assegurar o cumprimento de tratado: necessidade de ratificação pelo Congresso Nacional*".[48] The confusion arises from the wrong interpretation of the expression "decide definitively", included in the Brazilian Constitution of 1988 and others already mentioned, for example the Constitution of 1946, which was in force at the time of such *Opinion*.

The expression "decide definitively", an unhappy legacy of the first republican Constitution, does not imply in the Brazilian system the *ratification* of the treaty, which is an exclusive act of the Head of the Executive Power, responsible for the conduct of international relations, who is entitled to decide both on the convenience of starting negotiations and ratifying an international act already concluded; this only means that the Parliament is authorized to (1) accept the treaty signed by the Executive Power and (2) reject it, if deemed convenient, not being another meaning of the expression *approval*, as also explained by dictionaries. Therefore, the Parliament has powers to either *approve or reject* treaties submitted to it for consideration, and the Head of the Executive Power has powers to (discretionarily) *ratify them*, if approved by the Congress.

---

[48] Both published in: Cachapuz de Medeiros, Antônio Paulo (org.), *Pareceres dos consultores jurídicos do Itamaraty*, vol. IV (1946-1951), Brasilia: Federal Senate, 2000, p. 49-50 and p. 117-118, respectively. The same Legal Advisor, some years later, in his *Opinion* of September 20, 1949, referred to the parliamentary expression as "*homologation* by the National Congress" (*op. cit.*, p. 318-322), and also as "*approval* by the National Congress" (*op. cit.*, p. 323-326 and p. 401-414).

The expression *definitively* used in the Constitution must be interpreted under the theory of *useful effects*, according to which obscure or ambiguous legal rules must always be interpreted so as to produce the greatest sense and efficiency possible in relation to their purpose.[49] Therefore, knowing that it is the President of the Republic who really decides *definitively* on a treaty, once the agreement is approved by the Congress, we must ask this question: which is the *useful effect* that can be obtained from the expression then? The only possibility is to consider that the expression "definitively" is useful in case of *rejection* of the treaty by the Parliament. Thus, it must be understood that the National Congress only decides *definitively* on a treaty when it *rejects* the agreement, in which case the Executive Power cannot ratify it.[50] In case of approval, who decides *definitively* is the Head of the Executive Power, when ratifying or rejecting the treaty. If the treaty is not ratified, however, the President of the Republic exercises a right that is inherent in and characteristic of the State sovereignty, which does not constitute or involve any kind of unlawful act or penalty at an international level, which clearly shows the *definitiveness* of his political-discretionary decision. For this reason, the expression *decide definitively*, which, besides, is maintained today in Brazilian Constitutions, has been considered one of the most inappropriate among the expressions used in this area. Cachapuz de Medeiros, for example, considered it as "the most inappropriate, since the decision effectively definitive rests with the President of the Republic, who may or may not ratify international treaties, after they have been approved by the Congress".[51] Thus, the expression of the National Congress, following the rule of useful effects, is only definitive when it *disapproves* the text of the treaty previously signed, in which case the President of the Republic shall not be able to ratify the treaty.[52] However, if the Congress approved the treaty submitted to it for consideration, the Head of the Executive Power has the last word, and may or may not ratify the treaty, at his discretion,

---

49 In relation to the rule of useful effects, see Berlia, G., Contribution à l'interprétation des traités, cit., p. 306-311.

50 See Cachapuz de Medeiros, Antônio Paulo. *O Poder de celebrar tratados...*, cit., p. 118. In the same sense, see Rezek, José Francisco, As relações internacionais na Constituição da primeira República, *Arquivos do Ministério da Justiça*, No. 126, Jun/1973, p. 110-111.

51 Cachapuz de Medeiros, Antônio Paulo. *O poder de celebrar tratados...*, cit., p. 117.

52 See Fraga, Mirtô. *O conflito entre tratado internacional e norma de direito interno...*, cit., p. 57; and Mello, Celso D. de Albuquerque, *Direito constitucional internacional...*, cit., p. 292.

as he deems more convenient and appropriate. These criteria of *convenience* and *opportunity* – classic in Administrative Law – must govern the behavior and performance of the Executive Power in relation to the definitive conclusion (*ratification*) of a treaty already approved by the Parliament, mainly in those cases in which the parliamentary approval only occurred several years after the signature of the agreement, regardless of the reasons for such delay.

For this reason, it is worth clarifying, once and for all, that the National Congress *does not ratify* any kind of international act, although its *approval* represents the will of the whole Nation, which means the full realization of the democratic ideal. And the Congress does not ratify such acts because it has no outside voice, nor has it the power to establish international relations with other States. Actually, through the legislative decree our Federal Congress *authorizes* the ratification of the agreement, which is an exclusive (discretionary) act of the Head of the Executive Power. Therefore, when the legislative decree approves an international treaty, it does not "create" the right, and it does not affect the legal system. The international treaty continues being a treaty, and is not "transformed", *ipso facto*, into internal Law through the intervention of the Congress. In this area, the Parliament only approves or rejects the conventional text, so that the approval of the Legislative Power, in relation to the treaty, does not make it compulsory, since the President of the Republic, after that, may or may not ratify it, depending on his will.

> "Parliaments do not ratify international treaties. They only analyze them, authorizing or not the Executive Power to commit the State.
> Therefore, the ratification is an exclusive right of the Head of the Executive Power, by which he confirms to the other parties, definitively, the will of the State to comply with an international treaty.
> It is worth making clear that the approval of the Legislative Power does not make a treaty obligatory, because the Executive Power still has the right to ratify it nor not, as it deems more convenient.
> This is a universal rule, being unanimously understood that the decision to ratify rests with the same Power in whose name the treaties were signed.
> Basically, it is stated that, after some time has passed from the signature of the international agreement, the political circumstances may have changed, and the new situation may no longer recommend the commitment of the State".
> CACHAPUZ DE MEDEIROS, Antônio Paulo. *O poder legislativo e os tratados internacionais*. Porto Alegre: L&PM, 1983, p. 133.

It seems that a large number of national legal scholars has not properly understood this matter yet. Many authors still insist on mistakenly stating that the National Congress *ratifies* treaties.[53] It must be clarified that the *approval* of the Congress is one thing, and the *ratification* of the President of the Republic is another very different thing. The National Congress – it should be said again – *does not ratify* treaties. Who ratifies treaties is the Head of the Executive Power, that is, the President of the Republic. Without this presidential act there is no *valid* treaty to commit the Nation, both at an international and internal level. In addition, the approval of the treaty by the Legislative Power *does not force* its ratification.[54] If this were the case, the ratification would be unnecessary. The

---

53 This mistake seems to be even more rooted among tax jurists. Some of them, such as Ives Gandra da Silva Martins, even state that the treaty or convention does not produce internal effects, but the *legislative decree* approving them, since the Congress has powers to "decide definitively" on treaties (see *Temas de direito público*. São Paulo: Juarez de Oliveira, 2000, p. 89). The lesson of Sacha Calmon Navarro Coêlho is not different, which points out that "international treaties and conventions – which are acts concluded by the executive power through the President or plenipotentiary ministers – only revoke or modify tax legislation once approved by the National Congress, through legislative decrees, giving them substantially and formally the quality of law" (*Comentários à Constituição de 1988: sistema tributário*, 6. ed. Rio de Janeiro: Forense, 1997, p. 288). In addition, consider the words of Paulo de Barros Carvalho, for whom "international treaties and conventions do not have legal capacity to revoke or modify internal legislation, legislative decrees ratifying them do, which incorporate such treaties into the Brazilian legal order" (*Curso de direito tributário*, 18. ed. reviewed and updated. São Paulo: Saraiva, 2007, p. 79). This last tax jurist, as can be seen, apart from not granting "legal capacity" to treaties, as if they had no importance or value within our legal order, also understands that legislative decrees of the National Congress have *greater* legal stature than treaties (besides mistakenly stating that parliamentary decrees *ratify* treaties)!

54 Pedro Dallari is not right (for the reasons already explained) when he advocates the relationship between the ratification and the parliamentary approval of treaties, in these words: "As regards the third controversy mentioned above, on the related or discretionary nature of the presidential act of ratification or accession after the approval of the treaty by the National Congress, it can be said that the prevailing doctrine understanding – which is also adopted in the formalization of international agreements by Brazil – is that the legislative decree issued by the federal parliament is a mere authorization, not forcing the performance of any act by the Head of the Executive Power [in a note, he quotes Cachapuz de Medeiros when he states that the congressional approval "does not make a treaty obligatory, because the Executive Power has the right to ratify it nor not, as it deems more convenient"]. However, such understanding seems to contradict the emphasis with which the Constitution grants the National Congress competence to decide 'definitively' on treaties (Art. 49, I). Even though it appears in previous constitutional texts, what other meaning, considering the markedly democratizing guideline of the 1988 Constitution, may the expression 'definitively' have which is not the effective approval of the international treaty for its norms to be incorporated into the Brazilian

internal stage of the treaty-making process (legislative approval) cannot be confused with the *international* stage of the ratification, dealt with in the Vienna Convention on the Law of Treaties of 1969.

1.5.2 *The question of "charges or commitments encumbering the national patrimony"*

Finally, we should analyze the last part of item I of Art. 49 of the Constitution of 1988. Although some constitutional jurists – like José Afonso da Silva – see no "difficulty in the understanding of the text under analysis",[55] we think that Art. 49, I, *in fine*, of the Constitution is one of the most difficult provisions to be understood within the system of treaty approval and conclusion in Brazil, as will be explained below.

In the final part of Art. 49, I, the Constitution adds that international treaties, agreements or acts must involve "charges or commitments encumbering the national patrimony" to be subject to the approval of the National Congress. As can be noted, this phrasing was not the most appropriate, and its lack of clarity leads to important legal problems, such as the potential permission for *other international legal acts* to dodge parliamentary control. First of all, the expressions "charges", "commitments encumbering" and "national patrimony" used in the item being analyzed belong to the category of the so-called *indeterminate legal concepts*, which are difficult to interpret in the specific case and may be modified depending on the political situation and the circumstances the State is going through. These are *changing* expressions which do not attain a reasonable degree of certainty and stability necessary for the proper operation of the foreign affairs of the State.

It should be pointed out that we are dealing with international acts *stricto sensu* (that is, treaties with *long procedures*) and not with agreements *in simplified form*, which may not require (exceptionally, in the

---

legal order? What other effect may be derived from it which is not the obligation, for the President of the Republic, to perform the ratification or accession act? The possible absence of this international act would suggest a clear failure to comply with (*sic*) the decision of the National Congress" (*Constituição e tratados internacionais*. São Paulo: Saraiva, 2003, p. 96). It is clear that this (isolated) position of Pedro Dallari cannot be accepted, for all the reasons explained so far…

[55] See Silva, José Afonso da. *Comentário contextual à Constituição*, cit., p. 403.

cases already discussed) parliamentary approval, arising from the development of the referenced *extra legem* custom. We are analyzing the need for all treaties *stricto sensu* to be approved by the Legislative Power in order to be valid in Brazil.

At first, the final provision of Art. 49, I, of the Constitution of 1988, gives the false impression that not all international treaties (*stricto sensu*) concluded by the Executive Power are subject to parliamentary approval, but only those that involve "charges or commitments encumbering the national *patrimony*". And the difficulty increases when we discover the same Constitution, in another provision, states that the President of the Republic has powers to conclude international treaties, conventions and acts, (all) subject to the approval of the National Congress (Art. 84, VIII). Therefore, what would be the correct interpretation of these two provisions? Would those treaties that do not include charges or commitments encumbering the national patrimony be exempt from parliamentary approval?

The antinomy between Arts. 49, I and 84, VIII of the Constitution of 1988, is only apparent. As already explained, Art. 84, VIII, states that *all* international treaties, conventions and acts concluded by the Head of the Executive Power must be subject to the approval of the National Congress. Based on this provision, we should extensively interpret Art. 49, I, of the Constitution, considering the constituent legislator – according to Cachapuz de Medeiros – said less than he meant to: *lex minus dixit quam voluit*.[56] In accordance with this understanding, evidently the desire of the Constitutional Convention was to subject *all* international treaties, agreements or acts to the approval of the Legislative Power, and not only those that include charges or commitments encumbering the national patrimony. Therefore, the provision of Art. 84, VIII, of the Constitution prevails, which is more suitable for the national tradition and subjects *all* treaties signed in the name of the Nation to the approval of the National Congress.[57]

---

56 Cachapuz de Medeiros, Antônio Paulo. *O Poder de celebrar tratados...*, cit., p. 395.

57 See, in such regard, Mello, Celso D. de Albuquerque, *Direito constitucional internacional...*, cit., p. 293-294. To solve the apparent antinomy between the constitutional provisions mentioned above, Cachapuz de Medeiros uses the historical-teleological and logical-systematic methods and arrives at the following conclusion: "From the historical-teleological point of view, the only possible conclusion is that the constituent legislator wanted to establish the obligation of the congressional assent for [all] international treaties, *emphasizing* those that include financial charges, encumbrances [or] burdens

We arrive at the conclusion explained above analyzing the *purpose* of the combination of rules of Arts. 49, I and 84, VIII, of the Constitution, making a systematic and teleological interpretation of the constitutional system to conclude treaties. However, we could arrive at the same conclusion through a detailed literal interpretation of the rule of Art. 49, I, of the 1988 Constitution. If special consideration is given to the wording of this provision, it can be noted that it states that the National Congress shall have exclusive powers to "decide definitively on international treaties, agreements or *acts that result in charges or commitments encumbering the national patrimony*". Therefore, international treaties or agreements are not the ones that must result in charges or commitments encumbering the national patrimony for them to be, only in this case, subject to the approval of the Legislative Power. The "charges or commitments encumbering the national patrimony" mentioned in the Constitution are related to *international acts*, not the *treaties* and *agreements* mentioned in the constitutional text. This is suggested, of course, by the lack of punctuation: after the expression *international acts*, the Constitution does not include any dividing punctuation, that is, a *comma*, which would combine the last phrase ("charges or commitments encumbering the national patrimony") with the international treaties and agreements mentioned in the text. And if the constituent legislator decided to do that, it was because he desired to subject *all* international treaties and agreements, as well as *international acts that result in charges or commitments encumbering the national patrimony*, to the approval of the Federal Parliament. The generic expression "international acts", first added to the *treaties* and *agreements* by the text of the Constitution of 1967, and maintained by subsequent Constitutions, is aimed at all those instruments that, for any reason, did not receive the proper name of *treaties*. Therefore, the Constitution uses such expression as a true synonym of international agreement, and this never lead to the hypothesis that such addition would represent the obligation to submit to the Congress any act that was not an actual *treaty*.[58] However, if after

affecting the national patrimony. From the logical-systematic point of view, we should consider that these provisions belong to the same title of the Constitution (Organization of the Branches) and are like two sides of the same coin: Art. 84, VIII, grants the President of the Republic the power to conclude international treaties, conventions and acts, but states that *all* are subject to the approval of the National Congress; Art. 49, I, states that treaties, agreements or acts that result in charges or commitments encumbering the national patrimony must be approved by the Congress" [italics are ours] (*O Poder de celebrar tratados...*, cit., p. 397).

58 See Cachapuz de Medeiros, Antônio Paulo. *O Poder de celebrar tratados...*, cit., p. 398.

the expression "international acts" and before the last phrase referring to "charges or commitments encumbering the national patrimony", the constituent legislator had inserted a comma, the situation would be different. In this case, the "charges or commitments encumbering the national patrimony" would be linked to international treaties as well as international agreements or acts. But the Constitution – which it did well – did not intend it that way, as it preferred to subject *all* international treaties and agreements, *as well as* international acts that result in charges or commitments encumbering the national patrimony to the approval of the Legislative Power.

The conclusion at which we arrive is that Art. 49, I, *in fine*, of the 1988 Constitution distinguishes three situations: *a*) international treaties, whichever they are; *b*) international agreements, whichever they are (including here agreements in simplified form); and *c*) international acts that may result in charges or commitments encumbering the national patrimony. And, for the Constitution, *all of them* require congressional approval.

1.6 Internal procedure in the Houses of the National Congress

The National Congress, to analyze the feasibility of adhering to the treaties signed by the Executive Power, follows some internal stages that must be studied.[59]

In first place, the Legislative Power receives the *message* of the President of the Republic, accompanied by the Statement of Reasons (Exposição de Motivos – EM) of the Minister of Foreign Affairs, addressed to him, together with the full text of the treaty subject to approval. The above-mentioned *message*, headed by a notice of the Minister and Chief of Staff to the President, is sent to the First Secretary of the Chamber of Deputies, where its analysis shall begin, since by express constitutional determination "debates and votes on bills initiated by the President of the Republic (...) shall start in the Chamber of Deputies" (Art. 64).[60]

The matter is discussed and voted separately, beginning, as already stated, in the Chamber of Deputies. The approval, both in the Chamber

---

59 For further information see Pereira de Araújo, João Hermes, *A processualística dos atos internacionais*, cit., p. 180-188.

60 See Martins, Estevão Rezende. A apreciação de tratados e acordos internacionais pelo Congresso Nacional, cit., p. 264.

of Deputies and in the Senate, is done by a majority vote (simple, relative) of present members in both Houses, with the absolute majority of members present, according to the rule of Art. 47 of the Constitution. It shall only be considered approved by the Congress with the approval of *both* Houses, so that an "eventual disapproval within the Chamber of Deputies ends the process, there being no reasons to submit the question before the Senate in such circumstances".[61]

It shall be read in the Plenary Session, for Deputies to be informed of it in compliance with the principle of publicity. Then, a *process* is formed (which is called "Message"), with its own number, and that, under Art. 32, XV, *c*, of the Internal Regulations of the Chamber of Deputies, shall be sent to the Committee of Foreign Affairs. This Committee, after the analysis of the text of the treaty by a rapporteur designated from its members, assesses the report and issues an *opinion*. This opinion must include a *project* of legislative decree, which shall be subject to the approval of the Committee of Constitution, Justice and Citizenship (Art. 32, IV, of the Internal Regulations), which is in charge of analyzing the "constitutional, legal, judicial, regulatory and legislative technique aspects of projects, amendments or modifications subject to the approval of the Chamber or its committees". Once the project is approved by the Committees, it shall be subject to voting in Plenary Session. After the project is approved, in a single session, the final wording shall be submitted by the Committee of Constitution and Justice (Art. 32, IV, *q*). The final wording is approved and, then, the project is subject to the approval of the Federal Senate, according to Art. 65 of the Constitution[62]. Once the project is read and published, it shall be sent to the Committee of Foreign Affairs and National Defense, which is, in accordance with the provisions of the Internal Regulations of the Federal Senate, the competent Committee to analyze the "proposals referring to international acts and affairs" (Art. 103, I) and to "matters related to the United Nations and international entities of any nature" (Art. 103, VI).[63]

---

61 Rezek, José Francisco. *Direito dos tratados*, cit. p. 331.

62 *In litteris*: "A bill approved by one Chamber shall be reviewed by the other in a single round of discussion and voting; if the reviewing Chamber approves the bill, it shall be sent for enactment or promulgation, or if it is rejected, it shall be archived". Sole Paragraph. "If a bill is amended, it shall return to the Chamber that initiated it".

63 For further information see Martins, Estevão Rezende, A apreciação de tratados e acordos internacionais pelo Congresso Nacional, cit., p. 264-271.

An interesting question – which deserves better analysis – is related to the possibility of the project being approved *conclusively* by the thematic Committees of the Chamber of Deputies as well as the Federal Senate. In fact, the Constitution of 1988 gives powers to the Committees of the Chamber of Deputies and the Senate, based upon subjects over which they have competence, to "discuss and vote on bills in which, in accordance with the by-laws, the authority of the entire body is unnecessary, unless an objection is made by one-tenth of the members of the Chamber" (Art. 58, item 2, I). International treaties, in turn, are approved in the Parliament by a *legislative decree*, and not a *law*. It should even be investigated if the Constitution may be referring to *law* in a *broad* sense, in which case the approval of legislative decrees authorizing treaties may also be exempt from approval of the Plenary Session. In this sense, Márcio Garcia explains that: "In our opinion, however, this is a hypothesis which allows for a broad interpretation, except for the amendments to the Constitution. Otherwise, the constituent legislator would have excluded legislative decrees from the conclusive power of the Committees of the Congress. In lato sensu, the expression would also include projects of legislative decrees. Thus, there would be no confrontation with the constitutional text when the regulations set forth the exemption of approval by the Plenary Session of international treaties and agreements. (...) Consequently, the word 'law' in the constitutional provision in discussion contemplates, in our opinion, all the legislative expressions, except for the amendment to the Constitution" (Tratados e poder terminativo na Constituição de 1988. *Revista de Informação Legislativa*, year 45, No. 179, Brasilia: Federal Senate, Jul/Sep/2008, p. 238. According to this understanding (and also the cited author), constitutional *amendments* are not excluded from approval by the Plenary Session; thus, treaties on human rights adopted internally under Art. 5, item 3, of the Federal Constitution/88, shall never be approved conclusively by the Committees of the Congress, since they must *always* be discussed in Plenary Session. Finally, it should be pointed out that the dispensation of the Plenary Session in projects of legislative decrees approving treaties has never been used in Brazil. On the subject, see also Gabsch, Rodrigo d'Araujo, *Aprovação de tratados internacionais pelo Brasil...*, cit., p. 111-114.

In each of the Houses of the Congress it is possible to propose *amendments* to the projects submitted for approval. These amendments are strictly related to the project of legislative decree, never to the text of treaties submitted for approval, which cannot be modified. However, it is understood that mere formal corrections, such as a wording adjustment in the text, which do not affect the content of the project, do not require that it be returned to the Chamber for reconsideration. The reconsideration is obligatory only in case of modification *of the merits* (Art. 65, sole paragraph, Federal Constitution/88).

Once the analysis is concluded in the Committee of Foreign Affairs and National Defense, in the Senate, the project (when approved *not* conclusively) is ready to be included in the voting agenda of the Plenary Session. The approval in the Plenary Session is performed in a single session and without amendments, after which the text of the project of legislative decree (whose final wording is dispensed) is considered as definitively approved. The approval is followed by the *promulgation*, which is a prerogative of the President of the Federal Senate, who is the President of the National Congress, as set forth by Art. 57, item 5, of the Constitution.[64] Once the decree is promulgated, it shall be numbered (by the General Secretary of the Board of the Senate) and published in the *Official Gazette of the National Congress* and the *Official Gazette of the State*. However, attached to the legislative decree, it has been published in these two pieces of the official press, the text of the approved international treaty, which caused serious confusion by those who do not know the process of international acts, as they understand that this decree makes the treaty enter into force within the country. Thus, the correct procedure would be to publish the text of the treaty which has not been ratified yet, only in the *Official Gazette of the National Congress*, and publish in the *Official Gazette of the State* only those international acts whose immediate or future effectiveness is unquestionable, so as to avoid this kind of confusion.[65]

1.7 Brazilian practice for the entry into force of treaties

After the *legislative decree* is promulgated and published by the President of the Federal Senate, the Government is authorized to *ratify* the corresponding international treaty. From that moment, the procedures necessary for the entry into force, in the national legal system of international treaties subject to ratification, are set in motion. The truth is that, apart from the rules relating to the expression of consent by the State to be bound by the treaty, provided for in the Vienna Convention of 1969, there is also a *Brazilian practice* for the entry into force of international acts, as shall be explained in the following items.

1.7.1 Final agreement and deposit

The entry into force of *bilateral acts* may be performed both by the *exchange of information* and the *exchange of ratification letters*. When the entry into force is done through the first modality (exchange of information), a note may be promptly sent to the Embassy of the other party, certified by the Brazilian Government. If within the national territory there is no Embassy of the other party, the note is sent by the Embassy of Brazil, certified by the other party. In the last case, the notification is sent

---

[64] See Martins, Estevão Rezende. Idem, p. 269.

[65] See Pereira de Araújo, João Hermes. *A processualística dos atos internacionais*, cit., p. 187-188.

by the Brazilian Mission to the UN to the Mission of the other contracting party. If the entry into force is done through the *exchange of ratification instruments*, the procedure is interrupted until both parties finish the internal steps to approve the treaty, and only then the ceremony to exchange the respective instruments is performed. Two copies of the minutes (or protocol) stating the exchange of instruments are prepared, in the languages of both contracting parties or in a third language (in general, French), which are signed by the plenipotentiaries specifically designated for the exchange.[66]

The entry into force of *multilateral acts*, in turn, requires a procedure a bit more complex. In this case, once the legislative decree is published, the multilateral act must be *ratified* to enter into force. That is, after the signature of the treaty and subsequent approval by the National Congress, the ratification instrument of the Brazilian party must be *deposited* with the Government or international organization acting as a depositary.[67] The Vienna Convention of 1969 sets forth that the designation of the depositary of a treaty may be made by the negotiating States, either in the treaty itself or in some other manner. The depositary may be one or more States (usually the State where the treaty was signed), an international organization or the chief administrative officer of the organization (Art. 76, item 1). The Convention also clarifies that the functions of the depositary *are international in character* and that the depositary is under an obligation to act *impartially* in their performance (Art. 76, item 2); this means that the depositary, being international in character, must act in a *neutral* fashion between the parties, without making any value judgments (whether political, social, etc.) as to the instrument whose deposit was

---

66 See Accioly, Hildebrando. *Tratado de direito internacional público*, vol. I, cit., p. 594. See also Balladore Pallieri, G., *Diritto internazionale pubblico*, cit., p. 256-257; and Maresca, Adolfo, *Il diritto dei trattati...*, cit., p. 167-176.

67 Brazil is depositary of many relevant international treaties, for example, the Treaty of the Río de la Plata Basin (1969) and the Amazon Cooperation Treaty (1978). For a detailed study of the depositary of international treaties, see Rosenne, Shabtai, The depositary of international treaties, *American Journal of International Law*, vol. 61, N°. 4 (Oct. 1967), p. 923-945; and Rosenne, Shabtai, More on the depositary of international treaties, *American Journal of International Law*, vol. 64, No. 5 (Oct. 1970), p. 838-852. On the subject, see also Maresca, Adolfo, *Il diritto dei trattati...*, cit., p. 215-223; Rodas, João Grandino, *A publicidade dos tratados internacionais*, cit., p. 141-198; Remiro Brotons, Antonio, *Derecho internacional público*, vol. 2, cit., p. 109-111; Aust, Anthony, *Modern treaty law and practice*, cit., p. 261-274; and Villiger, Mark E., *Commentary on the 1969 Vienna Convention on the Law of Treaties*, cit., p. 924-933.

entrusted to them.[68] In the case of treaties concluded on the auspices of international organizations, the depositary shall be the same organization.

The depositary of treaties, according to the Vienna Convention, has the following duties: *a*) maintaining custody of the original text of the treaty and of any full powers delivered to the depositary; *b*) preparing certified copies of the original text and preparing any further text of the treaty in such additional languages as may be required by the treaty and transmitting them to the parties and to the States entitled to become parties to the treaty; *c*) receiving any signatures to the treaty and receiving and maintaining custody of any instruments, notifications and communications relating to it; *d*) examining whether the signature or any instrument, notification or communication relating to the treaty is in due and proper form and, if need be, bringing the matter to the attention of the State in question; *e*) informing the parties and the States entitled to become parties to the treaty of acts, notifications and communications relating to the treaty; *f*) informing the States entitled to become parties to the treaty when the number of signatures or of instruments of ratification, acceptance, approval or accession required for the entry into force of the treaty has been received or deposited; *g*) registering the treaty with the Secretariat of the United Nations; and *h*) performing the functions specified in other provisions of the present Convention. In the event of any difference appearing between a State and the depositary as to the performance of the latter's functions, the depositary shall bring the question to the attention of the signatory States and the contracting States or, where appropriate, of the competent organ of the international organization concerned (Art. 77, items 1 and 2).[69]

In summary, it is not the ratification itself which makes the treaty effective, but the *exchange* (bilateral treaties) or *deposit* (multilateral treaties) of the letter or ratification instruments at the place (for example, the State) established by the same treaty or with the corresponding international organization. Sometimes not even the deposit is sufficient, when

---

68 In this sense, see Villiger, Mark E., *Commentary on the 1969 Vienna Convention on the Law of Treaties*, cit., p. 930-931: "Thus, the depositary must perform its functions objectively and neutrally ('formally', 'notarially') without making any substantive or political appreciation".

69 See Remiro Brotons, Antonio. *Derecho internacional público*, vol. 2, cit., p. 110-111; De La Guardia, Ernesto, *Derecho de los tratados internacionales*, cit., p. 339-340; Reuter, Paul, *Introducción al derecho de los tratados*, cit., p. 88-89; and Villiger, Mark E., *Commentary on the 1969 Vienna Convention on the Law of Treaties*, cit., p. 941-945.

the treaty requires a certain number of deposits (or even deposit by all the parties) for the treaty to enter into force at an international level.[70]

1.7.2 *Promulgation*

After the ratification instrument is deposited with the Government or organization acting as depositary, the Brazilian practice, following the Portuguese tradition, has required that the President of the Republic – who is granted by the Constitution exclusive powers to conclude international treaties, conventions and acts (Art. 84, VIII) – issues an *execution decree*, promulgating and publishing in the *Official Gazette of the State* the content of the treaty. However, there is no rule in the Constitution of 1988 establishing this procedure, being the result of a *praxis* originated from the first treaty concluded by the Empire of Brazil. Indeed, the Treaty of Recognition of Independence and the Empire, signed with Portugal on August 29, 1825, was promulgated internally, after exchanging the ratification instruments, through a decree of April 10, 1826.

> *Decree*
>
> The Treaty signed in this Court, on the twenty-ninth day of August of last year by my plenipotentiaries and John VI, King of Portugal and Algarves, my august father, being mutually ratified, through which, finally ending the war that unfortunately was necessary between the two States, the total Independence of the Brazilian Nation was recognized, and the supreme dignity, to which I was elevated by the unanimous acclamation of the peoples, with the category of Constitutional Emperor, and its Perpetual Defender; be ordered that the aforementioned Treaty be given the most exact fulfillment and execution, as it is convenient for the sanctity of Treaties concluded between independent nations and inviolable good faith, with which they are signed, the Viscount of Inhambupe de Cima, of my Council of State, Minister and Secretary of Foreign Affairs, follow this order and make execute the treaty, issuing the corresponding announcements and printed copies for the competent positions of this Court and provinces of the Empire, with the most positive orders for them to be fulfilled and kept as stated therein. Palace of Rio de Janeiro, on the tenth day of April of one thousand, eight hundred and twenty-six.
>
> With the signature of YOUR IMPERIAL MAJESTY
>
> Viscount of Inhambupe
>
> *Treaty of Recognition of Independence and the Empire*
>
> *(Excerpts)*

---

[70] See Accioly, Hildebrando. *Tratado de direito internacional público*, vol. I, cit., p. 594; and De La Guardia, Ernesto, *Derecho de los tratados internacionales*, cit., p. 144-145.

In the name of the Most Holy and Indivisible Trinity

HIS MOST FAITHFUL MAJESTY Constantly cherishing in his royal mind the most lively wishes to reestablish peace, friendship and harmony between kindred nations whom the most sacred ties should conciliate and unite in perpetual alliance; to accomplish these important ends, promote general prosperity, assure political existence, and the future destinies of Portugal as well as Brazil; and desirous of removing at once all obstacles which might impede the said alliance, concord, and happiness of both States, by his diploma of the thirteenth of May of the current year, recognized Brazil as an independent Empire, and separated from the kingdoms of Portugal and Algarves, and his son PETER as Emperor, and freely ceding and transferring the sovereignty of the said Empire to the said son, and his legitimate successors, and taking only and reserving for his own person the same title.

And these august sovereigns accepting the mediation of HIS BRITANNIC MAJESTY for the adjustment of every question incident to the separation of the two States, have nominated plenipotentiaries, to wit [...].

And the said plenipotentiaries having seen and exchanged their respective powers, have agreed, in conformity with the principles expressed in this preamble, that the present Treaty be formed.

FIRST ARTICLE

HIS MOST FAITHFUL MAJESTY recognized Brazil as an independent Empire, and separated from the kingdoms of Portugal and Algarves; and his pre-eminently beloved and valued son PETER as Emperor, freely ceding and transferring the sovereignty of the said Empire to the said son and his legitimate successors, HIS FAITHFUL MAJESTY taking only, and reserving for his own person, the same title.

SECOND ARTICLE

HIS IMPERIAL MAJESTY, as an acknowledgment of the respect and love for his august father and lord, JOHN VI, consents that HIS MOST FAITHFUL MAJESTY shall take for himself the title of Emperor.

THIRD ARTICLE

HIS IMPERIAL MAJESTY promises not to admit propositions from any Portuguese colonies to unite themselves to the Empire of Brazil.

FOURTH ARTICLE

Henceforth, there shall be peace and alliance, and the most perfect friendship, between the Empire of Brazil and the kingdoms of Portugal and Algarves [...].

FIFTH ARTICLE

The subjects of the two nations, Brazilian and Portuguese, shall be considered and treated in the respective States, as those of the most favored and friendly nation, and their rights and property shall be religiously observed and protected, it remaining understood that the actual possessors of real estate shall remain in the peaceful possession of the same.

[...]

TENTH ARTICLE

The relations of commerce shall be immediately reestablished between the two nations, the Brazilian and the Portuguese; all merchandise paying reciprocally fifteen percent in duties of consumption provisionally; the duties on exportation and re-exportation remaining as before the separation.

ELEVENTH ARTICLE

Ratifications of the present Treaty shall be exchanged reciprocally in the city of Lisbon within five months, or sooner, if possible, computed from the day of the signature of the present Treaty.

[...]

Signed in the city of Rio de Janeiro on the twenty-ninth day of August of the year of our Lord Jesus Christ one thousand, eight hundred and twenty-five.

In the Brazilian system, the executive promulgation (which is *praxis* only among us) and the publication constitute the *integration stage* of the law effectiveness, as they attest its adoption by the Legislative Power, certify the existence of its text and finally, assert its imperative and enforceable value at an internal level.[71] In Brazil, all the treaties approved by the National Congress are *promulgated* executively (by presidential *decree*), which is valid as an act certifying the existence of the treaty; and after this promulgation, the international act is sent for *publication* in the *Official Gazette of the State*. In the *Official Gazette of the State*, there are *published*, without a previous promulgation act, only those treaties that dispense with the parliamentary approval and the ratification of the President of the Republic, for example, "executive agreements", whose publication in the *Official Gazette of the State* is authorized by the Minister of Foreign Affairs and effected by the International Act Division of the Itamaraty.[72]

The SFC has understood that the promulgation of the treaty is *necessary* for its internal applicability. For this reason, the SFC rejected the compliance with a *letter rogatory* issued by the Argentine Republic, in which it requested that Brazil granted the *exequatur* to the judgment rendered on preventive measure, under the allegation that the Convention on Execution of Preventive Measures, concluded by Brazil with the other countries of the Mercosur, in spite of being ratified, had not entered into force in Brazil yet because it lacked executive promulgation.[73] However, what is

71 Rodas, João Grandino. *A publicidade dos tratados internacionais*, cit., p. 200.

72 See Rezek, José Francisco. *Direito dos tratados*, cit., p. 385-387.

73 See Letter Rogatory No. 8.279, of the Argentine Republic, dated May 4, 1998, in *Court Gazette* of May 14, 1995, p. 34.

evident from that decision is the little importance that the SFC gave to the other signatory States of the Convention, since, once an international agreement is ratified, all the other signatory State which also ratified the treaty believed, with conviction, from that moment, that they could rely on the provisions included in the treaty, in case it was necessary. However, the President of the SFC preferred not to comply with said Convention at an internal level, invoking the thesis – which finally prevailed – that every international commitment, to be effective internally, must be *promulgated* by the Head of the Executive Power, through an execution decree.[74] It is only necessary to know what provision of the Constitution sets forth that, for ratified international treaties to be applicable at an internal level, there must be executive promulgation…

The supposed provision cannot be found, simply because it does not exist. No Brazilian Constitution ever included an express and specific provision establishing this procedure for the internal promulgation of treaties. There was no express rule ever, in the history of Brazilian constitutionalism, which established that international treaties ratified by the President of the Republic should be promulgated internally, through an executive decree, to be effective and applicable at an internal level.[75] International Law only needs to be *transformed* into internal Law when the constitutional text of the country so sets forth. If the Constitution states nothing about this, national courts are able to apply concluded treaties immediately, if they were self-applicable, from their ratification. In this case, the promulgation would be unnecessary, as there is no constitutional provision on this matter. In addition, it is incorrect to say that the lack of executive promulgation violates the principle of publicity, because once the treaty is ratified, it must be considered public from the date on which the National Congress approved it, through the *legislative decree*, which is included in the list of regulations of Art. 59 of the Constitution. Not to mention that the publication of any norm is exclusive competence of the President of the Republic. As José Carlos de Magalhães recalls, this "prerogative was also granted to the President of the Congress, as it can be seen, for example, in the veto override procedure, when the President does not approve the law within the term established in the Constitution. In this case, the approved project returns to the Legislative Power, and the President of the Congress is responsible for issuing a Legislative Decree,

---

74 See Magalhães, José Carlos de. *O Supremo Tribunal Federal e o direito internacional…*, cit., p. 70-72.

75 See Magalhães, José Carlos de. Idem, p. 74.

making the law effective within the country [Federal Constitution/88, Art. 66, item 7: 'If the law is not promulgated by the President of the Republic within forty-eight hours in the situations set out in items 3 and 5, the President of the Senate shall promulgate it, and if he does not do so within the same period, it shall be incumbent upon the Vice-President of the Senate to do so']. (...) Therefore, it is not true that the publicity of the legal norm is exclusive competence of the President of the Republic, since, in certain cases, this competence is also attributed to the President or Vice-President of the Senate".[76]

We understand that judges and courts, being aware of the treaty *already ratified* and *already effective* at an international level, may, of course, apply the treaty to the particular case, even if such instrument was not *promulgated* internally; it would be better if it were promulgated, but if that has not occurred yet and the judge, by any means, already *was aware* of the international force of the act and its *entry into force* in Brazil, may apply it, regardless of this last formality, which is more useful for the public in general (the *publication* is required for them to know national laws and rules) than the Judicial Power, which is *longa manus* of the State and has more access to what the Republic signed with other States at an international level. For this reason, Remiro Brotons observed that the current practice seems to "deny the obligation of State bodies not to apply, in each case, the provisions of a treaty which has not been duly published"; and finally he states that the practice has strengthened the idea "that the publication ends up being a mere condition for the *enforceability* of a treaty on people".[77] Apart from that, expecting that, after being signed, approved by the Parliament and ratified by the Government, the international treaty be subject, one more time, to a specific procedure of internal Law which "materializes" it and grants internal "applicability" which has no constitutional support.[78] However, the *Brazilian* practice in relation to treaties has followed the opposite current, in the sense that it requires the executive promulgation (and consequent publication) of treaties.[79]

---

76 Magalhães, José Carlos de. Idem, p. 80.

77 Remiro Brotons, Antonio. *Derecho internacional público*, vol. 2, cit., p. 269.

78 For a review of this system, in relation to the application of treaties by courts, see Reuter, Paul, *Introducción al derecho de los tratados*, cit., p. 34-38.

79 As regards treaties on *human rights* in particular, the promulgation *and publication* of the text are considered as dispensable, because they have "immediate application" in our legal system (according to Art. 5, item 1, of the Constitution) from their ratification. For

For some authors, such as Francisco Rezek, the promulgation decree is a result of the *praxis*, as old as independence and the first conventional acts of the Empire; it is called *decree* only because the acts of the Head of State usually have that name, and for no other reason.[80] However, others understand that the promulgation of international treaties comes from the constitutional provision stating that the President of the Republic has exclusive powers to approve, promulgate and order publication of laws, as well as issue decrees and regulations for their faithful execution (Art. 84, IV); in this case, the term *law* is used in its broader sense, understood as *positive source of law*. For this current, the promulgation of treaties is not, contrary to the common understanding, a mere established *practice*, but an implicit constitutional requirement. This is the position of Mirtô Fraga, for whom Brazilian Constitutions, when referring to the promulgation of *laws*, do so interpreting the term in a *broad sense*, which, in some case, is not complete with presidential approval. The author cites Art. 59, item 6, of the revoked Constitution, whose text established that "in the cases of Art. 44, after final approval, the *law* shall be promulgated by the President of the Federal Senate", concluding that, Art. 44 making reference to the matter which is *exclusive* competence of the National Congress and not constituting approval or veto, is because, consequently, it is not strictly a law.[81] The corresponding rule, in the current Constitution of 1988, is the above-mentioned Art. 66, item 7: "If the *law* is not promulgated by the President of the Republic within forty-eight hours in the situations set out in items 3 and 5, the President of the Senate shall promulgate it, and if he does not do so within the same period, it shall be incumbent upon the Vice-President of the Senate to do so".

With all due respect, we do not have the same opinion. For us, the internal effectiveness of a treaty does not require the presidential decree of promulgation. Now, the Constitution of 1988 sets forth that the President of the Republic has exclusive powers to approve, promulgate and order publication of *laws*, making no reference to the *treaties* concluded by Brazil. If the Constitution said nothing about this, it was because the internal promulga-

---

detailed information on this matter, see Mazzuoli, Valerio de Oliveira, *Direitos humanos, Constituição e os tratados internacionais...*, cit., p. 253-259; and Mazzuoli, Valerio de Oliveira, *Curso de direito internacional público*, cit., p. 896-927.

80 See Rezek, José Francisco. *Direito dos tratados*, cit., p. 385-386.

81 See Fraga, Mirtô. *O conflito entre tratado internacional e norma de direito interno...*, cit., p. 63. This same author, in a more recent study on the subject, reasserts this point of view. See Fraga, Mirtô. A obrigatoriedade do tratado na ordem interna, *Revista de Informação Legislativa*, year 41, No. 162, Brasilia: Federal Senate, Apr/Jun/2004, p. 316-317.

tion of an international commitment was considered unnecessary, a commitment which, technically, had already entered into force within the Country – as it was already *effective* at an international level – from the exchange or deposit of their ratification instruments (in case another date had not been provided for by the treaty). It would be a contradiction to admit that a State is obliged to execute a treaty at an international level, from its ratification, and that same treaty cannot be enforced internally because it lacks executive promulgation. It should be noted that the Brazilian Government itself has understood this in the same way, when, in the *recitals* preceding treaty promulgation decrees, it sets forth the date on which the international instrument entered into force in Brazil, meaning the date of exchange or deposit of the ratification instruments. Thus, the Brazilian Government is recognizing it also understands that the treaties promulgated by it enter into force in Brazil *before* the issuance of the promulgation decree, which is a mere internal formality, not important for Public International Law. For such purpose, see the following examples:

a) Decree No. 2.095, dated December 17, 1996, which promulgated the Buenos Aires Protocol on International Jurisdiction in Contractual Matters, concluded in Buenos Aires on August 5, 1994:

> "Considering the Brazilian Government deposited the Ratification Letter of the above-mentioned instrument on May 7, 1996, *which entered into force in Brazil on June 6, 1996*, in accordance with Article 16" (*Official Gazette of the State*, December 28, 1996, p. 27.299).

b) Decree No. 1.925, dated June 10, 1996, which promulgated the Inter-American Convention on Proof of and Information on Foreign Law, concluded in Montevideo, Uruguay, on May 8, 1979:

> "Considering the Brazilian Government deposited the ratification letter of the above-mentioned multilateral instrument on November 27, 1995, *which entered into force in Brazil on December 26, 1995*, in accordance with Article 15" (*Official Gazette of the State*, June 11, 1996, p. 10.235).

c) Decree No. 1.899, dated May 9, 1996, which promulgated the Inter-American Convention on Letters Rogatory of January 30, 1975:

> "Considering the promulgated convention was timely submitted to the National Congress, which approved it through Legislative Decree No. 61, dated April 19, 1995;
>
> Considering the Convention in question entered into force at an international level on January 16, 1976;

> Considering the Brazilian Government deposited the Ratification Letter of the above-mentioned multilateral instrument on November 27, 1995, *which entered into force in Brazil on December 27, 1995*, in accordance with Article 22" (*Official Gazette of the State*, May 10, 1996, p. 8.007).[82]

All this shows that even the Brazilian Government considers that the international treaty enters into force *before* its promulgation, exactly on the date of exchange or deposit of ratification instruments.

Besides, it cannot be stated that it would be difficult to know when the treaty enters into force at an international level, under the argument that only the depositary of the text is able to assess if the minimum *quorum* of ratifying or adhering countries was reached, or even if the *vacatio* established in the treaty already passed. Nowadays, notably due to media speed, there is no international fact of this nature that is not disclosed to the public almost immediately.

In summary, and not considering the many critics to its lack of necessity, the *decree of execution* is only "the internal legal act by which the Government of a State asserts or certifies the existence of a treaty concluded by it and compliance with the formalities required for its conclusion, and, apart from that, orders its performance within the limits of state competence".[83] That is, the issuance of the decree of execution aims at certifying and informing everybody that the international act *already exists* and that the constitutional formalities required for its conclusion were fulfilled.[84] This also shows that the international commitment is legally enforceable, and everybody is bound by it. From that moment, treaties become part of the internal legal system of the State and have internal applicability. The treaty shall be applicable as long as the signed commitment *has already entered into force* at an international level. This last observation is very important, since the treaty may never bind the Nation as to its performance because it has no international effectiveness. An international treaty that subjects its international effectiveness to a certain condition, such as a minimum number of ratifications, may never enter into force and, consequently, may never have any internal effects in rela-

---

82 Examples drawn from Magalhães, José Carlos de, *O Supremo Tribunal Federal e o direito internacional...*, cit., p. 77-78.

83 Accioly, Hildebrando. *Tratado de direito internacional público*, vol. I, cit., p. 602.

84 See Silva, José Afonso da. *Processo constitucional de formação das leis*, 2. ed. São Paulo: Malheiros, 2006, p. 233.

tion to ratifying States, even if they are promulgated and published internally, with an order of faithful performance.

The promulgation is not part of the legislative process. On the contrary: what is promulgated *already is* a legal rule, which can be inferred from the wording of Art. 66, item 7, of the Constitution of 1988, which states that: "If the *law* is not promulgated...". This clearly shows that the promulgation does not fall on the *project*, but the *rule* which is ready and concluded.[85] The same occurs with the promulgation of treaties, which also *already exist* before such promulgation, thus being incorrect to assert that the promulgated treaty *is transformed* into a rule of internal Law and is no longer a rule of International Law. What happens – Mirtô Fraga explains – is the following: "Once the treaty is signed, approved by the Legislative Power, and ratified by the Executive Power, it enters into force at an international level, as established in its own text. However, people and Courts must know it exists in order to comply with it and apply it, respectively. Through promulgation, the Head of the Executive Power only declares and solemnly certifies compliance with the formalities required for the regulatory act to be concluded".[86]

The executive decree of promulgation, signed by the President of the Republic, is also countersigned by the Minister for Foreign Affairs and accompanied by a copy of the complete text of the treaty.

1.7.3 Publication

For the legal rule to be considered as effectively promulgated, it is indispensable to *publish* the promulgation act in an official vehicle, giving notice to the public in general of the existence of the treaty.[87] Therefore, as only known rules are obligatory (and the publication allows to presume such knowledge), the ratified treaty shall only be effective within internal Law from the inclusion of the promulgated rule in the *Official Gazette of the State*, having attached the text of the treaty.[88] Now, if the promulgation

---

85 See Silva, José Afonso da. Idem, ibidem.

86 Fraga, Mirtô. *O conflito entre tratado internacional e norma de direito interno...*, cit., p. 64

87 Regarding the publication of laws in Brazil, see Silva, José Afonso da, *Processo constitucional de formação das leis*, cit., p. 248-259. As regards the publication (of treaties) in Spanish Law, see Remiro Brotons, Antonio, *Derecho internacional público*, vol. 2, cit., p. 266-273.

88 See Fraga, Mirtô. *O conflito entre tratado internacional e norma de direito interno...*, cit., p. 64.

act includes a presumption that the concluded treaty is valid, enforceable and potentially binding, as it was regularly concluded in compliance with the specific process set forth in the Constitution, and if through such act the Executive Power *informs* everybody that the international rule *already exists* as an act capable of binding its recipients, it would be completely useless not to give notice of such act to the people it affects, which can only be done through the *publication*.[89] However, bear in mind that it is not *the treaty* itself which is published, but its *promulgation act*, which has the text of the treaty attached.[90]

Like the promulgation, there is no express internal regulation in relation to the publication. However, there is an international regulation about this. The Havana Convention on Treaties of 1928, which is fully effective in Brazil, establishes in Art. 4 that treaties "shall be published *immediately* after exchange of ratifications", adding, however, that "the failure to discharge this international duty *shall affect neither* the force of treaties *nor* the fulfillment of obligations stipulated therein".

The Brazilian legal tradition has not conceived any rule (whether internal or international – and, in this last case, it is referring to treaties requiring congressional approval) without official publication, arising from treaties or internal regulations.[91] Besides, the *principle of publicity* is also valid in this case, when dealing with conventional rules ratified by the State. Nevertheless, the lack of publicity cannot be invoked to justify the violation of the treaty, as provided for in Art. 27 of the Vienna Convention of 1969.

> "States cannot invoke the lack of publication or promulgation as justification for their failure to comply with conventional obligations, as set forth in Art. 27 of the Vienna Convention. Even though it is true that a treaty which was not published is not binding upon individuals, in the sense of enforcing obligations, the truth is that they may invoke the treaty to demand rights arising from it.
> The need of publication (or promulgation) shall not be invoked for the internal effectiveness of treaties as an expression of distortion to the purity of the monistic principle (the so-called 'moderate monism'), since the essence of the monistic principle, as already stated, is only that treaties be effective as such, maintaining their nature, and not the dispensation of internal formalities for their full effectiveness".
> XAVIER, Alberto. *Direito tributário internacional do Brasil*, cit., p. 142.

---

89 For further information see Silva, José Afonso da, *Processo constitucional de formação das leis*, cit., p. 248-249; and Fraga, Mirtô, *O conflito entre tratado internacional e norma de direito interno…*, cit., p. 63-64.

90 See Silva, José Afonso da. *Processo constitucional de formação das leis*, cit., p. 249.

91 See Rezek, José Francisco. *Direito dos tratados*, cit., p. 385.

Finally, from the publication, treaties become part of the national legal system, "allowing their compliance by individuals and rulers, and their guarantee of effectiveness by the Judicial Power".[92] That is, the publication of the promulgation act is aimed at transmitting the content of the treaty to all its recipients, establishing also its entry into force. When they are silent in connection with this last purpose, they execute the provision of Art. 1 of the LINDB (Law of Introduction to Brazilian Law Rules), which grants forty-five days to this entry into force. This rule applies not only to laws, but also to all international acts containing rules intended for individuals, when the corresponding text does not specify another date for its entry into force. The *vacatio* is released for those administrative acts that only affect strictly internal matters of the Administration (which do not directly affect individuals).

As already stated by Charles Rousseau, in an extremely clear lesson, treaties "are *binding* by virtue of their ratification, *enforceable* by virtue of their promulgation and *applicable* due to their publication".[93] However, it should be clarified that all these provisions cannot turn International Law into internal Law, as already explained. A duly promulgated and published treaty is still a rule of International Law, according to a universally accepted standard. It is a mistake to state that the treaty is *transformed* into internal law with the promulgation act. This is what happens: the promulgated treaty has *force* of law or, if preferred, force *superior* to law, as it cannot be revoked by a subsequent internal rule, but this does not mean that the treaty is *transformed* into law with its promulgation. Therefore, there is no absolute identity between the treaty and the internal norm-setting procedure of the State, except for their binding effect, during the effective term. When we say that treaties are valid as internal *law*, we only mean that they have, *at least*, the same force as an internal legislative provision. But this is wrong too, as duly ratified treaties (any treaties) have supralegal value, since they revoke infra-constitutional legislation to the contrary and cannot be revoked by it.[94] Therefore, treaties being *similar* to laws, for purposes of their entry into force, the truth is that, if there are no other provisions, regulatory provisions related to the entry into force of legislative acts in Brazil are applied to treaties, which are included in the LINDB, especially those related to effectiveness and *vacatio legis*.

---

92 Rezek, José Francisco. Idem, p. 385.

93 Rousseau, Charles. *Principes généraux du droit international public*, t. I, cit., p. 403.

94 As it shall be seen below (Ch. 2, below), all treaties effective in Brazil have, at least, supra-legal status (although the SFC has understood differently).

In Brazil, promulgated and published international acts become part of the *Collection of Laws* of the Country. The Ministry of Foreign Affairs still publishes international acts to which Brazil is a party in the *Collection of International Acts*, which is also an official repository of treaties in our country.

1.8 Effects of the internal adoption of treaties in the national legal system

From the time they inter into force at an international level, treaties ratified by the State, promulgated and published, are incorporated into the internal legal system and, consequently, produce *effects* at an internal level. These instruments, once incorporated into Brazilian Law, began to follow, with very little variation, the same rules on force and effectiveness applicable to the other laws of the Country.

The first and most immediate effect generated by a treaty in the internal legal system is *revoking* all conflicting or incompatible provisions of infra-constitutional legislation (this includes, except for constitutional amendments, all other regulatory provisions which constitute the national legal system). Ordinary treaties (and not those treaties on human rights, which are constitutional in nature and level) revoke or modify all provisions that are below the Constitution, if they are incompatible with or expressly contrary to such treaties. There being incompatibility between the conventional provisions and the rules of internal Law, the possible antinomy is always solved in favor of the treaty, which is hierarchically superior to any infra-constitutional internal provision.

The revoking rule may be manifest (*express*) or implicit (*tacit* and *global*). It shall be manifest when it expressly sets forth the rule to be revoked; it shall be implicit when the subsequent rule is incompatible with the previous one (*tacit*) or when it completely regulates the matter dealt with by the previous law (*global*). These rules are valid both for subsequent treaties and for an internal legislative provision.

What cannot happen is the contrary: a treaty being revoked by a *subsequent law*. It would be illogical to admit that an international commitment may be revoked by subsequent legislation; it would be the same as allowing a State to unilaterally revoke an international commitment, when it is well-known that to do so is necessarily a formal act of *claim*. Besides, the thesis allowing the revocation of a treaty by subsequent internal law seems not to take into consideration that the violation of an international obligation results in the international responsibility of the

State. The criticism is related to the indifference that many people showed as to the serious problem of State *responsibility* in the international arena.

Another effect of treaties, internally, is authorizing individuals to claim, before ordinary courts, the satisfaction of the rights established in such treaties and compliance with the obligations arising from them. However, this shall only be possible in case it is verified, according to the content of the instrument, that it is truly intended for the citizen. A treaty protecting human rights that, by virtue of its nature, creates a subjective right for the citizen, may have its faithful performance demanded before an internal court, while a treaty addressed only and exclusively to the Government, to comply with a certain provision or to maintain a certain relationship with some State, certainly cannot have its effectiveness claimed, at court, by an individual. Only the other States would have, in this case, the right to claim the performance of the violated treaty.[95]

1.9 Public authorities responsible for the execution of treaties

At the end of this Chapter related to the constitutional procedural aspects of treaty conclusion, some considerations shall be expressed on the public authorities responsible for the execution of treaties.

What we can say here, very briefly, is that *all* public authorities (all State bodies) are responsible for the application of treaties at an internal level, because the obligation to comply with all the provisions of treaties rests with *the State* as a whole, in its capacity as *subject* of Public International Law.[96] Both the Executive Power and the Legislative and Judicial Powers, in the chart of their respective competencies, must guarantee the full execution of the international act in the internal sphere, under the penalty of international responsibility of the State.

However, the execution of a treaty within the scope of the State is not an essentially legal matter, but also (and especially) *political*. It is often required that public authorities take different measures to fully comply with the international act. Even changes in legislation may be required, as many treaties set forth (for example, treaties on human rights). This conventional determination is called *legislative adaptation (or adjustment)*.[97]

---

95 See Rezek, José Francisco. *Direito dos tratados*, cit., p. 394-395.

96 See Dinh, Daillier & Pellet. *Direito internacional público*, cit., p. 233.

97 On the subject, see Quadri, Rolando, Cours général de droit international public, *Recueil des Cours*, vol. 113 (1964-III), p. 297-302.

Consider, for example, Art. 2 of the American Convention on Human Rights: "Where the exercise of any of the rights or freedoms referred to in Article 1 is not already ensured by legislative or other provisions, the States Parties undertake to adopt, in accordance with their constitutional processes and the provisions of this Convention, such *legislative or other measures as may be necessary to give effect to those rights or freedoms*" [italics are ours].[98]

Compliance with the conventional obligations of adaptation or adjustment is verified, in general, resorting to the international responsibility of the State.[99] When the failure to comply with the treaty – as in the above-mentioned case of lack of legislative adaptation that guarantees the internal application of the agreement – is directly detrimental to citizens, the *internal* Judicial Power is responsible for solving the matter and condemning the State to make amends, and then (after exhausting internal resources), the victim may turn to an *international* court (principle of subsidiarity of international justice).

---

[98] See Mazzuoli, Valerio de Oliveira. *Comentários à Convenção Americana sobre Direitos Humanos* (*Pacto de San José da Costa Rica*), cit., p. 30-35.

[99] See Dinh, Daillier & Pellet. *Direito internacional público*, cit., p. 233.

Chapter 2

Conflict between Treaties and Rules of Internal Law

2.1 The case of Brazil

None of the provisions of the Federal Constitution of 1988 clearly established the hierarchical position of *ordinary* treaties in our internal Law. It left this matter to the opinion, necessarily fallible, of national legal scholars and case law, leaving them with a problem that should have been avoided by the legislator. This Chapter will deal with the hierarchy between *ordinary* (or *traditional*) international treaties and Brazilian internal laws.[100] For this purpose, it is important to analyze the position of the SFC on this topic and the discussions that until today national scholars have been held the in relation to the hierarchy between such treaties and internal laws. However, some parts of the text will also make reference to treaties on human rights, especially when studying the conventionality control of laws (see item 2.4, below).

The first observation to make when analyzing the conflict between (ordinary) international treaties and (infra-constitutional) internal laws is that the conflict between both rules can be solved, *a priori*, in two ways: in one of them, giving prevalence to treaties over infra-constitutional inter-

---

[100] The hierarchy of international treaties on human rights in Brazilian Law has been analyzed elsewhere, especially in Mazzuoli, Valerio de Oliveira, *Direitos humanos, Constituição e os tratados internacionais…*, cit., p. 233-325; and Mazzuoli, Valerio de Oliveira, *Curso de direito internacional público*, cit., p. 896-927. See also Mazzuoli, Valerio de Oliveira, *Tratados internacionais direitos humanos e direito interno*, cit., p. 80-128 and p. 178-226. In this last study, it was verified that the traditional criteria to solve antinomies (hierarchical, chronological and specialty) cannot be used when the conflict of rules involves a matter related to *human rights*.

nal law, for example, the French Constitution of 1958 (Art. 55), the Greek Constitution of 1975 (Art. 28, item 1) and the Peruvian Constitution of 1979 (Art. 101), providing the international commitment with full effectiveness, in spite of subsequent laws to the contrary; in the other, giving treaties *equal* treatment only, using as paradigm national laws and other provisions of equivalent level.[101] That is, if there is a conflict between a treaty and an internal law, the solution is to apply the *lex posterior derogat priori* criterion, a system found in SFC case law since 1977. In this sense, according to the SFC, once formalized, the treaty has force of *ordinary* law, and as such it may revoke contrary provisions or be repealed (lose effectiveness) by a subsequent law.[102] In other words, when dealing with ordinary international instruments (except for treaties on human rights), SFC case law has adopted the *treaty override* possibility in Brazilian Law, understanding that it is possible to repeal a treaty by virtue of a subsequent law. The so-called *treaty override* – (express or tacit) revocation of a treaty by an incompatible subsequent law – can be found to this day in the case law of our Supreme Court.[103]

In spite of this constitutional omission, regarding the conflict between international treaties and internal laws, for some decades Brazilian case law remained firm as to the superiority of International Law over internal Law, a position which was only modified from 1977, while judging the Extraordinary Appeal No. 80.004/SE, when it was established that in case of conflict between a treaty and an internal law the *most recent* rule should prevail, applying the *lex posterior derogat priori* principle. The discussion, in appellate jurisdiction, was about the conflict between the Decree-Law 427, of January 22, 1969, which created the obligatory registration of promissory notes with tax authorities, under penalty of nullity, and the Uniform Law for Bills of Exchange and Promissory Notes, approved by the Geneva Convention, previously ratified by the State of Brazil and with effectiveness recognized by the SFC. The whole dispute revolved around the nullity claim of Decree-Law 427/69, which required

---

101 See Rezek, José Francisco. *Direito internacional público...*, cit., p. 96-99.

102 See Resolution of the SFC, *RE* 80.004-SE, in *RTJ* 83/809 and following pages.

103 For detailed information on this matter, see Mazzuoli, Valerio de Oliveira, A opção do judiciário brasileiro em face dos conflitos entre tratados internacionais e leis internas, *Revista da AJURIS*, year XXVI, No. 81, vol. I (doctrine), Porto Alegre, Mar/2001, p. 306-325; and Mazzuoli, Valerio de Oliveira, O Supremo Tribunal Federal e os conflitos entre tratados internacionais e leis internas, *Revista de Informação Legislativa*, year 39, No. 154, Brasilia: Federal Senate, Apr/Jun/2002, p. 15-29.

the registration of promissory notes as a validity condition, within the lapsing period, with the competent authorities defined by the Ministry of Finance, a requirement not provided for or demanded by the Uniform Law of Geneva.

Even though it was decided by majority vote, with only one dissenting position, of Reporting Judge Xavier de Albuquerque, replaced by the designated Reporting Judge Cunha Peixoto, the majority votes in the Extraordinary Appeal mentioned above included arguments so different that it was difficult to know which of them prevailed before the Supreme Court. Setting aside old precedents that internal laws cannot repeal treaties previously concluded, the SFC preferred to follow the idea that there is no hierarchical prevalence between international treaties and internal laws and, thus, an international commitment could be revoked, without further consequences in internal Law, by subsequent ordinary legislation. Judges Cordeiro Guerra, Rodrigues Alckmin, Thompson Flores and Cunha Peixoto voted in the sense that treaties revoke previous internal laws *in the same way* as subsequent laws revoke treaties concluded before, according to the *lex posterior derogat priori* principle. The Court did not take into consideration that international treaties have their own revocation method, which is called denunciation, nor did it consider that the failure to comply internally with an international commitment results in the international responsibility of the State, apart from other serious consequences in foreign policy matters.[104]

For this reason, the observation of Amilcar de Castro cannot be applied, in which Judge Cunha Peixoto was based in his vote as designated reporting judge of *RE* 80.004/SE, that "a treaty is not a law; it is an international act which binds the people as a whole; which binds the government externally and not the people internally".[105] Now, this understanding presents an important aspect, which is the indifference with which the will of the Government is separated from the will of the Nation, or the power that emanates from the people, according to the rule of Art. 1, sole paragraph, of the Constitution of 1988, which follows previous Constitutions. If the power emanates from the people and that same people constitute the Government, it is because the authority of the State to commit the Na-

---

104 For further information see Magalhães, José Carlos de, *O Supremo Tribunal Federal e o direito internacional...*, cit., p. 58-60.

105 Castro, Amilcar de. *Direito internacional privado*, 5. ed. increased and updated by Osiris Rocha. Rio de Janeiro: Forense, 2001, p. 123-124.

tion at an international level is always *delegated* and not original. In other words, when the Constitution sets forth that "all power emanates from the people, who exercise it through elected representatives or directly", it is granting to the Brazilian people the *original jurisdiction*, and to the Government, the *delegated jurisdiction* in power matters. Therefore, it is unjustifiable to say that the treaty *binds the people considered as a whole*, because this does not explain why such obligation considered *as a whole* is not valid within the internal legal system. Thus, when the Head of the Executive Power commits the Nation at an international level, he does so with the power received from the people, not being necessary to say that the people make a commitment, through the Government, within the international sphere only, and not within the national sphere.[106]

The position of the SFC when judging the *RE* 80.004/SE, be said again, changed its previous point of view, which sustained the superiority of International Law over the Brazilian national system. Therefore, we are witnessing a true regression in this area. It should be noted that Philadelpho Azevedo published in 1945, when he still was a Judge of the SFC, a comment in which he showed the *unanimous* opinion of the Supreme Court, at that time, as to the *prevalence* of international treaties over infra-constitutional internal Law.[107]

2.2 Regulatory parity of ordinary treaties declared by the SFC

The conclusion at which the SFC arrived while judging the above-mentioned case (*RE* 80.004/SE) was that within the Brazilian legal system, in which treaties and conventions have a strict relation of *regulatory parity* with ordinary laws issued by the State, the norms of international treaties allows, as regards the hierarchy of sources, to place them on the same level and the same degree of effectiveness as our internal laws. The SFC understood that the Brazilian Constitution of that time, when dealing with its exclusive competence, would have placed international treaties ratified by Brazil on the same hierarchical level as infra-constitutional rules, which reflects *moderate monism*. Applying this reasoning to the constitutional text of 1988, it could be understood that, when the Constitution sets forth

---

106 For further information see Magalhães, José Carlos de, *O Supremo Tribunal Federal e o direito internacional...*, cit., p. 33-36 and 61.

107 See Rezek, José Francisco. *Direito dos tratados*, cit., p. 465-466. See Azevedo, Philadelpho. Os tratados e os interesses privados em face do direito brasileiro, *Boletim da Sociedade Brasileira de Direito Internacional*, vol. 1, Rio de Janeiro, 1945, p. 12-29.

that the SFC has powers to decide, on extraordinary appeal, cases decided in sole or last instance, "when the appealed decision declares a treaty *or* federal law unconstitutional", it would be placing on the same hierarchical level both legally effective provisions. Therefore, in case of conflict between the international rule and internal law, it would be applied the general principle related to rules with the same value, that is, the *chronological* criterion to solve antinomies, in which the most recent rule revokes the previous conflicting rule. In this way, any international treaty, ratified by Brazil and duly promulgated, would become part of our internal Law with status of federal ordinary law.[108]

This conclusion of the Distinguished Court, however, is very imprecise. Now, accepting that an international commitment may no longer be effective due to the issuance of a subsequent and conflicting law (*treaty override*) is allowing that a treaty may be unilaterally revoked by one of the States Parties, which is not legal or understandable. It would be easy to evade international agreements if, by virtue of internal legislative provisions, it were possible to modify such rules. If a State freely undertakes to comply with an international agreement, how could such State issue laws contrary to what was agreed? What would be the value of a treaty if, through an internal law, States could just decide not to apply it? It would be very simple to recognize that the failure to comply with a treaty internally could result in an international unlawful act, for which the State should take responsibility at an international level. In the reasons of the monocratic decision rendered by Judge Celso de Mello, in *HC* 77.631-5/SC, it is stated that a subsequent law may (and, therefore, it would be legitimate to do so) abrogate the rules of an international treaty, because otherwise this would be obstructing, "in evident contradiction to the supremacy of the Constitution (...), the exercise by the National Congress of its typical political-legal activity consisting of performing the legislative duty".

The reasoning of the Judge mentioned above introduced a subtly fallacious argument that is difficult to perceive, which deserves to be explained. When a State assumes an international commitment, *all* of the Nation makes a legal commitment, *all* of the community that forms the State, which includes its population and authorities (state power) locat-

108 See Decision No. 662-2, of the Extradition process judged by the SFC Full Bench, majority decision, on November 28, 1996 (*Court Gazette*, May 30, 1997, p. 23.176), Reporting Judge Celso de Mello.

ed in its territory. Only for practical purposes, the population and state authorities do not act jointly, and the foreign representation of the State mainly falls on the Head of the Executive Power. According to our Constitutional Law, the President of the Republic has exclusive competence to declare the will of the State at an international level, and the Legislative Power has exclusive competence to decide definitively on treaties, approving them or not (as deemed more convenient) before the ratification of the agreement or deposit of the ratification instruments with the competent body. The Judicial Power was not included in this process, which only acts in a later stage, in case of conflict resolution, as well as citizens, individually considered. However, even though it would not be practical, it could have been established otherwise, the Constitution anticipating the participation of the Judicial Power and also of individuals in the process to conclude international acts. Anyway, it would always be *the State*, as a unique and whole entity, which would assume a commitment at an international level, being of little importance which entity, according to the Constitution, has competence to conclude the agreement internationally. Thus, it is not possible to separate the many powers that form the State and introduce a sophism leading to think that some of them act to the detriment of the freedom of the powers of the others, because if they act in that way to commit the State at an international level, it is because the Constitution provided so. When the President of the Republic ratifies a treaty, he does not do so personally, but *in the name* of the State he governs; it is the Head of the Executive Power who acts, that is, who is *entitled* to commit the Nation internationally, but *from a legal point of view*, who does so is not the President of the Republic, but the *Brazilian State* represented by the President.[109] This destroys the allegation of the Supreme Court, presented while judging *HC* 77.631-5/SC, in the sense

---

109 For further details, see Vignali, Heber Arbuet & Arrighi, Jean Michel, Os vínculos entre o direito internacional público e os sistemas internos, cit., p. 416-417. In the words of Vignali and Arrighi: "Therefore, it is a fallacious argument to introduce the idea that it violates the Constitution because, when approving a treaty, some bodies (of the Executive Power) bind others (of the Legislative Power), limiting their powers. Actually, the sovereign Nation, when approving its Constitution, established a method to assume international commitments, which, once assumed according to the rules of the current constitutional regime, bind all the inhabitants and Powers of the State, in our understanding directly, without the need of 'transformation'; however, in this hypothesis, or if it is understood that they must be 'transformed', always without the possibility of being ignored by any body, except when the constitutional rule is explicitly violated" (Idem, ibidem).

that an internal law may derogate a treaty, under the penalty of obstructing the exercise by the National Congress of its "typical political-legal activity consisting of performing the legislative duty".

Now, frequently the purpose of an international treaty is precisely to influence situations that must be observed within the internal legal system of States. All treaties on human rights, for example, belong to that category, among many other examples that could be mentioned. The truth is that, when approving an international treaty, the Legislative Power implicitly undertakes not to issue conflicting laws, unless it intends to claim the treaty.

> "If Brazil, for example, signed a convention with Portugal, undertaking to recognize to Portuguese people residing here the same rights as citizens, the non-issuance of the regulations, by itself, would constitute an international unlawful act, which would be even more serious if, after the convention was signed, a legal rule was issued excluding Portuguese people, who are the beneficiaries of the equal treatment, from the right to submit applications for certain positions not reserved to people born in Brazil, for example. It is a contradiction to state that the Court must apply the subsequent law conflicting with the treaty and accept, at the same time, the responsibility of the State. It is free to sign contracts or stop doing so. Stating, as many people do, that the Executive Power cannot, by concluding the treaty, limit the competence and freedom of the Legislative Power would be valid if we were in the 18th century. At that time, the monarch embodied the State, and the sovereignty was vested in the figure of the ruler. With the advent of the French Revolution and liberal ideas, the sovereignty was transferred to the nation, represented by Assemblies. At that time, the pact, the agreement, was an act of the ruler, as opposed to the law, an act of national sovereignty. And as the power belonged to the people, the commitment signed by the sovereign could not bind the nation, which could act contrary to what had been agreed, in his name and without his consent. The obligatory approval, by the Legislative Power, of treaties signed by the Head of the State arose precisely from the democratization of the power. At present, accepting that the Legislative Power may, by law, contradict a treaty approved by it means, in summary, recognizing the predominance of Assemblies, in marked opposition to the constitutional provision that states the Powers of the State are harmonious and independent, without express authorization of the Constitution in that sense".
> FRAGA, Mirtô. *O conflito entre tratado internacional e norma de direito interno...*, cit., p. 83-84.

After the treaty is approved by the Congress and ratified by the President of the Republic, its regulatory provisions, with the publication of the text, become fully effective at an internal level. From this fact arises the connection of the State regarding the application of its rules, each of its Powers being responsible for the role they play in this process: the Legislative power is in charge of approving necessary laws, and refrain from voting on conflicting laws; the Executive Power has the responsibility of properly and exactly regulating them, making everything possible for their faithful execution; and the Judicial Power has the predominant role of applying treaties internally, as well as the laws regulating them, rejecting the application of conflicting national laws.[110]

If the National Congress consents to the contest of the commitment signed, it is because implicitly it recognizes that, if the agreement is ratified, it *cannot* issue conflicting rules in the future. Therefore, the Congress assumes a true *negative obligation*, namely, to refrain from legislating in opposition to the obligations assumed at an international level. Thus, recognizing that the Legislative Power may issue a law, revoking the treaty previously signed, means recognizing "the predominance of Assemblies, in opposition to the superior provision that states the Powers of the State are harmonious and independent".[111] If such laws were issued, they would never have force to prevent the internal application of a treaty previously concluded, since they have their own revocation method, which is the claim, governed by the rules of Public International Law. Therefore, these laws shall be invalid.

Even though the State has jurisdiction to decide the Law applicable to a certain factual situation, it must respect the principles and rules adopted by the international society, which are superior to it, limiting the power to legislate, under the penalty of suffering coercive measures that may be imposed by the organized international society. Constitutional review of laws, thus, apart from considering constitutional provisions related to the specific case, shall also respect commitments assumed by the State at an international level, as well as the principles of International Law generally accepted by the international society as a whole.[112]

On the other hand, admitting that the State, in its judicial capacity, may declare the revocation of an international commitment is the same as recognizing that other state bodies, other than the figure of the President of the Republic, provided for in the constitution, may indirectly denounce the commitment internationally signed, rendering it ineffective and inapplicable at an internal level. When not applying an international treaty due to the existence of a "subsequent law", the judge is implicitly creating a false and incoherent hierarchy between internal laws and international treaties, which is not expressly declared by the Constitution. For that rea-

110 See Fraga, Mirtô. *O conflito entre tratado internacional e norma de direito interno...*, cit., p. 84.

111 Fraga, Mirtô. Idem, p. 132.

112 See Magalhães, José Carlos de. *O Supremo Tribunal Federal e o direito internacional...*, cit., p. 32-33 and 62.

son, the judge cannot apply an internal law to the detriment of a current international treaty either.

The violation of the obligation to respect the principles and rules of International Law, through the powers of the State, results in its international responsibility, which certainly cannot be forgotten or pushed into the background when the Judicial Power renders a judgment related to such rules. In this case the *pacta sunt servanda* rule is valid, universally recognized as a guide for State foreign commitments, and expressly established in Art. 26 of the Vienna Convention on the Law of Treaties, according to which every treaty in force "is binding upon the parties to it and must be performed by them in good faith".

In brief, by reason of all the arguments explained, there is no doubt that *ordinary* international treaties in force in Brazil have a *supralegal* level in our legal system. Although ordinary treaties are inferior to the Constitution – even according to the constitutional provision that subjects treaties to constitutional review (Art. 102, III, *b*) – they cannot be revoked by a subsequent internal law, under the penalty of international responsibility of the State.

Some progress was made in the SFC, in relation to the conflict between treaties and internal laws, with the vote of Judge Sepúlveda Pertence, dated March 29, 2000, in *RHC* 79.785/RJ, in which he understood it was possible to consider treaties on *human rights* (and not others…) as documents with *supralegal* status (be repeated that, for us, any ordinary treaty already has that *supralegal* level, and the treaties on human rights have *constitutional* status and level). However, the thesis of the supralegal nature of treaties on human rights was even clearer in the SFC with the vote upon further review of Judge Gilmar Mendes, in the plenary session on November 22, 2006, while judging *RE* 466.343-1/SP, in which the question of civil imprisonment for debt in chattel mortgage agreements for a guaranty was being discussed.[113] Although he still considered that

[113] The Court, in this case in which Cezar Peluso was reporting Judge (judged definitively on December 3, 2008), expressly rejected this kind of personal coercion in chattel mortgage agreements for a guaranty, as we have always defended since the publication of our book *Prisão civil por dívida e o Pacto de San José da Costa Rica* (Rio de Janeiro: Forense, 2002, 228p.). The plenary session of December 3, 2008 was considered (even by present Judges) as an historic session, since from that moment, the Court changed its previous understanding that was in the sense of the full *constitutionality* of civil imprisonment for debt in cases of chattel mortgage agreements for a guaranty. Later on, with the issuance of Binding Abridgment No. 25 (dated December 16, 2009, *Official Gazette of the State* of

ordinary international treaties have a relation of regulatory parity (therefore, level of ordinary law) with the national legal system, Judge Gilmar Mendes defended the thesis that treaties on *human rights* would be in an intermediate hierarchical level: below the Constitution, but above all infra-constitutional legislation. In his opinion, "it seems more consistent the interpretation that grants *supralegal* nature to treaties and conventions on human rights", according to which "treaties on human rights would be infra-constitutional, however, due to their special quality in relation to the other international regulatory acts, they would also have *supralegal* nature". And concluded: "In other terms, treaties on human rights could not go above the supremacy of the Constitution, but they would have a special place reserved in the legal system. Placing these treaties on a level with ordinary legislation would mean underestimating their special value in the context of the human being protection system".[114]

2.3 Our opinion as to the position of the SFC

The thesis of the supralegal nature of treaties on human rights not approved by a qualified majority (defended, for example, by Judge Gilmar Mendes, in *RE* 466.343-1/SP) changes the equal status of such instru-

---

December 23, 2009, p. 1), the SFC definitively abolished in Brazil civil imprisonment of unfaithful depositories, regardless of the type of deposit, in these words: "Civil imprisonment of unfaithful depositories is against the law, regardless of the modality of deposit".

114 See vote upon further review of Judge Gilmar Mendes, in RE 466.343-1/SP, p. 21. See also Mendes, Gilmar Ferreira, A supralegalidade dos tratados internacionais de direitos humanos e a prisão civil do depositário infiel no Brasil, *Systemas: revista de ciências jurídicas e econômicas*, vol. 2, No.1 (2010), p. 64-100. It should be pointed out that on March 12, 2008, Judge Celso de Mello, in *HC* 87.585-8/TO, in which it was also being discussed the impossibility of civil imprisonment for debt by the application of the Pact of San José de Costa Rica, radically changed his previous opinion (as stated in the monocratic decision of *HC* 77.631-5/SC, published in the *Court Gazette* 158-E, of August 19, 1998, Section I, p. 35) to accept our thesis according to which treaties on human rights have status and level of constitutional rules in Brazil. The only point of disagreement with our position lies in the fact that Judge Celso de Mello accepted the thesis of the constitutional hierarchy of treaties on human rights *only* for instruments ratified until Constitutional Amendment No. 45/2004 (amendment that added item 3 to Art. 5 of the Constitution). In our opinion, treaties on human rights ratified by Brazil have constitutional status and level no matter when they were ratified, if before or after Constitutional Amendment No. 45/2004 (for further details on this matter see Mazzuoli, Valerio de Oliveira, *Curso de direito internacional público*, cit., p. 896-927). Regarding *ordinary* treaties, whose analysis is the purpose of this Chapter, the Judge continued to follow the traditional doctrine of the SFC, which places them on the same hierarchical level as ordinary legislation.

ments to the detriment of those instruments adopted internally by such majority, creating a "duplicity of legal regimes" improper for the current (internal and international) system for the protection of rights, because it establishes "categories" of treaties that have the same ethical basis. And this ethical basis is granted not by internal Law or any internal power (for example, Legislative Power), but the international system from which such treaties come. When creating the "categories" of treaties with *constitutional* and *supralegal* status (in case they are or are not approved by said qualified majority), the thesis of supralegality came to regulate *equal* instruments in totally *different* ways (that is, it changed the equal status of "equal" instruments), in marked opposition to the constitutional principle of *equality before the law*. For this reason, it is a mistake to place certain treaties on human rights *below* the Constitution and others (also on human rights) on the *same level* as the Constitution, under the penalty of subverting the whole conventional logic for the protection of such rights, for example, that situation in which an accessory instrument would be equivalent to a constitutional amendment, while the principal instrument would be in an inferior hierarchical level.

Therefore, even the modern position of the SFC, expressed in the vote upon further review of Judge Gilmar Mendes mentioned above, still is, in our opinion, insufficient. We think that *ordinary* international treaties ratified by the Brazilian State are placed at an *intermediate* hierarchical level, being below the Constitution, but above infra-constitutional legislation, not being revoked by a subsequent law (as they are not in a situation of regulatory parity with the other national laws).[115] Regarding treaties on human rights, we understand they have status of constitutional rule, regardless of their eventual qualified *quorum* of approval.[116] A similar result may be achieved applying the principle – today increasingly widespread in internal case law of other countries, and completely reaffirmed by international courts – of the *supremacy* of International Law

---

115 See, in that very sense, Accioly, Hildebrando, *Tratado de direito internacional público*, vol. I, cit., p. 547, who states the following: "As commitments assumed by the State in its relations with other States, treaties must be placed at a superior level in relation to the internal laws of the parties concluding them. Therefore, (...) they revoke previous conflicting laws; subsequent laws must not contradict the rules or principles established by them; and, finally, any internal law related to them must be interpreted, as far as possible, in accordance with previous conventional law". In Portuguese doctrine, see Pereira, André Gonçalves & Quadros, Fausto de, *Manual de direito internacional público*, cit., p. 121-124.

116 See Mazzuoli, Valerio de Oliveira. *Curso de direito internacional público*, cit., p. 913-924.

and the *prevalence* of its rules over all internal regulations, both previous and subsequent regulations.[117]

Considering this point of view – that, in general, international treaties have hierarchical superiority in relation to the other infra-constitutional rules, whether such superiority is *constitutional*, as in the case of treaties on human rights, or *supralegal*, as in the case of ordinary treaties – it can be concluded that state regulations must have not only *formal* (or *procedural*) limits, but also two *material* vertical limits, namely: *a*) the Constitution and treaties on human rights (because they have constitutional hierarchy); and *b*) ordinary international treaties with supralegal status. Thus, the (formal) compatibility of internal rules with the constitutional text no longer guarantees to the law *validity* within internal Law. In order to guarantee the validity (and consequent *effectiveness*) of a law, it must be materially compatible with the Constitution *and with* international treaties (on human rights or ordinary treaties) ratified and in force within the State. In other words, a certain internal law may even be considered to be *in force* (*existing*) because it was created following the rules of the legislative process established by the Constitution (and shall remain in published legislative compilations), but it shall not be *valid* if it contradicts treaties on human rights (which have constitutional hierarchy) or the other treaties to which the Federative Republic of Brazil is a party (which have supralegal status). For a law to have *force* and *validity* at the same time, it shall comply with a double material vertical compatibility, that is, the compatibility of the law (1) with the Constitution and treaties

---

117 See Vignali, Heber Arbuet & Arrighi, Jean Michel. Os vínculos entre o direito internacional público e os sistemas internos, cit., p. 420. In Germany, this is also the criterion adopted for most treaties ratified by this country (Art. 59, of the Fundamental Law: "Treaties governing political relations of the Federation or relate to matters of federal legislation shall require the approval or participation, in the form of a federal law, of the competent bodies in the corresponding matter of federal legislation", which shall prevail (even with immediate application, if they contain individual rights) over all regulations inferior to federal law, for example, rules created by Federated States and decrees issued by the government. This understanding is valid, in Germany, even for treaties on human rights, which is criticizable, because it allows for the application of the *lex posterior derogat legi priori* maxim in case of conflict between a treaty and subsequent federal law; but it is convenient to clarify that in said country, there are also doctrine currents that attribute constitutional level, at least, to the European Convention on Human Rights. For further information see Bank, Roland, Tratados internacionales de derechos humanos bajo el ordenamiento jurídico alemán, *Anuario de Derecho Constitucional Latinoamericano*, year 10, vol. II, Montevideo: Konrad-Adenauer-Stiftung, 2004, p. 721-734.

on human rights in force within the country and (2) with the other international instruments ratified by the Brazilian State.[118]

It is not possible to confuse *force* with *validity* (and consequent *effectiveness*) of legal rules, as the Kelsenian positivist model of legal teaching did; now, we must follow the lesson of Ferrajoli, who distinguishes both situations: a law *in force* is not necessarily *valid* and, in last instance, *effective*. In the future, for a rule to be *effective* and applied by the judge to a particular case, first it shall be *valid*, and to be valid first it shall be *in force*. In other words, the *force* (*existence*) does not depend on the *validity*, but the latter depends on the former, in the same way as the *effectiveness* depends on the validity (it is a set of values in which, first of all, we find the *force*, then the *validity* and, finally, the *effectiveness*).[119] For this reason, we do not accept the concepts of *validity* and *force* of Tercio Sampaio Ferraz Jr., for whom a *valid* rule is that which complied with the process of regulatory formation or production (which, for us, is a law *in force*), and a rule *in force* is that which was already *published*. The author defines force as a "term with which the time of validity of a rule is delimited" or, in other words, as "the valid rule (belonging to the system) whose authority may *already* be considered as immunized, making prescribed behaviors enforceable", concluding that a rule "may be valid without being in force, although a rule in force is always valid".[120] We do not agree (also based on Ferrajoli) with that understanding according to which a rule "may be valid without being in force", and that "a rule in force is always valid". In our opinion, a law formally *in force* (force and *formal existence* are exactly

---

118 All these legal instruments (international treaties and Constitution) comprise what the Italian doctrine calls "rules on legal production", which provide the "gross" act of formulation of the rule with the "institutional" quality of legislation. After analyzing this question, it is understood that a legal rule shall not be *valid* (even though it is *in force*) if it was not created in accordance with (at least) *some* of those rules on legal production (there are many types, but we are interested precisely in that related to the "content itself of future regulations", for example, "constitutional provisions [or conventional provisions, it may be added] which grant freedom rights to citizens"). For further information see Guastini, Riccardo, *Estudios de teoría constitucional*, Mexico, F.D.: UNAM, 2001, p. 85-97.

119 See Ferrajoli, Luigi. *Derechos y garantias: la ley del más débil*. Transl. by Perfecto Andrés Ibáñez and Andrea Greppi. Madrid: Trotta, 1999, p. 20-22. See also Ferrajoli, Luigi, *Direito e razão: teoria do garantismo penal*, 2. ed. (reviewed and extended), transl. by Ana Paula Zomer Sica (*et all.*), São Paulo: Revista dos Tribunais, 2006, p. 329-331.

120 Ferraz Jr., Tercio Sampaio. *Introdução ao estudo do direito: técnica, decisão, dominação*, 4. ed. (reviewed and extended), São Paulo: Atlas, 2003, p. 198.

the same[121]) is a law formulated by the Parliament in accordance with the rules of legislative process established by the Constitution; a *valid* law is a law *in force* materially compatible with the constitutional text and with the treaties (on human rights or not) ratified by the Government, that is, a law with respected authority protected against any attack (since it is compatible with the Constitution and treaties in force within the country).[122] Only having material vertical compatibility with both rules – the Constitution and treaties – the infra-constitutional law in question shall be *in force* and *valid* (and, possibly, *effective*). Otherwise, if the law does not go through the test of (material) vertical compatibility with the treaties, it shall have no validity (and no effectiveness) within internal Law, being rejected (not applied) by the judge in the particular case, in spite of being in force. Therefore, the lack of a definitive decision of the SFC as to the concentrated and diffuse control of constitutionality (in the last case, with the possibility of informing the Federal Senate so that it – by virtue of Art. 52, X of the Constitution – may suspend, in whole or in part, the effects of the law declared as unconstitutional by the SFC) maintains the *force* of laws in the country, which, however, shall not remain to be *valid* if they are materially incompatible with international treaties (on human rights or ordinary treaties) to which Brazil is a party.[123]

Some doubts may arise as to considering that *ordinary* treaties are instruments with supralegal status in Brazil. It could be objected that the Constitution did not set forth the hierarchy of those treaties in relation

---

121 In that very sense, see Ferrajoli, Luigi, *Derechos y garantías...*, cit., p. 21; and also Ferrajoli, Luigi, *Direito e razão...*, cit., p. 330.

122 For more information on the difference between *force* and *validity* of legal rules, see Guastini, Riccardo, *Estudios de teoría constitucional*, cit., p. 90-92.

123 There is an exceptional situation in which the declaration of unconstitutionality of a law affects its *force*, thus affecting its *validity* and consequent *effectiveness*. This is the case in which the law is declared as unconstitutional in its formal aspect. In this case, "it cannot be denied that such declaration of unconstitutionality affects (from that moment) the validity of the rule, but also its force. A law that did not follow the proper legislative procedure, after its formal unconstitutionality is declared (even though it is published in the Official Gazette), no longer in force. Although it is true that the declaration of material unconstitutionality does not affect this formal aspect (force), the same cannot be said as to formal unconstitutionality" (Gomes, Luiz Flávio. *Estado constitucional de direito e a nova pirâmide jurídica*. São Paulo: Premier Máxima, 2008, p. 77). In that very sense, see the lesson of Riccardo Guastini, for whom the *formal* invalidity "is a 'strong' invalidity, which, as a rule, results in the non-existence of the law" (*Estudios de teoría constitucional*, cit., p. 93).

to the other laws of the Republic. However, it suffices to verify, in a comparative study, some Brazilian legal provisions in order to conclude that our legal system favors the superiority of *any treaties* in the internal legal regime. One of those provisions is Art. 5 of the Criminal Code of Brazil, which has adopted this thesis since 1940, providing as follows: "Brazilian law shall be applied, *without prejudice to conventions, treaties and rules of international law*, to crimes committed in the national territory". This approach of criminal law, of superiority of international treaties over infra-constitutional legislation, was followed and reaffirmed, in 1941, by the Code of Criminal Procedure too, which set forth, in Art. 1(I), that the "criminal procedure shall be governed by this Code in all the Brazilian territory, *except for treaties, conventions and rules of international law*". Thus, such provision clearly intended to give to international treaties, in criminal procedural matters, a regulatory status superior to their own hierarchy. That is, if the criminal procedural law in Brazil is governed by the Code of Criminal Procedure, *except for treaties, conventions and rules of International Law*, this is because such instruments and rules of the Law of Nations prevail over infra-constitutional legislation, in relation to such matters. And if they *prevail* over the rules of the Code, evidently, this is because they are above them. In summary, these rules (Art. 5 of the Criminal Code and Art. 1(I), of the Code of Criminal Procedure) intended to expressly provide international treaties signed by the Brazilian State with a status of supralegality, since they prevail over ordinary criminal and criminal procedural legislation, respectively.

However, there is in Brazilian legislation another provision related to the supralegal status of ordinary treaties, which deserves to be mentioned. It is Art. 7 of Law 8.078, of September 11, 1990, which created the Consumer Protection and Defense Code, which argues the following:

> "The rights provided for in this Code *shall not exclude other rights arising from international treaties or conventions to which Brazil is signatory*, ordinary internal law, regulations issued by the competent administrative authorities or deriving from the general principles of law, analogy, customs, and equity".

As it can be easily noticed, such provision *separates* international treaties to which Brazil is a signatory from internal ordinary legislation, which clearly reflects the will of the national legislator to place international commitments assumed on a *superior* level as infra-constitutional ordinary legislation. If the intention of our legislator were to place international treaties on the same level as internal ordinary legislation, he would certainly not have made such a distinction. It sufficed to make reference to ordinary legislation only, which would include international treaties, if that were his desire. Therefore, as the provision separated international treaties from internal ordinary legislation, apart from making it clear that ordinary treaties are in a superior hierarchical position in relation to all infra-constitutional legislation, it also reinforced the idea that international treaties which protect human rights have status of constitutional rule, as a reinforcement of the idea expressed in item 2 of Art. 5 of the Constitution, which provides such treaties with that special nature; this is because consumer rights also belong to the group of fundamental human rights established in the Brazilian Constitution of 1988 (Art. 5, XXXII).

We should also highlight – because it is the *only* provision in Brazilian legislation that *expressly* grants superior hierarchy to treaties conflicting with a rule of internal Law – the wording of Art. 98 of the National Tax Code, according to which "international treaties and conventions revoke or modify internal tax legislation, *and shall be observed by subsequent legislation*". Through that rule, for example, state or municipal tax exemptions by way of treaties are guaranteed in Brazil.[124]

In summary, we come to the conclusion that any international treaty in force within Brazil has, at least, *supralegal* status, being below the Constitution and above all national laws (ordinary, complementary, etc.). On the other hand, treaties on *human rights* have *constitutional* status in Brazilian Law, regardless of the qualified approval of Art. 5, item 3, of the Constitution, solving an eventual conflict between such treaties and constitutional rules by the *pro homine* principle, which sets forth the application of the rule more favorable to the human being.[125]

2.4 Jurisdictional control of the conventionality of laws

As already stated, the Brazilian Constitution of 1988 gives treaties on human rights the same status and priority as constitutional rules, regardless of legislative approval by a qualified majority. That constitutional status of treaties on human rights is obtained from the interpretation *a contrario* of Art. 5, item 2, of the Constitution, which provides as follows:

---

[124] On the subject, see Mazzuoli, Valerio de Oliveira, Eficácia e aplicabilidade dos tratados em matéria tributária no direito brasileiro, *Revista Forense*, vol. 390, year 103, Rio de Janeiro, Mar/Apr/2007, p. 583-590.

[125] See Mazzuoli, Valerio de Oliveira. *Tratados internacionais direitos humanos e direito interno*, cit., p. 227-228.

> "The rights and guarantees established in this Constitution *do not exclude* others derived from the regime and principles adopted by it, or from *international treaties to which the Federative Republic of Brazil is a party*".

However, if they are approved by a qualified majority, such treaties shall be (once they are ratified and enter into force in the country) *equivalent* to constitutional amendments, as set forth by Art. 5, item 3, of the Constitution, added by Constitutional Amendment No. 45/2004:

> "International treaties and conventions on human rights approved by both Houses of the National Congress, in two different voting sessions, by three-fifths votes of their respective members, *shall be equivalent to Constitutional Amendments*".

From this innovation introduced by Constitutional Amendment 45, it arose (and gained visibility among us) a new type of control of the rules of internal Law: the control *of conventionality* of laws, which is the process of vertical adaptation (*material* in particular) of internal rules to provisions found in international conventions on human rights. Since treaties on human rights are *materially* constitutional (Art. 5, item 2) or *materially and formally* constitutional (Art. 5, item 3), it should be understood that the classic "control of constitutionality" must now share its space with this new kind of control ("of conventionality") of the formulation and application of internal regulations.[126]

It could be objected that the control *of constitutionality* is that control exercised in relation to treaties on human rights adopted internally in accordance with Art. 5, item 3, because they are equivalent to a constitutional *amendment*. In our opinion, the control *of constitutionality* itself may be performed only when there is confrontation with the *Constitution*. Even though treaties on human rights (materially *and formally* constitutional) are *equivalent to constitutional amendments*, this does not allow for reference to the control "of constitutionality" as the exercise of vertical adaptation performed by virtue of them, notably in case the constitutional text suffers no legislative violation (that is, in case the law *does not violate* the Constitution itself, but only the corresponding *treaty* on human rights). In brief, the expression "control of constitutionality" should be strictly reserved to cases of vertical (in)compatibility of laws with the Constitution, and the expression "control of conventionality" to cases of legislative (in)

---

[126] For detailed information on this matter, see Mazzuoli, Valerio de Oliveira, *O controle jurisdicional da convencionalidade das leis*, 2. ed. (reviewed, updated and extended), São Paulo: Revista dos Tribunais, 2011 (and all the bibliography specified there).

compatibility with treaties on human rights (formally constitutional or not) in force within the country.

2.4.1 *The doctrine of conventionality control in the Inter-American system*

In the Inter-American system of human rights, the theory on conventionality control appeared formally, for the first time, on September 26, 2006, when the Inter-American Court of Human Rights decided the *Case of Almonacid-Arellano et al. v. Chile*, and this was stated in paragraph 124 of the judgment:

> "The Court is aware that domestic judges and courts are bound to respect the rule of law, and therefore, they are bound to apply the provisions in force within the legal system. But when a State has ratified an international treaty such as the American Convention, its judges, as part of the State, are also bound by such Convention. This forces them to see that all the effects of the provisions embodied in the Convention are not adversely affected by the enforcement of laws which are contrary to its purpose and that have not had any legal effects since their inception. In other words, the Judiciary *must exercise a sort of 'conventionality control'* between the domestic legal provisions which are applied to specific cases and the American Convention on Human Rights. To perform this task, the Judiciary has to take into account not only the treaty, but also the interpretation thereof made by the Inter-American Court, which is the ultimate interpreter of the American Convention" [emphasis added].[127]

Therefore, this judgment is the case that formally inaugurates the doctrine of (internal) conventionality control within the American Continent.[128] It is also the case in which the intention of the Inter-American

---

[127] Inter-American Court of Human Rights, *Case of Almonacid-Arellano et al. v. Chile*, Preliminary Objections, Merits, Reparations and Costs, Judgment of September 26, 2006, Series C, No. 154.

[128] However, it should be noted that the expression "conventionality control" had already been used individually (in the same Court) before 2006. The first use of this expression (in the Inter-American regional system) is attributed to the concurring opinion of Judge Sérgio García Ramirez, in the *Case of Myrna Mack Chang v. Guatemala*, judged on November 25, 2003, paragraph 27, which says: "For the effects of the American Convention and of the exercise of the contentious jurisdiction of the Inter-American Court, the State is considered integrally, as a whole. Accordingly, responsibility is global, it concerns the State as a whole and cannot be subject to the division of authority established in domestic Law. At the international level, it is not possible to divide the State, to bind before the Court only one or some of its organs, to grant them representation of the State in the proceeding – without

Court is verified: that the conventionality control by local courts be considered as an actual question of international *public order*.[129]

> It should be pointed out that, for as long as it can be remembered (that is, from the time it began functioning, on July 18, 1978), the Inter-American Court has *controlled* the conventionality of the laws of States Parties to the American Convention, since this is exactly the function of an international court of human rights. What we should add is that the expression "conventionality control" formally appeared in the Inter-American system more than twenty years after the Court began functioning, from the moment in which discussions on this matter began to intensify. From that moment (since 2006), the Inter-American Court passed on the conventionality control obligation of these laws, primarily, to the Judicial Power of States Parties (which had not been expressly done so far).

Shortly after that, the Court referred again to the conventionality control, in the *Case of the Dismissed Congressional Employees v. Peru*, judged on November 24, 2006, reinforcing its previous understanding and highlighting some characteristics of this control. In paragraph 128 of the judgment, the Court established as follows:

> "When a State has ratified an international treaty such as the American Convention, the judges are also subject to it; this obliges them to ensure that the *effet util* of the Convention is not reduced or annulled by the application of laws contrary to its provisions, object and purpose. In other words, the organs of the Judiciary should exercise not only a control of constitutionality, but also of 'conventionality' *ex officio* between domestic norms and the American Convention, evidently in the context of their respective spheres of competence and the corresponding procedural regulations. This function should not be limited exclusively to the statements or actions of the plaintiffs in each specific case...".[130]

The imperative wording of the Court should be highlighted in the sense that it is a *duty* of the internal Judicial Power to control the con-

---

this representation affecting the whole State – and excluding other organs from this conventional regime of responsibility, leaving their actions outside the 'conventionality control' that involves the jurisdiction of the international Court" [italics are ours].

129 For an opinion on how this understanding has been adopted in many Latin American States, see Marinoni, Luiz Guilherme & Mazzuoli, Valerio de Oliveira (coord.), *Controle de convencionalidade: um panorama latino-americano (Brasil, Argentina, Chile, México, Peru, Uruguai)*, Brasilia: Gazeta Jurídica, 2013, 744p.

130 Inter-American Court of Human Rights, *Case of the Dismissed Congressional Employees (Aguado-Alfaro et al.) v. Peru*, Preliminary Objections, Merits, Reparations and Costs, Judgment of November 24, 2006, Series C, No. 158.

ventionality of its laws in relation to treaties on human rights in force within the country.[131] In the last phrase of the first passage quoted (*Case of Almonacid-Arellano et al. v. Chile*), according to which the Judicial Power "has to take into account not only the treaty, *but also the interpretation thereof made by the Inter-American Court*, which is the ultimate interpreter of the American Convention", it is also clear that the conventionality control exercised by national judges and courts shall be governed by the standards set forth by the "ultimate interpreter" of the Convention (that is, the Inter-American Court). This is reflected in the so-called *diffuse* conventionality control, because if the Court (be repeated: the "ultimate interpreter" of the Convention) does not limit such control to an *express request* of the parties in a particular case, and if, in turn, local judges and courts "must" take into account the interpretation of the treaty made by such Court, this means that the internal Judicial Power should not depend on the exclusive request of the parties, but control the conventionality of laws *ex officio,* as long as it has a particular case whose solution may be found in an international treaty on human rights to which the State is a party: *iura novit curia.*

It should be highlighted that *each and every* treaty on human rights is a paradigm for the conventionality control, and not only the American Convention (consider that the Court refers to an "international treaty *such as* the American Convention").[132] Therefore, it is a mistake to state – as some legal scholars do, who have recently studied this topic – that only the American Convention is a paradigm for the conventionality control of national rules; this understanding is reinforced by the wording of Art. 64, 1, of the American Convention itself, according to which the Member States of the Organization of American States "may consult the Court regarding the interpretation of this Convention *or of other treaties concerning the protection of human rights* in the American States..." [emphasis added]. The rights provided for in all these instruments, thus, form what may be called "conventionality block", similar to the well-known "consti-

[131] However, the application of treaties on human rights by the national Judicial Power must comply with the *pro homine* principle; that is, the national Judicial Power must apply the treaty even to the detriment of the Constitution of the State, provided the corresponding rule is *more beneficial* to the human being subject of rights.

[132] The Inter-American Court, in the *Case of Gómez Palomino v. Peru*, of November 22, 2005, controlled, for the first time, the conventionality of a treaty other that the American Convention; in this case, the *Inter-American Convention on Forced Disappearance of Persons*, approved in Belém do Pará (Brazil) in 1994, was used for control purposes.

tutionality block"; that is, they comprise a *corpus juris* of human rights that must be compulsorily respected by States Parties.

Finally, the denial of the Judicial Power to perform the diffuse conventionality control, under the argument that it was not requested by the parties or that it is not possible to exercise such control *ex officio*, is sufficient cause to bring about the international responsibility of the State for violation of human rights. It should also be pointed out that this obligation of internal judges to control the conventionality of laws shall exist even in those countries where singular judges do not have competence to perform the constitutionality control (countries that reserve this control only to the Supreme Court or a Constitutional Division of the Supreme Court, for example, Uruguay, Mexico and Costa Rica).[133]

However, it was in the *Case of Cabrera García and Montiel Flores v. Mexico*, judged on November 26, 2010, that the Inter-American Court (by unanimity of votes) definitively asserted its doctrine on the "conventionality control". From paragraph 225 through 233 of the judgment, the Court reaffirmed its consolidated case law on the subject, quoting (to reinforce its arguments) decisions from many Supreme Courts of Latin American countries that grant internal binding effects to the interpretations the Inter-American Court of Human Rights has made of the provisions of the American Convention. From this judgment, it became a *duty* of the Judicial Power of the States to control the conventionality of internal Law rules, and their denial to do so shall result in the international responsibility of the State.[134]

Another new rule related to the internal conventionality control was introduced in the judgment of the *Case of Gelman v. Uruguay*, of February 24, 2011, in which the Inter-American Court extended the internal duty

---

133 In these cases, even if internal judges do not have competence to control the constitutionality of laws, they shall (nevertheless) find the adequate means ("...in the context of their respective spheres of competence and the corresponding procedural regulations", as established by the Inter-American Court) to perform this control, by themselves or by submitting the process to the competent Court (or body of the Court). The internal Judicial Power cannot *refuse to control* the conventionality of laws, contradicting the decisions of the Inter-American Court in this sense, since the obligation to internally control the conventionality extends to *all* the bodies of the Judicial Power. For these countries, the best solution would be to amend the Constitution and adapt it to the decisions of the Inter-American Court.

134 See Inter-American Court of Human Rights, *Case of Cabrera García and Montiel Flores v. Mexico*, Preliminary Objections, Merits, Reparations and Costs, Judgment of November 26, 2010, Series C, No. 220.

of control, beyond the Judicial Power, to *all* the bodies of the State. In this judgment, apart from reaffirming the duty of the internal Judicial Power to control *prima facie* the conventionality of laws, the Court ordered that the other bodies of the State (especially those related to the administration of Justice, at all levels) have the *duty* to control the conventionality of internal rules as to international treaties on human rights in force in the State, particularly the American Convention. In fact, in paragraph 193 of the judgment, the Court established as follows:

> "When a State has ratified an international treaty such as the American Convention, all of its bodies, including its judges, are also subject to such a treaty, and this obligates them to ensure that the effects of the provisions of the Convention are not diminished by the application of norms contrary to its object and purpose. The Judicial Branch must exercise 'control of conformity with the Convention' *ex officio* of the harmonization of the domestic norms with the American Convention, evidently within the framework of their respective jurisdictions and the corresponding procedural rules. In this task, the Judicial Branch should bear in mind not only the treaty, but also the corresponding interpretation made by the Inter-American Court, the final interpreter of the American Convention".[135]

Therefore, Law operators must understand how this conventionality control is performed within the internal system. As already stated, in Brazil the Federal Constitution of 1988 gives treaties on human rights the same status and level as constitutional rules, regardless of legislative approval by a qualified majority (see Art. 5, items 2 and 3). For this reason, the Brazilian system accepts the *concentrated* and *diffuse* conventionality control of laws, as will be explained below.

2.4.2 Conventionality control in Brazilian Law

After analyzing the development of this matter in the Inter-American system, now we must understand *how the conventionality control is performed* in Brazilian Law. It should be pointed out that the emphasis to be placed on this subject is mainly related to the *jurisdictional* control of the conventionality of laws, without disregarding, however, that the Inter-American Court, in the *Case of Gelman v. Uruguay*, of February 24, 2011, extended such competence (and duty) of control to *all* the bodies of the State.

---

[135] Inter-American Court of Human Rights, *Case of Gelman v. Uruguay*, Merits and Reparations, Judgment of February 24, 2011, Series C, No. 221.

It should be clarified that this internal (national) control of the conventionality of internal rules is the *first* step to be taken, before any expression of an international court in such regard,[136] since international courts can only control the conventionality of an internal rule if the original Judicial Power did not perform such control, or did so insufficiently. Therefore, it is incorrect to think that only the *international* control of the conventionality of laws (performed by regional courts of human rights) would be the real conventionality control, because this reasoning holds the insuperable inconsistency of not recognizing that it is from the international courts themselves (for example, the Inter-American Court) that it leads to the *obligation* of internal judges and courts to control (first of all, before any international expression on the subject) the conventionality of their national rules. As is well-known, the international system to protect human rights *reinforces* or *complements* the protective system of internal Law, as explained in the *second whereas* of the American Convention, which sets forth that the conventional international protection is "reinforcing or complementing the protection provided by the domestic Law of the American States". For this reason, it is also important to study, apart from the Inter-American system, *our* (Brazilian) model of jurisdictional control of the conventionality of laws.

Let us begin by understanding the *concentrated* modality first, and then we will study the *diffuse* control.[137]

2.4.2.1 Concentrated control of conventionality

As regards the concentrated control of conventionality, the question to be answered are *how to apply it* before the SFC and which is the *legal basis* to exercise such control before the Supreme Court.

---

[136] See Inter-American Court of Human Rights, *Case of Almonacid-Arellano et al. v. Chile*, Preliminary Objections, Merits, Reparations and Costs, Judgment of September 26, 2006, Series C, No. 154, paragraph 124; *Case of the Dismissed Congressional Employees (Aguado-Alfaro et al.) v. Peru*, Preliminary Objections, Merits, Reparations and Costs, Judgment of November 24, 2006, Series C, No. 158, paragraph 128; and *Case of Cabrera García and Montiel Flores v. Mexico*, Preliminary Objections, Merits, Reparations and Costs, Judgment of November 26, 2010, Series C, No. 220, paragraphs 225-233.

[137] In the Brazilian doctrine, we systematized, for the first time, the application of the *concentrated* and *diffuse* controls of conventionality, and also the *supralegality* control. For detailed information on this matter, see Mazzuoli, Valerio de Oliveira, *O controle jurisdicional da convencionalidade das leis*, cit., p. 73-165.

Now, if the Constitution provides treaties on human rights with constitutional hierarchy, *equivalent to an amendment*, logically it must also guarantee the resources provided to any constitutional rule or amendment to protect against unauthorized attacks of infraconstitutional law. In this sense, we assert that it is totally possible to use concentrated control actions, such as the ADIn (which would invalidate the infra-constitutional rule due to *unconventionality*), the ADECON (which would guarantee to the infra-constitutional rule vertical compatibility with a formally constitutional treaty on human rights) or even the ADPF (which would make it possible to demand compliance with a "fundamental provision" found in a formally constitutional treaty on human rights), based not only on the constitutional text, but also on the treaties on human rights approved in accordance with Art. 5, item 3, of the Constitution and in force within the country. Thus, those legitimized to exercise the concentrated control (mentioned in Art. 103 of the Constitution) have many more resources at hand than before to invalidate an internal law incompatible with the treaties on human rights adopted internally with qualified *quorum*. Therefore, it can be said that treaties on human rights adopted internally by this qualified majority can be used as a means of concentrated control (of *conventionality*) of the rules of internal Law, apart from being used as paradigm for *diffuse* control.

In this way, the well-known Direct Action of Unconstitutionality (Ação Direta de Inconstitucionalidade, ADIn) would become an actual Direct Action *of Unconventionality*. Likewise, the Declaratory Action of Constitutionality (Ação Declaratória de Constitucionalidade, ADECON) would assume the role of a Declaratory Action *of Conventionality* (it would be necessary to bring this action when the infra-constitutional rule does not affect the Constitution in any way, but it is intended to guarantee its *compatibility* with a certain provision of a formally incorporated treaty on human rights equivalent to a constitutional amendment). In the same sense, the Allegation of Disobedience of a Fundamental Precept (Arguição de Descumprimento de Preceito Fundamental, ADPF) may be used to protect a "fundamental precept" of a treaty on human rights violated by infra-constitutional rules, even *municipal* laws and rules *prior* to the date on which such treaty was approved (and entered into force) with equivalent status as a constitutional amendment in Brazil.

The first action of abstract control proposed in Brazil to control the conventionality of a treaty on human rights (the *Convention on the Rights of Persons with Disabilities*, of 2007), adopted internally under Art. 5, item 3, of the Constitution, was precisely the ADPF (No. 182), of July 9, 2009. Its aim was to declare, with effectiveness *erga omnes* and binding effect, the invalidity of Art. 20, item 2, of Law 8.742/93, for not complying with the above-mentioned Convention, which uses the concept of "person with disabilities" in a broader sense and, therefore, more protective sense than the concept stated in the Law. In fact, the original wording of Art. 20, item 2, of Law 8.742/93 set forth as follows: "In order to grant this benefit, persons with disabilities are those who are disabled to lead an independent life and to work". In turn, Art. 1 of the Convention establishes, in a much broader sense, that persons with disabilities "include those who have long-term physical, mental, intellectual or sensory impairments which in interaction with various barriers may hinder their full and effective participation in society on an equal basis with others". It should be mentioned that the person who brought the action (General Attorney of the Republic) did not use, in the corresponding ADPF, the expression "conventionality control", as would be advisable, just stating that the Convention, after it was adopted internally with equivalent status as a constitutional amendment, is included in the "Brazilian constitutionality block" (claim page 1). This ADPF (even before it was decided) lost its purpose, since Law 12,470/11, modifying Art. 20, item 2, of Law 8.742/93, granted to the expression "persons with disabilities" the *exact* same meaning as the Convention (therefore, it can be said that there was a *legislative* control of conventionality of such Law, as it was feared that the proposed ADPF would be accepted by the SFC).

We must also mention the Direct Action of Unconstitutionality by Omission (Ação Direta de Inconstitucionalidade por Omissão, ADO), provided for in Art. 103, item 2, of the Constitution, which can be brought in any case that an *internal law is missing* that would be necessary for a conventional rule to become effective. In this case, the SFC may declare the *unconventionality by omission* of a measure to make effective an international rule on human rights in force in Brazil and previously approved by a qualified majority, informing the competent Power to take the necessary steps and, if an administrative body is involved, to do so in thirty days.

Regarding legislative omissions, it becomes (from that moment) perfectly applicable the constitutional injunctive relief to correct regulatory omissions that prevent the exercise of a right or freedom included in a treaty on human rights adopted internally with qualified *quorum*, since the constitutional provision guarantees the use of such remedy "whenever the lack of regulatory provisions makes the exercise of *constitutional* rights and liberties [including constitutional rules by comparison, as is the case of treaties *equivalent* to constitutional amendments] and the prerogatives inherent in nationality, sovereignty and citizenship unfeasible" (Art. 5, LXXI).

In summary, what should be defended is the following: when the constitutional text (in Art. 102, I, *a*) sets forth that the SFC has primary responsibility for "safeguarding the Constitution", with powers to decide, as matters of original jurisdiction, direct actions of unconstitutionality

(ADIn) of a law or federal or state regulatory act, or declaratory actions of constitutionality (ADECON) of a law or federal regulatory act, it is authorizing those specifically legitimated to bring such actions (mentioned in Art. 103 of the Constitution) to take such measures whenever the *Constitution* or *any rules equivalent to it* (such as, for example, treaties on human rights adopted internally with qualified *quorum*) are violated by infra-constitutional rules. From the Constitutional Amendment No. 45/04, it is necessary to understand that the expression "safeguarding the Constitution", used in Art. 102, I, *a*, includes, apart from the text of the Constitution itself, constitutional rules by comparison, as is the case of the above-mentioned treaties on human rights. Therefore, even though the Constitution says nothing as to a certain right, and being that same right provided for in a treaty on human rights *constitutionalized* in accordance with Art. 5, item 3, the SFC has powers to exercise the concentrated control of constitutionality/conventionality (for example, ADIn) to adapt the infra-constitutional rule to the provisions of the constitutionalized treaty.

2.4.2.2 *Diffuse control of conventionality*

Treaties on human rights not adopted internally by the qualified majority analyzed above shall (only) be paradigm of *diffuse* control of conventionality (because, in our opinion, treaties on human rights not approved by this qualified majority are only *materially constitutional*, in contrast to treaties approved by such majority, which have material *and formal* status of constitutional rules). Thus, to exercise control through an action (concentrated control), treaties on human rights must be approved in accordance with Art. 5, item 3, of the Federal Constitution/88 (that is, they must be *equivalent* to constitutional amendments); and to exercise control through a motion (diffuse control), these treaties must be ratified and effective at an internal level, since, by virtue of Art. 5, item 2, of the aforementioned Constitution, they already have status of constitutional rule.[138]

Thus, the *diffuse* control of conventionality is that control to be exercised by all judges and courts of the country, at the request of the parties

138 In Part IV, Ch. I, Section I, item 8, of our *Curso de direito internacional público* (8. ed. 2014, cit.), the reader finds a detailed explanation of the reason why treaties on human rights not adopted internally in accordance with Art. 5, item 3, of the Constitution have status of (materially) constitutional rule, and which are the differences between "*status* of constitutional rule" and "*equivalent* to constitutional amendment".

or *ex officio*. Since *all* treaties on human rights in force in Brazil have a materially constitutional level, it is an *obligation* of local judges and courts (including the SFC, for example, when it decides an Extraordinary Appeal, *Habeas Corpus*, etc.) to invalidate internal laws – provided they are *less beneficial* than the corresponding treaty on human rights, in accordance with the *pro homine* principle – conflicting with international rules on human rights accepted by Brazil (by a formal *ratification*) at an international level. In this case, also as an example of what happens in the diffuse control of constitutionality, the judicial decision invalidating an internal law due to the provision of a treaty only produces effects *inter partes*, that is, only between the parties to the particular case.

It should be pointed out that the *diffuse* control of conventionality exists among us from the promulgation of the Constitution, on October 5, 1988, and from the entry into force of treaties on human rights ratified by Brazil after such date, even though no national doctrine has made reference (so far) to that terminology. It is so true that the diffuse control of conventionality exists from the promulgation of the Constitution that the text of Art. 105, III, *a*, of the Constitution of 1988 – considering as an example the control in the SCJ – expressly sets forth that this court has the power to "decide, on special appeal, cases decided in sole or last instance by the Federal Regional Courts or by courts of the States, Federal District and Territories, when the appealed decision *is contrary to a treaty* or federal law, or denies the effectiveness thereof".[139] On the other hand, the *concentrated* control of conventionality was introduced on December 8, 2004, with the promulgation of the Constitutional Amendment No. 45.

As already stated, the Inter-American Court has understood (since 2006, when it judged the *Case of Almonacid-Arellano et al. v. Chile*) that the conventionality control performed by local courts is a duty arising from international *ordre public*, which cannot be avoided by any reason, under the penalty of international responsibility of the State.

---

[139] Art. 105, III, a, of the Constitution may also be used for the SCJ to perform the *supralegality control* of internal laws in relation to *ordinary* international treaties that are above such laws. In the previous example, we refer to the control performed by the SCJ as diffuse control *of conventionality* (expression reserved to treaties with constitutional hierarchy) as it is supposed to deal with the compatibility of laws with a treaty *on human rights*. However, if the analysis of the SCJ refers to an *ordinary* treaty, in this case the control performed is a *supralegality control*, as will be explained below (item 2.4.3).

In brief, in the current Brazilian Law all treaties comprising the conventional *corpus juris* of human rights to which the State is a party are used as paradigm for the conventionality control of internal rules, with the specifications established above: *a*) treaties on human rights adopted internally with qualified *quorum* (*equivalent* to constitutional amendments) are paradigm of concentrated control (apart from *diffuse* control, of course), corresponding, for example, a ADIn in the SFC in order to invalidate an infra-constitutional rule incompatible with them; *b*) treaties on human rights that only have "status of constitutional rule" (not being "*equivalent* to constitutional amendments", because they are not approved by the qualified majority of Art. 5, item 3) are paradigm only of *diffuse* control of conventionality, and any judge or court may base on them to declare a conflicting law *invalid*.

2.4.3 Control of supralegality

As regards the topic of conventionality control, there is still one last aspect to be highlighted, related to *ordinary* international treaties. Would they also be paradigm for the conventionality control of laws? First of all, it is known (contrary to what the SFC still thinks) that ordinary international treaties (those dealing with topics other than human rights) also have status superior to internal laws. Even though they are not placed on a level with constitutional rules, ordinary conventional instruments (as we always assert, based on Art. 27 of the Vienna Convention on the Law of Treaties of 1969) have *supralegal* hierarchy in our country, because they cannot be revoked by a subsequent internal law, as is also shown by several provisions of Brazilian legislation, among them Art. 98 of the National Tax Code mentioned before. In this last case, such (ordinary) treaties may also be used as paradigm to control infra-constitutional rules, since they are placed above them, with the only difference (in relation to treaties on human rights) that they shall not be used as paradigm of *conventionality* control (expression reserved for treaties with constitutional status), but of *supralegality* control of infra-constitutional rules. Thus, laws contrary to ordinary treaties are *invalid* for violating the hierarchy principle, because such treaties (being supralegal) are above them.[140]

---

140 For further information see Mazzuoli, Valerio de Oliveira, *O controle jurisdicional da convencionalidade das leis*, cit., p. 154-159.

It is evident that it may be thought (and this reasoning would not be wrong) that any control involving the adaptation of a national rule to an international *treaty* (regardless of its nature, on human rights or not) would be a *conventionality* control. This is true, there being no problems with this reasoning; any international convention (using the expression "convention" in a generic sense, including a "treaty", "agreement", etc.) is paradigm of conventionality control *lato sensu*. We prefer to define the control *of conventionality* as that control exercised exclusively in relation to treaties on human rights (which, in Brazil, may have status of, or be "equivalent" to, constitutional amendment), considering that, in the light of case law of international courts, this expression is not used when trying to adapt the obligations of the State to *ordinary* treaties. Another reason why we prefer to reserve the expression "control of conventionality" to the adaptation of internal rules to treaties on human rights (only) is not forgetting that these treaties have the same hierarchy as constitutional rules (that is why the neologism "conventionality" is similar to "constitutionality"); in this sense, the expression "control of conventionality" would be side-by-side with the expression "control of constitutionality". Thus, we thought it was more appropriate to differentiate between the name of the control having as paradigm ordinary treaties ("control of supralegality") and that related to treaties on human rights ("control of conventionality"). However, to be repeated, it is not technically incorrect to refer to the "control of conventionality" as the vertical adaptation of internal rules to *any international treaties* (on human rights or not) ratified by the government and in force within the State.

Such supralegality control is always exercised through a motion, that is, it is always *diffuse*; on the contrary, the *conventionality* control may be *diffused* or *concentrated*, the last case when the treaty on human rights was approved in accordance with Art. 5, item 3, of the Constitution and entered into force in Brazil (meaning: once *ratified*...) with equivalent status as a constitutional amendment.

In conclusion, what we can verify (from this moment) is that in current Brazilian Law there are *six types* of control of internal rules, namely: 1) control of legality (for example, adapting a decree to an ordinary law); 2) control of supralegality (exercised in relation to *ordinary* treaties); 3) concentrated control of constitutionality; 4) diffuse control of constitutionality; 5) concentrated control of conventionality (for treaties on human rights *equivalent* to constitutional amendments); and 6) diffuse control of conventionality (for all treaties on human rights in force within the country). For this reason, the justifications generally made to violate conventional obligations assumed by the State are absolutely *ineffective* in the light of Public International Law (especially, International Law of Human Rights) and now, also of the Brazilian constitutional system itself, which has been incorporated into these new (and up to that moment, barely known) means to control internal Law rules.

2.5 Some sensitive issues on the application of treaties in Brazil

At the end of this Chapter, some consideration must be given to the problems existing in Brazil as to the application of international acts.

First of all, the difficulty should be highlighted of the national Judicial Power (especially ordinary courts) to deal with the application of international acts, notably when no conventional protection is mentioned in the exordium, and from the analysis of the particular case it is understood that the judge should know and apply a certain treaty. Now, when a treaty is incorporated into the national legal system, it becomes part of the internal set of rules, and the Judicial Power must apply such treaty as if it was an internal law, even if it were not claimed by the parties: *jura novit curia*.

The powers of the State should know that the difficulty for Brazil to conclude an international commitment is, at least, the same as the necessary steps to implement norm-setting procedures. When the country assumes a commitment in relation to the performance of what it concluded internationally, it is considered to be bound by the terms of the commitment signed, being obliged to apply it as it applies any internal rule, not being enough the fact that treaties (any of them) in force here have, at least, the status of a supralegal rule (therefore, they may revoke previous internal legislation, but may not be revoked by a subsequent law).[141] From the moment the Republic assumes an international commitment, through a treaty ratified by it, courts must (compulsorily) respect and enforce such obligations assumed at an international level, under the penalty of committing an international unlawful act, arising from the unjustified violation of the treaty, which causes great constraints to the country internationally, together with a significant discredit before the other States with which Brazil concluded such agreement.

The role of the Judicial Power, as to the effective and correct application of treaties in Brazil is, as may be perceived, of fundamental importance. For this reason, national judges and courts must be familiar

---

141 We already explained that this is not the (current) position of the SFC, which understands that *only* treaties on *human rights* have supra legal hierarchy (see *RHC* 79,785/RJ, vote of Judge Sepúlveda Pertence, judged on March 29, 2000; and *RE* 466.343-1/SP, vote upon further review of Judge Gilmar Mendes, judged on December 3, 2008); but we also explained that this understanding is wrong (it contradicts the best doctrine and does not respect Art. 27 of the Vienna Convention on the Law of Treaties, in force within Brazil since the publication of Decree 7.030, of December 14, 2009).

with international instruments ratified by the Brazilian State, for them to be properly applied, mainly in relation to treaties that protect human rights, which have constitutional status and level.[142] But the responsibility of the Judicial Power must be integrated with that of the Legislative Power which, when it approves a treaty, undertakes not to issue subsequent conflicting laws, under the penalty of international responsibility, and also with the obligations assumed by the Executive Power at an international level, which historically was always in charge of international relations.

The harmonious integration of the powers of the State with regard to the application of treaties ratified by the State, apart from the constitutional obligation, arises from the good faith international practice that States must have in relation to each other in their mutual relationships. If the State is not satisfied with the ratified convention, it may claim the corresponding treaty without using legislative procedures aimed at obstructing its internal performance and application. This is a great inconvenience for interested parties who really need to see the treaty properly applied, for example, by the Judicial Power. Either the internal legislation is modified to be adapted to the content of the international commitment signed, or the agreement is claimed, as the case may be.

These are very sensitive issues that the Law of Treaties faces in relation to the incorporation and application of these international instruments in Brazil. For this reason, they deserve serious thought and analysis by experts in public international law and also by constitutional jurists, who must understand the modern international and constitutional system of treaty incorporation and application and their effectiveness in our internal legal system.

International treaties are based on the free and combined will of States, and that freedom of international performance must be safeguarded at any price, by internal powers, because treaties transform public international law into a complex of rules governing the international society, transforming it into a dynamic, representative and expressively authentic law. Therefore, there is no way of reversing the course of history and the evolution of international law, which has found in international treaties, mainly in open multilateral treaties, its most concrete and secure source.

---

142 See Mazzuoli, Valerio de Oliveira. *O controle jurisdicional da convencionalidade das leis*, cit., p. 25-71; and Mazzuoli, Valerio de Oliveira, *Curso de direito internacional público*, cit., p. 896-927.

References

Accioly, Hildebrando. A ratificação e a promulgação dos tratados em face da Constituição Federal brasileira. *Boletim da Sociedade Brasileira de Direito Internacional*, n. 7, Rio de Janeiro, jan./jun./1948, p. 5-11.

________. Ainda o problema da ratificação dos tratados, em face da Constituição Federal Brasileira. *Boletim da Sociedade Brasileira de Direito Internacional*, n. 11/12, Rio de Janeiro, jan./dez./1950, p. 95-108.

________. *Tratado de direito internacional público*, vol. I, 2. ed. Rio de Janeiro: MRE, 1956.

________; Nascimento e Silva, Geraldo Eulálio. *Manual de direito internacional público*, 13. ed. São Paulo: Saraiva, 1998.

Ago, Roberto. Droit des traités à la lumière de la Convention de Vienne. *Recueil des Cours*, vol. 134 (1971-III), p. 297-331.

Akehurst, Michael. The hierarchy of the sources of international law. *The British Yearbook of International Law*, vol. 47 (1974-75), p. 273-285.

Alland, Denis (coord.). *Droit international public*. Paris: PUF, 2000.

Almeida, Paula Wojcikiewicz; Pereira, Maíra Fajardo Linhares. Revisitando os efeitos da assinatura de um tratado internacional: da obrigação de boa-fé à sujeição internacional do Estado. *Revista Direito GV*, vol. 9, n. 1, São Paulo, jan./jun./2013, p. 171-197.

Amaral Júnior, Alberto do. *Curso de direito internacional público*, 2. ed. São Paulo: Atlas, 2011.

Anzilotti, Dionisio. *Cours de droit international*. Transl. by Gilbert Gidel. Paris: Editions Panthéon-Assas, 1999 (*Collection Les Introuvables*).

Atay, Ender Ethem. La conclusion des traités internationaux et les systèmes constitutionnels. *Journal of the Faculty of Law of Gazi University*, vol. 1, n. 1, Ankara, jun./1997, p. 153-195.

Aust, Anthony. *Modern treaty law and practice*, 4th printing. Cambridge: Cambridge University Press, 2004.

________. Amendment of treaties. In: Orakhelashvili, Alexander & Williams, Sarah (eds.). *40 years of the Vienna Convention on the Law of Treaties*. London: BIICL, 2010, p. 41-54.

Azevedo, Philadelpho. Os tratados e os interesses privados em face do direito brasileiro. *Boletim da Sociedade Brasileira de Direito Internacional*, vol. 1, Rio de Janeiro, 1945, p. 12-29.

Balladore Pallieri, G. La formation des traités dans la pratique internationale contemporaine. *Recueil des Cours*, vol. 74 (1949-I), p. 465-545.

________. *Diritto internazionale pubblico*, 6. ed. rifatta. Milano: Giuffrè, 1952.

BANK, Roland. Tratados internacionales de derechos humanos bajo el ordenamiento jurídico alemán. *Anuario de Derecho Constitucional Latinoamericano*, 10º año, t. II, Montevideo: Konrad-Adenauer-Stiftung, 2004, p. 721-734.

BAPTISTA, Luiz Olavo; MAZZUOLI, Valerio de Oliveira (orgs.). *Doutrinas essenciais de direito internacional*. São Paulo: Revista dos Tribunais, 2012 (5 vols.).

BARBALHO, João. *Constituição Federal Brasileira: comentários*, 2. ed. corrigida e aum. Rio de Janeiro: F. Briguiet Editores, 1924.

BARDONNET, Daniel. Frontières terrestres et frontières maritimes. *Annuaire Français de Droit International*, vol. 35 (1989), p. 1-64.

BARILE, Giuseppe. La structure de l'ordre juridique international: règles générales et règles conventionnelles. *Recueil des Cours*, vol. 161 (1978-III), p. 9-126.

________. The protection of human rights in article 60, paragraph 5 of the Vienna Convention on the Law of Treaties. *International law at the time of its codification: essays in honour of Roberto Ago*, vol. II. Milano: Giuffré, 1987, p. 3-14.

BARILE, Paolo; CHELI, Enzo; GRASSI, Stefano. *Istituzioni di diritto pubblico*, 8. ed. Padova: CEDAM, 1998.

BASDEVANT, Jules. La conclusion et la rédaction des traités et des instruments diplomatiques autres que les traités. *Recueil des Cours*, vol. 15 (1926-V), p. 535-643.

BASTID, Suzanne. *Les traités dans la vie internationale: conclusion et effets*. Paris: Économica, 1985.

BEAUMONT, Paul R. Reflections on the relevance of public international law to private international law treaty making. *Recueil des Cours*, vol. 340 (2009), p. 9-61.

BERGBOHM, Carl. *Staatsverträge und Gesetze als Quellen des Völkerrechts*. Dorpat: C. Mattiesen, 1876.

BERGSTEN, Eric E. *Community law in the french courts: the law of treaties in modern attire*. The Hague: Martinus Nijhoff, 1973.

BERLIA, G. Contribution à l'interprétation des traités. *Recueil des Cours*, vol. 114 (1965-I), p. 283-333.

BERNARDES, Maurício da Costa Carvalho; CHADID, Gustavo Teixeira; CARNEIRO, Paulo Camargo. A Convenção de Viena de 1986 sobre direito dos tratados entre Estados e organizações internacionais e entre organizações internacionais: estado atual da matéria no direito internacional público. In: CANÇADO TRINDADE, Antônio Augusto (org.). *A nova dimensão do direito internacional*. Brasília: Instituto Rio Branco, 2003, p. 173-200.

BERNHARDT, Rudolf. Interpretation and implied (tacit) modification of treaties: comments on Arts. 27, 28, 29 and 38 of the ILC's 1966 Draft Articles on the Law of Treaties. *Zeitschrift für ausländisches öffentliches Recht und Völkerrecht*, vol. 27, n. 3, Berlin (1967), p. 491-506.

BEVILÁQUA, Clóvis. *Direito público internacional: a synthese dos princípios e a contribuição do Brasil*, t. II. Rio de Janeiro: Francisco Alves, 1911.

________. Denúncia de tratado e saída do Brasil da Sociedade das Nações. In: CACHAPUZ DE MEDEIROS, Antônio Paulo (org.). *Pareceres dos consultores jurídicos do Itamaraty*, vol. II (1913-1934). Brasília: Senado Federal, 2000, p. 347-348.

BEXTER, R. R. Treaties and customs. *Recueil des Cours*, vol. 129 (1970-I), p. 27-105.

BIANCHI, Andrea. Human rigths and the magic of *jus cogens*. *European Journal of International Law*, vol. 19, n. 3 (2008), p. 491-508.

BILDER, Richard B. Beyond compliance: helping nations to cooperate. In: SHELTON, Dinah (ed.). *Commitment and compliance: the role of non-binding norms in the international legal system*. Oxford: Oxford University Press, 2000, p. 65-73.

BISHOP JR., William W. Reservations to treaties. *Recueil des Cours*, vol. 103 (1961-II), p. 245-341.

BLASER, Cornelia Rabl. *Die* clausula rebus sic stantibus *im Völkerrecht*. Zürich: Dike, 2012.

BLIX, Hans. *Treaty-making power*. London: Stevens & Sons, 1960.

BOYLE, Alan. Reflections on the treaty as a law-making instrument. In: ORAKHELASHVILI, Alexander & WILLIAMS, Sarah (eds.). *40 years of the Vienna Convention on the Law of Treaties*. London: BIICL, 2010, p. 1-28.

BRADLEY, Curtis A. Unratified treaties, domestic politics, and the U.S. Constitution. *Harvard International Law Journal*, vol. 48, n. 2 (2007), p. 307-336.

BRANT, Leonardo Nemer Caldeira. *A Corte Internacional de Justiça e a construção do direito internacional*. Belo Horizonte: CEDIN, 2005.

BRASIL. Ministério das Relações Exteriores. *Atos internacionais – Prática diplomática brasileira – Manual de procedimentos*. Brasília: DAI/MRE, 2008.

BRICHAMBAUT, Marc Perrin de; DOBELLE, Jean-François; COULÉE, Frédérique. *Leçons de droit international public*, 2. ed. Paris: Dalloz, 2011.

BRIERLY, J. L. *Direito internacional*, 2. ed. Transl. by M. R. Crucho de Almeida. Lisboa: Fundação Calouste Gulbenkian, 1968.

BROWNLIE, Ian. *Princípios de direito internacional público*. Transl. by Maria Manuela Farrajota (*et all.*). Lisboa: Fundação Calouste Gulbenkian, 1997.

BUERGENTHAL, Thomas; GROS ESPIELL, Héctor; GROSSMAN, Claudio; MAIER, Harold G. *Manual de derecho internacional público*. México, D.F.: Fondo de Cultura Económica, 1994.

CACHAPUZ DE MEDEIROS, Antônio Paulo. *O poder legislativo e os tratados internacionais*. Porto Alegre: L&PM, 1983.

________. *O poder de celebrar tratados: competência dos poderes constituídos para a celebração de tratados, à luz do direito internacional, do direito comparado e do direito constitucional brasileiro*. Porto Alegre: Sergio Antonio Fabris, 1995.

________. (org.) *Desafios do direito internacional contemporâneo*. Brasília: Fundação Alexandre de Gusmão, 2007.

________. A Constituição de 1988 e o poder de celebrar tratados. *Revista de Informação Legislativa*, ano 45, n. 179, Brasília: Senado Federal, jul./set./2008, p. 89-126.

CAHIER, Philippe. *Étude des accords de siège conclus entre les organisations internationales et les États où elles résident*. Milano: Giuffrè, 1959.

________. La violation du droit interne relatif à la competence pour conclure des traités comme cause de nullité des traités. *Rivista di Diritto Internazionale*, vol. 54, fasc. 2 (1971), p. 226-245.

________. Le problème des effets des traités à l'égard des états tiers. *Recueil des Cours*, vol. 143 (1974-III), p. 589-736.

CALATAYUD, Esperanza Orihuela. *Los tratados internacionales y su aplicación en el tiempo: consideraciones sobre el efecto inicial de las disposiciones convencionales*. Madrid: Dykinson, 2004.

CALSING, Maria de Assis. *O tratado internacional e sua aplicação no Brasil.* Dissertação de Mestrado em Direito. Brasília: UnB/Faculdade de Estudos Sociais Aplicados, 1984.

CAMPOS, Francisco. *Direito constitucional*, vol. II. Rio de Janeiro: Freitas Bastos, 1956.

CANÇADO TRINDADE, Antônio Augusto. Reavaliação das fontes do direito internacional público ao início da década de oitenta. *Revista de Informação Legislativa*, ano 18, n. 69, Brasília: Senado Federal, jan./mar./1981, p. 91-134.

________. *Direito das organizações internacionais*, 2. ed. (reviewed and updated). Belo Horizonte: Del Rey, 2002.

________. Direito dos tratados e direito das organizações internacionais. Capacidade de celebrar tratados. Projetos de codificação da Comissão de Direito Internacional da ONU. Posições do Brasil. In: CACHAPUZ DE MEDEIROS, Antônio Paulo (org.). *Pareceres dos Consultores Jurídicos do Itamaraty*, vol. VIII (1985-1990). Brasília: Senado Federal, 2004, p. 210-236.

________. Projeto de decreto legislativo sobre suspensão da vigência dos atos internacionais ainda não aprovados pelo Congresso Nacional: elementos para a tomada de posição do Itamaraty. In: CACHAPUZ DE MEDEIROS, Antônio Paulo (org.). *Pareceres dos Consultores Jurídicos do Itamaraty*, vol. VIII (1985-1990). Brasília: Senado Federal, 2004, p. 493-496.

________. (org.). *Repertório da prática brasileira do direito internacional público (período 1899-1918)*, 2. ed. Brasília: Fundação Alexandre de Gusmão, 2012.

CANNIZZARO, Enzo (ed.). *The law of treaties beyond the Vienna Convention*. Oxford: Oxford University Press, 2011.

CANOTILHO, J. J. Gomes; MENDES, Gilmar Ferreira; SARLET, Ingo Wolfgang; STRECK, Lenio Luiz (coord.). *Comentários à Constituição do Brasil.* São Paulo: Saraiva/Almedina, 2013.

CAPALDO, Giuliana Zicardi. *La competenza a denunciare i trattati internazionali: contributo allo studio del treaty power*. Napoli: Edizioni Scientifiche Italiane, 1983.

CAPOTORTI, Francesco. L'extinction et la suspension des traités. *Recueil des Cours*, vol. 134 (1971-III), p. 417-587.

CARNEIRO, Levi. Acordo por troca de notas e aprovação pelo Congresso Nacional. *Boletim da Sociedade Brasileira de Direito Internacional*, n. 13/14, Rio de Janeiro, jan./dez./1951, p. 129-134.

________. Acordos sobre compra de tecidos. Necessidade de ratificação pelo Congresso Nacional. In: CACHAPUZ DE MEDEIROS, Antônio Paulo (org.). *Pareceres dos Consultores Jurídicos do Itamaraty*, vol. IV (1946-1951). Brasília: Senado Federal, 2000, p. 49-50.

________. Acordo mediante notas reversais para assegurar o cumprimento de tratado: necessidade de ratificação pelo Congresso Nacional. In: CACHAPUZ DE MEDEIROS,

Antônio Paulo (org.). *Pareceres dos Consultores Jurídicos do Itamaraty*, vol. IV (1946-1951). Brasília: Senado Federal, 2000, p. 117-118.

Carreau, Dominique. *Droit international*, 8. ed. Paris: A. Pedone, 2004.

Carter, Barry E.; Trimble, Phillip R.; Weiner, Allen S. *International law*, 5. ed. New York: Wolters Kluwer, 2007.

Casolari, Federico. *L'incorporazione del diritto internazionale nell'ordinamento dell'Unione Europea*. Milano: Giuffrè, 2008.

Cassese, Antonio. *Diritto internazionale* (a cura di Paola Gaeta). Bologna: Il Mulino, 2006.

Castro, Amilcar de. *Direito internacional privado*, 5. ed. (updated and extended by Osiris Rocha). Rio de Janeiro: Forense, 2001.

Cavaglieri, Arrigo. Règles générales du droit de la paix. *Recueil des Cours*, vol. 26 (1929-I), p. 311-585.

Caviedes, Antonio Poch de. De la clause *rebus sic stantibus* à la clause de révision dans les conventions internationales. *Recueil des Cours*, vol. 118 (1966-II), p. 105-208.

Cervo, Amado Luiz. *O parlamento brasileiro e as relações exteriores (1826-1889)*. Brasília: Editora UnB, 1981.

Chanaki, Athina. *L'adaptation des traités dans le temps*. Bruxelles: Bruylant, 2013.

Chiu, Hungdah. *The capacity of international organizations to conclude treaties, and the special legal aspects of the treaties so concluded*. The Hague: Martinus Nijhoff, 1966.

Clève, Clèmerson Merlin. *A fiscalização abstrata de constitucionalidade no direito brasileiro*. São Paulo: Revista dos Tribunais, 1995.

Coccia, Massimo. Reservations to multilateral treaties on human rights. *California Western International Law Journal*, vol. 15, n. 1 (1985), p. 1-51.

Coêlho, Sacha Calmon Navarro. *Curso de direito tributário*, 8. ed. (reviewed and updated). Rio de Janeiro: Forense, 2005.

Combacau, Jean; Sur, Serge. *Droit international public*, 6. ed. Paris: Montchrestien, 2004.

Conforti, Benedetto. *The law and practice of the United Nations*, 3. ed. (reviewed). Leiden: Martinus Nijhoff, 2005.

________; Labella, Angelo. Invalidity and termination of treaties: the role of national courts. *European Journal of International Law*, vol. 44 (1990), p. 44-66.

Corriente Córdoba, José Antonio. *Valoración jurídica de los preámbulos de los tratados internacionales*. Pamplona: Universidad de Navarra, 1973.

Corten, Olivier; Klein, Pierre (eds.). *The Vienna Conventions on the Law of Treaties: a commentary*. Oxford: Oxford University Press, 2011 (2 vols.).

Cot, Jean-Pierre. La conduite subséquente des parties a un traité. *Revue Générale de Droit International Public*, vol. 70, Paris (1966), p. 632-666.

Coulée, Frédérique. La codification du droit international: les cas des réserves aux traités internationaux. In: Brichambaut, Dobelle & Coulée. *Leçons de droit international public*, 2. ed. Paris: Dalloz, 2011, p. 307-334.

CRANDALL, Samuel B. *Treaties: their making and enforcement*, 2. ed. Washington, D.C.: John Byrne & Company, 1916.

CRAWFORD, James. *The International Law Commission's Articles on State Responsibility: introduction, text and commentaries*. Cambridge: Cambridge University Press, 2002.

________. *Brownlie's principles of public international law*, 8. ed. Oxford: Oxford University Press, 2012.

CREIFELDS, Carl. *Rechtswörterbuch*, 17 ed. München: C. H. Beck, 2002.

D'ASPREMONT, Jean. The International Court of Justice and tacit conventionality. *Questions of International Law*, Zoom-in vol. 18 (2015), p. 3-17.

DALLARI, Pedro B. A. *Constituição e tratados internacionais*. São Paulo: Saraiva, 2003.

DANIEL, José. La Convention de Vienne de 1969 sur le droit des traités et le droit humanitaire. *Revue Internationale de la Croix-Rouge*, vol. 54 (July 1972), p. 401-414.

DANILENKO, G. M. *Law-making in the international community*. Dordrecht: Martinus Nijhoff, 1993.

DAUDET, Yves. Actualités de la codification du droit international. *Recueil des Cours*, vol. 303 (2003), p. 9-118.

DAUDT, Gabriel Pithan. *Reservas aos tratados internacionais de direitos humanos: o conflito entre a eficácia e a promoção dos direitos humanos*. Porto Alegre: Sergio Antonio Fabris, 2006.

DAVIDSON, Scott (ed.). *The law of treaties*. Trowbridge: Ashgate/Dartmouth, 2004.

DE LA GUARDIA, Ernesto. *Derecho de los tratados internacionales*. Buenos Aires: Ábaco, 1997.

DEL VECCHIO, Giorgio. *El derecho internacional y el problema de la paz*. Barcelona: BOSCH, 1959.

DINH, Nguyen Quoc; DAILLIER, Patrick; PELLET, Alain. *Direito internacional público*, 2. ed. Transl. by Vítor Marques Coelho. Lisboa: Fundação Calouste Gulbenkian, 2003.

DINSTEIN, Yoram. The interaction between customary international law and treaties. *Recueil des Cours*, vol. 322 (2006), p. 243-427.

DUBOUIS, Louis. L'erreur en droit international public. *Annuaire Français de Droit International*, vol. 9 (1963), p. 191-227.

DUPUY, Pierre-Marie. *Soft law* and the international law of the environment. *Michigan Journal of International Law*, vol. 12 (Winter 1991), p. 420-435.

________. *Droit international public*, 7. ed. Paris: Dalloz, 2004.

DUPUY, René Jean. Codification et règlement des différends: les débats de Vienne sur les procédures de règlement. *Annuaire Français de Droit International*, vol. 15 (1969), p. 70-90.

DORMOY, Daniel. *Droit des organisations internationales*. Paris: Dalloz, 1995.

EDWARDS JR., Richard W. Reservations to treaties: the Belilos case and the work of the International Law Commission. *University of Toledo Law Review*, vol. 31 (2000), p. 195-207.

EHRLICH, Ludwik. L'interprétation des traités. *Recueil des Cours*, vol. 24 (1928-IV), p. 1-145.

ELIAS, Taslim Olawale. Problems concerning the validity of treaties. *Recueil des Cours*, vol. 134 (1971-III), p. 333-416.

ENGELEN, Frank. *Interpretation of tax treaties under international law*. Amsterdam: IBDF, 2004.

EUSTATHIADES, Konstantinos Th. *Unratified codification conventions: lecture delivered on 11 July 1973* (Gilberto Amado Memorial Lecture). Geneva: United Nations Publ., 1973.

FARINHA, João de Deus Pinheiro. Interpretação dos tratados e das convenções. *Tribuna da Justiça*, Fundão (Portugal), fev./1985, p. 7-10.

FERRAJOLI, Luigi. *Derechos y garantias: la ley del más débil*. Transl. by Perfecto Andrés Ibáñez e Andrea Greppi. Madrid: Trotta, 1999.

________. *Direito e razão: teoria do garantismo penal*, 2. ed. (reviewed and updated). Transl. by Ana Paula Zomer Sica (*et all.*). São Paulo: Revista dos Tribunais, 2006.

________. *A soberania no mundo moderno: nascimento e crise do Estado nacional*. Transl. by Carlo Coccioli e Márcio Lauria Filho. São Paulo: Martins Fontes, 2007.

FERRAZ JR., Tercio Sampaio. *Introdução ao estudo do direito: técnica, decisão, dominação*, 4. ed. (reviewed and extended). São Paulo: Atlas, 2003.

FIORATI, Jete Jane. Jus cogens*: as normas imperativas de direito internacional público como modalidade extintiva dos tratados internacionais*. Franca: Ed. Unesp, 2002.

FITZMAURICE, Gerald Gray. Do treaties need ratification? *British Yearbook of International Law*, vol. 15 (1934), p. 113-137.

FITZMAURICE, Malgosia. Third parties and the law of treaties. *Max Planck Yearbook of United Nations Law*, vol. 6, n. 1 (2002), p. 37-127.

________. The practical working of the law of treaties. In: EVANS, Malcolm D. (ed.). *International law*, 3rd ed. Oxford: Oxford University Press, 2010, p. 172-200.

________; ELIAS, Olufemi. *Contemporary issues in the law of treaties*. Utrecht: Eleven, 2005.

________; ________; MERKOURIS, Panos (eds.). *Treaty interpretation and the Vienna Convention on the Law of Treaties: 30 years on*. Leiden: Martinus Nijhoff, 2010 (Queen Mary Studies in International Law).

FLEISCHHAUER, Carl-August. The United Nations treaty series. In: DINSTEIN, Yoram (ed.). *International law at a time of perplexity: essays in honour of Shabtai Rosenne*. Dordrecht: Martinus Nijhoff, 1989, p. 131-148.

FOCARELLI, Carlo. I limiti dello *jus cogens* nella giurisprudenza più recente. *Rivista di Diritto Internazionale*, vol. 90, n. 3 (2007), p. 637-656.

FORLATI, Serena. *Diritto dei trattati e responsabilità internazionale*. Milano: Giuffrè, 2005.

FOX, Hazel. Article 31(3) (a) and (b) of the Vienna Convention and the *Kasikili/Sedudu Island* Case. In: FITZMAURICE, Malgosia, ELIAS, Olufemi & MERKOURIS, Panos (eds.). *Treaty interpretation and the Vienna Convention on the Law of Treaties: 30 years on*. Leiden: Martinus Nijhoff, 2010, p. 59-74.

FRAGA, Mirtô. *O conflito entre tratado internacional e norma de direito interno: estudo analítico da situação do tratado na ordem jurídica brasileira*. Rio de Janeiro: Forense, 1998.

FRANCA FILHO, Marcílio Toscano; MIALHE, Jorge Luís; JOB, Ulisses da Silveira (orgs.). *Epitácio Pessoa e a codificação do direito internacional*. Porto Alegre: Sergio Antonio Fabris, 2013.

FRIEDRICH, Tatyana Scheila. *As normas imperativas de direito internacional público* jus cogens. Belo Horizonte: Fórum, 2004.

GABSCH, Rodrigo d'Araujo. *Aprovação de tratados internacionais pelo Brasil: possíveis opções para acelerar o seu processo*. Brasília: Fundação Alexandre de Gusmão, 2010.

GAJA, Giorgio. *Jus cogens* beyond the Vienna convention. *Recueil des Cours*, vol. 172 (1981-III), p. 271-316.

GAMBLE JR., John King. Reservations to multilateral treaties: a macroscopic view of State practice. *American Journal of International Law*, vol. 74, n. 2 (April 1980), p. 272-394.

GARCIA, Eugênio Vargas. *O Brasil e a Liga das Nações (1919-1926)*, 2. ed. Porto Alegre: Ed. UFRGS, 2005.

GARCIA, Márcio Pereira Pinto. Tratados e poder terminativo na Constituição de 1988. *Revista de Informação Legislativa*, ano 45, n. 179, Brasília: Senado Federal, jul./set./2008, p. 233-240.

________. *A terminação de tratado e o Poder Legislativo à vista do direito internacional, do direito comparado e do direito constitucional internacional brasileiro*. Rio de Janeiro: Renovar, 2011.

GARDINER, Richard K. *Treaty interpretation*. New York: Oxford University Press, 2008.

________. The role of preparatory work in treaty interpretation. In: ORAKHELASHVILI, Alexander & WILLIAMS, Sarah (eds.). *40 years of the Vienna Convention on the Law of Treaties*. London: BIICL, 2010, p. 97-116.

GOETZ, Walter (coord.). *Historia Universal*, t. I. Transl. by Manuel García Morente. Madrid: Espasa-Calpe, 1945.

GOMAA, Mohammed M. *Suspension or termination of treaties on grounds of breach*. The Hague: Martinus Nijhoff, 1996.

GOMES, Luiz Flávio. *Estado constitucional de direito e a nova pirâmide jurídica*. São Paulo: Premier Máxima, 2008.

GÓMEZ ROBLEDO, Antonio. Le *ius cogens* international: sa genèse, sa nature, ses fonctions. Recueil des Cours, vol. 172 (1981-III), p. 9-218.

________. *El* ius cogens *internacional: estudio histórico-crítico*. México, D.F.: UNAM, 2003.

GOUVEIA, Jorge Bacelar. *Manual de direito internacional público*, 3. ed. (updated and extended). Coimbra: Almedina, 2008.

GÖZLER, Kemal. La question de la supériorité des normes de droit international sur la Constitution. *Ankara Üniversitesi Hukuk Fakültesi Dergisi*, vol. 45, n.ºs 1-4, 1996, p. 195-211.

GREIG, D. W. *Intertemporality and the law of treaties*. London: BIICL, 2001.

________. *Invalidity and the law of treaties*. London: BIICL, 2006.

GRNCHALLA-WESIERSKI, Tadensz. A framework for understanding "soft law". *McGill Law Journal*, vol. 30 (1984), p. 38-88.

GUASTINI, Riccardo. *Estudios de teoría constitucional*. México, D.F.: UNAM, 2001.

GUGGENHEIM, Paul. Contribution à l'histoire des sources du droit des gens. *Recueil des Cours*, vol. 94 (1958-II), p. 1-84.

HANNIKAINEN, Lauri. *Peremptory norms (*jus cogens*) in international law: historical development, criteria, present status*. Helsinki: Finnish Lawyers' Publishing, 1988.

HARASZTI, György. *Some fundamental problems of the law of treaties*. Budapest: Akadémiai Kiadó, 1973.

________. Treaties and the fundamental change of circumstances. *Recueil des Cours*, vol. 146 (1975-III), p. 1-94.

HEILBORN, Paul. Les sources du droit international. *Recueil des Cours*, vol. 11 (1926-I), p. 1-64.

HOLLIS, Duncan B. (ed.). *The Oxford guide to treaties*. Oxford: Oxford University Press, 2012.

HOLLOWAY, Kaye. *Modern trends in treaty law: constitutional law, reservations and the three modes of legislation*. London: Stevens & Sons, 1967.

HUBER, Jean. *Le droit de conclure des traités internationaux*. Montreux: Ganguin & Laubsher, 1951.

HUMPHREY, John P. The implementation of international human rights law. *New York Law School Review*, vol. 24 (1978), p. 31-33.

HURD, Ian. *International organizations: politics, law, practice*. Cambridge: Cambridge University Press, 2011.

JAYME, Erik. Identité culturelle et intégration: le droit international privé postmoderne. *Recueil des Cours*, vol. 251 (1995), p. 9-267.

JENKS, Clarence Wilfred. *A new world of law? A study of the creative imagination in international law*. London: Longmans, 1969.

JONAS, David S.; SAUNDERS, Thomas N. The object and purpose of a treaty: three interpretive methods. *Vanderbilt Journal of Transnational Law*, vol. 43, n. 3 (2010), p. 565-609.

JONES, J. Mervyn. *Full powers and ratification*. Cambridge: Cambridge University Press, 1946.

KAMTO, Maurice. La volonté de l'État en droit international. *Recueil des Cours*, vol. 310 (2004), p. 9-428.

KEARNEY, Richard D.; DALTON, Robert E. The treaty on treaties. *American Journal of International Law*, vol. 64, n. 3 (July 1970), p. 495-561.

KELSEN, Hans. *Principles of international law*. New York: Rinehart & Company, 1952.

________. *Teoria geral do direito e do Estado*. Transl. by Luís Carlos Borges. São Paulo: Martins Fontes, 1990.

KITCHEN, K. A. *Pharaoh Triumphant: the life and times of Ramesses II*, 2. ed. Cairo, Egypt: American University in Cairo Press (*et all.*), 1997.

KLABBERS, Jan. *The concept of treaty in international law*. The Hague: Kluwer Law International, 1996.

________. Some problems regarding the object and purpose of treaties. *The Finnish Yearbook of International Law*, vol. VIII (1997), p. 138-160.

________. How to defeat a treaty's object and purpose pending entry into force: toward manifest intent. *Vanderbilt Journal of Transnational Law*, vol. 34, n. 2 (2001), p. 283-335.

________. Not re-visiting the concept of treaty. In: ORAKHELASHVILI, Alexander & WILLIAMS, Sarah (eds.). *40 years of the Vienna Convention on the Law of Treaties*. London: BIICL, 2010, p. 29-40.

________; LEFEBER, René (eds.). *Essays on the law of treaties: a collection of essays in honour of Bert Vierdag*. Dordrecht: Martinus Nijhoff, 1998.

KOH, Jean Kyongun. Reservations to multilateral treaties: how international legal doctrine reflects world vision. *Harvard International Law Journal*, vol. 23, n. 1 (1982), p. 71-116.

KOLB, Robert. *Jus cogens*, intangibilité, intransgressibilité, dérogation "positive" et "négative". *Revue Générale de Droit International Public*, vol. 109, n. 2, Paris (2005), p. 305-329.

________. Principles as sources of international law (with special reference to good faith). *Netherlands International Law Review*, vol. 53, n. 1 (2006), p. 1-36.

KONTOU, Nancy. *The termination and revision of treaties in the light of new customary international law*. Oxford: Clarendon Presss, 1995.

KORKELIA, Konstantin. New challenges to the regime of reservations under the International Covenant on Civil and Political Rights. *European Journal of International Law*, vol. 13, n. 2 (2002), p. 437-477.

KRAUS, Herbert. Système et fonctions des traités internationaux. *Recueil des Cours*, vol. 50 (1934-IV), p. 311-400.

KRÜGER, Herbert. Völkerrecht im Bundesstaat. *Um Recht und Gerechtigkeit*: Festgabe für Erich Kaufmann zu seinem 70, Geburtstage, 21 September 1950; überreicht von Freunden, Verehrern und Schülern. Stuttgart und Köln: W. Kohlhammer Verlag, 1950, p. 239-248.

LA ROSA, Rosanna; PANELLA, Lina; ZANGHÌ, Claudio (orgs.). *I trattati internazionali e il parlamento italiano: repertorio dei trattati conclusi dall'Italia (l'intervento del Parlamento nella procedura di ratifica ed esecuzione dal 1948)*. Milano: Giuffrè, 1988 (2 vols.).

LACHARRIÉRE, Guy de. Aspects récents de la clause de la nation la plus favorisée. *Annuaire Français de Droit International*, vol. 7 (1961), p. 107-117.

LACHS, Manfred. Lê développement et les fonctions des traités multilatéraux. *Recueil des Cours*, vol. 92 (1957-II), p. 229-341.

LANTIS, Jeffrey S. *The life and death of international treaties: double-edged diplomacy and the politics of ratification in comparative perspective*. New York: Oxford University Press, 2009.

LAUTERPACHT, Hersch. Les travaux préparatoires et l'interprétation des traités. *Recueil des Cours*, vol. 48 (1934-II), p. 709-817.

________. *The development of international law by the International Court*. London: Stevens & Sons, 1958.

Leary, Virginia A. *International labour conventions and national law*. Dordrecht: Martinus Nijhoff, 1982.

Lijnzaad, Liesbeth. *Reservations to UN-human rights treaties: ratify and ruin?* Dordrecht: Martinus Nijhoff, 1995.

Lim, Chin; Elias, Olufemi. The role of treaties in the contemporary international legal order. *Nordic Journal of International Law*, vol. 66 (1997), p. 1-21.

Linderfalk, Ulf. *On the interpretation of treaties: the modern international law as expressed in the 1969 Vienna Convention on the Law of Treaties*. Dordrecht: Springer, 2007.

________. The effect of *jus cogens* norms: whoever opened Pandora's Box, did you ever think about the consequences? *European Journal of International Law*, vol. 18, n. 5 (2007), p. 853-871.

Lindgren Alves, J. A. *Os direitos humanos como tema global*. São Paulo: Perspectiva, 1994.

Magalhães, José Carlos de. *O Supremo Tribunal Federal e o direito internacional: uma análise crítica*. Porto Alegre: Livraria do Advogado Editora, 2000.

Maresca, Adolfo. *Il diritto dei trattati: la convenzione codificatrice di Vienna del 23 maggio 1969*. Milano: Giuffrè, 1971.

Marinoni, Luiz Guilherme; Mazzuoli, Valerio de Oliveira (coord.). *Controle de convencionalidade: um panorama latino-americano (Brasil, Argentina, Chile, México, Peru, Uruguai)*. Brasília: Gazeta Jurídica, 2013.

Marković, Milan. Les traites inegaux en droit international. *Jugoslovenska Revija za Međunarodno Pravo*, n.s 2-3 (1970), p. 264-284.

Martins, Estevão Rezende. A apreciação de tratados e acordos internacionais pelo Congresso Nacional. In: Cançado Trindade, Antônio Augusto (ed.). *A incorporação das normas internacionais de proteção dos direitos humanos no direito brasileiro*, 2. ed. San José/Brasília: IIDH (*et all.*), 1996, p. 263-271.

Martins, Pedro Baptista. *Da unidade do direito e da supremacia do direito internacional*. Rio de Janeiro: Forense, 1998.

Mazzuoli, Valerio de Oliveira. A opção do judiciário brasileiro em face dos conflitos entre tratados internacionais e leis internas. *Revista da AJURIS*, ano XXVI, n. 81, Tomo I (doutrina), Porto Alegre, mar./2001, p. 306-325.

________. O poder legislativo e os tratados internacionais: o *treaty-making power* na Constituição brasileira de 1988. *Revista de Informação Legislativa*, ano 38, n. 150, Brasília: Senado Federal, abr./jun./2001, p. 27-53.

________. O Supremo Tribunal Federal e os conflitos entre tratados internacionais e leis internas. *Revista de Informação Legislativa*, ano 39, n. 154, Brasília: Senado Federal, abr./jun./2002, p. 15-29.

________. *Prisão civil por dívida e o Pacto de San José da Costa Rica: especial enfoque para os contratos de alienação fiduciária em garantia*. Rio de Janeiro: Forense, 2002.

________. *Direitos humanos, Constituição e os tratados internacionais: estudo analítico da situação e aplicação do tratado na ordem jurídica brasileira*. São Paulo: Juarez de Oliveira, 2002.

________. *Natureza jurídica e eficácia dos acordos* stand-by *com o FMI*. São Paulo: Revista dos Tribunais, 2005.

________. Eficácia e aplicabilidade dos tratados em matéria tributária no direito brasileiro. *Revista Forense*, vol. 390, ano 103, Rio de Janeiro, mar./abr./2007, p. 583-590.

________. *Comentários à Convenção Americana sobre Direitos Humanos (Pacto de San José da Costa Rica)*, 3. ed. (reviewed, updated and extended). São Paulo: Revista dos Tribunais, 2010 (co-authored with Luiz Flávio Gomes).

________. *Tratados internacionais de direitos humanos e direito interno*. São Paulo: Saraiva, 2010.

________. *Coletânea de direito internacional – Constituição Federal*, 9. ed. (reviewed, updated and extended). São Paulo: Revista dos Tribunais, 2011.

________. *O controle jurisdicional da convencionalidade das leis*, 2. ed. (reviewed, updated and extended). São Paulo: Revista dos Tribunais, 2011.

________. *Tribunal Penal Internacional e o direito brasileiro*, 3. ed. (reviewed, updated and extended). São Paulo: Revista dos Tribunais, 2011.

________. Vícios do consentimento e nulidade dos tratados à luz da Convenção de Viena sobre o Direito dos Tratados de 1969. *Revista dos Tribunais*, vol. 914, ano 100, São Paulo, dez./2011, p. 185-197.

________. Algumas questões jurídicas sobre a formação e aplicação do costume internacional. *Revista dos Tribunais*, vol. 921, ano 101, São Paulo, jul./2012, p. 259-278.

________. Apontamentos sobre o direito dos tratados no Projeto de Código de Direito Internacional Público de Epitácio Pessoa. In: FRANCA FILHO, Marcílio Toscano; MIALHE, Jorge Luís; JOB, Ulisses da Silveira (orgs.). *Epitácio Pessoa e a codificação do direito internacional*. Porto Alegre: Sergio Antonio Fabris, 2013.

________. Comentário ao artigo 5.º, § 3.º. In: CANOTILHO, J. J. Gomes; MENDES, Gilmar Ferreira; SARLET, Ingo Wolfgang; STRECK, Lenio Luiz (coord.). *Comentários à Constituição do Brasil*. São Paulo: Saraiva/Almedina, 2013, p. 518-524.

________. Comentário ao artigo 49, I. In: CANOTILHO, J. J. Gomes; MENDES, Gilmar Ferreira; SARLET, Ingo Wolfgang; STRECK, Lenio Luiz (coord.). *Comentários à Constituição do Brasil*. São Paulo: Saraiva/Almedina, 2013, p. 1018-1022.

________. Comentário ao artigo 52, V. In: CANOTILHO, J. J. Gomes; MENDES, Gilmar Ferreira; SARLET, Ingo Wolfgang; STRECK, Lenio Luiz (coord.). *Comentários à Constituição do Brasil*. São Paulo: Saraiva/Almedina, 2013, p. 1054-1058.

________. Comentário ao artigo 84, VIII. In: CANOTILHO, J. J. Gomes; MENDES, Gilmar Ferreira; SARLET, Ingo Wolfgang; STRECK, Lenio Luiz (coord.). *Comentários à Constituição do Brasil*. São Paulo: Saraiva/Almedina, 2013, p. 1241-1246.

________. *Curso de direito internacional público*, 8. ed. (reviewed, updated and extended). São Paulo: Revista dos Tribunais, 2014.

________; ALONSO MASSA, Diego Luis. Analysis of the Decision rendered by the U.S. Supreme Court in *Re BG Group plc v. Republic of Argentina*: do all roads lead to Rome? *Journal of International Arbitration*, vol. 32, n. 2 (2015), p. 215–236.

MCDOUGAL, Myres S. The International Law Commission's Draft Articles upon interpretation: textuality *redivivus*. *American Journal of International Law*, vol. 61, n. 4 (Oct. 1967), p. 992-1000.

MCNAIR, Arnold Duncan. La terminaison et la dissolution des traités. *Recueil des Cours*, vol. 22 (1928-II), p. 459-538.

________. L'application et l'interprétation des traités d'après la jurisprudence britannique. *Recueil des Cours*, vol. 43 (1933-I), p. 247-307.

________. Les effets de la guerre sur les traités. *Recueil des Cours*, vol. 59 (1937-I), p. 523-585.

________. *The law of treaties*. Oxford: Clarendon Press, 1961.

MCNEILL, John H. International agreements: recent U.S.-UK practice concerning the Memorandum of Understanding. *American Journal of International Law*, vol. 88, n. 4 (Oct. 1994), p. 821-826.

MCRAE, Donald M. The legal effect of interpretative declarations. *British Yearbook of International Law*, vol. 49 (1978), p. 155-173.

MEIRA MATTOS, Adherbal. *Direito internacional público*, 2. ed. (updated and extended). Rio de Janeiro: Renovar, 2002.

MELLO, Celso D. de Albuquerque. *Ratificação de tratados: estudo de direito internacional e constitucional*. Rio de Janeiro: Freitas Bastos, 1966.

________. Os tratados na Constituição. In: *Tendências atuais do direito público: estudos em homenagem ao Professor Afonso Arinos de Melo Franco*. Rio de Janeiro: Forense, 1976, p. 121-166.

________. Constituição e relações internacionais. In: DOLINGER, Jacob (org.). *A nova Constituição e o direito internacional*. Rio de Janeiro: Freitas Bastos, 1987, p. 19-38.

________. *Direito constitucional internacional: uma introdução*, 2. ed. (reviewed). Rio de Janeiro: Renovar, 2000.

________. *Curso de direito internacional público*, vol. 1, 15. ed. (reviewed and extended). Rio de Janeiro: Renovar, 2004.

MELO FRANCO, Afonso Arinos. *Estudos de direito constitucional*. Rio de Janeiro: Forense, 1957.

________. *Curso de direito constitucional brasileiro*, vol. II. Rio de Janeiro: Forense, 1960.

MENDELSON, Maurice H. The formation of customary international law. *Recueil des Cours*, vol. 272 (1998), p. 155-410.

MENDES, Gilmar Ferreira. *Jurisdição constitucional: o controle abstrato de normas no Brasil e na Alemanha*, 5. ed. São Paulo: Saraiva, 2005.

________. A supralegalidade dos tratados internacionais de direitos humanos e a prisão civil do depositário infiel no Brasil. *Systemas: revista de ciências jurídicas e econômicas*, vol. 2, n. 1 (2010), p. 64-100.

MERON, Theodor. Article 46 of the Vienna Convention on the Law of Treaties (*ultra vires* treaties): some recent cases. *British Yearbook of International Law*, vol. 49 (1978), p. 175-199.

MERTSCH, Anneliese Quast. *Provisionally applied treaties: their binding force and legal nature*. Leiden: Brill, 2012.

MESTRE, Achille. Les traités et le droit interne. *Recueil des Cours*, vol. 38 (1931-IV), p. 233-306.

MIRANDA, Jorge. Nos 60 anos da Declaração Universal dos Direitos do Homem: uma perspectiva constitucional portuguesa. *Polis – Revista de Estudos Jurídico-Políticos*, n. 17, Lisboa, 2009, p. 13-25.

________. *Curso de direito internacional público*, 5. ed. (reviewed and updated). Cascais: Princípia, 2012.

MIRKINE-GUETZÉVITCH, Boris. Droit international et droit constitutionnel. *Recueil des Cours*, vol. 38 (1931-IV), p. 307-465.

MONROY CABRA, Marco Gerardo. *Derecho de los tratados*, 2. ed. Bogotá: Leyer, 1995.

MORGENSTERN, Felice. The Convention on the Law of Treaties between States and International Organizations or between International Organizations. In: DINSTEIN, Yoram (ed.). *International law at a time of perplexity: essays in honour of Shabtai Rosenne*. Dordrecht: Martinus Nijhoff, 1989, p. 435-447.

MYERS, Denys P. The names and scope of treaties. *American Journal of International Law*, vol. 51, n. 3 (July 1957), p. 574-605.

NAHLIK, S. E. The grounds of invalidity and termination of treaties. *American Journal of International Law*, vol. 65, n. 5 (Oct. 1971), p. 736-756.

NASCIMENTO E SILVA, Geraldo Eulálio. *Conferência de Viena sobre o direito dos tratados*. Brasília: MRE, 1971.

________. Le facteur temps et les traités. *Recueil des Cours*, vol. 154 (1977-I), p. 215-298.

________. The 1986 Vienna Convention and the treaty-making power of international organizations. *German Yearbook of International Law*, vol. 29 (1987), p. 68-85.

NASSER, Salem Hikmat. *Fontes e normas do direito internacional: um estudo sobre a* soft law. São Paulo: Atlas, 2005.

NISOT, Joseph. A propos du projet de la Commission du Droit International des Nations Unies relative au droit des traités. *Revue Générale de Droit International Public*, n. 2, Paris (1967), p. 309-324.

NOZARI, Fariborz. *Unequal treaties in international law*. Stockholm: S-Byran Sundt & Co., 1971.

OLIVER, Covey T. The enforcement of treaties by a Federal State. *Recueil des Cours*, vol. 141 (1974-I), p. 417-508.

ORAKHELASHVILI, Alexander; WILLIAMS, Sarah (eds.). *40 years of the Vienna Convention on the Law of Treaties*. London: BIICL, 2010.

PAISANT, Marcel. Les droits de la France au Niger (avec trois cartes). *Revue Générale du Droit International Public*, vol. 5, Paris (1898), p. 5-37.

PALCHETTI, Paolo. Article 18 of the 1969 Vienna Convention: a vague and ineffective obligation or a useful means for strengthening legal cooperation? In: CANNIZZARO,

Enzo (ed.). *The law of treaties beyond the Vienna Convention*. Oxford: Oxford University Press, 2011, p. 25-36.

Palmer, Richard E. *Hermenêutica*. Transl. by Maria Luísa Ribeiro Ferreira. Lisboa: Edições 70, 1969.

Paulus, Andreas L. *Jus cogens* in a time of hegemony and fragmentation: an attempt at a re-appraisal. *Nordic Journal of International Law*, vol. 74 (2005), p. 297-334.

Pauwelyn, Joost. *Conflict of norms in public international law: how WTO law relates to other rules of international law*. Cambridge: Cambridge University Press, 2003.

Pereira, André Gonçalves; Quadros, Fausto de. *Manual de direito internacional público*, 3. ed. (reviewed and extended), (8th reprint). Coimbra: Almedina, 2009.

Pereira, Lafayette Rodrigues. *Princípios de direito internacional*, t 1. Rio de Janeiro: Jacintho Ribeiro dos Santos, 1903.

Pereira de Araújo, João Hermes. *A processualística dos atos internacionais*. Rio de Janeiro: Ministério das Relações Exteriores/Seção de Publicações, 1958.

Pessoa, Epitácio. *Projeto de Código de Direito Internacional Público*. Rio de Janeiro: Imprensa Nacional, 1911.

Piérola y Balta, Nicolás de. Las convenciones de Viena sobre el derecho de los tratados: algunas consideraciones. *Revista Peruana de Derecho Internacional*, vol. 43, n. 103, Lima, enero/junio/1994.

Pinto, Roger. La réforme du Congrés. *Revue du Droit Public et de la Science Politique*, t. 66. Paris: LGDJ, 1950.

Piombo, Horacio Daniel. *Teoría general de la publicidad y tratados internacionales: análisis normativo, fáctico y dikelógico*. Buenos Aires: Depalma, 1977.

Pontes de Miranda, Francisco Cavalcanti. *Comentários à Constituição de 1946*, vol. II, 2. ed. São Paulo: Max Limonad, 1946.

________. *Comentários à Constituição de 1967 com a Emenda n. 1 de 1969*, t. III, 2. ed. São Paulo: Revista dos Tribunais, 1970.

________. *Comentários à Constituição de 1967 com a Emenda n. 1 de 1969*, t. III, 3. ed. Rio de Janeiro: Forense, 1987.

Prieto, Vicente. *Diritto dei rapporti tra Chiesa e società civile*. Roma: Edizioni Università della Santa Croce, 2008.

Quadri, Rolando. Cours général de droit international public. *Recueil des Cours*, vol. 113 (1964-III), p. 237-483.

Rangel, Vicente Marotta. Integração das convenções de Genebra no direito brasileiro. *Revista do Instituto de Pesquisas e Estudos Jurídico-Econômico-Sociais*, ano II, n. 3, Bauru, jan./mar./1967, p. 195-266.

________. Emendas dos tratados internacionais. In: Cachapuz de Medeiros, Antônio Paulo (org.). *Pareceres dos consultores jurídicos do Itamaraty*, vol. IX (1990-2000). Brasília: Fundação Alexandre de Gusmão, 2009, p. 85-95.

Redgwell, Catherine. Reservations to treaties and human rights: Committee general comment n. 24(52). *International and Comparative Law Quarterly*, vol. 46 (1997), p. 390-405.

REISMAN, Michael W. Unratified treaties and other unperfected acts in international law: constitutional functions. *Vanderbilt Journal of Transnational Law*, vol. 35, n. 3 (2002), p. 729-747.

REMIRO BROTONS, Antonio. *Derecho internacional público*, vol. 2 (*Derecho de los tratados*). Madrid: Tecnos, 1987.

________; RIQUELME CORTADO, Rosa; ORIHUELA CALATAYUD, Esperanza; DÍEZ-HOCHLEITNER, Javier; PÉREZ-PRAT DURBAN, Luis. *Derecho internacional*. Valencia: Tirant lo Blanch, 2007.

REUTER, Paul. *Institutions internationales*, 8. ed. Paris: PUF, 1975.

________. Le traité international, acte et norme. *Archives de Philosophie du Droit*, t. 32. Paris: Sirey, 1987, p. 111-117.

________. *Le développement de l'ordre juridique international: écrits de droit international*. Paris: Economica, 1995.

________. *Introducción al derecho de los tratados*, 1. ed. (em espanhol) revisada por Peter Haggenmacher. Transl. by Eduardo L. Suárez. México, D.F.: Fondo de Cultura Económica, 1999.

REZEK, José Francisco. As relações internacionais na Constituição da primeira República. *Arquivos do Ministério da Justiça*, n. 126, jun./1973, p. 107-112.

________. *Direito dos tratados*. Rio de Janeiro: Forense, 1984.

________. *Direito internacional público: curso elementar*, 9. ed. (reviewed). São Paulo: Saraiva, 2002.

________. Parlamento e tratados: o modelo constitucional do Brasil. *Revista de Informação Legislativa*, ano 41, n. 162, Brasília: Senado Federal, abr./jun./2004, p. 121-148.

________. Efeitos do tratado internacional sobre terceiros: o artigo 35 da Convenção de Viena. In: TIBÚRCIO, Carmen; BARROSO, Luís Roberto (orgs.). *O direito internacional contemporâneo: estudos em homenagem ao Professor Jacob Dolinger*. Rio de Janeiro: Renovar, 2006, p. 491-504.

RIQUELME CORTADO, Rosa. *Las reservas a los tratados: lagunas y ambigüedades del Régimen de Viena*. Murcia: Universidad de Murcia, 2004.

RODAS, João Grandino. Os acordos em forma simplificada. *Revista da Faculdade de Direito da Universidade de São Paulo*, vol. LXVIII, fasc. I (1973), p. 319-340.

________. *Jus cogens* em direito internacional. *Revista da Faculdade de Direito da Universidade de São Paulo*, vol. LXIX, fasc. II (1974), p. 125-136.

________. *A publicidade dos tratados internacionais*. São Paulo: Revista dos Tribunais, 1980.

________. A constituinte e os tratados internacionais. *Revista dos Tribunais*, vol. 624, São Paulo, out./1987, p. 43-51.

________. *Tratados internacionais*. São Paulo: Revista dos Tribunais, 1991.

RODRIGUES, Carlos Calero. O trabalho de codificação do direito internacional nas Nações Unidas. *Boletim da Sociedade Brasileira de Direito Internacional*, n. 101/103, Brasília, jan./jun./1996, p. 23-31.

RODRIGUES, Luís Barbosa. *A interpretação dos tratados internacionais*, 2. ed. (reviewed). Lisboa: Associação Acadêmica da Faculdade de Direito, 2002.

RODRIGUES, José Honório; SEITENFUS, Ricardo. *Uma história diplomática do Brasil (1531-1945)*. Rio de Janeiro: Civilização Brasileira, 1995.

ROGOFF, Martin A. The international legal obligations of signatories to an ungratified treaty. *Maine Law Review*, vol. 32, n. 12 (1980), p. 263-299.

RONZITTI, Natalino. La disciplina dello *jus cogens* nella Convenzione di Vienna sul Diritto dei Trattati. In: *Comunicazioni e Studi*, vol. 15. Milano: Giuffrè, 1978, p. 243-299.

ROSENNE, Shabtai. The depositary of international treaties. *American Journal of International Law*, vol. 61, n. 4 (Oct. 1967), p. 923-945.

________. More on the depositary of international treaties. *American Journal of International Law*, vol. 64, n. 5 (Oct. 1970), p. 838-852.

________. *The law of treaties: a guide to the legislative history of the Vienna Convention*. Leiden: Sijthoff, 1970.

________. The settlement of treaty disputes under the Vienna Convention of 1969. *Zeitschrift für ausländisches öffentliches Recht und Völkerrecht*, vol. 31 (1971), p. 1-62.

ROUCOUNAS, Emmanuel. Engagements parallèles et contradictoires. *Recueil des Cours*, vol. 206 (1987-VI), p. 9-287.

ROUSSEAU, Charles. *Principes généraux du droit international public*, t. I (Introduction, Sources). Paris: A. Pedone, 1944.

RUDA, J. M. Reservations to treaties. *Recueil des Cours*, vol. 146 (1975-III), p. 95-218.

SADAT-AKHAVI, Seyed Ali. *Methods of resolving conflicts between treaties*. Leiden: Brill Academic Publishers, 2003.

SAGÜÉS, Néstor Pedro. *Teoría de la Constitución*. Buenos Aires: Astrea, 2004.

SALERNO, Francesco. Treaties esbablishing objective regimes. In: CANNIZZARO, Enzo (ed.). *The law of treaties beyond the Vienna Convention*. Oxford: Oxford University Press, 2011, p. 225-243.

SALMON, Jean. Les antinomies en droit international public. In : PERELMAN, Chaïm (ed.). *Les antinomies en droit*. Bruxelles: Bruylant, 1965, p. 285-314.

SBOLCI, Luigi. *Obblighi di procedura nell'estinzione dei trattati*. Padova: CEDAM, 2008.

________. Supplementary means of interpretation. In: CANNIZZARO, Enzo (ed.). *The law of treaties beyond the Vienna Convention*. Oxford: Oxford University Press, 2011, p. 145-163.

SCHNEIDER, J. W. *Treaty-making power of international organizations*. Genève: Droz, 1963 (Travaux de Droit, d'Économie et de Sociologie, n. 12).

SCOTT, David C. Presidential power to "un-sign" treaties. *The University of Chicago Law Review*, vol. 69, n. 3 (2002), p. 1447-1477.

SEIDL-HOENVELDERN, Ignaz. Hierarchy of treaties. In: KLABBERS, Jan; LEFEBER, René (eds.). *Essays on the law of treaties: a collection of essays in honour of Bert Vierdag*. Dordrecht: Martinus Nijhoff, 1998, p. 7-18.

SEITENFUS, Ricardo. *Manual das organizações internacionais*, 4. ed. (reviewed, updated and extended). Porto Alegre: Livraria do Advogado, 2005.

SEPÚLVEDA, César. *Derecho internacional*, 26. ed. México, D.F.: Porrúa, 2009.

SÈROUSSI, Roland. *Introdução ao direito inglês e norte-americano*. Transl. by Renata Maria Parreira Cordeiro. São Paulo: Landy, 2001.

SETTE CÂMARA, José. *The ratification of international treaties*. Toronto: The Ontario Publishing Company Limited, 1949.

SHAW, Malcolm N. *Direito internacional*. Transl. by Marcelo Brandão Cipolla (*et all.*) São Paulo: Martins Fontes, 2010.

SHELTON, Dinah. Normative hierarchy in international law. *American Journal of International Law*, vol. 100, n. 2 (April 2006), p. 291-323.

SIBERT, Marcel. Quelques aspects de l'organisation et de la technique des conférences internationales. *Recueil des Cours*, vol. 48 (1934-II), p. 387-457.

SILVA, José Afonso da. *Comentário contextual à Constituição*, 2. ed. São Paulo: Malheiros, 2006.

________. *Processo constitucional de formação das leis*, 2. ed. São Paulo: Malheiros, 2006.

SIMMA, Bruno. From bilateralism to community interest in international law. *Recueil des Cours*, vol. 250 (1994-VI), p. 293-321.

________; HERNÁNDEZ, Gleider I. Legal consequences of an impermissible reservation to a human rights treaty: where do we stand? In: CANNIZZARO, Enzo (ed.). *The law of treaties beyond the Vienna Convention*. Oxford: Oxford University Press, 2011, p. 60-85.

SINCLAIR, Ian. *The Vienna Convention on the Law of Treaties*, 2. ed. Manchester: Manchester University Press, 1984 (Melland Schill monographs in international law).

________. The impact of the unratified codification convention. In: BOS, Adriaan & SIBLESZ, Hugo (eds.). *Realism in law-making: essays on international law in honour of William Riphagen*. Dordrecht: Martinus Nijhoff, 1986, p. 211-229.

SOARES, Guido Fernando Silva. "Agreements" – "Executive Agreements" – "Gentlemen's Agreements". In: FRANÇA, R. Limongi (coord.). *Enciclopédia Saraiva do Direito*, vol. 5. São Paulo: Saraiva, 1977, p. 247-248.

________. Os acordos administrativos e sua validade no Brasil. *Revista Forense*, vol. 272, Rio de Janeiro, 1980, p. 57-76.

________. The treaty-making process under the 1988 Federal Constitution of Brazil. *Chicago-Kent Law Review*, vol. 67, n. 2 (1991), p. 495-513.

________. *Curso de direito internacional público*, vol. 1. São Paulo: Atlas, 2002.

________. *Direito internacional do meio ambiente: emergência, obrigações e responsabilidades*, 2. ed. São Paulo: Atlas, 2003.

SOHN, Louis B. Settlement of disputes relating to the interpretation and application of treaties. *Recueil des Cours*, vol. 150 (1976-II), p. 195-294.

SPINEDI, Marina. From one codification to another: bilateralism and multilateralism in the genesis of the codification of the law of treaties and the law of State responsibility. *European Journal of International Law*, vol. 13, n. 5 (2002), p. 1099-1125.

SUR, Serge; COMBACAU, Jean. *Droit international public*, 6. ed. Paris: Montchrestien, 2004.

SÜSSEKIND, Arnaldo. *Direito internacional do trabalho*, 2. ed. (updated and extended). São Paulo: LTr, 1987.

SZABÓ, Marcel (ed.). *State responsibility and the law of treaties*. The Hague: Eleven International, 2010.

SZTUCKI, Jerzy. Jus cogens *and the Vienna Convention on the Law of Treaties: a critical appraisal*. New York: Springer-Verlag, 1974.

TAMS, Christian J. *Enforcing obligations* erga omnes *in international law*. Cambridge: Cambridge University Press, 2005.

TAUBE, Michel de. L'inviolabilité des traités. *Recueil des Cours*, vol. 32 (1930-II), p. 291-389.

TAVARES, Francisco de Assis Maciel. *Ratificação de tratados internacionais*. Rio de Janeiro: Lumen Juris, 2003.

THIRLWAY, Hugh. The law and procedure of the International Court of Justice, 1960-1989 (Part Four). *British Year Book of International Law*, vol. 63 (1992), p. 1-96.

TORRES BERNÁRDEZ, Santiago. La obra de desarrollo progresivo y codificación del derecho internacional llevada a cabo por Naciones Unidas. In: *ONU, año XX (1946-1966)*. Madrid: Tecnos, 1966, p. 199-248.

TREVES, Tullio. Une nouvelle technique dans la codification du droit international: le comité de redaction de la conference sur le droit de la mer. *Annuaire Français de Droit International*, vol. 27 (1981), p. 65-85.

TUCKER, Henry St. George. *Limitations on the treaty-making power under the Constitution of the United States*. Boston: Litte & Brown, 1915.

TUNKIN, Grigory. International law in the international system. *Recueil des Cours*, vol. 147 (1975-IV), p. 1-218.

VALLADÃO, Haroldo. Aprovação de Ajustes Internacionais pelo Congresso Nacional. *Boletim da Sociedade Brasileira de Direito Internacional*, Rio de Janeiro, jan./dez./1950, p. 95-108.

VALTICOS, Nicolas. Nature et portée juridique de la ratification des conventions internationales du travail. In: DINSTEIN, Yoram (ed.). *International law at a time of perplexity: essays in honour of Shabtai Rosenne*. Dordrecht: Martinus Nijhoff, 1989, p. 987-1004.

VAMVOUKOS, Athanassios. *Termination of treaties in international law: the doctrines of* rebus sic stantibus *and* desuetude. Oxford: Clarendon Press, 1985.

VELLOSO, Carlos Mário da Silva. Os tratados na jurisprudência do Supremo Tribunal Federal. *Revista de Informação Legislativa*, ano 41, n. 162, Brasília: Senado Federal, abr./jun./2004, p. 35-45.

VERDROSS, Alfred; SIMMA, Bruno. *Universelles Völkerrecht: Theorie und Praxis*, 3. ed. Berlin: Duncker & Humblot, 1984.

VERHOEVEN, Joe. Sur les "bons" et les "mauvais" emplois du *jus cogens*. *III Anuário Brasileiro de Direito Internacional*, vol. I. Belo Horizonte: CEDIN, 2006, p. 133-160.

________. Invalidity of treaties: anything new in/under the Vienna Conventions? In: CANNIZZARO, Enzo (ed.). *The law of treaties beyond the Vienna Convention*. Oxford: Oxford University Press, 2011, p. 297-319.

VIEGAS, Vera Lúcia. *Ius cogens* e o tema da nulidade dos tratados. *Revista de Informação Legislativa*, ano 36, n. 144, Brasília: Senado Federal, out./dez./1999, p. 181-196.

VIGNALI, Heber Arbuet; ARRIGHI, Jean Michel. Os vínculos entre o direito internacional público e os sistemas internos. *Revista de Informação Legislativa*, ano 29, n. 115, Brasília: Senado Federal, jul./set./1992, p. 413-420.

VILLIGER, Mark E. *Customary international law and treaties: a study of their interactions and interrelations with special consideration of the 1969 Vienna Convention on the Law of Treaties*. Dordrecht: Martinus Nijhoff, 1985.

________. *Commentary on the 1969 Vienna Convention on the Law of Treaties*. Leiden: Martinus Nijhoff, 2009.

________. The 1969 Vienna Convention on the Law of Treaties: 40 years after. *Recueil des Cours*, vol. 344 (2009), p. 9-192.

WEI, Su. Reservation to treaties and some practical issues. *Asian Yearbook of International Law*, vol. 7 (1997), p. 105-139.

WETZEL, Ralf Günter; RAUSCHNING, Dietrich. *The Vienna Convention on the Law of Treaties: travaux préparatoires*. Frankfurt: A. Metzner, 1978.

WHEATON, Henry. *Elements of international law*, 6th english edition, revised throughout, considerably enlarged and re-written by A. Berriedale Keith, D.C.L., D.Litt. London: Stevens & Sons, 1929 (2 vols.).

WILCOX, Francis O. *The ratification of international conventions: a study of the relationship of the ratification process to the development of international legislation*. London: George Allen & Unwin Ltd., 1935.

WOLFKE, Karol. Treaties and custom: aspects of interrelation. In: KLABBERS, Jan; LEFEBER, René (eds.). *Essays on the law of treaties: a collection of essays in honour of Bert Vierdag*. Dordrecht: Martinus Nijhoff, 1998, p. 31-40.

WOLFRUM, Rüdiger; RÖBEN, Volker (eds.). *Developments of international law in treaty-making*. Berlin: Springer, 2005 (Beiträge zum ausländischen öffentlichen Recht und Völkerrecht 177).

XAVIER, Alberto. *Direito tributário internacional do Brasil*, 6. ed. (updated and extended). Rio de Janeiro: Forense, 2005.

________; XAVIER, Helena de Araújo Lopes. Tratados: superioridade hierárquica em relação à lei face à Constituição Federal de 1988. *Revista de Direito Tributário*, n. 66, São Paulo, jan./1996, p. 30-48.

YASSEEN, Mustafa Kamil. L'interprétation des traités d'après la convention de Vienne sur le droit des traités. *Recueil des Cours*, vol. 151 (1976-III), p. 1-114.

ZEMANEK, Karl. *Das Vertragsrecht der internationalen Organisationen*. Wien: Springer, 1957.

ZOLLER, Elizabeth. *La bonne foi en droit international public*. Paris: A. Pedone, 1977.

ZOLO, Danilo. *La justicia de los vencedores: de Nuremberg a Bagdad*. Transl. by Elena Bossi. Madrid: Trotta, 2007.

Annexes

Annex I

Havana Convention on Treaties (1928)*

Entry into force: 29 August 1929

The governments of the American States being desirous of clearly fixing the rules which must govern the treaties they may sign among themselves, have decided to establish them in a convention, and to that end have appointed the following plenipotentiaries:

[Here follow the names of the plenipotentiaries]

Who, having exchanged their respective full powers and found them to be in good and due form, have agreed on the following:

Article 1

Treaties will be concluded by the competent authorities of the States or by their representatives, according to their respective internal law.

Article 2

The written form is an essential condition of treaties.

The confirmation, prorogation, renewal or continuance, shall also be made in writing unless other stipulations have been made.

Article 3

The authentic interpretation of treaties, when considered necessary by the contracting parties, shall likewise be in writing.

Article 4

Treaties shall be published immediately after exchange of ratifications. The failure to discharge this international duty shall affect neither the force of treaties nor the fulfillment of obligations stipulated therein.

---

* Adopted by the Sixth International Conference of American States, Havana, 20 February 1928. The French, Portuguese and Spanish versions of this Convention are also authoritative. The English version reproduced here is from the English version of the Final Act of the Sixth International Conference of American States, p. 135. See, also, 22 *American Journal of International Law*, Supp. (1928), p. 138-142. On April 1, 1935, the Convention was in force for Brazil, Dominican Republic, Haiti, Nicaragua and Panama.

Article 5

Treaties are obligatory only after ratification by the contracting States, even though this condition is not stipulated in the full powers of the negotiators or does not appear in the treaty itself.

Article 6

Ratification must be unconditional and must embrace the entire treaty. It must be made in writing pursuant to the legislation of the State.

In case the ratifying State makes reservations to the treaty it shall become effective when the other contracting party informed of the reservations expressly accepts them, or having failed to reject them formally, should perform action implying its acceptance.

In international treaties celebrated between different Sates, a reservation made by one of them in the act of ratification affects only the application of the clause in question in the relation of the other contracting States with the State making the reservation.

Article 7

Refusal to ratify or the formulation of a reservation are acts inherent in national sovereignty and as such constitute the exercise of a right which violates no international stipulation or good form. In case of refusal it shall be communicated to the other contracting parties.

Article 8

Treaties shall become effective from the date of exchange or deposit of ratification, unless some other date has been agreed upon through an express provision.

Article 9

The acceptance or the non-acceptance of provisions in a treaty, for the benefit of a third State which was not a contracting party, depends exclusively upon the latter's decision.

Article 10

No state can relieve itself of the obligations of a treaty or modify its stipulations except by the agreement, secured through peaceful means, of the other contracting parties.

Article 11

Treaties shall continue in effect even though the internal constitution of the contracting States has been modified. If the organization of the State should be changed in such a manner as to render impossible the execution of treaties, because of division of territory or other like reasons, treaties shall be adapted to the new conditions.

Article 12

Whenever a treaty becomes impossible of execution through the fault of the party entering into the obligation, or through circumstances which at the moment of concluding it were under control of this party and unknown to the other party, the former shall be responsible for damages resulting from its non-execution.

Article 13

The execution of a treaty may, through express stipulation or by virtue of special agreement, be placed wholly or partly under the guaranty of one or more States.

The guarantor State can intervene in the execution of the treaty only by virtue of a request by one of the interested parties and then only under the conditions which were stipulated for intervention. When intervention takes place, only such measures may be employed by the guarantor State as are sanctioned by international law, and without requirements of greater scope than those of the State which has been guaranteed.

Article 14

Treaties cease to be effective;

a) When the stipulated obligation has been fulfilled.

b) When the length of time for which it was made has expired.

c) When the resolutory condition has been fulfilled.

d) By agreement between the parties.

e) By renunciation of the party exclusively entitled to a benefit thereunder.

f) By total or partial denunciation, if agreed upon.

g) When it becomes incapable of execution.

Article 15

The caducity of a treaty may also be declared when it is permanent and of non-continuous application, on condition that the causes which originated it have disappeared and when it may logically be deduced that they will not reappear in the future.

The contracting party invoking this caducity may, upon not obtaining the consent of the other party or parties, appeal to arbitration, the contracted obligation to remain in force if a favorable award is not obtained and while the decision is being made.

Article 16

Obligations contracted in treaties shall be sanctioned in cases of non-compliance and when all diplomatic negotiations have been exhausted without success, by decision of a court of justice or an arbitral tribunal, within the limits and according to the procedure in use at the time in which the infraction is alleged.

Article 17

Treaties whose denunciation may have been agreed upon and those establishing rules of international law, can be denounced only in the manner provided thereby.

In the absence of such a stipulation, a treaty may be denounced by any contracting State, which State shall notify the others of this decision, provided it has complied with all obligations covenanted therein.

In this event the treaty shall become ineffective, as far as the denouncing State is concerned, one year after the last notification, and will continue in force for any other signatory States, if any.

Article 18

Two or more States may agree that their relations are to be governed by rules other than those established in general conventions celebrated by them with other States.

This precept applies not only to future treaties but also to those in effect at the time of concluding this convention.

Article 19

A State not participating in the making of a treaty may adhere to the same if none other of the contracting parties be opposed, its adherence to be communicated to all. The adherence shall be deemed final unless made with express reservation of ratification.

Article 20

The present convention does not affect obligations previously undertaken by contracting parties through international agreements.

Article 21

After being signed, the present Convention shall be submitted to the ratification of the signatory States. The Government of Cuba is charged with transmitting authentic certified copies to the Governments for the aforementioned purpose of ratification. The instrument of ratification shall be deposited in the archives of the Pan American Union in Washington, the Union to notify the signatory governments of said deposit. Such notification shall be considered as an exchange of ratifications. This Convention shall remain open to the adherence of non-signatory States.

In witness whereof, the Plenipotentiaries sign the present Convention in Spanish, English, French and Portuguese, in the city of Havana, the 20th day of February, 1928.

RESERVATION OF THE DELEGATION OF MEXICO

The Delegation of Mexico regardless of the contrary vote it wishes to formulate with respect to several articles in the Conventions on Public International Law already adopted, will sign them making as sole reservation one relative to Article 13, which it does not accept, of the Convention on Treaties.

RESERVATION OF THE DELEGATION OF EL SALVADOR

The Delegation of El Salvador not only casts its negative vote to Article 13, but it also votes against the Convention and does not sign it.

RESERVATIONS OF THE DELEGATION OF BOLIVIA

In the opinion of the Delegation of Bolivia the condition of becoming incapable of execution to which section *g)* of Article 14 refers, also arises among others in the following cases:

I. When the facts and circumstances which gave origin or served as a basis to the treaty have been fundamentally modified;

II. When its execution becomes contrary to the nature of things;

III. When it becomes incompatible with the existence, independence or dignity of a State;

IV. When it becomes ruinous to its wealth or its commerce.

The reservation which Bolivia makes to Article 15 is to the effect that not only treaties of non-continuous application, as provided in said article, are subject to a declaration of caducity, but that the same should apply to all kinds of treaties, whatever their nature or denomination, even to those so-called definitive treaties which like every human covenant are liable to error, since there is nothing immutable and eternal.

Annex II

Vienna Convention on the Law of Treaties (1969)*

Entry into force: 27 January 1980

The States Parties to the present Convention,

Considering the fundamental role of treaties in the history of international relations,

Recognizing the ever-increasing importance of treaties as a source of international law and as a means of developing peaceful co-operation among nations, whatever their constitutional and social systems,

Noting that the principles of free consent and of good faith and the *pacta sunt servanda* rule are universally recognized,

Affirming that disputes concerning treaties, like other international disputes, should be settled by peaceful means and in conformity with the principles of justice and international law,

Recalling the determination of the peoples of the United Nations to establish conditions under which justice and respect for the obligations arising from treaties can be maintained,

Having in mind the principles of international law embodied in the Charter of the United Nations, such as the principles of the equal rights and self-determination of peoples, of the sovereign equality and independence of all States, of non-interference in the domestic affairs of States, of the prohibition of the threat or use of force and of universal respect for, and observance of, human rights and fundamental freedoms for all,

Believing that the codification and progressive development of the law of treaties achieved in the present Convention will promote the purposes of the United Nations set forth in the Charter, namely, the maintenance of international peace and security, the development of friendly relations and the achievement of co-operation among nations,

---

* Authentic texts: English, French, Chinese, Russian and Spanish. Registered *ex officio* on 27 January 1980, No. 18232.

Affirming that the rules of customary international law will continue to govern questions not regulated by the provisions of the present Convention,

Have agreed as follows:

PART I
INTRODUCTION

Article 1
Scope of the present Convention

The present Convention applies to treaties between States.

Article 2
Use of terms

1. For the purposes of the present Convention:

(a) "treaty" means an international agreement concluded between States in written form and governed by international law, whether embodied in a single instrument or in two or more related instruments and whatever its particular designation;

(b) "ratification", "acceptance", "approval" and "accession" mean in each case the international act so named whereby a State establishes on the international plane its consent to be bound by a treaty;

(c) "full powers" means a document emanating from the competent authority of a State designating a person or persons to represent the State for negotiating, adopting or authenticating the text of a treaty, for expressing the consent of the State to be bound by a treaty, or for accomplishing any other act with respect to a treaty;

(d) "reservation" means a unilateral statement, however phrased or named, made by a State, when signing, ratifying, accepting, approving or acceding to a treaty, whereby it purports to exclude or to modify the legal effect of certain provisions of the treaty in their application to that State;

(e) "negotiating State" means a State which took part in the drawing up and adoption of the text of the treaty;

(f) "contracting State" means a State which has consented to be bound by the treaty, whether or not the treaty has entered into force;

(g) "party" means a State which has consented to be bound by the treaty and for which the treaty is in force;

(h) "third State" means a State not a party to the treaty;

(i) "international organization" means an intergovernmental organization.

2. The provisions of paragraph 1 regarding the use of terms in the present Convention are without prejudice to the use of those terms or to the meanings which may be given to them in the internal law of any State.

Article 3
International agreements not within the scope of the present Convention

The fact that the present Convention does not apply to international agreements concluded between States and other subjects of international law or between such other subjects of international law, or to international agreements not in written form, shall not affect:

(a) the legal force of such agreements;

(b) the application to them of any of the rules set forth in the present Convention to which they would be subject under international law independently of the Convention;

(c) the application of the Convention to the relations of States as between themselves under international agreements to which other subjects of international law are also parties.

Article 4
Non-retroactivity of the present Convention

Without prejudice to the application of any rules set forth in the present Convention to which treaties would be subject under international law independently of the Convention, the Convention applies only to treaties which are concluded by States after the entry into force of the present Convention with regard to such States.

Article 5
Treaties constituting international organizations and treaties adopted within an international organization

The present Convention applies to any treaty which is the constituent instrument of an international organization and to any treaty adopted within an international organization without prejudice to any relevant rules of the organization.

PART II
CONCLUSION AND ENTRY INTO FORCE OF TREATIES

SECTION 1
CONCLUSION OF TREATIES

Article 6
Capacity of States to conclude treaties

Every State possesses capacity to conclude treaties.

Article 7
Full powers

1. A person is considered as representing a State for the purpose of adopting or authenticating the text of a treaty or for the purpose of expressing the consent of the State to be bound by a treaty if:

(a) he produces appropriate full powers; or

(b) it appears from the practice of the States concerned or from other circumstances that their intention was to consider that person as representing the State for such purposes and to dispense with full powers.

2. In virtue of their functions and without having to produce full powers, the following are considered as representing their State:

(a) Heads of State, Heads of Government and Ministers for Foreign Affairs, for the purpose of performing all acts relating to the conclusion of a treaty;

(b) heads of diplomatic missions, for the purpose of adopting the text of a treaty between the accrediting State and the State to which they are accredited;

(c) representatives accredited by States to an international conference or to an international organization or one of its organs, for the purpose of adopting the text of a treaty in that conference, organization or organ.

Article 8

Subsequent confirmation of an act performed without authorization

An act relating to the conclusion of a treaty performed by a person who cannot be considered under article 7 as authorized to represent a State for that purpose is without legal effect unless afterwards confirmed by that State.

Article 9

Adoption of the text

1. The adoption of the text of a treaty takes place by the consent of all the States participating in its drawing up except as provided in paragraph 2.

2. The adoption of the text of a treaty at an international conference takes place by the vote of two-thirds of the States present and voting, unless by the same majority they shall decide to apply a different rule.

Article 10

Authentication of the text

The text of a treaty is established as authentic and definitive:

(a) by such procedure as may be provided for in the text or agreed upon by the States participating in its drawing up; or

(b) failing such procedure, by the signature, signature ad referendum or initialling by the representatives of those States of the text of the treaty or of the Final Act of a conference incorporating the text.

Article 11

Means of expressing consent to be bound by a treaty

The consent of a State to be bound by a treaty may be expressed by signature, exchange of instruments constituting a treaty, ratification, acceptance, approval or accession, or by any other means if so agreed.

Article 12

Consent to be bound by a treaty expressed by signature

1. The consent of a State to be bound by a treaty is expressed by the signature of its representative when:

(a) the treaty provides that signature shall have that effect;

(b) it is otherwise established that the negotiating States were agreed that signature should have that effect; or

(c) the intention of the State to give that effect to the signature appears from the full powers of its representative or was expressed during the negotiation.

2. For the purposes of paragraph 1:

(a) the initialling of a text constitutes a signature of the treaty when it is established that the negotiating States so agreed;

(b) the signature ad referendum of a treaty by a representative, if confirmed by his State, constitutes a full signature of the treaty.

Article 13
Consent to be bound by a treaty expressed by an exchange of instruments constituting a treaty

The consent of States to be bound by a treaty constituted by instruments exchanged between them is expressed by that exchange when:

(a) the instruments provide that their exchange shall have that effect; or

(b) it is otherwise established that those States were agreed that the exchange of instruments should have that effect

Article 14
Consent to be bound by a treaty expressed by ratification, acceptance or approval

1. The consent of a State to be bound by a treaty is expressed by ratification when:

(a) the treaty provides for such consent to be expressed by means of ratification;

(b) it is otherwise established that the negotiating States were agreed that ratification should be required;

(c) the representative of the State has signed the treaty subject to ratification; or

(d) the intention of the State to sign the treaty subject to ratification appears from the full powers of its representative or was expressed during the negotiation.

2. The consent of a State to be bound by a treaty is expressed by acceptance or approval under conditions similar to those which apply to ratification.

Article 15
Consent to be bound by a treaty expressed by accession

The consent of a State to be bound by a treaty is expressed by accession when:

(a) the treaty provides that such consent may be expressed by that State by means of accession;

(b) it is otherwise established that the negotiating States were agreed that such consent may be expressed by that State by means of accession; or

(c) all the parties have subsequently agreed that such consent may be expressed by that State by means of accession.

Article 16
Exchange or deposit of instruments of ratification, acceptance, approval or accession

Unless the treaty otherwise provides, instruments of ratification, acceptance, approval or accession establish the consent of a State to be bound by a treaty upon:

(a) their exchange between the contracting States;

(b) their deposit with the depositary; or

(c) their notification to the contracting States or to the depositary, if so agreed.

Article 17
Consent to be bound by part of a treaty and choice of differing provisions

1. Without prejudice to articles 19 to 23, the consent of a State to be bound by part of a treaty is effective only if the treaty so permits or the other contracting States so agree.

2. The consent of a State to be bound by a treaty which permits a choice between differing provisions is effective only if it is made clear to which of the provisions the consent relates.

Article 18
Obligation not to defeat the object and purpose of a treaty prior to its entry into force

A State is obliged to refrain from acts which would defeat the object and purpose of a treaty when:

(a) it has signed the treaty or has exchanged instruments constituting the treaty subject to ratification, acceptance or approval, until it shall have made its intention clear not to become a party to the treaty; or

(b) it has expressed its consent to be bound by the treaty, pending the entry into force of the treaty and provided that such entry into force is not unduly delayed.

SECTION 2
RESERVATIONS

Article 19
Formulation of reservations

A State may, when signing, ratifying, accepting, approving or acceding to a treaty, formulate a reservation unless:

(a) the reservation is prohibited by the treaty;

(b) the treaty provides that only specified reservations, which do not include the reservation in question, may be made; or

(c) in cases not falling under sub-paragraphs *(a)* and *(b)*, the reservation is incompatible with the object and purpose of the treaty.

Article 20
Acceptance of and objection to reservations

1. A reservation expressly authorized by a treaty does not require any subsequent acceptance by the other contracting States unless the treaty so provides.

2. When it appears from the limited number of the negotiating States and the object and purpose of a treaty that the application of the treaty in its entirety between all the parties is an essential condition of the consent of each one to be bound by the treaty, a reservation requires acceptance by all the parties.

3. When a treaty is a constituent instrument of an international organization and unless it otherwise provides, a reservation requires the acceptance of the competent organ of that organization.

4. In cases not falling under the preceding paragraphs and unless the treaty otherwise provides:

(a) acceptance by another contracting State of a reservation constitutes the reserving State a party to the treaty in relation to that other State if or when the treaty is in force for those States;

(b) an objection by another contracting State to a reservation does not preclude the entry into force of the treaty as between the objecting and reserving States unless a contrary intention is definitely expressed by the objecting State;

(c) an act expressing a State's consent to be bound by the treaty and containing a reservation is effective as soon as at least one other contracting State has accepted the reservation.

5. For the purposes of paragraphs 2 and 4 and unless the treaty otherwise provides, a reservation is considered to have been accepted by a State if it shall have raised no objection to the reservation by the end of a period of twelve months after it was notified of the reservation or by the date on which it expressed its consent to be bound by the treaty, whichever is later.

Article 21
Legal effects of reservations and of objections to reservations

1. A reservation established with regard to another party in accordance with articles 19, 20 and 23:

(a) modifies for the reserving State in its relations with that other party the provisions of the treaty to which the reservation relates to the extent of the reservation; and

(b) modifies those provisions to the same extent for that other party in its relations with the reserving State.

2. The reservation does not modify the provisions of the treaty for the other parties to the treaty inter se.

3. When a State objecting to a reservation has not opposed the entry into force of the treaty between itself and the reserving State, the provisions to which the reservation relates do not apply as between the two States to the extent of the reservation.

Article 22
Withdrawal of reservations and of objections to reservations

1. Unless the treaty otherwise provides, a reservation may be withdrawn at any time and the consent of a State which has accepted the reservation is not required for its withdrawal.

2. Unless the treaty otherwise provides, an objection to a reservation may be withdrawn at any time.

3. Unless the treaty otherwise provides, or it is otherwise agreed:

(a) the withdrawal of a reservation becomes operative in relation to another contracting State only when notice of it has been received by that State;

(b) the withdrawal of an objection to a reservation becomes operative only when notice of it has been received by the State which formulated the reservation.

Article 23
Procedure regarding reservations

1. A reservation, an express acceptance of a reservation and an objection to a reservation must be formulated in writing and communicated to the contracting States and other States entitled to become parties to the treaty.

2. If formulated when signing the treaty subject to ratification, acceptance or approval, a reservation must be formally confirmed by the reserving State when expressing its consent to be bound by the treaty. In such a case the reservation shall be considered as having been made on the date of its confirmation.

3. An express acceptance of, or an objection to, a reservation made previously to confirmation of the reservation does not itself require confirmation.

4. The withdrawal of a reservation or of an objection to a reservation must be formulated in writing.

SECTION 3
ENTRY INTO FORCE AND PROVISIONAL APPLICATION OF TREATIES

Article 24
Entry into force

1. A treaty enters into force in such manner and upon such date as it may provide or as the negotiating States may agree.

2. Failing any such provision or agreement, a treaty enters into force as soon as consent to be bound by the treaty has been established for all the negotiating States.

3. When the consent of a State to be bound by a treaty is established on a date after the treaty has come into force, the treaty enters into force for that State on that date, unless the treaty otherwise provides.

4. The provisions of a treaty regulating the authentication of its text, the establishment of the consent of States to be bound by the treaty, the manner or date of its entry into force, reservations, the functions of the depositary and other matters

arising necessarily before the entry into force of the treaty apply from the time of the adoption of its text.

Article 25
Provisional application

1. A treaty or a part of a treaty is applied provisionally pending its entry into force if:

(a) the treaty itself so provides; or

(b) the negotiating States have in some other manner so agreed.

2. Unless the treaty otherwise provides or the negotiating States have otherwise agreed, the provisional application of a treaty or a part of a treaty with respect to a State shall be terminated if that State notifies the other States between which the treaty is being applied provisionally of its intention not to become a party to the treaty.

PART III
OBSERVANCE, APPLICATION AND INTERPRETATION OF TREATIES

SECTION 1
OBSERVANCE OF TREATIES

Article 26
Pacta sunt servanda

Every treaty in force is binding upon the parties to it and must be performed by them in good faith.

Article 27
Internal law and observance of treaties

A party may not invoke the provisions of its internal law as justification for its failure to perform a treaty. This rule is without prejudice to article 46.

SECTION 2
APPLICATION OF TREATIES

Article 28
Non-retroactivity of treaties

Unless a different intention appears from the treaty or is otherwise established, its provisions do not bind a party in relation to any act or fact which took place or any situation which ceased to exist before the date of the entry into force of the treaty with respect to that party.

Article 29
Territorial scope of treaties

Unless a different intention appears from the treaty or is otherwise established, a treaty is binding upon each party in respect of its entire territory.

Article 30
Application of successive treaties relating to the same subject-matter

1. Subject to Article 103 of the Charter of the United Nations, the rights and obligations of States parties to successive treaties relating to the same subject-matter shall be determined in accordance with the following paragraphs.

2. When a treaty specifies that it is subject to, or that it is not to be considered as incompatible with, an earlier or later treaty, the provisions of that other treaty prevail.

3. When all the parties to the earlier treaty are parties also to the later treaty but the earlier treaty is not terminated or suspended in operation under article 59, the earlier treaty applies only to the extent that its provisions are compatible with those of the latter treaty.

4. When the parties to the later treaty do not include all the parties to the earlier one:

(a) as between States parties to both treaties the same rule applies as in paragraph 3;

(b) as between a State party to both treaties and a State party to only one of the treaties, the treaty to which both States are parties governs their mutual rights and obligations.

5. Paragraph 4 is without prejudice to article 41, or to any question of the termination or suspension of the operation of a treaty under article 60 or to any question of responsibility which may arise for a State from the conclusion or application of a treaty, the provisions of which are incompatible with its obligations towards another State under another treaty.

SECTION 3
INTERPRETATION OF TREATIES

Article 31
General rule of interpretation

1. A treaty shall be interpreted in good faith in accordance with the ordinary meaning to be given to the terms of the treaty in their context and in the light of its object and purpose.

2. The context for the purpose of the interpretation of a treaty shall comprise, in addition to the text, including its preamble and annexes:

(a) any agreement relating to the treaty which was made between all the parties in connexion with the conclusion of the treaty;

(b) any instrument which was made by one or more parties in connexion with the conclusion of the treaty and accepted by the other parties as an instrument related to the treaty.

3. There shall be taken into account, together with the context:

(a) any subsequent agreement between the parties regarding the interpretation of the treaty or the application of its provisions;

(b) any subsequent practice in the application of the treaty which establishes the agreement of the parties regarding its interpretation;

(c) any relevant rules of international law applicable in the relations between the parties.

4. A special meaning shall be given to a term if it is established that the parties so intended.

Article 32
Supplementary means of interpretation

Recourse may be had to supplementary means of interpretation, including the preparatory work of the treaty and the circumstances of its conclusion, in order to confirm the meaning resulting from the application of article 31, or to determine the meaning when the interpretation according to article 31:

(a) leaves the meaning ambiguous or obscure; or

(b) leads to a result which is manifestly absurd or unreasonable.

Article 33
Interpretation of treaties authenticated in two or more languages

1. When a treaty has been authenticated in two or more languages, the text is equally authoritative in each language, unless the treaty provides or the parties agree that, in case of divergence, a particular text shall prevail.

2. A version of the treaty in a language other than one of those in which the text was authenticated shall be considered an authentic text only if the treaty so provides or the parties so agree.

3. The terms of the treaty are presumed to have the same meaning in each authentic text.

4. Except where a particular text prevails in accordance with paragraph 1, when a comparison of the authentic texts discloses a difference of meaning which the application of articles 31 and 32 does not remove, the meaning which best reconciles the texts, having regard to the object and purpose of the treaty, shall be adopted.

SECTION 4
TREATIES AND THIRD STATES

Article 34
General rule regarding third States

A treaty does not create either obligations or rights for a third State without its consent.

Article 35
Treaties providing for obligations for third States

An obligation arises for a third State from a provision of a treaty if the parties to the treaty intend the provision to be the means of establishing the obligation and the third State expressly accepts that obligation in writing.

Article 36
Treaties providing for rights for third States

1. A right arises for a third State from a provision of a treaty if the parties to the treaty intend the provision to accord that right either to the third State, or to a group of States to which it belongs, or to all States, and the third State assents thereto. Its assent shall be presumed so long as the contrary is not indicated, unless the treaty otherwise provides.

2. A State exercising a right in accordance with paragraph 1 shall comply with the conditions for its exercise provided for in the treaty or established in conformity with the treaty.

Article 37
Revocation or modification of obligations or rights of third States

1. When an obligation has arisen for a third State in conformity with article 35, the obligation may be revoked or modified only with the consent of the parties to the treaty and of the third State, unless it is established that they had otherwise agreed.

2. When a right has arisen for a third State in conformity with article 36, the right may not be revoked or modified by the parties if it is established that the right was intended not to be revocable or subject to modification without the consent of the third State.

Article 38
Rules in a treaty becoming binding on third States through international custom

Nothing in articles 34 to 37 precludes a rule set forth in a treaty from becoming binding upon a third State as a customary rule of international law, recognized as such.

PART IV
AMENDMENT AND MODIFICATION OF TREATIES

Article 39
General rule regarding the amendment of treaties

A treaty may be amended by agreement between the parties. The rules laid down in Part II apply to such an agreement except in so far as the treaty may otherwise provide.

Article 40
Amendment of multilateral treaties

1. Unless the treaty otherwise provides, the amendment of multilateral treaties shall be governed by the following paragraphs.

2. Any proposal to amend a multilateral treaty as between all the parties must be notified to all the contracting States, each one of which shall have the right to take part in:

(a) the decision as to the action to be taken in regard to such proposal;

(b) the negotiation and conclusion of any agreement for the amendment of the treaty.

3. Every State entitled to become a party to the treaty shall also be entitled to become a party to the treaty as amended.

4. The amending agreement does not bind any State already a party to the treaty which does not become a party to the amending agreement; article 30, paragraph 4(b), applies in relation to such State.

5. Any State which becomes a party to the treaty after the entry into force of the amending agreement shall, failing an expression of a different intention by that State:

(a) be considered as a party to the treaty as amended; and

(b) be considered as a party to the unamended treaty in relation to any party to the treaty not bound by the amending agreement.

Article 41
Agreements to modify multilateral treaties between certain of the parties only

1. Two or more of the parties to a multilateral treaty may conclude an agreement to modify the treaty as between themselves alone if:

(a) the possibility of such a modification is provided for by the treaty; or

(b) the modification in question is not prohibited by the treaty and:

(i) does not affect the enjoyment by the other parties of their rights under the treaty or the performance of their obligations;

(ii) does not relate to a provision, derogation from which is incompatible with the effective execution of the object and purpose of the treaty as a whole.

2. Unless in a case falling under paragraph 1*(a)* the treaty otherwise provides, the parties in question shall notify the other parties of their intention to conclude the agreement and of the modification to the treaty for which it provides.

PART V
INVALIDITY, TERMINATION AND SUSPENSION OF THE OPERATION OF TREATIES

SECTION 1
GENERAL PROVISIONS

Article 42
Validity and continuance in force of treaties

1. The validity of a treaty or of the consent of a State to be bound by a treaty may be impeached only through the application of the present Convention.

2. The termination of a treaty, its denunciation or the withdrawal of a party, may take place only as a result of the application of the provisions of the treaty or of the present Convention. The same rule applies to suspension of the operation of a treaty.

Article 4
Obligations imposed by international law independently of a treaty

The invalidity, termination or denunciation of a treaty, the withdrawal of a party from it, or the suspension of its operation, as a result of the application of the present

Convention or of the provisions of the treaty, shall not in any way impair the duty of any State to fulfil any obligation embodied in the treaty to which it would be subject under international law independently of the treaty.

Article 44
Separability of treaty provisions

1. A right of a party, provided for in a treaty or arising under article 56, to denounce, withdraw from or suspend the operation of the treaty may be exercised only with respect to the whole treaty unless the treaty otherwise provides or the parties otherwise agree.

2. A ground for invalidating, terminating, withdrawing from or suspending the operation of a treaty recognized in the present Convention may be invoked only with respect to the whole treaty except as provided in the following paragraphs or in article 60.

3. If the ground relates solely to particular clauses, it may be invoked only with respect to those clauses where:

(a) the said clauses are separable from the remainder of the treaty with regard to their application;

(b) it appears from the treaty or is otherwise established that acceptance of those clauses was not an essential basis of the consent of the other party or parties to be bound by the treaty as a whole; and

(c) continued performance of the remainder of the treaty would not be unjust.

4. In cases falling under articles 49 and 50 the State entitled to invoke the fraud or corruption may do so with respect either to the whole treaty or, subject to paragraph 3, to the particular clauses alone.

5. In cases falling under articles 51, 52 and 53, no separation of the provisions of the treaty is permitted.

Article 45
Loss of a right to invoke a ground for invalidating, terminating, withdrawing from or suspending the operation of a treaty

A State may no longer invoke a ground for invalidating, terminating, withdrawing from or suspending the operation of a treaty under articles 46 to 50 or articles 60 and 62 if, after becoming aware of the facts:

(a) it shall have expressly agreed that the treaty is valid or remains in force or continues in operation, as the case may be; or

(b) it must by reason of its conduct be considered as having acquiesced in the validity of the treaty or in its maintenance in force or in operation, as the case may be.

SECTION 2
INVALIDITY OF TREATIES

Article 46
Provisions of internal law regarding competence to conclude treaties

1. A State may not invoke the fact that its consent to be bound by a treaty has been expressed in violation of a provision of its internal law regarding competence to conclude

treaties as invalidating its consent unless that violation was manifest and concerned a rule of its internal law of fundamental importance.

2. A violation is manifest if it would be objectively evident to any State conducting itself in the matter in accordance with normal practice and in good faith.

Article 47
Specific restrictions on authority to express the consent of a State

If the authority of a representative to express the consent of a State to be bound by a particular treaty has been made subject to a specific restriction, his omission to observe that restriction may not be invoked as invalidating the consent expressed by him unless the restriction was notified to the other negotiating States prior to his expressing such consent.

Article 48
Error

1. A State may invoke an error in a treaty as invalidating its consent to be bound by the treaty if the error relates to a fact or situation which was assumed by that State to exist at the time when the treaty was concluded and formed an essential basis of its consent to be bound by the treaty.

2. Paragraph 1 shall not apply if the State in question contributed by its own conduct to the error or if the circumstances were such as to put that State on notice of a possible error.

3. An error relating only to the wording of the text of a treaty does not affect its validity; article 79 then applies.

Article 49
Fraud

If a State has been induced to conclude a treaty by the fraudulent conduct of another negotiating State, the State may invoke the fraud as invalidating its consent to be bound by the treaty.

Article 50
Corruption of a representative of a State

If the expression of a State's consent to be bound by a treaty has been procured through the corruption of its representative directly or indirectly by another negotiating State, the State may invoke such corruption as invalidating its consent to be bound by the treaty.

Article 51
Coercion of a representative of a State

The expression of a State's consent to be bound by a treaty which has been procured by the coercion of its representative through acts or threats directed against him shall be without any legal effect.

Article 52
Coercion of a State by the threat or use of force

A treaty is void if its conclusion has been procured by the threat or use of force in violation of the principles of international law embodied in the Charter of the United Nations.

Article 53
Treaties conflicting with a peremptory norm of general international law (*jus cogens*)

A treaty is void if, at the time of its conclusion, it conflicts with a peremptory norm of general international law. For the purposes of the present Convention, a peremptory norm of general international law is a norm accepted and recognized by the international community of States as a whole as a norm from which no derogation is permitted and which can be modified only by a subsequent norm of general international law having the same character.

SECTION 3
TERMINATION AND SUSPENSION OF THE OPERATION OF TREATIES

Article 54
Termination of or withdrawal from a treaty under its provisions or by consent of the parties

The termination of a treaty or the withdrawal of a party may take place:

(a) in conformity with the provisions of the treaty; or

(b) at any time by consent of all the parties after consultation with the other contracting States.

Article 55
Reduction of the parties to a multilateral treaty below the number necessary for its entry into force

Unless the treaty otherwise provides, a multilateral treaty does not terminate by reason only of the fact that the number of the parties falls below the number necessary for its entry into force.

Article 56
Denunciation of or withdrawal from a treaty containing no provision regarding termination, denunciation or withdrawal

1. A treaty which contains no provision regarding its termination and which does not provide for denunciation or withdrawal is not subject to denunciation or withdrawal unless:

(a) it is established that the parties intended to admit the possibility of denunciation or withdrawal; or

(b) a right of denunciation or withdrawal may be implied by the nature of the treaty.

2. A party shall give not less than twelve months' notice of its intention to denounce or withdraw from a treaty under paragraph 1.

Article 57
Suspension of the operation of a treaty under its provisions or by consent of the parties

The operation of a treaty in regard to all the parties or to a particular party may be suspended:

(a) in conformity with the provisions of the treaty; or

(b) at any time by consent of all the parties after consultation with the other contracting States.

Article 58
Suspension of the operation of a multilateral treaty by agreement between certain of the parties only

1. Two or more parties to a multilateral treaty may conclude an agreement to suspend the operation of provisions of the treaty, temporarily and as between themselves alone, if:

(a) the possibility of such a suspension is provided for by the treaty; or

(b) the suspension in question is not prohibited by the treaty and:

(i) does not affect the enjoyment by the other parties of their rights under the treaty or the performance of their obligations;

(ii) is not incompatible with the object and purpose of the treaty.

2. Unless in a case falling under paragraph 1*(a)* the treaty otherwise provides, the parties in question shall notify the other parties of their intention to conclude the agreement and of those provisions of the treaty the operation of which they intend to suspend.

Article 59
Termination or suspension of the operation of a treaty implied by conclusion of a later treaty

1. A treaty shall be considered as terminated if all the parties to it conclude a later treaty relating to the same subject-matter and:

(a) it appears from the later treaty or is otherwise established that the parties intended that the matter should be governed by that treaty; or

(b) the provisions of the later treaty are so far incompatible with those of the earlier one that the two treaties are not capable of being applied at the same time.

2. The earlier treaty shall be considered as only suspended in operation if it appears from the later treaty or is otherwise established that such was the intention of the parties.

Article 60
Termination or suspension of the operation of a treaty as a consequence of its breach

1. A material breach of a bilateral treaty by one of the parties entitles the other to invoke the breach as a ground for terminating the treaty or suspending its operation in whole or in part.

2. A material breach of a multilateral treaty by one of the parties entitles:

(a) the other parties by unanimous agreement to suspend the operation of the treaty in whole or in part or to terminate it either:

(i) in the relations between themselves and the defaulting State, or

(ii) as between all the parties;

(b) a party specially affected by the breach to invoke it as a ground for suspending the operation of the treaty in whole or in part in the relations between itself and the defaulting State;

(c) any party other than the defaulting State to invoke the breach as a ground for suspending the operation of the treaty in whole or in part with respect to itself if the treaty is of such a character that a material breach of its provisions by one party radically changes the position of every party with respect to the further performance of its obligations under the treaty.

3. A material breach of a treaty, for the purposes of this article, consists in:

(a) a repudiation of the treaty not sanctioned by the present Convention; or

(b) the violation of a provision essential to the accomplishment of the object or purpose of the treaty.

4. The foregoing paragraphs are without prejudice to any provision in the treaty applicable in the event of a breach.

5. Paragraphs 1 to 3 do not apply to provisions relating to the protection of the human person contained in treaties of a humanitarian character, in particular to provisions prohibiting any form of reprisals against persons protected by such treaties.

Article 61
Supervening impossibility of performance

1. A party may invoke the impossibility of performing a treaty as a ground for terminating or withdrawing from it if the impossibility results from the permanent disappearance or destruction of an object indispensable for the execution of the treaty. If the impossibility is temporary, it may be invoked only as a ground for suspending the operation of the treaty.

2. Impossibility of performance may not be invoked by a party as a ground for terminating, withdrawing from or suspending the operation of a treaty if the impossibility is the result of a breach by that party either of an obligation under the treaty or of any other international obligation owed to any other party to the treaty.

Article 62
Fundamental change of circumstances

1. A fundamental change of circumstances which has occurred with regard to those existing at the time of the conclusion of a treaty, and which was not foreseen by the parties, may not be invoked as a ground for terminating or withdrawing from the treaty unless:

(a) the existence of those circumstances constituted an essential basis of the consent of the parties to be bound by the treaty; and

(b) the effect of the change is radically to transform the extent of obligations still to be performed under the treaty.

2. A fundamental change of circumstances may not be invoked as a ground for terminating or withdrawing from a treaty:

(a) if the treaty establishes a boundary; or

(b) if the fundamental change is the result of a breach by the party invoking it either of an obligation under the treaty or of any other international obligation owed to any other party to the treaty.

3. If, under the foregoing paragraphs, a party may invoke a fundamental change of circumstances as a ground for terminating or withdrawing from a treaty it may also invoke the change as a ground for suspending the operation of the treaty.

Article 63
Severance of diplomatic or consular relations

The severance of diplomatic or consular relations between parties to a treaty does not affect the legal relations established between them by the treaty except in so far as the existence of diplomatic or consular relations is indispensable for the application of the treaty.

Article 64
Emergence of a new peremptory norm of general international law (*jus cogens*)

If a new peremptory norm of general international law emerges, any existing treaty which is in conflict with that norm becomes void and terminates.

SECTION 4
PROCEDURE

Article 65
Procedure to be followed with respect to invalidity, termination, withdrawal from or suspension of the operation of a treaty

1. A party which, under the provisions of the present Convention, invokes either a defect in its consent to be bound by a treaty or a ground for impeaching the validity of a treaty, terminating it, withdrawing from it or suspending its operation, must notify the other parties of its claim. The notification shall indicate the measure proposed to be taken with respect to the treaty and the reasons therefor.

2. If, after the expiry of a period which, except in cases of special urgency, shall not be less than three months after the receipt of the notification, no party has raised any objection, the party making the notification may carry out in the manner provided in article 67 the measure which it has proposed.

3. If, however, objection has been raised by any other party, the parties shall seek a solution through the means indicated in article 33 of the Charter of the United Nations.

4. Nothing in the foregoing paragraphs shall affect the rights or obligations of the parties under any provisions in force binding the parties with regard to the settlement of disputes.

5. Without prejudice to article 45, the fact that a State has not previously made the notification prescribed in paragraph 1 shall not prevent it from making such notification in answer to another party claiming performance of the treaty or alleging its violation.

Article 66
Procedures for judicial settlement, arbitration and conciliation

If, under paragraph 3 of article 65, no solution has been reached within a period of 12 months following the date on which the objection was raised, the following procedures shall be followed:

(a) any one of the parties to a dispute concerning the application or the interpretation of articles 53 or 64 may, by a written application, submit it to the International Court of Justice for a decision unless the parties by common consent agree to submit the dispute to arbitration;

(b) any one of the parties to a dispute concerning the application or the interpretation of any of the other articles in Part V of the present Convention may set in motion the procedure specified in the Annex to the Convention by submitting a request to that effect to the Secretary-General of the United Nations.

Article 67
Instruments for declaring invalid, terminating, withdrawing from or suspending the operation of a treaty

1. The notification provided for under article 65 paragraph 1 must be made in writing.

2. Any act declaring invalid, terminating, withdrawing from or suspending the operation of a treaty pursuant to the provisions of the treaty or of paragraphs 2 or 3 of article 65 shall be carried out through an instrument communicated to the other parties. If the instrument is not signed by the Head of State, Head of Government or Minister for Foreign Affairs, the representative of the State communicating it may be called upon to produce full powers.

Article 68
Revocation of notifications and instruments provided for in articles 65 and 67

A notification or instrument provided for in articles 65 or 67 may be revoked at any time before it takes effect.

SECTION 5
CONSEQUENCES OF THE INVALIDITY, TERMINATION OR SUSPENSION OF THE OPERATION OF A TREATY

Article 69
Consequences of the invalidity of a treaty

1. A treaty the invalidity of which is established under the present Convention is void. The provisions of a void treaty have no legal force.

2. If acts have nevertheless been performed in reliance on such a treaty:

(a) each party may require any other party to establish as far as possible in their mutual relations the position that would have existed if the acts had not been performed;

(b) acts performed in good faith before the invalidity was invoked are not rendered unlawful by reason only of the invalidity of the treaty.

3. In cases falling under articles 49, 50, 51 or 52, paragraph 2 does not apply with respect to the party to which the fraud, the act of corruption or the coercion is imputable.

4. In the case of the invalidity of a particular State's consent to be bound by a multilateral treaty, the foregoing rules apply in the relations between that State and the parties to the treaty.

Article 70
Consequences of the termination of a treaty

1. Unless the treaty otherwise provides or the parties otherwise agree, the termination of a treaty under its provisions or in accordance with the present Convention:

(a) releases the parties from any obligation further to perform the treaty;

(b) does not affect any right, obligation or legal situation of the parties created through the execution of the treaty prior to its termination.

2. If a State denounces or withdraws from a multilateral treaty, paragraph 1 applies in the relations between that State and each of the other parties to the treaty from the date when such denunciation or withdrawal takes effect.

Article 71
Consequences of the invalidity of a treaty which conflicts with a peremptory norm of general international law

1. In the case of a treaty which is void under article 53 the parties shall:

(a) eliminate as far as possible the consequences of any act performed in reliance on any provision which conflicts with the peremptory norm of general international law; and

(b) bring their mutual relations into conformity with the peremptory norm of general international law.

2. In the case of a treaty which becomes void and terminates under article 64, the termination of the treaty:

(a) releases the parties from any obligation further to perform the treaty;

(b) does not affect any right, obligation or legal situation of the parties created through the execution of the treaty prior to its termination; provided that those rights, obligations or situations may thereafter be maintained only to the extent that their maintenance is not in itself in conflict with the new peremptory norm of general international law.

Article 72
Consequences of the suspension of the operation of a treaty

1. Unless the treaty otherwise provides or the parties otherwise agree, the suspension of the operation of a treaty under its provisions or in accordance with the present Convention:

(a) releases the parties between which the operation of the treaty is suspended from the obligation to perform the treaty in their mutual relations during the period of the suspension;

(b) does not otherwise affect the legal relations between the parties established by the treaty.

2. During the period of the suspension the parties shall refrain from acts tending to obstruct the resumption of the operation of the treaty.

PART VI
MISCELLANEOUS PROVISIONS

Article 73
Cases of State succession, State responsibility and outbreak of hostilities

The provisions of the present Convention shall not prejudge any question that may arise in regard to a treaty from a succession of States or from the international responsibility of a State or from the outbreak of hostilities between States.

Article 74
Diplomatic and consular relations and the conclusion of treaties

The severance or absence of diplomatic or consular relations between two or more States does not prevent the conclusion of treaties between those States. The conclusion of a treaty does not in itself affect the situation in regard to diplomatic or consular relations.

Article 75
Case of an aggressor State

The provisions of the present Convention are without prejudice to any obligation in relation to a treaty which may arise for an aggressor State in consequence of measures taken in conformity with the Charter of the United Nations with reference to that State's aggression.

PART VII
DEPOSITARIES, NOTIFICATIONS, CORRECTIONS AND REGISTRATION

Article 76
Depositaries of treaties

1. The designation of the depositary of a treaty may be made by the negotiating States, either in the treaty itself or in some other manner. The depositary may be one or more States, an international organization or the chief administrative officer of the organization.

2. The functions of the depositary of a treaty are international in character and the depositary is under an obligation to act impartially in their performance. In particular, the fact that a treaty has not entered into force between certain of the parties or that a difference has appeared between a State and a depositary with regard to the performance of the latter's functions shall not affect that obligation.

Article 77
Functions of depositaries

1. The functions of a depositary, unless otherwise provided in the treaty or agreed by the contracting States, comprise in particular:

(a) keeping custody of the original text of the treaty and of any full powers delivered to the depositary;

(b) preparing certified copies of the original text and preparing any further text of the treaty in such additional languages as may be required by the treaty and transmitting them to the parties and to the States entitled to become parties to the treaty;

(c) receiving any signatures to the treaty and receiving and keeping custody of any instruments, notifications and communications relating to it;

(d) examining whether the signature or any instrument, notification or communication relating to the treaty is in due and proper form and, if need be, bringing the matter to the attention of the State in question;

(e) informing the parties and the States entitled to become parties to the treaty of acts, notifications and communications relating to the treaty;

(f) informing the States entitled to become parties to the treaty when the number of signatures or of instruments of ratification, acceptance, approval or accession required for the entry into force of the treaty has been received or deposited;

(g) registering the treaty with the Secretariat of the United Nations;

(h) performing the functions specified in other provisions of the present Convention.

2. In the event of any difference appearing between a State and the depositary as to the performance of the latter's functions, the depositary shall bring the question to the attention of the signatory States and the contracting States or, where appropriate, of the competent organ of the international organization concerned.

Article 78
Notifications and communications

Except as the treaty or the present Convention otherwise provide, any notification or communication to be made by any State under the present Convention shall:

(a) if there is no depositary, be transmitted direct to the States for which it is intended, or if there is a depositary, to the latter;

(b) be considered as having been made by the State in question only upon its receipt by the State to which it was transmitted or, as the case may be, upon its receipt by the depositary;

(c) if transmitted to a depositary, be considered as received by the State for which it was intended only when the latter State has been informed by the depositary in accordance with article 77, paragraph 1*(e)*.

Article 79
Correction of errors in texts or in certified copies of treaties

1. Where, after the authentication of the text of a treaty, the signatory States and the contracting States are agreed that it contains an error, the error shall, unless they decide upon some other means of correction, be corrected:

(a) by having the appropriate correction made in the text and causing the correction to be initialled by duly authorized representatives;

(b) by executing or exchanging an instrument or instruments setting out the correction which it has been agreed to make; or

(c) by executing a corrected text of the whole treaty by the same procedure as in the case of the original text.

2. Where the treaty is one for which there is a depositary, the latter shall notify the signatory States and the contracting States of the error and of the proposal to correct it and shall specify an appropriate time-limit within which objection to the proposed correction may be raised. If, on the expiry of the time-limit:

(a) no objection has been raised, the depositary shall make and initial the correction in the text and shall execute a *procès-verbal* of the rectification of the text and communicate a copy of it to the parties and to the States entitled to become parties to the treaty;

(b) an objection has been raised, the depositary shall communicate the objection to the signatory States and to the contracting States.

3. The rules in paragraphs 1 and 2 apply also where the text has been authenticated in two or more languages and it appears that there is a lack of concordance which the signatory States and the contracting States agree should be corrected.

4. The corrected text replaces the defective text *ab initio*, unless the signatory States and the contracting States otherwise decide.

5. The correction of the text of a treaty that has been registered shall be notified to the Secretariat of the United Nations.

6. Where an error is discovered in a certified copy of a treaty, the depositary shall execute a *procès-verbal* specifying the rectification and communicate a copy of it to the signatory States and to the contracting States.

Article 80
Registration and publication of treaties

1. Treaties shall, after their entry into force, be transmitted to the Secretariat of the United Nations for registration or filing and recording, as the case may be, and for publication.

2. The designation of a depositary shall constitute authorization for it to perform the acts specified in the preceding paragraph.

PART VIII
FINAL PROVISIONS

Article 81
Signature

The present Convention shall be open for signature by all States Members of the United Nations or of any of the specialized agencies or of the International Atomic Energy Agency or parties to the Statute of the International Court of Justice, and by any other State invited by the General Assembly of the United Nations to become a party to the Convention, as follows: until 30 November 1969, at the Federal Ministry for Foreign Affairs of the Republic of Austria, and subsequently, until 30 April 1970, at United Nations Headquarters, New York.

Article 82
Ratification

The present Convention is subject to ratification. The instruments of ratification shall be deposited with the Secretary-General of the United Nations.

Article 83
Accession

The present Convention shall remain open for accession by any State belonging to any of the categories mentioned in article 81. The instruments of accession shall be deposited with the Secretary-General of the United Nations.

Article 84
Entry into force

1. The present Convention shall enter into force on the thirtieth day following the date of deposit of the thirty-fifth instrument of ratification or accession.

2. For each State ratifying or acceding to the Convention after the deposit of the thirty-fifth instrument of ratification or accession, the Convention shall enter into force on the thirtieth day after deposit by such State of its instrument of ratification or accession.

Article 85
Authentic texts

The original of the present Convention, of which the Chinese, English, French, Russian and Spanish texts are equally authentic, shall be deposited with the Secretary-General of the United Nations.

IN WITNESS WHEREOF the undersigned Plenipotentiaries, being duly authorized thereto by their respective Governments, have signed the present Convention.

DONE at Vienna, this twenty-third day of May, one thousand nine hundred and sixty-nine.

ANNEX

1. A list of conciliators consisting of qualified jurists shall be drawn up and maintained by the Secretary-General of the United Nations. To this end, every State which is a Member of the United Nations or a party to the present Convention shall be invited to nominate two conciliators, and the names of the persons so nominated shall constitute the list. The term of a conciliator, including that of any conciliator nominated to fill a casual vacancy, shall be five years and may be renewed. A conciliator whose term expires shall continue to fulfil any function for which he shall have been chosen under the following paragraph.

2. When a request has been made to the Secretary-General under article 66, the Secretary-General shall bring the dispute before a conciliation commission constituted as follows:

The State or States constituting one of the parties to the dispute shall appoint:

(a) one conciliator of the nationality of that State or of one of those States, who may or may not be chosen from the list referred to in paragraph 1; and

(b) one conciliator not of the nationality of that State or of any of those States, who shall be chosen from the list.

The State or States constituting the other party to the dispute shall appoint two conciliators in the same way. The four conciliators chosen by the parties shall be appointed within sixty days following the date on which the Secretary-General receives the request.

The four conciliators shall, within sixty days following the date of the last of their own appointments, appoint a fifth conciliator chosen from the list, who shall be chairman.

If the appointment of the chairman or of any of the other conciliators has not been made within the period prescribed above for such appointment, it shall be made by the Secretary-General within sixty days following the expiry of that period. The appointment of the chairman may be made by the Secretary-General either from the list or from the membership of the International Law Commission. Any of the periods within which appointments must be made may be extended by agreement between the parties to the dispute.

Any vacancy shall be filled in the manner prescribed for the initial appointment.

3. The Conciliation Commission shall decide its own procedure. The Commission, with the consent of the parties to the dispute, may invite any party to the treaty to submit to it its views orally or in writing. Decisions and recommendations of the Commission shall be made by a majority vote of the five members.

4. The Commission may draw the attention of the parties to the dispute to any measures which might facilitate an amicable settlement.

5. The Commission shall hear the parties, examine the claims and objections, and make proposals to the parties with a view to reaching an amicable settlement of the dispute.

6. The Commission shall report within twelve months of its constitution. Its report shall be deposited with the Secretary-General and transmitted to the parties to the dispute. The report of the Commission, including any conclusions stated therein regarding the facts or questions of law, shall not be binding upon the parties and it shall have no other character than that of recommendations submitted for the consideration of the parties in order to facilitate an amicable settlement of the dispute.

7. The Secretary-General shall provide the Commission with such assistance and facilities as it may require. The expenses of the Commission shall be borne by the United Nations.

Annex III

Vienna Convention on the Law of Treaties between States and International Organizations or between International Organizations (1986)*

The Parties to the present Convention,

Considering the fundamental role of treaties in the history of international relations,

Recognizing the consensual nature of treaties and their ever-increasing importance as a source of international law,

Noting that the principles of free consent and of good faith and the *pacta sunt servanda* rule are universally recognized,

Affirming the importance of enhancing the process of codification and progressive development of international law at a universal level,

Believing that the codification and progressive development of the rules relating to treaties between States and international organizations or between international organizations are means of enhancing legal order in international relations and of serving the purposes of the United Nations,

Having in mind the principles of international law embodied in the Charter of the United Nations, such as the principles of the equal rights and self-determination of peoples, of the sovereign equality and independence of all States, of non-interference in the domestic affairs of States, of the prohibition of the threat or use of force and of universal respect for, and observance of, human rights and fundamental freedoms for all,

Bearing in mind the provisions of the Vienna Convention on the Law of Treaties of 1969,

Recognizing the relationship between the law of treaties between States and the law of treaties between States and international organizations or between international organizations,

---

* Not yet in force. See *Official Records of the United Nations Conference on the Law of Treaties between States and International Organizations or between International Organizations*, vol. II (United Nations publication, Sales No. E.94.V.5).

Considering the importance of treaties between States and international organizations or between international organizations as a useful means of developing international relations and ensuring conditions for peaceful cooperation among nations, whatever their constitutional and social systems,

Having in mind the specific features of treaties to which international organizations are parties as subjects of international law distinct from States,

Noting that international organizations possess the capacity to conclude treaties which is necessary for the exercise of their functions and the fulfillment of their purposes,

Recognizing that the practice of international organizations in concluding treaties with States or between themselves should be in accordance with their constituent instruments,

Affirming that nothing in the present Convention should be interpreted as affecting those relations between an international organization and its members which are regulated by the rules of the organization,

Affirming also that disputes (concerning treaties, like other international disputes, should be settled, in conformity with the Charter of the United Nations, by peaceful means and in conformity with the principles of justice and international law,

Affirming also that the rules of customary international law will continue to govern questions not regulated by the provisions of the present Convention.

Have agreed as follows:

PART I
INTRODUCTION

Article 1
Scope of the present Convention

The present Convention applies to:

(a) treaties between one or more States and one or more international organizations, and

(b) treaties between international organizations.

Article 2
Use of terms

1. For the purposes of the present Convention:

(a) "treaty" means an international agreement governed by international law and concluded in written form:

(i) between one or more States and one or more international organizations; or

(ii) between international organizations, whether that agreement is embodied in a single instrument or in two or more related instruments and whatever its particular designation;

(b) "ratification" means the international act so named whereby a State establishes on the international plane its consent to be bound by a treaty;

(b bis) "act of formal confirmation" means an international act corresponding to that of ratification by a State, whereby an international organization establishes on the international plane its consent to be bound by a treaty;

(b ter) "acceptance", "approval" and "accession" mean in each case the international act so named whereby a State or an international organization establishes on the international plane its consent to be bound by a treaty;

(c) "full powers" means a document emanating from the competent authority of a State or from the competent organ of an international organization designating a person or persons to represent the State or the organization for negotiating, adopting or authenticating the text of a treaty, for expressing the consent of the State or of the organization to be bound by a treaty, or for accomplishing any other act with respect to a treaty;

(d) "reservation" means a unilateral statement, however phrased or named, made by a State or by an international organization when signing, ratifying, formally confirming, accepting, approving or acceding to a treaty, whereby it purports to exclude or to modify the legal effect of certain provisions of the treaty in their application to that State or to that organization;

(e) "negotiating State" and "negotiating organization" mean respectively:

(i) a State, or

(ii) an international organization, which took part in the drawing up and adoption of the text of the treaty;

(f) "contracting State" and "contracting organization" mean respectively:

(i) a State, or

(ii) an international organization, which has consented to be bound by the treaty, whether or not the treaty has entered into force;

(g) "party" means a State or an international organization which has consented to be bound by the treaty and for which the treaty is in force;

(h) "third State" and "third organization" mean respectively:

(i) a State, or

(ii) an international organization, not a party to the treaty;

(i) "international organization" means an intergovernmental organization;

(j) "rules of the organization" means, in particular, the constituent instruments, decisions and resolutions adopted in accordance with them, and established practice of the organization.

2. The provisions of paragraph 1 regarding the use of terms in the present Convention are without prejudice to the use of those terms or to the meanings which may be given to them in the internal law of any State or in the rules of any international organization.

Article 3
International agreements not within the scope of the present Convention

The fact that the present Convention does not apply:

(i) to international agreements to which one or more States, one or more international organizations and one or more subjects of international law other than States or organizations are parties;

(ii) to international agreements to which one or more international organizations and one or more subjects of international law other than States or organizations are parties;

(iii) to international agreements not in written form between one or more States and one or more international organizations, or between international organizations; or

(iv) to international agreements between subjects of international law other than States or international organizations;

shall not affect:

(a) the legal force of such agreements;

(b) the application to them of any of the rules set forth in the present Convention to which they would be subject under international law independently of the Convention;

(c) the application of the Convention to the relations between States and international organizations or to the relations of organizations as between themselves, when those relations are governed by international agreements to which other subjects of international law are also parties.

Article 4
Non-retroactivity of the present Convention

Without prejudice to the application of any rules set forth in the present Convention to which treaties between one or more States and one or more international organizations or between international organizations would be subject under international law independently of the Convention, the Convention applies only to such treaties concluded after the entry into force of the present Convention with regard to those States and those organizations.

Article 5
Treaties constituting international organizations and treaties adopted within an international organization

The present Convention applies to any treaty between one or more States and one or more international organizations which is the constituent instrument of an international organization and to any treaty adopted within an international organization, without prejudice to any relevant rules of the organization.

PART II
CONCLUSION AND ENTRY INTO FORCE OF TREATIES

SECTION 1
CONCLUSION OF TREATIES

Article 6
Capacity of international organizations to conclude treaties

The capacity of an international organization to conclude treaties is governed by the rules of that organization.

Article 7
Full powers

1. A person is considered as representing a State for the purpose of adopting or authenticating the text of a treaty or for the purpose of expressing the consent of the State to be bound by a treaty if:

(a) that person produces appropriate full powers; or

(b) it appears from practice or from other circumstances that it was the intention of the States and international organizations concerned to consider that person as representing the State for such purposes without having to produce full powers.

2. In virtue of their functions and without having to produce full powers, the following are considered as representing their State:

(a) Heads of State, Heads of Government and Ministers for Foreign Affairs, for the purpose of performing all acts relating to the conclusion of a treaty between one or more States and one or more international organizations;

(b) representatives accredited by States to an international conference, for the purpose of adopting the text of a treaty between States and international organizations;

(c) representatives accredited by States to an international organization or one of its organs, for the purpose of adopting the text of a treaty in that organization or organ;

(d) heads of permanent missions to an international organization, for the purpose of adopting the text of a treaty between the accrediting States and that organization.

3. A person is considered as representing an international organization for the purpose of adopting or authenticating the text of a treaty, or expressing the consent of that organization to be bound by a treaty if:

(a) that person produces appropriate full powers; or

(b) it appears from the circumstances that it was the intention of the States and international organizations concerned to consider that person as representing the organization for such purposes, in accordance with the rules of the organization, without having to produce full powers.

Article 8
Subsequent confirmation of an act performed without authorization

An act relating to the conclusion of a treaty performed by a person who cannot be considered under article 7 as authorized to represent a State or an international organization for that purpose is without legal effect unless afterwards confirmed by that State or that organization.

Article 9
Adoption of the text

1. The adoption of the text of a treaty takes place by the consent of all the states and international organizations or, as the case may be, all the organizations participating in its drawing up except as provided in paragraph 2.

2. The adoption of the text of a treaty at an international conference takes place in accordance with the procedure agreed upon by the participants in that conference. If,

however, no agreement is reached on any such procedure, the adoption of the text shall take place by the vote of two-thirds of the participants present and voting unless by the same majority they shall decide to apply a different rule.

Article 10
Authentication of the text

1. The text of a treaty between one or more States and one or more international organizations is established as authentic and definitive:

(a) by such procedure as may be provided for in the text or agreed upon by the States and organizations participating in its drawing up; or

(b) failing such procedure, by the signature, signature ad referendum or initialling by the representatives of those States and those organizations of the text of the treaty or of the Final Act of a conference incorporating the text.

2. The text of a treaty between international organizations is established as authentic and definitive:

(a) by such procedure as may be provided for in the text or agreed upon by the organizations participating in its drawing up; or

(b) failing such procedure, by the signature, signature ad referendum or initialling by the representatives of those organizations of the text of the treaty or of the Final Act of a conference incorporating the text.

Article 11
Means of expressing consent to be bound by a treaty

1. The consent of a State to be bound by a treaty may be expressed by signature, exchange of instruments constituting a treaty, ratification, acceptance, approval or accession, or by any other means if so agreed.

2. The consent of an international organization to be bound by a treaty may be expressed by signature, exchange of instruments constituting a treaty, act of formal confirmation, acceptance, approval or accession, or by any other means if so agreed.

Article 12
Consent to be bound by a treaty expressed by signature

1. The consent of a State or of an international organization to be bound by a treaty is expressed by the signature of the representative of that State or of that organization when:

(a) the treaty provides that signature shall have that effect;

(b) it is otherwise established that the negotiating States and negotiating organizations or, as the case any be, the negotiating organizations were agreed that signature should have that effect; or

(c) the intention of the State or organization to give that effect to the signature appears from the full powers of its representative or was expressed during the negotiation.

2. For the purposes of paragraph 1:

(a) the initialling of a text constitutes a signature of the treaty when it is established that the negotiating States and negotiating organizations or, as the case may be, the negotiating organizations so agreed;

(b) the signature ad referendum of a treaty by the representative of a State or an international organization, if confirmed by his State or organization, constitutes a full signature of the treaty.

Article 13
Consent to be bound by a treaty expressed by an exchange of instruments constituting a treaty

The consent of States or of international organizations to be bound by a treaty constituted by instruments exchanged between them is expressed by that exchange when:

(a) the instruments provide that their exchange shall have that effect; or

(b) it is otherwise established that those States and those organizations or, as the case may be, those organizations were agreed that the exchange of instruments should have that effect.

Article 14
Consent to be bound by a treaty expressed by ratification, act of formal confirmation, acceptance or approval

1. The consent of a State to be bound by at treaty is expressed by ratification when;

(a) the treaty provides for such consent to be expressed by means of ratification;

(b) it is otherwise established that the negotiating States and negotiating organizations were agreed that ratification should be required;

(c) the representative of the State has signed the treaty subject to ratification; or

(d) the intention of the State to sign the treaty subject to ratification appears from the full powers of its representative or was expressed during the negotiation.

2. The consent of an international organization to be bound by a treaty is expressed by an act of formal confirmation when:

(a) the treaty provides for such consent to be expressed by means of an act of formal confirmation;

(b) it is otherwise established that the negotiating States and negotiating organizations or, as the case may be, the negotiating organizations were agreed that an act of formal confirmation should be required;

(c) the representative of the organization has signed the treaty subject to an act of formal confirmation; or

(d) the intention of the organization to sign the treaty subject to an act of formal confirmation appears from the full powers of its representative or was expressed during the negotiation.

3. The consent of a State or of an international organization to be bound by a treaty is expressed by acceptance or approval under conditions similar to those which apply to ratification or, as the case may be, to an act of formal confirmation.

Article 15
Consent to be bound by a treaty expressed by accession

The consent of a State or of an international organization to be bound by a treaty is expressed by accession when:

(a) the treaty provides that such consent may be expressed by that State or that organization by means of accession;

(b) it is otherwise established that the negotiating States and negotiating organizations or, as the case may be, the negotiating organizations were agreed that such consent may be expressed by that State or that organization by means of accession; or

(c) all the parties have subsequently agreed that such consent may be expressed by that State or that organization by means of accession.

Article 16
Exchange or deposit of instruments of ratification, formal confirmation, acceptance, approval or accession

1. Unless the treaty otherwise provides, instruments of ratification, instruments relating to an act of formal confirmation or instruments of acceptance, approval or accession establish the consent of a State or of an international organization to be bound by treaty between one or more States and one or more international organizations upon:

(a) their exchange between the contracting States and contracting organizations;

(b) their deposit with the depositary; or

(c) their notification to the contracting States and to the contracting organizations or to the depositary, if so agreed.

2. Unless the treaty otherwise provides, instruments relating to an act of formal confirmation or instruments of acceptance, approval or accession establish the consent of an international organization to be bound by a treaty between international organizations upon:

(a) their exchange between the contracting organizations;

(b) their deposit with the depositary; or

(c) their notification to the contracting organizations or to the depositary, if so agreed.

Article 17
Consent to be bound by part of a treaty and choice of differing provisions

1. Without prejudice to articles 19 to 23, the consent of a State or of an international organization to be bound by part of a treaty is effective only if the treaty so permits, or if the contracting States and contracting organizations or, as the case may be, the contracting organizations so agree.

2. The consent of a State or of an international organization to be bound by a treaty which permits a choice between differing provisions is effective only if it is made clear to which of the provisions the consent relates.

Article 18
Obligation not to defeat the object and purpose of a treaty prior to its entry into force

A State or an international organization is obliged to refrain from acts which would defeat the object and purpose of a treaty when:

(a) that State or that organization has signed the treaty or has exchanged instruments constituting the treaty subject to ratification, act of formal confirmation, acceptance or approval, until that State or that organization shall have made its intention clear not to become a party to the treaty; or

(b) that State or that organization has expressed its consent to be bound by the treaty, pending the entry into force of the treaty and provided that such entry into force is not unduly delayed.

SECTION 2
RESERVATIONS

Article 19
Formulation of reservations

A State or an international organization may, when signing, ratifying, formally confirming, accepting, approving or acceding to a treaty, formulate a reservation unless:

(a) the reservation is prohibited by the treaty;

(b) the treaty provides that only specified reservations, which do not include the reservation in question, may be made; or

(c) in cases not falling under sub-paragraphs *(a)* and *(b)*, the reservation is incompatible with the object and purpose of the treaty.

Article 20
Acceptance of and objection to reservations

1. A reservation expressly authorized by a treaty does not require any subsequent acceptance by the contracting States and contracting organizations or, as the case may be, by the contracting organizations unless the treaty so provides.

2. When it appears from the limited number of the negotiating States and negotiating organizations or, as the case may be, of the negotiating organizations and the object and purpose of a treaty that the application of the treaty in its entirety between all the parties is an essential condition of the consent of each one to be bound by the treaty, a reservation requires acceptance by all the parties.

3. When a treaty is a constituent instrument of an international organization and unless it otherwise provides, a reservation requires the acceptance of the competent organ of that organization.

4. In cases not falling under the preceding paragraphs and unless the treaty otherwise provides:

(a) acceptance of a reservation by a contracting State or by a contracting organization constitutes the reserving State or international organization a party to the treaty in relation to the accepting State or organization if or when the treaty is in force for the reserving State or organization and for the accepting State or organization;

(b) an objection by a contracting State or by a contracting organization to a reservation does not preclude the entry into force of the treaty as between the objecting State or international organization and the reserving State or organization unless a contrary intention is definitely expressed by the objecting State or organization;

(c) an act expressing the consent of a State or of an international organization to be bound by the treaty and containing a reservation is effective as soon as at least one contracting State or one contracting organization has accepted the reservation.

5. For the purposes of paragraphs 2 and 4 and unless the treaty otherwise provides, a reservation is considered to have been accepted by a State or an international organization if it shall have raised no objection to the reservation by the end of a period of twelve months after it was notified of the reservation or by the date on which it expressed its consent to be bound by the treaty, whichever is later.

Article 21

Legal effects of reservations and of objections to reservations

1. A reservation established with regard to another party in accordance with articles 19, 20 and 23:

(a) modifies for the reserving State or international organization in its relations with that other party the provisions of the treaty to which the reservation relates to the extent of the reservation; and

(b) modifies those provisions to the same extent for that other party in its relations with the reserving State or international organization.

2. The reservation does not modify the provisions of the treaty for the other parties to the treaty inter se.

3. When a State or an international organization objecting to a reservation has not opposed the entry into force of the treaty between itself and the reserving State or organization, the provisions to which the reservation relates do not apply as between the reserving State or organization and the objecting State or organization to the extent of the reservation.

Article 22

Withdrawal of reservations and of objections to reservations

1. Unless the treaty otherwise provides, a reservation may be withdrawn at any time and the consent of a State or of an international organization which has accepted the reservation is not required for its withdrawal.

2. Unless the treaty otherwise provides, an objection to a reservation may be withdrawn at any time.

3. Unless the treaty otherwise provides, or it is otherwise agreed:

(a) the withdrawal of a reservation becomes operative in relation to a contracting State or a contracting organization only when notice of it has been received by that State or that organization;

(b) the withdrawal of an objection to a reservation becomes operative only when notice of it has been received by the State or international organization which formulated the reservation.

Article 23
Procedure regarding reservations

1. A reservation, an express acceptance of a reservation and an objection to a reservation must be formulated in writing and communicated to the contracting States and contracting organizations and other States and international organizations entitled to become parties to the treaty.

2. If formulated when signing the treaty subject to ratification, act of formal confirmation, acceptance or approval, a reservation must be formally confirmed by the reserving State or international organization when expressing its consent to be bound by the treaty. In such a case the reservation shall be considered as having been made on the date of its confirmation.

3. An express acceptance of, or an objection to, a reservation made previously to confirmation of the reservation does not itself require confirmation.

4. The withdrawal of a reservation or of an objection to a reservation must be formulated in writing.

SECTION 3
ENTRY INTO FORCE AND PROVISIONAL APPLICATION OF TREATIES

Article 24
Entry into force

1. A treaty enters into force in such manner and upon such date as it may provide or as the negotiating States and negotiating organizations or, as the case may be, the negotiating organizations may agree.

2. Failing any such provision or agreement, a treaty enters into force as soon as consent to be bound by the treaty has been established for all the negotiating States and negotiating organizations or, as the case may be, all the negotiating organizations.

3. When the consent of a State or of an international organization to be bound by a treaty is established on a date after the treaty has come into force, the treaty enters into force for that State or that organization on that date, unless the treaty otherwise provides.

4. The provisions of a treaty regulating the authentication of its text, the establishment of consent to be bound by the treaty, the manner or date of its entry into force, reservations, the functions of the depositary and other matters arising necessarily before the entry into force of the treaty apply from the time of the adoption of its text.

Article 25
Provisional application

1. A treaty or a part of a treaty is applied provisionally pending its entry into force if:

(a) the treaty itself so provides; or

(b) the negotiating States and negotiating organizations or, as the case may be, the negotiating organizations have in some other manner so agreed.

2. Unless the treaty otherwise provides or the negotiating States and negotiating organizations or, as the case may be, the negotiating organizations have otherwise agreed, the provisional application of a treaty or a part of a treaty with respect to a State or an international organization shall be terminated if that State or that organization notifies the States and organizations with regard to which the treaty is being applied provisionally of its intention not to become a party to the treaty.

PART III
OBSERVANCE, APPLICATION AND INTERPRETATION OF TREATIES

SECTION 1
OBSERVANCE OF TREATIES

Article 26
Pacta sunt servanda

Every treaty in force is binding upon the parties to it and must be performed by them in good faith.

Article 27
Internal law of States, rules of international organizations and observance of treaties

1. A State party to a treaty may not invoke the provisions of its internal law as justification for its failure to perform the treaty.

2. An international organization party to a treaty may not invoke the rules of the organization as justification for its failure to perform the treaty.

3. The rules contained in the preceding paragraphs are without prejudice to article 46.

SECTION 2
APPLICATION OF TREATIES

Article 28
Non-retroactivity of treaties

Unless a different intention appears from the treaty or is otherwise established, its provisions do not bind a party in relation to any act or fact which took place or any situation which ceased to exist before the date of the entry into force of the treaty with respect to that party.

Article 29
Territorial scope of treaties

Unless a different intention appears from the treaty or is otherwise established, a treaty between one or more States and one or more international organizations is binding upon each State party in respect of its entire territory.

Article 30
Application of successive treaties relating to the same subject-matter

1. The rights and obligations of States and international organizations parties to successive treaties relating to the same subject-matter shall be determined in accordance with the following paragraphs.

2. When a treaty specifies that it is subject to, or that it is not to be considered as incompatible with, an earlier or later treaty, the provisions of that other treaty prevail.

3. When all the parties to the earlier treaty are parties also to the later treaty but the earlier treaty is not terminated or suspended in operation under article 59, the earlier treaty applies only to the extent that its provisions are compatible with those of the later treaty.

4. When the parties to the later treaty do not include all the parties to the earlier one:

(a) as between two parties, each of which is a party to both treaties, the same rule applies as in paragraph 3;

(b) as between at party to both treaties and a party to only one of the treaties, the treaty to which both are parties governs their mutual rights and obligations.

5. Paragraph 4 is without prejudice to article 41, or to any question of the termination or suspension of the operation of a treaty under article 60 or to any question of responsibility which may arise for a State or for an international organization from the conclusion or application of a treaty the provisions of which are incompatible with its obligations towards a State or an organization under another treaty.

6. The preceding paragraphs are without prejudice to the fact that, in the event of a conflict between obligations under the Charter of the United Nations and obligations under a treaty, the obligations under the Charter shall prevail.

SECTION 3
INTERPRETATION OF TREATIES

Article 31
General rule of interpretation

1. A treaty shall be interpreted in good faith in accordance with the ordinary meaning to be given to the terms of the treaty in their context and in the light of its object and purpose.

2. The context for the purpose of the interpretation of a treaty shall comprise, in addition to the text, including its preamble and annexes:

(a) any agreement relating to the treaty which was made between all the parties in connection with the conclusion of the treaty;

(b) any instrument which was made by one or more parties in connection with the conclusion of the treaty and accepted by the other parties as an instrument related to the treaty.

3. There shall be taken into account, together with the context:

(a) any subsequent agreement between the parties regarding the interpretation of the treaty or the application of its provisions;

(b) any subsequent practice in the application of the treaty which establishes the agreement of the parties regarding its interpretation;

(c) any relevant rules of international law applicable in the relations between the parties.

4. A special meaning shall be given to a term if it is established that the parties so intended.

Article 32
Supplementary means of interpretation

Recourse may be had to supplementary means of interpretation, including the preparatory work of the treaty and the circumstances of its conclusion, in order to confirm the meaning resulting from the application of article 31, or to determine the meaning when the interpretation according to article 31:

(a) leaves the meaning ambiguous or obscure; or

(b) leads to a result which is manifestly absurd or unreasonable.

Article 33
Interpretation of treaties authenticated in two or more languages

1. When a treaty has been authenticated in two or more languages, the text is equally authoritative in each language, unless the treaty provides or the parties agree that, in case of divergence, a particular text shall prevail.

2. A version of the treaty in a language other than one of those in which the text was authenticated shall be considered an authentic text only if the treaty so provides or the parties so agree.

3. The terms of a treaty are presumed to have the same meaning in each authentic text.

4. Except where a particular text prevails in accordance with paragraph 1, when a comparison of the authentic texts discloses a difference of meaning which the application of articles 31 and 32 does not remove, the meaning which best reconciles the texts, having regard to the object and purpose of the treaty, shall be adopted.

SECTION 4
TREATIES AND THIRD STATES OR THIRD ORGANIZATIONS

Article 34
General rule regarding third States and third organizations

A treaty does not create either obligations or rights for a third State or a third organization without the consent of that State or that organization.

Article 35
Treaties providing for obligations for third States or third organizations

An obligation arises for a third State or a third organization from a provision of a treaty if the parties to the treaty intend the provision to be the means of establishing the obligation and the third State or the third organization expressly accepts that obligation in writing. Acceptance by the third organization of such an obligation shall be governed by the rules of that organization.

Article 36
Treaties providing for rights for third States or third organizations

1. A right arises for a third State from a provision of a treaty if the parties to the treaty intend the provision to accord that right either to the third State, or to a group of States to which it belongs, or to all States, and the third State assents thereto. Its assent shall be presumed so long as the contrary is not indicated, unless the treaty otherwise provides.

2. A right arises for a third organization from a provision of a teaty if the parties to the treaty intend the provision to accord that right either to the third organization, or to a group of international organizations to which it belongs, or to all organizations, and the third organization assents thereto. Its assent shall be governed by the rules of the organization.

3. A State or an international organization exercising a right in accordance with paragraph 1 or 2 shall comply with the conditions for its exercise provided for in the treaty or established in conformity with the treaty.

Article 37
Revocation or modification of obligations or rights of third States or third organizations

1. When an obligation has arisen for a third State or a third organization in conformity with article 35, the obligation may be revoked or modified only with the consent of the parties to the treaty and of the third State or the third organization, unless it is established that they had otherwise agreed.

2. When a right has arisen for a third State or a third organization in conformity with article 36, the right may not be revoked or modified by the parties if it is established that the right was intended not to be revocable or subject to modification without the consent of the third State or the third organization.

3. The consent of an international organization party to the treaty or of a third organization, as provided for in the foregoing paragraphs, shall be governed by the rules of that organization.

Article 38
Rules in a treaty becoming binding on third States or third organizations through international custom

Nothing in articles 34 to 37 precludes a rule set forth in a treaty from becoming binding upon a third State or a third organization as a customary rule of international law, recognized as such.

PART IV
AMENDMENT AND MODIFICATION OF TREATIES

Article 39
General rule regarding the amendment of treaties

1. A treaty may be amended by agreement between the parties. The rules laid down in Part II apply to such an agreement except in so far as the treaty may otherwise provide.

2. The consent of an international organization to an agreement provided for in paragraph 1 shall be governed by the rules of that organization.

Article 40
Amendment of multilateral treaties

1. Unless the treaty otherwise provides, the amendment of multilateral treaties shall be governed by the following paragraphs.

2. Any proposal to amend a multilateral treaty as between all the parties must be notified to all the contracting States and all the contracting organizations, each one of which shall have the right to take part in:

(a) the decision as to the action to be taken in regard to such proposal;

(b) the negotiation and conclusion of any agreement for the amendment of the treaty.

3. Every State or international organization entitled to become a party to the treaty shall also be entitled to become a party to the treaty as amended.

4. The amending agreement does not bind any State or international organization already a party to the treaty which does not become a party to the amending agreement; article 30, paragraph 4*(b)*, applies in relation to such State or organization.

5. Any State or international organization which becomes a party to the treaty after the entry into force of the amending agreement shall, failing an expression of a different intention by that State or that organization:

(a) be considered as a party to the treaty as amended; and

(b) be considered as a party to the unamended treaty in relation to any party to the treaty not bound by the amending agreement.

Article 41
Agreements to modify multilateral treaties between certain of the parties only

1. Two or more of the parties to a multilateral treaty may conclude an agreement to modify the treaty as between themselves alone if:

(a) the possibility of such a modification is provided for by the treaty; or (b) the modification in question is not prohibited by the treaty and:

(i) does not affect the enjoyment by the other parties of their rights under the treaty or the performance of their obligations;

(ii) does not relate to a provision, derogation from which is incompatible with the effective execution of the object and purpose of the treaty as a whole.

2. Unless in a case falling under paragraph 1*(a)* the treaty otherwise provides, the parties in question shall notify the other parties of their intention to conclude the agreement and of the modification to the treaty for which it provides.

PART V
INVALIDITY, TERMINATION AND SUSPENSION OF THE OPERATION OF TREATIES

SECTION 1
GENERAL PROVISIONS

Article 42
Validity and continuance in force of treaties

1. The validity of a treaty or of the consent of a State or an international organization to be bound by a treaty may be impeached only through the application of the present Convention.

2. The termination of a treaty, its denunciation or the withdrawal of a party, may take place only as a result of the application of the provisions of the treaty or of the present Convention. The same rule applies to suspension of the operation of a treaty.

Article 43
Obligations imposed by international law independently of a treaty

The invalidity, termination or denunciation of a treaty, the withdrawal of a party from it, or the suspension of its operation, as a result of the application of the present Convention or of the provisions of the treaty, shall not in any way impair the duty of any State or of any international organization to fulfil any obligation embodied in the treaty to which that State or that organization would be subject under international law independently of the treaty.

Article 44
Separability of treaty provisions

1. A right of a party, provided for in a treaty or arising under article 56, to denounce, withdraw from or suspend the operation of the treaty may be exercised only with respect to the whole treaty unless the treaty otherwise provides or the parties otherwise agree.

2. A ground for invalidating, terminating, withdrawing from or suspending the operation of a treaty recognized in the present Convention may be invoked only with respect to the whole treaty except as provided in the following paragraphs or in article 60.

3. If the ground relates solely to particular clauses, it may be invoked only with respect to those clauses where:

(a) the said clauses are separable from the remainder of the treaty with regard to their application;

(b) it appears from the treaty or is otherwise established that acceptance of those clauses was not an essential basis of the consent of the other party or parties to be bound by the treaty as a whole; and

(c) continued performance of the remainder of the treaty would not be unjust.

4. In cases falling under articles 49 and 50, the State or international organization entitled to invoke the fraud or corruption may do so with respect either to the whole treaty or, subject to paragraph 3, to the particular clauses alone.

5. In cases falling under articles 51, 52 and 53, no separation of the provisions of the treaty is permitted.

Article 45
Loss of a right to invoke a ground for invalidating, terminating, withdrawing from or suspending the operation of a treaty

1. A State may no longer invoke a ground for invalidating, terminating, withdrawing from or suspending the operation of a treaty under articles 46 to 50 or articles 60 and 62 if, after becoming aware of the facts:

(a) it shall have expressly agreed that the treaty is valid or remains in force or continues in operation, as the case may be; or

(b) it must by reason of its conduct be considered as having acquiesced in the validity of the treaty or in its maintenance in force or in operation, as the case may be.

2. An international organization may no longer invoke a ground for invalidating, terminating, withdrawing from or suspending the operation of a treaty under articles 46 to 50 or articles 60 and 62 if, after becoming aware of the facts:

(a) it shall have expressly agreed that the treaty is valid or remains in force or continues in operation, as the case may be; or

(b) it must by reason of the conduct of the competent organ be considered as having renounced the right to invoke that ground.

SECTION 2
INVALIDITY OF TREATIES

Article 46
Provisions of internal law of a State and rules of an international organization regarding competence to conclude treaties

1. A State may not invoke the fact that its consent to be bound by a treaty has been expressed in violation of a provision of its internal law regarding competence to conclude treaties as invalidating its consent unless that violation was manifest and concerned a rule of its internal law of fundamental importance.

2. An international organization may not invoke the fact that its consent to be bound by a treaty has been expressed in violation of the rules of the organization regarding competence to conclude treaties as invalidating its consent unless that violation was manifest and concerned a rule of fundamental importance.

3. A violation is manifest if it would be objectively evident to any State or any international organization conducting itself in the matter in accordance with the normal practice of States and, where appropriate, of international organizations and in good faith.

Article 47
Specific restrictions on authority to express the consent of a State or an international organization

If the authority of a representative to express the consent of a State or of an international organization to be bound by a particular treaty has been made subject to a specific restriction, his omission to observe that restriction may not be invoked as invalidating the consent expressed by him unless the restriction was notified to the negotiating States and negotiating organizations prior to his expressing such consent.

Article 48
Error

1. A State or an international organization may invoke an error in a treaty as invalidating its consent to be bound by the treaty if the error relates to a fact or situation which was assumed by that State or that organization to exist at the time when the treaty was concluded and formed an essential basis of the consent of that State or that organization to be bound by the treaty.

2. Paragraph 1 shall not apply if the State or international organization in question contributed by its own conduct to the error or if the circumstances were such as to put that State or that organization on notice of a possible error.

3. An error relating only to the wording of the text of a treaty does not affect its validity; article 80 then applies.

Article 49
Fraud

A State or an international organization induced to conclude a treaty by the fraudulent conduct of a negotiating State or a negotiating organization may invoke the fraud as invalidating its consent to be bound by the treaty.

Article 50
Corruption of a representative of a State or of an international organization

A State or an international organization the expression of whose consent to be bound by a treaty has been procured through the corruption of its representative directly or indirectly by a negotiating State or a negotiating organization may invoke such corruption as invalidating its consent to be bound by the treaty.

Article 51
Coercion of a representative of a State or of an international organization

The expression by a State or an international organization of consent to be bound by a treaty which has been procured by the coercion of the representative of that State or that organization through acts or threats directed against him shall be without any legal effect.

Article 52
Coercion of a State or of an international organization by the threat or use of force

A treaty is void if its conclusion has been procured by the threat or use of force in violation of the principles of international law embodied in the Charter of the United Nations.

Article 53
Treaties conflicting with a peremptory norm of general international law (*jus cogens*)

A treaty is void if, at the time of its conclusion, it conflicts with a peremptory norm of general international law. For the purposes of the present Convention, a peremptory norm of general international law is a norm accepted and recognized by the international community of States as a whole as a norm from which no derogation is permitted and which can be modified only by a subsequent norm of general international law having the same character.

SECTION 3
TERMINATION AND SUSPENSION OF THE OPERATION OF TREATIES

Article 54
Termination of or withdrawal from a treaty under its provisions or by consent of the parties

The termination of a treaty or the withdrawal of a party may take place:

(a) in conformity with the provisions of the treaty; or

(b) at any time by consent of all the parties after consultation with the contracting States and contracting organizations.

Article 55
Reduction of the parties to a multilateral treaty below the number necessary for its entry into force

Unless the treaty otherwise provides, a multilateral treaty does not terminate by reason only of the fact that the number of the parties falls below the number necessary for its entry into force.

Article 56
Denunciation of or withdrawal from a treaty containing no provision regarding termination, denunciation or withdrawal

1. A treaty which contains no provision regarding its termination and which does not provide for denunciation or withdrawal is not subject to denunciation or withdrawal unless:

(a) it is established that the parties intended to admit the possibility of denunciation or withdrawal; or

(b) a right of denunciation or withdrawal may be implied by the nature of the treaty.

2. A party shall give not less than twelve months' notice of its intention to denounce or withdraw from a treaty under paragraph 1.

Article 57

Suspension of the operation of a treaty under its provisions or by consent of the parties

The operation of a treaty in regard to all the parties or to a particular party may be suspended:

(a) in conformity with the provisions of the treaty; or

(b) at any time by consent of all the parties after consultation with the contracting States and contracting organizations.

Article 58

Suspension of the operation of a multilateral treaty by agreement between certain of the parties only

1. Two or more parties to a multilateral treaty may conclude an agreement to suspend the operation of provisions of the treaty, temporarily and as between themselves alone, if:

(a) the possibility of such a suspension is provided for by the treaty; or

(b) the suspension in question is not prohibited by the treaty and:

(i) does not affect the enjoyment by the other parties of their rights under the treaty or the performance of their obligations;

(ii) is not incompatible with the object and purpose of the treaty.

2. Unless in a case falling under paragraph 1 *(a)* the treaty otherwise provides, the parties in question shall notify the other parties of their intention to conclude the agreement and of those provisions of the treaty the operation of which they intend to suspend.

Article 59

Termination or suspension of the operation of a treaty implied by conclusion of a later treaty

1. A treaty shall be considered as terminated if all the parties to it conclude a later treaty relating to the same subject-matter and:

(a) it appears from the later treaty or is otherwise established that the parties intended that the matter should be governed by that treaty; or

(b) the provisions of the later treaty are so far incompatible with those of the earlier one that the two treaties are not capable of being applied at the same time.

2. The earlier treaty shall be considered as only suspended in operation if it appears from the later treaty or is otherwise established that such was the intention of the parties.

Article 60

Termination or suspension of the operation of a treaty as a consequence of its breach

1. A material breach of a bilateral treaty by one of the parties entitles the other to invoke the breach as a ground for terminating the treaty or suspending its operation in whole or in part.

2. A material breach of a multilateral treaty by one of the parties entitles:

(a) the other parties by unanimous agreement to suspend the operation of the treaty in whole or in part or to terminate it either:

(i) in the relations between themselves and the defaulting State or international organization, or

(ii) as between all the parties;

(b) a party specially affected by the breach to invoke it as a ground for suspending the operation of the treaty in whole or in part in the relations between itself and the defaulting State or international organization;

(c) any party other than the defaulting State or international organization to invoke the breach as a ground for suspending the operation of the treaty in whole or in part with respect to itself if the treaty is of such a character that a material breach of its provisions by one party radically changes the position of every party with respect to the further performance of its obligations under the treaty.

3. A material breach of a treaty, for the purposes of this article, consists in;

(a) a repudiation of the treaty not sanctioned by the present Convention; or

(b) the violation of a provision essential to the accomplishment of the object or purpose of the treaty.

4. The foregoing paragraphs are without prejudice to any provision in the treaty applicable in the event of a breach.

5. Paragraphs 1 to 3 do not apply to provisions relating to the protection of the human person contained in treaties of a humanitarian character, in particular to provisions prohibiting any form of reprisals against persons protected by such treaties.

Article 61
Supervening impossibility of performance

1. A party may invoke the impossibility of performing a treaty as a ground for terminating or withdrawing from it if the impossibility results from the permanent disappearance or destruction of an object indispensable for the execution of the treaty. If the impossibility is temporary, it may be invoked only as a ground for suspending the operation of the treaty.

2. Impossibility of performance may not be invoked by a party as a ground for terminating, withdrawing from or suspending the operation of a treaty if the impossibility is the result of a breach by that party either of an obligation under the treaty or of any other international obligation owed to any other party to the treaty.

Article 62
Fundamental change of circumstances

1. A fundamental change of circumstances which has occurred with regard to those existing at the time of the conclusion of a treaty, and which was not foreseen by the parties, may not be invoked as a ground for terminating or withdrawing from the treaty unless:

(a) the existence of those circumstances constituted an essential basis of the consent of the parties to be bound by the treaty; and

(b) the effect of the change is radically to transform the extent of obligations still to be performed under the treaty.

2. A fundamental change of circumstances may not be invoked as a ground for terminating or withdrawing from a treaty between two or more States and one or more international organizations if the treaty establishes a boundary.

3. A fundamental change of circumstances may not be invoked as a ground for terminating or withdrawing from a treaty if the fundamental change is the result of a breach by the party invoking it either of an obligation under the treaty or of any other international obligation owed to any other party to the treaty.

4. If, under the foregoing paragraphs, a party may invoke a fundamental change of circumstances as a ground for terminating or withdrawing from a treaty it may also invoke the change as a ground for suspending the operation of the treaty.

Article 63
Severance of diplomatic or consular relations

The severance of diplomatic or consular relations between States parties to a treaty between two or more States and one or more international organizations does not affect the legal relations established between those States by the treaty except in so far as the existence of diplomatic or consular relations is indispensable for the application of the treaty.

Article 64
Emergence of a new peremptory norm of general international law (*jus cogens*)

If a new peremptory norm of general international law emerges, any existing treaty which is in conflict with that norm becomes void and terminates.

SECTION 4
PROCEDURE

Article 65
Procedure to be followed with respect to invalidity, termination, withdrawal from or suspension of the operation of a treaty

1. A party which, under the provisions of the present Convention, invokes either a defect in its consent to be bound by a treaty or a ground for impeaching the validity of a treaty, terminating it, withdrawing from it or suspending its operation, must notify the other parties of its claim. The notification shall indicate the measure proposed to be taken with respect to the treaty and the reasons therefor.

2. If, after the expiry of a period which, except in cases of special urgency, shall not be less than three months after the receipt of the notification, no party has raised any objection, the party making the notification may carry out in the manner provided in article 67 the measure which it has proposed.

3. If, however, objection has been raised by any other party, the parties shall seek a solution through the means indicated in Article 33 of the Charter of the United Nations.

4. The notification or objection made by an international organization shall be governed by the rules of that organization.

5. Nothing in the foregoing paragraphs shall affect the rights or obligations of the parties under any provisions in force binding the parties with regard to the settlement of disputes.

6. Without prejudice to article 45, the fact that a State or an international organization has not previously made the notification prescribed in paragraph 1 shall not prevent it from making such notification in answer to another party claiming performance of the treaty or alleging its violation.

Article 66
Procedures for judicial settlement, arbitration and conciliation

1. If, under paragraph 3 of article 65, no solution has been reached within a period of twelve months following the date on which the objection was raised, the procedures specified in the following paragraphs shall be followed.

2. With respect to a dispute concerning the application or the interpretation of article 53 or 64:

(a) if a State is a party to the dispute with one or more States, it may, by a written application, submit the dispute to the International Court of Justice for a decision;

(b) if a State is a party to the dispute to which one or more international organizations are parties, the State may, through a Member State of the United Nations if necessary, request the General Assembly or the Security Council or, where appropriate, the competent organ of an international organization which is a party to the dispute and is authorized in accordance with Article 96 of the Charter of the United Nations, to request an advisory opinion of the International Court of Justice in accordance with article 65 of the Statute of the Court;

(c) if the United Nations or an international organization that is authorized in accordance with Article 96 of the Charter of the United Nations is a party to the dispute, it may request an advisory opinion of the International Court of Justice in accordance with article 65 of the Statute of the Court;

(d) if an international organization other than those referred to in sub-paragraph *(c)* is a party to the dispute, it may, through a Member State of the United Nations, follow the procedure specified in sub-paragraph *(b)*;

(e) the advisory opinion given pursuant to sub-paragraph *(b)*, *(c)* or *(d)* shall be accepted as decisive by all the parties to the dispute concerned;

(f) if the request under sub-paragraph *(b)*, *(c)* or *(d)* for an advisory opinion of the Court is not granted, any one of the parties to the dispute may, by written notification to the other party or parties, submit it to arbitration in accordance with the provisions of the Annex to the present Convention.

3. The provisions of paragraph 2 apply unless all the parties to a dispute referred to in that paragraph by common consent agree to submit the dispute to an arbitration procedure, including the one specified in the Annex to the present Convention.

4. With respect to a dispute concerning the application or the interpretation of any of the articles in Part V, other than articles 53 and 64, of the present Convention, any one of the parties to the dispute may set in motion the conciliation procedure specified in the Annex to the Convention by submitting a request to that effect to the Secretary-General of the United Nations.

Article 67
Instruments for declaring invalid, terminating, withdrawing from or suspending the operation of a treaty

1. The notification provided for under article 65, paragraph 1 must be made in writing.

2. Any act declaring invalid, terminating, withdrawing from or suspending the operation of a treaty pursuant to the provisions of the treaty or of paragraphs 2 or 3 of article 65 shall be carried out through an instrument communicated to the other parties. If the instrument emanating from a State is not signed by the Head of State, Head of Government or Minister for Foreign Affairs, the representative of the State communicating it may be called upon to produce full powers. If the instrument emanates from an international organization, the representative of the organization communicating it may be called upon to produce full powers.

Article 68
Revocation of notifications and instruments provided for in articles 65 and 67

A notification or instrument provided for in articles 65 or 67 may be revoked at any time before it takes effect.

SECTION 5
CONSEQUENCES OF THE INVALIDITY TERMINATION OR SUSPENSION OF THE OPERATION OF A TREATY

Article 69
Consequences of the invalidity of a treaty

1. A treaty the invalidity of which is established under the present Convention is void. The provisions of a void treaty have no legal force.

2. If acts have nevertheless been performed in reliance on such a treaty:

(a) each party may require any other party to establish as far as possible in their mutual relations the position that would have existed if the acts had not been performed;

(b) acts performed in good faith before the invalidity was invoked are not rendered unlawful by reason only of the invalidity of the treaty.

3. In cases falling under articles 49, 50, 51 or 52, paragraph 2 does not apply with respect to the party to which the fraud, the act of corruption or the coercion is imputable.

4. In the case of the invalidity of the consent of a particular State or a particular international organization to be bound by a multilateral treaty, the foregoing rules apply in the relations between that State or that organization and the parties to the treaty.

Article 70
Consequences of the termination of a treaty

1. Unless the treaty otherwise provides or the parties otherwise agree, the termination of a treaty under its provisions or in accordance with the present Convention:

(a) releases the parties from any obligation further to perform the treaty;

(b) does not affect any right, obligation or legal situation of the parties created through the execution of the treaty prior to its termination.

2. If it State or an international organization denounces or withdraws from a multilateral treaty, paragraph 1 applies in the relations between that State or that organization and each of the other parties to the treaty from the date when such denunciation or withdrawal takes effect.

Article 71
Consequences of the invalidity of a treaty which conflicts with a peremptory norm of general international law

1. In the case of a treaty which is void under article 53 the parties shall:

(a) eliminate as far as possible the consequences of any act performed in reliance on any provision which conflicts with the peremptory norm of general international law; and

(b) bring their mutual relations into conformity with the peremptory norm of general international law.

2. In the case of a treaty which becomes void and terminates under article 64, the termination of the treaty:

(a) releases the parties from any obligation further to perform the treaty;

(b) does not affect any right, obligation or legal situation of the parties created through the execution of the treaty prior to its termination; provided that those rights, obligations or situations may thereafter be maintained only to the extent that their maintenance is not in itself in conflict with the new peremptory norm of general international law.

Article 72
Consequences of the suspension of the operation of a treaty

1. Unless the treaty otherwise provides or the parties otherwise agree, the suspension of the operation of a treaty under its provisions or in accordance with the present Convention:

(a) releases the parties between which the operation of the treaty is suspended from the obligation to perform the treaty in their mutual relations during the period of the suspension;

(b) does not otherwise affect the legal relations between the parties established by the treaty.

2. During the period of the suspension the parties shall refrain from acts tending to obstruct the resumption of the operation of the treaty.

PART VI
MISCELLANEOUS PROVISIONS

Article 73
Relationship to the Vienna Convention on the Law of Treaties

As between States parties to the Vienna Convention on the Law of Treaties of 1969, the relations of those States under a treaty between two or more States and one or more international organizations shall be governed by that Convention.

Article 74
Questions not prejudged by the present Convention

1. The provisions of the present Convention shall not prejudge any question that may arise in regard to a treaty between one or more States and one or more international organizations from a succession of States or from the international responsibility of a State or from the outbreak of hostilities between States.

2. The provisions of the present Convention shall not prejudge any question that may arise in regard to a treaty from the international responsibility of an international organization, from the termination of the existence of the organization or from the termination of participation by a State in the membership of the organization.

3. The provisions of the present Convention shall not prejudge any question that may arise in regard to the establishment of obligations and rights for States members of an international organization under a treaty to which that organization is a party.

Article 75
Diplomatic and consular relations and the conclusion of treaties

The severance or absence of diplomatic or consular relations between two or more States does not prevent the conclusion of treaties between two or more of those States and one or more international organizations. The conclusion of such a treaty does not in itself affect the situation in regard to diplomatic or consular relations.

Article 76
Case of an aggressor State

The provisions of the present Convention are without prejudice to any obligation in relation to a treaty between one or more States and one or more international organizations which may arise for an aggressor State in consequence of measures taken in conformity with the Charter of the United Nations with reference to that State's aggression.

PART VII
DEPOSITARIES, NOTIFICATIONS, CORRECTIONS AND REGISTRATION

Article 77
Depositaries of treaties

1. The designation of the depositary of a treaty may be made by the negotiating States and negotiating organizations or, as the case may be, the negotiating organizations, either

in the treaty itself or in some other manner. The depositary may be one or more States, an international organization or the chief administrative officer of the organization.

2. The functions of the depositary of a treaty are international in character and the depositary is under an obligation to act impartially in their performance. In particular, the fact that a treaty has not entered into force between certain of the parties or that a difference has appeared between a State or an international organization and a depositary with regard to the performance of the latter's functions shall not affect that obligation.

Article 78
Functions of depositaries

1. The functions of a depositary, unless otherwise provided in the treaty or agreed by the contracting States and contracting organizations or, as the case may be, by the contracting organizations, comprise in particular:

(a) keeping custody of the original text of the treaty and of any full powers delivered to the depositary;

(b) preparing certified copies of the original text and preparing any further text of the treaty in such additional languages as may be required by the treaty and transmitting them to the parties and to the States and international orgaizations entitled to become parties to the treaty;

(c) receiving any signatures to the treaty and receiving and keeping custody of any instruments, notifications and communications relating to it;

(d) examining whether the signature or any instrument, notification or communication relating to the treaty is in due and proper form and, if need be, bringing the matter to the attention of the State or international organization in question;

(e) informing the parties and the States and international organizations entitled to become parties to the treaty of acts, notifications and communications relating to the treaty;

(f) informing the States and international organizations entitled to become parties to the treaty when the number of signatures or of instruments of ratification, instruments relating to an act of formal confirmation, or of instruments of acceptance, approval or accession required for the entry into force of the treaty has been received or deposited;

(g) registering the treaty with the Secretariat of the United Nations;

(h) performing the functions specified in other provisions of the present Convention.

2. In the event of any difference appearing between a State or an international organization and the depositary as to the performance of the latter's functions, the depositary shall bring the question to the attention of:

(a) the signatory States and organizations and the contracting States and contracting organizations; or

(b) where appropriate, the competent organ of the international organization concerned.

Article 79
Notifications and communications

Except as the treaty or the present Convention otherwise provide, any notification or communication to be made by any State or any international organization under the present Convention shall:

(a) if there is no depositary, be transmitted direct to the States and organizations for which it is intended, or if there is a depositary, to the latter;

(b) be considered as having been nude by the State or organization in question only upon its receipt by the State or organization to which it was transmitted or, as the case may be, upon its receipt by the depositary;

(c) if transmitted to a depositary, be considered as received by the State or organization for which it was intended only when the latter State or organization has been informed by the depositary in accordance with article 78, paragraph 1*(e)*.

Article 80
Correction of errors in texts or in certified copies of treaties

1. Where, after the authentication of the text of a treaty, the signatory States and international organizations and the contracting States and contracting organizations are agreed that it contains an error, the error shall, unless those States and organizations decide upon some other means of correction, be corrected:

(a) by having the appropriate correction made in the text and causing the correction to be initialled by duly authorized representatives;

(b) by executing or exchanging an instrument or instruments setting out the correction which it has been agreed to make; or

(c) by executing a corrected text of the whole treaty by the same procedure as in the case of the original text.

2. Where the treaty is one for which there is a depositary, the latter shall notify the signatory States and international organizations and the contracting States and contracting organizations of the error and of the proposal to correct it and shall specify an appropriate time-limit within which objection to the proposed correction may be raised. If, on the expiry of the time-limit:

(a) no objection has been raised, the depositary shall make and initial the correction in the text and shall execute a *procès-verbal* of the rectification of the text and communicate a copy of it to the parties and to the States and organizations entitled to become parties to the treaty;

(b) an objection has been raised, the depositary shall communicate the objection to the signatory States and organizations and to the contracting States and contracting organizations.

3. The rules in paragraphs 1 and 2 apply also where the text has been authenticated in two or more languages and it appears that there is a lack of concordance which the signatory States and international organizations and the contracting States and contracting organizations agree should be corrected.

4. The corrected text replaces the defective text *ab initio*, unless the signatory States and international organizations and the contracting States and contracting organizations otherwise decide.

5. The correction of the text of a treaty that has been registered shall be notified to the Secretariat of the United Nations.

6. Where an error is discovered in a certified copy of a treaty, the depositary shall execute a *procès-verbal* specifying the rectification and communicate a copy of it to the signatory States and international organizations and to the contracting States and contracting organizations.

Article 81
Registration and publication of treaties

1. Treaties shall, after their entry into force, be transmitted to the Secretariat of the United Nations for registration or filing and recording, as the case may be, and for publication.

2. The designation of a depositary shall constitute authorization for it to perform the acts specified in the preceding paragraph.

PART VIII
FINAL PROVISIONS

Article 82
Signature

The present Convention shall be open for signature until 31 December 1986 at the Federal Ministry for Foreign Affairs of the Republic of Austria, and subsequently, until 30 June 1987, at United Nations Headquarters, New York by:

(a) all States;

(b) Namibia, represented by the United Nations Council for Namibia;

(c) international organizations invited to participate in the United Nations Conference on the Law of Treaties between States and International Organizations or between International Organizations.

Article 83
Ratification or act of formal confirmation

The present Convention is subject to ratification by States and by Namibia, represented by the United Nations Council for Namibia, and to acts of formal confirmation by international organizations. The instruments of ratification and those relating to acts of formal confirmation shall be deposited with the Secretary-General of the United Nations.

Article 84
Accession

1. The present Convention shall remain open for accession by any State, by Namibia, represented by the United Nations Council for Namibia, and by any international organization which has the capacity to conclude treaties.

2. An instrument of accession of an international organization shall contain a declaration that it has the capacity to conclude treaties.

3. The instruments of accession shall be deposited with the Secretary-General of the United Nations.

Article 85
Entry into force

1. The present Convention shall enter into force on the thirtieth day following the date of deposit of the thirty-fifth instrument of ratification or accession by States or by Namibia, represented by the United Nations Council for Namibia.

2. For each State or for Namibia, represented by the United Nations Council for Namibia, ratifying or acceding to the Convention after the condition specified in paragraph 1 has been fulfilled, the Convention shall enter into force on the thirtieth day after deposit by such State or by Namibia of its instrument of ratification or accession.

3. For each international organization depositing an instrument relating to an act of formal confirmation or an instrument of accession, the Convention shall enter into force on the thirtieth day after such deposit, or at the date the Convention enters into force pursuant to paragraph 1, whichever is later.

Article 86
Authentic texts

The original of the present Convention, of which the Arabic, Chinese, English, French, Russian and Spanish texts are equally authentic, shall be deposited with the Secretary-General of the United Nations.

IN WITNESS WHEREOF the undersigned Plenipotentiaries, being duly authorized by their respective Governments, and duly authorized representatives of the United Nations Council for Namibia and of international organizations have signed the present Convention.

DONE at VIENNA this twenty-first day of March one thousand nine hundred and eighty-six.

ANNEX
ARBITRATION AND CONCILIATION PROCEDURES ESTABLISHED IN APPLICATION OF ARTICLE 66

I. ESTABLISHMENT OF THE ARBITRAL TRIBUNAL OR CONCILIATION COMMISSION

1. A list consisting of qualified jurists, from which the parties to a dispute may choose the persons who are to constitute an arbitral tribunal or, as the case may be, a conciliation commission, shall be drawn up and maintained by the Secretary-General of the United Nations. To this end, every State which is a Member of the United Nations and every party to the present Convention shall be invited to nominate two persons, and the names of the persons so nominated shall constitute the list, a copy of which shall be transmitted to the President of the International Court of Justice. The term of office of a person on the list, including that of any person nominated to fill a casual vacancy, shall be five years and may be renewed. A person whose term expires shall continue to fulfil any function for which he shall have been chosen under the following paragraphs.

2. When notification has been made under article 66, paragraph 2, sub-paragraph (f), or agreement on the procedure in the present Annex has been reached under

paragraph 3, the dispute shall be brought before an arbitral tribunal. When a request has been made to the Secretary-General under article 66, paragraph 4, the Secretary-General shall bring the dispute before a conciliation commission. Both the arbitral tribunal and the conciliation commission shall be constituted as follows:

The States, international organizations or, as the case may be, the States and organizations which constitute one of the parties to the dispute shall appoint by common consent:

(a) one arbitrator or, as the case may be, one conciliator, who may or may not be chosen from the list referred to in paragraph 1; and

(b) one arbitrator or, as the case may be, one conciliator, who shall be chosen from among those included in the list and shall not be of the nationality of any of the States or nominated by any of the organizations which constitute that party to the dispute, provided that a dispute between two international organizations is not considered by nationals of one and the same State.

The States, international organizations or, as the case may be, the States and organizations which constitute the other party to the dispute shall appoint two arbitrators or, as the case may be, two conciliators, in the same way. The four persons chosen by the parties shall be appointed within sixty days following the date on which the other party to the dispute receives notification under article 66, paragraph 2, sub-paragraph *(f)*, or on which the agreement on the procedure in the present Annex under paragraph 3 is reached, or on which the Secretary-General receives the request for conciliation.

The four persons so chosen shall, within sixty days following the date of the last of their own appointments, appoint from the list a fifth arbitrator or, as the case may be, conciliator, who shall be chairman.

If the appointment of the chairman, or any of the arbitrators or, as the case may be, conciliators, has not been made within the period prescribed above for such appointment, it shall be made by the Secretary-General of the United Nations within sixty days following the expiry of that period. The appointment of the chairman may be made by the Secretary-General either from the list or from the membership of the International Law Commission. Any of the periods within which appointments must be made may be extended by agreement between the parties to the dispute. If the United Nations is a party or is included in one of the parties to the dispute, the Secretary-General shall transmit the above-mentioned request to the President of the International Court of Justice, who shall perform the functions conferred upon the Secretary-General under this sub-paragraph.

Any vacancy shall be filled in the manner prescribed for the initial appointment.

The appointment of arbitrators or conciliators by an international organization provided for in paragraphs 1 and 2 shall be governed by the rules of that organization.

II. FUNCTIONING OF THE ARBITRAL TRIBUNAL

3. Unless the parties to the dispute otherwise agree, the Arbitral Tribunal shall decide its own procedure, assuring to each party to the dispute a full opportunity to be heard and to present its case.

4. The Arbitral Tribunal, with the consent of the parties to the dispute, may invite any interested State or international organization to submit to it its views orally or in writing.

5. Decisions of the Arbitral Tribunal shall be adopted by a majority vote of the members. In the event of an equality of votes, the vote of the Chairman shall be decisive.

6. When one of the parties to the dispute does not appear before the Tribunal or fails to defend its case, the other party may request the Tribunal to continue the proceedings and to make its award. Before making its award, the Tribunal must satisfy itself not only that it has jurisdiction over the dispute but also that the claim is well founded in fact and law.

7. The award of the Arbitral Tribunal shall be confined to the subject-matter of the dispute and state the reasons on which it is based. Any member of the Tribunal may attach a separate or dissenting opinion to the award.

8. The award shall be final and without appeal. It shall be complied with by all parties to the dispute.

9. The Secretary-General shall provide the Tribunal with such assistance and facilities as it may require. The expenses of the Tribunal shall be borne by the United Nations.

III. FUNCTIONING OF THE CONCILIATION COMMISSION

10. The Conciliation Commission shall decide its own procedure. The Commission, with the consent of the parties to the dispute, may invite any party to the treaty to submit to it its views orally or in writing. Decisions and recommendations of the Commission shall be made by a majority vote of the five members.

11. The Commission may draw the attention of the parties to the dispute to any measures which might facilitate an amicable settlement.

12. The Commission shall hear the parties, examine the claims and objections, and make proposals to the parties with a view to reaching an amicable settlement of the dispute.

13. The Commission shall report within twelve months of its constitution. Its report shall be deposited with the Secretary-General and transmitted to the parties to the dispute. The report of the Commission, including any conclusions stated therein regarding the facts or questions of law, shall not be binding upon the parties and it shall have no other character than that of recommendations submitted for the consideration of the parties in order to facilitate an amicable settlement of the dispute.

14. The Secretary-General shall provide the Commission with such assistance and facilities as it may require. The expenses of the Commission shall be borne by the United Nations.

Annex IV

Official Status of the 1969 Vienna Convention on the Law of Treaties*

Entry into force: 27 January 1980, in accordance with article 84(1)

Registration: 27 January 1980, No. 18232

Status: Signatories: 45. Parties: 114

Text: United Nations, *Treaty Series*, vol. 1155, p. 331.

Note: The Convention was adopted on 22 May 1969 and opened for signature on 23 May 1969 by the United Nations Conference on the Law of Treaties. The Conference was convened pursuant to General Assembly resolutions 2166 (XXI) 1 of 5 December 1966 and 2287 (XXII)[2] of 6 December 1967. The Conference held two sessions, both at the Neue Hofburg in Vienna, the first session from 26 March to 24 May 1968 and the second session from 9 April to 22 May 1969. In addition to the Convention, the Conference adopted the Final Act and certain declarations and resolutions, which are annexed to that Act. By unanimous decision of the Conference, the original of the Final Act was deposited in the archives of the Federal Ministry for Foreign Affairs of Austria. The text of the Final Act is included in document A/CONF.39/11/Add.2.

Participant	***Signature***	***Ratification, Accession(a), Succession(d)***
Afghanistan	23 May 1969	
Albania		27 Jun 2001 a
Algeria		8 Nov 1988 a
Andorra		5 Apr 2004 a
Argentina	23 May 1969	5 Dec 1972
Armenia		17 May 2005 a
Australia		13 Jun 1974 a

* See *Multilateral treaties deposited with the Secretary-General: status as at 31 December 2010*. New York: United Nations Publication, 2011 (Chapter XXIII, Law of Treaties). In: [https://treaties.un.org/pages/ParticipationStatus.aspx]. Status of the Convention as of 13 December 2015.

Participant	***Signature***	***Ratification, Accession(a), Succession(d)***
Austria		30 Apr 1979 a
Barbados	23 May 1969	24 Jun 1971
Belarus		1 May 1986 a
Belgium		1 Sep 1992 a
Bolivia (Plurinational State of)	23 May 1969	
Bosnia and Herzegovina[3]		1 Sep 1993 d
Brazil	23 May 1969	25 Sep 2009
Bulgaria		21 Apr 1987 a
Burkina Faso		25 May 2006 a
Cambodia	23 May 1969	
Cameroon		23 Oct 1991 a
Canada		14 Oct 1970 a
Central African Republic		10 Dec 1971 a
Chile	23 May 1969	9 Apr 1981
China[4]		3 Sep 1997 a
Colombia	23 May 1969	10 Apr 1985
Congo	23 May 1969	12 Apr 1982
Costa Rica	23 May 1969	22 Nov 1996
Côte d'Ivoire	23 Jul 1969	
Croatia[3]		12 Oct 1992 d
Cuba		9 Sep 1998 a
Cyprus		28 Dec 1976 a
Czech Republic[5]		22 Feb 1993 d
Democratic Republic of the Congo		25 Jul 1977 a
Denmark	18 Apr 1970	1 Jun 1976
Dominican Republic		1 Apr 2010 a
Ecuador	23 May 1969	11 Feb 2005
Egypt		11 Feb 1982 a
El Salvador	16 Feb 1970	
Estonia		21 Oct 1991 a
Ethiopia	30 Apr 1970	
Finland	23 May 1969	19 Aug 1977
Gabon		5 Nov 2004 a
Georgia		8 Jun 1995 a
Germany[6,7]	30 Apr 1970	21 Jul 1987
Ghana	23 May 1969	
Greece		30 Oct 1974 a
Guatemala	23 May 1969	21 Jul 1997
Guinea		16 Sep 2005 a
Guyana	23 May 1969	15 Sep 2005
Haiti		25 Aug 1980 a

Participant	Signature	Ratification, Accession(a), Succession(d)
Holy See	30 Sep 1969	25 Feb 1977
Honduras	23 May 1969	20 Sep 1979
Hungary		19 Jun 1987 a
Iran (Islamic Republic of)	23 May 1969	
Ireland		7 Aug 2006 a
Italy	22 Apr 1970	25 Jul 1974
Jamaica	23 May 1969	28 Jul 1970
Japan		2 Jul 1981 a
Kazakhstan		5 Jan 1994 a
Kenya	23 May 1969	
Kiribati		15 Sep 2005 a
Kuwait		11 Nov 1975 a
Kyrgyzstan		11 May 1999 a
Lao People's Democratic Republic		31 Mar 1998 a
Latvia		4 May 1993 a
Lesotho		3 Mar 1972 a
Liberia	23 May 1969	29 Aug 1985
Libya		22 Dec 2008 a
Liechtenstein		8 Feb 1990 a
Lithuania		15 Jan 1992 a
Luxembourg	4 Sep 1969	23 May 2003
Madagascar	23 May 1969	
Malawi		23 Aug 1983 a
Malaysia		27 Jul 1994 a
Maldives		14 Sep 2005 a
Mali		31 Aug 1998 a
Malta		26 Sep 2012 a
Mauritius		18 Jan 1973 a
Mexico	23 May 1969	25 Sep 1974
Mongolia		16 May 1988 a
Montenegro[8]		23 Oct 2006 d
Morocco	23 May 1969	26 Sep 1972
Mozambique		8 May 2001 a
Myanmar		16 Sep 1998 a
Nauru		5 May 1978 a
Nepal	23 May 1969	
Netherlands[9]		9 Apr 1985 a
New Zealand	29 Apr 1970	4 Aug 1971
Niger		27 Oct 1971 a
Nigeria	23 May 1969	31 Jul 1969
Oman		18 Oct 1990 a

Participant	***Signature***	***Ratification, Accession(a), Succession(d)***
Pakistan	29 Apr 1970	
Panama		28 Jul 1980 a
Paraguay		3 Feb 1972 a
Peru	23 May 1969	14 Sep 2000
Philippines	23 May 1969	15 Nov 1972
Poland		2 Jul 1990 a
Portugal		6 Feb 2004 a
Republic of Korea[10]	27 Nov 1969	27 Apr 1977
Republic of Moldova		26 Jan 1993 a
Russian Federation		29 Apr 1986 a
Rwanda		3 Jan 1980 a
Saudi Arabia		14 Apr 2003 a
Senegal		11 Apr 1986 a
Serbia[3]		12 Mar 2001 d
Slovakia[5]		28 May 1993 d
Slovenia[3]		6 Jul 1992 d
Solomon Islands		9 Aug 1989 a
Spain		16 May 1972 a
St. Vincent and the Grenadines		27 Apr 1999 a
State of Palestine		2 Apr 2014 a
Sudan	23 May 1969	18 Apr 1990
Suriname		31 Jan 1991 a
Sweden	23 Apr 1970	4 Feb 1975
Switzerland		7 May 1990 a
Syrian Arab Republic		2 Oct 1970 a
Tajikistan		6 May 1996 a
The former Yugoslav Republic of Macedonia[3]		8 Jul 1999 d
Timor-Leste		8 Jan 2013 a
Togo		28 Dec 1979 a
Trinidad and Tobago	23 May 1969	
Tunisia		23 Jun 1971 a
Turkmenistan		4 Jan 1996 a
Ukraine		14 May 1986 a
United Kingdom of Great Britain and Northern Ireland	20 Apr 1970	25 Jun 1971
United Republic of Tanzania		12 Apr 1976 a
United States of America	24 Apr 1970	
Uruguay	23 May 1969	5 Mar 1982
Uzbekistan		12 Jul 1995 a
Viet Nam		10 Oct 2001 a
Zambia	23 May 1969	

Declarations and Reservations

(Unless otherwise indicated, the declarations and reservations were made upon ratification, accession or succession.)

Afghanistan

Upon signature:

"Afghanistan's understanding of article 62 (fundamental change of circumstances) is as follows:

"Sub-paragraph 2*(a)* of this article does not cover unequal and illegal treaties, or any treaties which were contrary to the principle of self-determination. This view was also supported by the Expert Consultant in his statement of 11 May 1968 in the Committee of the Whole and on 14 May 1969 (doc. A/CONF.39/L.40) to the Conference."

Algeria

Declaration:

The accession of the People's Democratic Republic of Algeria to the present Convention does not in any way mean recognition of Israel.

This accession shall not be interpreted as involving the establishment of relations of any kind whatever with Israel.

Reservation:

The Government of the People's Democratic Republic of Algeria considers that the competence of the International Court of Justice cannot be exercised with respect to a dispute such as that envisaged in article 66 *(a)* at the request of one of the parties alone.

It declares that, in each case, the prior agreement of all the parties concerned is necessary for the dispute to be submitted to the said Court.

Argentina

(a) The Argentine Republic does not regard the rule contained in article 45 *(b)* as applicable to it inasmuch as the rule in question provides for the renunciation of rights in advance.

(b) The Argentine Republic does not accept the idea that a fundamental change of circumstances which has occurred with regard to those existing at the time of the conclusion of a treaty, and which was not foreseen by the parties, may be invoked as a ground for terminating or withdrawing from the treaty; moreover, it objects to the reservations made by Afghanistan, Morocco and Syria with respect to article 62, paragraph 2*(a)*, and to any reservations to the same effect as those of the States referred to which may be made in the future with respect to article 62.

The application of this Convention to territories whose sovereignty is a subject of dispute between two or more States, whether or not they are parties to it, cannot be deemed to imply a modification, renunciation or abandonment of the position heretofore maintained by each of them.

Armenia[11]

13 July 2006

Reservation:

"The Republic of Armenia does not consider itself bound by the provisions of article 66 of the Vienna Convention on the Law of Treaties and declares that for any dispute among the Contracting Parties concerning the application or the interpretation of any article of part V of the Convention to be submitted to the International Court of Justice for a decision or to the Conciliation Commission for consideration the consent of all the parties to the dispute is required in each separate case."

Belarus

[Same reservations and declaration, identical in essence, mutatis mutandis, *as the one made by the Russian Federation.]*

Belgium[12]

21 June 1993

Reservation:

The Belgian State will not be bound by articles 53 and 64 of the Convention with regard to any party which, in formulating a reservation concerning article 66 (*a*), objects to the settlement procedure established by this article.

Bolivia (Plurinational State of)

Upon signature:

1. The shortcomings of the Vienna Convention on the Law of Treaties are such as to postpone the realization of the aspirations of mankind.

2. Nevertheless, the rules endorsed by the Convention do represent significant advances, based on the principles of international justice which Bolivia has traditionally supported.

Brazil

Reservation:

...with a reservation to articles 25 and 66.

Bulgaria[13]

Declaration:

The People's Republic of Bulgaria considers it necessary to underline that articles 81 and 83 of the Convention, which preclude a number of States from becoming parties to it, are of an unjustifiably restrictive character. These provisions are incompatible with the very nature of the Convention, which is of a universal character and should be open for accession by all States.

Canada

"In acceding to the Vienna Convention on the Law of Treaties, the Government of Canada declares its understanding that nothing in article 66 of the Convention is intended to exclude the jurisdiction of the International Court of Justice where such jurisdiction exists under the provisions of any treaty in force binding the parties with regard to the settlement of disputes. In relation to states parties to the Vienna Convention which accept as compulsory the jurisdiction of the International Court of Justice, the Government of Canada declares that it does not regard the provisions of article 66 of the Vienna Convention as providing 'some other method of peaceful settlement' within the meaning of paragraph 2*(a)* of the declaration of the Government of Canada accepting as compulsory the jurisdiction of the International Court of Justice which was deposited with the Secretary-General of the United Nations on April 7, 1970."

Chile

Reservation:

The Republic of Chile declares its adherence to the general principle of the immutability of treaties, without prejudice to the right of States to stipulate, in particular, rules which modify this principle, and for this reason formulates a reservation relating to the provisions of article 62, paragraphs 1 and 3, of the Convention, which it considers inapplicable to Chile.

China

Reservation:

1. The People's Republic of China makes its reservation to article 66 of the said Convention.

Declaration:

2. The signature to the said Convention by the Taiwan authorities on 27 April 1970 in the name of "China" is illegal and therefore null and void.

Colombia

Reservation:

With regard to article 25, Colombia formulates the reservation that the Political Constitution of Colombia does not recognize the provisional application of treaties; it is the responsibility of the National Congress to approve or disapprove any treaties and conventions which the Government concludes with other States or with international legal entities.

Costa Rica[14]

Reservations and declarations made upon signature and confirmed upon ratification:

1. With regard to articles 11 and 12, the delegation of Costa Rica wishes to make a reservation to the effect that the Costa Rican system of constitutional law does not authorize any form of consent which is not subject to ratification by the Legislative Assembly.

2. With regard to article 25, it wishes to make a reservation to the effect that the Political Constitution of Costa Rica does not permit the provisional application of treaties, either.

3. With regard to article 27, it interprets this article as refer ring to secondary law and not to the provisions of the Political Constitution.

4. With regard to article 38, its interpretation is that no customary rule of general international law shall take precedence over any rule of the Inter-American System to which, in its view, this Convention is supplementary.

Cuba

Reservation:

The Government of the Republic of Cuba enters an explicit reservation to the procedure established under article 66 of the Convention, since it believes that any dispute should be settled by any means adopted by agreement between the parties to the dispute; the Republic of Cuba therefore cannot accept solutions which provide means for one of the parties, without the consent of the other to submit the dispute to procedures for judicial settlement, arbitration and conciliation.

Declaration:

The Government of the Republic of Cuba declares that the Vienna Convention on the Law of Treaties essentially codified and systematized the norms that had been established by custom and other sources of international law concerning negotiation, signature, ratification, entry into force, termination and other stipulations relating to international treaties; hence, those provisions, owing to their compulsory character, by virtue of having been established by universally recognized sources of international law, particularly those relating to invalidity, termination and suspension of the application of treaties, are applicable [to] any treaty negotiated by the Republic of Cuba prior to the aforesaid convention, essentially, treaties, covenants and concessions negotiated under conditions of inequality or which disregard or diminish its sovereignty and territorial integrity.

Czech Republic[5]

Denmark

As between itself and any State which formulates, wholly or in part, a reservation relating to the provisions of article 66 of the Convention concerning the compulsory settlement of certain disputes, Denmark will not consider itself bound by those provisions of part V of the Convention, according to which the procedures for settlement set forth in article 66 are not to apply in the event of reservations formulated by other States.

Ecuador

Upon signature:

In signing this Convention, Ecuador has not considered it necessary to make any reservation in regard to article 4 of the Convention because it understands that the rules referred to in the first part of article 4 include the principle of the peaceful settlement of disputes, which is set forth in Article 2, paragraph 3 of the Charter of the United Nations and which, as *jus cogens*, has universal and mandatory force.

Ecuador also considers that the first part of article 4 is applicable to existing treaties. It wishes to place on record, in this form, its view that the said article 4 incorporates the indisputable principle that, in cases where the Convention codifies rules of *lex lata*, these rules, as pre-existing rules, may be invoked and applied to treaties signed before the entry into force of this Convention, which is the instrument codifying the rules.

Upon ratification:

In ratifying this Convention, Ecuador wishes to place on record its adherence to the principles, norms and methods of peaceful settlement of disputes provided for in the Charter of the United Nations and in other international instruments on the subject, which have been expressly included in the Ecuadorian legal system in article 4, paragraph 3, of the Political Constitution of the Republic.

Finland[15]

"Finland also declares that as to its relation with any State which has made or makes a reservation to the effect that this State will not be bound by some or all of the provisions of article 66, Finland will consider itself bound neither by those procedural provisions nor by the substantive provisions of part V of the Convention to which the procedures provided for in article 66 do not apply as a result of the said reservation."

Germany[7]

Upon signature:

"The Federal Republic of Germany reserves the right, upon ratifying the Vienna Convention on the Law of Treaties, to state its views on the declarations made by other States upon signing or ratifying or acceding to that Convention and to make reservations regarding certain provisions of the said Convention."

Upon ratification:

(...)

2. The Federal Republic of Germany assumes that the jurisdiction of the International Court of Justice brought about by consent of States outside the Vienna Convention on the Law of Treaties cannot be excluded by invoking the provisions of article 66 (*b*) of the Convention.

3. The Federal Republic of Germany interprets "measures taken in conformity with the Charter of the United Nations", as referred to in article 75, to mean future decisions by the Security Council of the United Nations in conformity with Chapter VII of the Charter for the maintenance of international peace and security.

Guatemala[16]

Upon signature:

Reservations:

I. Guatemala cannot accept any provision of this Convention which would prejudice its rights and its claim to the Territory of Belize.

II. Guatemala will not apply articles [...], 25 and 66 in so far as they are contrary to the provisions of the Constitution of the Republic.

III. Guatemala will apply the provision contained in article 38 only in cases where it considers that it is in the national interest to do so.

Upon ratification:

Reservations:

(*a*) The Republic of Guatemala formally confirms reservations I and III which it formulated upon signing the [said Convention], to the effect, respectively, that Guatemala could not accept any provision of the Convention which would prejudice its rights and its claim to the territory of Belize and that it would apply the provision contained in article 38 of the Convention only in cases where it considered that it was in the national interest to do so;

(*b*) With respect to reservation II, which was formulated on the same occasion and which indicated that the Republic of Guatemala would not apply articles [...], 25 and 66 of the [said Convention] insofar as they were contrary to the Constitution, Guatemala states:

(*b*) (I) That it confirms the reservation with respect to the non-application of articles 25 and 66 of the Convention, insofar as both are incompatible with provisions of the Political Constitution currently in force;

(*b*) (II) [...]

Guatemala's consent to be bound by a treaty is subject to compliance with the requirements and procedures established in its Political Constitution. For Guatemala, the signature or initialling of a treaty by its representative is always understood to be *ad referendum* and subject, in either case, to confirmation by its Government.

(*c*) A reservation is hereby formulated with respect to article 27 of the Convention, to the effect that the article is understood to refer to the provisions of the secondary legislation of Guatemala and not to those of its Political Constitution, which take precedence over any law or treaty.

Hungary[17]

Kuwait

The participation of Kuwait in this Convention does not mean in any way recognition of Israel by the Government of the State of Kuwait and that furthermore, no treaty relations will arise between the State of Kuwait and Israel.

Mongolia[18]

Declarations:

1. The Mongolian People's Republic declares that it reserves the right to take any measures to safeguard its interests in the case of the non-observance by other States of the provisions of the Vienna Convention on the Law of Treaties.

2. The Mongolian People's Republic deems it appropriate to draw attention to the discriminatory nature of article 81 and 83 of the Vienna Convention on the Law of Treaties and declares that the Convention should be open for accession by all States.

Morocco

Reservation made upon signature and confirmed upon ratification:

1. Morocco interprets paragraph 2*(a)* of article 62 (Fundamental change of circumstances) as not applying to unlawful or inequitable treaties, or to any treaty contrary to the principle of self-determination. Morocco's views on paragraph 2*(a)* were supported by the Expert Consultant in his statements in the Committee of the Whole on

11 May1968 and before the Conference in plenary on 14 May 1969 (see Document A/CONF.39/L.40).

2. It shall be understood that Morocco's signature of this Convention does not in any way imply that it recognized Israel. Furthermore, no treaty relationships will be established between Morocco and Israel.

Netherlands

Declaration:

"The Kingdom of the Netherlands does not regard the provisions of Article 66 (*b*) of the Convention as providing 'some other method of peaceful settlement' within the meaning of the declaration of the Kingdom of the Netherlands accepting as compulsory the jurisdiction of the International Court of Justice which was deposited with the Secretary-General of the United Nations on 1 August 1956."

New Zealand

Declaration:

"The Government of New Zealand declares its understanding that nothing in article 66 of the Convention is intended to exclude the jurisdiction of the International Court of Justice where such jurisdiction exists under the provisions of any treaty in force binding the parties with regard to the settlement of disputes. In relations to states parties to the Vienna Convention which accept as compulsory the jurisdiction of the International Court of Justice, the Government of New Zealand declares that it will not regard the provisions of article 66 of the Vienna Convention as providing 'some other method of peaceful settlement' within the meaning of this phrase where it appears in the declaration of the Government of New Zealand accepting as compulsory the jurisdiction of the International Court of Justice, which was deposited with the Secretary-General of the League of Nations on 8 April 1940."

Oman

Declaration:

According to the understanding of the Government of the Sultanate of Oman the implementation of paragraph (2) of article (62) of the said Convention does not include those Treaties which are contrary to the right to self-determination.

Peru[19]

Reservation:

For the Government of Peru, the application of articles 11, 12 and 25 of the Convention must be understood in accordance with, and subject to, the process of treaty signature, approval, ratification, accession and entry into force stipulated by its constitutional provisions.

Portugal

Declaration:

"Article 66 of the Vienna of the Convention is inextricably linked with the provisions of Part V to which it relates. Therefore, Portugal declares that as to its relation with any

State which has made or makes a reservation to the effect that this State will not be bound by some or all of the provisions of article 66, it will consider itself bound neither by those procedural norms nor by the substantive norms of Part V of the Convention to which the procedures provided for in Article 66 do not apply as a result of the said reservation. However, Portugal does not object to the entry into force of the remaining of the Convention between the Portuguese Republic and such a State and considers that the absence of treaty relations between itself and that State with regard to all or certain norms of Part V will not in any way impair the latter to fulfil any obligation embodied in those provisions to which it is subject under international law in dependently of the Convention".

Russian Federation

The Union of Soviet Socialist Republics does not consider itself bound by the provisions of article 66 of the Vienna Convention on the Law of Treaties and declares that, in order for any dispute among the Contracting Parties concerning the application or the interpretation of articles 53 or 64 to be submitted to the International Court of Justice for a decision or for any dispute concerning the application or interpretation of any other articles in Part V of the Convention to be submitted for consideration by the Conciliation Commission, the consent of all the parties to the dispute is required in each separate case, and that the conciliators constituting the Conciliation Commission may only be persons appointed by the parties to the dispute by common consent.

The Union of Soviet Socialist Republics will consider that it is not obligated by the provisions of article 20, paragraph 3 or of article 45*(b)* of the Vienna Convention on the Law of Treaties, since they are contrary to established international practice.

Declaration:

The Union of Soviet Socialist Republics declares that it reserves the right to take any measures to safeguard its interests in the event of the non-observance by other States of the provisions of the Vienna Convention on the Law of Treaties.

Saudi Arabia

Reservation:

"... with a reservation regarding Article 66 so that the recourse to judgement or to arbitration should be preceded by agreement between the two countries concerned."

Slovakia[5]

Syrian Arab Republic

A – Acceptance of this Convention by the Syrian Arab Republic and ratification of it by its Government shall in no way signify recognition of Israel and cannot have as a result the establishment with the latter of any contact governed by the provisions of this Convention.

B – The Syrian Arab Republic considers that article 81 is not in conformity with the aims and purposes of the Convention in that it does not allow all States, without distinction or discrimination, to become parties to it.

C – The Government of the Syrian Arab Republic does not in any case accept the non-applicability of the principle of a fundamental change of circumstances with regard to treaties establishing boundaries, referred to in article 62, paragraph 2*(a)*, inasmuch as it regards this as a flagrant violation of an obligatory norm which forms part of general international law and which recognizes the right of peoples to self-determination.

D – The Government of the Syrian Arab Republic interprets the provisions in article 52 as follows:

The expression "the threat or use of force" used in this article extends also to the employment of economic, political, military and psychological coercion and to all types of coercion constraining a State to conclude a treaty against its wishes or its interests.

E – The accession of the Syrian Arab Republic to this Convention and the ratification of it by its Government shall not apply to the Annex to the Convention, which concerns obligatory conciliation.

Tunisia

The dispute referred to in article 66 (*a*) requires the consent of all parties thereto in order to be submitted to the International Court of Justice for a decision.

Ukraine

[Same reservations and declaration, identical in essence, mutatis mutandis, as the one made by the Union of Soviet Socialist Republics.]

United Kingdom of Great Britain and Northern Ireland[20]

Upon signature:

"In signing the Vienna Convention on the Law of Treaties, the Government of the United Kingdom of Great Britain and Northern Ireland declare their understanding that nothing in article 66 of the Convention is intended to oust the jurisdiction of the International Court of Justice where such jurisdiction exists under any provisions in force binding the parties with regard to the settlement of disputes. In particular, and in relation to States parties to the Vienna Convention which accept as compulsory the jurisdiction of the International Court of Justice, the Government of the United Kingdom declare that they will not regard the provisions of sub-paragraph *(b)* of article 66 of the Vienna Convention as providing 'some other method of peaceful settlement' within the meaning of sub-paragraph *(i) (a)* of the Declaration of the Government of the United Kingdom accepting as compulsory the jurisdiction of the International Court of Justice which was deposited with the Secretary-General of the United Nations on the 1st of January 1969.

The Government of the United Kingdom, while reserving their position for the time being with regard to other declarations and reservations made by various States on signing the Convention, consider it necessary to state that the United Kingdom does not accept that Guatemala has any rights or any valid claim in respect of the territory of British Honduras."

Upon ratification:

It is [the United Kingdom's] understanding that nothing in Article 66 of the Convention is intended to oust the jurisdiction of the International Court of Justice where such jurisdiction exists under any provisions in force binding the parties with regard to the settlement of disputes. In particular, and in relation to States parties to the

Vienna Convention which accept as compulsory the jurisdiction of the International Court, the United Kingdom will not regard the provisions of sub-paragraph *(b)* of Article 66 of the Vienna Convention on the Law of Treaties as providing 'some other method of peaceful settlement' within the meaning of sub-paragraph *(i) (a)* of the Declaration of the Government of the United Kingdom which was deposited with the Secretary-General of the United Nations on the 1st of January 1969.

United Republic of Tanzania

"Article 66 of the Convention shall not be applied to the United Republic of Tanzania by any State which enters a reservation on any provision of part V or the whole of that part of the Convention."

Viet Nam

Reservation:

"Acceeding to this Convention, the Socialist Republic of Vietnam makes its reservation to article 66 of the said Convention."

Objections

(Unless otherwise indicated the objections were made upon ratification, accession or succession.)

Algeria

The Government of the People's Democratic Republic of Algeria, dedicated to the principle of the inviolability of the frontiers inherited on accession to independence, expresses an objection to the reservation entered by the Kingdom of Morocco with regard to paragraph 2*(a)* of article 62 of the Convention.

Austria

16 September 1998

With respect to the reservations made by Guatemala upon ratification:

"Austria is of the view that the Guatemalan reservations refer almost exclusively to general rules of [the said Convention] many of which are solidly based on international customary law. The reservations could call into question well-established and universally accepted norms. Austria is of the view that the reservations also raise doubts as to their compatibility with the object and purpose of the [said Convention]. Austria therefore objects to these reservations. This objection does not preclude the entry into force of the [said Convention] between Austria and Guatemala."

Canada

22 October 1971

"...Canada does not consider itself in treaty relations with the Syrian Arab Republic in respect of those provisions of the Vienna Convention on the Law of Treaties to which the compulsory conciliation procedures set out in the annex to that Convention are applicable."

Chile

The Republic of Chile formulates an objection to the reservations which have been made or may be made in the future relating to article 62, paragraph 2, of the Convention.

Denmark

With regard to reservations made by Guatemala upon ratification:

"These reservations refer to general rules of [the said Convention], many of which are solidly based on customary international law. The reservation – if accepted – could call to question well established and universally accepted norms.

It is the opinion of the Government of Denmark that the reservations are not compatible with the object and purpose of [said Convention].

It is in the common interest of States that treaties to which they have chosen to become Parties are respected, as to their object and purpose, by all Parties and that States are prepared to undertake any legislative changes necessary to comply with their obligations under the treaties.

The Government of Denmark therefore objects to the aforesaid reservations made by the Government of Guatemala to [the said Convention]. This objection does not preclude the entry into force of [the said Convention] between Guatemala and Denmark and will thus enter into force between Guatemala and Denmark without Guatemala benefitting from these reservations."

Egypt

The Arab Republic of Egypt does not consider itself bound by part V of the Convention *vis-à-vis* States which formulate reservations concerning the procedures for judicial settlement and compulsory arbitration set forth in article 66 and in the annex to the Convention, and it rejects reservations made to the provisions of part V of the Convention.

Finland

16 September 1998

With regard to reservations made by Guatemala upon ratification:

"These reservations which consist of general references to national law and which do not clearly specify the extent of the derogation from the provisions of the Convention, may create serious doubts about the Commitment of the reserving State as to the object and purpose of the Convention and may contribute to undermining the basis of international treaty law. In addition, the Government of Finland considers the reservation to article 27 of the Convention particularly problematic as it is a well-established rule of customary international law. The Government of Finland would like to recall that according to article 19 *c* of the [said] Convention, a reservation incompatible with the object and purpose of the Convention shall not be permitted.

The Government of Finland therefore objects to these reservations made by the Government of Guatemala to the [said] Convention.

This objection does not preclude the entry into force of the Convention between Guatemala and Finland. The Convention will thus become operative between the two States without Guatemala benefitting from these reservations."

Germany[7]

1. The Federal Republic of Germany rejects the reservations made by Tunisia, the Union of Soviet Socialist Republics, the Byelorussian Soviet Socialist Republic, the Ukrainian Soviet Socialist Republic and the German Democratic Republic and with regard to article 66 of the Vienna Convention on the Law of Treaties as incompatible with the object and purpose of the said Convention. In this connection it wishes to point out that, as stressed on numerous other occasions, the Government of the Federal Republic of Germany considers articles 53 and 64 to be inextricably linked to article 66 (*a*).

Objections, identical in essence, *mutatis mutandis*, were also formulated by the Government of the Federal Republic of Germany in regard to reservations made by various states, as follows:

(i) 27 January 1988: in respect of reservations formulated by Bulgaria, the Hungarian People's Republic and the Czechoslovak Socialist Republic.

(ii) 21 September 1988: in respect of the reservation made by Mongolia;

(iii) 30 January 1989: in respect of the reservation made by Algeria.

12 June 2002

With respect to the reservation made by Viet Nam upon accession:

"The Government of the Federal Republic of Germany has examined the reservation to article 66 of the Vienna Convention on the Law of Treaties made by the Government of the Socialist Republic of Vietnam at the time of its accession to the Convention. The Government of the Federal Republic of Germany considers that the dispute settlement procedure provided for by article 66 is inextricably linked with the provisions of Part V of the Convention and was indeed the basis on which the Vienna Conference accepted elements of Part V. The dispute settlement set forth in article 66 therefore is an essential part of the Convention.

The Government of the Republic of Germany is thus of the view that the reservation excluding that procedures for judicial settlement, arbitration and conciliation to be followed incase of a dispute, raises doubts as to the full commitment of the Socialist Republic of Vietnam to the object and purpose of the Vienna Convention on the Law of Treaties.

The Government of the Republic of Germany, therefore, objects to the reservation made by the Government of the Socialist Republic of Vietnam.

This objection does not preclude the entry into force of the Convention between the Federal Republic of Germany and the Socialist Republic of Vietnam".

Israel

16 March 1970

"The Government of Israel has noted the political character of paragraph 2 in the declaration made by the Government of Morocco on that occasion. In the view of the Government of Israel, this Convention is not the proper place for making such political pronouncements. Moreover, that declaration cannot in any way affect the obligations of Morocco already existing under general international law or under particular treaties.

The Government of Israel will, in so far as concerns the substance of the matter, adopt towards the Government of Morocco an attitude of complete reciprocity."

16 November 1970

[With respect of declaration "A" made by the Syrian Arab Republic, same declaration, in essence, as the one above.]

Japan

"1. The Government of Japan objects to any reservation in tended to exclude the application, wholly or in part, of the pro-visions of article 66 and the Annex concerning the obligatory procedures for settlement of disputes and does not consider Japan to be in treaty relations with any State which has formulated or will formulate such reservation, in respect of those provisions of Part V of the Convention regarding which the application of the obligatory procedures mentioned above are to be excluded as a result of the said reservation. Accordingly, the treaty relations between Japan and the Syrian Arab Republic will not include those provisions of Part V of the Convention to which the conciliation procedure in the Annex applies and the treaty relations between Japan and Tunisia will not include articles 53 and 64 of the Convention.

2. The Government of Japan does not accept the interpretation of article 52 put forward by the Government of the Syrian Arab Republic, since that interpretation does not correctly reflect the conclusions reached at the Conference of Vienna on the subject of coercion."

3 April 1987

"[In view of its declaration made upon accession] ...the Government of Japan objects to the reservations made by the Governments of the German Democratic Republic and the Union of Soviet Socialist Republics to article 66 and the Annex of the Convention and reaffirms the position of Japan that [it] will not be in treaty relations with the above States in respect of the provisions of Part V of the Convention.

2. The Government of Japan objects to the reservation made by the Government of the Union of Soviet Socialist Republics to article 20, paragraph 3.

3. The Government of Japan objects to the declarations made by the Governments of the German Democratic Republic and the Union of Soviet Socialist Republics reserving their right to take any measures to safeguard their interests in the event of the non-observance by other States of the provisions of the Convention."

Netherlands

"The Kingdom of the Netherlands is of the opinion that the provisions regarding the settlement of disputes, as laid down in Article 66 of the Convention, are an important part of the Convention and that they cannot be separated from the substantive rules with which they are connected. Consequently, the Kingdom of the Netherlands considers it necessary to object to any reservation which is made by another State and whose aim is to exclude the application, wholly or in part, of the provisions regarding the settlement of disputes. While not objecting to the entry into force of the Convention between the Kingdom of the Netherlands and such a State, the Kingdom of the Netherlands considers that their treaty relations will not include the provisions of Part V of the Convention with regard to which the application of the procedures regarding the settlement of disputes, as laid down in Article 66, wholly or in part is excluded.

The Kingdom of the Netherlands considers that the absence of treaty relations between the Kingdom of the Netherlands and such a State with regard to all or certain provisions of Part V will not in any way impair the duty of the latter to fulfil any obligation embodied in those provisions to which it is subject under international law independently of the Convention.

For the reasons set out above, the Kingdom of the Netherlands objects to the reservation of the Syrian Arab Republic, according to which its accession to the Convention shall not include the Annex, and to the reservation of Tunisia, according to which the submission to the International Court of Justice of a dispute referred to in Article 66 (*a*) requires the consent of all parties there to. Accordingly, the treaty relations between the Kingdom of the Netherlands and the Syrian Arab Republic will not include the provisions to which the conciliation procedure in the Annex applies and the treaty relations between the Kingdom of the Netherlands and Tunisia will not include Article 53 and 64 of the Convention."

Objections, identical in essence, *mutatis mutandis*, were also formulated by the Government of the Netherlands in regard to reservations made by various states, as follows:

(i) 25 September 1987: in respect of reservations formulated by the Union of Soviet Socialist Republics, the Byelorussian Soviet Socialist Republic, the Ukrainian Soviet Socialist Republic and the German Democratic Republic;

(ii) 14 July 1988: in respect of reservations made by the Government of Bulgaria, Czechoslovakia and Hungary;

(iii) 28 July 1988: in respect of one of the reservations made by Mongolia;

(iv) 30 January 1989: in respect of the reservation made by Algeria.

(v) 14 September 1998: in respect of the reservation to article 66 made by Guatemala."

15 November 1999

In regard to the reservation made by Cuba upon accession:

"In conformity with the terms of the objections the Kingdom of the Netherlands must be deemed to have objected to the reservation, excluding wholly or in part the procedures for the settlement of disputes, contained in article 66 of the Convention, as formulated by Cuba. Accordingly, the treaty relations between the Kingdom of the Netherlands and Cuba under the Convention do not include any of the provisions contained in Part V of the Convention. The Kingdom of the Netherlands reiterates that the absence of treaty relations between itself and Cuba in respect of Part V of the Convention will not in any way impair the duty of Cuba to fulfil any obligation embodied in those provisions to which it is subject under international law independent of the Convention."

11 October 2001

In regard to the reservation made by Peru upon ratification:

"The Government of the Kingdom of the Netherlands has examined the reservation made by the Government of Peru at the time of its ratification of the Vienna Convention on the Law of Treaties. The Government of the Kingdom of the Netherlands notes that the articles 11, 12 and 25 of the Convention are being made subject to a general reservation referring to the contents of existing legislation in Peru.

The Government of the Kingdom of the Netherlands is of the view that, in the absence of further clarification, this reservation raises doubts as to the commitment of Peru as to the object and purpose of the Convention and would like to recall that, according to customary international law as codified in the Vienna Convention on the Law of Treaties, a reservation incompatible with the object and purpose of a treaty shall not be permitted.

It is in the common interest of States that treaties to which they have chosen to become parties are respected as to their object and purpose by all Parties and that States are prepared to undertake any legislative changes necessary to comply with their obligations under the treaties.

The Government of the Kingdom of the Netherlands therefore objects to the aforesaid reservation made by the Government of Peru to the Vienna Convention on the Law of Treaties.

This objection shall not preclude the entry into force of the Convention between the Kingdom of the Netherlands and Peru."

4 December 2001

In regard to the reservation made by Viet Nam upon accession:

"The Government of the Kingdom of the Netherlands has examined the reservation with regard to article 66 made by the Government of the Socialist Republic of Viet Nam at the time of its accession to the Vienna Convention on the Law of Treaties, concluded on 23 May 1969, and refers to the objections formulated by the Kingdom of the Netherlands upon its accession to the above-mentioned Convention on 9 April 1985.

In conformity with the terms of the objections the Kingdom of the Netherlands must be deemed to have objected to the reservation formulated by the Socialist Republic of Viet Nam, excluding wholly the procedures for the settlement of disputes contained in article 66 of the Convention. Accordingly, the treaty relations between the Kingdom of the Netherlands and the Socialist Republic of Viet Nam under the Convention do not include any of the provisions contained in Part V of the Convention.

The Kingdom of the Netherlands stresses that the absence of treaty relations between itself and the Socialist Republic of Viet Nam in respect of Part V of the Convention will not in any way impair the duty of Viet Nam to fulfil any obligation embodied in those provisions, to which it is bound under international law, independent of the Convention."

New Zealand

14 October 1971

"...The New Zealand Government objects to the reservation entered by the Government of Syria to the obligatory conciliation procedures contained in the Annex to the Vienna Convention on the Law of Treaties and does not accept the entry into force of the Convention as between New Zealand and Syria."

10 August 1972

"...The New Zealand Government objects to the reservation entered by the Government of Tunisia in respect of Article 66 (*a*) of the Convention and does not consider New Zealand to be in treaty relations with Tunisia in respect of those provisions of the Convention to which the dispute settlement procedure provided for in Article 66 (*a*) is applicable."

Sweden

4 February 1975

"Article 66 of the Convention contains certain provisions regarding procedures for judicial settlement, arbitration and conciliation. According to these provisions a dispute concerning the application or the interpretation of articles 53 or 64, which deal with the so called *jus cogens*, may be submitted to the International Court of Justice. If the dispute concerns the application or the interpretation of any of the other articles in Part V of the Convention, the conciliation procedure specified in the Annex to the Convention may be set in motion.

The Swedish Government considers that these provisions regarding the settlement of disputes are an important part of the Convention and that they cannot be separated from the substantive rules with which they are connected. Consequently, the Swedish Government considers it necessary to raise objections to any reservation which is made by another State and whose aim is to exclude the application, wholly or in part, of the provisions regarding the settlement of disputes. While not objecting to the entry into force of the Convention between Sweden and such a State, the Swedish Government considers that their treaty relations will not include either the procedural provision in respect of which a reservation has been made or the substantive provisions to which that procedural provision relates.

For the reasons set out above, the Swedish Government objects to the reservation of the Syrian Arab Republic, according to which its accession to the Convention shall not include the Annex, and to the reservation of Tunisia, according to which the dispute referred to in article 66 (*a*) requires the consent of all parties thereto in order to be submitted to the International Court of Justice for a decision. In view of these reservations, the Swedish Government considers, *firstly*, that the treaty relations between Sweden and the Syrian Arab Republic will not include those provisions of Part V of the Convention to which the conciliation procedure in the Annex applies and, *secondly*, that the treaty relations between Sweden and Tunisia will not include articles 53 and 64 of the Convention.

The Swedish Government has also taken note of the declaration of the Syrian Arab Republic, according to which it interprets the expression 'the threat or use of force' as used in article 52 of the Convention so as to extend also to the employment of economic, political, military and psychological coercion and to all types of coercion constraining a State to conclude a treaty against its wishes or its interests. On this point, the Swedish Government observes that since article 52 refers to threat or use of force in violation of the principles of international law embodied in the Charter of the United Nations, it should be interpreted in the light of the practice which has developed or will develop on the basis of the Charter."

16 September 1998

With regard to reservations made by Guatemala upon ratification:

"The Government of Sweden is of the view that these reservations raise doubts as to their compatibility with the object and purpose of the Convention. The reservations refer almost exclusively to general rules of the Vienna Convention on the Law of Treaties, many of which are solidly based on customary international law. The reservations could call into question well established and universally accepted norms.

The Government of Sweden notes in particular that the Government of Guatemala has entered a reservation that it would apply the provisions contained in article 38 of the Convention only in cases where it considered that it was in the national interest to do so; and furthermore a reservation with respect to article 27 of the Convention, to the effect that the article is understood to refer to the provisions of the secondary legislation of Guatemala and not to those of its Political Constitution, which take precedence over any law or treaty.

It is in the common interest of States that treaties to which they have chosen to become parties are respected, as to their object and purpose, by all parties and that States are prepared to undertake any legislative changes necessary to comply with their obligations under the treaties.

The Government of Sweden therefore objects to the aforesaid reservations made by the Government of Guatemala to the [said] Convention.

This objection does not preclude the entry into force of the Convention between Guatemala and Sweden. The Convention will thus become operative between the two States without Guatemala benefiting from this reservation."

17 November 1999

With regard to the reservation made by Cuba upon accession:

"The Government of Sweden wishes to recall its statements of the 4th of February 1975, made in connection with its ratification of the Convention, relating to the accession of the Syrian Arab Republic and the Republic of Tunisia respectively, which reads as follows: 'Article 66 of the Convention contains certain provisions regarding procedures for judicial settlement, arbitration and conciliation. According to these provisions a dispute concerning the application or the interpretation of articles 53 or 64, which deal with the so called *jus cogens*, may be submitted to the International Court of Justice. If the dispute concerns the application or the interpretation of any of the other articles in Part V of the Convention, the conciliation procedure specified in the Annex to the Convention may be set in motion. The Swedish Government considers that these provisions regarding the settlement of disputes are an important part of the Convention and that they cannot be separated from the substantive rules with which they are connected. Consequently, the Swedish Government considers it necessary to raise objections to any reservation which is made by another State and whose aim is to exclude the application, wholly in part, of the provisions regarding the settlement of disputes. While not objecting to the entry into force of the Convention between Sweden and such a State, the Swedish Government considers that their treaty relations will not include either the procedural provision in respect of which a reservation has been made or the substantive provisions to which that procedural provision relates.' For the reasons set out above, which also apply to the reservation made by the Republic of Cuba, the Swedish Government objects to the reservation entered by the Government of the Republic of Cuba to the Vienna Convention on the Law of Treaties."

25 July 2001

With regard to the reservation made by Peru upon ratification:

"The Government of Sweden has examined the reservation made by Peru at the time of its ratification of the Vienna Convention on the Law of Treaties.

The Government of Sweden notes that articles 11, 12 and 25 of the Convention are being made subject to a general reservation referring to the contents of existing legislation in Peru.

The Government of Sweden is of the view that, in the absence of further clarification, this reservation raises doubts as to the commitment of Peru to the object and purpose of the Convention and would like to recall that, according to customary international law as codified in the Vienna Convention on the Law of Treaties, a reservation incompatible with the object and purpose of a treaty shall not be permitted.

It is in the common interest of States that treaties to which they have chosen to become parties are respected as to their object and purpose, by all parties, and that States are prepared to undertake any legislative changes necessary to comply with their obligations under the treaties.

The Government of Sweden therefore objects to the aforesaid reservation by the Government of Peru to the Vienna Convention on the Law of Treaties.

This objection shall not preclude the entry into force of the Convention between Peru and Sweden. The Convention enters into force in its entirety between the two States, without Peru benefiting from its reservation."

United Kingdom of Great Britain and Northern Ireland

"The United Kingdom does not accept that the interpretation of Article 52 put forward by the Government of Syria correctly reflects the conclusions reached at the Conference of Vienna on the subject of coercion; the Conference dealt with this matter by adopting a Declaration on this subject which forms part of the Final Act;

The United Kingdom objects to the reservation entered by the Government of Syria in respect of the Annex to the Convention and does not accept the entry into force of the Convention as between the United Kingdom and Syria;

With reference to a reservation in relation to the territory of British Honduras made by Guatemala on signing the Convention, the United Kingdom does not accept that Guatemala has any rights or any valid claim with respect to that territory;

The United Kingdom fully reserves its position in other respects with regard to the declarations made by various States on signature, to some of which the United Kingdom would object, if they were to be confirmed on ratification."

22 June 1972

"...The United Kingdom objects to the reservation entered by the Government of Tunisia in respect of Article 66 (*a*) of the Convention and does not accept the entry into force of the Convention as between the United Kingdom and Tunisia."

7 December 1977

"The Government of the United Kingdom of Great Britain and Northern Ireland note that the instrument of ratification of the Government of Finland, which was deposited with the Secretary-General on 19 August 1977, contains a declaration relating to paragraph 2 of article 7 of the Convention. The Government of the United Kingdom wish to inform the Secretary-General that they do not regard that declaration as in any way affecting the interpretation or application of article 7."

5 June 1987

"The Government of the United Kingdom of Great Britain and Northern Ireland object to the reservation entered by the Government of the Union of Soviet Socialist Republics by which it rejects the application of article 66 of the Convention. Article 66 provides in certain circumstances for the compulsory settlement of disputes by the International Court of Justice (in the case of disputes concerning the application or interpretation of articles 53 or 64) or by a conciliation procedure (in the case of the rest of Part V of the Convention). These provisions are inextricably linked with the provisions of Part V to which they relate. Their inclusion was the basis on which those parts of Part V which represent progressive development of international law were accepted by the Vienna Conference. Accordingly the United Kingdom does not consider that the treaty relations between it and the Soviet Union include Part V of the Convention.

With respect to any other reservation the intention of which is to exclude the application, in whole or in part, of the provisions of article 66, to which the United Kingdom has already objected or which is made after the reservation by the Government of the Union of Soviet Socialist Republics, the United Kingdom will not consider its treaty relations with the State which has formulated or will formulate such a reservation as including those provisions of Part V of the Convention with regard to which the application of article 66 is rejected by the reservation.

The instrument of accession deposited by the Union of Soviet Socialist Republics included also a declaration that it reserves the right to take 'any measures' to safeguard its interests in the event of the non-observance by other States of the provisions of the Convention. The purpose and scope of this statement is unclear; but, given that the Union of Soviet Socialist Republics has rejected the application of article 66 of the Convention, it would seem to apply rather to acts by Parties to the Convention in respect of treaties where such acts are in breach of the Convention. In such circumstances a State would not be limited in its response to the measures in article 60: under customary international law it would be entitled to take other measures, provided always that they are reasonable and in proportion to the breach."

11 October 1989

With regard to the reservation made by Algeria upon accession:

"The Government of the United Kingdom wish in this context to recall their declaration of 5 June 1987 [in respect of the accession of the Union of Soviet Socialist Republics] which in accordance with its terms applies to the reservations mentioned above, and will similarly apply to any like reservations which any other State may formulate."

19 November 1999

With regard to the reservation made by Cuba upon accession:

"The Government of the United Kingdom of Great Britain and Northern Ireland objects to the reservation [...]. The Government of the United Kingdom wishes in this context to recall their declaration of 5 June 1987 (in respect of the accession of the Union of Soviet Socialist Republics) which in accordance with its terms applies to the reservation mentioned above, and will apply similarly to any like reservation which any other State may formulate. Accordingly the United Kingdom does not consider that the treaty relations between it and the Republic of Cuba include Part V of the Convention."

22 July 2002

With regard to the reservation made by Viet Nam upon accession:

"The instrument of accession deposited by the Government of the Socialist Republic of Vietnam contains a reservation in respect of article 66 of the Convention. The United Kingdom objects to the reservation entered by the Socialist Republic of Vietnam in respect of article 66 and does not accept the entry into force of the Convention as between the United Kingdom and the Socialist Republic of Vietnam."

United States of America

26 May 1971

The Government of the United States of America objects to reservation E of the Syrian instrument of accession:

"In the view of the United States Government that reservation is incompatible with the object and purpose of the Convention and undermines the principle of impartial settlement of disputes concerning the invalidity, termination, and suspension of the operation of treaties, which was the subject of extensive negotiation at the Vienna Conference.

The United States Government intends, at such time as it may become a party to the Vienna Convention on the Law of Treaties, to reaffirm its objection to the foregoing reservation and to reject treaty relations with the Syrian Arab Republic under all provisions in Part V of the Convention with regard to which the Syrian Arab Republic has rejected the obligatory conciliation procedures set forth in the Annex to the Convention.

The United States Government is also concerned about Syrian reservation C declaring that the Syrian Arab Republic does not accept the non-applicability of the principle of a fundamental change of circumstances with regard to treaties establishing boundaries, as stated in Article 62, 2 (*a*), and Syrian reservation D concerning its interpretation of the expression 'the threat or use of force' in Article 52. However, in view of the United States Government's intention to reject treaty relations with the Syrian Arab Republic under all provisions in Part V to which reservations C and D relate, we do not consider it necessary at this time to object formally to those reservations.

The United States Government will consider that the absence of treaty relations between the United States of America and the Syrian Arab Republic with regard to certain provisions in Part V will not in any way impair the duty of the latter to fulfil any obligation embodied in those provisions to which it is subject under international law independently of the Vienna Convention on the Law of Treaties."

29 September 1972

"… The United States of America objects to the reservation by Tunisia to paragraph *(a)* of Article 66 of the Vienna Convention on the Law of Treaties regarding a dispute as to the interpretation or application of Article 53 or 64. The right of a party to invoke the provisions of Article 53 or 64 is inextricably linked with the provisions of Article 42 regarding impeachment of the validity of a treaty and paragraph *(a)* of Article 66 regarding the right of any party to submit to the International Court of Justice for decision any dispute concerning the application or the interpretation of Article 53 or 64.

Accordingly, the United States Government intends, at such time as it becomes a party to the Convention, to reaffirm its objection to the Tunisian reservation and declare that it will not consider that Article 53 or 64 of the Convention is in force between the United States of America and Tunisia."

Notifications made under the Annex (paragraphs 1 and 2) (List of conciliators nominated for the purpose of constituting a conciliation commission) (For the list of conciliators whose nomination was not renewed, see note 21 hereinafter).[21]

Participant	*Nominations*	*Date of deposit of notification with the Secretary-General*
Austria[22]	Ambassador Helmut Türk	8 Jan 2001
Austria[22]	Professor Karl Zemanek	8 Jan 2001
Croatia	Dr. Stanko Nick	14 Dec 1992
Croatia	Professor Dr. Budislav Vukas	14 Dec 1992
Denmark[22]	Prof. Isi Foighel	7 Mar 1995
Denmark[22]	Ambassador Skjold Gustav Mellbin	7 Mar 1995
Germany	Prof. Dr. Wolff Heintschel von Heinegg	12 Mar 2001
Germany	Dr. Andreas Zimmermann	12 March 2001
Paraguay	Dr. Luis María Ramírez Boettner	22 Sep 1994
Paraguay	Dr. Jerónimo Irala Burgos	22 Sept 1994
Portugal	Professor Wladimir Brito	5 Oct 2011
Portugal	Professor Francisco Ferreira de Almelda	5 Oct 2011

Participant	***Nominations***	***Date of deposit of notification with the Secretary-General***
Slovakia	Dr. Igor Grexa, Director-General for Legal and Consular Affairs, Ministry of Foreign Affairs of Slovakia	9 Jul 2004
Spain	Sr. D. José Antonio Pastor Ridruejo	3 Jan 2001
Spain	Sr. D. Aurelio Pérez Giralda	3 Jan 2001
Sweden[22]	Mr. Hans Danelius	17 Feb 1994
Sweden[22]	Mr. Love Gustav-Adolf Kellberg	17 Feb 1994
Switzerland	Mr. Lucius Caflisch, Judge at the European Court of Human Rights	6 March 2008
Switzerland	Mr. Walter Kälin, Professor of Public Law and International Law at the University of Berne	6 March 2008
The former Yugoslav Republic of Macedonia	Mrs. Elena Andreevska, Director of the Directorate on International Law	3 Mar 1999
The former Yugoslav Republic of Macedonia	Mr. Goran Stevcevski, Director of the Directorate on International Law	27 April 2011

End Note:

1. Official Records of the General Assembly, Twenty-first Session, Supplement No. 16 (A/6316), p. 95.

2. bid., Twenty-second Session, Supplement No. 16 (A/6716), p. 80.

3. The former Yugoslavia had signed and ratified the Convention on 23 May 1969 and 27 August 1970, respectively. See also note 1 under "Bosnia and Herzegovina", "Croatia", "former Yugoslavia", "Slovenia", "The Former Yugoslav Republic of Macedonia" and "Yugoslavia" in the "Historical Information" section in the front matter of this volume.

4. Signed on behalf of the Republic of China on 27 April 1970. See note concerning signatures, ratifications, accessions, etc., on behalf of China (note 1 under "China" in the "Historical Information" section in the front matter of this volume).

In a communication addressed to the Secretary-General with reference to the above-mentioned signature, the Permanent Mission of the Union of Soviet Socialist Republics stated that the said signature was irregular since the so-called "Government of China" represented no one and had no right to speak on behalf of China, there being only one Chinese State in the world-the People's Republic of China.

The Permanent Mission of Bulgaria to the United Nations later addressed to the Secretary-General a similar communication.

In two letters addressed to the Secretary-General in regard to the above-mentioned communications, the Permanent Representative of China to the United Nations stated that the Republic of China, a sovereign State and Member of the United Nations, had attended the United Nations Conference on the Law of Treaties in 1968 and 1969, contributed to the formulation of the Convention concerned and signed it, and that "any statements or reservations to the said Convention that are incompatible with or derogatory to the legitimate position of the Government of the Republic of China shall in no way affect the rights and obligations of the Republic of China as a signatory of the said Convention".

5. Czechoslovakia had acceded to the Convention on 29 July 1987, with a reservation. By a communication received on 19 October 1990, the Government of Czechoslovakia notified the Secretary-General of its decision to withdraw the reservation made upon accession with respect to article 66 of the Convention, which reads as follows:

The Czechoslovak Socialist Republic does not consider itself bound by the provisions of article 66 of the Convention and declares that, in accordance with the principle of sovereign equality of States, for any dispute to be submitted to the International Court of Justice or to a conciliation procedure, the consent of all the parties to the dispute is required in each separate case.

See also note 1 under "Czech Republic" and note 1 under "Slovakia" in the "Historical Information" section in the front matter of this volume.

6. See note 1 under "Germany" in the "Historical Information" section in the front matter of this volume.

7. The German Democratic Republic had acceded to the Convention on 20 October 1986 with the following reservation and declarations:

Reservation:

The German Democratic Republic does not consider itself bound by the provisions of article 66 of the Convention.

In order to submit a dispute concerning the application or the interpretation of article 53 or 64 to the International Court of Justice for a decision or to submit a dispute on the application or the interpretation of any of the other articles of Part V of the Convention to the Conciliation Commission for consideration it shall be necessary in every single case to have the consent of all Parties to the dispute. The members of the Conciliation commission shall be appointed jointly by the Parties to the dispute.

Declarations:

The German Democratic Republic declares that it reserves itself the right to take measures to protect its interests in the case that other States would not comply with the provisions of the Convention.

The German Democratic Republic holds the view that the provisions of articles 81 and 83 of the Convention are in contradiction to the principle according to which any State, the policy of which is guided by the purposes and principles of the United Nations Charter, has the right to become a Party to Conventions affecting the interests of all States.

See also note 2 under "Germany" in the "Historical Information" section in the front matter of this volume.

8. See note 1 under "Montenegro" in the "Historical Information" section in the front matter of this volume.

9. See note 1 under "Netherlands" regarding Aruba/Netherlands Antilles in the "Historical Information" section in the front matter of this volume.

10. With reference to this signature, communications have been addressed to the Secretary-General by the Permanent Missions to the United Nations of Bulgaria, Mongolia and the Union of Soviet Socialist Republics, stating that the said signature was illegal inasmuch as the South Korean authorities could not under any circumstances speak on behalf of Korea.

In a communication addressed to the Secretary-General the Permanent Observer of the Republic of Korea to the United Nations declared that the above-mentioned statement by the Permanent Mission of the Union of Soviet Socialist Republics was without legal foundation and therefore neither affected the legitimate act of signing the Convention by the Government of the Republic of Korea nor prejudiced the rights and obligations of the Republic of Korea under it. He further stated that "in this connexion, it should be noted that the General Assembly of the United Nations declared at its third session and has continuously reaffirmed thereafter that the Government of the Republic of Korea is the only lawful Government in Korea".

Subsequently, in a communication received on 24 October 2002, the Government of Bulgaria informed the Secretary-General of the following:

"...upon signature of the above Convention by the Republic of Korea, in 1971, the Government of the People's Republic of Bulgaria[,] in [a] communication addressed to the Secretary-General with reference to the above-mentioned signature, ... stated that its Government considered the said signature was illegal inasmuch as the South Korean authorities could not speak on behalf of Korea.

Now therefore [the Government of the Republic of Bulgaria declares] that the Government of the Republic of Bulgaria, having reviewed the said declaration, hereby withdraws the same."

11. Within a period of one year from the date of the depositary notification transmitting the reservation (i.e. 13 July 2005), none of the Contracting Parties to the said Convention had notified the Secretary-General of an objection either to the deposit itself or to the procedure envisaged. Consequently, the reservation in question was accepted for deposit upon the above-stipulated one year period, that is on 13 July 2006.

12. On 18 February 1993, the Government of Belgium notified the Secretary-General that its instrument of accession should have specified that the said accession was made subject to the said reservation. None of the Contracting Parties to the Agreement having notified the Secretary-General of an objection either to the deposit itself or to the procedure envisaged, within a period of 90 days from the date its circulation (23 March 1993), the reservation is deemed to have been accepted.

13. In a notification received on 6 May 1994, the Government of Bulgaria notified the Secretary-General that it had decided to withdraw the reservation made upon accession with regard to article 66 (*a*), which read as follows:

The People's Republic of Bulgaria does not consider itself bound by the provision of article 66, paragraph *a)* of the Convention, according to which any one of the parties to a dispute concerning the application or the interpretation of article 53 or 64 may, by a written application, submit it to the International Court of Justice for a decision unless the parties by common consent agree to submit the dispute to arbitration. The

Government of the People's Republic of Bulgaria states that for the submission of such a dispute to the International Court of Justice for a decision, the preliminary consent of all parties to the dispute is needed.

14. In this regard, on 13 October 1998, the Secretary-General received from the Government of the United Kingdom of Great Britain and Northern Ireland the following communication: "The Government of the United Kingdom object to the reservation entered by Costa Rica in respect of article 27 and reiterate their observation in respect of the similar reservation entered by the Republic of Guatemala."

15. On 20 April 2001, the Government of Finland informed the Secretary-General that it had decided to withdraw its declaration in respect of article 7(2) made upon ratification. The text of the declaration reads as follows:

"Finland declares its understanding that nothing in paragraph 2 of article 7 of the Convention is intended to modify any provisions of internal law in force in any Contracting State concerning competence to conclude treaties. Under the Constitution of Finland the competence to conclude treaties is given to the President of the Republic, who also decides on the issuance of full powers to the Head of Government and the Minister for Foreign Affairs."

16. On 15 March 2007, the Government of Guatemala informed the Secretary-General of that it had decided the following:

"Withdraw in their entirety the reservations formulated by the Republic of Guatemala on 23 May 1969 and confirmed upon 14 May 1997 to Articles 11 and 12 of the Vienna Convention on the Law of Treaties."

The text of the reservations made upon signature and ratification read as follows:

Upon signature:

Reservations:

I. Guatemala cannot accept any provision of this Convention which would prejudice its rights and its claim to the Territory of Belize.

II. Guatemala will not apply articles 11, 12, 25 and 66 in so far as they are contrary to the provisions of the Constitution of the Republic.

III. Guatemala will apply the provision contained in article 38 only in cases where it considers that it is in the national interest to do so.

Upon ratification:

Reservations:

(*a*) The Republic of Guatemala formally confirms reservations I and III which it formulated upon signing the [said Convention], to the effect, respectively, that Guatemala could not accept any provision of the Convention which would prejudice its rights and its claim to the territory of Belize and that it would apply the provision contained in article 38 of the Convention only in cases where it considered that it was in the national interest to do so;

(*b*) With respect to reservation II, which was formulated on the same occasion and which indicated that the Republic of Guatemala would not apply articles 11,12, 25 and 66 of the [said Convention] insofar as they were contrary to the Constitution, Guatemala states: (*b*) (I) That it confirms the reservation with respect to the non-application of articles 25 and 66 of the Convention, insofar as both are incompatible with provisions of the Political Constitution currently in force; (*b*) (II) That it also confirms the reservation with respect to the non-application of articles 11 and 12 of the Convention.

Guatemala's consent to be bound by a treaty subject to compliance with the requirements and procedures established in its Political Constitution. For Guatemala, the signature or initialling of a treaty by its representative is always understood to be ad referendum and subject, in either case, to confirmation by its Government.

(*c*) A reservation is hereby formulated with respect to article 27 of the Convention, to the effect that the article is understood to refer to the provisions of the secondary legislation of Guatemala and not to those of its Political Constitution, which take precedence over any law or treaty.

In will be recalled that the Secretary-General received communications in regard to the said reservations from the various States on the dates indicated hereinafter:

Germany (21 September 1998):

These reservations refer almost exclusively to general rules of the Convention many of which are solidly based on customary international law. The reservations could call into question well-established and universally-accepted norms of international law, especially insofar as the reservations concern articles 27 and 38 of the Convention. The Government of the Federal Republic of Germany is of the view that the reservations also raise doubts as to their compatibility with the object and purpose of the Convention. The Government of the Federal Republic of Germany therefore objects to these reservations. This objection does not preclude the entry into force of the Convention between Germany and Guatemala.

Belgium (30 September 1998):

The reservations entered by Guatemala essentially concern general rules laid down in the [said Convention], many of which form part of customary international law. These reservations could call into question firmly established and universally accepted norms. The Kingdom of Belgium therefore raises an objection to the reservations. This objection does not prevent the [said Convention] from taking effect between the Kingdom of Belgium and Guatemala.

United Kingdom of Great Britain and Northen Ireland (13 October 1998):

"The Government of the United Kingdom of Great Britain and Northern Ireland object to the reservation entered by the Republic of Guatemala in respect of article 27, and wish to observe that the customary international law rule set out in that article applies to constitutional as well as to other internal laws. The Government of the United Kingdom object also to the reservation entered by the Republic of Guatemala in respect of article 38, by which the Republic of Guatemala seek subjective application of the rule of customary international law set out in that article. The Government of the United Kingdom wish to recall their declaration of 5 June 1987 (in respect of the accession of the Union of Soviet Socialist Republics), which, in accordance with its terms, applies to the reservation entered by the Republic of Guatemala in respect of article 66 and will similarly apply to any like reservation which any other State may formulate."

17. In a communication received on 8 December 1989, the Government of Hungary notified the Secretary-General that it had decided to withdraw as from that date, its reservation regarding article 66 made upon accession which reservation reads as follows:

The Hungarian People's Republic does not consider itself bound by the provisions of article 66 of the Vienna Convention on the Law of Treaties and declares that submission of a dispute concerning the application or the interpretation of article 53 or 64 to the International Court of Justice for a decision or submission of a dispute concerning the application or the interpretation of any articles in Part V of the Convention to a conciliation commission for consideration shall be subject to the consent of all the parties to the dispute and that the conciliators constituting the conciliation commission shall have been nominated exclusively with the common consent of the parties to the dispute.

18. In a communication received on 19 July 1990, the Government of Mongolia notified the Secretary-General of its decision to withdraw the reservation made upon accession, which reads as follows:

1. The Mongolian People's Republic does not consider itself bound by the provisions of article 66 of the Convention.

The Mongolian People's Republic declares that submission of any dispute concerning the application or the interpretation of articles 53 and 64 to the International Court of Justice for a decision as well as submission of any dispute concerning the application or the interpretation of any other articles in Part V of the Convention to a conciliation commission for consideration shall be subject to the consent of all the parties to the dispute in each separate case, and that the conciliators constituting the conciliation commission shall be appointed by the parties to the dispute by common consent.

2. The Mongolian People's Republic is not obligated by the provisions of article 45 (*b*) of the Vienna Convention on the Law of Treaties, since they are contrary to established international practice.

19. On 14 November 2001, the Secretary-General received from the Government of Austria the following communication:

"Austria has examined the reservation made by the Government of Peru at the time of its ratification of the Vienna Convention on the Law of Treaties, regarding the application of articles 11, 12 and 25 of the Convention.

The fact that Peru is making the application of the said articles subject to a general reservation referring to the contents of existing national legislation, in the absence of further clarification raises doubts as to the commitment of Peru to the object and purpose of the Convention. According to customary international law as codified in the Vienna Convention on the Law of Treaties, a reservation incompatible with the object and purpose of a treaty shall not be permitted. In Austria's view the reservation in question is therefore inadmissible to the extent that its application could negatively affect the compliance by Peru with its obligations under articles 11, 12 and 25 of the Convention.

For these reasons, Austria objects to the reservation made by the Government of Peru to the Vienna Convention on the Law of Treaties.

This objection shall not preclude the entry into force of the Convention in its entirety between Peru and Austria, without Peru benefiting from its reservation."

In this regard, the Secretary-General received, on 21 January 2002, from the Government of Peru the following communication:

[The Government of Peru refers to the communication made by the Government of Austria relating to the reservation made by Peru upon ratification]. In this document, Member States are informed of a communication from the Government of Austria stating its objection to the reservation entered in respect of the Vienna Convention on the Law of Treaties by the Government of Peru on 14 September 2000 when depositing the corresponding instrument of ratification.

As the [Secretariat] is aware, article 20, paragraph 5, of the Vienna Convention states that "a reservation is considered to have been accepted by a State if it shall have raised no objection to the reservation by the end of a period of twelve months after it was notified of the reservation (...)". The ratification and reservation by Peru in respect of the Vienna Convention were communicated to Member States on 9 November 2000.

Since the communication from the Austrian Government was received by the Secretariat on 14 November 2001 and circulated to Member States on 28 November 2001, the Peruvian Mission is of the view that there is tacit acceptance on the part of the Austrian Government of the reservation entered by Peru, the 12-month period referred to in article 20, paragraph 5, of the Vienna Convention having elapsed without any objection being raised. The Peruvian Government considers the communication from the Austrian Government as being without legal effect, since it was not submitted in a timely manner.

20. On 24 February 1998, the Secretary-General received from the Government of Guatemala the following communication:

Guatemala maintains a territorial dispute over the illegal occupation of part of its territory by the Government of the United Kingdom of Great Britain and Northern Ireland, succeeded by the Government of Belize, and Guatemala therefore continues to assert a valid claim based on international law which must be settled by restoring to it the territory which historically and legally belongs to it.

21. The nomination of the conciliators listed hereinafter was not renewed after five years. For the date of their nomination and their titles, see the preceding editions of the present publication:

State:	***Conciliators:***
Australia	Mr. Patrick Brazil
Austria	Professorr Stephen Verosta, Dr. Helmut Tuerk, Dr. Karl Zemanek
Cyprus	M. Criton Tornaritis, Mr. Michalakis Triantafillides, Mrs. Stella Soulioti
Denmark	Ambassador Paul Fischer
Finland	Professor Isi Foighel, Professor Erik Castrén
Germany	Professor Thomas Oppermann (German Democratic Republic), Professor Günther Jaenicke (German Democratic Republic)
Iran (Islamic Republic of)	Mr. Morteza Kalantarian

State:	***Conciliators:***
Italy	Professor Riccardo Monaco, Professor Luigi Ferrari-Bravo
Japan	Professor Shigejiro Tabata, Judge Masato Fujisaki
Kenya	Mr. John Maximian Nazareth
	Mr. S. Amos Wako
Mexico	Mr. Antonio Gomez Robledo, Mr. César Sepúlveda, Ambassador Alfonso de Rosenzweig-Diáz
Morocco	Mr. Abdelaziz Amine Filali, Mr. Ibrahim Keddara, Mr. Abdelaziz Benjelloun
Netherlands	Professor W. Riphagen, Professor A.M. Stuyt,
Panama	Mr. Jorge E. Illueca, Mr. Nanader A. Pitty Velasquez
Spain	Professor Julio Diego González Campos, Professor Manuel Diez de Velasco Vallejo
Sweden	Mr. Gunnar Lagergren, Mr. Ivan Wallenberg
United Kingdom of Great Britain and Northern Ireland	Professor R.Y. Jennings, Sir Ian Sinclaire
Yugoslavia (former)	Dr. Milan Bulajic, Dr. Milivoj Despot, Dr. Budislav Vukas, Dr. Borut Bohte

22. Designation renewed on that date for a term of five years.

Annex V

Guide to Practice on Reservations to Treaties (2011)

Adopted by the International Law Commission at its sixty-third session, in 2011, and submitted to the General Assembly as a part of the Commission's report covering the work of that session (A/66/10, para. 75). The report will appear in *Yearbook of the International Law Commission*, 2011, vol. II, Part Two.

1. Definitions

1.1 Definition of reservations

1. "Reservation" means a unilateral statement, however phrased or named, made by a State or an international organization when signing, ratifying, formally confirming, accepting, approving or acceding to a treaty, or by a State when making a notification of succession to a treaty, whereby the State or organization purports to exclude or to modify the legal effect of certain provisions of the treaty in their application to that State or to that international organization.

2. Paragraph 1 is to be interpreted as including reservations which purport to exclude or to modify the legal effect of certain provisions of a treaty, or of the treaty as a whole with respect to certain specific aspects, in their application to the State or to the international organization which formulates the reservation.

1.1.1 Statements purporting to limit the obligations of their author

A unilateral statement formulated by a State or an international organization at the time when that State or that organization expresses its consent to be bound by a treaty, by which its author purports to limit the obligations imposed on it by the treaty, constitutes a reservation.

1.1.2 Statements purporting to discharge an obligation by equivalent means

A unilateral statement formulated by a State or an international organization at the time when that State or that organization expresses its consent to be bound by a treaty, by which that State or that organization purports to discharge an obligation pursuant to the treaty in a manner different from, but considered by the author of the statement to be equivalent to that imposed by the treaty, constitutes a reservation.

1.1.3 Reservations relating to the territorial application of the treaty

A unilateral statement by which a State purports to exclude the application of some provisions of a treaty, or of the treaty as a whole with respect to certain specific aspects, to a territory to which they would be applicable in the absence of such a statement constitutes a reservation.

1.1.4 Reservations formulated when extending the territorial application of a treaty

A unilateral statement by which a State, when extending the application of a treaty to a territory, purports to exclude or to modify the legal effect of certain provisions of the treaty in relation to that territory constitutes a reservation.

1.1.5 Reservations formulated jointly

The joint formulation of a reservation by several States or international organizations does not affect the unilateral character of that reservation.

1.1.6 Reservations formulated by virtue of clauses expressly authorizing the exclusion or the modification of certain provisions of a treaty

A unilateral statement made by a State or an international organization when that State or organization expresses its consent to be bound by a treaty, in accordance with a clause expressly authorizing the parties or some of them to exclude or to modify the legal effect of certain provisions of the treaty with regard to the party that has made the statement, constitutes a reservation expressly authorized by the treaty.

1.2 Definition of interpretative declarations

"Interpretative declaration" means a unilateral statement, however phrased or named, made by a State or an international organization, whereby that State or that organization purports to specify or clarify the meaning or scope of a treaty or of certain of its provisions.

1.2.1 Interpretative declarations formulated jointly

The joint formulation of an interpretative declaration by several States or international organizations does not affect the unilateral character of that interpretative declaration.

1.3 Distinction between reservations and interpretative declarations

The character of a unilateral statement as a reservation or as an interpretative declaration is determined by the legal effect that its author purports to produce.

1.3.1 Method of determining the distinction between reservations and interpretative declarations

To determine whether a unilateral statement formulated by a State or an international organization in respect of a treaty is a reservation or an interpretative declaration, the statement should be interpreted in good faith in accordance with the ordinary meaning to be given to its terms, with a view to identifying there from the intention of its author, in light of the treaty to which it refers.

1.3.2 Phrasing and name

The phrasing or name of a unilateral statement provides an indication of the purported legal effect.

1.3.3 Formulation of a unilateral statement when a reservation is prohibited

When a treaty prohibits reservations to all or certain of its provisions, a unilateral statement formulated in respect of those provisions by a State or an international organization shall be presumed not to constitute a reservation. Such a statement nevertheless constitutes a reservation if it purports to exclude or modify the legal effect of certain provisions of the treaty, or of the treaty as a whole with respect to certain specific aspects, in their application to its author.

1.4 Conditional interpretative declarations

1. A conditional interpretative declaration is a unilateral statement formulated by a State or an international organization when signing, ratifying, formally confirming, accepting, approving or acceding to a treaty, or by a State when making a notification of succession to a treaty, whereby the State or international organization subjects its consent to be bound by the treaty to a specific interpretation of the treaty or of certain provisions thereof.

2. Conditional interpretative declarations are subject to the rules applicable to reservations.

1.5 Unilateral statements other than reservations and interpretative declarations

Unilateral statements formulated in relation to a treaty which are not reservations nor interpretative declarations (including conditional interpretative declarations) are outside the scope of the present Guide to Practice.

1.5.1 Statements of non-recognition

A unilateral statement by which a State indicates that its participation in a treaty does not imply recognition of an entity which it does not recognize is outside the scope of the present Guide to Practice even if it purports to exclude the application of the treaty between the declaring State and the non-recognized entity.

1.5.2 Statements concerning modalities of implementation of a treaty at the internal level

A unilateral statement formulated by a State or an international organization whereby that State or that organization indicates the manner in which it intends to implement a treaty at the internal level, without affecting its rights and obligations towards the other contracting States or contracting organizations, is outside the scope of the present Guide to Practice.

1.5.3 Unilateral statements made under a clause providing for options

1. A unilateral statement made by a State or an international organization, in accordance with a clause in a treaty permitting the parties to accept an obligation that is not otherwise imposed by the treaty, or permitting them to choose between two or more provisions of the treaty, is outside the scope of the present Guide to Practice.

2. A restriction or condition contained in a statement by which a State or an international organization accepts, by virtue of a clause in a treaty, an obligation that is not otherwise imposed by the treaty does not constitute a reservation.

1.6 Unilateral statements in respect of bilateral treaties

1.6.1 "Reservations" to bilateral treaties

A unilateral statement, however phrased or named, formulated by a State or an international organization after initialling or signature but prior to entry into force of a bilateral treaty, by which that State or that organization purports to obtain from the other party a modification of the provisions of the treaty, does not constitute a reservation within the meaning of the present Guide to Practice.

1.6.2 Interpretative declarations in respect of bilateral treaties

Guidelines 1.2 and 1.4 are applicable to interpretative declarations in respect of both multilateral and bilateral treaties.

1.6.3 Legal effect of acceptance of an interpretative declaration made in respect of a bilateral treaty by the other party

The interpretation resulting from an interpretative declaration made in respect of a bilateral treaty by a State or an international organization party to the treaty and accepted by the other party constitutes an authentic interpretation of that treaty.

1.7 Alternatives to reservations and interpretative declarations

1.7.1 Alternatives to reservations

In order to achieve results comparable to those effected by reservations, States or international organizations may also have recourse to alternative procedures, such as:

- the insertion in the treaty of a clause purporting to limit its scope or application;
- the conclusion of an agreement, under a specific provision of a treaty, by which two or more States or international organizations purport to exclude or modify the legal effect of certain provisions of the treaty as between themselves.

1.7.2 Alternatives to interpretative declarations

In order to specify or clarify the meaning or scope of a treaty or certain of its provisions, States or international organizations may also have recourse to procedures other than interpretative declarations, such as:

- the insertion in the treaty of provisions purporting to interpret the treaty;
- the conclusion of a supplementary agreement to the same end, simultaneously or subsequently to the conclusion of the treaty.

1.8 Scope of definitions

The definitions of unilateral statements included in the present Part are without prejudice to the validity and legal effects of such statements under the rules applicable to them.

2. Procedure

2.1 Form and notification of reservations

2.1.1 Form of reservations

A reservation must be formulated in writing.

2.1.2 Statement of reasons for reservations

A reservation should, to the extent possible, indicate the reasons why it is being formulated.

2.1.3 Representation for the purpose of formulating a reservation at the international level

1. Subject to the usual practices followed in international organizations which are depositaries of treaties, a person is considered as representing a State or an international organization for the purpose of formulating a reservation if:

(*a*) that person produces appropriate full powers for the purposes of adopting or authenticating the text of the treaty with regard to which the reservation is formulated or expressing the consent of the State or organization to be bound by the treaty; or (*b*) it appears from practice or from other circumstances that it was the intention of the States and international organizations concerned to consider that person as representing the State or the international organization for such purposes without having to produce full powers.

2. In virtue of their functions and without having to produce full powers, the following are considered as representing their State for the purpose of formulating a reservation at the international level:

(*a*) Heads of State, Heads of Government and Ministers for Foreign Affairs;

(*b*) representatives accredited by States to an international conference, for the purpose of formulating a reservation to a treaty adopted at that conference;

(*c*) representatives accredited by States to an international organization or one of its organs, for the purpose of formulating a reservation to a treaty adopted in that organization or organ;

(*d*) heads of permanent missions to an international organization, for the purpose of formulating a reservation to a treaty between the accrediting States and that organization.

2.1.4 Absence of consequences at the international level of the violation of internal rules regarding the formulation of reservations

1. The competent authority and the procedure to be followed at the internal level for formulating a reservation are determined by the internal law of each State or the relevant rules of each international organization.

2. A State or an international organization may not invoke the fact that a reservation has been formulated in violation of a provision of the internal law of that State or the rules of that organization regarding competence and the procedure for formulating reservations for the purpose of invalidating the reservation.

2.1.5 Communication of reservations

1. A reservation must be communicated in writing to the contracting States and contracting organizations and other States and international organizations entitled to become parties to the treaty.

2. A reservation to a treaty in force which is the constituent instrument of an international organization must also be communicated to such organization.

2.1.6 Procedure for communication of reservations

1. Unless otherwise provided in the treaty or agreed by the contracting States and contracting organizations, the communication of a reservation to a treaty shall be transmitted:

(i) if there is no depositary, directly by the author of the reservation to the contracting States and contracting organizations and other States and international organizations entitled to become parties to the treaty; or

(ii) if there is a depositary, to the latter, which shall notify the States and international organizations for which it is intended as soon as possible.

2. The communication of a reservation shall be considered as having been made with regard to a State or an international organization only upon receipt by that State or organization.

3. The communication of a reservation to a treaty by means other than a diplomatic note or depositary notification, such as electronic mail or facsimile, must be confirmed within an appropriate period of time by such a note or notification. In such case, the reservation is considered as having been formulated at the date of the initial communication.

2.1.7 Functions of depositaries

1. The depositary shall examine whether a reservation to a treaty formulated by a State or an international organization is in due and proper form and, if need be, bring the matter to the attention of the State or international organization concerned.

2. In the event of any difference appearing between a State or an international organization and the depositary as to the performance of the latter's functions, the depositary shall bring the question to the attention of:

(*a*) the signatory States and organizations and the contracting States and contracting organizations; or

(*b*) where appropriate, the competent organ of the international organization concerned.

2.2 Confirmation of reservations

2.2.1 Formal confirmation of reservations formulated when signing a treaty

If formulated when signing a treaty subject to ratification, act of formal confirmation, acceptance or approval, a reservation must be formally confirmed by the reserving State or international organization when expressing its consent to be bound by the treaty. In such a case, the reservation shall be considered as having been formulated on the date of its confirmation.

2.2.2 Instances of non-requirement of confirmation of reservations formulated when signing a treaty

A reservation formulated when signing a treaty does not require subsequent confirmation when a State or an international organization expresses by signature its consent to be bound by the treaty.

2.2.3 Reservations formulated upon signature when a treaty expressly so provides

Where the treaty expressly provides that a State or an international organization may formulate a reservation when signing the treaty, such a reservation does not require formal confirmation by the reserving State or international organization when expressing its consent to be bound by the treaty.

2.2.4 Form of formal confirmation of reservations

The formal confirmation of a reservation must be made in writing.

2.3 Late formulation of reservations

A State or an international organization may not formulate a reservation to a treaty after expressing its consent to be bound by the treaty, unless the treaty otherwise provides or none of the other contracting States and contracting organizations opposes the late formulation of the reservation.

2.3.1 Acceptance of the late formulation of a reservation

Unless the treaty otherwise provides or the well-established practice followed by the depositary differs, the late formulation of a reservation shall only be deemed to have been accepted if no contracting State or contracting organization has opposed such formulation after the expiry of the twelve-month period following the date on which notification was received.

2.3.2 Time period for formulating an objection to a reservation that is formulated late

An objection to a reservation that is formulated late must be made within twelve months of the acceptance, in accordance with guideline 2.3.1, of the late formulation of the reservation.

2.3.3 Limits to the possibility of excluding or modifying the legal effect of a treaty by means other than reservations

A contracting State or a contracting organization cannot exclude or modify the legal effect of provisions of the treaty by:

(*a*) the interpretation of an earlier reservation; or

(*b*) a unilateral statement made subsequently under a clause providing for options.

2.3.4 Widening of the scope of a reservation

The modification of an existing reservation for the purpose of widening its scope is subject to the rules applicable to the late formulation of a reservation. If such a modification is opposed, the initial reservation remains unchanged.

2.4 Procedure for interpretative declarations

2.4.1 Form of interpretative declarations

An interpretative declaration should preferably be formulated in writing.

2.4.2 Representation for the purpose of formulating interpretative declarations

An interpretative declaration must be formulated by a person who is considered as representing a State or an international organization for the purpose of adopting or authenticating the text of a treaty or expressing the consent of the State or international organization to be bound by a treaty.

2.4.3 Absence of consequences at the international level of the violation of internal rules regarding the formulation of interpretative declarations

1. The competent authority and the procedure to be followed at the internal level for formulating an interpretative declaration are determined by the internal law of each State or the relevant rules of each international organization.

2. A State or an international organization may not invoke the fact that an interpretative declaration has been formulated in violation of a provision of the internal law of that State or the rules of that organization regarding competence and the procedure for formulating interpretative declarations for the purpose of invalidating the declaration.

2.4.4 Time at which an interpretative declaration may be formulated

Without prejudice to the provisions of guidelines 1.4 and 2.4.7, an interpretative declaration may be formulated at any time.

2.4.5 Communication of interpretative declarations

The communication of written interpretative declarations should follow the procedure established in guidelines 2.1.5, 2.1.6 and 2.1.7.

2.4.6 Non-requirement of confirmation of interpretative declarations formulated when signing a treaty

An interpretative declaration formulated when signing a treaty does not require subsequent confirmation when a State or an international organization expresses its consent to be bound by the treaty.

2.4.7 Late formulation of an interpretative declaration

Where a treaty provides that an interpretative declaration may be formulated only at specified times, a State or an international organization may not formulate an interpretative declaration concerning that treaty subsequently, unless none of the other contracting States and contracting organizations objects to the late formulation of the interpretative declaration.

2.4.8 Modification of an interpretative declaration

Unless the treaty otherwise provides, an interpretative declaration may be modified at any time.

2.5 Withdrawal and modification of reservations and interpretative declarations

2.5.1 Withdrawal of reservations

Unless the treaty otherwise provides, a reservation may be withdrawn at any time without the consent of a State or of an international organization which has accepted the reservation being required for its withdrawal.

2.5.2 Form of withdrawal

The withdrawal of a reservation must be formulated in writing.

2.5.3 Periodic review of the usefulness of reservations

1. States or international organizations which have formulated one or more reservations to a treaty should undertake a periodic review of such reservations and consider withdrawing those which no longer serve their purpose.

2. In such a review, States and international organizations should devote special attention to the aim of preserving the integrity of multilateral treaties and, where relevant, consider the usefulness of retaining the reservations, in particular in relation to developments in their internal law since the reservations were formulated.

2.5.4 Representation for the purpose of withdrawing a reservation at the international level

1. Subject to the usual practices followed in international organizations which are depositaries of treaties, a person is considered as representing a State or an international organization for the purpose of withdrawing a reservation made on behalf of a State or an international organization if:

(*a*) that person produces appropriate full powers for the purpose of that withdrawal; or

(*b*) it appears from practice or from other circumstances that it was the intention of the States and international organizations concerned to consider that person as representing the State or the international organization for such purpose without having to produce full powers.

2. In virtue of their functions and without having to produce full powers, the following are considered as representing a State for the purpose of withdrawing a reservation at the international level on behalf of that State:

(*a*) Heads of State, Heads of Government and Ministers for Foreign Affairs;

(*b*) representatives accredited by States to an international organization or one of its organs, for the purpose of withdrawing a reservation to a treaty adopted in that organization or organ;

(*c*) heads of permanent missions to an international organization, for the purpose of withdrawing a reservation to a treaty between the accrediting States and that organization.

2.5.5 Absence of consequences at the international level of the violation of internal rules regarding the withdrawal of reservations

1. The competent authority and the procedure to be followed at the internal level for withdrawing a reservation are determined by the internal law of each State or the relevant rules of each international organization.

2. A State or an international organization may not invoke the fact that a reservation has been withdrawn in violation of a provision of the internal law of that State or the rules of that organization regarding competence and the procedure for the withdrawal of reservations for the purpose of invalidating the withdrawal.

2.5.6 Communication of withdrawal of a reservation

The procedure for communicating the withdrawal of a reservation follows the rules applicable to the communication of reservations contained in guidelines 2.1.5, 2.1.6 and 2.1.7.

2.5.7 Effects of withdrawal of a reservation

1. The withdrawal of a reservation entails the full application of the provisions to which the reservation relates in the relations between the State or international organization which withdraws the reservation and all the other parties, whether they had accepted the reservation or objected to it.

2. The withdrawal of a reservation entails the entry into force of the treaty in the relations between the State or international organization which withdraws the reservation and a State or international organization which had objected to the reservation and opposed the entry into force of the treaty between itself and the reserving State or international organization by reason of that reservation.

2.5.8 Effective date of withdrawal of a reservation

Unless the treaty otherwise provides, or it is otherwise agreed, the withdrawal of a reservation becomes operative in relation to a contracting State or a contracting organization only when notice of it has been received by that State or that organization.

2.5.9 Cases in which the author of a reservation may set the effective date of withdrawal of the reservation

The withdrawal of a reservation becomes operative on the date set by the State or international organization which withdraws the reservation, where:

(*a*) that date is later than the date on which the other contracting States or contracting organizations received notification of it; or

(*b*) the withdrawal does not add to the rights of the withdrawing State or international organization, in relation to the other contracting States or contracting organizations.

2.5.10 Partial withdrawal of reservations

1. The partial withdrawal of a reservation limits the legal effect of the reservation and achieves a more complete application of the provisions of the treaty, or of the treaty

as a whole, in the relations between the withdrawing State or international organization and the other parties to the treaty.

2. The partial withdrawal of a reservation is subject to the same rules on form and procedure as a total withdrawal and becomes operative on the same conditions.

2.5.11 Effect of a partial withdrawal of a reservation

1. The partial withdrawal of a reservation modifies the legal effect of the reservation to the extent provided by the new formulation of the reservation. Any objection formulated to the reservation continues to have effect as long as its author does not withdraw it, insofar as the objection does not apply exclusively to that part of the reservation which has been withdrawn.

2. No new objection may be formulated to the reservation resulting from the partial withdrawal, unless that partial withdrawal has a discriminatory effect.

2.5.12 Withdrawal of interpretative declarations

An interpretative declaration may be withdrawn at any time by an authority considered as representing the State or international organization for that purpose, following the same procedure applicable to its formulation.

2.6 Formulation of objections

2.6.1 Definition of objections to reservations

"Objection" means a unilateral statement, however phrased or named, made by a State or an international organization in response to a reservation formulated by another State or international organization, whereby the former State or organization purports to preclude the reservation from having its intended effects or otherwise opposes the reservation.

2.6.2 Right to formulate objections

A State or an international organization may formulate an objection to a reservation irrespective of the permissibility of the reservation.

2.6.3 Author of an objection

An objection to a reservation may be formulated by:

(i) any contracting State or contracting organization; and

(ii) any State or international organization that is entitled to become a party to the treaty, in which case the objection does not produce any legal effect until the State or international organization has expressed its consent to be bound by the treaty.

2.6.4 Objections formulated jointly

The joint formulation of an objection by several States or international organizations does not affect the unilateral character of that objection.

2.6.5 Form of objections

An objection must be formulated in writing.

2.6.6 Right to oppose the entry into force of the treaty *vis-à-vis* the author of the reservation

A State or an international organization that formulates an objection to a reservation may oppose the entry into force of the treaty as between itself and the author of the reservation.

2.6.7 Expression of intention to preclude the entry into force of the treaty

When a State or an international organization formulating an objection to a reservation intends to preclude the entry into force of the treaty as between itself and the reserving State or international organization, it shall definitely express its intention before the treaty would otherwise enter into force between them.

2.6.8 Procedure for the formulation of objections

Guidelines 2.1.3, 2.1.4, 2.1.5, 2.1.6 and 2.1.7 are applicable *mutatis mutandis* to objections.

2.6.9 Statement of reasons for objections

An objection should, to the extent possible, indicate the reasons why it is being formulated.

2.6.10 Non-requirement of confirmation of an objection formulated prior to formal confirmation of a reservation

An objection to a reservation formulated by a State or an international organization prior to confirmation of the reservation in accordance with guideline 2.2.1 does not itself require confirmation.

2.6.11 Confirmation of an objection formulated prior to the expression of consent to be bound by a treaty

An objection formulated prior to the expression of consent to be bound by the treaty does not need to be formally confirmed by the objecting State or international organization at the time it expresses its consent to be bound if that State or that organization was a signatory to the treaty when it formulated the objection; it must be confirmed if the State or international organization had not signed the treaty.

2.6.12 Time period for formulating objections

Unless the treaty otherwise provides, a State or an international organization may formulate an objection to a reservation within a period of twelve months after it was notified of the reservation or by the date on which such State or international organization expresses its consent to be bound by the treaty, whichever is later.

2.6.13 Objections formulated late

An objection to a reservation formulated after the end of the time period specified in guideline 2.6.12 does not produce all the legal effects of an objection formulated within that time period.

2.7 Withdrawal and modification of objections to reservations

2.7.1 Withdrawal of objections to reservations

Unless the treaty otherwise provides, an objection to a reservation may be withdrawn at any time.

2.7.2 Form of withdrawal of objections to reservations

The withdrawal of an objection to a reservation must be formulated in writing.

2.7.3 Formulation and communication of the withdrawal of objections to reservations

Guidelines 2.5.4, 2.5.5 and 2.5.6 are applicable *mutatis mutandis* to the withdrawal of objections to reservations.

2.7.4 Effect on reservation of withdrawal of an objection

A State or an international organization that withdraws an objection formulated to a reservation is presumed to have accepted that reservation.

2.7.5 Effective date of withdrawal of an objection

Unless the treaty otherwise provides, or it is otherwise agreed, the withdrawal of an objection to a reservation becomes operative only when notice of it has been received by the State or international organization which formulated the reservation.

2.7.6 Cases in which the author of an objection may set the effective date of withdrawal of the objection

The withdrawal of an objection becomes operative on the date set by its author where that date is later than the date on which the reserving State or international organization received notice of it.

2.7.7 Partial withdrawal of an objection

1. Unless the treaty otherwise provides, a State or an international organization may partially withdraw an objection to a reservation.

2. The partial withdrawal of an objection is subject to the same rules on form and procedure as a total withdrawal and becomes operative on the same conditions.

2.7.8 Effect of a partial withdrawal of an objection

The partial withdrawal modifies the legal effects of the objection on the treaty relations between the author of the objection and the author of the reservation to the extent provided by the new formulation of the objection.

2.7.9 Widening of the scope of an objection to a reservation

1. A State or an international organization which has made an objection to a reservation may widen the scope of that objection during the time period referred to in guideline 2.6.12.

2. Such a widening of the scope of the objection cannot have an effect on the existence of treaty relations between the author of the reservation and the author of the objection.

2.8 Formulation of acceptances of reservations

2.8.1 Forms of acceptance of reservations

The acceptance of a reservation may arise from a unilateral statement to this effect or from silence of a contracting State or contracting organization during the periods specified in guideline 2.6.12.

2.8.2 Tacit acceptance of reservations

Unless the treaty otherwise provides, a reservation is considered to have been accepted by a State or an international organization if it shall have raised no objection to the reservation within the time period provided for in guideline 2.6.12.

2.8.3 Express acceptance of reservations

A State or an international organization may, at any time, expressly accept a reservation formulated by another State or international organization.

2.8.4 Form of express acceptance of reservations

The express acceptance of a reservation must be formulated in writing.

2.8.5 Procedure for formulating express acceptance of reservations

Guidelines 2.1.3, 2.1.4, 2.1.5, 2.1.6 and 2.1.7 apply *mutatis mutandis* to express acceptances.

2.8.6 Non-requirement of confirmation of an acceptance formulated prior to formal confirmation of a reservation

An express acceptance of a reservation formulated by a State or an international organization prior to confirmation of the reservation in accordance with guideline 2.2.1 does not itself require confirmation.

2.8.7 Unanimous acceptance of reservations

In the event of a reservation requiring unanimous acceptance by some or all States or international organizations which are parties or entitled to become parties to the treaty, such acceptance, once obtained, is final.

2.8.8 Acceptance of a reservation to the constituent instrument of an international organization

When a treaty is a constituent instrument of an international organization and unless it otherwise provides, a reservation requires the acceptance of the competent organ of that organization.

2.8.9 Organ competent to accept a reservation to a constituent instrument

Subject to the rules of the organization, competence to accept a reservation to a constituent instrument of an international organization belongs to the organ competent to:

- decide on the admission of a member to the organization; or
- amend the constituent instrument; or
- interpret this instrument.

2.8.10 Modalities of the acceptance of a reservation to a constituent instrument

1. Subject to the rules of the organization, the acceptance by the competent organ of the organization shall not be tacit. However, the admission of the State or the international organization which is the author of the reservation is tantamount to the acceptance of that reservation.

2. For the purposes of the acceptance of a reservation to the constituent instrument of an international organization, the individual acceptance of the reservation by States or international organizations that are members of the organization is not required.

2.8.11 Acceptance of a reservation to a constituent instrument that has not yet entered into force

In the case set forth in guideline 2.8.8 and where the constituent instrument has not yet entered into force, a reservation is considered to have been accepted if no signatory State or signatory international organization has raised an objection to that reservation within a period of twelve months after they were notified of that reservation. Such a unanimous acceptance, once obtained, is final.

2.8.12 Reaction by a member of an international organization to a reservation to its constituent instrument

Guideline 2.8.10 does not preclude States or international organizations that are members of an international organization from taking a position on the permissibility or appropriateness of a reservation to a constituent instrument of the organization. Such an opinion is in itself devoid of legal effects.

2.8.13 Final nature of acceptance of a reservation

The acceptance of a reservation cannot be withdrawn or amended.

2.9 Formulation of reactions to interpretative declarations

2.9.1 Approval of an interpretative declaration

"Approval" of an interpretative declaration means a unilateral statement made by a State or an international organization in reaction to an interpretative declaration in respect of a treaty formulated by another State or another international organization, whereby the former State or organization expresses agreement with the interpretation formulated in that declaration.

2.9.2 Opposition to an interpretative declaration

"Opposition" to an interpretative declaration means a unilateral statement made by a State or an international organization in reaction to an interpretative declaration in respect of a treaty formulated by another State or another international organization, whereby the former State or organization disagrees with the interpretation formulated in the interpretative declaration, including by formulating an alternative interpretation.

2.9.3 Recharacterization of an interpretative declaration

1. "Recharacterization" of an interpretative declaration means a unilateral statement made by a State or an international organization in reaction to an interpretative declaration in respect of a treaty formulated by another State or another international organization, whereby the former State or organization purports to treat the declaration as a reservation.

2. A State or an international organization that intends to treat an interpretative declaration as a reservation should take into account guidelines 1.3 to 1.3.3.

2.9.4 Right to formulate approval or opposition, or to recharacterize

An approval, opposition or recharacterization in respect of an interpretative declaration may be formulated at any time by any contracting State or any contracting organization and by any State or any international organization that is entitled to become a party to the treaty.

2.9.5 Form of approval, opposition and recharacterization

An approval, opposition or recharacterization in respect of an interpretative declaration should preferably be formulated in writing.

2.9.6 Statement of reasons for approval, opposition and recharacterization

An approval, opposition or recharacterization in respect of an interpretative declaration should, to the extent possible, indicate the reasons why it is being formulated.

2.9.7 Formulation and communication of approval, opposition or recharacterization

Guidelines 2.1.3, 2.1.4, 2.1.5, 2.1.6 and 2.1.7 are applicable *mutatis mutandis* to an approval, opposition or recharacterization in respect of an interpretative declaration.

2.9.8 Non-presumption of approval or opposition

1. An approval of, or an opposition to, an interpretative declaration shall not be presumed.

2. Notwithstanding guidelines 2.9.1 and 2.9.2, an approval of an interpretative declaration or an opposition thereto may be inferred, in exceptional cases, from the conduct of the States or international organizations concerned, taking into account all relevant circumstances.

2.9.9 Silence with respect to an interpretative declaration

An approval of an interpretative declaration shall not be inferred from the mere silence of a State or an international organization.

3. Permissibility of reservations and interpretative declarations

3.1 Permissible reservations

A State or an international organization may, when signing, ratifying, formally confirming, accepting, approving or acceding to a treaty, formulate a reservation unless:

(*a*) the reservation is prohibited by the treaty;

(*b*) the treaty provides that only specified reservations, which do not include the reservation in question, may be made; or

(*c*) in cases not falling under subparagraphs *(a)* and *(b)*, the reservation is incompatible with the object and purpose of the treaty.

3.1.1 Reservations prohibited by the treaty

A reservation is prohibited by the treaty if it contains a provision:

(*a*) prohibiting all reservations;

(*b*) prohibiting reservations to specified provisions to which the reservation in question relates; or

(*c*) prohibiting certain categories of reservations including the reservation in question.

3.1.2 Definition of specified reservations

For the purposes of guideline 3.1, the expression "specified reservations" means reservations that are expressly envisaged in the treaty to certain provisions of the treaty or to the treaty as a whole with respect to certain specific aspects.

3.1.3 Permissibility of reservations not prohibited by the treaty

Where the treaty prohibits the formulation of certain reservations, a reservation which is not prohibited by the treaty may be formulated by a State or an international organization only if it is not incompatible with the object and purpose of the treaty.

3.1.4 Permissibility of specified reservations

Where the treaty envisages the formulation of specified reservations without defining their content, a reservation may be formulated by a State or an international organization only if it is not incompatible with the object and purpose of the treaty.

3.1.5 Incompatibility of a reservation with the object and purpose of the treaty

A reservation is incompatible with the object and purpose of the treaty if it affects an essential element of the treaty that is necessary to its general tenour, in such a way that the reservation impairs the *raison d'être* of the treaty.

3.1.5.1 Determination of the object and purpose of the treaty

The object and purpose of the treaty is to be determined in good faith, taking account of the terms of the treaty in their context, in particular the title and the preamble of the treaty. Recourse may also be had to the preparatory work of the treaty and the circumstances of its conclusion and, where appropriate, the subsequent practice of the parties.

3.1.5.2 Vague or general reservations

A reservation shall be worded in such a way as to allow its meaning to be understood, in order to assess in particular its compatibility with the object and purpose of the treaty.

3.1.5.3 Reservations to a provision reflecting a customary rule

The fact that a treaty provision reflects a rule of customary international law does not in itself constitute an obstacle to the formulation of a reservation to that provision.

3.1.5.4 Reservations to provisions concerning rights from which no derogation is permissible under any circumstances

A State or an international organization may not formulate a reservation to a treaty provision concerning rights from which no derogation is permissible under any circumstances, unless the reservation in question is compatible with the essential rights and obligations arising out of that treaty. In assessing that compatibility, account shall be taken of the importance which the parties have conferred upon the rights at issue by making them non-derogable.

3.1.5.5 Reservations relating to internal law

A reservation by which a State or an international organization purports to exclude or to modify the legal effect of certain provisions of a treaty or of the treaty as a whole in order to preserve the integrity of specific rules of the internal law of that State or of specific rules of that organization in force at the time of the formulation of the reservation may be formulated only insofar as it does not affect an essential element of the treaty nor its general tenour.

3.1.5.6 Reservations to treaties containing numerous interdependent rights and obligations

To assess the compatibility of a reservation with the object and purpose of a treaty containing numerous interdependent rights and obligations, account shall be taken of that interdependence as well as the importance that the provision to which the reservation relates has within the general tenour of the treaty, and the extent of the impact that the reservation has on the treaty.

3.1.5.7 Reservations to treaty provisions concerning dispute settlement or the monitoring of the implementation of the treaty

A reservation to a treaty provision concerning dispute settlement or the monitoring of the implementation of the treaty is not, in itself, incompatible with the object and purpose of the treaty, unless:

(i) the reservation purports to exclude or modify the legal effect of a provision of the treaty essential to its *raison d'être*; or

(ii) the reservation has the effect of excluding the reserving State or international organization from a dispute settlement or treaty implementation monitoring mechanism with respect to a treaty provision that it has previously accepted, if the very purpose of the treaty is to put such a mechanism into effect.

3.2 Assessment of the permissibility of reservations

The following may assess, within their respective competences, the permissibility of reservations to a treaty formulated by a State or an international organization:

- contracting States or contracting organizations;
- dispute settlement bodies;
- treaty monitoring bodies.

3.2.1 Competence of the treaty monitoring bodies to assess the permissibility of reservations

1. A treaty monitoring body may, for the purpose of discharging the functions entrusted to it, assess the permissibility of reservations formulated by a State or an international organization.

2. The assessment made by such a body in the exercise of this competence has no greater legal effect than that of the act which contains it.

3.2.2 Specification of the competence of treaty monitoring bodies to assess the permissibility of reservations

When providing bodies with the competence to monitor the application of treaties, States or international organizations should specify, where appropriate, the nature and the limits of the competence of such bodies to assess the permissibility of reservations.

3.2.3 Consideration of the assessments of treaty monitoring bodies

States and international organizations that have formulated reservations to a treaty establishing a treaty monitoring body shall give consideration to that body's assessment of the permissibility of the reservations.

3.2.4 Bodies competent to assess the permissibility of reservations in the event of the establishment of a treaty monitoring body

When a treaty establishes a treaty monitoring body, the competence of that body is without prejudice to the competence of the contracting States or contracting organizations to assess the permissibility of reservations to that treaty, or to that of dispute settlement bodies competent to interpret or apply the treaty.

3.2.5 Competence of dispute settlement bodies to assess the permissibility of reservations

When a dispute settlement body is competent to adopt decisions binding upon the parties to a dispute, and the assessment of the permissibility of a reservation is necessary for the discharge of such competence by that body, such assessment is, as an element of the decision, legally binding upon the parties.

3.3 Consequences of the non-permissibility of a reservation

3.3.1 Irrelevance of distinction among the grounds for non-permissibility

A reservation formulated notwithstanding a prohibition arising from the provisions of the treaty or notwithstanding its incompatibility with the object and purpose of the treaty is impermissible, without there being any need to distinguish between the consequences of these grounds for non-permissibility.

3.3.2 Non-permissibility of reservations and international responsibility

The formulation of an impermissible reservation produces its consequences pursuant to the law of treaties and does not engage the international responsibility of the State or international organization which has formulated it.

3.3.3 Absence of effect of individual acceptance of a reservation on the permissibility of the reservation

Acceptance of an impermissible reservation by a contracting State or by a contracting organization shall not affect the impermissibility of the reservation.

3.4 Permissibility of reactions to reservations

3.4.1 Permissibility of the acceptance of a reservation

Acceptance of a reservation is not subject to any condition of permissibility.

3.4.2 Permissibility of an objection to a reservation

An objection to a reservation by which a State or an international organization purports to exclude in its relations with the author of the reservation the application of provisions of the treaty to which the reservation does not relate is only permissible if:

(1) the provisions thus excluded have a sufficient link with the provisions to which the reservation relates; and

(2) the objection would not defeat the object and purpose of the treaty in the relations between the author of the reservation and the author of the objection.

3.5 Permissibility of an interpretative declaration

A State or an international organization may formulate an interpretative declaration unless the interpretative declaration is prohibited by the treaty.

3.5.1 Permissibility of an interpretative declaration which is in fact a reservation

If a unilateral statement which appears to be an interpretative declaration is in fact a reservation, its permissibility must be assessed in accordance with the provisions of guidelines 3.1 to 3.1.5.7.

3.6 Permissibility of reactions to interpretative declarations

An approval of, opposition to, or recharacterization of, an interpretative declaration shall not be subject to any conditions for permissibility.

4. Legal effects of reservations and interpretative declarations

4.1 Establishment of a reservation with regard to another State or international organization

A reservation formulated by a State or an international organization is established with regard to a contracting State or a contracting organization if it is permissible and was formulated in accordance with the required form and procedures, and if that contracting State or contracting organization has accepted it.

4.1.1 Establishment of a reservation expressly authorized by a treaty

1. A reservation expressly authorized by a treaty does not require any subsequent acceptance by the other contracting States and contracting organizations, unless the treaty so provides.

2. A reservation expressly authorized by a treaty is established with regard to the other contracting States and contracting organizations if it was formulated in accordance with the required form and procedures.

4.1.2 Establishment of a reservation to a treaty which has to be applied in its entirety

When it appears, from the limited number of negotiating States and organizations and the object and purpose of the treaty, that the application of the treaty in its entirety between all the parties is an essential condition of the consent of each one to be bound by the treaty, a reservation to this treaty is established with regard to the other contracting States and contracting organizations if it is permissible and was formulated in accordance with the required form and procedures, and if all the contracting States and contracting organizations have accepted it.

4.1.3 Establishment of a reservation to a constituent instrument of an international organization

When a treaty is a constituent instrument of an international organization, a reservation to this treaty is established with regard to the other contracting States and contracting organizations if it is permissible and was formulated in accordance with the required form and procedures, and if it has been accepted in conformity with guidelines 2.8.8 to 2.8.11.

4.2 Effects of an established reservation

4.2.1 Status of the author of an established reservation

As soon as a reservation is established in accordance with guidelines 4.1 to 4.1.3, its author becomes a contracting State or contracting organization to the treaty.

4.2.2 Effect of the establishment of a reservation on the entry into force of a treaty

1. When a treaty has not yet entered into force, the author of a reservation shall be included in the number of contracting States and contracting organizations required for the treaty to enter into force once the reservation is established.

2. The author of the reservation may however be included at a date prior to the establishment of the reservation in the number of contracting States and contracting organizations required for the treaty to enter into force, if no contracting State or contracting organization is opposed.

4.2.3 Effect of the establishment of a reservation on the status of the author as a party to the treaty

The establishment of a reservation constitutes its author a party to the treaty in relation to contracting States and contracting organizations in respect of which the reservation is established if or when the treaty is in force.

4.2.4 Effect of an established reservation on treaty relations

1. A reservation established with regard to another party excludes or modifies for the reserving State or international organization in its relations with that other party the legal effect of the provisions of the treaty to which the reservation relates or of the treaty as a whole with respect to certain specific aspects, to the extent of the reservation.

2. To the extent that an established reservation excludes the legal effect of certain provisions of a treaty, the author of that reservation has neither rights nor obligations under those provisions in its relations with the other parties with regard to which the reservation is established. Those other parties shall likewise have neither rights nor obligations under those provisions in their relations with the author of the reservation.

3. To the extent that an established reservation modifies the legal effect of certain provisions of a treaty, the author of that reservation has rights and obligations under those provisions, as modified by the reservation, in its relations with the other parties with regard to which the reservation is established. Those other parties shall have rights and obligations under those provisions, as modified by the reservation, in their relations with the author of the reservation.

4.2.5 Non-reciprocal application of obligations to which a reservation relates

Insofar as the obligations under the provisions to which the reservation relates are not subject to reciprocal application in view of the nature of the obligations or the object and purpose of the treaty, the content of the obligations of the parties other than the author of the reservation remains unaffected. The content of the obligations of those parties likewise remains unaffected when reciprocal application is not possible because of the content of the reservation.

4.2.6 Interpretation of reservations

A reservation is to be interpreted in good faith, taking into account the intention of its author as reflected primarily in the text of the reservation, as well as the object and purpose of the treaty and the circumstances in which the reservation was formulated.

4.3 Effect of an objection to a valid reservation

Unless the reservation has been established with regard to an objecting State or organization, the formulation of an objection to a valid reservation precludes the reservation from having its intended effects as against that State or international organization.

4.3.1 Effect of an objection on the entry into force of the treaty as between the author of the objection and the author of a reservation

An objection by a contracting State or by a contracting organization to a valid reservation does not preclude the entry into force of the treaty as between the objecting State or organization and the reserving State or organization, except in the case mentioned in guideline 4.3.5.

4.3.2 Effect of an objection to a reservation that is formulated late

If a contracting State or a contracting organization to a treaty objects to a reservation whose late formulation has been unanimously accepted in accordance with guideline 2.3.1, the treaty shall enter into or remain in force in respect of the reserving State or international organization without the reservation being established.

4.3.3 Entry into force of the treaty between the author of a reservation and the author of an objection

The treaty enters into force between the author of a valid reservation and the objecting contracting State or contracting organization as soon as the author of the reservation has become a contracting State or a contracting organization in accordance with guideline 4.2.1 and the treaty has entered into force.

4.3.4 Non-entry into force of the treaty for the author of a reservation when unanimous acceptance is required

If the establishment of a reservation requires the acceptance of the reservation by all the contracting States and contracting organizations, any objection by a contracting State or by a contracting organization to a valid reservation precludes the entry into force of the treaty for the reserving State or organization.

4.3.5 Non-entry into force of the treaty as between the author of a reservation and the author of an objection with maximum effect

An objection by a contracting State or a contracting organization to a valid reservation precludes the entry into force of the treaty as between the objecting State or organization and the reserving State or organization, if the objecting State or organization has definitely expressed an intention to that effect in accordance with guideline 2.6.7.

4.3.6 Effect of an objection on treaty relations

1. When a State or an international organization objecting to a valid reservation has not opposed the entry into force of the treaty between itself and the reserving State or organization, the provisions to which the reservation relates do not apply as between the author of the reservation and the objecting State or organization, to the extent of the reservation.

2. To the extent that a valid reservation purports to exclude the legal effect of certain provisions of the treaty, when a contracting State or a contracting organization has raised an objection to it but has not opposed the entry into force of the treaty between itself and the author of the reservation, the objecting State or organization and the author of the reservation are not bound, in their treaty relations, by the provisions to which the reservation relates.

3. To the extent that a valid reservation purports to modify the legal effect of certain provisions of the treaty, when a contracting State or a contracting organization has raised an objection to it but has not opposed the entry into force of the treaty between itself and the author of the reservation, the objecting State or organization and the author of the reservation are not bound, in their treaty relations, by the provisions of the treaty as intended to be modified by the reservation.

4. All the provisions of the treaty other than those to which the reservation relates shall remain applicable as between the reserving State or organization and the objecting State or organization.

4.3.7 Effect of an objection on provisions other than those to which the reservation relates

1. A provision of the treaty to which the reservation does not relate, but which has a sufficient link with the provisions to which the reservation does relate, is not applicable in the treaty relations between the author of the reservation and the author of an objection formulated in accordance with guideline 3.4.2.

2. The reserving State or international organization may, within a period of twelve months following the notification of an objection which has the effect referred to in

paragraph 1, oppose the entry into force of the treaty between itself and the objecting State or organization. In the absence of such opposition, the treaty shall apply between the author of the reservation and the author of the objection to the extent provided by the reservation and the objection.

4.3.8 Right of the author of a valid reservation not to comply with the treaty without the benefit of its reservation

The author of a valid reservation is not required to comply with the provisions of the treaty without the benefit of its reservation.

4.4 Effect of a reservation on rights and obligations independent of the treaty

4.4.1 Absence of effect on rights and obligations under other treaties

A reservation, acceptance of a reservation or objection to a reservation neither modifies nor excludes any rights and obligations of their authors under other treaties to which they are parties.

4.4.2 Absence of effect on rights and obligations under customary international law

A reservation to a treaty provision which reflects a rule of customary international law does not of itself affect the rights and obligations under that rule, which shall continue to apply as such between the reserving State or organization and other States or international organizations which are bound by that rule.

4.4.3 Absence of effect on a peremptory norm of general international law (*jus cogens*)

1. A reservation to a treaty provision which reflects a peremptory norm of general international law (*jus cogens*) does not affect the binding nature of that norm, which shall continue to apply as such between the reserving State or organization and other States or international organizations.

2. A reservation cannot exclude or modify the legal effect of a treaty in a manner contrary to a peremptory norm of general international law.

4.5 Consequences of an invalid reservation

4.5.1 Nullity of an invalid reservation

A reservation that does not meet the conditions of formal validity and permissibility set out in Parts 2 and 3 of the Guide to Practice is null and void, and therefore devoid of any legal effect.

4.5.2 Reactions to a reservation considered invalid

1. The nullity of an invalid reservation does not depend on the objection or the acceptance by a contracting State or a contracting organization.

2. Nevertheless, a State or an international organization which considers that a reservation is invalid should formulate a reasoned objection as soon as possible.

4.5.3 Status of the author of an invalid reservation in relation to the treaty

1. The status of the author of an invalid reservation in relation to a treaty depends on the intention expressed by the reserving State or international organization on whether it intends to be bound by the treaty without the benefit of the reservation or whether it considers that it is not bound by the treaty.

2. Unless the author of the invalid reservation has expressed a contrary intention or such an intention is otherwise established, it is considered a contracting State or a contracting organization without the benefit of the reservation.

3. Notwithstanding paragraphs 1 and 2, the author of the invalid reservation may express at any time its intention not to be bound by the treaty without the benefit of the reservation.

4. If a treaty monitoring body expresses the view that a reservation is invalid and the reserving State or international organization intends not to be bound by the treaty without the benefit of the reservation, it should express its intention to that effect within a period of twelve months from the date at which the treaty monitoring body made its assessment.

4.6 Absence of effect of a reservation on the relations between the other parties to the treaty

A reservation does not modify the provisions of the treaty for the other parties to the treaty *inter se.*

4.7 Effect of interpretative declarations

4.7.1 Clarification of the terms of the treaty by an interpretative declaration

1. An interpretative declaration does not modify treaty obligations. It may only specify or clarify the meaning or scope which its author attributes to a treaty or to certain provisions thereof and may, as appropriate, constitute an element to be taken into account in interpreting the treaty in accordance with the general rule of interpretation of treaties.

2. In interpreting the treaty, account shall also be taken, as appropriate, of the approval of, or opposition to, the interpretative declaration, by other contracting States or contracting organizations.

4.7.2 Effect of the modification or the withdrawal of an interpretative declaration

The modification or the withdrawal of an interpretative declaration may not produce the effects provided for in draft guideline 4.7.1 to the extent that other contracting States or contracting organizations have relied upon the initial declaration.

4.7.3 Effect of an interpretative declaration approved by all the contracting States and contracting organizations

An interpretative declaration that has been approved by all the contracting States and contracting organizations may constitute an agreement regarding the interpretation of the treaty.

5. Reservations, acceptances of reservations, objections to reservations, and interpretative declarations in cases of succession of States

5.1 Reservations in cases of succession of States

5.1.1 Newly independent States

1. When a newly independent State establishes its status as a party or as a contracting State to a multilateral treaty by a notification of succession, it shall be considered as maintaining any reservation to that treaty which was applicable at the date of the succession of States in respect of the territory to which the succession of States relates unless, when making the notification of succession, it expresses a contrary intention or formulates a reservation which relates to the same subject matter as that reservation.

2. When making a notification of succession establishing its status as a party or as a contracting State to a multilateral treaty, a newly independent State may formulate a reservation unless the reservation is one the formulation of which would be excluded by the provisions of subparagraph *(a)*, *(b)* or *(c)* of guideline 3.1.

3. When a newly independent State formulates a reservation in conformity with paragraph 2, the relevant rules set out in Part 2 (Procedure) of the Guide to Practice apply in respect of that reservation.

4. For the purposes of this Part of the Guide to Practice, "newly independent State" means a successor State the territory of which immediately before the date of the succession of States was a dependent territory for the international relations of which the predecessor State was responsible.

5.1.2 Uniting or separation of States

1. Subject to the provisions of guideline 5.1.3, a successor State which is a party to a treaty as the result of a uniting or separation of States shall be considered as maintaining any reservation to the treaty which was applicable at the date of the succession of States in respect of the territory to which the succession of States relates, unless it expresses its intention not to maintain one or more reservations of the predecessor State at the time of the succession.

2. A successor State which is a party to a treaty as the result of a uniting or separation of States may neither formulate a new reservation nor widen the scope of a reservation that is maintained.

3. When a successor State formed from a uniting or separation of States makes a notification whereby it establishes its status as a contracting State to a treaty which, at the date of the succession of States, was not in force for the predecessor State but to which the predecessor State was a contracting State, that State shall be considered as maintaining any reservation to the treaty which was applicable at the date of the succession of States in respect of the territory to which the succession of States relates, unless it expresses a contrary intention when making the notification or formulates a reservation which relates to the same subject matter as that reservation. That successor State may formulate a new reservation to the treaty.

4. A successor State may formulate a reservation in accordance with paragraph 3 only if the reservation is one the formulation of which would not be excluded by the provisions of subparagraph *(a)*, *(b)* or *(c)* of guideline 3.1. The relevant rules set out in Part 2 (Procedure) of the Guide to Practice apply in respect of that reservation.

5.1.3 Irrelevance of certain reservations in cases involving a uniting of States

When, following a uniting of two or more States, a treaty in force at the date of the succession of States in respect of any of them continues in force in respect of the successor State, such reservations as may have been formulated by any such State which, at the date of the succession of States, was a contracting State in respect of which the treaty was not in force shall not be maintained.

5.1.4 Maintenance of the territorial scope of reservations formulated by the predecessor State

Subject to the provisions of guideline 5.1.5, a reservation considered as being maintained in conformity with guideline 5.1.1, paragraph 1, or guideline 5.1.2, paragraph

1 or 3, shall retain the territorial scope that it had at the date of the succession of States, unless the successor State expresses a contrary intention.

5.1.5 Territorial scope of reservations in cases involving a uniting of States

1. When, following a uniting of two or more States, a treaty in force at the date of the succession of States in respect of only one of the States forming the successor State becomes applicable to a part of the territory of that State to which it did not apply previously, any reservation considered as being maintained by the successor State shall apply to that territory unless:

(*a*) the successor State expresses a contrary intention when making the notification extending the territorial scope of the treaty; or

(*b*) the nature or purpose of the reservation is such that the reservation cannot be extended beyond the territory to which it was applicable at the date of the succession of States.

2. When, following a uniting of two or more States, a treaty in force at the date of the succession of States in respect of two or more of the uniting States becomes applicable to a part of the territory of the successor State to which it did not apply at the date of the succession of States, no reservation shall extend to that territory unless:

(*a*) an identical reservation has been formulated by each of those States in respect of which the treaty was in force at the date of the succession of States;

(*b*) the successor State expresses a different intention when making the notification extending the territorial scope of the treaty; or

(*c*) a contrary intention otherwise becomes apparent from the circumstances surrounding that State's succession to the treaty.

3. A notification purporting to extend the territorial scope of a reservation in accordance with paragraph 2(*b*) shall be without effect if such an extension would give rise to the application of contradictory reservations to the same territory.

4. The provisions of paragraphs 1 to 3 apply *mutatis mutandis* to reservations considered as being maintained by a successor State that is a contracting State, following a uniting of States, to a treaty which was not in force for any of the uniting States at the date of the succession of States but to which one or more of those States were contracting States at that date, when the treaty becomes applicable to a part of the territory of the successor State to which it did not apply at the date of the succession of States.

5.1.6 Territorial scope of reservations of the successor State in cases of succession involving part of territory

When, as a result of a succession of States involving part of the territory of a State, a treaty to which the successor State is a contracting State becomes applicable to that territory, any reservation to the treaty formulated previously by that State shall also apply to that territory as from the date of the succession of States unless:

(*a*) the successor State expresses a contrary intention; or

(*b*) it appears from the reservation that its scope was limited to the territory of the successor State that was within its borders prior to the date of the succession of States, or to a part of this territory.

5.1.7 Timing of the effects of non-maintenance by a successor State of a reservation formulated by the predecessor State

The non-maintenance, in conformity with guideline 5.1.1 or 5.1.2, by the successor State of a reservation formulated by the predecessor State becomes operative in relation to another contracting State or a contracting organization only when notice of it has been received by that State or organization.

5.1.8 Late formulation of a reservation by a successor State

A reservation shall be considered as late if it is formulated:

(*a*) by a newly independent State after it has made a notification of succession to the treaty;

(*b*) by a successor State other than a newly independent State after it has made a notification establishing its status as a contracting State to a treaty which, at the date of the succession of States, was not in force for the predecessor State but in respect of which the predecessor State was a contracting State; or

(*c*) by a successor State other than a newly independent State in respect of a treaty which, following the succession of States, continues in force for that State.

5.2 Objections to reservations in cases of succession of States

5.2.1 Maintenance by the successor State of objections formulated by the predecessor State

Subject to the provisions of guideline 5.2.2, a successor State shall be considered as maintaining any objection formulated by the predecessor State to a reservation formulated by a contracting State or contracting organization, unless it expresses a contrary intention at the time of the succession.

5.2.2 Irrelevance of certain objections in cases involving a uniting of States

1. When, following a uniting of two or more States, a treaty in force at the date of the succession of States in respect of any of them continues in force in respect of the State so formed, such objections to a reservation as may have been formulated by any of those States in respect of which the treaty was not in force on the date of the succession of States shall not be maintained.

2. When, following a uniting of two or more States, the successor State is a contracting State to a treaty to which it has maintained reservations in conformity with guideline 5.1.1 or 5.1.2, objections to a reservation made by another contracting State or a contracting organization shall not be maintained if the reservation is identical or equivalent to a reservation which the successor State itself has maintained.

5.2.3 Maintenance of objections to reservations of the predecessor State

When a reservation formulated by the predecessor State is considered as being maintained by the successor State in conformity with guideline 5.1.1 or 5.1.2, any objection to that reservation formulated by another contracting State or by a contracting organization shall be considered as being maintained in respect of the successor State.

5.2.4 Reservations of the predecessor State to which no objections have been made

When a reservation formulated by the predecessor State is considered as being maintained by the successor State in conformity with guideline 5.1.1 or 5.1.2, a State or an international organization that had not formulated an objection to the reservation in respect of the predecessor State may not object to it in respect of the successor State, unless:

(*a*) the time period for formulating an objection has not yet expired at the date of the succession of States and the objection is made within that time period; or

(*b*) the territorial extension of the treaty radically changes the conditions for the operation of the reservation.

5.2.5 Right of a successor State to formulate objections to reservations

1. When making a notification of succession establishing its status as a contracting State, a newly independent State may, in accordance with the relevant guidelines, formulate an objection to reservations formulated by a contracting State or a contracting organization, even if the predecessor State made no such objection.

2. A successor State, other than a newly independent State, shall also have the right provided for in paragraph 1 when making a notification establishing its status as a contracting State to a treaty which, at the date of the succession of States, was not in force for the predecessor State but in respect of which the predecessor State was a contracting State.

3. The right referred to in paragraphs 1 and 2 is nonetheless excluded in the case of treaties falling under guidelines 2.8.7 and 4.1.2.

5.2.6 Objections by a successor State other than a newly independent State in respect of which a treaty continues in force

A successor State, other than a newly independent State, in respect of which a treaty continues in force following a succession of States may not formulate an objection to a reservation to which the predecessor State had not objected, unless the time period for formulating an objection has not yet expired at the date of the succession of States and the objection is made within that time period.

5.3 Acceptances of reservations in cases of succession of States

5.3.1 Maintenance by a newly independent State of express acceptances formulated by the predecessor State

When a newly independent State establishes its status as a contracting State to a treaty, it shall be considered as maintaining any express acceptance by the predecessor State of a reservation formulated by a contracting State or by a contracting organization, unless it expresses a contrary intention within twelve months of the date of the notification of succession.

5.3.2 Maintenance by a successor State other than a newly independent State of express acceptances formulated by the predecessor State

1. A successor State, other than a newly independent State, in respect of which a treaty continues in force following a succession of States shall be considered as maintaining any express acceptance by the predecessor State of a reservation formulated by a contracting State or by a contracting organization.

2. When making a notification of succession establishing its status as a contracting State to a treaty which, on the date of the succession of States, was not in force for the predecessor State but to which the predecessor State was a contracting State, a successor

State other than a newly independent State shall be considered as maintaining any express acceptance by the predecessor State of a reservation formulated by a contracting State or by a contracting organization, unless it expresses a contrary intention within twelve months of the date of the notification of succession.

5.3.3 Timing of the effects of non-maintenance by a successor State of an express acceptance formulated by the predecessor State

The non-maintenance, in conformity with guideline 5.3.1 or guideline 5.3.2, paragraph 2, by the successor State of the express acceptance by the predecessor State of a reservation formulated by a contracting State or a contracting organization becomes operative in relation to a contracting State or a contracting organization only when notice of it has been received by that State or that organization.

5.4 Legal effects of reservations, acceptances and objections in cases of succession of States

1. Reservations, acceptances and objections considered as being maintained pursuant to the guidelines contained in this Part of the Guide to Practice shall continue to produce their legal effects in conformity with the provisions of Part 4 of the Guide.

2. Part 4 of the Guide to Practice is also applicable, *mutatis mutandis*, to new reservations, acceptances and objections formulated by a successor State in conformity with the provisions of the present Part of the Guide.

5.5 Interpretative declarations in cases of succession of States

1. A successor State should clarify its position concerning interpretative declarations formulated by the predecessor State. In the absence of such clarification, a successor State shall be considered as maintaining the interpretative declarations of the predecessor State.

2. Paragraph 1 is without prejudice to cases in which the successor State has demonstrated, by its conduct, its intention to maintain or to reject an interpretative declaration formulated by the predecessor State.

Annex

Conclusions on the reservations dialogue

The International Law Commission,

Recalling the provisions on reservations to treaties contained in the Vienna Convention on the Law of Treaties and the Vienna Convention on the Law of Treaties between States and International Organizations or between International Organizations,

Taking into account the seventeenth report[1] presented by the Special Rapporteur on the topic "Reservations to treaties", which addresses the question of the reservations dialogue,

Bearing in mind the need to achieve a satisfactory balance between the objectives of safeguarding the integrity of multilateral treaties and securing the widest possible participation therein,

---

1 A/CN.4/647, paras. 2 to 68.

Recognizing the role that reservations to treaties may play in achieving this balance,

Concerned at the number of reservations that appear incompatible with the limits imposed by the law of treaties, in particular article 19 of the Vienna Conventions on the Law of Treaties,

Aware of the difficulties raised by the assessment of the validity of reservations,

Convinced of the usefulness of a pragmatic dialogue with the author of a reservation,

Welcoming the efforts made in recent years, including within the framework of international organizations and human rights treaty bodies, to encourage such a dialogue,

I. Considers that:

1. States and international organizations intending to formulate reservations should do so as precisely and narrowly as possible, consider limiting their scope and ensure that they are not incompatible with the object and purpose of the treaty to which they relate;

2. In formulating a unilateral statement, States and international organizations should indicate whether it amounts to a reservation and, if so, explain why the reservation is deemed necessary and the effect it will have on the fulfilment by its author of its obligations under the treaty;

3. Statements of reasons by the author of a reservation are important for the assessment of the validity of the reservation, and States and international organizations should state the reason for any modification of a reservation;

4. States and international organizations should periodically review their reservations with a view to limiting their scope or withdrawing them where appropriate;

5. The concerns about reservations that are frequently expressed by States and international organizations, as well as monitoring bodies, may be useful for the assessment of the validity of reservations;

6. States and international organizations, as well as monitoring bodies, should explain to the author of a reservation the reasons for their concerns about the reservation and, where appropriate, request any clarification that they deem useful;

7. States and international organizations, as well as monitoring bodies, if they deem it useful, should encourage the withdrawal of reservations, the reconsideration of the need for a reservation or the gradual reduction of the scope of a reservation through partial withdrawals;

8. States and international organizations should address the concerns and reactions of other States, international organizations and monitoring bodies and take them into account, to the extent possible, with a view to reconsidering, modifying or withdrawing a reservation;

9. States and international organizations, as well as monitoring bodies, should cooperate as closely as possible in order to exchange views on reservations in respect of which concerns have been raised and coordinate the measures to be taken; and

II. Recommends that:

The General Assembly call upon States and international organizations, as well as monitoring bodies, to initiate and pursue such a reservations dialogue in a pragmatic and transparent manner.

List of Other Published Works of the Author

Published books:

Curso de direito internacional público. 9. ed. São Paulo: Revista dos Tribunais, 2015.

Curso de direitos humanos. 2. ed. São Paulo: Método, 2015.

Direito internacional privado: curso elementar. Rio de Janeiro: Forense, 2015.

Direito internacional público: parte geral. 8. ed. São Paulo: Revista dos Tribunais, 2014.

Direito internacional: tratados e direitos humanos fundamentais na ordem jurídica brasileira. Rio de Janeiro: América Jurídica, 2001.

Direitos humanos e cidadania à luz do novo direito internacional. Campinas: Minelli, 2002.

Direitos humanos, Constituição e os tratados internacionais: estudo analítico da situação e aplicação do tratado na ordem jurídica brasileira. São Paulo: Juarez de Oliveira, 2002.

Natureza jurídica e eficácia dos acordos stand-by *com o FMI*. São Paulo: Revista dos Tribunais, 2005.

O controle jurisdicional da convencionalidade das leis. 3. ed. São Paulo: Revista dos Tribunais, 2013.

Os sistemas regionais de proteção dos direitos humanos: uma análise comparativa dos sistemas interamericano, europeu e africano. São Paulo: Revista dos Tribunais, 2011.

Por um tribunal de justiça para a Unasul: a necessidade de uma corte de justiça para a América do Sul sob os paradigmas do Tribunal de Justiça da União Europeia e da Corte Centro-Americana de Justiça. Brasília: Senado Federal, 2014.

Prisão civil por dívida e o Pacto de San José da Costa Rica: especial enfoque para os contratos de alienação fiduciária em garantia. Rio de Janeiro: Forense, 2002.

Tratados internacionais de direitos humanos e direito interno. São Paulo: Saraiva, 2010.

Tratados internacionais: com comentários à Convenção de Viena de 1969. 2. ed. São Paulo: Juarez de Oliveira, 2004.

Tribunal Penal Internacional e o direito brasileiro. 3. ed. São Paulo: Revista dos Tribunais, 2012.

Co-autorship:

Acumulação de cargos públicos: uma questão de aplicação da Constituição (co-author: Waldir Alves). São Paulo: Revista dos Tribunais, 2013.

Comentários à Convenção Americana sobre Direitos Humanos – Pacto de San José da Costa Rica. 4. ed. (co-author: Luiz Flávio Gomes). São Paulo: Revista dos Tribunais, 2013.

Direito supraconstitucional: do absolutismo ao Estado Constitucional e Humanista de Direito. 2. ed. (co-author: Luiz Flávio Gomes). São Paulo: Revista dos Tribunais, 2013.

Teoria tridimensional das integrações supranacionais: uma análise comparativa dos sistemas e modelos de integração da Europa e América Latina (co-author: Michele Carducci). Rio de Janeiro: Forense, 2014.

Co-autorship and coordination:

O novo direito internacional do meio ambiente. Curitiba: Juruá, 2011.

Co-autorship and co-coordination:

Controle de convencionalidade: um panorama latino-americano (with Luiz Guilherme Marinoni). Brasília: Gazeta Jurídica, 2013.

Crimes da ditadura militar: uma análise à luz da jurisprudência atual da Corte Interamericana de Direitos Humanos (with Luiz Flávio Gomes). São Paulo: Revista dos Tribunais, 2011.

Direito à liberdade religiosa: desafios e perspectivas para o século XXI (with Aldir Guedes Soriano). Belo Horizonte: Fórum, 2009.

Direito da integração regional: diálogo entre jurisdições na América Latina (with Eduardo Biacchi Gomes). São Paulo: Saraiva, 2015.

Direito internacional dos direitos humanos: estudos em homenagem à Professora Flávia Piovesan (with Maria de Fátima Ribeiro). Curitiba: Juruá, 2004.

Doutrinas essenciais de direito internacional, 5 vols. (with Luiz Olavo Baptista). São Paulo: Revista dos Tribunais, 2012.

Novas perspectivas do direito ambiental brasileiro: visões interdisciplinares (with Carlos Teodoro José Hugueney Irigaray). Cuiabá: Cathedral, 2009.

Novas vertentes do direito do comércio internacional (with Jete Jane Fiorati). Barueri: Manole, 2003.

Novos estudos de direito internacional contemporâneo, 2 vols. (with Helena Aranda Barrozo and Márcia Teshima). Londrina: EDUEL, 2008.

O Brasil e os acordos econômicos internacionais: perspectivas jurídicas e econômicas à luz dos acordos com o FMI (with Roberto Luiz Silva). São Paulo: Ed. RT, 2003.

Organization:

Coletânea de direito internacional e Constituição Federal. 13. ed. São Paulo: Revista dos Tribunais, 2015.

Cód.: 1214215

Gráfica Santuário – 2016/01